REVISED EDITION

GOOD
AND
EVIL

The Ultimate Comic Book
Action Bible

MICHAEL PEARL

Our desire is that after reading *Good and Evil®* you will be motivated to read the entire Bible and that it will come alive to you. Make it a daily habit to read a portion of the Bible and then pray that God will help you understand and apply it.

Good and Evil® The Ultimate Comic Book Action Bible is licensed to:

Good and Evil International, Inc.
1000 Pearl Road
Pleasantville, TN 37033-1796

All scripture quotations are taken from The Holy Bible, King James Version, the written Word of God to English-speaking people. *Good and Evil®* is God's Word adapted into story form.

Print ISBN: 978-1-61644-086-2

1. Bible 2. Old Testament 3. New Testament 4. Jesus 5. Religion 6. Christianity
7. Salvation 8. Graphic Novel
I. Pearl, Michael II. Good and Evil® The Ultimate Comic Book Action Bible

Good and Evil® The Ultimate Comic Book Action Bible may be purchased at special quantity discounts for sales promotions, gifts, fundraising, book clubs, or educational purposes for churches, prison ministries, schools and universities. Rights and Licensing Agreements are available. For more information, contact Mel Cohen (mel@comicbook.bible).

Printed in China

CONTENTS

THE STORY

CREDITS

Author: Michael Pearl

Artist: Danny Bulanadi

Coloration: Clint Cearley

Good and Evil® The Ultimate Comic Book Action Bible is a Bible storybook meant to draw readers of all ages to the Bible. Most of the content in *Good and Evil®* is not directly quoted from scripture so we encourage you to read the scripture references at the bottom of each page and look them up in your Bible.

INTRODUCTION

A MODERN MARVEL FOR MISSIONS

With the arrival of a new millennium, evangelist and author Michael Pearl arrived at a new vision for spreading the Gospel. To address the problems of communicating to divergent language groups and to reading-disadvantaged people, he dreamed of delivering the message of Christ via a "graphic novel" format.

Although Michael and his wife Debi had supported various missions for more than 40 years, Michael's concern over the obstacles in cross-cultural communications peaked when the Pearls' daughter began ministering to a primitive tribe on a remote mountain in Papua New Guinea. She needed some form of simple Bible story art that could speak clearly to the Kumboi tribe, but the only art available at the time was either poorly done or too expensive. Their daughter's immediate need connected with Michael Pearl's vision, and he, in turn, connected with the astounding talent and experience of Marvel Comics' artist Danny Bulanadi.

God had been at work in Danny's life, and Danny had become a born again Christian a few years prior to Michael's contacting him. No longer comfortable with the comic art he was producing, Danny had quit work for Marvel and taken a job as a night watchman in San Francisco. Michael offered Danny a renewed opportunity in comic-style art, and together, they crafted *Good and Evil*, this Genesis to Revelation graphic-novel-style presentation of God's work of saving mankind from sin. Once Michael and Danny created the black and white version, they joined forces with illustrator Clint Cearley to add the amazing color that brings this book to life.

Although a few familiar Bible stories are not included (David and Goliath, for instance), this chronological presentation of Old Testament history delivers all the background you need to grasp the reality of the God of Abraham, Isaac, Jacob, and the New Testament Apostles, as well as the necessity of salvation through Jesus Christ. Since the release of its first edition in 2008, Good and Evil has entertained and educated English-speaking readers, and true to the original intent, it has also established a remarkable track record of cross-cultural communication. The book now ministers to people in more than 40 languages—Spanish, Ukrainian, Lao, Thai, Hmong, Burmese, Cebuano, Karen, and Wa, to name a few—and has been produced as a 13-episode animated video. What's more, Good and Evil is welcomed in places otherwise closed to the Gospel. The engaging, high-energy artwork appeals even to Hindus and Muslims and can be found on the shelves of some of the world's most remote roadside stands.

In 2015, Michael Pearl's dream for this piece led to the creation of Good and Evil International, an organization committed to the wider distribution of the Good and Evil book and DVD and to developing other innovative Gospel products leveraging twenty-first century technologies. Thanks to Good and Evil, modern missions will never be the same, and as you dive into the biblical adventure that follows, you'll marvel at what you find.

The original version of each Good and Evil story is recorded in the Bible. Scripture references corresponding to these graphic accounts are noted at the bottom of each page, so you can look them up and read the stories from the Bible itself.

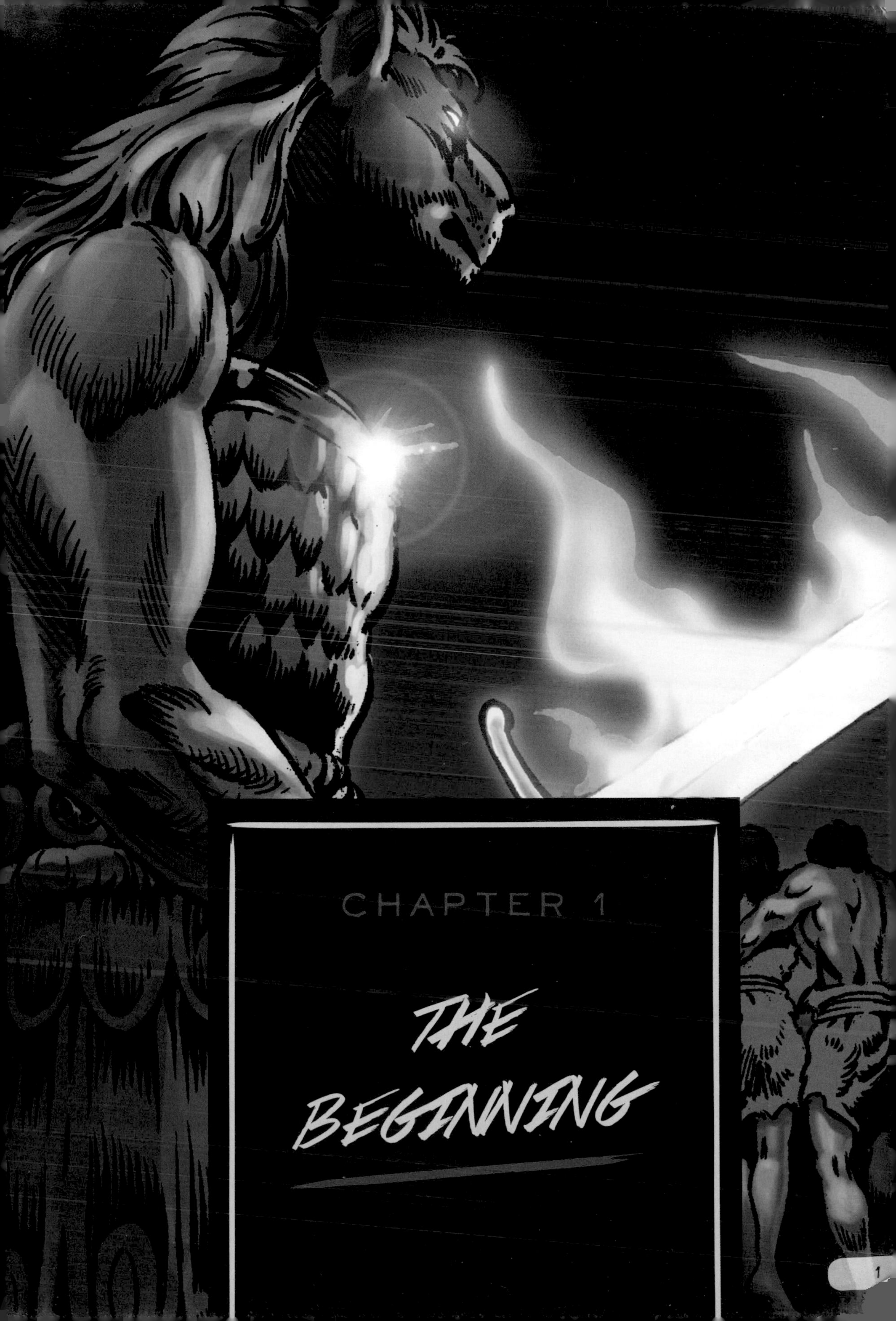

CHAPTER 1

THE BEGINNING

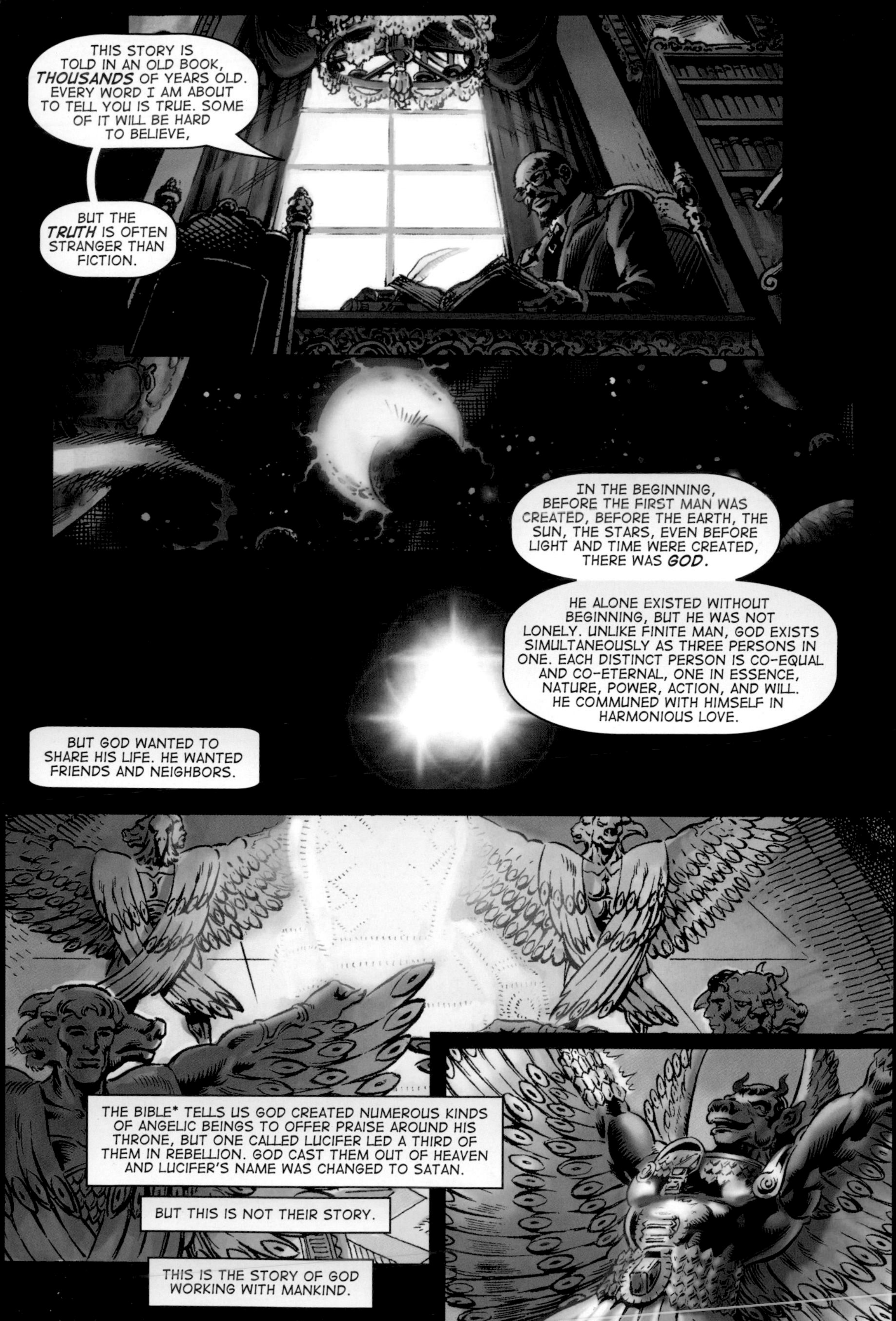
THIS STORY IS TOLD IN AN OLD BOOK, **THOUSANDS** OF YEARS OLD. EVERY WORD I AM ABOUT TO TELL YOU IS TRUE. SOME OF IT WILL BE HARD TO BELIEVE,
BUT THE **TRUTH** IS OFTEN STRANGER THAN FICTION.
IN THE BEGINNING, BEFORE THE FIRST MAN WAS CREATED, BEFORE THE EARTH, THE SUN, THE STARS, EVEN BEFORE LIGHT AND TIME WERE CREATED, THERE WAS **GOD**.
HE ALONE EXISTED WITHOUT BEGINNING, BUT HE WAS NOT LONELY. UNLIKE FINITE MAN, GOD EXISTS SIMULTANEOUSLY AS THREE PERSONS IN ONE. EACH DISTINCT PERSON IS CO-EQUAL AND CO-ETERNAL, ONE IN ESSENCE, NATURE, POWER, ACTION, AND WILL. HE COMMUNED WITH HIMSELF IN HARMONIOUS LOVE.
BUT GOD WANTED TO SHARE HIS LIFE. HE WANTED FRIENDS AND NEIGHBORS.
THE BIBLE* TELLS US GOD CREATED NUMEROUS KINDS OF ANGELIC BEINGS TO OFFER PRAISE AROUND HIS THRONE, BUT ONE CALLED LUCIFER LED A THIRD OF THEM IN REBELLION. GOD CAST THEM OUT OF HEAVEN AND LUCIFER'S NAME WAS CHANGED TO SATAN.
BUT THIS IS NOT THEIR STORY.
THIS IS THE STORY OF GOD WORKING WITH MANKIND.

ISAIAH 45:18 - *SEE PAGE 322 FOR A BRIEF DESCRIPTION OF THE BOOK CALLED THE BIBLE. FOR MORE INFORMATION ABOUT SATAN, SEE: ISAIAH 14:12-14; EZEKIEL 28:13-19; MATTHEW 25:41; LUKE 10:18; REVELATION 12:4, 20:2

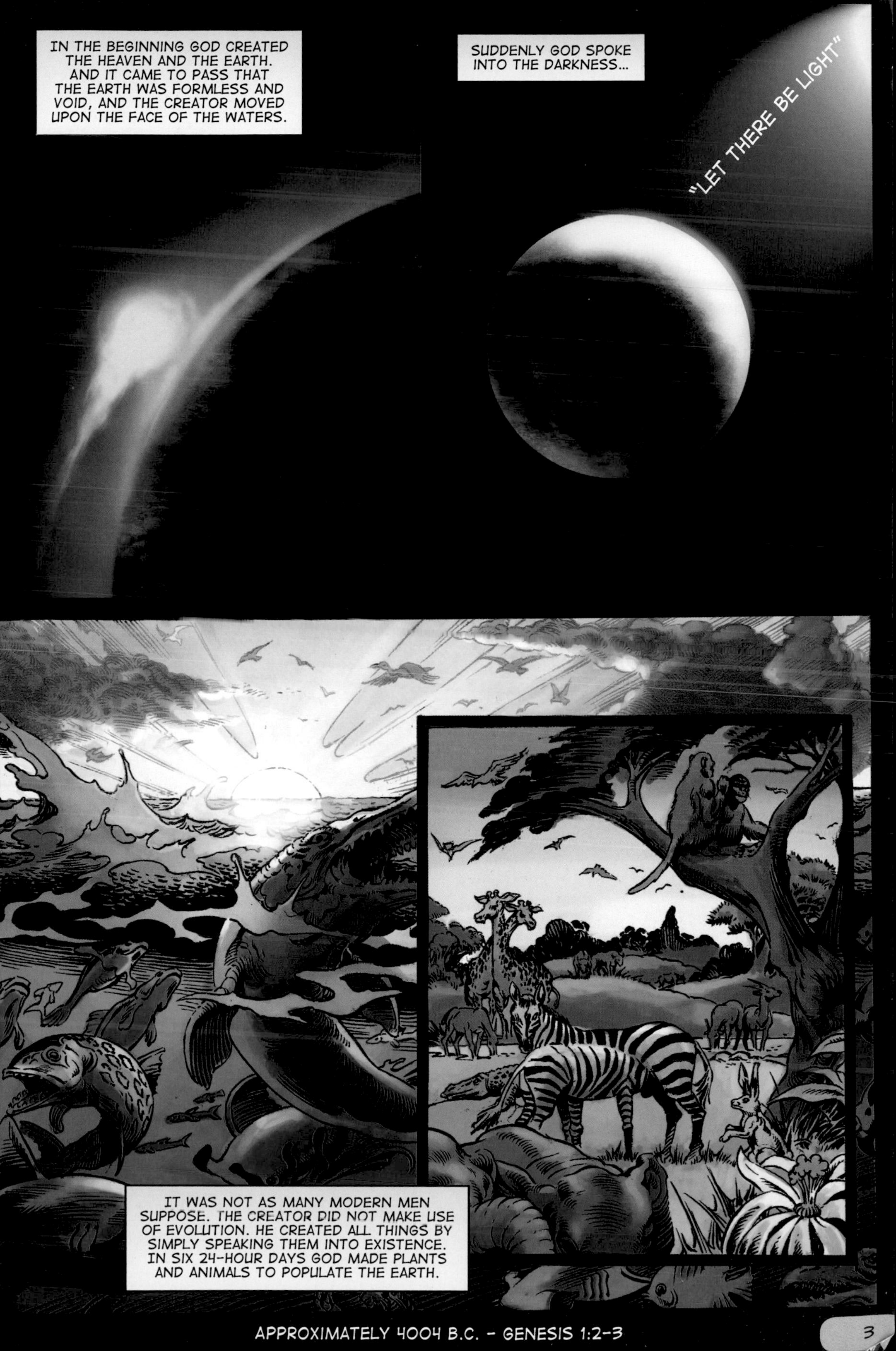
IN THE BEGINNING GOD CREATED THE HEAVEN AND THE EARTH. AND IT CAME TO PASS THAT THE EARTH WAS FORMLESS AND VOID, AND THE CREATOR MOVED UPON THE FACE OF THE WATERS.
SUDDENLY GOD SPOKE INTO THE DARKNESS...
"LET THERE BE LIGHT"
IT WAS NOT AS MANY MODERN MEN SUPPOSE. THE CREATOR DID NOT MAKE USE OF EVOLUTION. HE CREATED ALL THINGS BY SIMPLY SPEAKING THEM INTO EXISTENCE. IN SIX 24-HOUR DAYS GOD MADE PLANTS AND ANIMALS TO POPULATE THE EARTH.

APPROXIMATELY 4004 B.C. - GENESIS 1:2-3

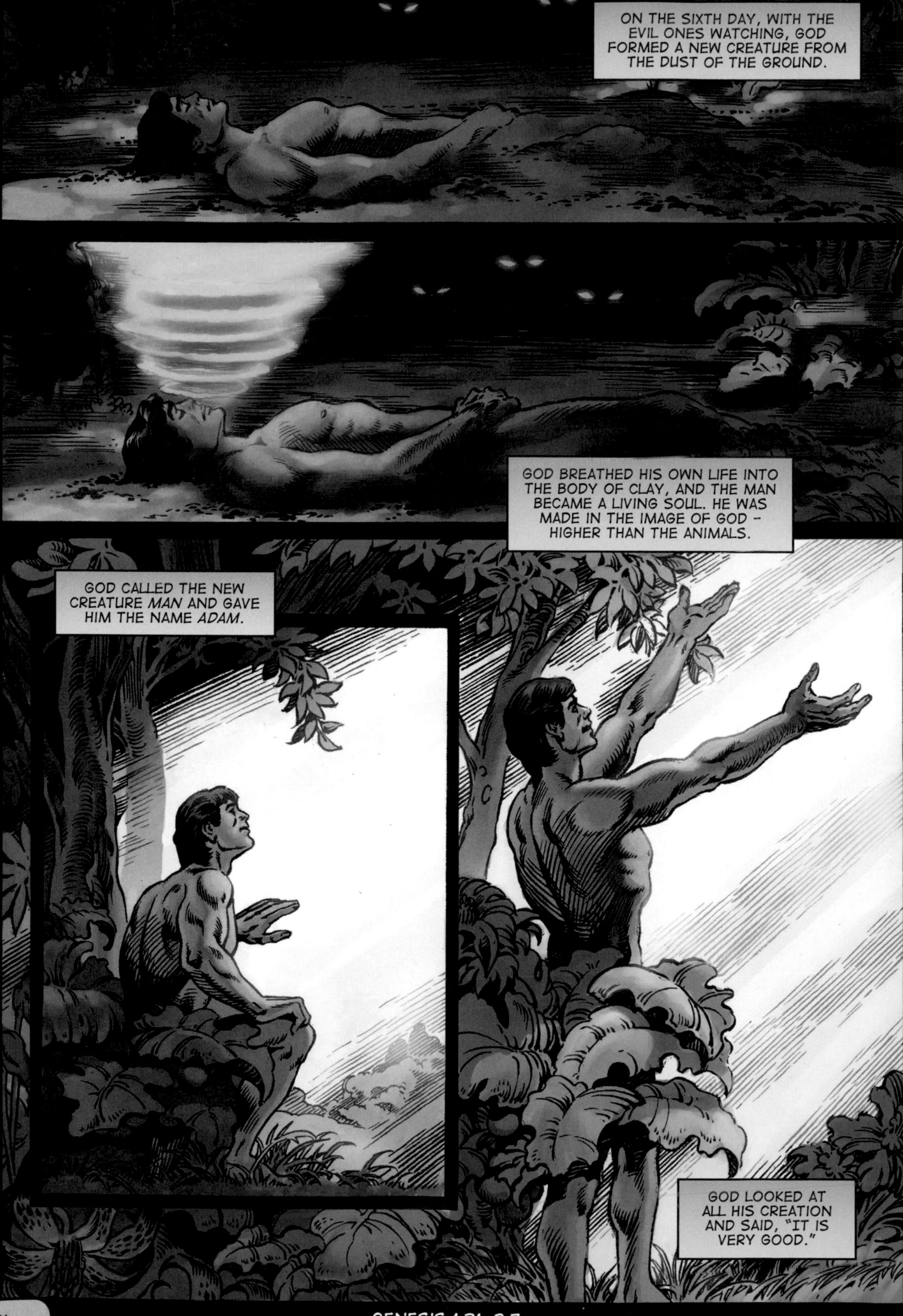
ON THE SIXTH DAY, WITH THE EVIL ONES WATCHING, GOD FORMED A NEW CREATURE FROM THE DUST OF THE GROUND.
GOD BREATHED HIS OWN LIFE INTO THE BODY OF CLAY, AND THE MAN BECAME A LIVING SOUL. HE WAS MADE IN THE IMAGE OF GOD - HIGHER THAN THE ANIMALS.
GOD CALLED THE NEW CREATURE *MAN* AND GAVE HIM THE NAME *ADAM*.
GOD LOOKED AT ALL HIS CREATION AND SAID, "IT IS VERY GOOD."

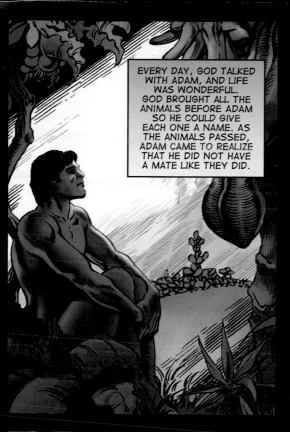

EVERY DAY, GOD TALKED WITH ADAM, AND LIFE WAS WONDERFUL. GOD BROUGHT ALL THE ANIMALS BEFORE ADAM SO HE COULD GIVE EACH ONE A NAME. AS THE ANIMALS PASSED, ADAM CAME TO REALIZE THAT HE DID NOT HAVE A MATE LIKE THEY DID.

AND GOD SAID...

I WILL MAKE A MATE TO HELP ADAM.

GOD CAUSED ADAM TO EXPERIENCE A DEEP SLEEP AND THEN TOOK A RIB FROM HIS SIDE. WITH THE RIB, GOD FASHIONED A BEAUTIFUL WOMAN TO BE ADAM'S LOVING HELPER.

GOD WOKE ADAM AND BROUGHT THE WOMAN TO HIM. HE TOLD THEM TO HAVE CHILDREN AND REPLENISH THE EARTH, AND ADAM CALLED HIS BEAUTIFUL NEW WIFE "EVE."

THEY WERE BOTH NAKED, BUT, LIKE CHILDREN, THEY WERE NOT AWARE OF IT.

SHE IS BONE OF MY BONE AND FLESH OF MY FLESH.

SATAN, THE EVIL ONE, WATCHED.

THEY WERE HAPPY IN THE GARDEN. THERE WAS NO SIN, NO HUNGER; IT GOT NEITHER TOO HOT NOR TOO COLD.

GOD SPOKE OF THE TREES, SAYING...

YOU MAY EAT OF ALL THE TREES IN THE GARDEN, BUT DO NOT EAT FROM THIS ONE TREE IN THE MIDDLE OF THE GARDEN, FOR IN THE DAY YOU EAT YOU WILL DIE.

GENESIS 1:28, 2:2, 16-22, 25

5

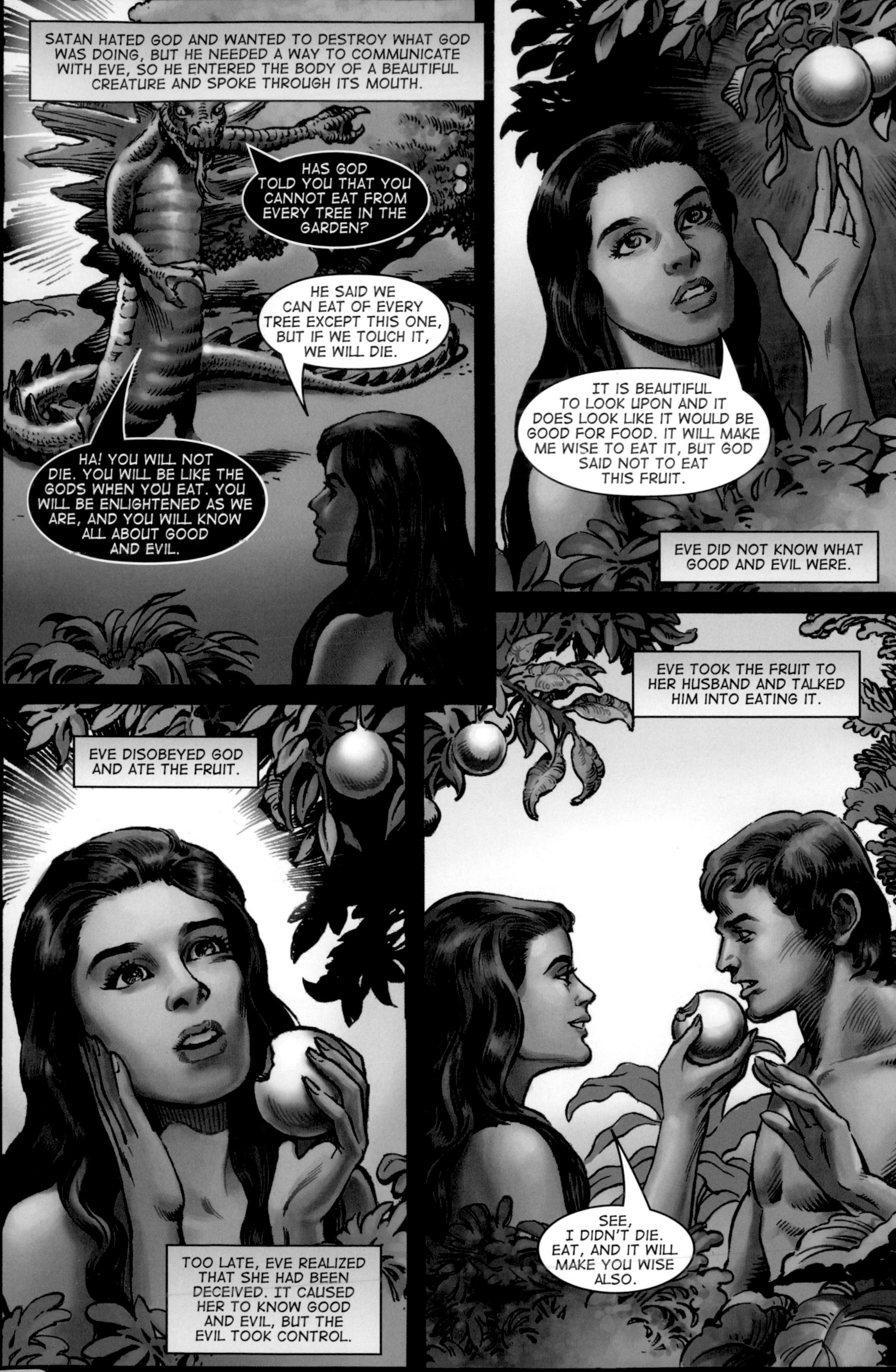
SATAN HATED GOD AND WANTED TO DESTROY WHAT GOD WAS DOING, BUT HE NEEDED A WAY TO COMMUNICATE WITH EVE, SO HE ENTERED THE BODY OF A BEAUTIFUL CREATURE AND SPOKE THROUGH ITS MOUTH.
HAS GOD TOLD YOU THAT YOU CANNOT EAT FROM EVERY TREE IN THE GARDEN?
HE SAID WE CAN EAT OF EVERY TREE EXCEPT THIS ONE, BUT IF WE TOUCH IT, WE WILL DIE.
HA! YOU WILL NOT DIE. YOU WILL BE LIKE THE GODS WHEN YOU EAT. YOU WILL BE ENLIGHTENED AS WE ARE, AND YOU WILL KNOW ALL ABOUT GOOD AND EVIL.
IT IS BEAUTIFUL TO LOOK UPON AND IT DOES LOOK LIKE IT WOULD BE GOOD FOR FOOD. IT WILL MAKE ME WISE TO EAT IT, BUT GOD SAID NOT TO EAT THIS FRUIT.
EVE DID NOT KNOW WHAT GOOD AND EVIL WERE.
EVE DISOBEYED GOD AND ATE THE FRUIT.
TOO LATE, EVE REALIZED THAT SHE HAD BEEN DECEIVED. IT CAUSED HER TO KNOW GOOD AND EVIL, BUT THE EVIL TOOK CONTROL.
EVE TOOK THE FRUIT TO HER HUSBAND AND TALKED HIM INTO EATING IT.
SEE, I DIDN'T DIE. EAT, AND IT WILL MAKE YOU WISE ALSO.

GENESIS 3:1-6; REVELATION 20:2

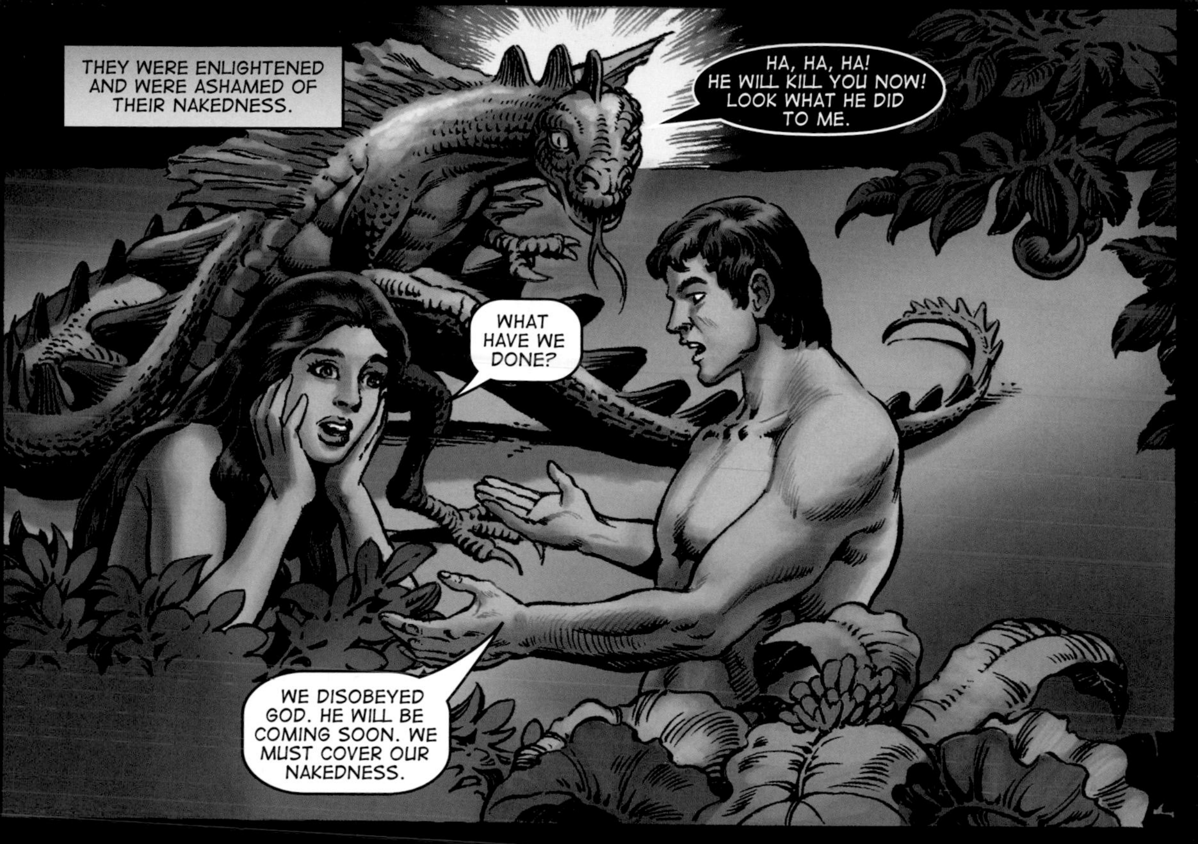
THEY WERE ENLIGHTENED AND WERE ASHAMED OF THEIR NAKEDNESS.
HA, HA, HA! HE WILL KILL YOU NOW! LOOK WHAT HE DID TO ME.
WHAT HAVE WE DONE?
WE DISOBEYED GOD. HE WILL BE COMING SOON. WE MUST COVER OUR NAKEDNESS.

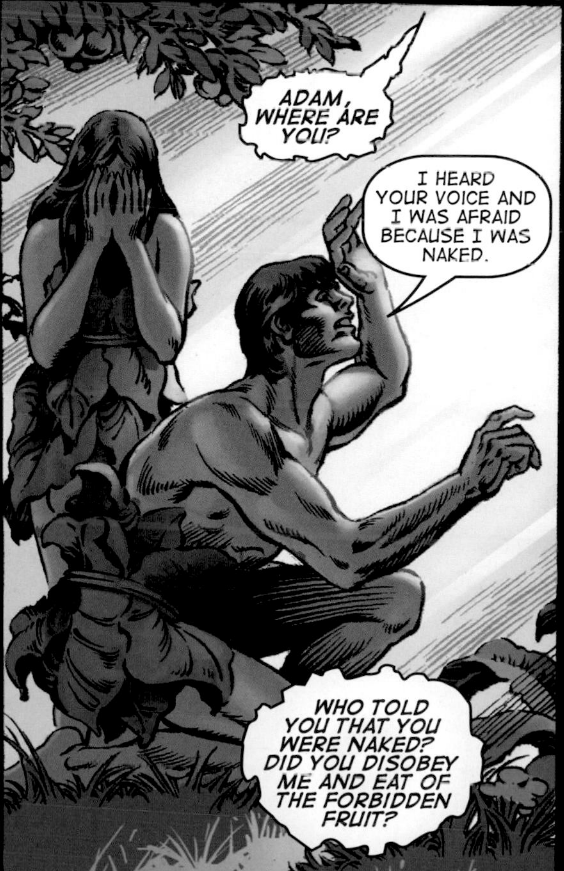
ADAM, WHERE ARE YOU?
I HEARD YOUR VOICE AND I WAS AFRAID BECAUSE I WAS NAKED.
WHO TOLD YOU THAT YOU WERE NAKED? DID YOU DISOBEY ME AND EAT OF THE FORBIDDEN FRUIT?

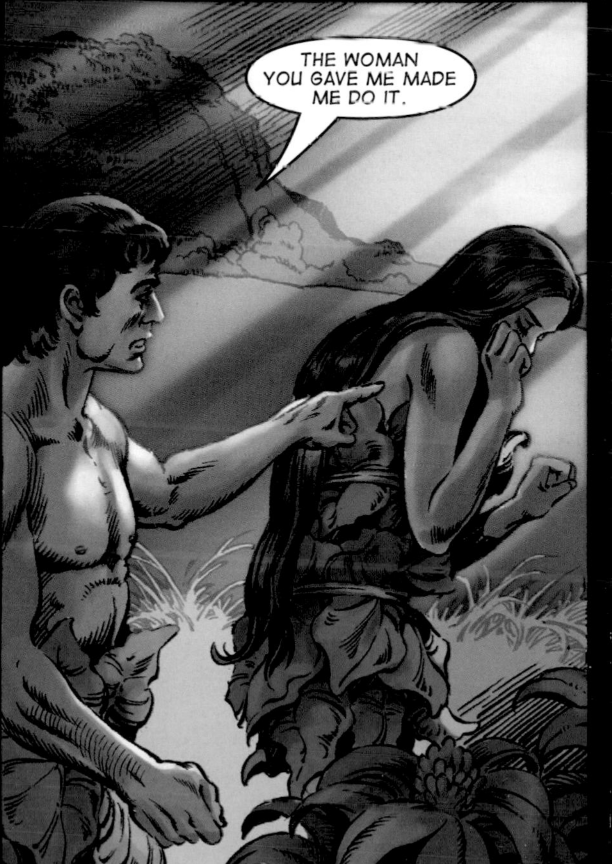
THE WOMAN YOU GAVE ME MADE ME DO IT.

GENESIS 3:6-12

HISSSSS...

THE SERPENT DECEIVED ME. HE TOLD ME I WOULDN'T DIE, THAT I WOULD BE LIKE YOU, BUT I AM NOT LIKE YOU. I FEEL AWFUL.

SO GOD CURSED THE SERPENT AND SAID UNTO HIM...

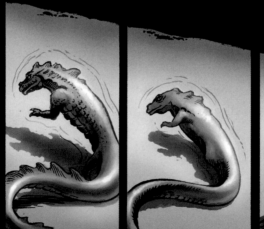

BECAUSE YOU HAVE DONE THIS, I WILL MAKE YOU CRAWL ON YOUR BELLY AND GET DUST IN YOUR MOUTH.

I WILL MAKE YOUR SEED AND THE WOMAN'S CHILD TO BE ENEMIES. YOUR SEED WILL BRUISE THE HEEL OF THE WOMAN'S CHILD, BUT HE WILL BRUISE YOUR HEAD.

HERE IS PROMISE OF A FUTURE BATTLE. A TIME WILL COME WHEN THE WOMAN'S SEED WILL DEFEAT SATAN. THIS PERSON WILL REDEEM MANKIND BACK TO GOD AND DELIVER THEM FROM THE CURSE OF SIN AND DEATH.

GOD COULD HAVE DESTROYED LUCIFER AND ALL HIS ANGELS IN JUST A MOMENT'S TIME, BUT HE ALLOWED THEM TO LIVE AS A TEST FOR THE HUMAN RACE. WILL MEN FOLLOW GOD, OR WILL THEY FOLLOW SATAN IN HIS REBELLION?

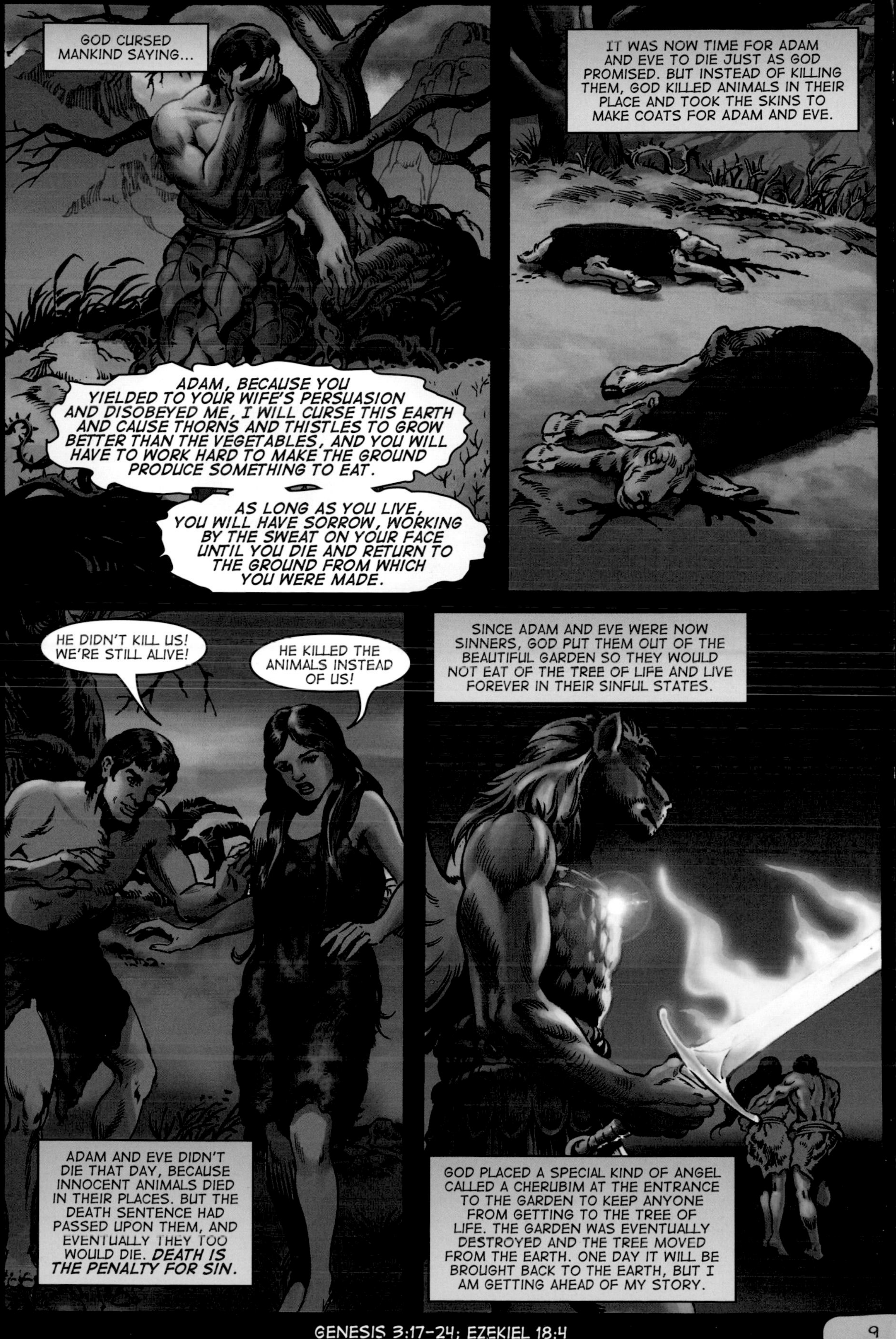
GOD CURSED MANKIND SAYING...
ADAM, BECAUSE YOU YIELDED TO YOUR WIFE'S PERSUASION AND DISOBEYED ME, I WILL CURSE THIS EARTH AND CAUSE THORNS AND THISTLES TO GROW BETTER THAN THE VEGETABLES, AND YOU WILL HAVE TO WORK HARD TO MAKE THE GROUND PRODUCE SOMETHING TO EAT.
AS LONG AS YOU LIVE, YOU WILL HAVE SORROW, WORKING BY THE SWEAT ON YOUR FACE UNTIL YOU DIE AND RETURN TO THE GROUND FROM WHICH YOU WERE MADE.
IT WAS NOW TIME FOR ADAM AND EVE TO DIE JUST AS GOD PROMISED. BUT INSTEAD OF KILLING THEM, GOD KILLED ANIMALS IN THEIR PLACE AND TOOK THE SKINS TO MAKE COATS FOR ADAM AND EVE.
HE DIDN'T KILL US! WE'RE STILL ALIVE!
HE KILLED THE ANIMALS INSTEAD OF US!
ADAM AND EVE DIDN'T DIE THAT DAY, BECAUSE INNOCENT ANIMALS DIED IN THEIR PLACES. BUT THE DEATH SENTENCE HAD PASSED UPON THEM, AND EVENTUALLY THEY TOO WOULD DIE. DEATH IS THE PENALTY FOR SIN.
SINCE ADAM AND EVE WERE NOW SINNERS, GOD PUT THEM OUT OF THE BEAUTIFUL GARDEN SO THEY WOULD NOT EAT OF THE TREE OF LIFE AND LIVE FOREVER IN THEIR SINFUL STATES.
GOD PLACED A SPECIAL KIND OF ANGEL CALLED A CHERUBIM AT THE ENTRANCE TO THE GARDEN TO KEEP ANYONE FROM GETTING TO THE TREE OF LIFE. THE GARDEN WAS EVENTUALLY DESTROYED AND THE TREE MOVED FROM THE EARTH. ONE DAY IT WILL BE BROUGHT BACK TO THE EARTH, BUT I AM GETTING AHEAD OF MY STORY.

GENESIS 3:17-24; EZEKIEL 18:4

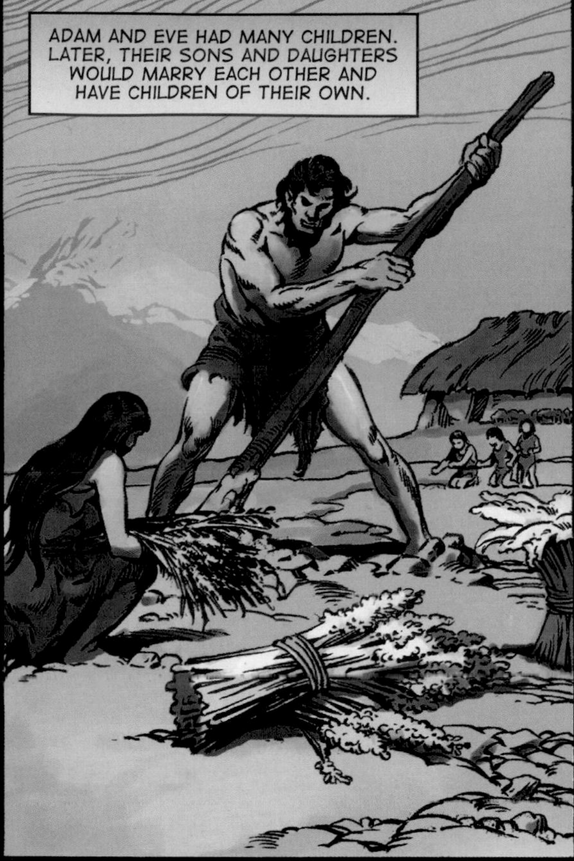
ADAM AND EVE HAD MANY CHILDREN. LATER, THEIR SONS AND DAUGHTERS WOULD MARRY EACH OTHER AND HAVE CHILDREN OF THEIR OWN.

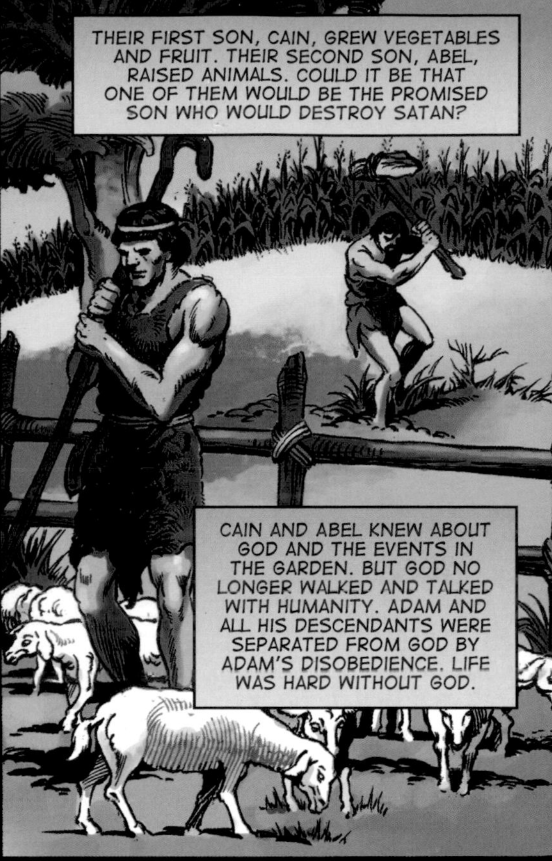
THEIR FIRST SON, CAIN, GREW VEGETABLES AND FRUIT. THEIR SECOND SON, ABEL, RAISED ANIMALS. COULD IT BE THAT ONE OF THEM WOULD BE THE PROMISED SON WHO WOULD DESTROY SATAN?
CAIN AND ABEL KNEW ABOUT GOD AND THE EVENTS IN THE GARDEN. BUT GOD NO LONGER WALKED AND TALKED WITH HUMANITY. ADAM AND ALL HIS DESCENDANTS WERE SEPARATED FROM GOD BY ADAM'S DISOBEDIENCE. LIFE WAS HARD WITHOUT GOD.

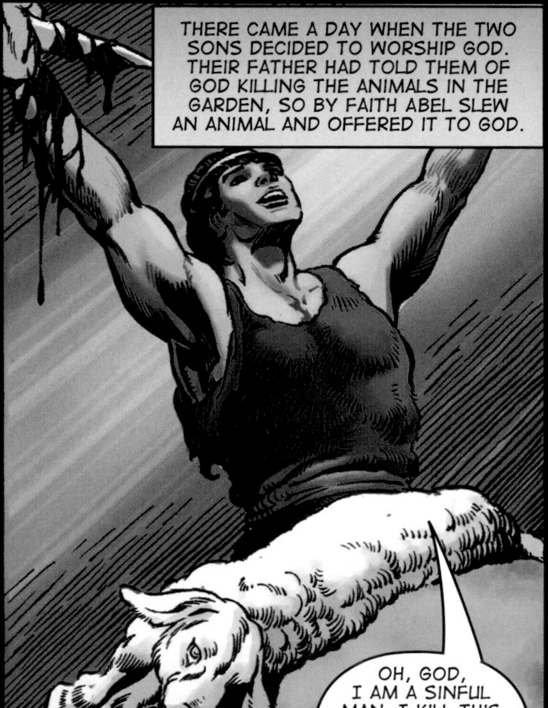
THERE CAME A DAY WHEN THE TWO SONS DECIDED TO WORSHIP GOD. THEIR FATHER HAD TOLD THEM OF GOD KILLING THE ANIMALS IN THE GARDEN, SO BY FAITH ABEL SLEW AN ANIMAL AND OFFERED IT TO GOD.
OH, GOD, I AM A SINFUL MAN; I KILL THIS LAMB AND OFFER IT TO YOU IN THE PLACE OF MY OWN DEATH.

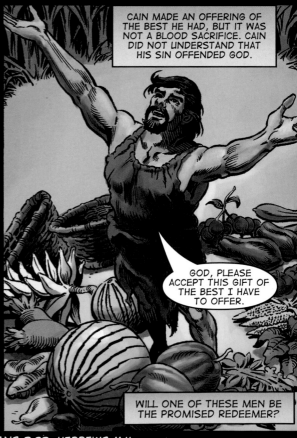

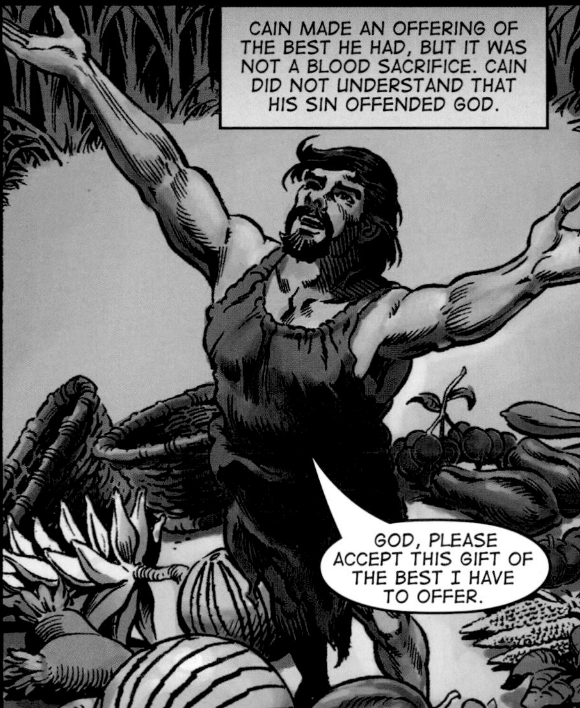
CAIN MADE AN OFFERING OF THE BEST HE HAD, BUT IT WAS NOT A BLOOD SACRIFICE. CAIN DID NOT UNDERSTAND THAT HIS SIN OFFENDED GOD.
GOD, PLEASE ACCEPT THIS GIFT OF THE BEST I HAVE TO OFFER.
WILL ONE OF THESE MEN BE THE PROMISED REDEEMER?

GENESIS 4:1-4; ROMANS 3:23; HEBREWS 11:4

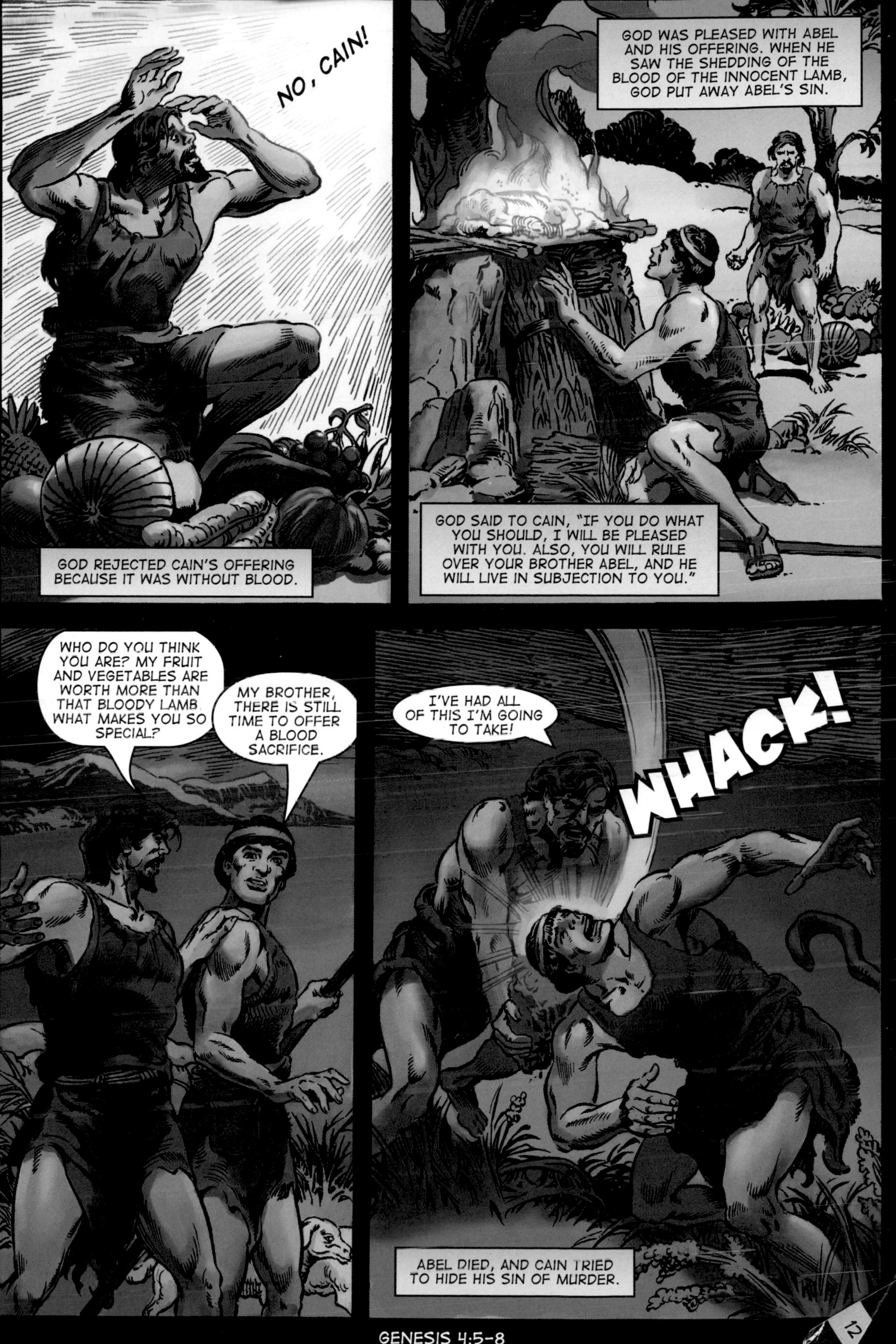
NO, CAIN!
GOD REJECTED CAIN'S OFFERING BECAUSE IT WAS WITHOUT BLOOD.
GOD WAS PLEASED WITH ABEL AND HIS OFFERING. WHEN HE SAW THE SHEDDING OF THE BLOOD OF THE INNOCENT LAMB, GOD PUT AWAY ABEL'S SIN.
GOD SAID TO CAIN, "IF YOU DO WHAT YOU SHOULD, I WILL BE PLEASED WITH YOU. ALSO, YOU WILL RULE OVER YOUR BROTHER ABEL, AND HE WILL LIVE IN SUBJECTION TO YOU."
WHO DO YOU THINK YOU ARE? MY FRUIT AND VEGETABLES ARE WORTH MORE THAN THAT BLOODY LAMB. WHAT MAKES YOU SO SPECIAL?
MY BROTHER, THERE IS STILL TIME TO OFFER A BLOOD SACRIFICE.
I'VE HAD ALL OF THIS I'M GOING TO TAKE!
WHACK!
ABEL DIED, AND CAIN TRIED TO HIDE HIS SIN OF MURDER.

GENESIS 4:5-8

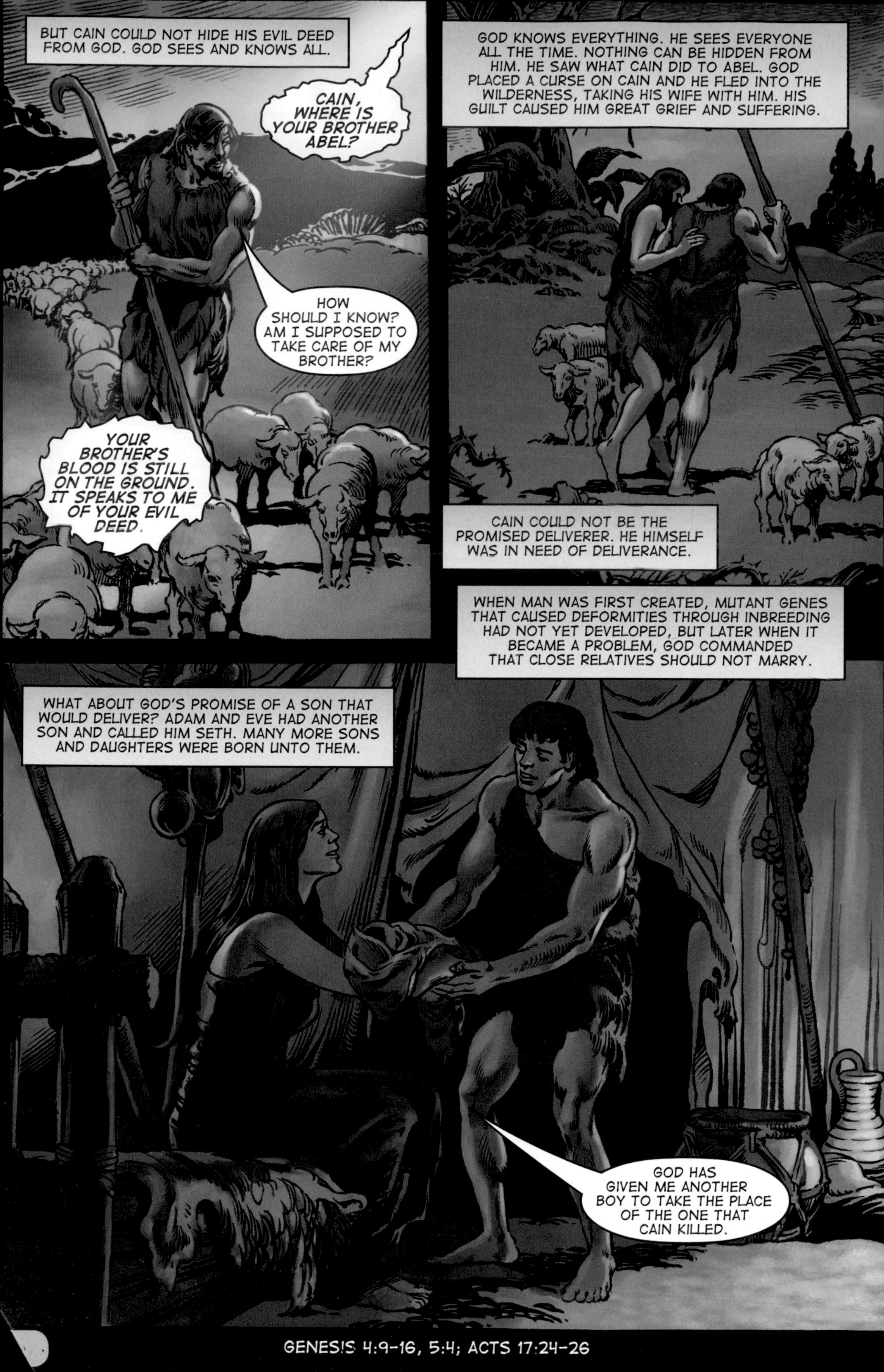
BUT CAIN COULD NOT HIDE HIS EVIL DEED FROM GOD. GOD SEES AND KNOWS ALL.
CAIN, WHERE IS YOUR BROTHER ABEL?
HOW SHOULD I KNOW? AM I SUPPOSED TO TAKE CARE OF MY BROTHER?
YOUR BROTHER'S BLOOD IS STILL ON THE GROUND. IT SPEAKS TO ME OF YOUR EVIL DEED.
GOD KNOWS EVERYTHING. HE SEES EVERYONE ALL THE TIME. NOTHING CAN BE HIDDEN FROM HIM. HE SAW WHAT CAIN DID TO ABEL. GOD PLACED A CURSE ON CAIN AND HE FLED INTO THE WILDERNESS, TAKING HIS WIFE WITH HIM. HIS GUILT CAUSED HIM GREAT GRIEF AND SUFFERING.
CAIN COULD NOT BE THE PROMISED DELIVERER. HE HIMSELF WAS IN NEED OF DELIVERANCE.
WHEN MAN WAS FIRST CREATED, MUTANT GENES THAT CAUSED DEFORMITIES THROUGH INBREEDING HAD NOT YET DEVELOPED, BUT LATER WHEN IT BECAME A PROBLEM, GOD COMMANDED THAT CLOSE RELATIVES SHOULD NOT MARRY.
WHAT ABOUT GOD'S PROMISE OF A SON THAT WOULD DELIVER? ADAM AND EVE HAD ANOTHER SON AND CALLED HIM SETH. MANY MORE SONS AND DAUGHTERS WERE BORN UNTO THEM.
GOD HAS GIVEN ME ANOTHER BOY TO TAKE THE PLACE OF THE ONE THAT CAIN KILLED.

GENESIS 4:9-16, 5:4; ACTS 17:24-26

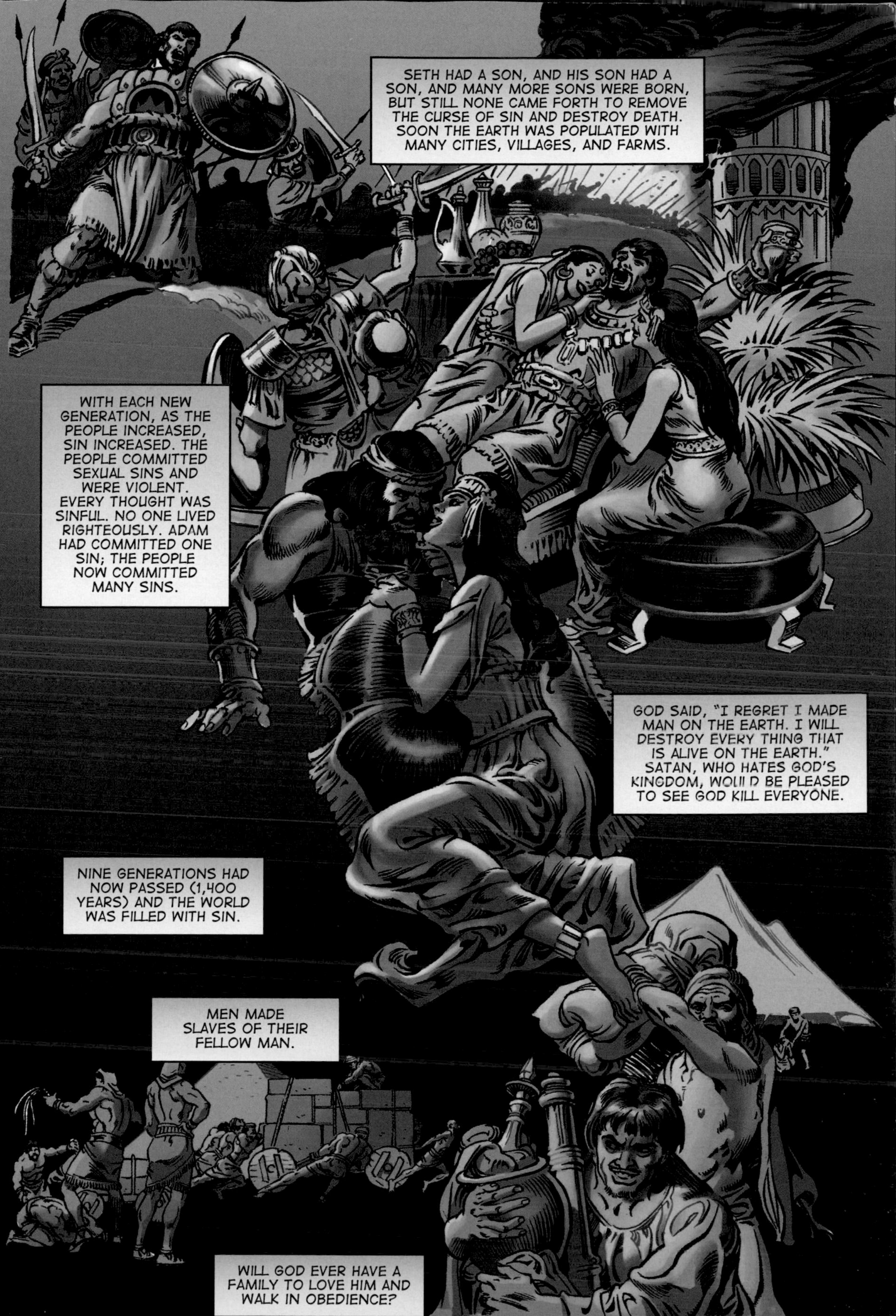
SETH HAD A SON, AND HIS SON HAD A SON, AND MANY MORE SONS WERE BORN, BUT STILL NONE CAME FORTH TO REMOVE THE CURSE OF SIN AND DESTROY DEATH. SOON THE EARTH WAS POPULATED WITH MANY CITIES, VILLAGES, AND FARMS.
WITH EACH NEW GENERATION, AS THE PEOPLE INCREASED, SIN INCREASED. THE PEOPLE COMMITTED SEXUAL SINS AND WERE VIOLENT. EVERY THOUGHT WAS SINFUL. NO ONE LIVED RIGHTEOUSLY. ADAM HAD COMMITTED ONE SIN; THE PEOPLE NOW COMMITTED MANY SINS.
GOD SAID, "I REGRET I MADE MAN ON THE EARTH. I WILL DESTROY EVERY THING THAT IS ALIVE ON THE EARTH." SATAN, WHO HATES GOD'S KINGDOM, WOULD BE PLEASED TO SEE GOD KILL EVERYONE.
NINE GENERATIONS HAD NOW PASSED (1,400 YEARS) AND THE WORLD WAS FILLED WITH SIN.
MEN MADE SLAVES OF THEIR FELLOW MAN.
WILL GOD EVER HAVE A FAMILY TO LOVE HIM AND WALK IN OBEDIENCE?

GENESIS 6:5-7; ROMANS 5:12

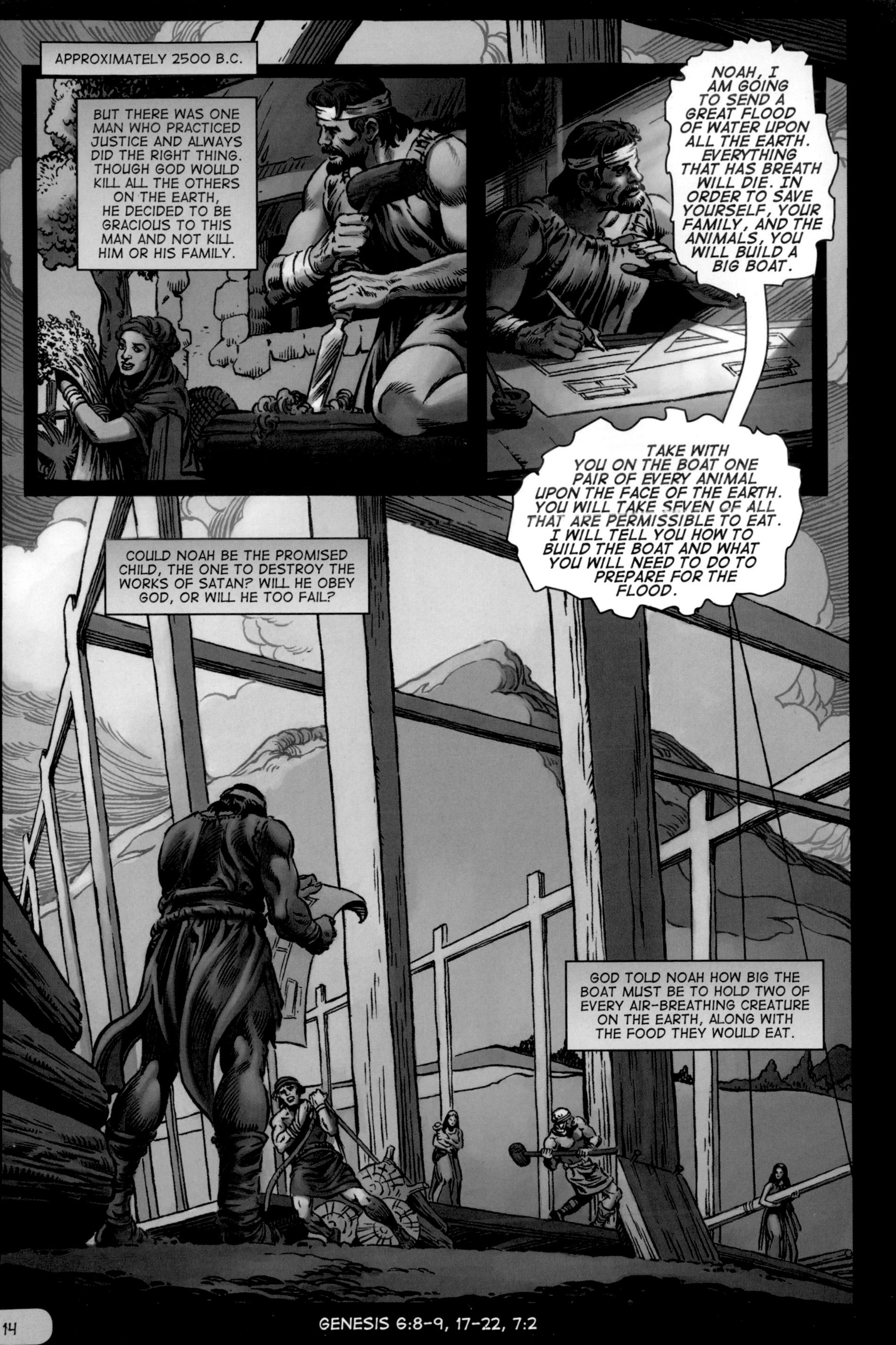
APPROXIMATELY 2500 B.C.
BUT THERE WAS ONE MAN WHO PRACTICED JUSTICE AND ALWAYS DID THE RIGHT THING. THOUGH GOD WOULD KILL ALL THE OTHERS ON THE EARTH, HE DECIDED TO BE GRACIOUS TO THIS MAN AND NOT KILL HIM OR HIS FAMILY.
NOAH, I AM GOING TO SEND A GREAT FLOOD OF WATER UPON ALL THE EARTH. EVERYTHING THAT HAS BREATH WILL DIE. IN ORDER TO SAVE YOURSELF, YOUR FAMILY, AND THE ANIMALS, YOU WILL BUILD A BIG BOAT.
TAKE WITH YOU ON THE BOAT ONE PAIR OF EVERY ANIMAL UPON THE FACE OF THE EARTH. YOU WILL TAKE SEVEN OF ALL THAT ARE PERMISSIBLE TO EAT. I WILL TELL YOU HOW TO BUILD THE BOAT AND WHAT YOU WILL NEED TO DO TO PREPARE FOR THE FLOOD.
COULD NOAH BE THE PROMISED CHILD, THE ONE TO DESTROY THE WORKS OF SATAN? WILL HE OBEY GOD, OR WILL HE TOO FAIL?
GOD TOLD NOAH HOW BIG THE BOAT MUST BE TO HOLD TWO OF EVERY AIR-BREATHING CREATURE ON THE EARTH, ALONG WITH THE FOOD THEY WOULD EAT.

GENESIS 6:8-9, 17-22, 7:2

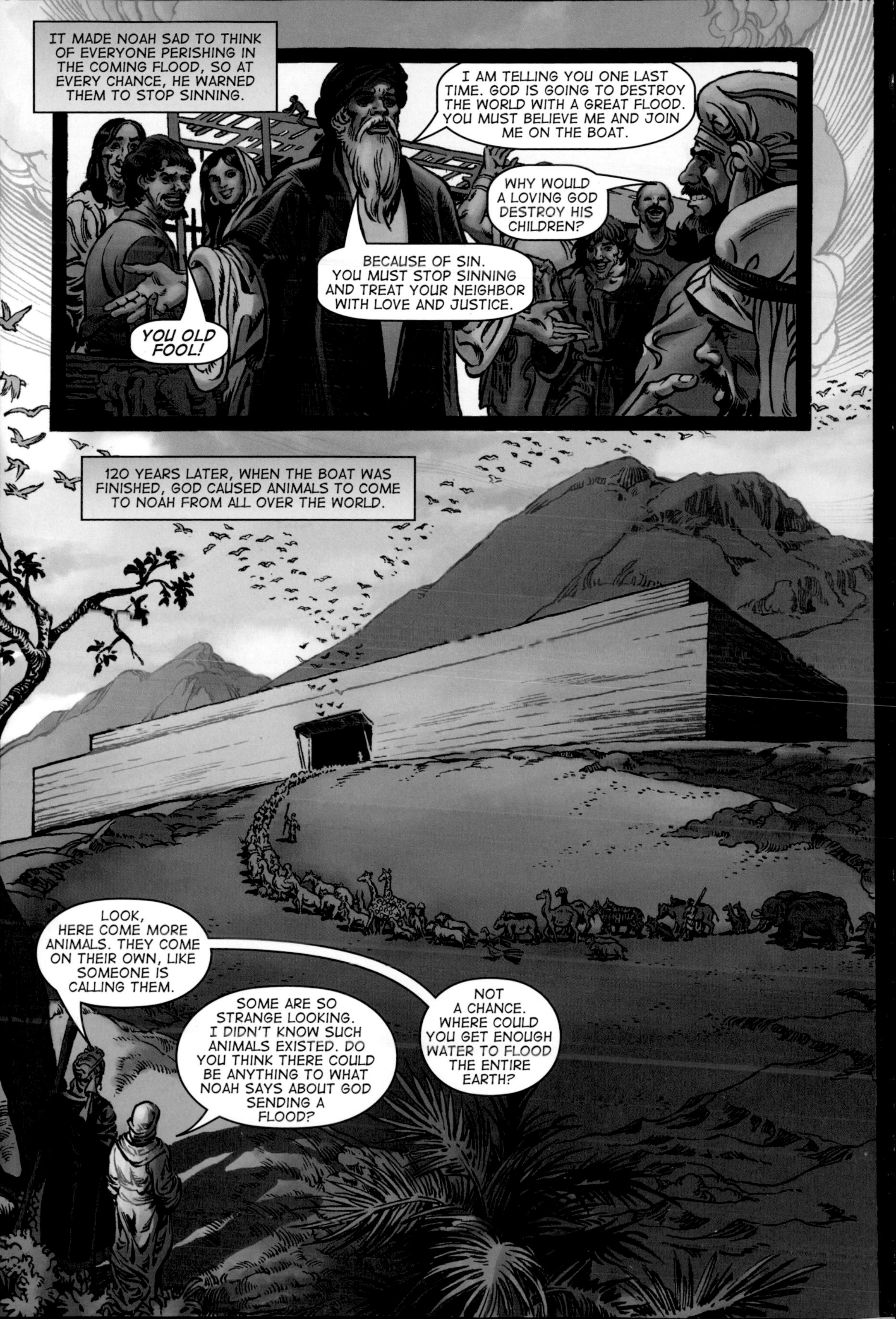
IT MADE NOAH SAD TO THINK OF EVERYONE PERISHING IN THE COMING FLOOD, SO AT EVERY CHANCE, HE WARNED THEM TO STOP SINNING.
I AM TELLING YOU ONE LAST TIME. GOD IS GOING TO DESTROY THE WORLD WITH A GREAT FLOOD. YOU MUST BELIEVE ME AND JOIN ME ON THE BOAT.
WHY WOULD A LOVING GOD DESTROY HIS CHILDREN?
BECAUSE OF SIN. YOU MUST STOP SINNING AND TREAT YOUR NEIGHBOR WITH LOVE AND JUSTICE.
YOU OLD FOOL!
120 YEARS LATER, WHEN THE BOAT WAS FINISHED, GOD CAUSED ANIMALS TO COME TO NOAH FROM ALL OVER THE WORLD.
LOOK, HERE COME MORE ANIMALS. THEY COME ON THEIR OWN, LIKE SOMEONE IS CALLING THEM.
SOME ARE SO STRANGE LOOKING. I DIDN'T KNOW SUCH ANIMALS EXISTED. DO YOU THINK THERE COULD BE ANYTHING TO WHAT NOAH SAYS ABOUT GOD SENDING A FLOOD?
NOT A CHANCE. WHERE COULD YOU GET ENOUGH WATER TO FLOOD THE ENTIRE EARTH?

GENESIS 7:7–9; 2 PETER 2:5

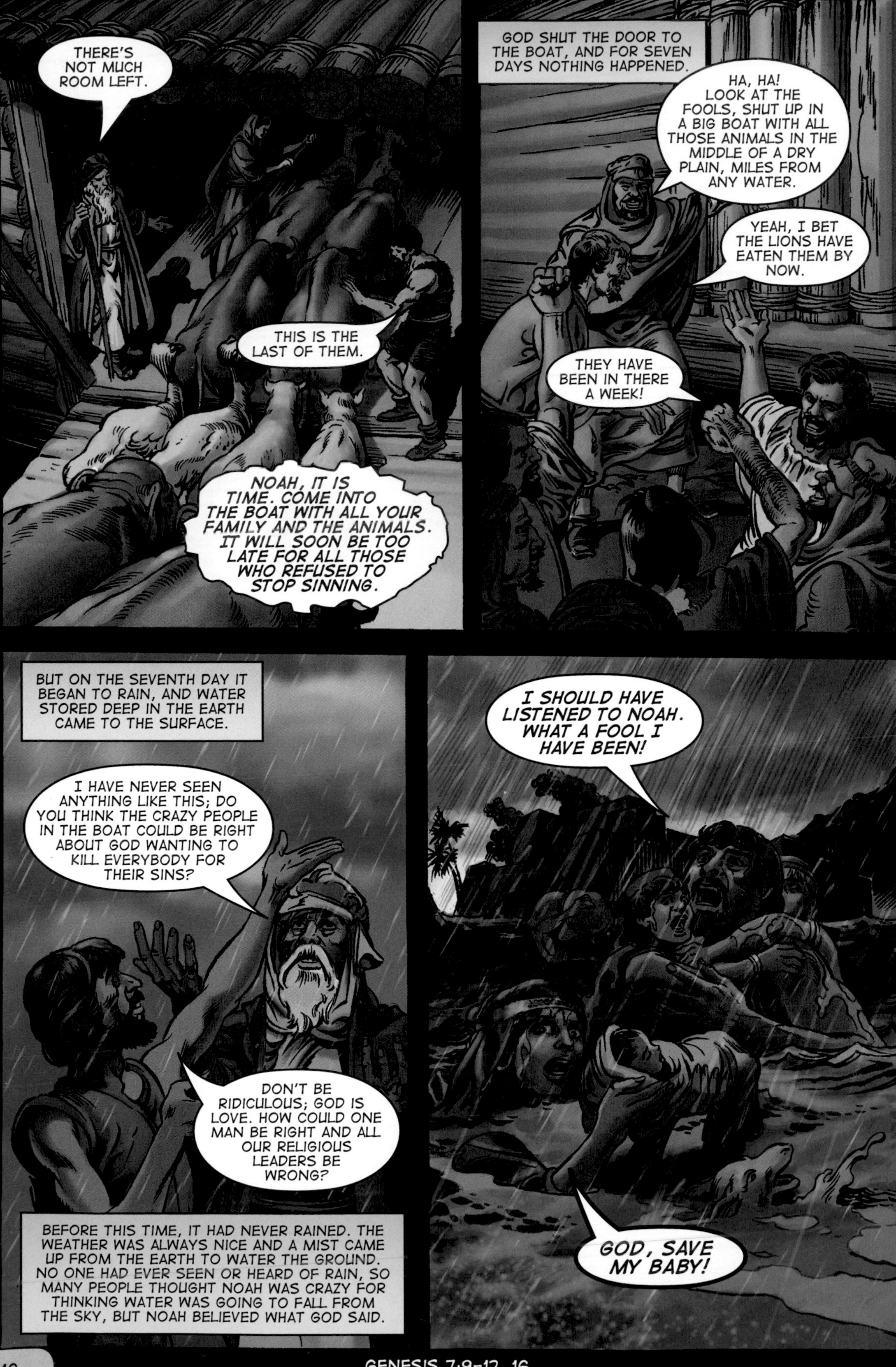
THERE'S NOT MUCH ROOM LEFT.
THIS IS THE LAST OF THEM.
NOAH, IT IS TIME. COME INTO THE BOAT WITH ALL YOUR FAMILY AND THE ANIMALS. IT WILL SOON BE TOO LATE FOR ALL THOSE WHO REFUSED TO STOP SINNING.
GOD SHUT THE DOOR TO THE BOAT, AND FOR SEVEN DAYS NOTHING HAPPENED.
HA, HA! LOOK AT THE FOOLS, SHUT UP IN A BIG BOAT WITH ALL THOSE ANIMALS IN THE MIDDLE OF A DRY PLAIN, MILES FROM ANY WATER.
YEAH, I BET THE LIONS HAVE EATEN THEM BY NOW.
THEY HAVE BEEN IN THERE A WEEK!
BUT ON THE SEVENTH DAY IT BEGAN TO RAIN, AND WATER STORED DEEP IN THE EARTH CAME TO THE SURFACE.
I HAVE NEVER SEEN ANYTHING LIKE THIS; DO YOU THINK THE CRAZY PEOPLE IN THE BOAT COULD BE RIGHT ABOUT GOD WANTING TO KILL EVERYBODY FOR THEIR SINS?
DON'T BE RIDICULOUS; GOD IS LOVE. HOW COULD ONE MAN BE RIGHT AND ALL OUR RELIGIOUS LEADERS BE WRONG?
BEFORE THIS TIME, IT HAD NEVER RAINED. THE WEATHER WAS ALWAYS NICE AND A MIST CAME UP FROM THE EARTH TO WATER THE GROUND. NO ONE HAD EVER SEEN OR HEARD OF RAIN, SO MANY PEOPLE THOUGHT NOAH WAS CRAZY FOR THINKING WATER WAS GOING TO FALL FROM THE SKY, BUT NOAH BELIEVED WHAT GOD SAID.
I SHOULD HAVE LISTENED TO NOAH. WHAT A FOOL I HAVE BEEN!
GOD, SAVE MY BABY!

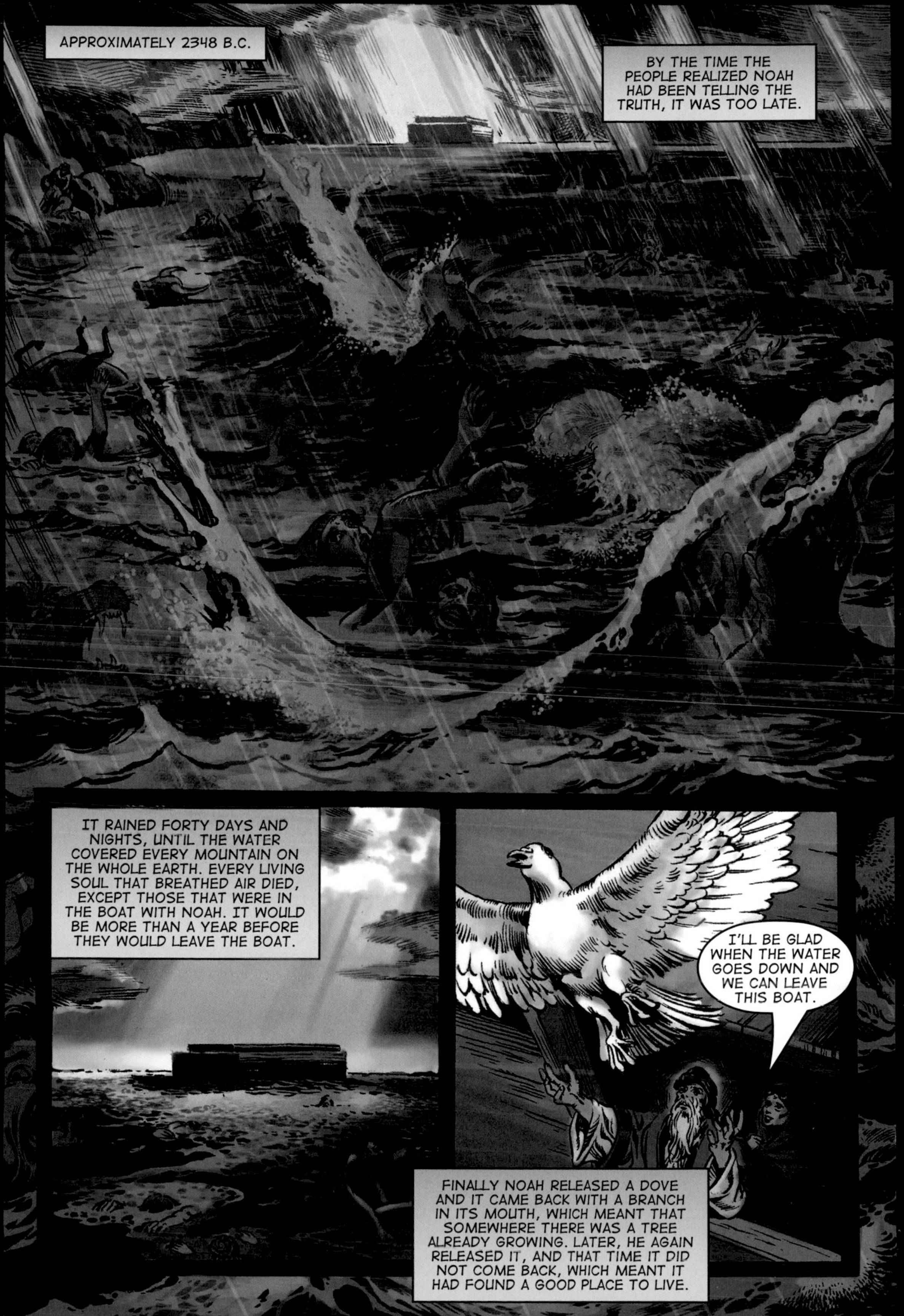
APPROXIMATELY 2348 B.C.
BY THE TIME THE PEOPLE REALIZED NOAH HAD BEEN TELLING THE TRUTH, IT WAS TOO LATE.
IT RAINED FORTY DAYS AND NIGHTS, UNTIL THE WATER COVERED EVERY MOUNTAIN ON THE WHOLE EARTH. EVERY LIVING SOUL THAT BREATHED AIR DIED, EXCEPT THOSE THAT WERE IN THE BOAT WITH NOAH. IT WOULD BE MORE THAN A YEAR BEFORE THEY WOULD LEAVE THE BOAT.
I'LL BE GLAD WHEN THE WATER GOES DOWN AND WE CAN LEAVE THIS BOAT.
FINALLY NOAH RELEASED A DOVE AND IT CAME BACK WITH A BRANCH IN ITS MOUTH, WHICH MEANT THAT SOMEWHERE THERE WAS A TREE ALREADY GROWING. LATER, HE AGAIN RELEASED IT, AND THAT TIME IT DID NOT COME BACK, WHICH MEANT IT HAD FOUND A GOOD PLACE TO LIVE.

GENESIS 7:12, 19–23, 8:9–12

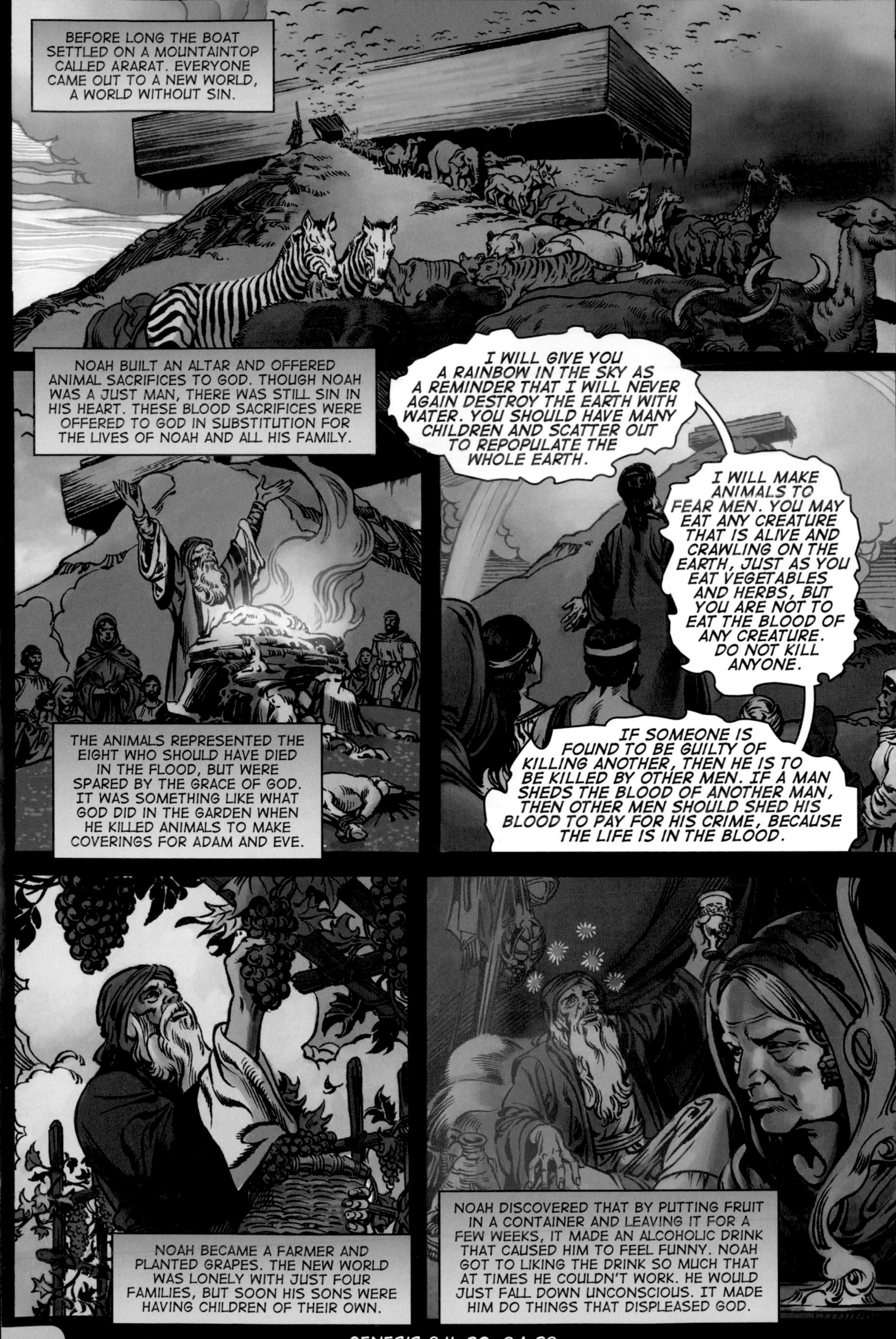
BEFORE LONG THE BOAT SETTLED ON A MOUNTAINTOP CALLED ARARAT. EVERYONE CAME OUT TO A NEW WORLD, A WORLD WITHOUT SIN.
NOAH BUILT AN ALTAR AND OFFERED ANIMAL SACRIFICES TO GOD. THOUGH NOAH WAS A JUST MAN, THERE WAS STILL SIN IN HIS HEART. THESE BLOOD SACRIFICES WERE OFFERED TO GOD IN SUBSTITUTION FOR THE LIVES OF NOAH AND ALL HIS FAMILY.
THE ANIMALS REPRESENTED THE EIGHT WHO SHOULD HAVE DIED IN THE FLOOD, BUT WERE SPARED BY THE GRACE OF GOD. IT WAS SOMETHING LIKE WHAT GOD DID IN THE GARDEN WHEN HE KILLED ANIMALS TO MAKE COVERINGS FOR ADAM AND EVE.
I WILL GIVE YOU A RAINBOW IN THE SKY AS A REMINDER THAT I WILL NEVER AGAIN DESTROY THE EARTH WITH WATER. YOU SHOULD HAVE MANY CHILDREN AND SCATTER OUT TO REPOPULATE THE WHOLE EARTH.
I WILL MAKE ANIMALS TO FEAR MEN. YOU MAY EAT ANY CREATURE THAT IS ALIVE AND CRAWLING ON THE EARTH, JUST AS YOU EAT VEGETABLES AND HERBS, BUT YOU ARE NOT TO EAT THE BLOOD OF ANY CREATURE. DO NOT KILL ANYONE.
IF SOMEONE IS FOUND TO BE GUILTY OF KILLING ANOTHER, THEN HE IS TO BE KILLED BY OTHER MEN. IF A MAN SHEDS THE BLOOD OF ANOTHER MAN, THEN OTHER MEN SHOULD SHED HIS BLOOD TO PAY FOR HIS CRIME, BECAUSE THE LIFE IS IN THE BLOOD.
NOAH BECAME A FARMER AND PLANTED GRAPES. THE NEW WORLD WAS LONELY WITH JUST FOUR FAMILIES, BUT SOON HIS SONS WERE HAVING CHILDREN OF THEIR OWN.
NOAH DISCOVERED THAT BY PUTTING FRUIT IN A CONTAINER AND LEAVING IT FOR A FEW WEEKS, IT MADE AN ALCOHOLIC DRINK THAT CAUSED HIM TO FEEL FUNNY. NOAH GOT TO LIKING THE DRINK SO MUCH THAT AT TIMES HE COULDN'T WORK. HE WOULD JUST FALL DOWN UNCONSCIOUS. IT MADE HIM DO THINGS THAT DISPLEASED GOD.

GENESIS 8:4, 20, 9:1-29

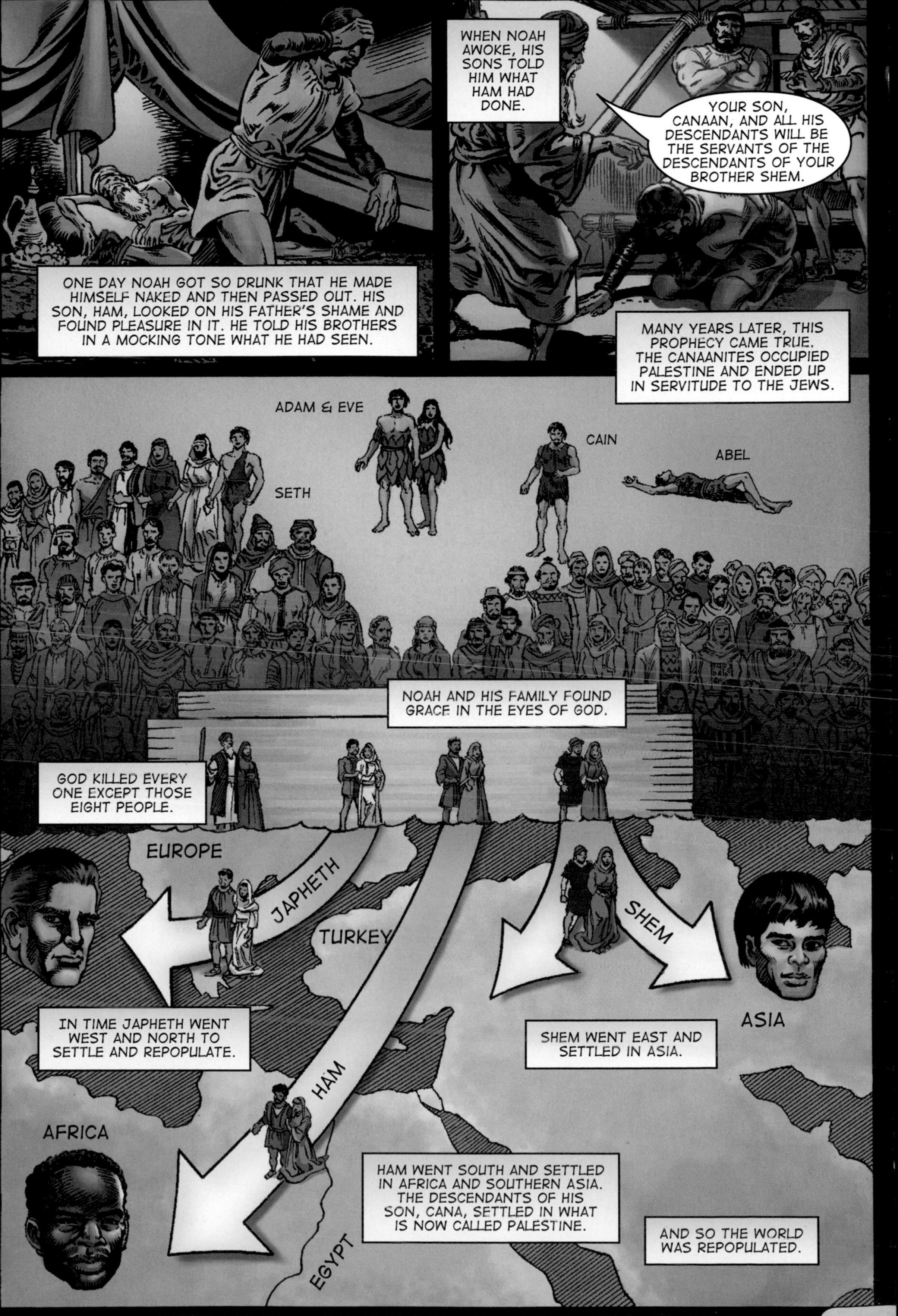
ONE DAY NOAH GOT SO DRUNK THAT HE MADE HIMSELF NAKED AND THEN PASSED OUT. HIS SON, HAM, LOOKED ON HIS FATHER'S SHAME AND FOUND PLEASURE IN IT. HE TOLD HIS BROTHERS IN A MOCKING TONE WHAT HE HAD SEEN.
WHEN NOAH AWOKE, HIS SONS TOLD HIM WHAT HAM HAD DONE.
YOUR SON, CANAAN, AND ALL HIS DESCENDANTS WILL BE THE SERVANTS OF THE DESCENDANTS OF YOUR BROTHER SHEM.
MANY YEARS LATER, THIS PROPHECY CAME TRUE. THE CANAANITES OCCUPIED PALESTINE AND ENDED UP IN SERVITUDE TO THE JEWS.
ADAM & EVE
CAIN
ABEL
SETH
NOAH AND HIS FAMILY FOUND GRACE IN THE EYES OF GOD.
GOD KILLED EVERY ONE EXCEPT THOSE EIGHT PEOPLE.
EUROPE
JAPHETH
TURKEY
SHEM
ASIA
IN TIME JAPHETH WENT WEST AND NORTH TO SETTLE AND REPOPULATE.
SHEM WENT EAST AND SETTLED IN ASIA.
HAM
AFRICA
HAM WENT SOUTH AND SETTLED IN AFRICA AND SOUTHERN ASIA. THE DESCENDANTS OF HIS SON, CANA, SETTLED IN WHAT IS NOW CALLED PALESTINE.
AND SO THE WORLD WAS REPOPULATED.
EGYPT

GENESIS 9:21-27; 1 CHRONICLES 4:40; PSALMS 78:51, 105:23,27, 106:22

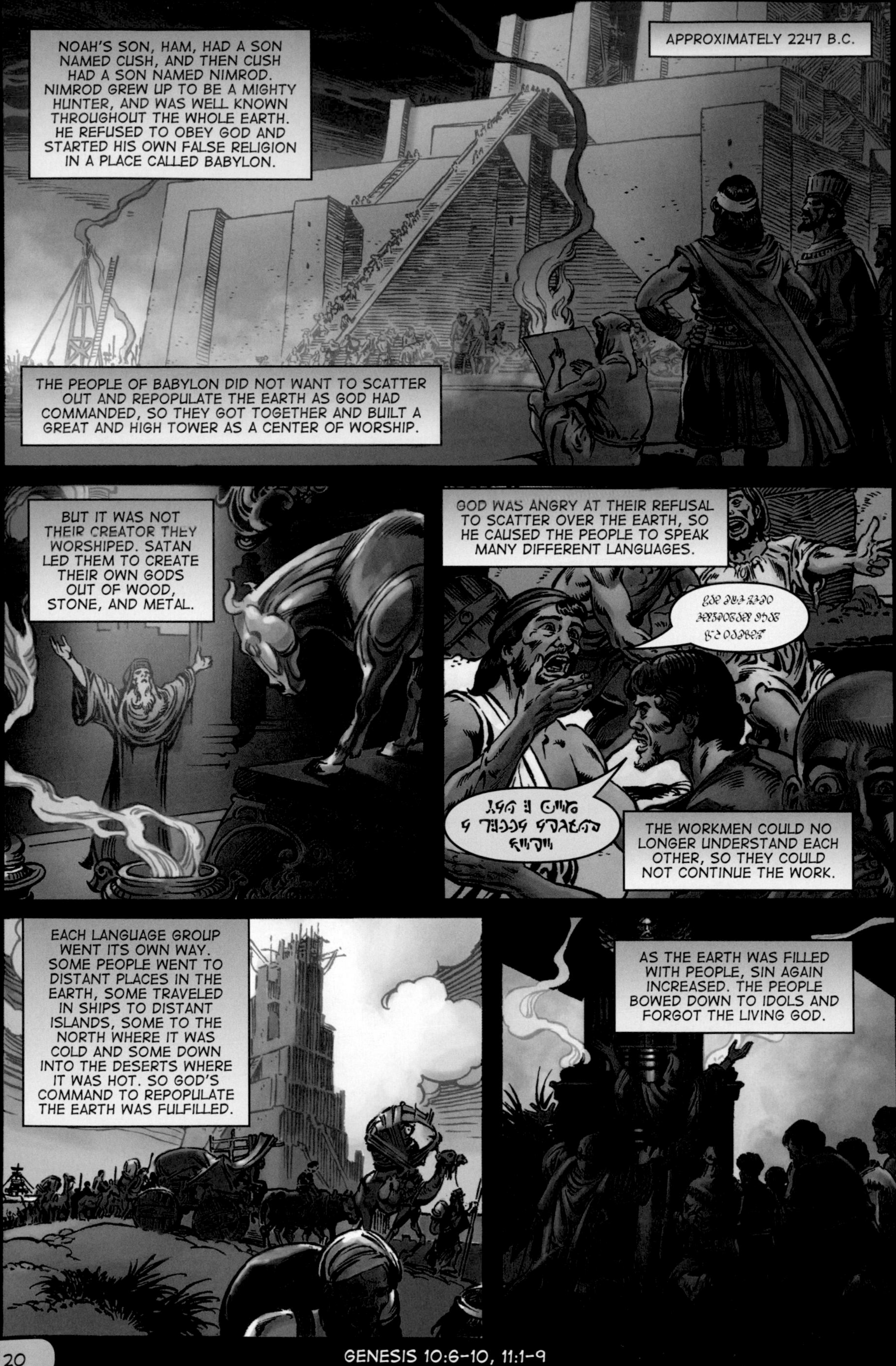
APPROXIMATELY 2247 B.C.
NOAH'S SON, HAM, HAD A SON NAMED CUSH, AND THEN CUSH HAD A SON NAMED NIMROD. NIMROD GREW UP TO BE A MIGHTY HUNTER, AND WAS WELL KNOWN THROUGHOUT THE WHOLE EARTH. HE REFUSED TO OBEY GOD AND STARTED HIS OWN FALSE RELIGION IN A PLACE CALLED BABYLON.
THE PEOPLE OF BABYLON DID NOT WANT TO SCATTER OUT AND REPOPULATE THE EARTH AS GOD HAD COMMANDED, SO THEY GOT TOGETHER AND BUILT A GREAT AND HIGH TOWER AS A CENTER OF WORSHIP.
BUT IT WAS NOT THEIR CREATOR THEY WORSHIPED. SATAN LED THEM TO CREATE THEIR OWN GODS OUT OF WOOD, STONE, AND METAL.
GOD WAS ANGRY AT THEIR REFUSAL TO SCATTER OVER THE EARTH, SO HE CAUSED THE PEOPLE TO SPEAK MANY DIFFERENT LANGUAGES.
THE WORKMEN COULD NO LONGER UNDERSTAND EACH OTHER, SO THEY COULD NOT CONTINUE THE WORK.
EACH LANGUAGE GROUP WENT ITS OWN WAY. SOME PEOPLE WENT TO DISTANT PLACES IN THE EARTH, SOME TRAVELED IN SHIPS TO DISTANT ISLANDS, SOME TO THE NORTH WHERE IT WAS COLD AND SOME DOWN INTO THE DESERTS WHERE IT WAS HOT. SO GOD'S COMMAND TO REPOPULATE THE EARTH WAS FULFILLED.
AS THE EARTH WAS FILLED WITH PEOPLE, SIN AGAIN INCREASED. THE PEOPLE BOWED DOWN TO IDOLS AND FORGOT THE LIVING GOD.

GENESIS 10:6-10, 11:1-9

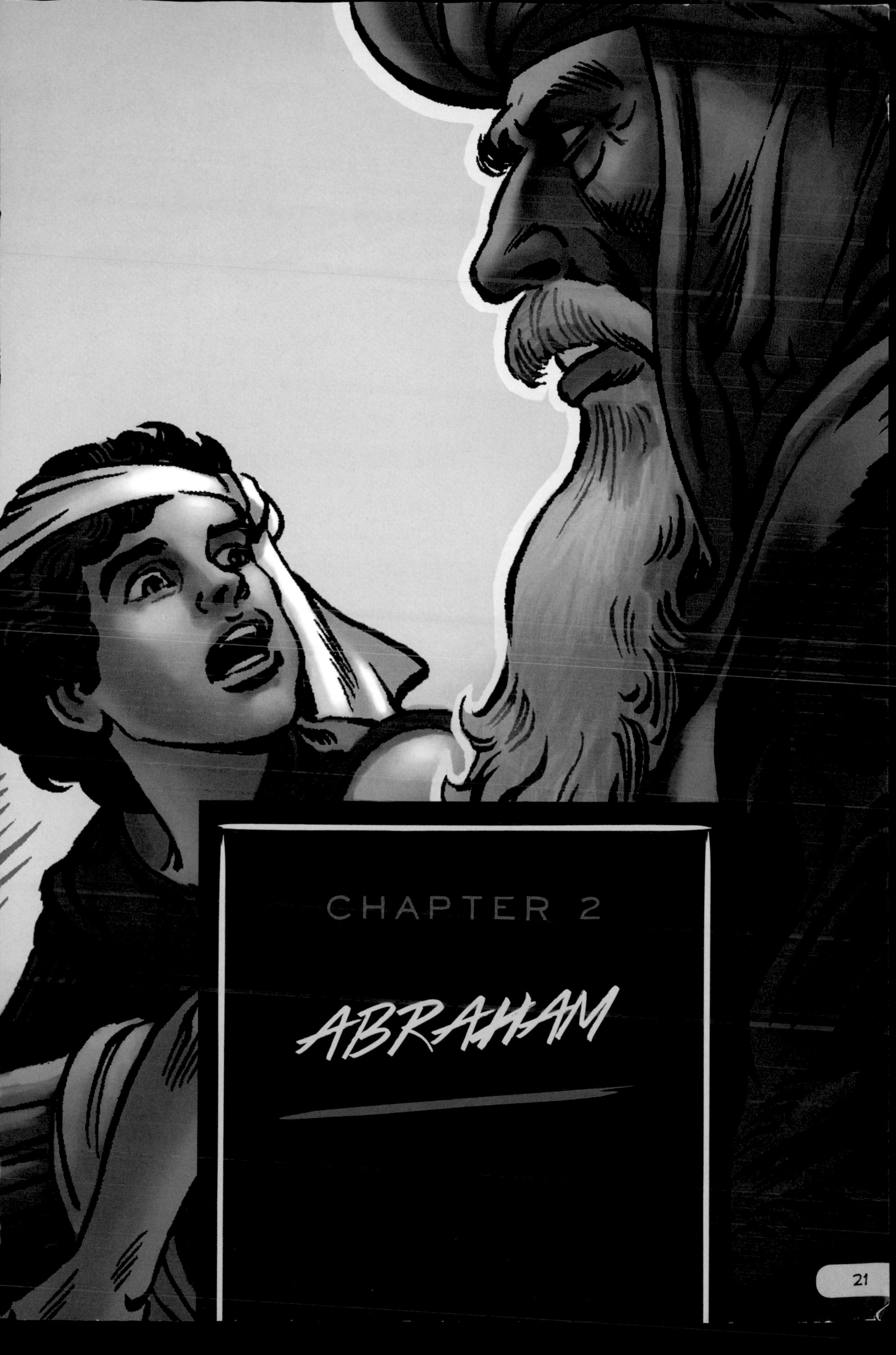

CHAPTER 2

ABRAHAM

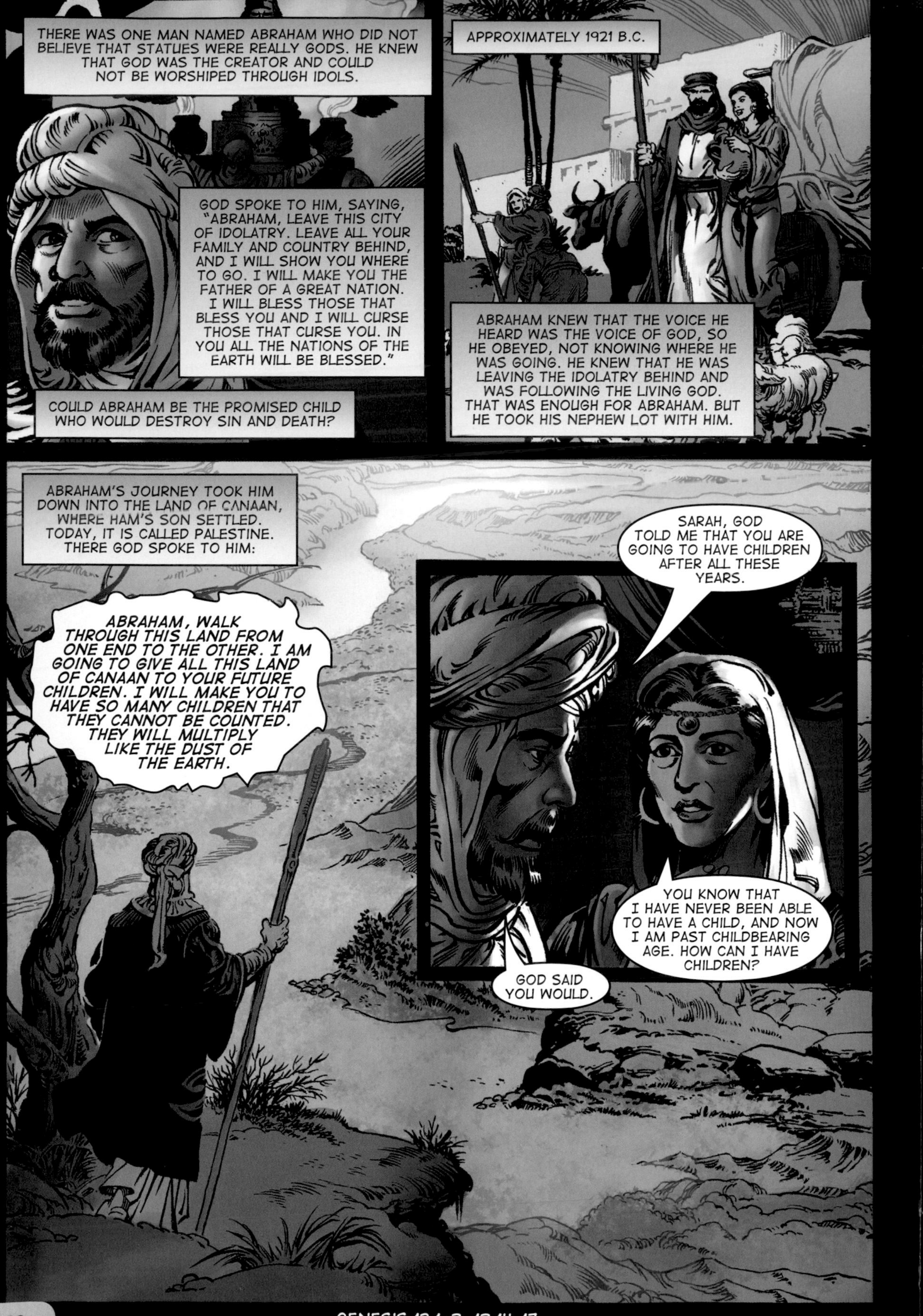
THERE WAS ONE MAN NAMED ABRAHAM WHO DID NOT BELIEVE THAT STATUES WERE REALLY GODS. HE KNEW THAT GOD WAS THE CREATOR AND COULD NOT BE WORSHIPED THROUGH IDOLS.
GOD SPOKE TO HIM, SAYING, "ABRAHAM, LEAVE THIS CITY OF IDOLATRY. LEAVE ALL YOUR FAMILY AND COUNTRY BEHIND, AND I WILL SHOW YOU WHERE TO GO. I WILL MAKE YOU THE FATHER OF A GREAT NATION. I WILL BLESS THOSE THAT BLESS YOU AND I WILL CURSE THOSE THAT CURSE YOU. IN YOU ALL THE NATIONS OF THE EARTH WILL BE BLESSED."
COULD ABRAHAM BE THE PROMISED CHILD WHO WOULD DESTROY SIN AND DEATH?
APPROXIMATELY 1921 B.C.
ABRAHAM KNEW THAT THE VOICE HE HEARD WAS THE VOICE OF GOD, SO HE OBEYED, NOT KNOWING WHERE HE WAS GOING. HE KNEW THAT HE WAS LEAVING THE IDOLATRY BEHIND AND WAS FOLLOWING THE LIVING GOD. THAT WAS ENOUGH FOR ABRAHAM. BUT HE TOOK HIS NEPHEW LOT WITH HIM.
ABRAHAM'S JOURNEY TOOK HIM DOWN INTO THE LAND OF CANAAN, WHERE HAM'S SON SETTLED. TODAY, IT IS CALLED PALESTINE. THERE GOD SPOKE TO HIM:
ABRAHAM, WALK THROUGH THIS LAND FROM ONE END TO THE OTHER. I AM GOING TO GIVE ALL THIS LAND OF CANAAN TO YOUR FUTURE CHILDREN. I WILL MAKE YOU TO HAVE SO MANY CHILDREN THAT THEY CANNOT BE COUNTED. THEY WILL MULTIPLY LIKE THE DUST OF THE EARTH.
SARAH, GOD TOLD ME THAT YOU ARE GOING TO HAVE CHILDREN AFTER ALL THESE YEARS.
YOU KNOW THAT I HAVE NEVER BEEN ABLE TO HAVE A CHILD, AND NOW I AM PAST CHILDBEARING AGE. HOW CAN I HAVE CHILDREN?
GOD SAID YOU WOULD.

GENESIS 12:1-3, 13:14-17

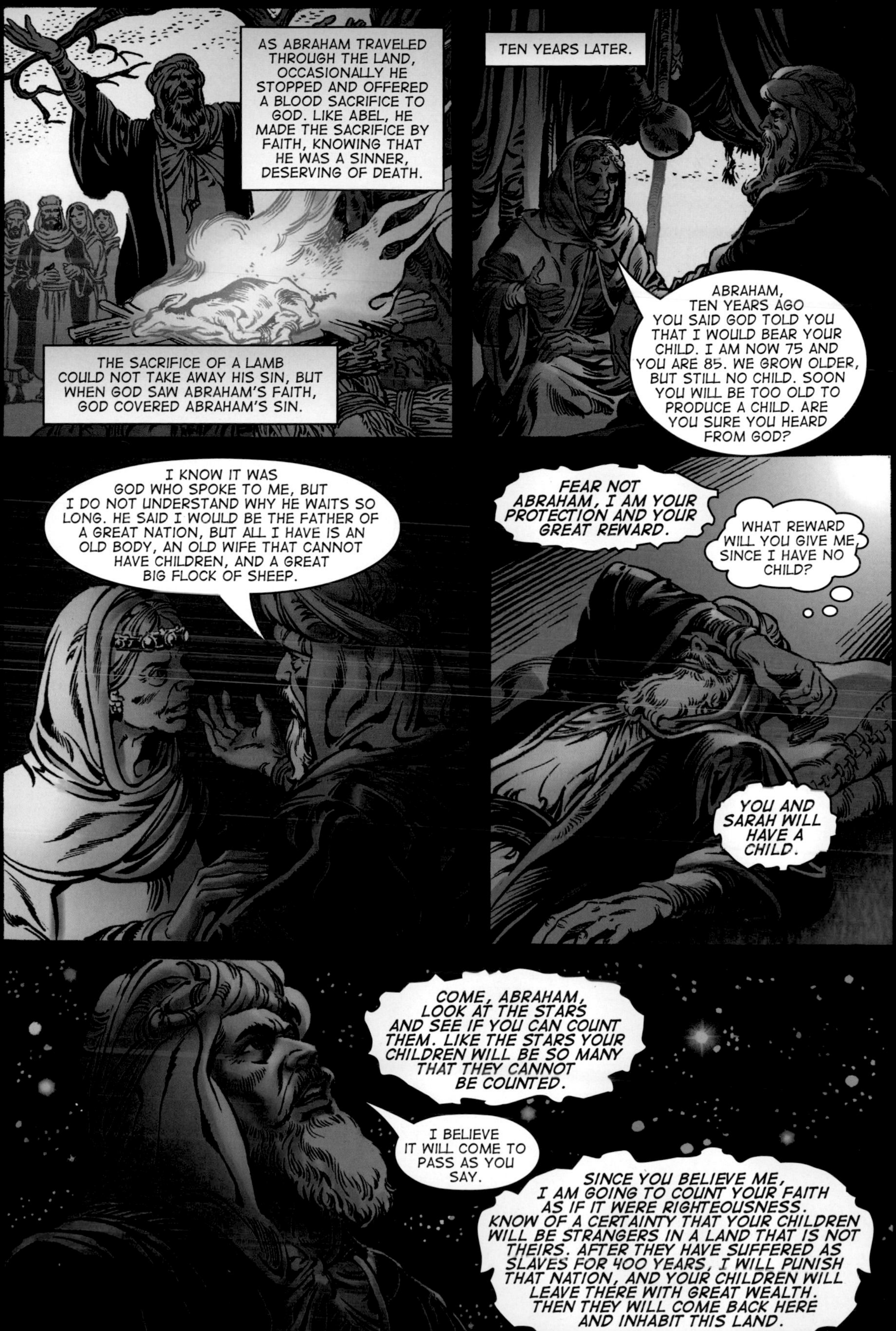
AS ABRAHAM TRAVELED THROUGH THE LAND, OCCASIONALLY HE STOPPED AND OFFERED A BLOOD SACRIFICE TO GOD. LIKE ABEL, HE MADE THE SACRIFICE BY FAITH, KNOWING THAT HE WAS A SINNER, DESERVING OF DEATH.
THE SACRIFICE OF A LAMB COULD NOT TAKE AWAY HIS SIN, BUT WHEN GOD SAW ABRAHAM'S FAITH, GOD COVERED ABRAHAM'S SIN.
TEN YEARS LATER.
ABRAHAM, TEN YEARS AGO YOU SAID GOD TOLD YOU THAT I WOULD BEAR YOUR CHILD. I AM NOW 75 AND YOU ARE 85. WE GROW OLDER, BUT STILL NO CHILD. SOON YOU WILL BE TOO OLD TO PRODUCE A CHILD. ARE YOU SURE YOU HEARD FROM GOD?
I KNOW IT WAS GOD WHO SPOKE TO ME, BUT I DO NOT UNDERSTAND WHY HE WAITS SO LONG. HE SAID I WOULD BE THE FATHER OF A GREAT NATION, BUT ALL I HAVE IS AN OLD BODY, AN OLD WIFE THAT CANNOT HAVE CHILDREN, AND A GREAT BIG FLOCK OF SHEEP.
FEAR NOT ABRAHAM, I AM YOUR PROTECTION AND YOUR GREAT REWARD.
WHAT REWARD WILL YOU GIVE ME, SINCE I HAVE NO CHILD?
YOU AND SARAH WILL HAVE A CHILD.
COME, ABRAHAM, LOOK AT THE STARS AND SEE IF YOU CAN COUNT THEM. LIKE THE STARS YOUR CHILDREN WILL BE SO MANY THAT THEY CANNOT BE COUNTED.
I BELIEVE IT WILL COME TO PASS AS YOU SAY.
SINCE YOU BELIEVE ME, I AM GOING TO COUNT YOUR FAITH AS IF IT WERE RIGHTEOUSNESS. KNOW OF A CERTAINTY THAT YOUR CHILDREN WILL BE STRANGERS IN A LAND THAT IS NOT THEIRS. AFTER THEY HAVE SUFFERED AS SLAVES FOR 400 YEARS, I WILL PUNISH THAT NATION, AND YOUR CHILDREN WILL LEAVE THERE WITH GREAT WEALTH. THEN THEY WILL COME BACK HERE AND INHABIT THIS LAND.

GENESIS 15:1-6, 13-14

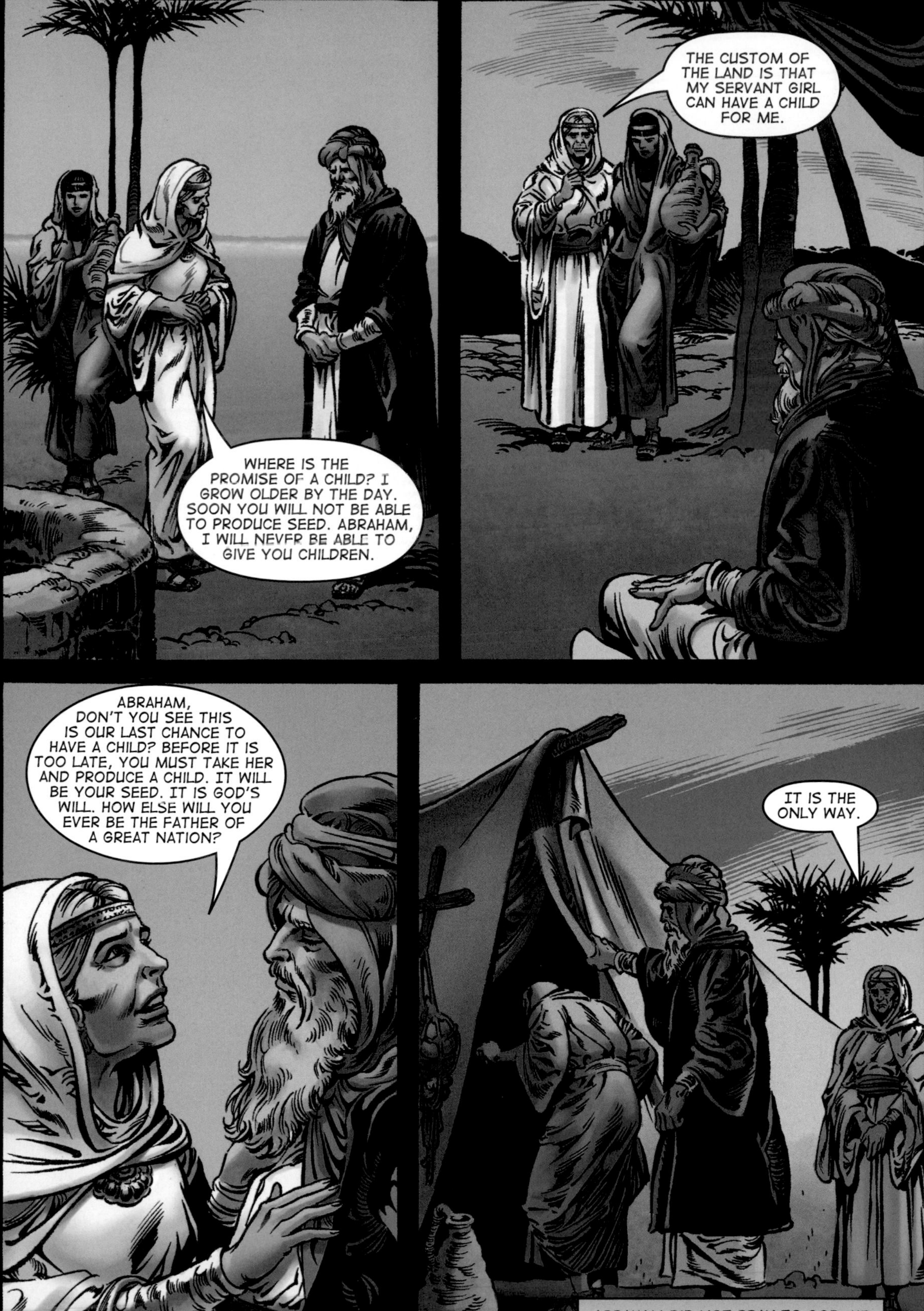
WHERE IS THE PROMISE OF A CHILD? I GROW OLDER BY THE DAY. SOON YOU WILL NOT BE ABLE TO PRODUCE SEED. ABRAHAM, I WILL NEVER BE ABLE TO GIVE YOU CHILDREN.
THE CUSTOM OF THE LAND IS THAT MY SERVANT GIRL CAN HAVE A CHILD FOR ME.
ABRAHAM, DON'T YOU SEE THIS IS OUR LAST CHANCE TO HAVE A CHILD? BEFORE IT IS TOO LATE, YOU MUST TAKE HER AND PRODUCE A CHILD. IT WILL BE YOUR SEED. IT IS GOD'S WILL. HOW ELSE WILL YOU EVER BE THE FATHER OF A GREAT NATION?
IT IS THE ONLY WAY.
ABRAHAM DID NOT PRAY TO GOD. HE FORGOT THE PROMISE OF GOD AND OBEYED THE VOICE OF HIS WIFE.

SEVERAL MONTHS LATER.

I AM GOING TO HAVE ABRAHAM'S CHILD.

WHEN HAGAR KNEW THAT SHE CARRIED ABRAHAM'S CHILD, SHE BECAME PROUD AND DESPISED SARAH. SARAH GREW UNHAPPY WITH JEALOUSY.

SARAH MADE HAGAR WORK HARD AND TREATED HER UNKINDLY. GOD NEVER INTENDED FOR A MAN TO HAVE TWO WIVES OR TO HAVE CHILDREN THROUGH A CONCUBINE.

WHEN YOU ARE FINISHED WITH THE WATER, YOU CAN SPLIT THE FIREWOOD.

HAGAR MADE PLANS TO RUN AWAY.

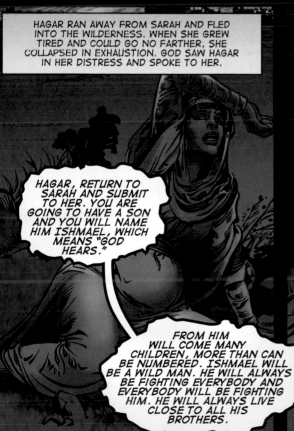

HAGAR RAN AWAY FROM SARAH AND FLED INTO THE WILDERNESS. WHEN SHE GREW TIRED AND COULD GO NO FARTHER, SHE COLLAPSED IN EXHAUSTION. GOD SAW HAGAR IN HER DISTRESS AND SPOKE TO HER.

HAGAR, RETURN TO SARAH AND SUBMIT TO HER. YOU ARE GOING TO HAVE A SON AND YOU WILL NAME HIM ISHMAEL, WHICH MEANS "GOD HEARS."

FROM HIM WILL COME MANY CHILDREN, MORE THAN CAN BE NUMBERED. ISHMAEL WILL BE A WILD MAN. HE WILL ALWAYS BE FIGHTING EVERYBODY AND EVERYBODY WILL BE FIGHTING HIM. HE WILL ALWAYS LIVE CLOSE TO ALL HIS BROTHERS.

HAGAR RETURNED HOME AND IN TIME THE CHILD WAS BORN.

GOD TOLD ME THAT SINCE THIS CHILD IS ABRAHAM'S, HE WOULD BE THE FATHER OF MANY NATIONS.

ISHMAEL LATER BECAME THE FATHER OF ALL ARABIC NATIONS.

GENESIS 16:4-16

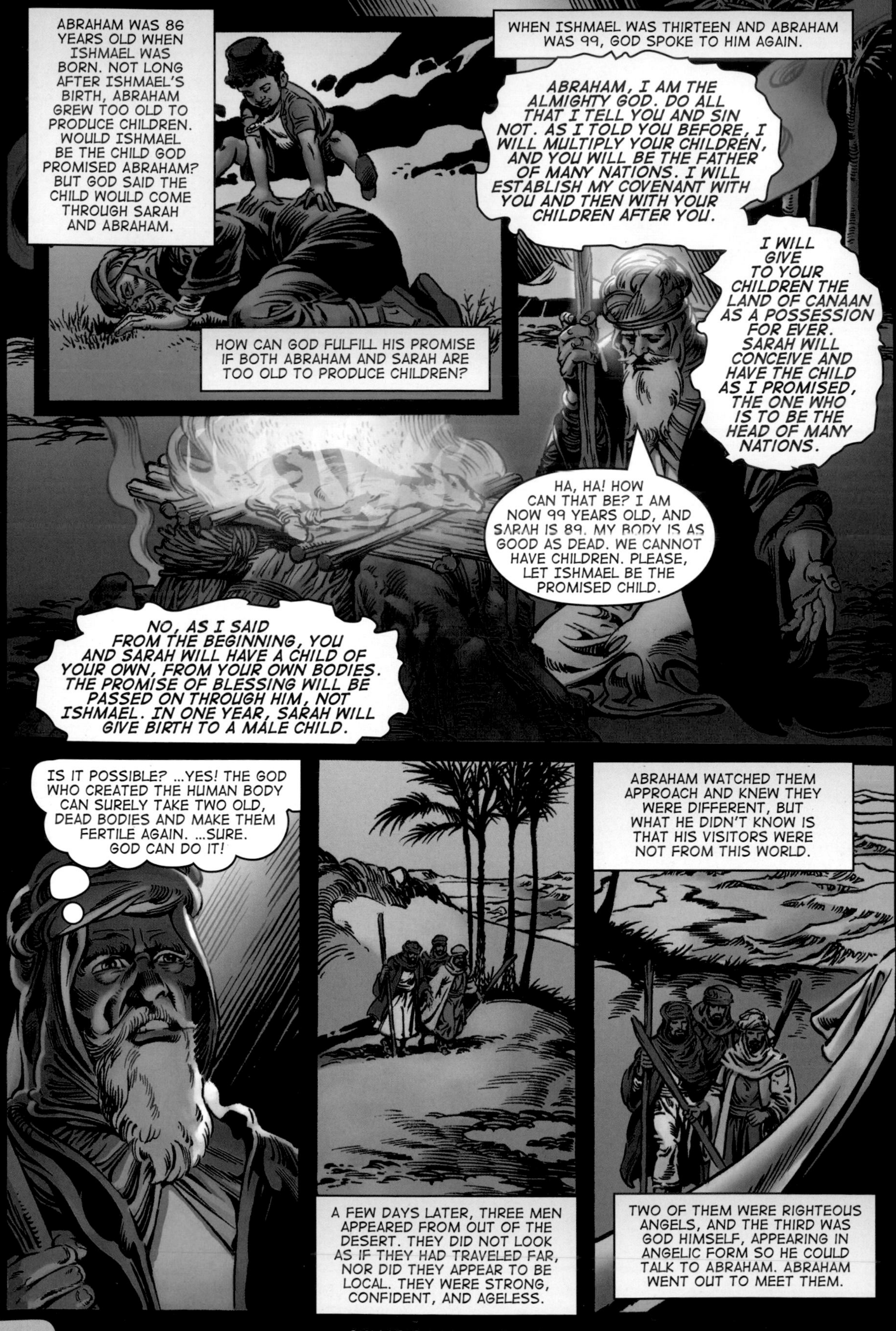

ABRAHAM WAS 86 YEARS OLD WHEN ISHMAEL WAS BORN. NOT LONG AFTER ISHMAEL'S BIRTH, ABRAHAM GREW TOO OLD TO PRODUCE CHILDREN. WOULD ISHMAEL BE THE CHILD GOD PROMISED ABRAHAM? BUT GOD SAID THE CHILD WOULD COME THROUGH SARAH AND ABRAHAM.
HOW CAN GOD FULFILL HIS PROMISE IF BOTH ABRAHAM AND SARAH ARE TOO OLD TO PRODUCE CHILDREN?
WHEN ISHMAEL WAS THIRTEEN AND ABRAHAM WAS 99, GOD SPOKE TO HIM AGAIN.
ABRAHAM, I AM THE ALMIGHTY GOD. DO ALL THAT I TELL YOU AND SIN NOT. AS I TOLD YOU BEFORE, I WILL MULTIPLY YOUR CHILDREN, AND YOU WILL BE THE FATHER OF MANY NATIONS. I WILL ESTABLISH MY COVENANT WITH YOU AND THEN WITH YOUR CHILDREN AFTER YOU.
I WILL GIVE TO YOUR CHILDREN THE LAND OF CANAAN AS A POSSESSION FOR EVER. SARAH WILL CONCEIVE AND HAVE THE CHILD AS I PROMISED, THE ONE WHO IS TO BE THE HEAD OF MANY NATIONS.
HA, HA! HOW CAN THAT BE? I AM NOW 99 YEARS OLD, AND SARAH IS 89. MY BODY IS AS GOOD AS DEAD. WE CANNOT HAVE CHILDREN. PLEASE, LET ISHMAEL BE THE PROMISED CHILD.
NO, AS I SAID FROM THE BEGINNING, YOU AND SARAH WILL HAVE A CHILD OF YOUR OWN, FROM YOUR OWN BODIES. THE PROMISE OF BLESSING WILL BE PASSED ON THROUGH HIM, NOT ISHMAEL. IN ONE YEAR, SARAH WILL GIVE BIRTH TO A MALE CHILD.
IS IT POSSIBLE? ...YES! THE GOD WHO CREATED THE HUMAN BODY CAN SURELY TAKE TWO OLD, DEAD BODIES AND MAKE THEM FERTILE AGAIN. ...SURE. GOD CAN DO IT!
A FEW DAYS LATER, THREE MEN APPEARED FROM OUT OF THE DESERT. THEY DID NOT LOOK AS IF THEY HAD TRAVELED FAR, NOR DID THEY APPEAR TO BE LOCAL. THEY WERE STRONG, CONFIDENT, AND AGELESS.
ABRAHAM WATCHED THEM APPROACH AND KNEW THEY WERE DIFFERENT, BUT WHAT HE DIDN'T KNOW IS THAT HIS VISITORS WERE NOT FROM THIS WORLD.
TWO OF THEM WERE RIGHTEOUS ANGELS, AND THE THIRD WAS GOD HIMSELF, APPEARING IN ANGELIC FORM SO HE COULD TALK TO ABRAHAM. ABRAHAM WENT OUT TO MEET THEM.

GENESIS 17:1-21, 18:1-2

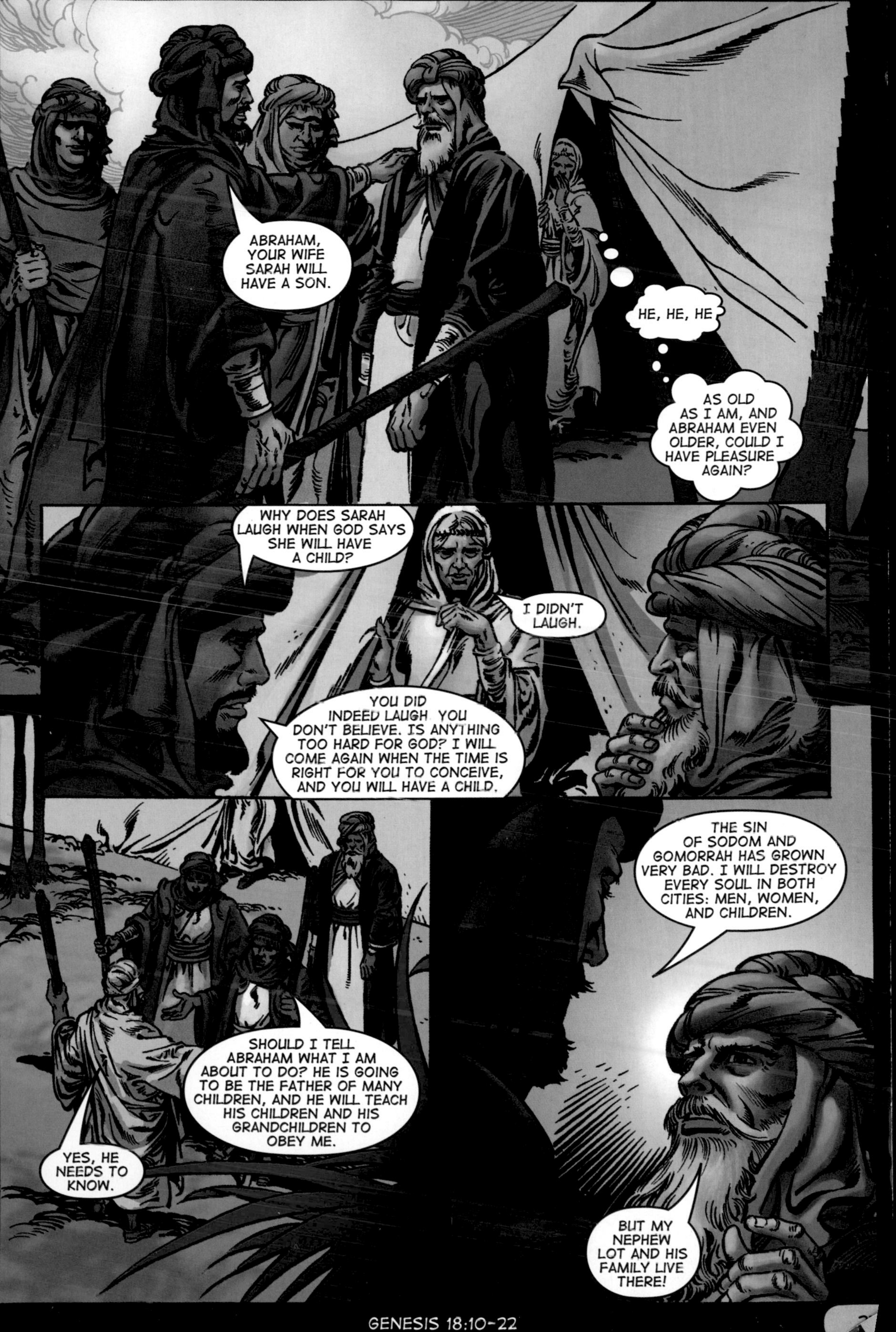
ABRAHAM, YOUR WIFE SARAH WILL HAVE A SON.
HE, HE, HE
AS OLD AS I AM, AND ABRAHAM EVEN OLDER, COULD I HAVE PLEASURE AGAIN?
WHY DOES SARAH LAUGH WHEN GOD SAYS SHE WILL HAVE A CHILD?
I DIDN'T LAUGH.
YOU DID INDEED LAUGH. YOU DON'T BELIEVE. IS ANYTHING TOO HARD FOR GOD? I WILL COME AGAIN WHEN THE TIME IS RIGHT FOR YOU TO CONCEIVE, AND YOU WILL HAVE A CHILD.
SHOULD I TELL ABRAHAM WHAT I AM ABOUT TO DO? HE IS GOING TO BE THE FATHER OF MANY CHILDREN, AND HE WILL TEACH HIS CHILDREN AND HIS GRANDCHILDREN TO OBEY ME.
YES, HE NEEDS TO KNOW.
THE SIN OF SODOM AND GOMORRAH HAS GROWN VERY BAD. I WILL DESTROY EVERY SOUL IN BOTH CITIES: MEN, WOMEN, AND CHILDREN.
BUT MY NEPHEW LOT AND HIS FAMILY LIVE THERE!

GENESIS 18:10-22

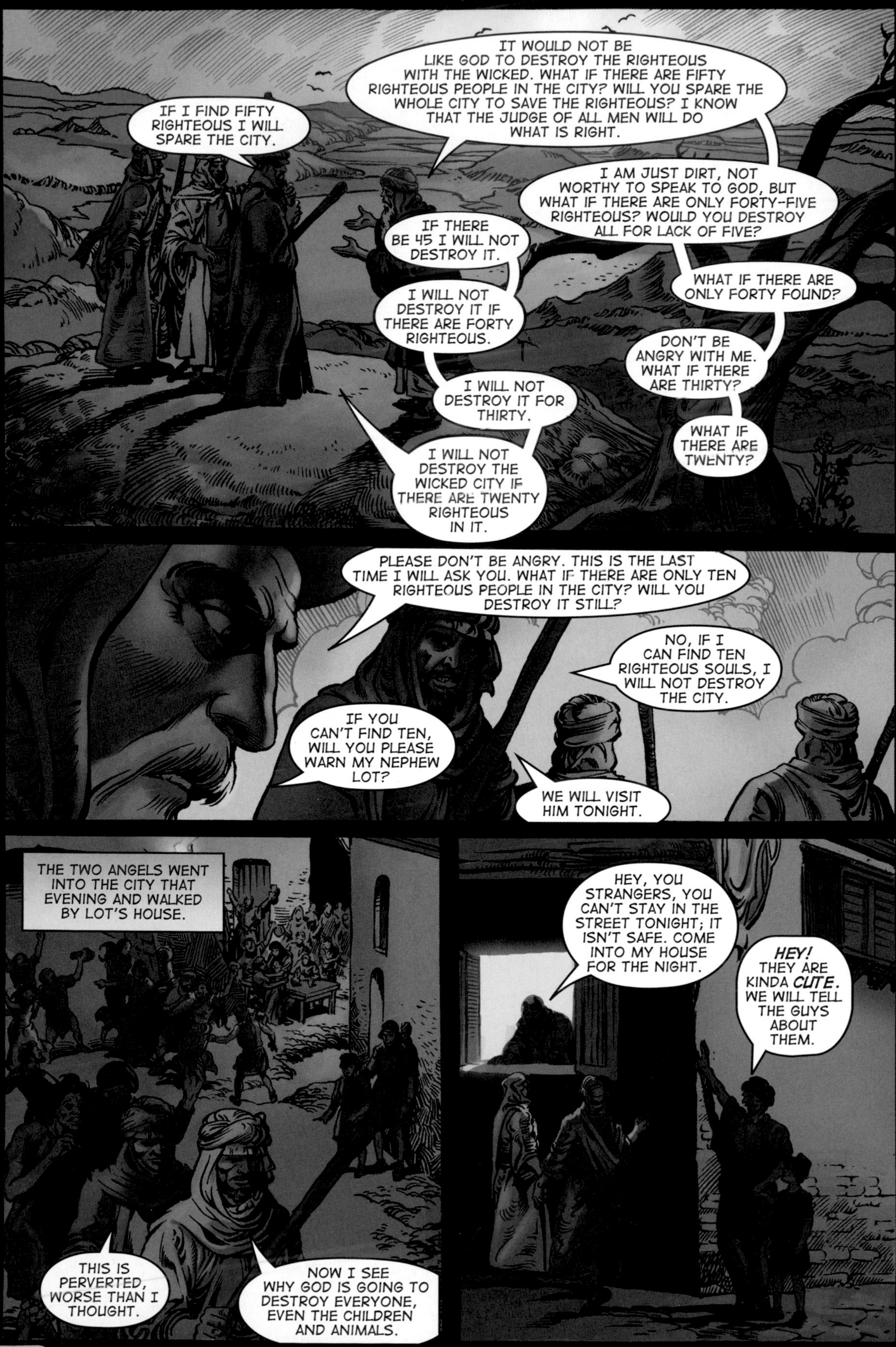
IF I FIND FIFTY RIGHTEOUS I WILL SPARE THE CITY.
IT WOULD NOT BE LIKE GOD TO DESTROY THE RIGHTEOUS WITH THE WICKED. WHAT IF THERE ARE FIFTY RIGHTEOUS PEOPLE IN THE CITY? WILL YOU SPARE THE WHOLE CITY TO SAVE THE RIGHTEOUS? I KNOW THAT THE JUDGE OF ALL MEN WILL DO WHAT IS RIGHT.
I AM JUST DIRT, NOT WORTHY TO SPEAK TO GOD, BUT WHAT IF THERE ARE ONLY FORTY-FIVE RIGHTEOUS? WOULD YOU DESTROY ALL FOR LACK OF FIVE?
IF THERE BE 45 I WILL NOT DESTROY IT.
WHAT IF THERE ARE ONLY FORTY FOUND?
I WILL NOT DESTROY IT IF THERE ARE FORTY RIGHTEOUS.
DON'T BE ANGRY WITH ME. WHAT IF THERE ARE THIRTY?
I WILL NOT DESTROY IT FOR THIRTY.
WHAT IF THERE ARE TWENTY?
I WILL NOT DESTROY THE WICKED CITY IF THERE ARE TWENTY RIGHTEOUS IN IT.
PLEASE DON'T BE ANGRY. THIS IS THE LAST TIME I WILL ASK YOU. WHAT IF THERE ARE ONLY TEN RIGHTEOUS PEOPLE IN THE CITY? WILL YOU DESTROY IT STILL?
NO, IF I CAN FIND TEN RIGHTEOUS SOULS, I WILL NOT DESTROY THE CITY.
IF YOU CAN'T FIND TEN, WILL YOU PLEASE WARN MY NEPHEW LOT?
WE WILL VISIT HIM TONIGHT.
THE TWO ANGELS WENT INTO THE CITY THAT EVENING AND WALKED BY LOT'S HOUSE.
THIS IS PERVERTED, WORSE THAN I THOUGHT.
NOW I SEE WHY GOD IS GOING TO DESTROY EVERYONE, EVEN THE CHILDREN AND ANIMALS.
HEY, YOU STRANGERS, YOU CAN'T STAY IN THE STREET TONIGHT; IT ISN'T SAFE. COME INTO MY HOUSE FOR THE NIGHT.
HEY! THEY ARE KINDA CUTE. WE WILL TELL THE GUYS ABOUT THEM.

GENESIS 18:23–19:2

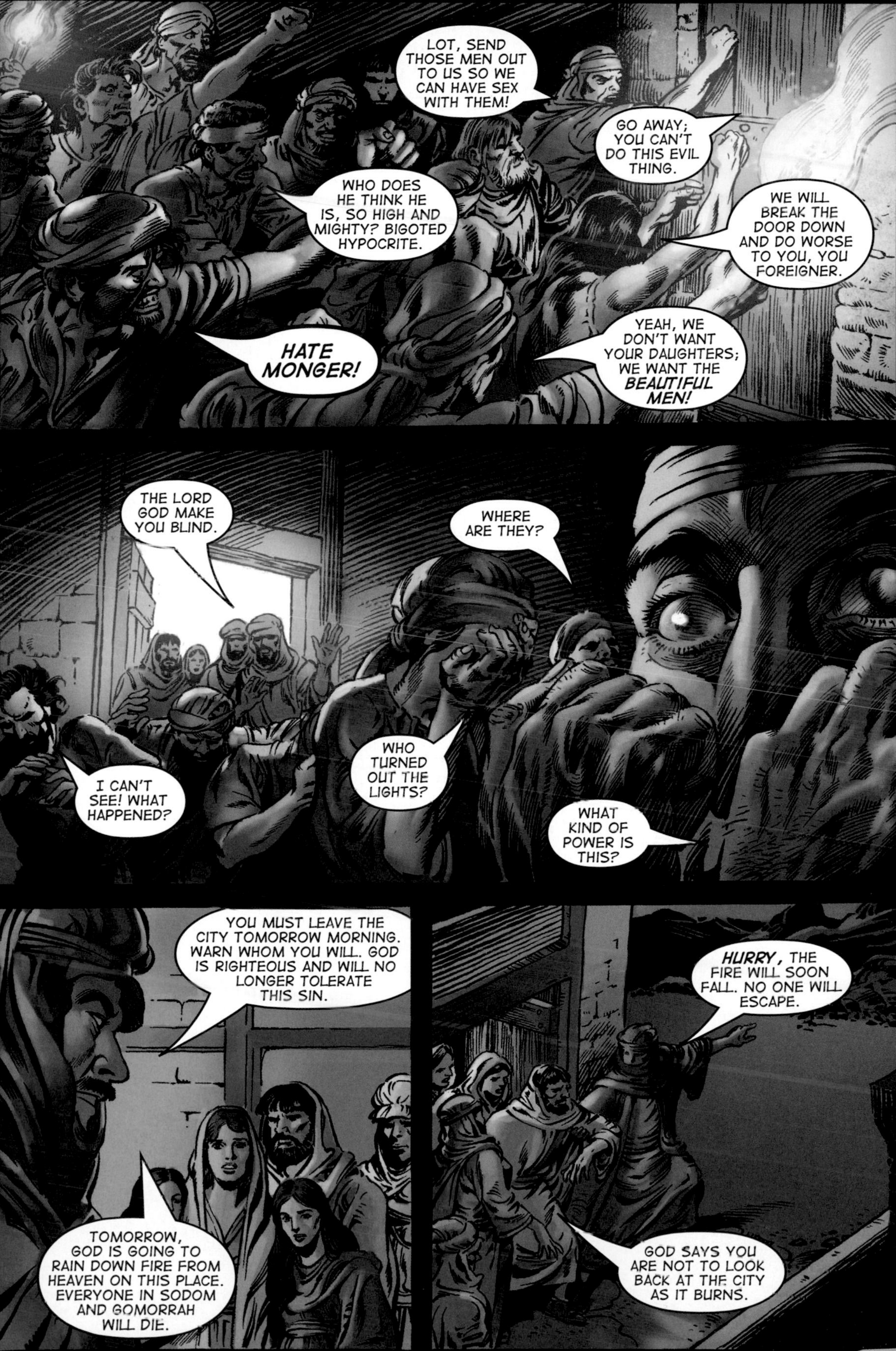
LOT, SEND THOSE MEN OUT TO US SO WE CAN HAVE SEX WITH THEM!
GO AWAY; YOU CAN'T DO THIS EVIL THING.
WHO DOES HE THINK HE IS, SO HIGH AND MIGHTY? BIGOTED HYPOCRITE.
WE WILL BREAK THE DOOR DOWN AND DO WORSE TO YOU, YOU FOREIGNER.
HATE MONGER!
YEAH, WE DON'T WANT YOUR DAUGHTERS; WE WANT THE BEAUTIFUL MEN!
THE LORD GOD MAKE YOU BLIND.
WHERE ARE THEY?
I CAN'T SEE! WHAT HAPPENED?
WHO TURNED OUT THE LIGHTS?
WHAT KIND OF POWER IS THIS?
YOU MUST LEAVE THE CITY TOMORROW MORNING. WARN WHOM YOU WILL. GOD IS RIGHTEOUS AND WILL NO LONGER TOLERATE THIS SIN.
TOMORROW, GOD IS GOING TO RAIN DOWN FIRE FROM HEAVEN ON THIS PLACE. EVERYONE IN SODOM AND GOMORRAH WILL DIE.
HURRY, THE FIRE WILL SOON FALL. NO ONE WILL ESCAPE.
GOD SAYS YOU ARE NOT TO LOOK BACK AT THE CITY AS IT BURNS.

GENESIS 19:4-17

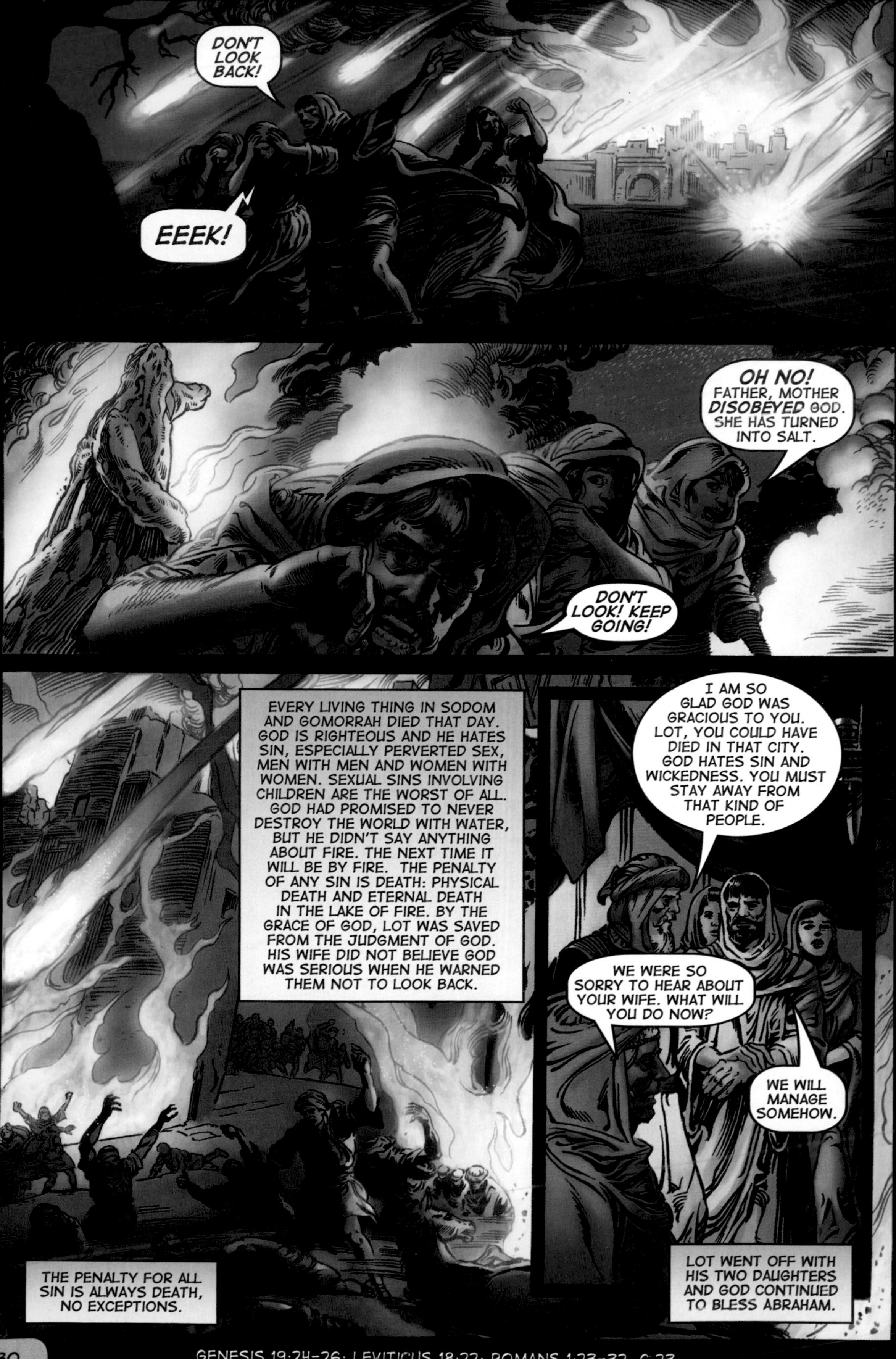
DON'T LOOK BACK!
EEEK!
OH NO! FATHER, MOTHER DISOBEYED GOD. SHE HAS TURNED INTO SALT.
DON'T LOOK! KEEP GOING!
EVERY LIVING THING IN SODOM AND GOMORRAH DIED THAT DAY. GOD IS RIGHTEOUS AND HE HATES SIN, ESPECIALLY PERVERTED SEX, MEN WITH MEN AND WOMEN WITH WOMEN. SEXUAL SINS INVOLVING CHILDREN ARE THE WORST OF ALL. GOD HAD PROMISED TO NEVER DESTROY THE WORLD WITH WATER, BUT HE DIDN'T SAY ANYTHING ABOUT FIRE. THE NEXT TIME IT WILL BE BY FIRE. THE PENALTY OF ANY SIN IS DEATH: PHYSICAL DEATH AND ETERNAL DEATH IN THE LAKE OF FIRE. BY THE GRACE OF GOD, LOT WAS SAVED FROM THE JUDGMENT OF GOD. HIS WIFE DID NOT BELIEVE GOD WAS SERIOUS WHEN HE WARNED THEM NOT TO LOOK BACK.
THE PENALTY FOR ALL SIN IS ALWAYS DEATH, NO EXCEPTIONS.
I AM SO GLAD GOD WAS GRACIOUS TO YOU. LOT, YOU COULD HAVE DIED IN THAT CITY. GOD HATES SIN AND WICKEDNESS. YOU MUST STAY AWAY FROM THAT KIND OF PEOPLE.
WE WERE SO SORRY TO HEAR ABOUT YOUR WIFE. WHAT WILL YOU DO NOW?
WE WILL MANAGE SOMEHOW.
LOT WENT OFF WITH HIS TWO DAUGHTERS AND GOD CONTINUED TO BLESS ABRAHAM.

GENESIS 19:24-26; LEVITICUS 18:22; ROMANS 1:23-32, 6:23;
1 CORINTHIANS 6:9-11; REVELATION 21:8

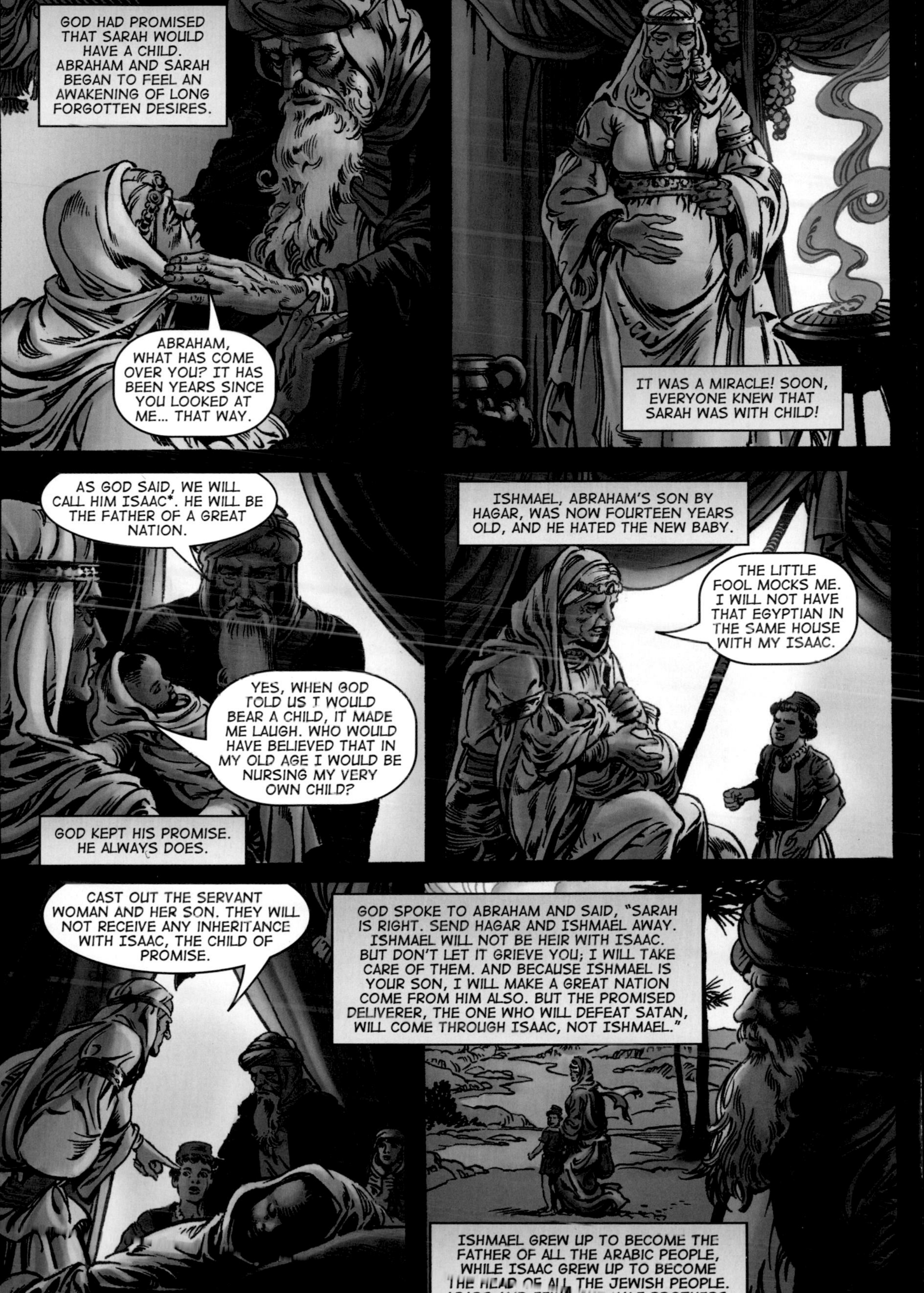
GOD HAD PROMISED THAT SARAH WOULD HAVE A CHILD. ABRAHAM AND SARAH BEGAN TO FEEL AN AWAKENING OF LONG FORGOTTEN DESIRES.
ABRAHAM, WHAT HAS COME OVER YOU? IT HAS BEEN YEARS SINCE YOU LOOKED AT ME... THAT WAY.
IT WAS A MIRACLE! SOON, EVERYONE KNEW THAT SARAH WAS WITH CHILD!
AS GOD SAID, WE WILL CALL HIM ISAAC*. HE WILL BE THE FATHER OF A GREAT NATION.
YES, WHEN GOD TOLD US I WOULD BEAR A CHILD, IT MADE ME LAUGH. WHO WOULD HAVE BELIEVED THAT IN MY OLD AGE I WOULD BE NURSING MY VERY OWN CHILD?
GOD KEPT HIS PROMISE. HE ALWAYS DOES.
ISHMAEL, ABRAHAM'S SON BY HAGAR, WAS NOW FOURTEEN YEARS OLD, AND HE HATED THE NEW BABY.
THE LITTLE FOOL MOCKS ME. I WILL NOT HAVE THAT EGYPTIAN IN THE SAME HOUSE WITH MY ISAAC.
CAST OUT THE SERVANT WOMAN AND HER SON. THEY WILL NOT RECEIVE ANY INHERITANCE WITH ISAAC, THE CHILD OF PROMISE.
GOD SPOKE TO ABRAHAM AND SAID, "SARAH IS RIGHT. SEND HAGAR AND ISHMAEL AWAY. ISHMAEL WILL NOT BE HEIR WITH ISAAC. BUT DON'T LET IT GRIEVE YOU; I WILL TAKE CARE OF THEM. AND BECAUSE ISHMAEL IS YOUR SON, I WILL MAKE A GREAT NATION COME FROM HIM ALSO. BUT THE PROMISED DELIVERER, THE ONE WHO WILL DEFEAT SATAN, WILL COME THROUGH ISAAC, NOT ISHMAEL."
ISHMAEL GREW UP TO BECOME THE FATHER OF ALL THE ARABIC PEOPLE, WHILE ISAAC GREW UP TO BECOME THE HEAD OF ALL THE JEWISH PEOPLE. ARABS AND JEWS ARE HALF BROTHERS.

GENESIS 21:1-3, 9-14

*THE NAME ISAAC MEANS LAUGHTER.

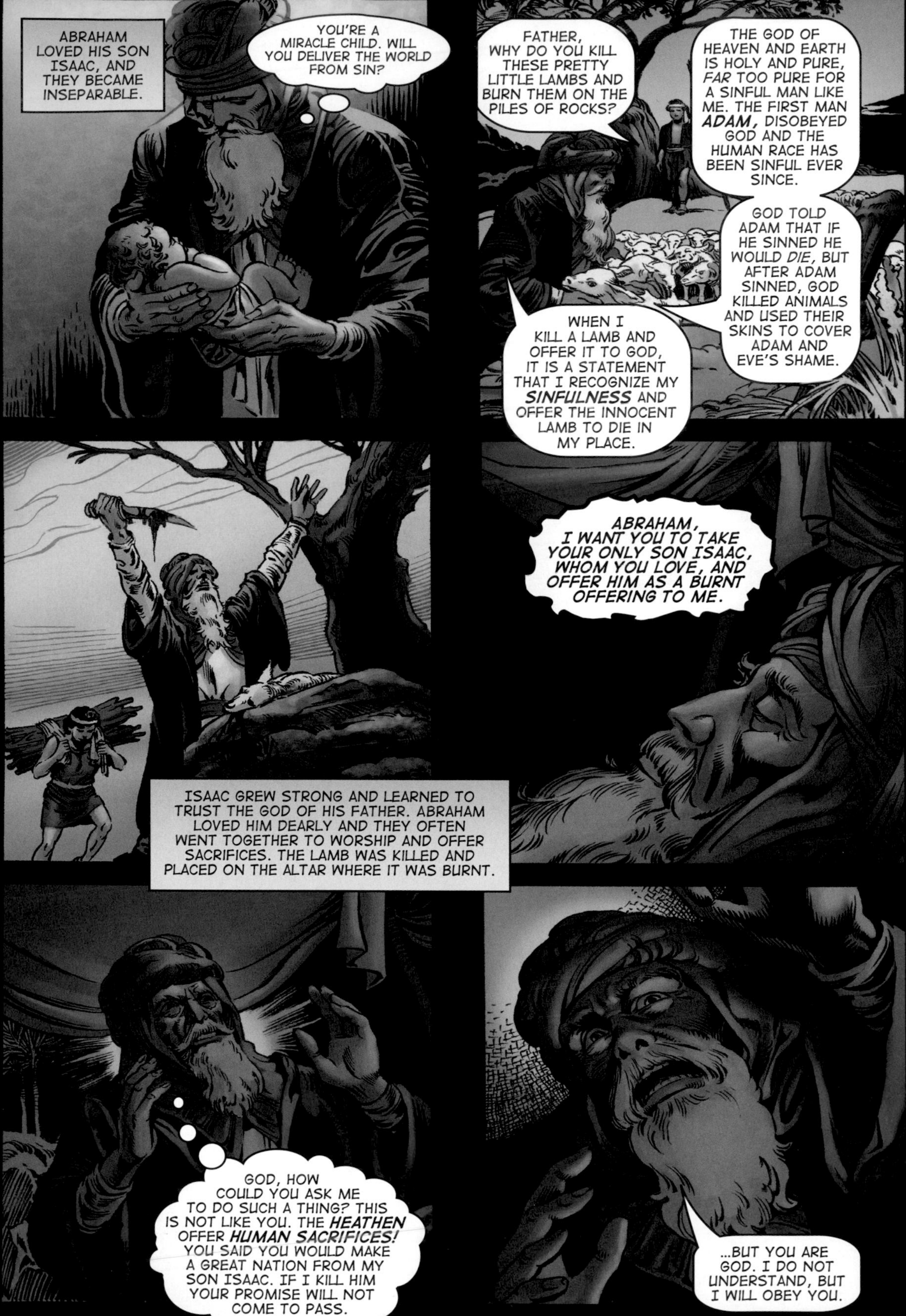
ABRAHAM LOVED HIS SON ISAAC, AND THEY BECAME INSEPARABLE.
YOU'RE A MIRACLE CHILD. WILL YOU DELIVER THE WORLD FROM SIN?
FATHER, WHY DO YOU KILL THESE PRETTY LITTLE LAMBS AND BURN THEM ON THE PILES OF ROCKS?
THE GOD OF HEAVEN AND EARTH IS HOLY AND PURE, *FAR* TOO PURE FOR A SINFUL MAN LIKE ME. THE FIRST MAN **ADAM,** DISOBEYED GOD AND THE HUMAN RACE HAS BEEN SINFUL EVER SINCE.
GOD TOLD ADAM THAT IF HE SINNED HE WOULD *DIE,* BUT AFTER ADAM SINNED, GOD KILLED ANIMALS AND USED THEIR SKINS TO COVER ADAM AND EVE'S SHAME.
WHEN I KILL A LAMB AND OFFER IT TO GOD, IT IS A STATEMENT THAT I RECOGNIZE MY ***SINFULNESS*** AND OFFER THE INNOCENT LAMB TO DIE IN MY PLACE.
ISAAC GREW STRONG AND LEARNED TO TRUST THE GOD OF HIS FATHER. ABRAHAM LOVED HIM DEARLY AND THEY OFTEN WENT TOGETHER TO WORSHIP AND OFFER SACRIFICES. THE LAMB WAS KILLED AND PLACED ON THE ALTAR WHERE IT WAS BURNT.
ABRAHAM, I WANT YOU TO TAKE YOUR ONLY SON ISAAC, WHOM YOU LOVE, AND OFFER HIM AS A BURNT OFFERING TO ME.
GOD, HOW COULD YOU ASK ME TO DO SUCH A THING? THIS IS NOT LIKE YOU. THE ***HEATHEN*** OFFER ***HUMAN SACRIFICES!*** YOU SAID YOU WOULD MAKE A GREAT NATION FROM MY SON ISAAC. IF I KILL HIM YOUR PROMISE WILL NOT COME TO PASS.
...BUT YOU ARE GOD. I DO NOT UNDERSTAND, BUT I WILL OBEY YOU.

GENESIS 22:2; ROMANS 5:12

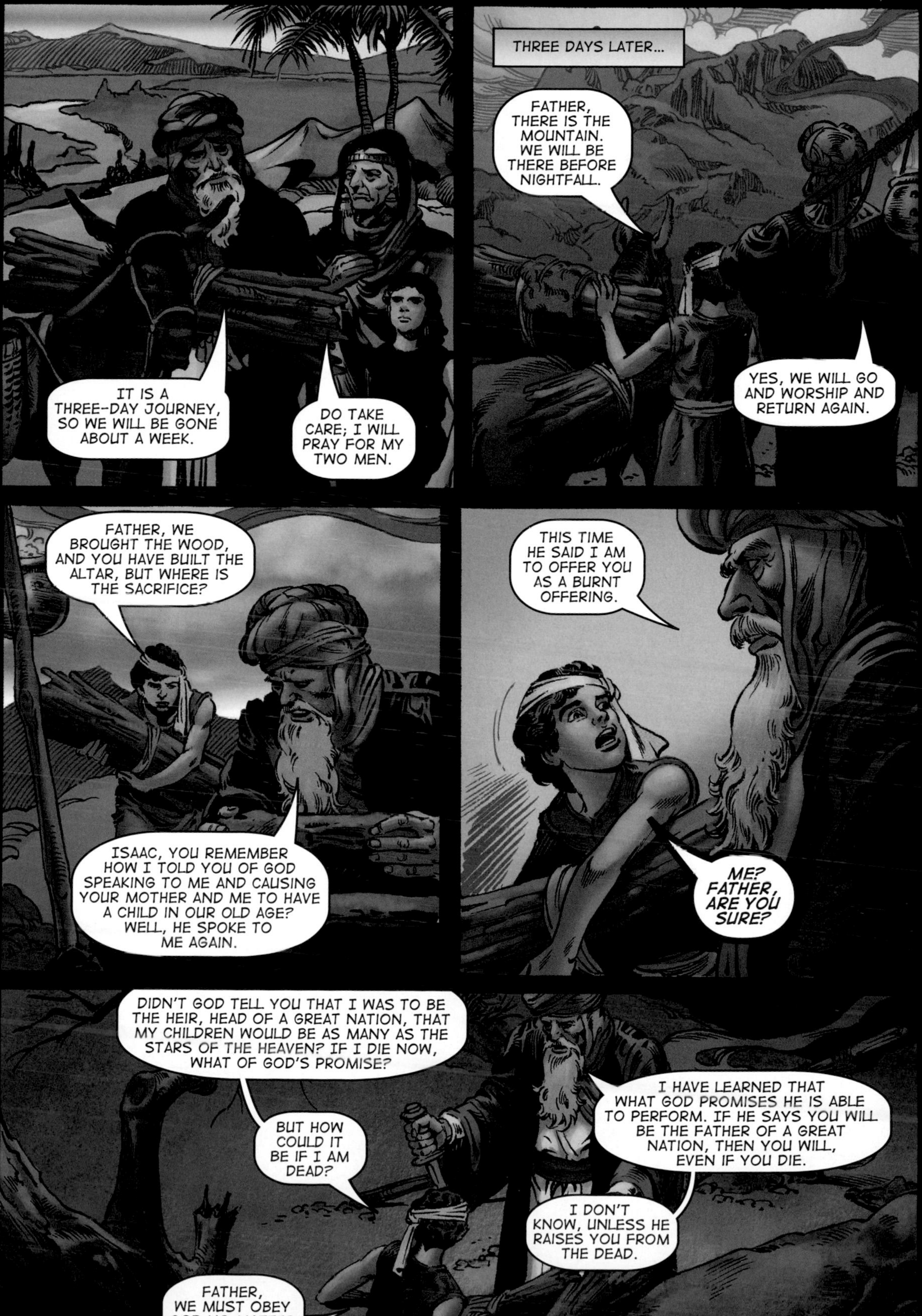
IT IS A THREE-DAY JOURNEY, SO WE WILL BE GONE ABOUT A WEEK.
DO TAKE CARE; I WILL PRAY FOR MY TWO MEN.
THREE DAYS LATER...
FATHER, THERE IS THE MOUNTAIN. WE WILL BE THERE BEFORE NIGHTFALL.
YES, WE WILL GO AND WORSHIP AND RETURN AGAIN.
FATHER, WE BROUGHT THE WOOD, AND YOU HAVE BUILT THE ALTAR, BUT WHERE IS THE SACRIFICE?
ISAAC, YOU REMEMBER HOW I TOLD YOU OF GOD SPEAKING TO ME AND CAUSING YOUR MOTHER AND ME TO HAVE A CHILD IN OUR OLD AGE? WELL, HE SPOKE TO ME AGAIN.
THIS TIME HE SAID I AM TO OFFER YOU AS A BURNT OFFERING.
ME? FATHER, ARE YOU SURE?
DIDN'T GOD TELL YOU THAT I WAS TO BE THE HEIR, HEAD OF A GREAT NATION, THAT MY CHILDREN WOULD BE AS MANY AS THE STARS OF THE HEAVEN? IF I DIE NOW, WHAT OF GOD'S PROMISE?
BUT HOW COULD IT BE IF I AM DEAD?
I HAVE LEARNED THAT WHAT GOD PROMISES HE IS ABLE TO PERFORM. IF HE SAYS YOU WILL BE THE FATHER OF A GREAT NATION, THEN YOU WILL, EVEN IF YOU DIE.
I DON'T KNOW, UNLESS HE RAISES YOU FROM THE DEAD.
FATHER, WE MUST OBEY GOD NO MATTER WHAT.

GENESIS 22:3–9

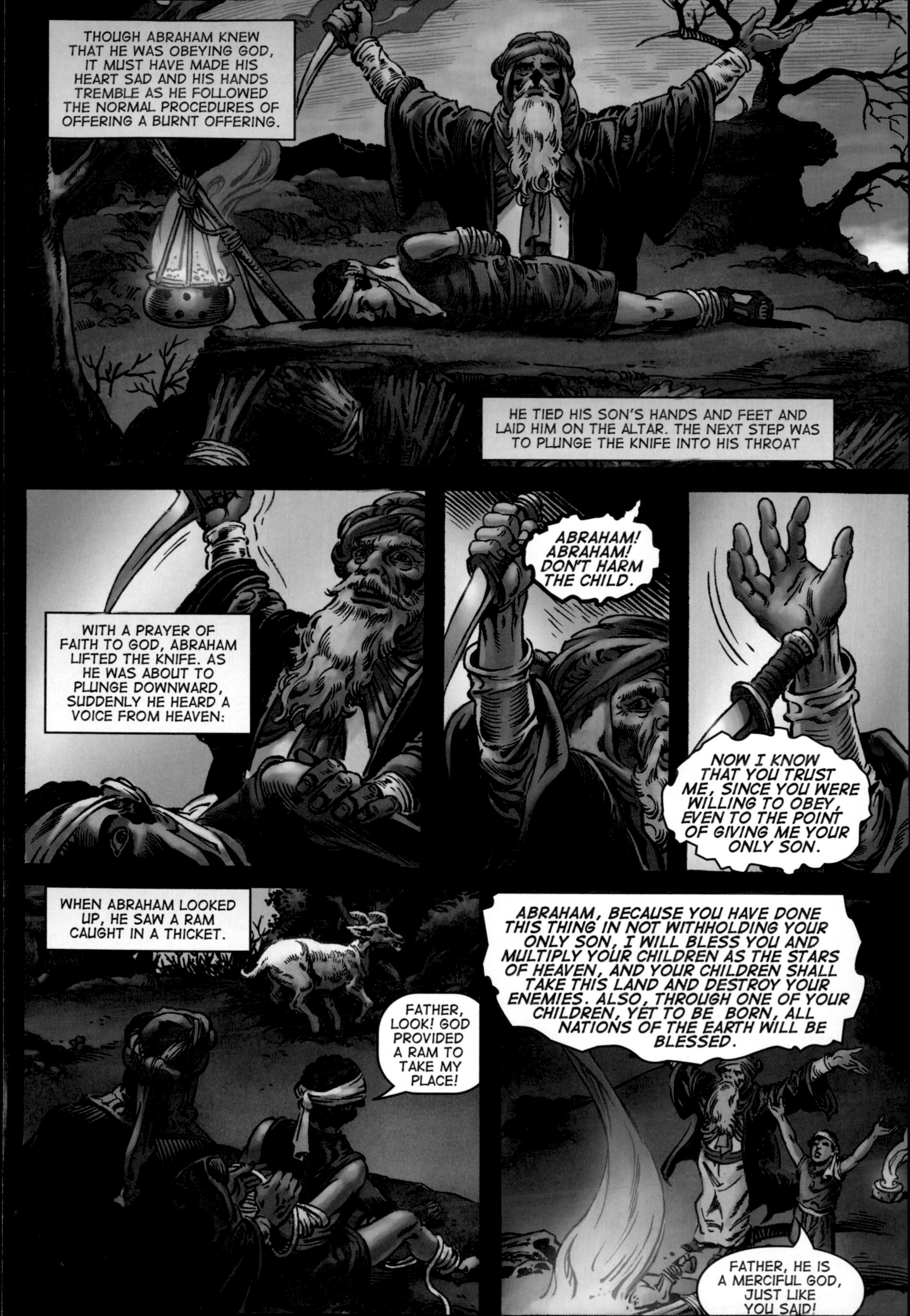
THOUGH ABRAHAM KNEW THAT HE WAS OBEYING GOD, IT MUST HAVE MADE HIS HEART SAD AND HIS HANDS TREMBLE AS HE FOLLOWED THE NORMAL PROCEDURES OF OFFERING A BURNT OFFERING.
HE TIED HIS SON'S HANDS AND FEET AND LAID HIM ON THE ALTAR. THE NEXT STEP WAS TO PLUNGE THE KNIFE INTO HIS THROAT
WITH A PRAYER OF FAITH TO GOD, ABRAHAM LIFTED THE KNIFE. AS HE WAS ABOUT TO PLUNGE DOWNWARD, SUDDENLY HE HEARD A VOICE FROM HEAVEN:
ABRAHAM! ABRAHAM! DON'T HARM THE CHILD.
NOW I KNOW THAT YOU TRUST ME, SINCE YOU WERE WILLING TO OBEY, EVEN TO THE POINT OF GIVING ME YOUR ONLY SON.
WHEN ABRAHAM LOOKED UP, HE SAW A RAM CAUGHT IN A THICKET.
FATHER, LOOK! GOD PROVIDED A RAM TO TAKE MY PLACE!
ABRAHAM, BECAUSE YOU HAVE DONE THIS THING IN NOT WITHHOLDING YOUR ONLY SON, I WILL BLESS YOU AND MULTIPLY YOUR CHILDREN AS THE STARS OF HEAVEN, AND YOUR CHILDREN SHALL TAKE THIS LAND AND DESTROY YOUR ENEMIES. ALSO, THROUGH ONE OF YOUR CHILDREN, YET TO BE BORN, ALL NATIONS OF THE EARTH WILL BE BLESSED.
FATHER, HE IS A MERCIFUL GOD, JUST LIKE YOU SAID!

GENESIS 22:9–18; HEBREWS 11:17–19

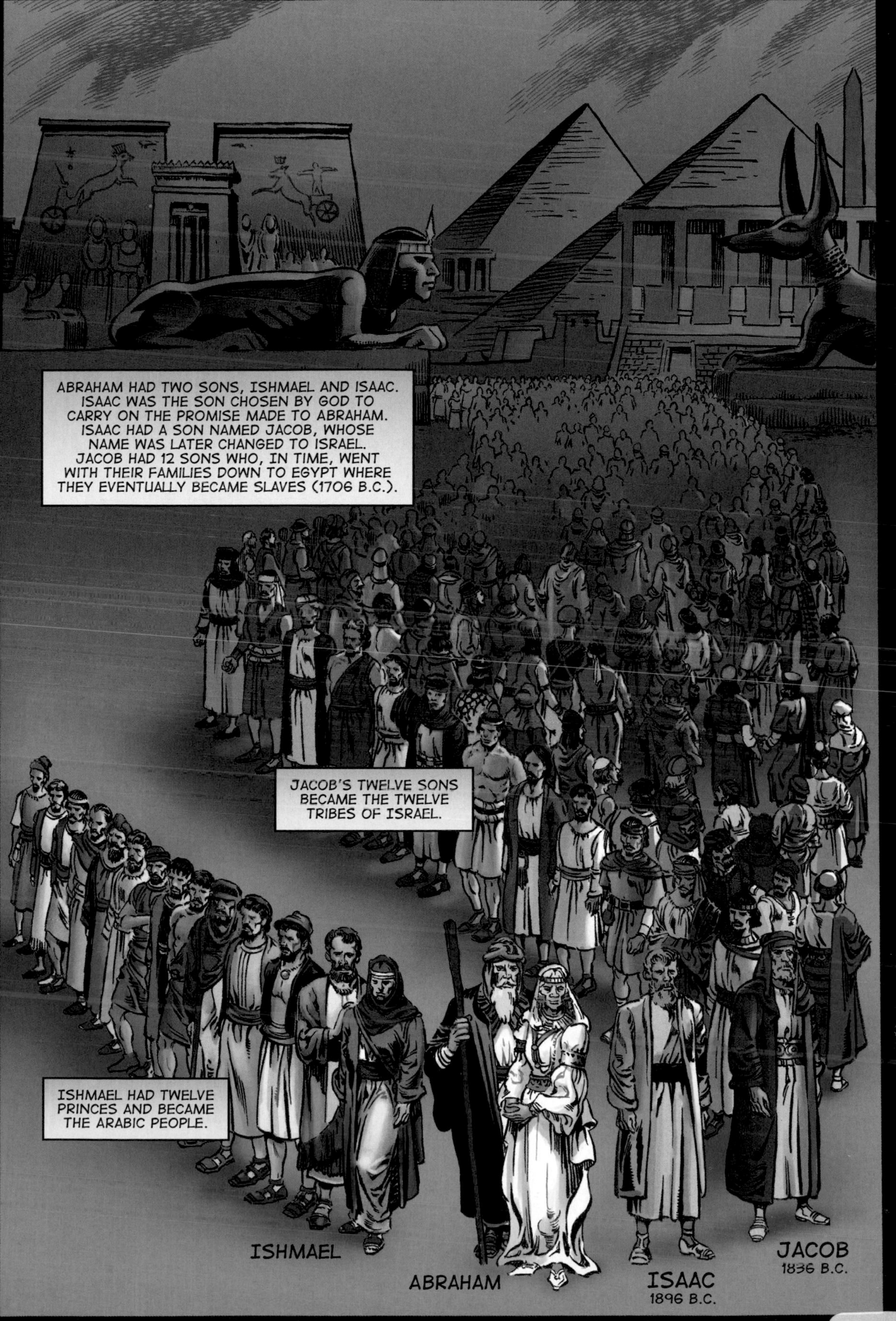
ABRAHAM HAD TWO SONS, ISHMAEL AND ISAAC. ISAAC WAS THE SON CHOSEN BY GOD TO CARRY ON THE PROMISE MADE TO ABRAHAM. ISAAC HAD A SON NAMED JACOB, WHOSE NAME WAS LATER CHANGED TO ISRAEL. JACOB HAD 12 SONS WHO, IN TIME, WENT WITH THEIR FAMILIES DOWN TO EGYPT WHERE THEY EVENTUALLY BECAME SLAVES (1706 B.C.).
JACOB'S TWELVE SONS BECAME THE TWELVE TRIBES OF ISRAEL.
ISHMAEL HAD TWELVE PRINCES AND BECAME THE ARABIC PEOPLE.
ISHMAEL
ABRAHAM
ISAAC
1896 B.C.
JACOB
1836 B.C.

GENESIS 21:5, 13, 24:67, 25:12-18, 21-26, 29:23-30

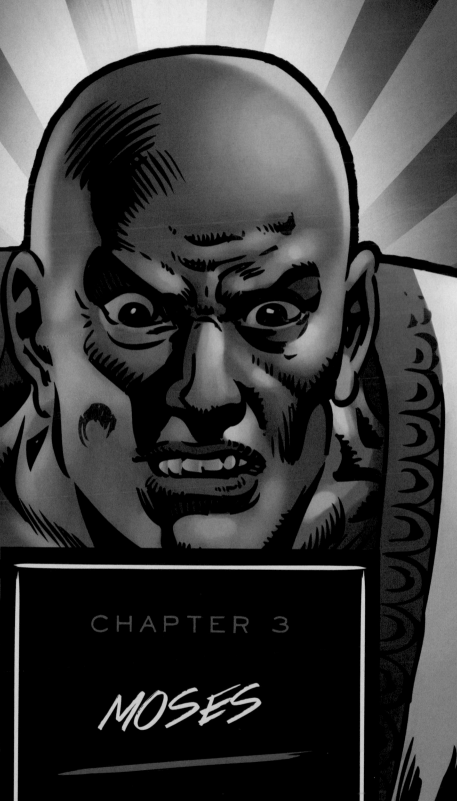

CHAPTER 3

MOSES

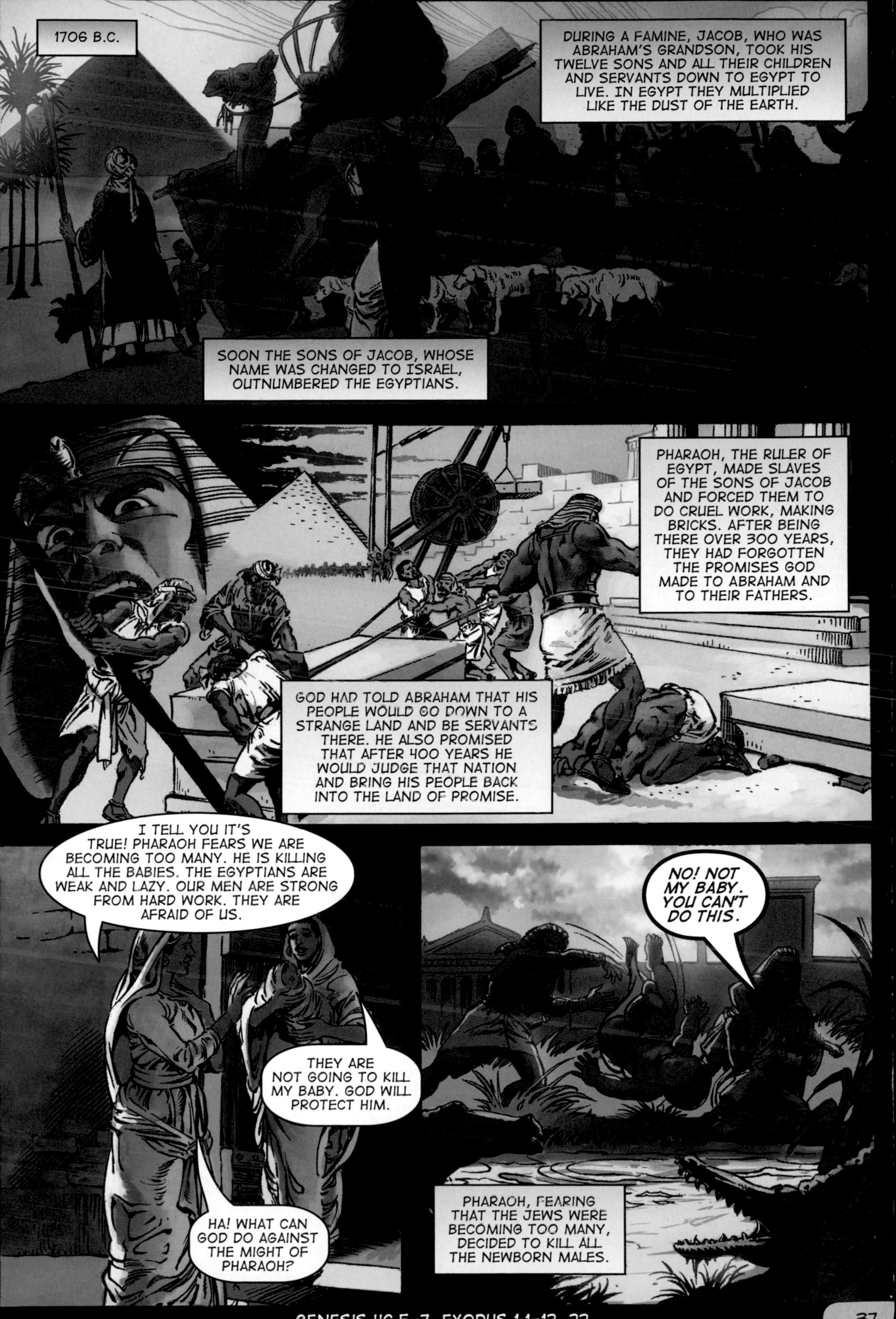

1706 B.C.
DURING A FAMINE, JACOB, WHO WAS ABRAHAM'S GRANDSON, TOOK HIS TWELVE SONS AND ALL THEIR CHILDREN AND SERVANTS DOWN TO EGYPT TO LIVE. IN EGYPT THEY MULTIPLIED LIKE THE DUST OF THE EARTH.
SOON THE SONS OF JACOB, WHOSE NAME WAS CHANGED TO ISRAEL, OUTNUMBERED THE EGYPTIANS.
PHARAOH, THE RULER OF EGYPT, MADE SLAVES OF THE SONS OF JACOB AND FORCED THEM TO DO CRUEL WORK, MAKING BRICKS. AFTER BEING THERE OVER 300 YEARS, THEY HAD FORGOTTEN THE PROMISES GOD MADE TO ABRAHAM AND TO THEIR FATHERS.
GOD HAD TOLD ABRAHAM THAT HIS PEOPLE WOULD GO DOWN TO A STRANGE LAND AND BE SERVANTS THERE. HE ALSO PROMISED THAT AFTER 400 YEARS HE WOULD JUDGE THAT NATION AND BRING HIS PEOPLE BACK INTO THE LAND OF PROMISE.
I TELL YOU IT'S TRUE! PHARAOH FEARS WE ARE BECOMING TOO MANY. HE IS KILLING ALL THE BABIES. THE EGYPTIANS ARE WEAK AND LAZY. OUR MEN ARE STRONG FROM HARD WORK. THEY ARE AFRAID OF US.
THEY ARE NOT GOING TO KILL MY BABY. GOD WILL PROTECT HIM.
HA! WHAT CAN GOD DO AGAINST THE MIGHT OF PHARAOH?
NO! NOT MY BABY. YOU CAN'T DO THIS.
PHARAOH, FEARING THAT THE JEWS WERE BECOMING TOO MANY, DECIDED TO KILL ALL THE NEWBORN MALES.

GENESIS 46:5-7; EXODUS 1:1-12, 22

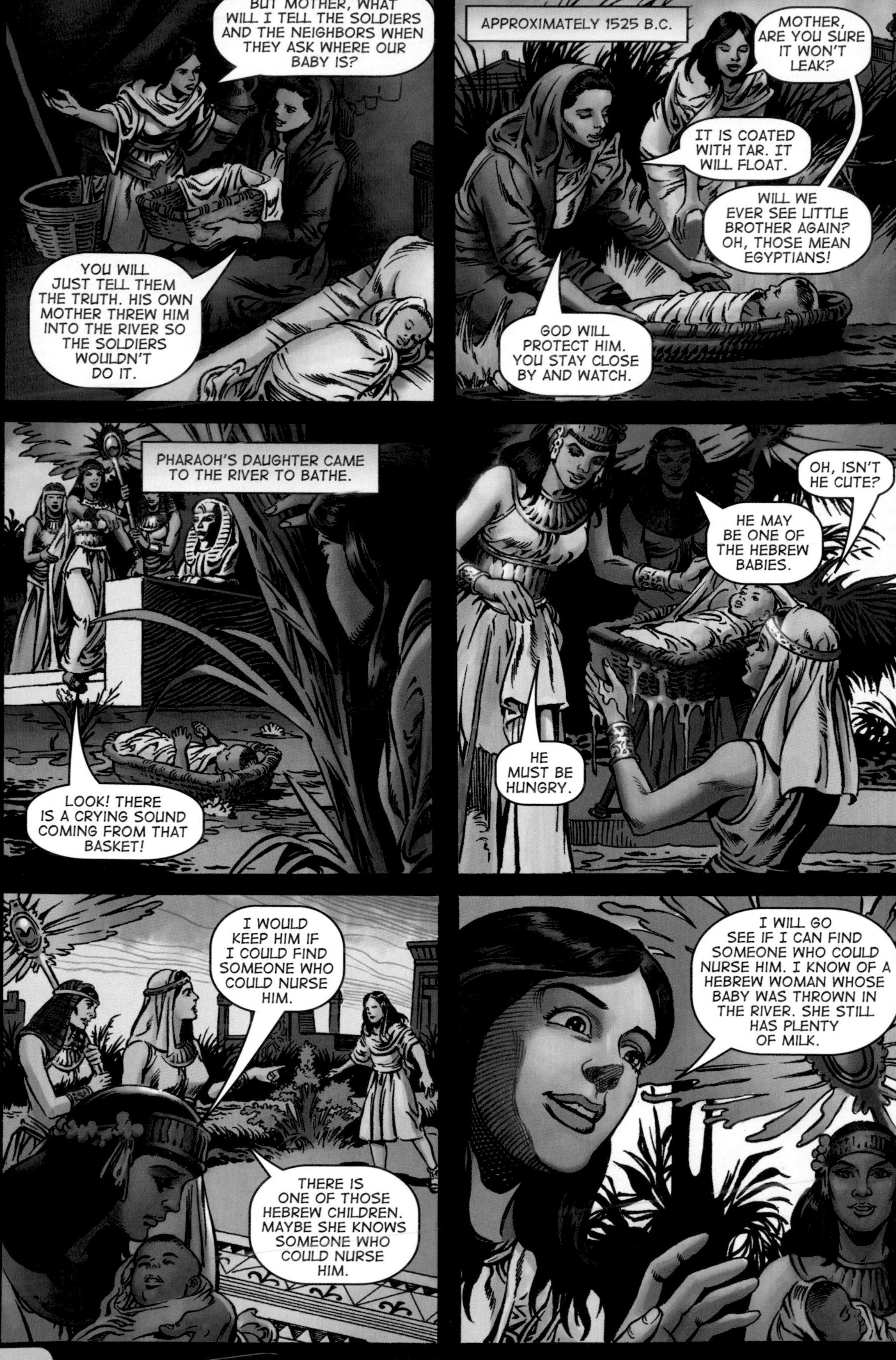
BUT MOTHER, WHAT WILL I TELL THE SOLDIERS AND THE NEIGHBORS WHEN THEY ASK WHERE OUR BABY IS?
YOU WILL JUST TELL THEM THE TRUTH. HIS OWN MOTHER THREW HIM INTO THE RIVER SO THE SOLDIERS WOULDN'T DO IT.
APPROXIMATELY 1525 B.C.
MOTHER, ARE YOU SURE IT WON'T LEAK?
IT IS COATED WITH TAR. IT WILL FLOAT.
WILL WE EVER SEE LITTLE BROTHER AGAIN? OH, THOSE MEAN EGYPTIANS!
GOD WILL PROTECT HIM. YOU STAY CLOSE BY AND WATCH.
PHARAOH'S DAUGHTER CAME TO THE RIVER TO BATHE.
LOOK! THERE IS A CRYING SOUND COMING FROM THAT BASKET!
OH, ISN'T HE CUTE?
HE MAY BE ONE OF THE HEBREW BABIES.
HE MUST BE HUNGRY.
I WOULD KEEP HIM IF I COULD FIND SOMEONE WHO COULD NURSE HIM.
THERE IS ONE OF THOSE HEBREW CHILDREN. MAYBE SHE KNOWS SOMEONE WHO COULD NURSE HIM.
I WILL GO SEE IF I CAN FIND SOMEONE WHO COULD NURSE HIM. I KNOW OF A HEBREW WOMAN WHOSE BABY WAS THROWN IN THE RIVER. SHE STILL HAS PLENTY OF MILK.

EXODUS 2:3-9

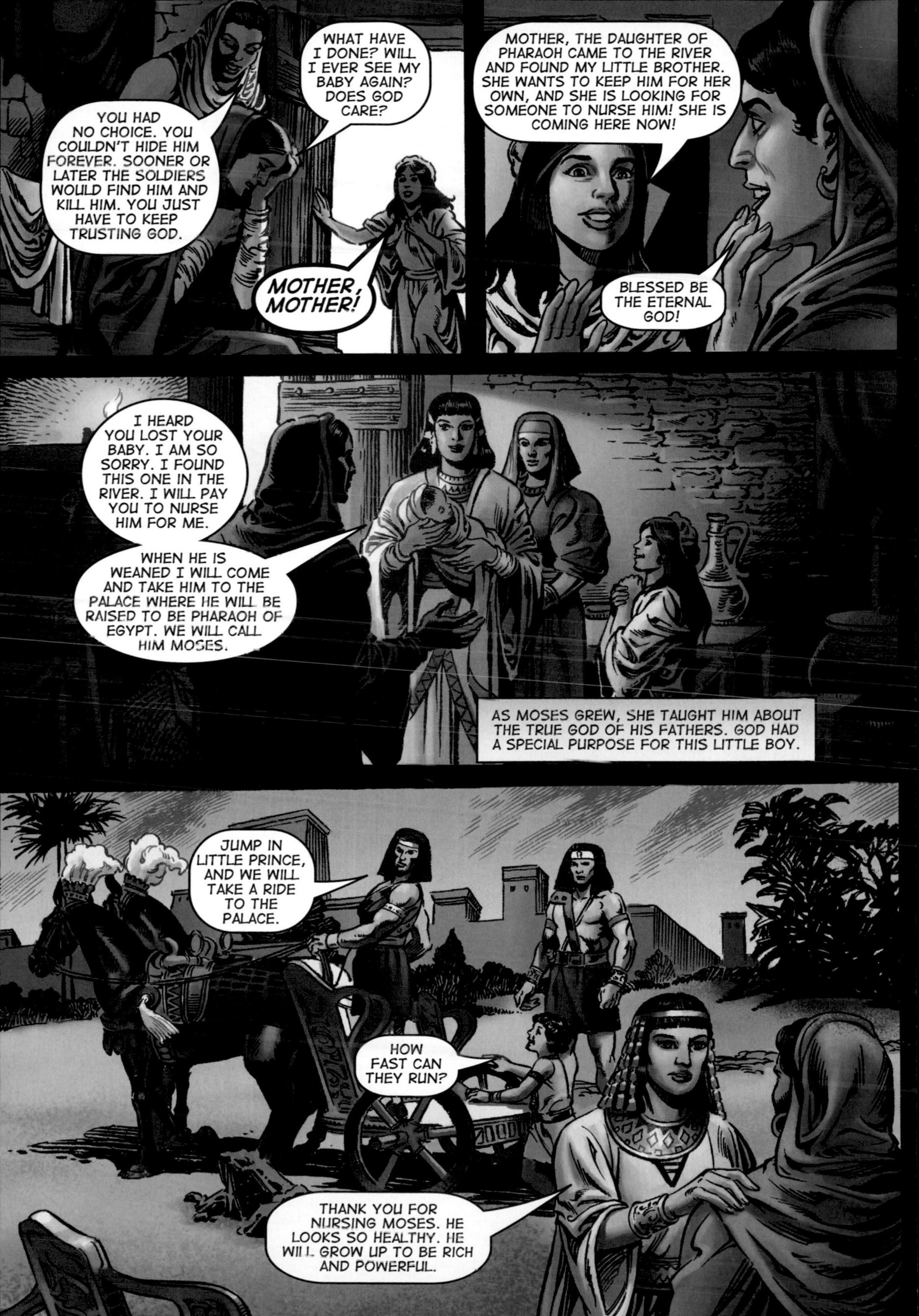
WHAT HAVE I DONE? WILL I EVER SEE MY BABY AGAIN? DOES GOD CARE?
YOU HAD NO CHOICE. YOU COULDN'T HIDE HIM FOREVER. SOONER OR LATER THE SOLDIERS WOULD FIND HIM AND KILL HIM. YOU JUST HAVE TO KEEP TRUSTING GOD.
MOTHER, MOTHER!
MOTHER, THE DAUGHTER OF PHARAOH CAME TO THE RIVER AND FOUND MY LITTLE BROTHER. SHE WANTS TO KEEP HIM FOR HER OWN, AND SHE IS LOOKING FOR SOMEONE TO NURSE HIM! SHE IS COMING HERE NOW!
BLESSED BE THE ETERNAL GOD!
I HEARD YOU LOST YOUR BABY. I AM SO SORRY. I FOUND THIS ONE IN THE RIVER. I WILL PAY YOU TO NURSE HIM FOR ME.
WHEN HE IS WEANED I WILL COME AND TAKE HIM TO THE PALACE WHERE HE WILL BE RAISED TO BE PHARAOH OF EGYPT. WE WILL CALL HIM MOSES.
AS MOSES GREW, SHE TAUGHT HIM ABOUT THE TRUE GOD OF HIS FATHERS. GOD HAD A SPECIAL PURPOSE FOR THIS LITTLE BOY.
JUMP IN LITTLE PRINCE, AND WE WILL TAKE A RIDE TO THE PALACE.
HOW FAST CAN THEY RUN?
THANK YOU FOR NURSING MOSES. HE LOOKS SO HEALTHY. HE WILL GROW UP TO BE RICH AND POWERFUL.

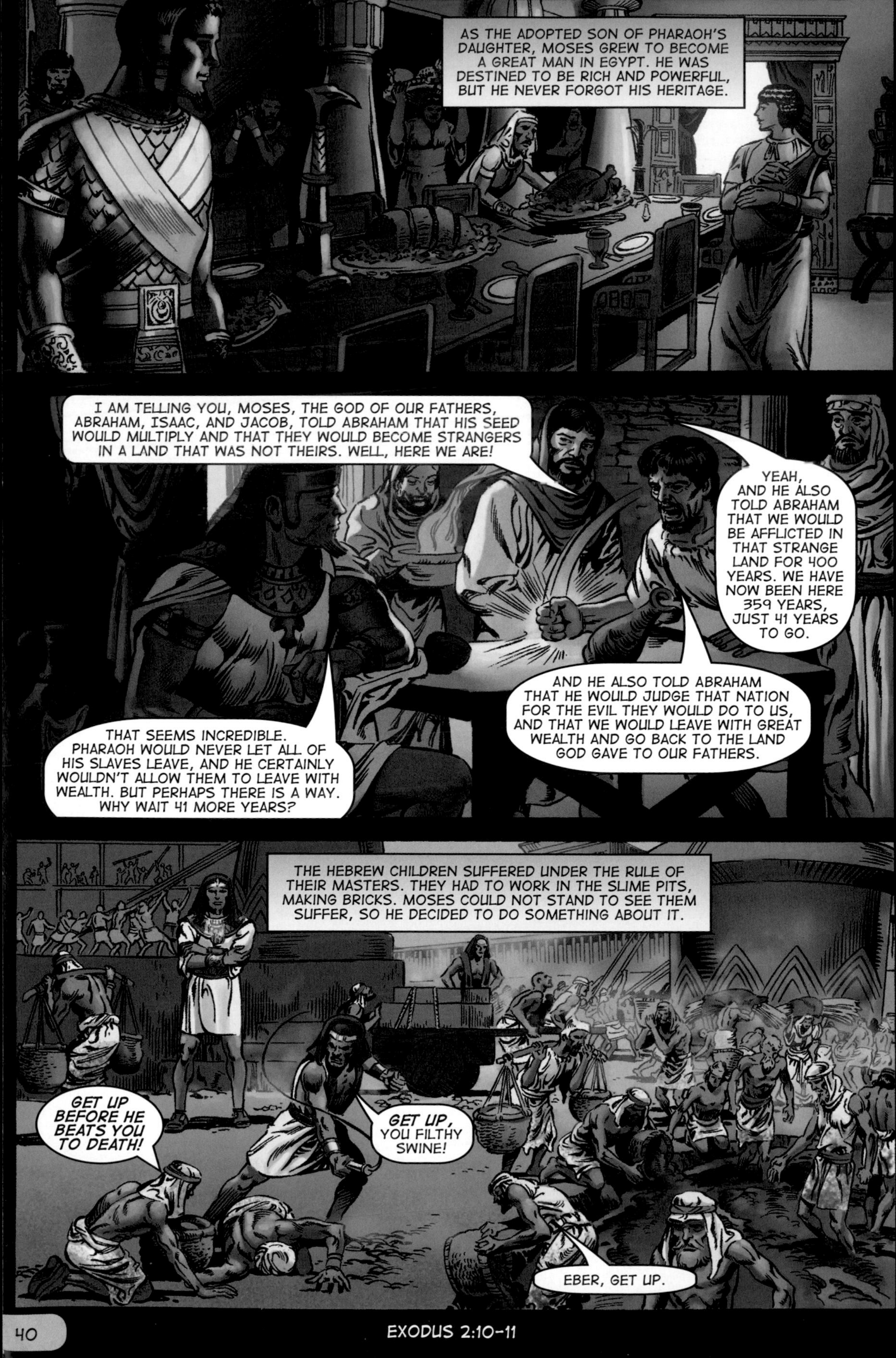
AS THE ADOPTED SON OF PHARAOH'S DAUGHTER, MOSES GREW TO BECOME A GREAT MAN IN EGYPT. HE WAS DESTINED TO BE RICH AND POWERFUL, BUT HE NEVER FORGOT HIS HERITAGE.
I AM TELLING YOU, MOSES, THE GOD OF OUR FATHERS, ABRAHAM, ISAAC, AND JACOB, TOLD ABRAHAM THAT HIS SEED WOULD MULTIPLY AND THAT THEY WOULD BECOME STRANGERS IN A LAND THAT WAS NOT THEIRS. WELL, HERE WE ARE!
YEAH, AND HE ALSO TOLD ABRAHAM THAT WE WOULD BE AFFLICTED IN THAT STRANGE LAND FOR 400 YEARS. WE HAVE NOW BEEN HERE 359 YEARS, JUST 41 YEARS TO GO.
AND HE ALSO TOLD ABRAHAM THAT HE WOULD JUDGE THAT NATION FOR THE EVIL THEY WOULD DO TO US, AND THAT WE WOULD LEAVE WITH GREAT WEALTH AND GO BACK TO THE LAND GOD GAVE TO OUR FATHERS.
THAT SEEMS INCREDIBLE. PHARAOH WOULD NEVER LET ALL OF HIS SLAVES LEAVE, AND HE CERTAINLY WOULDN'T ALLOW THEM TO LEAVE WITH WEALTH. BUT PERHAPS THERE IS A WAY. WHY WAIT 41 MORE YEARS?
THE HEBREW CHILDREN SUFFERED UNDER THE RULE OF THEIR MASTERS. THEY HAD TO WORK IN THE SLIME PITS, MAKING BRICKS. MOSES COULD NOT STAND TO SEE THEM SUFFER, SO HE DECIDED TO DO SOMETHING ABOUT IT.
GET UP BEFORE HE BEATS YOU TO DEATH!
GET UP, YOU FILTHY SWINE!
EBER, GET UP.

EXODUS 2:10-11

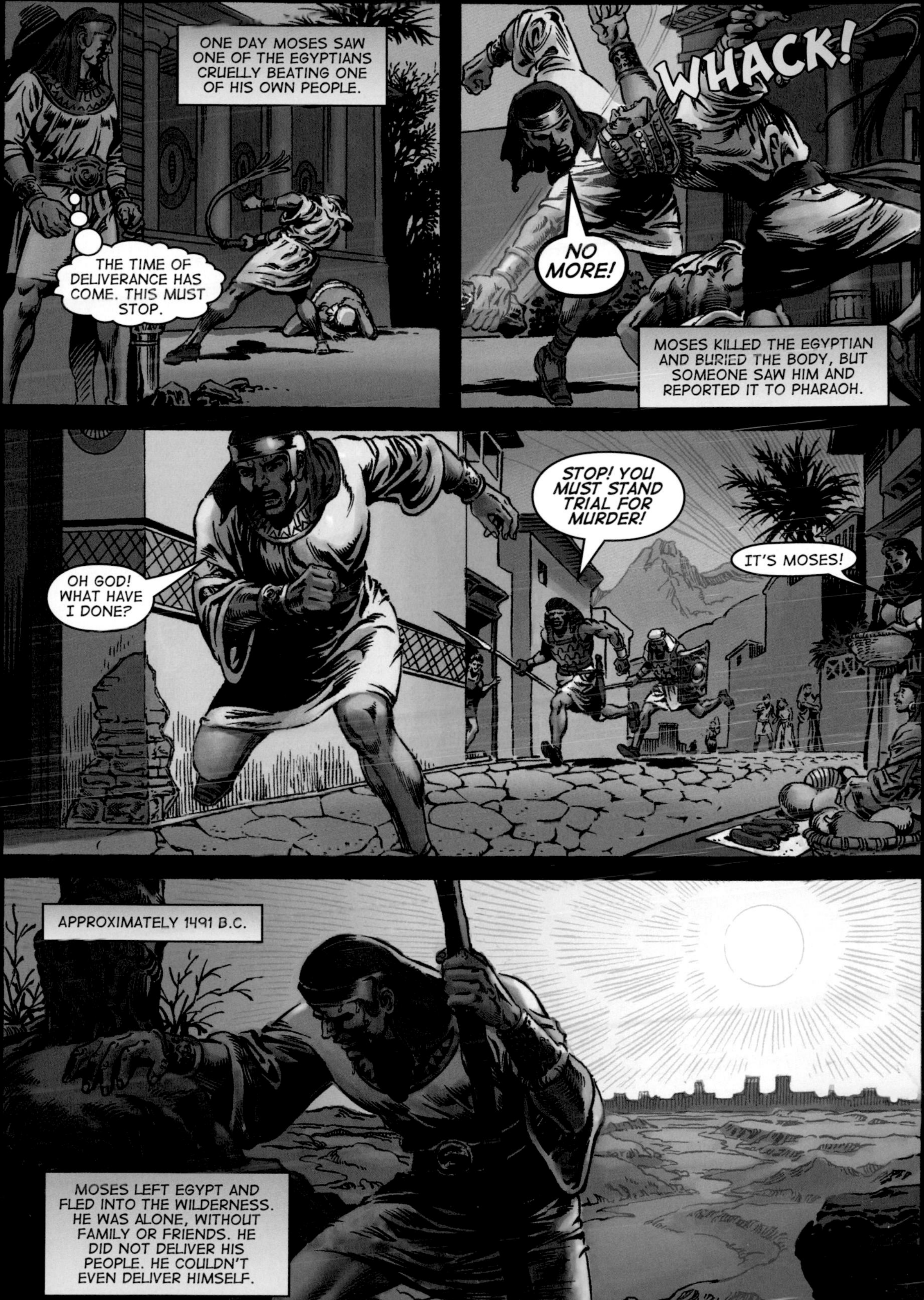
ONE DAY MOSES SAW ONE OF THE EGYPTIANS CRUELLY BEATING ONE OF HIS OWN PEOPLE.
THE TIME OF DELIVERANCE HAS COME. THIS MUST STOP.
WHACK!
NO MORE!
MOSES KILLED THE EGYPTIAN AND BURIED THE BODY, BUT SOMEONE SAW HIM AND REPORTED IT TO PHARAOH.
STOP! YOU MUST STAND TRIAL FOR MURDER!
IT'S MOSES!
OH GOD! WHAT HAVE I DONE?
APPROXIMATELY 1491 B.C.
MOSES LEFT EGYPT AND FLED INTO THE WILDERNESS. HE WAS ALONE, WITHOUT FAMILY OR FRIENDS. HE DID NOT DELIVER HIS PEOPLE. HE COULDN'T EVEN DELIVER HIMSELF.

EXODUS 2:11–15

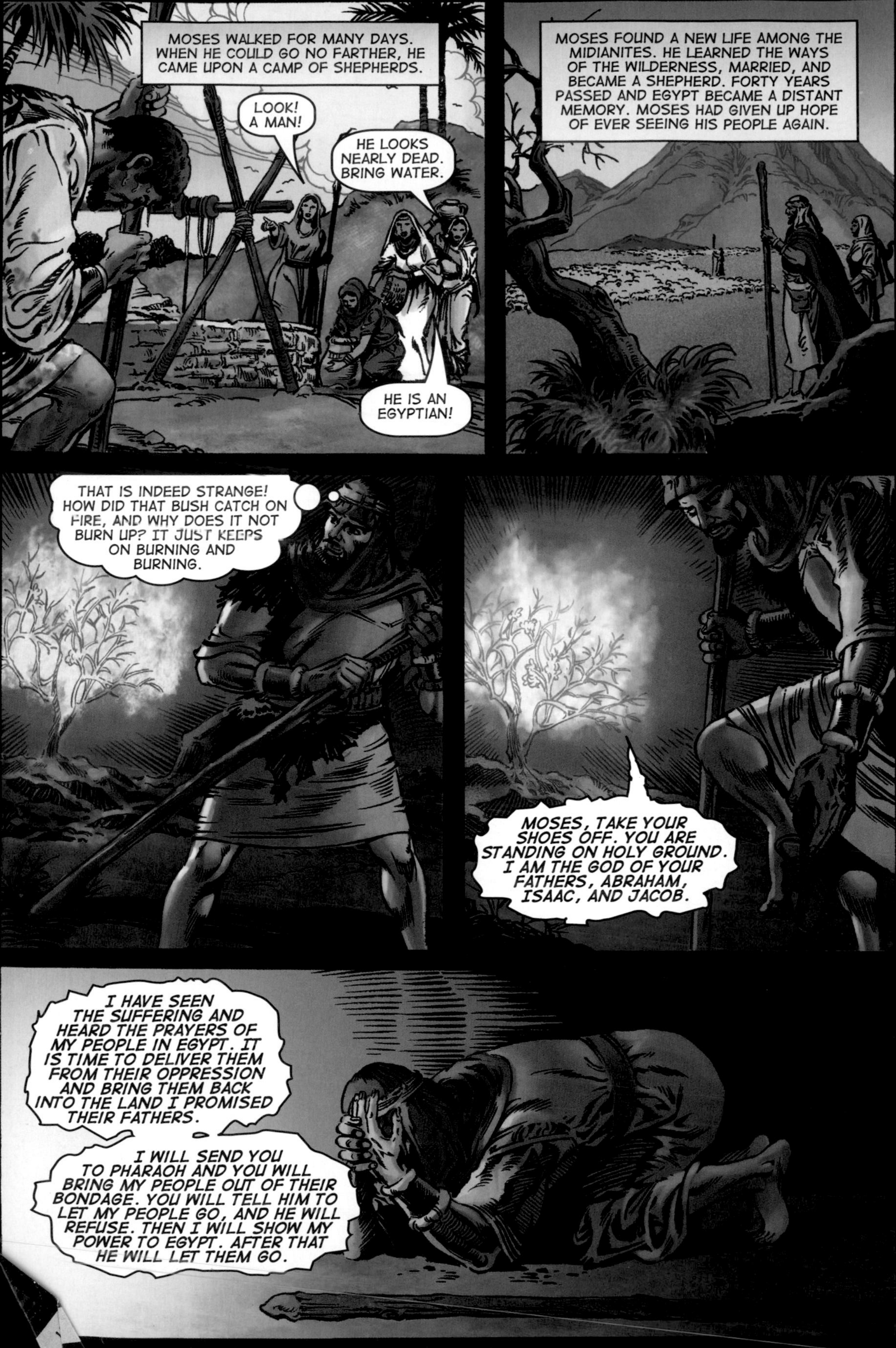
MOSES WALKED FOR MANY DAYS. WHEN HE COULD GO NO FARTHER, HE CAME UPON A CAMP OF SHEPHERDS.
LOOK! A MAN!
HE LOOKS NEARLY DEAD. BRING WATER.
HE IS AN EGYPTIAN!
MOSES FOUND A NEW LIFE AMONG THE MIDIANITES. HE LEARNED THE WAYS OF THE WILDERNESS, MARRIED, AND BECAME A SHEPHERD. FORTY YEARS PASSED AND EGYPT BECAME A DISTANT MEMORY. MOSES HAD GIVEN UP HOPE OF EVER SEEING HIS PEOPLE AGAIN.
THAT IS INDEED STRANGE! HOW DID THAT BUSH CATCH ON FIRE, AND WHY DOES IT NOT BURN UP? IT JUST KEEPS ON BURNING AND BURNING.
MOSES, TAKE YOUR SHOES OFF. YOU ARE STANDING ON HOLY GROUND. I AM THE GOD OF YOUR FATHERS, ABRAHAM, ISAAC, AND JACOB.
I HAVE SEEN THE SUFFERING AND HEARD THE PRAYERS OF MY PEOPLE IN EGYPT. IT IS TIME TO DELIVER THEM FROM THEIR OPPRESSION AND BRING THEM BACK INTO THE LAND I PROMISED THEIR FATHERS.
I WILL SEND YOU TO PHARAOH AND YOU WILL BRING MY PEOPLE OUT OF THEIR BONDAGE. YOU WILL TELL HIM TO LET MY PEOPLE GO, AND HE WILL REFUSE. THEN I WILL SHOW MY POWER TO EGYPT. AFTER THAT HE WILL LET THEM GO.

EXODUS 2:16–3:10

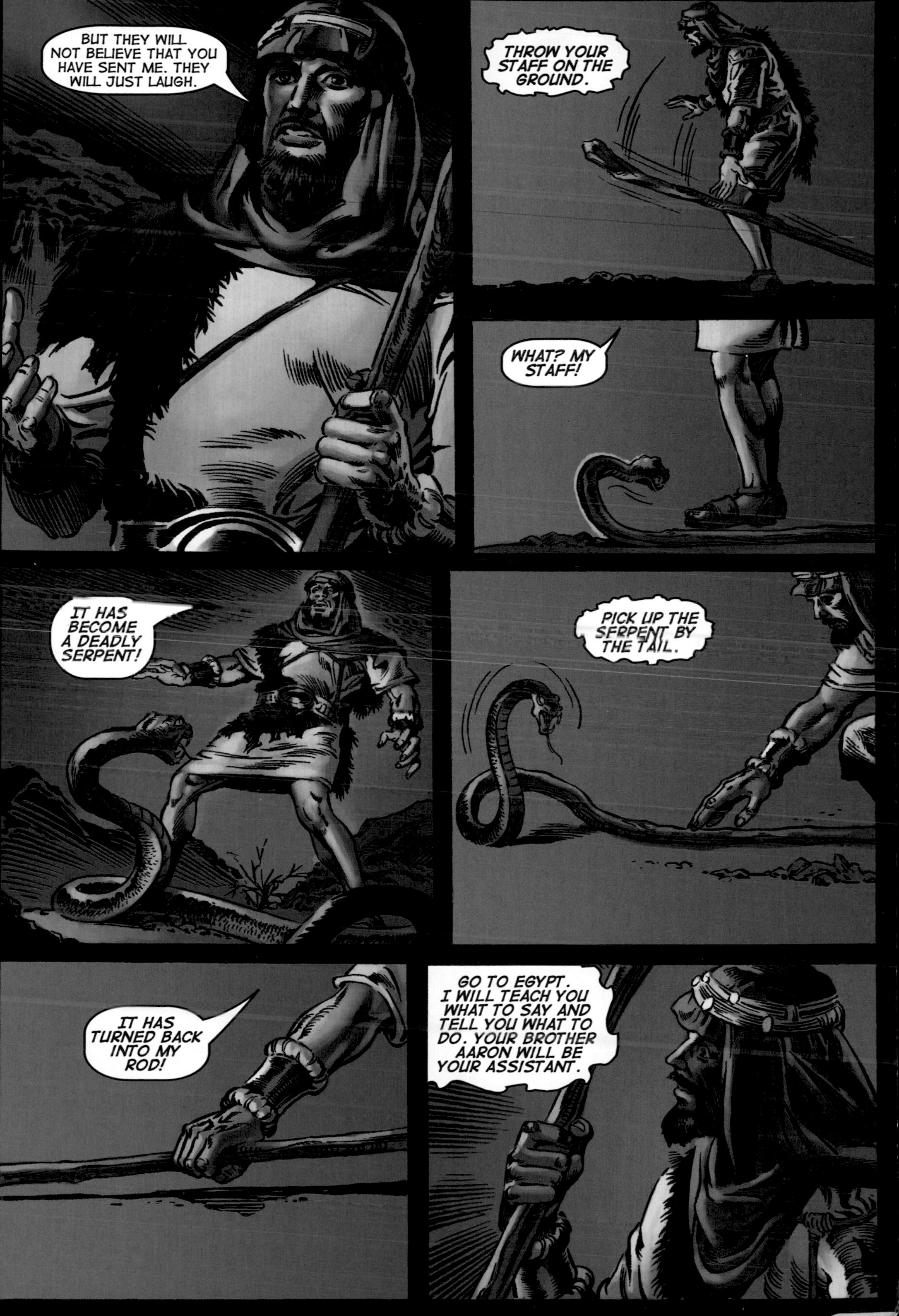
BUT THEY WILL NOT BELIEVE THAT YOU HAVE SENT ME. THEY WILL JUST LAUGH.
THROW YOUR STAFF ON THE GROUND.
WHAT? MY STAFF!
IT HAS BECOME A DEADLY SERPENT!
PICK UP THE SERPENT BY THE TAIL.
IT HAS TURNED BACK INTO MY ROD!
GO TO EGYPT. I WILL TEACH YOU WHAT TO SAY AND TELL YOU WHAT TO DO. YOUR BROTHER AARON WILL BE YOUR ASSISTANT.

EXODUS 4:1-4, 12-16

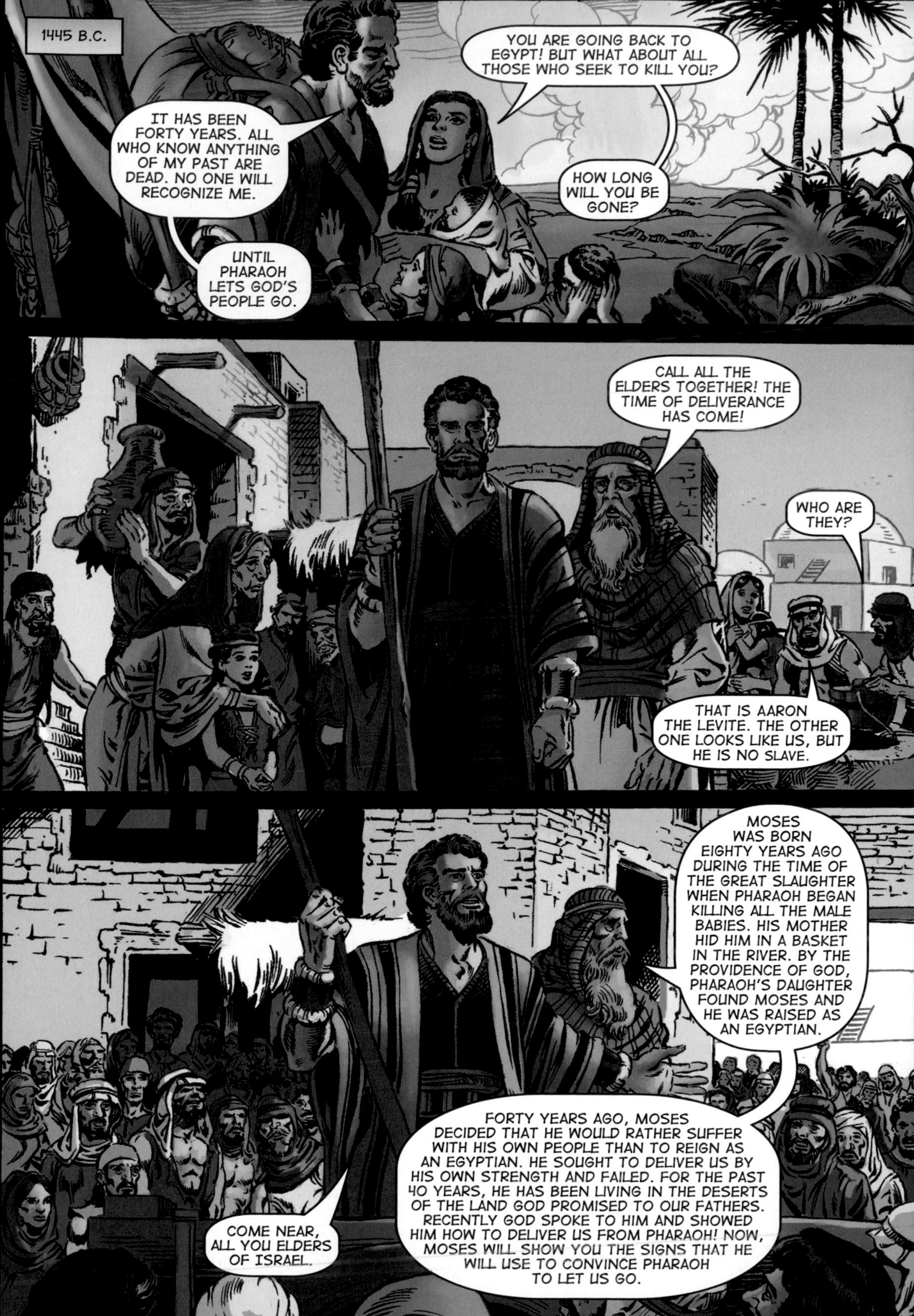
1445 B.C.
IT HAS BEEN FORTY YEARS. ALL WHO KNOW ANYTHING OF MY PAST ARE DEAD. NO ONE WILL RECOGNIZE ME.
YOU ARE GOING BACK TO EGYPT! BUT WHAT ABOUT ALL THOSE WHO SEEK TO KILL YOU?
HOW LONG WILL YOU BE GONE?
UNTIL PHARAOH LETS GOD'S PEOPLE GO.
CALL ALL THE ELDERS TOGETHER! THE TIME OF DELIVERANCE HAS COME!
WHO ARE THEY?
THAT IS AARON THE LEVITE. THE OTHER ONE LOOKS LIKE US, BUT HE IS NO SLAVE.
MOSES WAS BORN EIGHTY YEARS AGO DURING THE TIME OF THE GREAT SLAUGHTER WHEN PHARAOH BEGAN KILLING ALL THE MALE BABIES. HIS MOTHER HID HIM IN A BASKET IN THE RIVER. BY THE PROVIDENCE OF GOD, PHARAOH'S DAUGHTER FOUND MOSES AND HE WAS RAISED AS AN EGYPTIAN.
FORTY YEARS AGO, MOSES DECIDED THAT HE WOULD RATHER SUFFER WITH HIS OWN PEOPLE THAN TO REIGN AS AN EGYPTIAN. HE SOUGHT TO DELIVER US BY HIS OWN STRENGTH AND FAILED. FOR THE PAST 40 YEARS, HE HAS BEEN LIVING IN THE DESERTS OF THE LAND GOD PROMISED TO OUR FATHERS. RECENTLY GOD SPOKE TO HIM AND SHOWED HIM HOW TO DELIVER US FROM PHARAOH! NOW, MOSES WILL SHOW YOU THE SIGNS THAT HE WILL USE TO CONVINCE PHARAOH TO LET US GO.
COME NEAR, ALL YOU ELDERS OF ISRAEL.

EXODUS 4:29-31

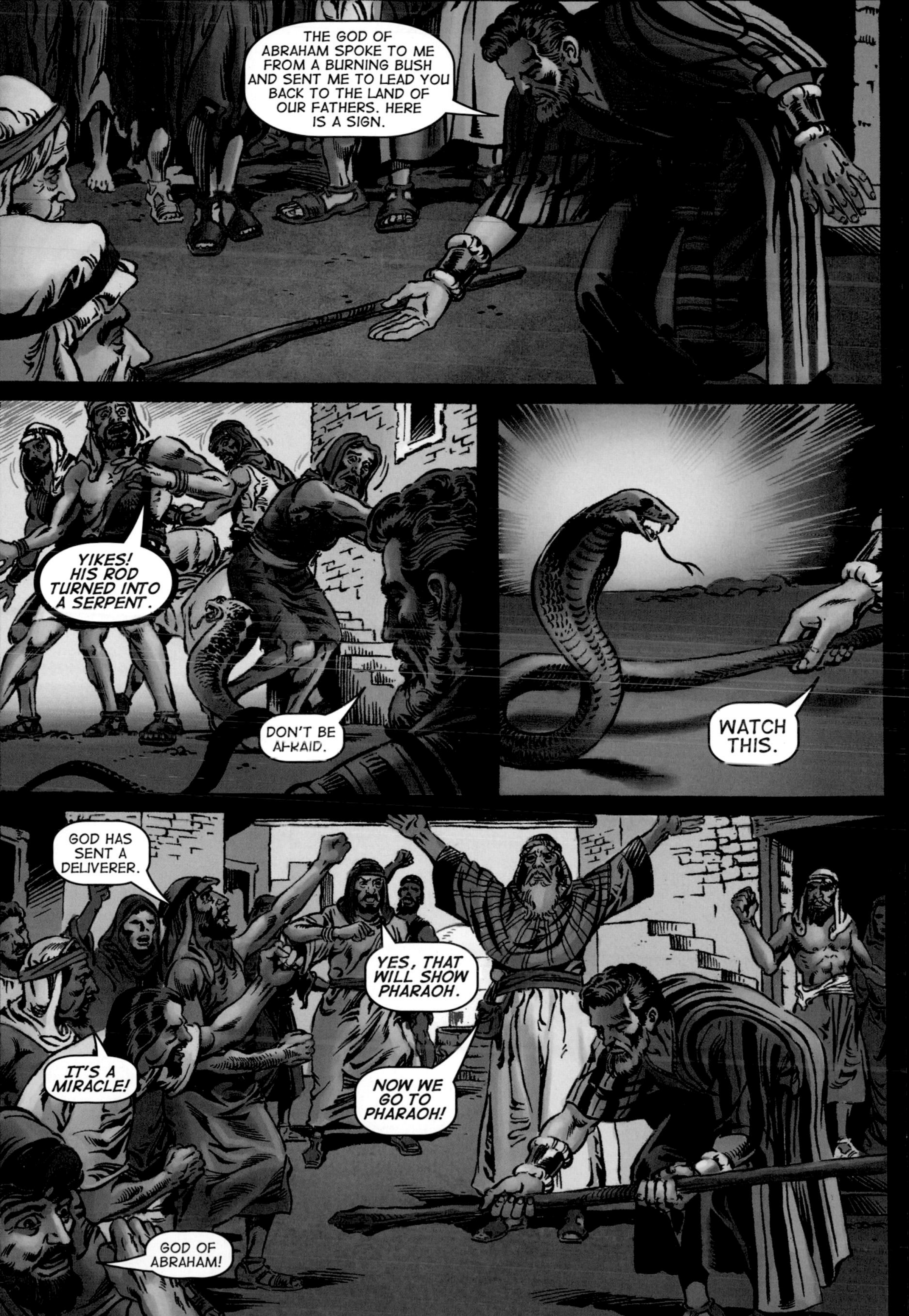
THE GOD OF ABRAHAM SPOKE TO ME FROM A BURNING BUSH AND SENT ME TO LEAD YOU BACK TO THE LAND OF OUR FATHERS. HERE IS A SIGN.
YIKES! HIS ROD TURNED INTO A SERPENT.
DON'T BE AFRAID.
WATCH THIS.
GOD HAS SENT A DELIVERER.
YES, THAT WILL SHOW PHARAOH.
IT'S A MIRACLE!
NOW WE GO TO PHARAOH!
GOD OF ABRAHAM!

EXODUS 4:17, 30

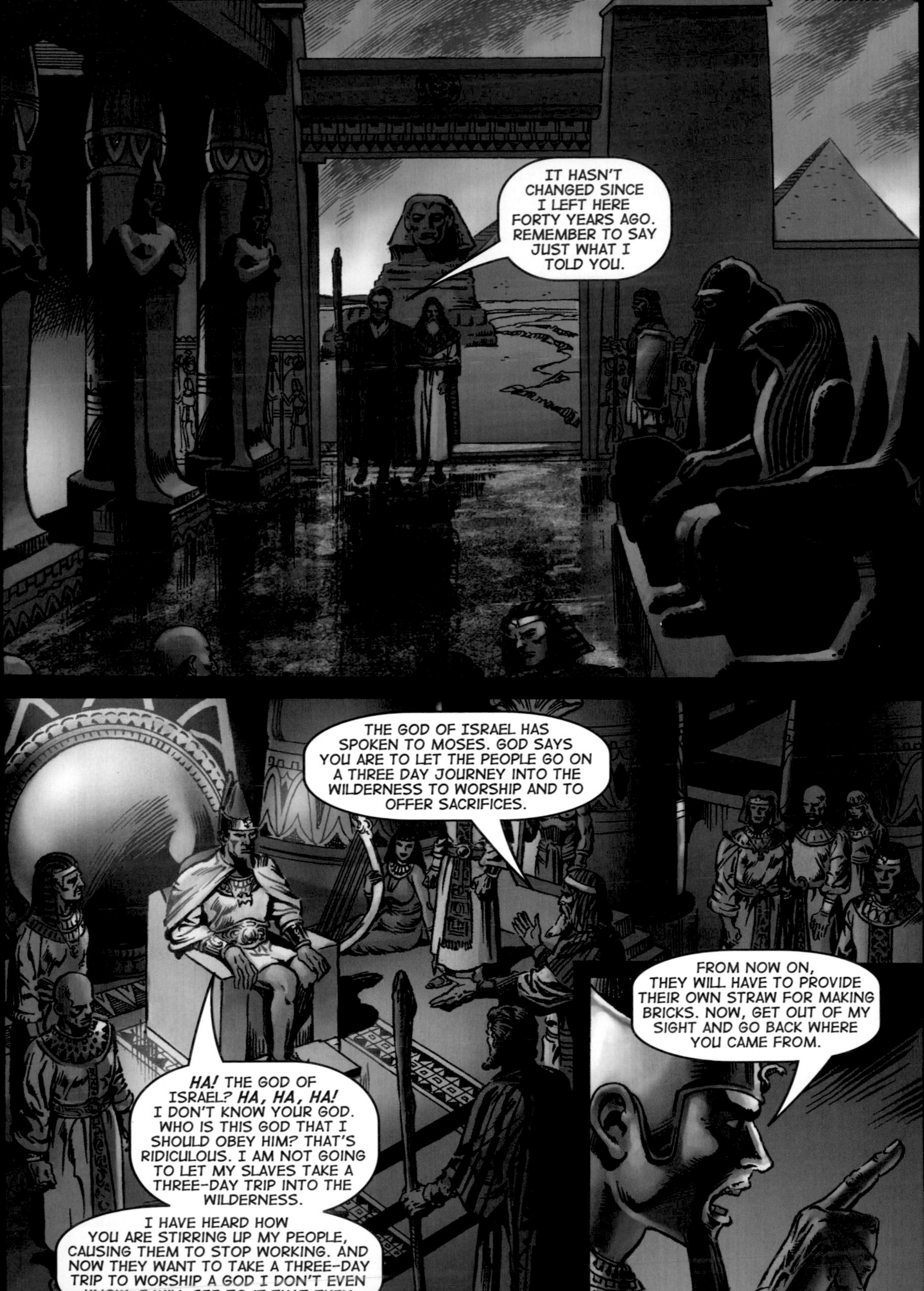
IT HASN'T CHANGED SINCE I LEFT HERE FORTY YEARS AGO. REMEMBER TO SAY JUST WHAT I TOLD YOU.
THE GOD OF ISRAEL HAS SPOKEN TO MOSES. GOD SAYS YOU ARE TO LET THE PEOPLE GO ON A THREE DAY JOURNEY INTO THE WILDERNESS TO WORSHIP AND TO OFFER SACRIFICES.
HA! THE GOD OF ISRAEL? HA, HA, HA! I DON'T KNOW YOUR GOD. WHO IS THIS GOD THAT I SHOULD OBEY HIM? THAT'S RIDICULOUS. I AM NOT GOING TO LET MY SLAVES TAKE A THREE-DAY TRIP INTO THE WILDERNESS.
I HAVE HEARD HOW YOU ARE STIRRING UP MY PEOPLE, CAUSING THEM TO STOP WORKING. AND NOW THEY WANT TO TAKE A THREE-DAY TRIP TO WORSHIP A GOD I DON'T EVEN KNOW. I WILL SEE TO IT THAT THEY HAVE MORE WORK TO DO.
FROM NOW ON, THEY WILL HAVE TO PROVIDE THEIR OWN STRAW FOR MAKING BRICKS. NOW, GET OUT OF MY SIGHT AND GO BACK WHERE YOU CAME FROM.

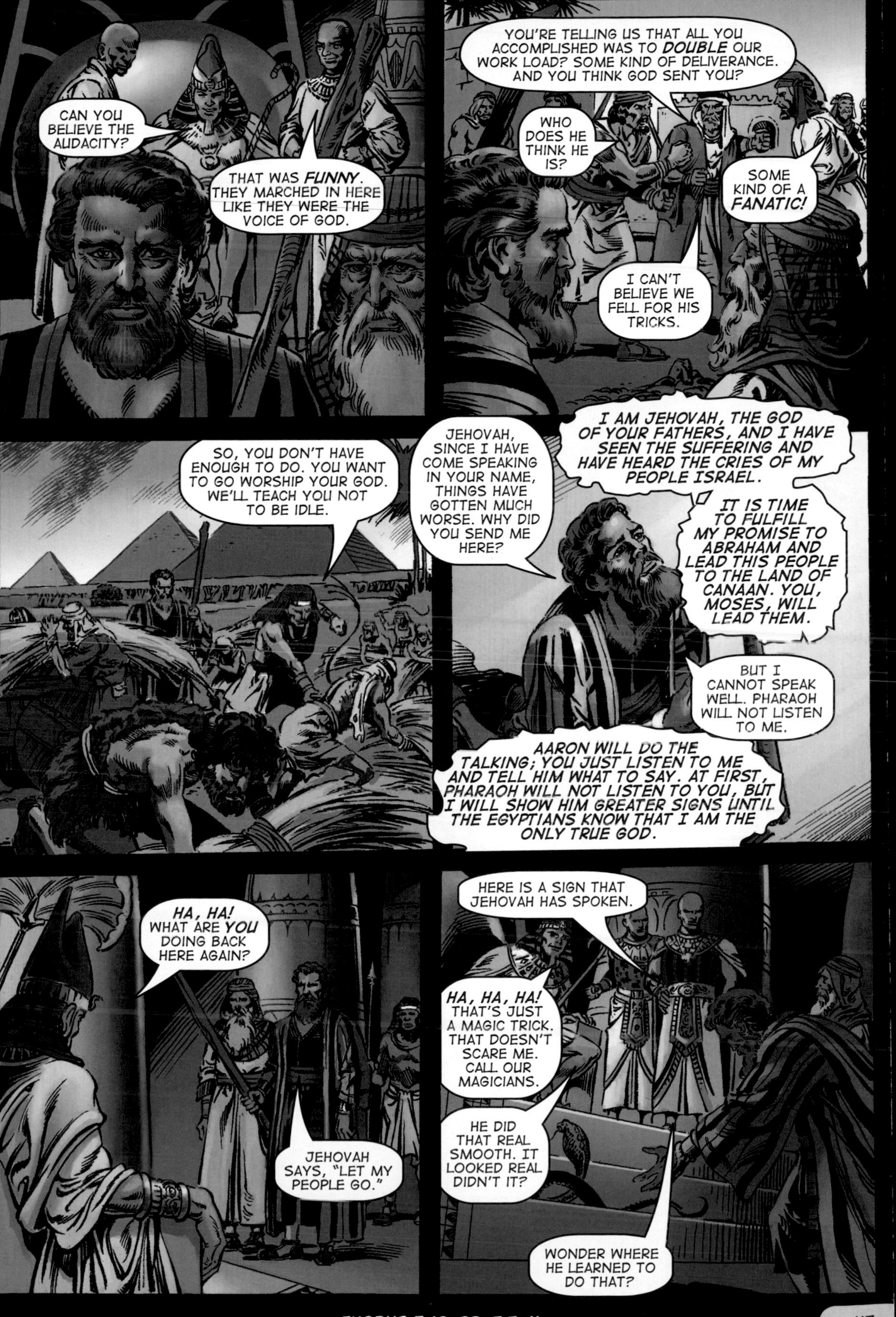
CAN YOU BELIEVE THE AUDACITY?
THAT WAS FUNNY. THEY MARCHED IN HERE LIKE THEY WERE THE VOICE OF GOD.
YOU'RE TELLING US THAT ALL YOU ACCOMPLISHED WAS TO DOUBLE OUR WORK LOAD? SOME KIND OF DELIVERANCE. AND YOU THINK GOD SENT YOU?
WHO DOES HE THINK HE IS?
SOME KIND OF A FANATIC!
I CAN'T BELIEVE WE FELL FOR HIS TRICKS.
SO, YOU DON'T HAVE ENOUGH TO DO. YOU WANT TO GO WORSHIP YOUR GOD. WE'LL TEACH YOU NOT TO BE IDLE.
JEHOVAH, SINCE I HAVE COME SPEAKING IN YOUR NAME, THINGS HAVE GOTTEN MUCH WORSE. WHY DID YOU SEND ME HERE?
I AM JEHOVAH, THE GOD OF YOUR FATHERS, AND I HAVE SEEN THE SUFFERING AND HAVE HEARD THE CRIES OF MY PEOPLE ISRAEL.
IT IS TIME TO FULFILL MY PROMISE TO ABRAHAM AND LEAD THIS PEOPLE TO THE LAND OF CANAAN. YOU, MOSES, WILL LEAD THEM.
BUT I CANNOT SPEAK WELL. PHARAOH WILL NOT LISTEN TO ME.
AARON WILL DO THE TALKING; YOU JUST LISTEN TO ME AND TELL HIM WHAT TO SAY. AT FIRST, PHARAOH WILL NOT LISTEN TO YOU, BUT I WILL SHOW HIM GREATER SIGNS UNTIL THE EGYPTIANS KNOW THAT I AM THE ONLY TRUE GOD.
HA, HA! WHAT ARE YOU DOING BACK HERE AGAIN?
JEHOVAH SAYS, "LET MY PEOPLE GO."
HERE IS A SIGN THAT JEHOVAH HAS SPOKEN.
HA, HA, HA! THAT'S JUST A MAGIC TRICK. THAT DOESN'T SCARE ME. CALL OUR MAGICIANS.
HE DID THAT REAL SMOOTH. IT LOOKED REAL DIDN'T IT?
WONDER WHERE HE LEARNED TO DO THAT?

EXODUS 5:10-23, 7:7-11

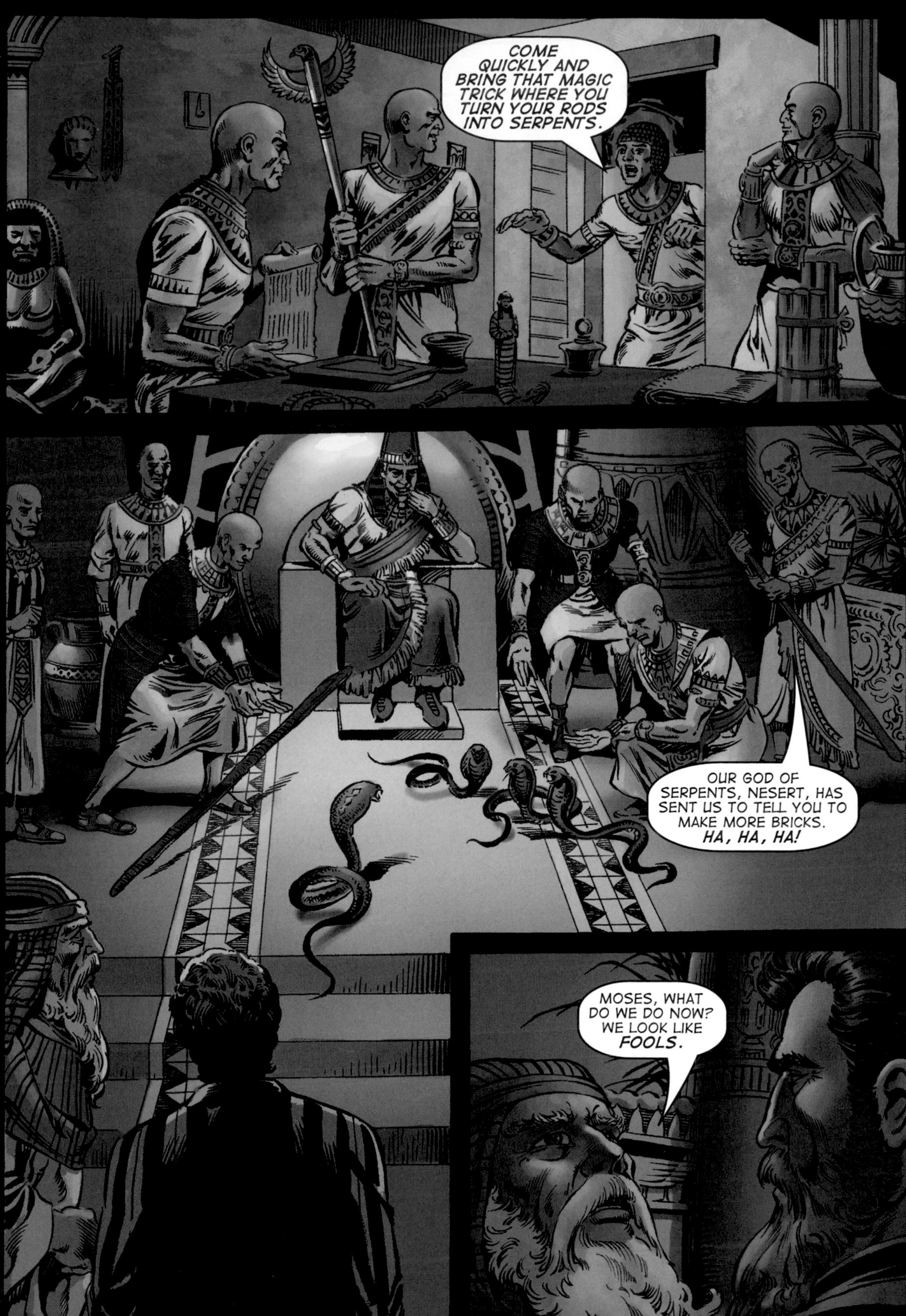
COME QUICKLY AND BRING THAT MAGIC TRICK WHERE YOU TURN YOUR RODS INTO SERPENTS.
OUR GOD OF SERPENTS, NESERT, HAS SENT US TO TELL YOU TO MAKE MORE BRICKS. HA, HA, HA!
MOSES, WHAT DO WE DO NOW? WE LOOK LIKE FOOLS.

LOOK! HIS SERPENT WANTS TO FIGHT OURS.

HIS SERPENT IS EATING ONE OF OURS!

IT SWALLOWED OUR SERPENT COMPLETELY!

DON'T TELL ME IT IS GOING TO TRY TO EAT *ANOTHER* ONE! OUR SERPENT GOD, NESERT, WILL BE *ANGRY.*

I CAN'T BELIEVE IT! HIS SERPENT HAS EATEN EVERY ONE OF OURS.

HOW COULD THIS BE?

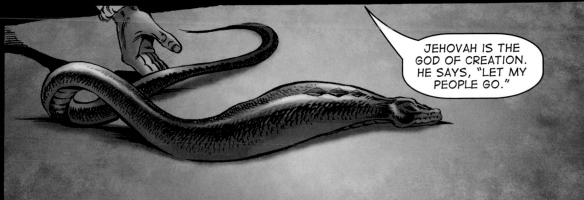

JEHOVAH IS THE GOD OF CREATION. HE SAYS, "LET MY PEOPLE GO."

EXODUS 7:12

49

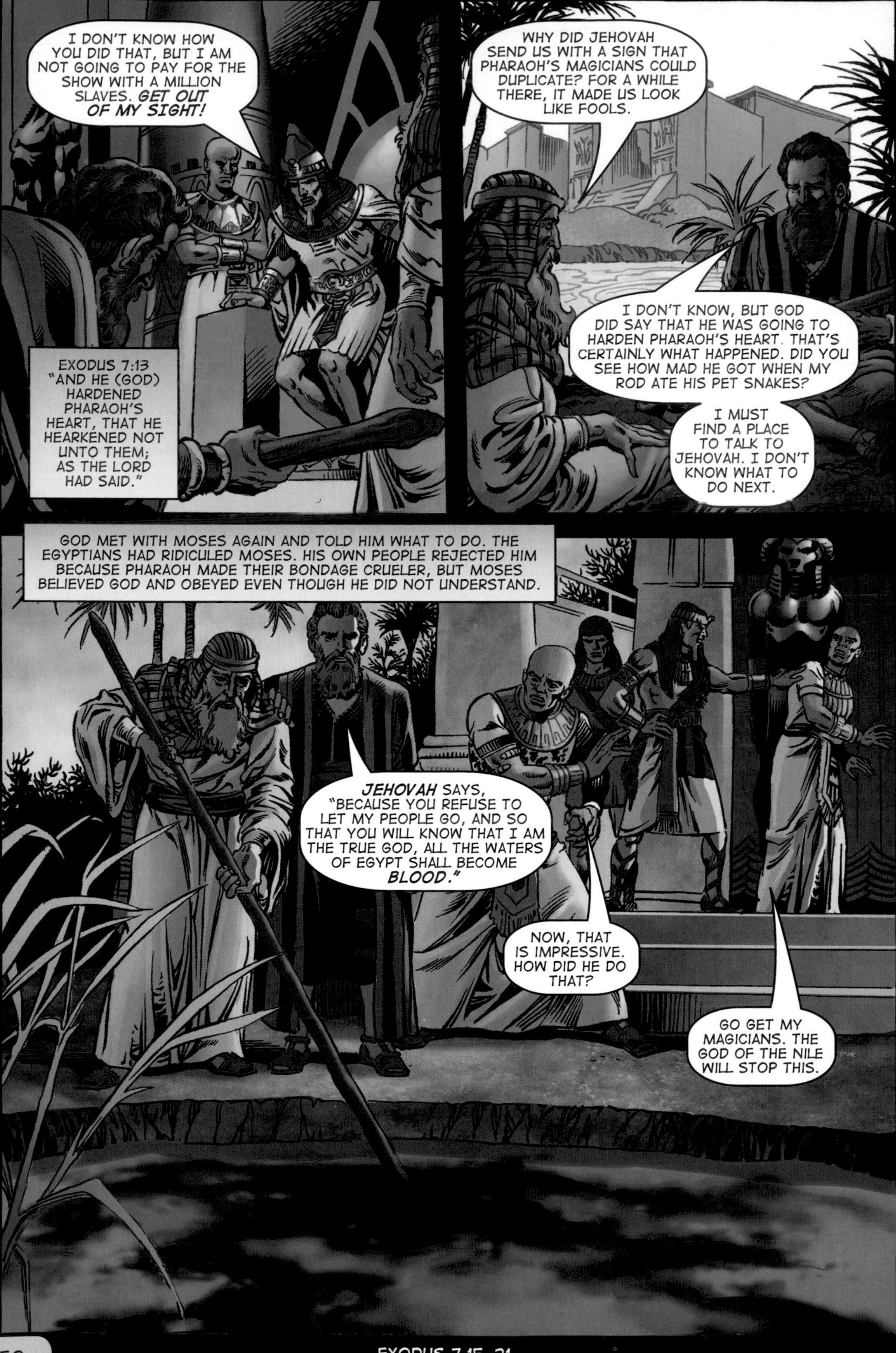
I DON'T KNOW HOW YOU DID THAT, BUT I AM NOT GOING TO PAY FOR THE SHOW WITH A MILLION SLAVES. GET OUT OF MY SIGHT!
EXODUS 7:13 "AND HE (GOD) HARDENED PHARAOH'S HEART, THAT HE HEARKENED NOT UNTO THEM; AS THE LORD HAD SAID."
WHY DID JEHOVAH SEND US WITH A SIGN THAT PHARAOH'S MAGICIANS COULD DUPLICATE? FOR A WHILE THERE, IT MADE US LOOK LIKE FOOLS.
I DON'T KNOW, BUT GOD DID SAY THAT HE WAS GOING TO HARDEN PHARAOH'S HEART. THAT'S CERTAINLY WHAT HAPPENED. DID YOU SEE HOW MAD HE GOT WHEN MY ROD ATE HIS PET SNAKES?
I MUST FIND A PLACE TO TALK TO JEHOVAH. I DON'T KNOW WHAT TO DO NEXT.
GOD MET WITH MOSES AGAIN AND TOLD HIM WHAT TO DO. THE EGYPTIANS HAD RIDICULED MOSES. HIS OWN PEOPLE REJECTED HIM BECAUSE PHARAOH MADE THEIR BONDAGE CRUELER, BUT MOSES BELIEVED GOD AND OBEYED EVEN THOUGH HE DID NOT UNDERSTAND.
JEHOVAH SAYS, "BECAUSE YOU REFUSE TO LET MY PEOPLE GO, AND SO THAT YOU WILL KNOW THAT I AM THE TRUE GOD, ALL THE WATERS OF EGYPT SHALL BECOME BLOOD."
NOW, THAT IS IMPRESSIVE. HOW DID HE DO THAT?
GO GET MY MAGICIANS. THE GOD OF THE NILE WILL STOP THIS.

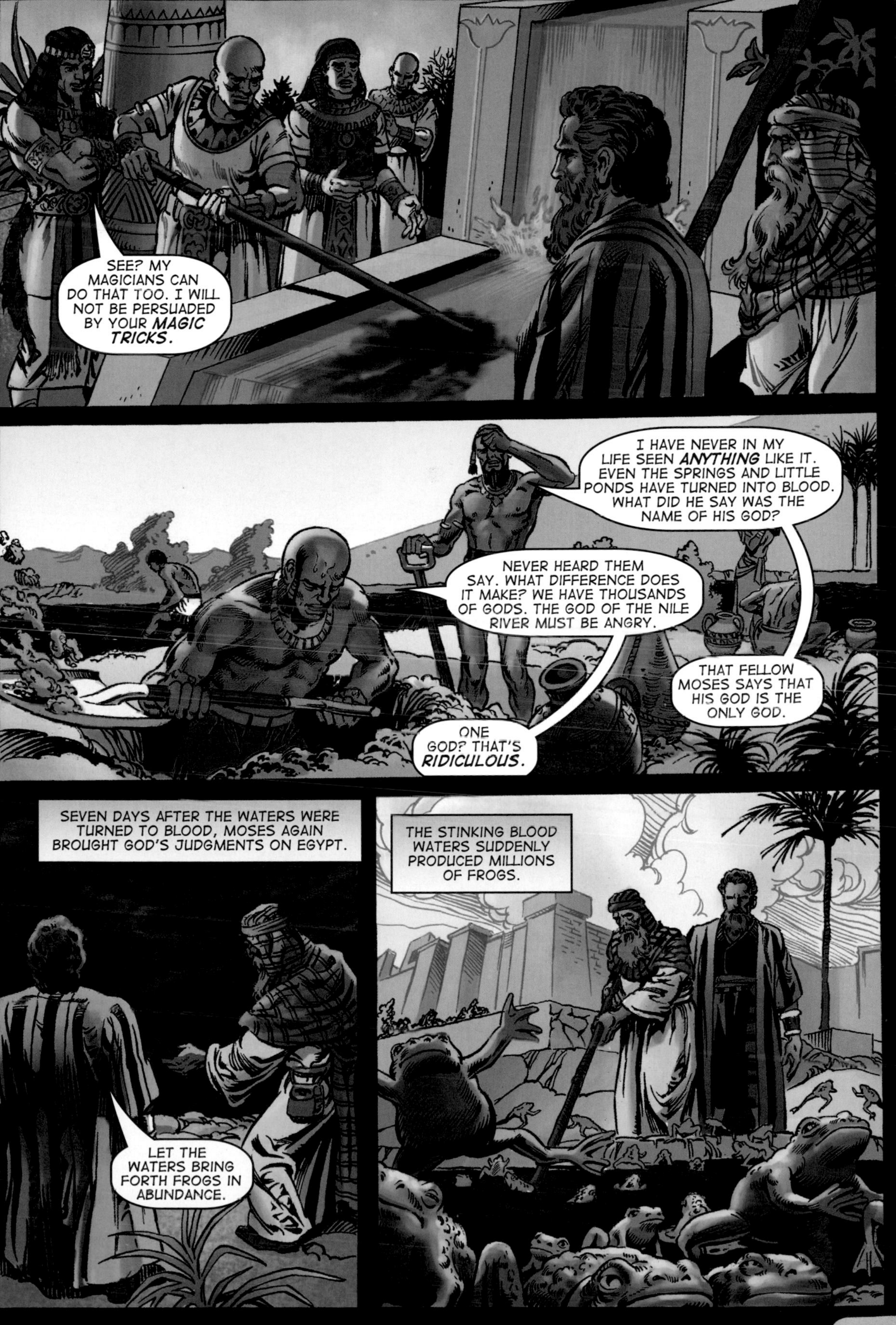
SEE? MY MAGICIANS CAN DO THAT TOO. I WILL NOT BE PERSUADED BY YOUR MAGIC TRICKS.
I HAVE NEVER IN MY LIFE SEEN ANYTHING LIKE IT. EVEN THE SPRINGS AND LITTLE PONDS HAVE TURNED INTO BLOOD. WHAT DID HE SAY WAS THE NAME OF HIS GOD?
NEVER HEARD THEM SAY. WHAT DIFFERENCE DOES IT MAKE? WE HAVE THOUSANDS OF GODS. THE GOD OF THE NILE RIVER MUST BE ANGRY.
THAT FELLOW MOSES SAYS THAT HIS GOD IS THE ONLY GOD.
ONE GOD? THAT'S RIDICULOUS.
SEVEN DAYS AFTER THE WATERS WERE TURNED TO BLOOD, MOSES AGAIN BROUGHT GOD'S JUDGMENTS ON EGYPT.
LET THE WATERS BRING FORTH FROGS IN ABUNDANCE.
THE STINKING BLOOD WATERS SUDDENLY PRODUCED MILLIONS OF FROGS.

EXODUS 7:21-25, 8:6

MY HOUSE IS FULL OF FROGS.

ALL OF EGYPT IS FILLED WITH FROGS. *THE GODS ARE ANGRY!*

WHERE ARE OUR PRIESTS? CAN'T THEY DO SOMETHING?

EIIIII!

PHARAOH, SEE, WE MAGICIANS CAN MAKE FROGS TOO.

WHY ARE THEY MAKING *MORE* FROGS? DIDN'T THAT FELLOW MOSES GIVE US ENOUGH? NOW PHARAOH GIVES US MORE.

WHY DON'T YOU LET THEM GO INTO THE WILDERNESS AS THEY ASKED? WE CAN'T STAND MUCH MORE OF THIS.

CALL MOSES. TELL HIM I WANT TO TALK.

YES MASTER, AS YOU SAY.

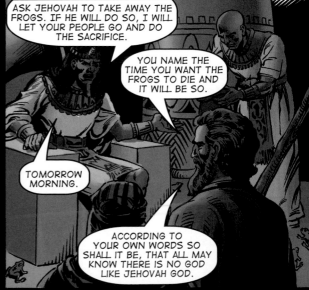

ASK JEHOVAH TO TAKE AWAY THE FROGS. IF HE WILL DO SO, I WILL LET YOUR PEOPLE GO AND DO THE SACRIFICE.

YOU NAME THE TIME YOU WANT THE FROGS TO DIE AND IT WILL BE SO.

TOMORROW MORNING.

ACCORDING TO YOUR OWN WORDS SO SHALL IT BE, THAT ALL MAY KNOW THERE IS NO GOD LIKE JEHOVAH GOD.

EXODUS 8:7-10

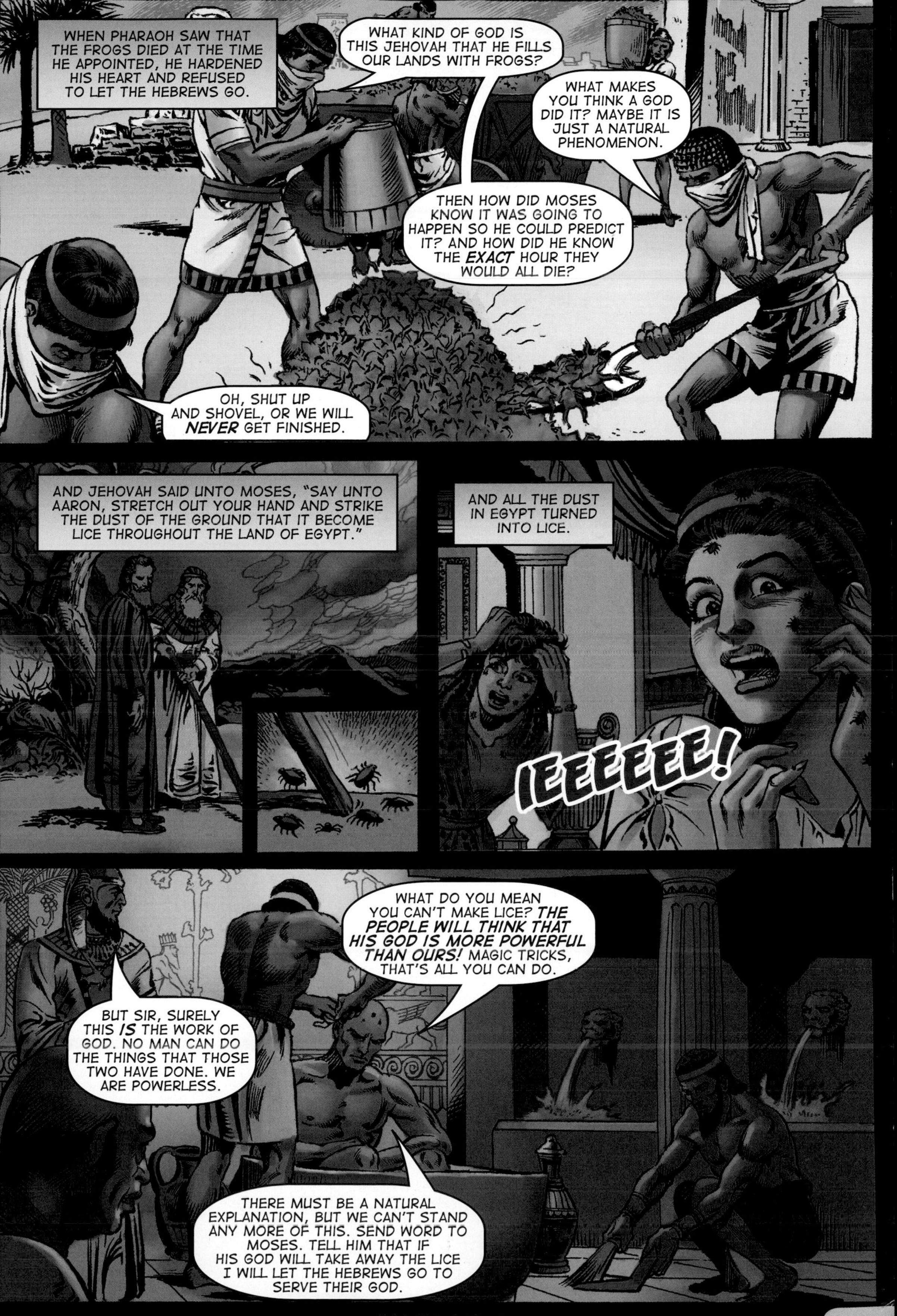
WHEN PHARAOH SAW THAT THE FROGS DIED AT THE TIME HE APPOINTED, HE HARDENED HIS HEART AND REFUSED TO LET THE HEBREWS GO.
WHAT KIND OF GOD IS THIS JEHOVAH THAT HE FILLS OUR LANDS WITH FROGS?
WHAT MAKES YOU THINK A GOD DID IT? MAYBE IT IS JUST A NATURAL PHENOMENON.
THEN HOW DID MOSES KNOW IT WAS GOING TO HAPPEN SO HE COULD PREDICT IT? AND HOW DID HE KNOW THE EXACT HOUR THEY WOULD ALL DIE?
OH, SHUT UP AND SHOVEL, OR WE WILL NEVER GET FINISHED.
AND JEHOVAH SAID UNTO MOSES, "SAY UNTO AARON, STRETCH OUT YOUR HAND AND STRIKE THE DUST OF THE GROUND THAT IT BECOME LICE THROUGHOUT THE LAND OF EGYPT."
AND ALL THE DUST IN EGYPT TURNED INTO LICE.
IEEEEEE!
WHAT DO YOU MEAN YOU CAN'T MAKE LICE? THE PEOPLE WILL THINK THAT HIS GOD IS MORE POWERFUL THAN OURS! MAGIC TRICKS, THAT'S ALL YOU CAN DO.
BUT SIR, SURELY THIS IS THE WORK OF GOD. NO MAN CAN DO THE THINGS THAT THOSE TWO HAVE DONE. WE ARE POWERLESS.
THERE MUST BE A NATURAL EXPLANATION, BUT WE CAN'T STAND ANY MORE OF THIS. SEND WORD TO MOSES. TELL HIM THAT IF HIS GOD WILL TAKE AWAY THE LICE I WILL LET THE HEBREWS GO TO SERVE THEIR GOD.

EXODUS 8:13-19

THE LICE ARE GONE, BUT I CANNOT LET THE SLAVES GO. AFTER ALL, WHAT ELSE COULD HIS GOD DO?

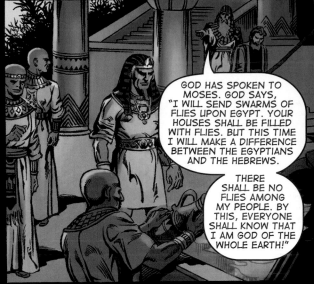

GOD HAS SPOKEN TO MOSES. GOD SAYS, "I WILL SEND SWARMS OF FLIES UPON EGYPT. YOUR HOUSES SHALL BE FILLED WITH FLIES. BUT THIS TIME I WILL MAKE A DIFFERENCE BETWEEN THE EGYPTIANS AND THE HEBREWS.

THERE SHALL BE NO FLIES AMONG MY PEOPLE. BY THIS, EVERYONE SHALL KNOW THAT I AM GOD OF THE WHOLE EARTH!"

DADDY, WHY CAN'T OUR PRIESTS *STOP* THIS MAN? WHERE IS THEIR *POWER?*

I DON'T KNOW ANYTHING ABOUT RELIGION. I JUST MIND MY OWN BUSINESS.

IT IS JUST AS HE SAID; *THERE ARE NO FLIES AMONG THE HEBREWS!* THIS MUST BE THE WORK OF THEIR GOD.

GO FIND MOSES.

GO THEN, AND SACRIFICE TO YOUR GOD, BUT *DO NOT* LEAVE THE LAND OF EGYPT.

WE MUST GO AT LEAST THREE DAYS' JOURNEY.

I SAID YOU CAN GO, BUT YOU CANNOT GO VERY FAR. NOW TALK TO YOUR GOD AND ASK HIM TO TAKE AWAY THESE STINKING FLIES.

THERE IS NOT ONE FLY LEFT ALIVE IN ALL EGYPT. NOW THAT IS A MIRACLE.

SHUT UP. YOU SOUND AS IF YOU ARE BEGINNING TO BELIEVE THE BABBLER.

AGAIN PHARAOH HARDENED HIS HEART AND REFUSED TO LET THE PEOPLE GO.

EXODUS 8:20-32

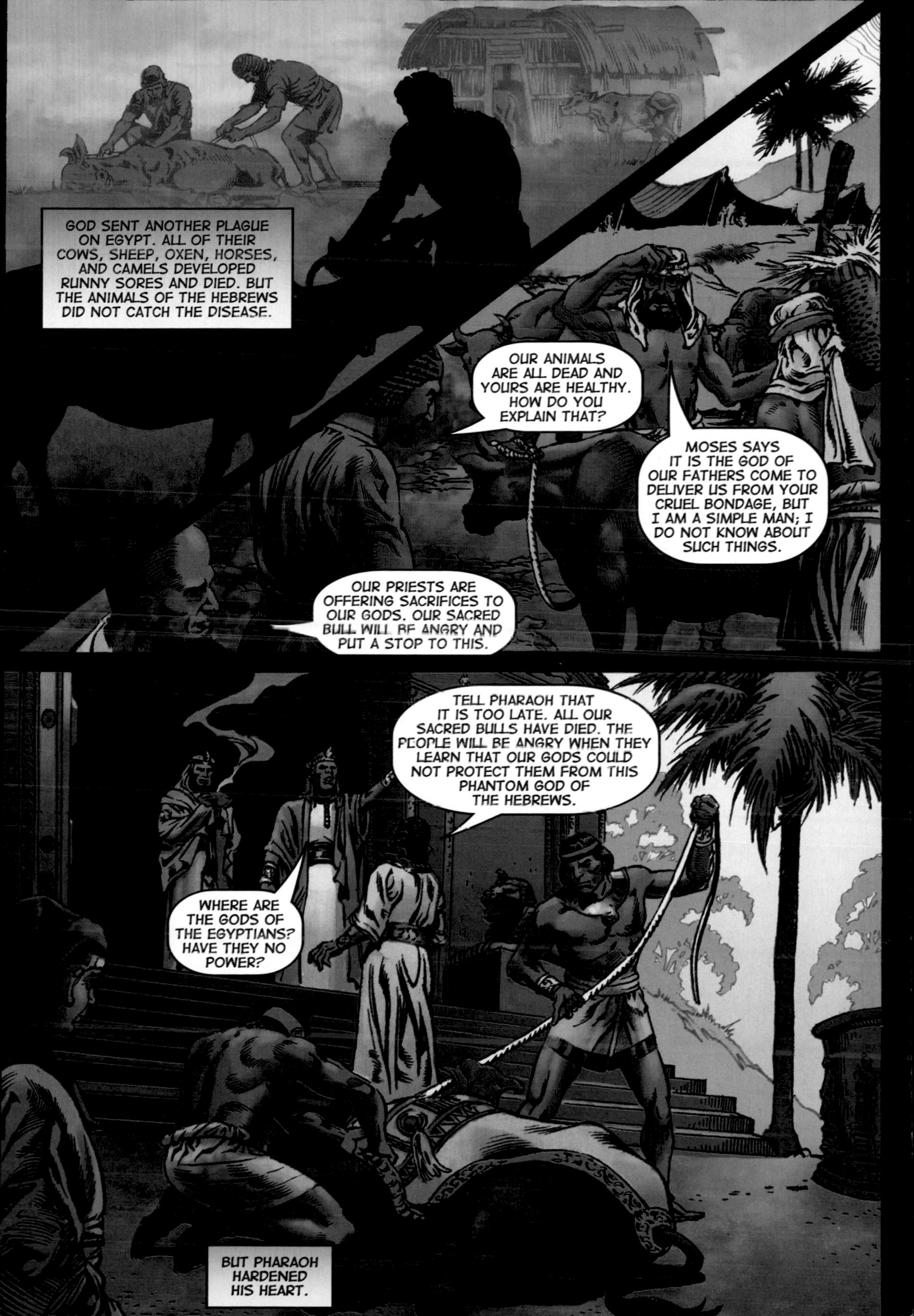
GOD SENT ANOTHER PLAGUE ON EGYPT. ALL OF THEIR COWS, SHEEP, OXEN, HORSES, AND CAMELS DEVELOPED RUNNY SORES AND DIED. BUT THE ANIMALS OF THE HEBREWS DID NOT CATCH THE DISEASE.
OUR ANIMALS ARE ALL DEAD AND YOURS ARE HEALTHY. HOW DO YOU EXPLAIN THAT?
MOSES SAYS IT IS THE GOD OF OUR FATHERS COME TO DELIVER US FROM YOUR CRUEL BONDAGE, BUT I AM A SIMPLE MAN; I DO NOT KNOW ABOUT SUCH THINGS.
OUR PRIESTS ARE OFFERING SACRIFICES TO OUR GODS. OUR SACRED BULL WILL BE ANGRY AND PUT A STOP TO THIS.
TELL PHARAOH THAT IT IS TOO LATE. ALL OUR SACRED BULLS HAVE DIED. THE PEOPLE WILL BE ANGRY WHEN THEY LEARN THAT OUR GODS COULD NOT PROTECT THEM FROM THIS PHANTOM GOD OF THE HEBREWS.
WHERE ARE THE GODS OF THE EGYPTIANS? HAVE THEY NO POWER?
BUT PHARAOH HARDENED HIS HEART.

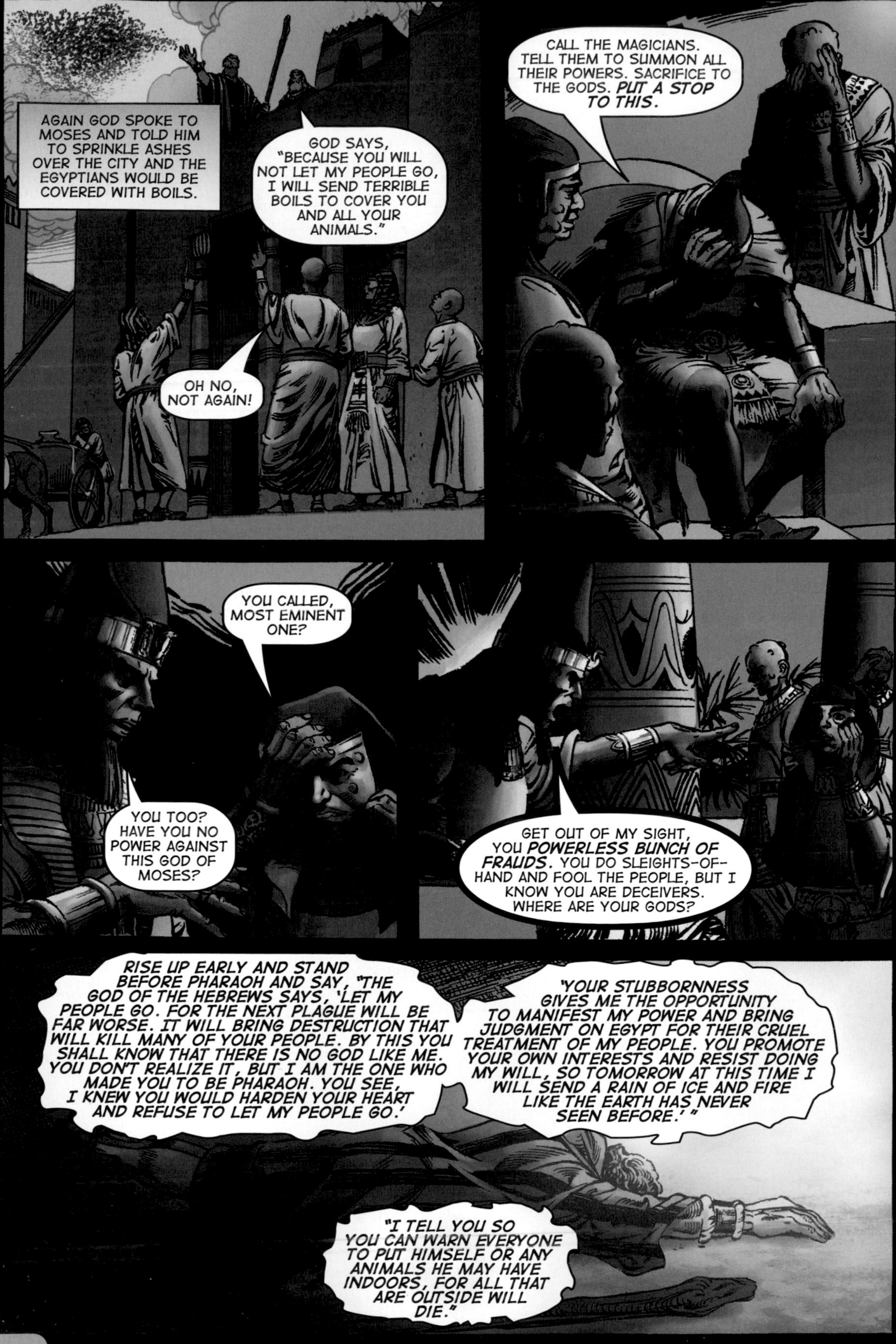
AGAIN GOD SPOKE TO MOSES AND TOLD HIM TO SPRINKLE ASHES OVER THE CITY AND THE EGYPTIANS WOULD BE COVERED WITH BOILS.
GOD SAYS, "BECAUSE YOU WILL NOT LET MY PEOPLE GO, I WILL SEND TERRIBLE BOILS TO COVER YOU AND ALL YOUR ANIMALS."
OH NO, NOT AGAIN!
CALL THE MAGICIANS. TELL THEM TO SUMMON ALL THEIR POWERS. SACRIFICE TO THE GODS. *PUT A STOP TO THIS*.
YOU CALLED, MOST EMINENT ONE?
YOU TOO? HAVE YOU NO POWER AGAINST THIS GOD OF MOSES?
GET OUT OF MY SIGHT, YOU **POWERLESS BUNCH OF FRAUDS**. YOU DO SLEIGHTS-OF-HAND AND FOOL THE PEOPLE, BUT I KNOW YOU ARE DECEIVERS. WHERE ARE YOUR GODS?
RISE UP EARLY AND STAND BEFORE PHARAOH AND SAY, "THE GOD OF THE HEBREWS SAYS, 'LET MY PEOPLE GO. FOR THE NEXT PLAGUE WILL BE FAR WORSE. IT WILL BRING DESTRUCTION THAT WILL KILL MANY OF YOUR PEOPLE. BY THIS YOU SHALL KNOW THAT THERE IS NO GOD LIKE ME. YOU DON'T REALIZE IT, BUT I AM THE ONE WHO MADE YOU TO BE PHARAOH. YOU SEE, I KNEW YOU WOULD HARDEN YOUR HEART AND REFUSE TO LET MY PEOPLE GO.'
"YOUR STUBBORNNESS GIVES ME THE OPPORTUNITY TO MANIFEST MY POWER AND BRING JUDGMENT ON EGYPT FOR THEIR CRUEL TREATMENT OF MY PEOPLE. YOU PROMOTE YOUR OWN INTERESTS AND RESIST DOING MY WILL, SO TOMORROW AT THIS TIME I WILL SEND A RAIN OF ICE AND FIRE LIKE THE EARTH HAS NEVER SEEN BEFORE.' "
"I TELL YOU SO YOU CAN WARN EVERYONE TO PUT HIMSELF OR ANY ANIMALS HE MAY HAVE INDOORS, FOR ALL THAT ARE OUTSIDE WILL DIE."

EXODUS 9:8-19

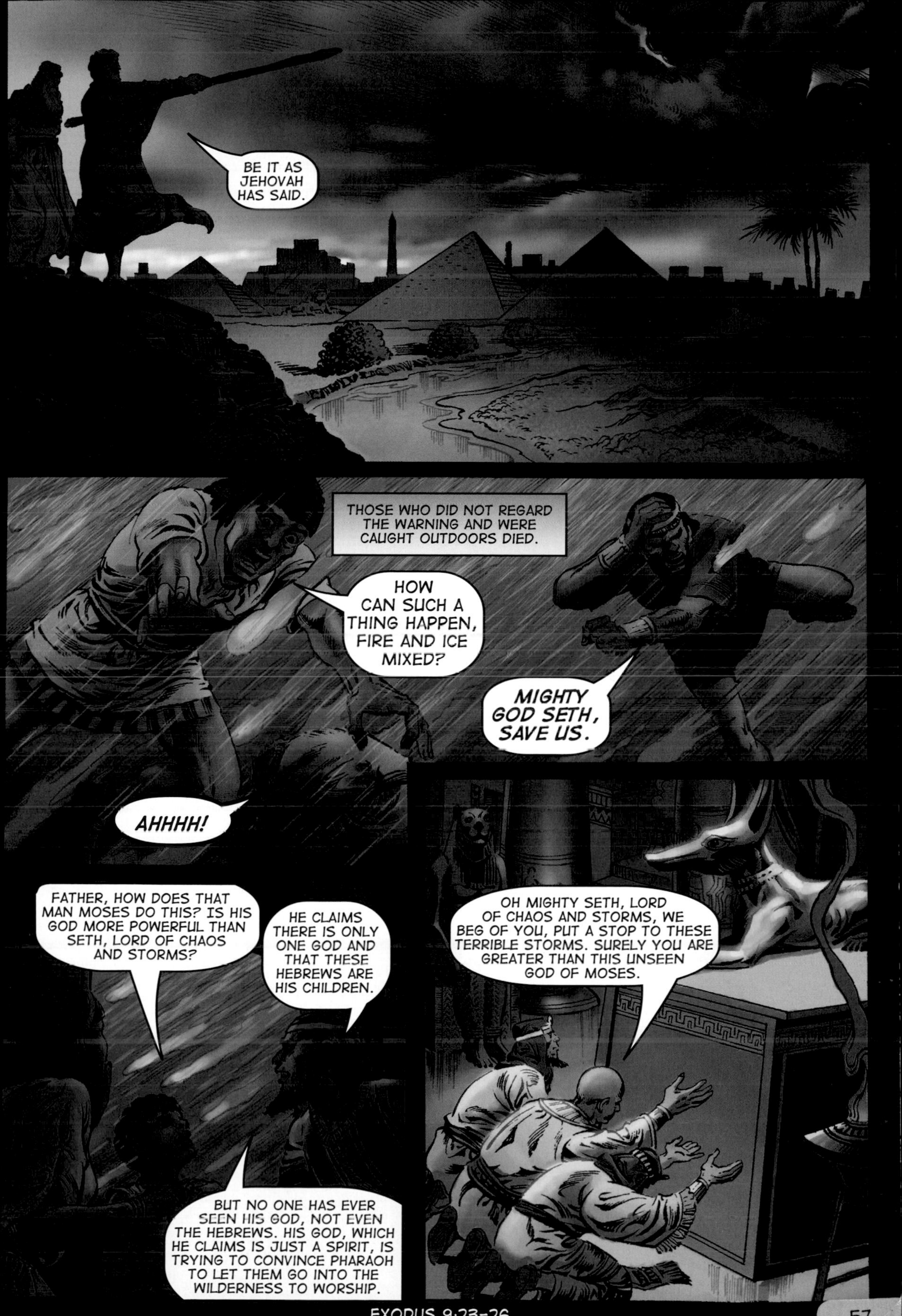
BE IT AS JEHOVAH HAS SAID.
THOSE WHO DID NOT REGARD THE WARNING AND WERE CAUGHT OUTDOORS DIED.
HOW CAN SUCH A THING HAPPEN, FIRE AND ICE MIXED?
MIGHTY GOD SETH, SAVE US.
AHHHH!
FATHER, HOW DOES THAT MAN MOSES DO THIS? IS HIS GOD MORE POWERFUL THAN SETH, LORD OF CHAOS AND STORMS?
HE CLAIMS THERE IS ONLY ONE GOD AND THAT THESE HEBREWS ARE HIS CHILDREN.
BUT NO ONE HAS EVER SEEN HIS GOD, NOT EVEN THE HEBREWS. HIS GOD, WHICH HE CLAIMS IS JUST A SPIRIT, IS TRYING TO CONVINCE PHARAOH TO LET THEM GO INTO THE WILDERNESS TO WORSHIP.
OH MIGHTY SETH, LORD OF CHAOS AND STORMS, WE BEG OF YOU, PUT A STOP TO THESE TERRIBLE STORMS. SURELY YOU ARE GREATER THAN THIS UNSEEN GOD OF MOSES.

EXODUS 9:23-26

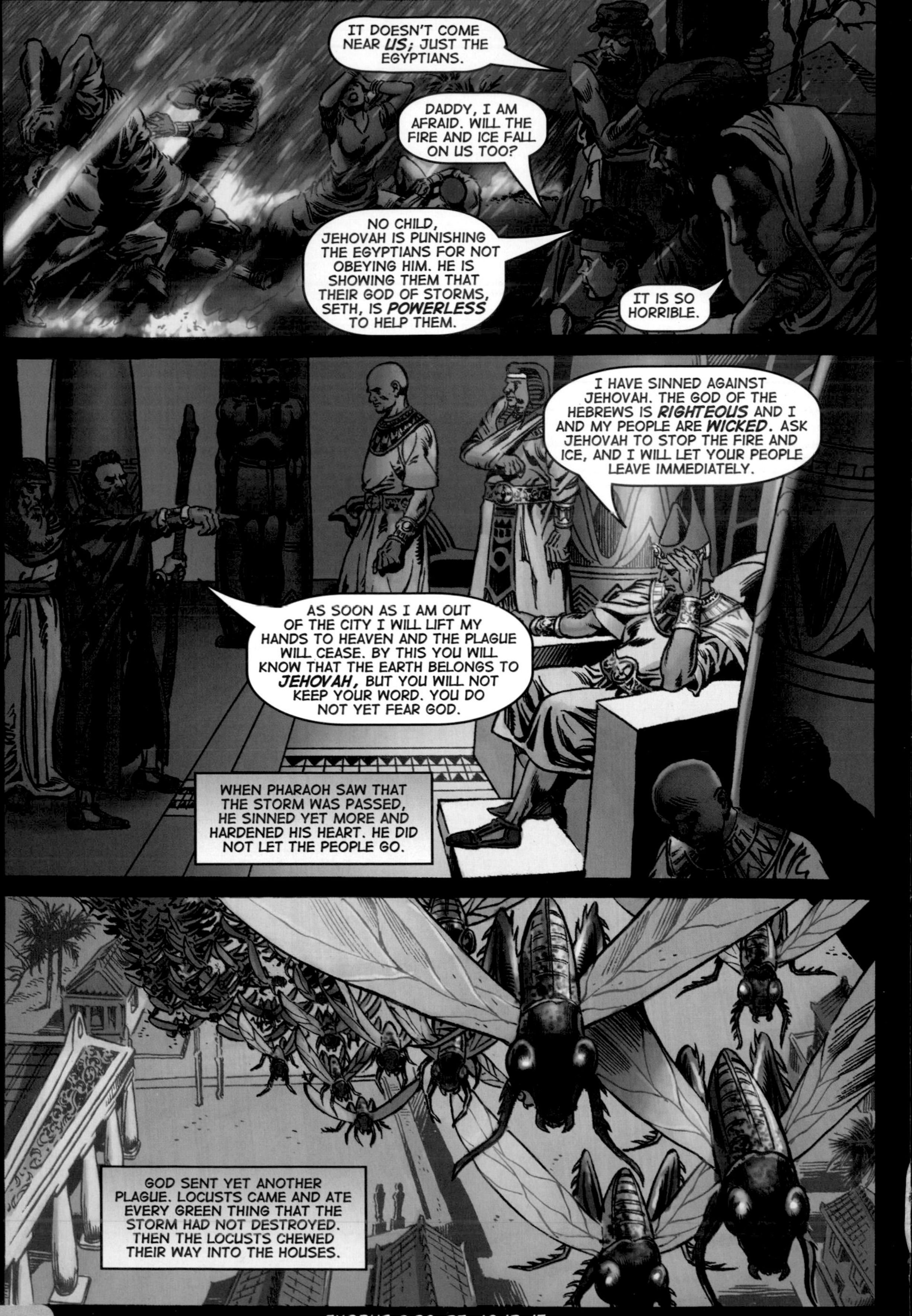
IT DOESN'T COME NEAR US; JUST THE EGYPTIANS.
DADDY, I AM AFRAID. WILL THE FIRE AND ICE FALL ON US TOO?
NO CHILD, JEHOVAH IS PUNISHING THE EGYPTIANS FOR NOT OBEYING HIM. HE IS SHOWING THEM THAT THEIR GOD OF STORMS, SETH, IS POWERLESS TO HELP THEM.
IT IS SO HORRIBLE.
I HAVE SINNED AGAINST JEHOVAH. THE GOD OF THE HEBREWS IS RIGHTEOUS AND I AND MY PEOPLE ARE WICKED. ASK JEHOVAH TO STOP THE FIRE AND ICE, AND I WILL LET YOUR PEOPLE LEAVE IMMEDIATELY.
AS SOON AS I AM OUT OF THE CITY I WILL LIFT MY HANDS TO HEAVEN AND THE PLAGUE WILL CEASE. BY THIS YOU WILL KNOW THAT THE EARTH BELONGS TO JEHOVAH, BUT YOU WILL NOT KEEP YOUR WORD. YOU DO NOT YET FEAR GOD.
WHEN PHARAOH SAW THAT THE STORM WAS PASSED, HE SINNED YET MORE AND HARDENED HIS HEART. HE DID NOT LET THE PEOPLE GO.
GOD SENT YET ANOTHER PLAGUE. LOCUSTS CAME AND ATE EVERY GREEN THING THAT THE STORM HAD NOT DESTROYED. THEN THE LOCUSTS CHEWED THEIR WAY INTO THE HOUSES.

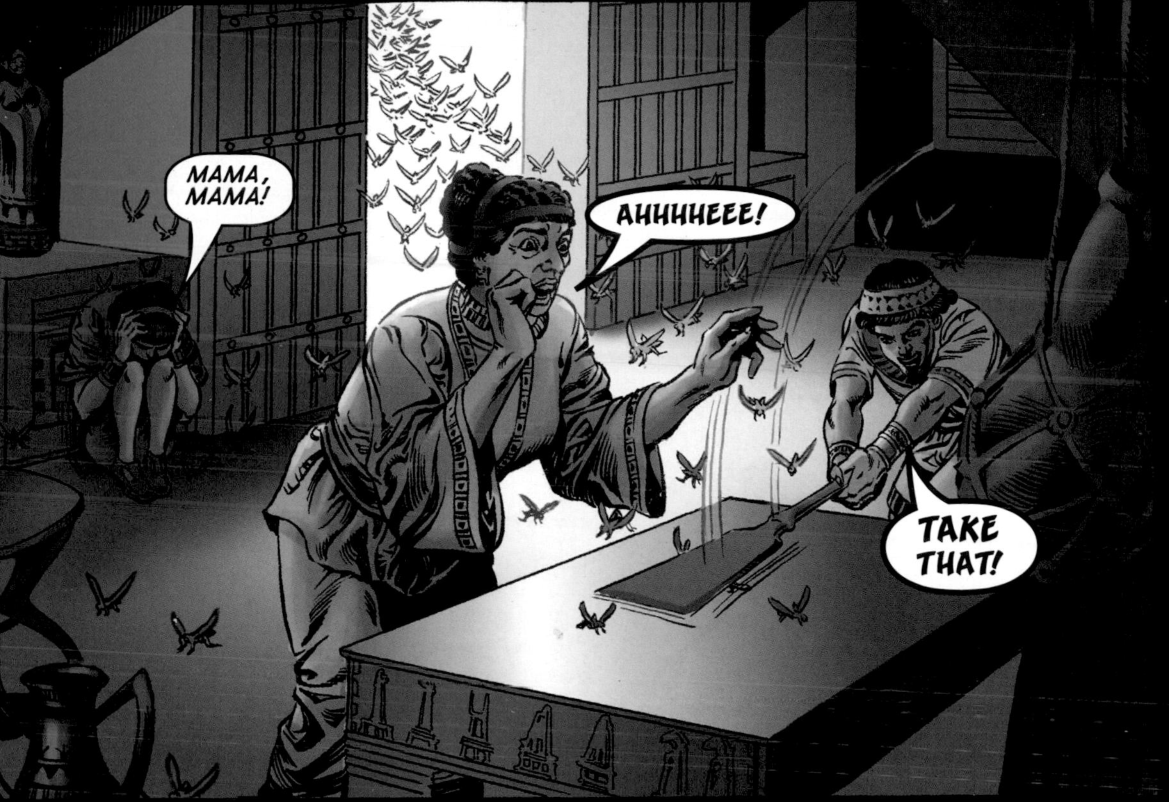
MAMA, MAMA!
AHHHHEEE!
TAKE THAT!

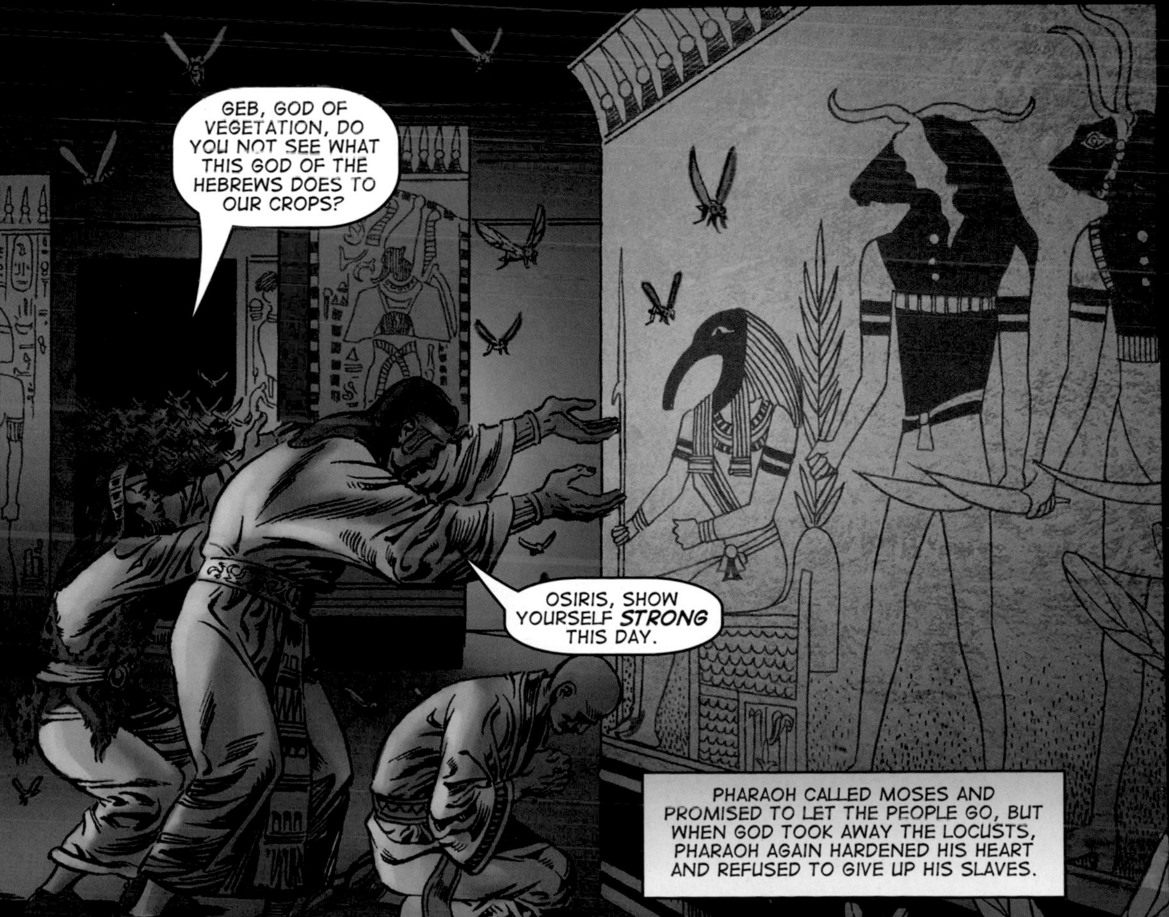
GEB, GOD OF VEGETATION, DO YOU NOT SEE WHAT THIS GOD OF THE HEBREWS DOES TO OUR CROPS?
OSIRIS, SHOW YOURSELF STRONG THIS DAY.
PHARAOH CALLED MOSES AND PROMISED TO LET THE PEOPLE GO, BUT WHEN GOD TOOK AWAY THE LOCUSTS, PHARAOH AGAIN HARDENED HIS HEART AND REFUSED TO GIVE UP HIS SLAVES.

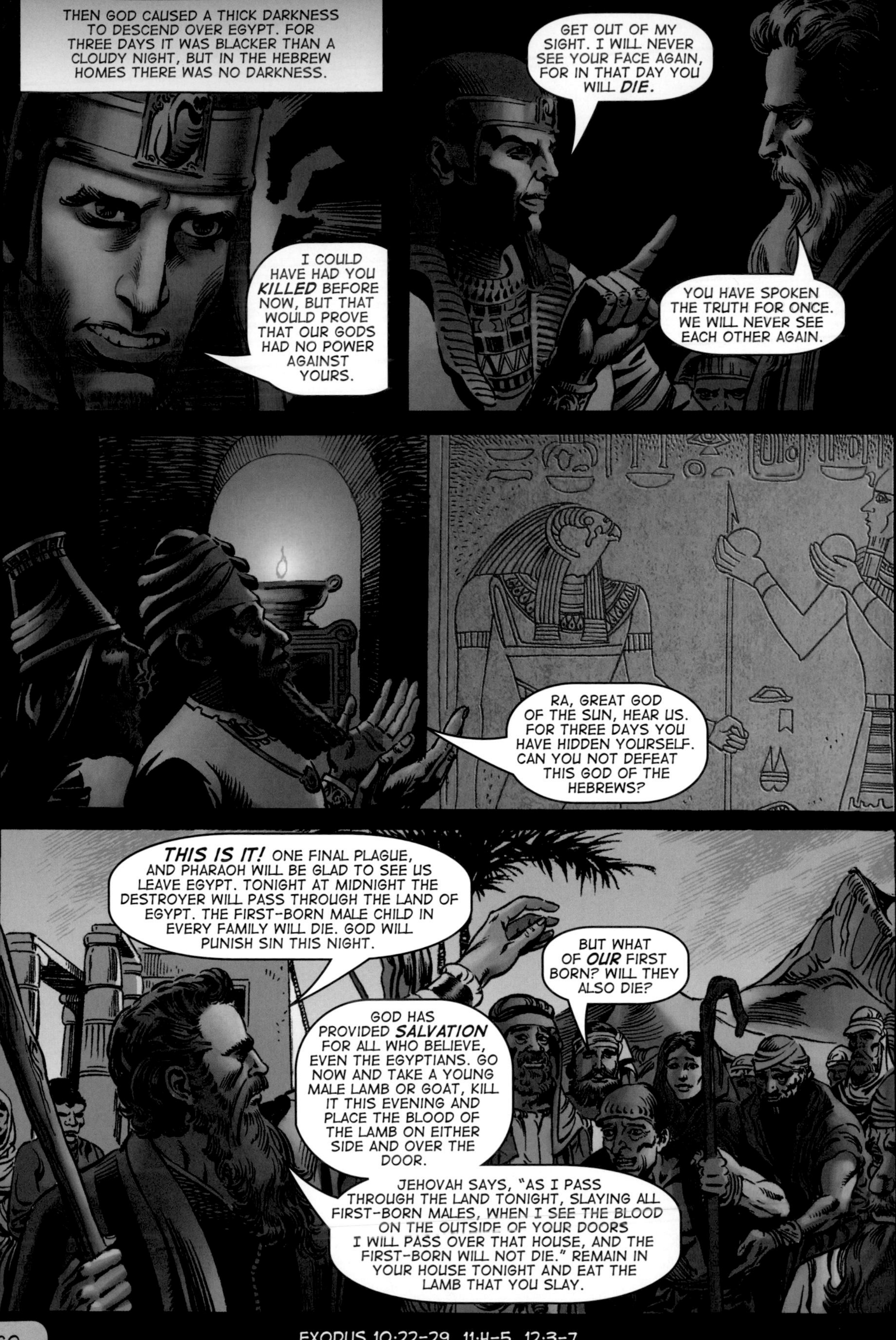
THEN GOD CAUSED A THICK DARKNESS TO DESCEND OVER EGYPT. FOR THREE DAYS IT WAS BLACKER THAN A CLOUDY NIGHT, BUT IN THE HEBREW HOMES THERE WAS NO DARKNESS.
I COULD HAVE HAD YOU KILLED BEFORE NOW, BUT THAT WOULD PROVE THAT OUR GODS HAD NO POWER AGAINST YOURS.
GET OUT OF MY SIGHT. I WILL NEVER SEE YOUR FACE AGAIN, FOR IN THAT DAY YOU WILL DIE.
YOU HAVE SPOKEN THE TRUTH FOR ONCE. WE WILL NEVER SEE EACH OTHER AGAIN.
RA, GREAT GOD OF THE SUN, HEAR US. FOR THREE DAYS YOU HAVE HIDDEN YOURSELF. CAN YOU NOT DEFEAT THIS GOD OF THE HEBREWS?
THIS IS IT! ONE FINAL PLAGUE, AND PHARAOH WILL BE GLAD TO SEE US LEAVE EGYPT. TONIGHT AT MIDNIGHT THE DESTROYER WILL PASS THROUGH THE LAND OF EGYPT. THE FIRST-BORN MALE CHILD IN EVERY FAMILY WILL DIE. GOD WILL PUNISH SIN THIS NIGHT.
BUT WHAT OF OUR FIRST BORN? WILL THEY ALSO DIE?
GOD HAS PROVIDED SALVATION FOR ALL WHO BELIEVE, EVEN THE EGYPTIANS. GO NOW AND TAKE A YOUNG MALE LAMB OR GOAT, KILL IT THIS EVENING AND PLACE THE BLOOD OF THE LAMB ON EITHER SIDE AND OVER THE DOOR.
JEHOVAH SAYS, “AS I PASS THROUGH THE LAND TONIGHT, SLAYING ALL FIRST-BORN MALES, WHEN I SEE THE BLOOD ON THE OUTSIDE OF YOUR DOORS I WILL PASS OVER THAT HOUSE, AND THE FIRST-BORN WILL NOT DIE.” REMAIN IN YOUR HOUSE TONIGHT AND EAT THE LAMB THAT YOU SLAY.

EXODUS 10:22-29, 11:4-5, 12:3-7

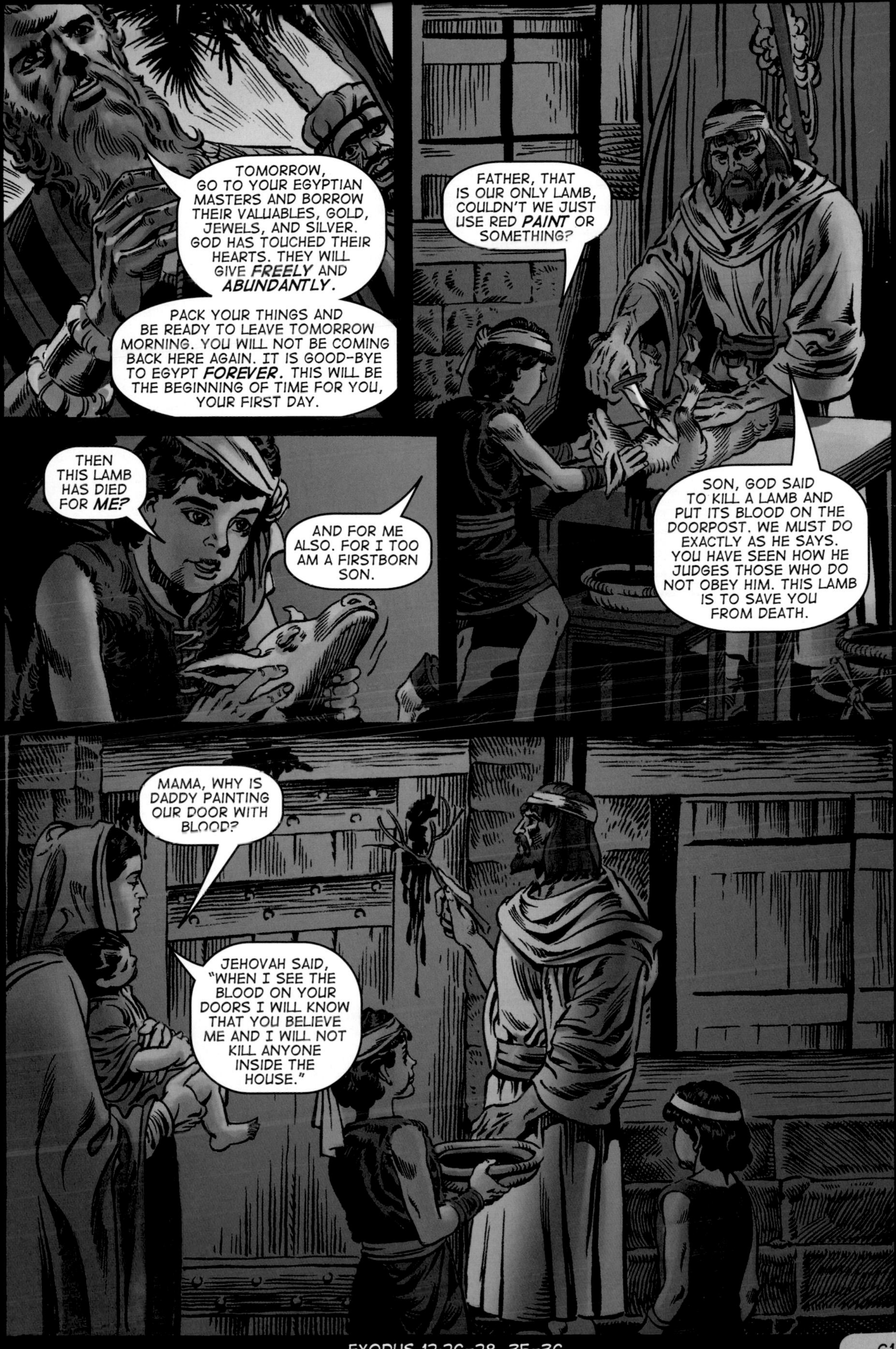
TOMORROW, GO TO YOUR EGYPTIAN MASTERS AND BORROW THEIR VALUABLES, GOLD, JEWELS, AND SILVER. GOD HAS TOUCHED THEIR HEARTS. THEY WILL GIVE FREELY AND ABUNDANTLY.
PACK YOUR THINGS AND BE READY TO LEAVE TOMORROW MORNING. YOU WILL NOT BE COMING BACK HERE AGAIN. IT IS GOOD-BYE TO EGYPT FOREVER. THIS WILL BE THE BEGINNING OF TIME FOR YOU, YOUR FIRST DAY.
FATHER, THAT IS OUR ONLY LAMB, COULDN'T WE JUST USE RED PAINT OR SOMETHING?
SON, GOD SAID TO KILL A LAMB AND PUT ITS BLOOD ON THE DOORPOST. WE MUST DO EXACTLY AS HE SAYS. YOU HAVE SEEN HOW HE JUDGES THOSE WHO DO NOT OBEY HIM. THIS LAMB IS TO SAVE YOU FROM DEATH.
THEN THIS LAMB HAS DIED FOR ME?
AND FOR ME ALSO. FOR I TOO AM A FIRSTBORN SON.
MAMA, WHY IS DADDY PAINTING OUR DOOR WITH BLOOD?
JEHOVAH SAID, "WHEN I SEE THE BLOOD ON YOUR DOORS I WILL KNOW THAT YOU BELIEVE ME AND I WILL NOT KILL ANYONE INSIDE THE HOUSE."

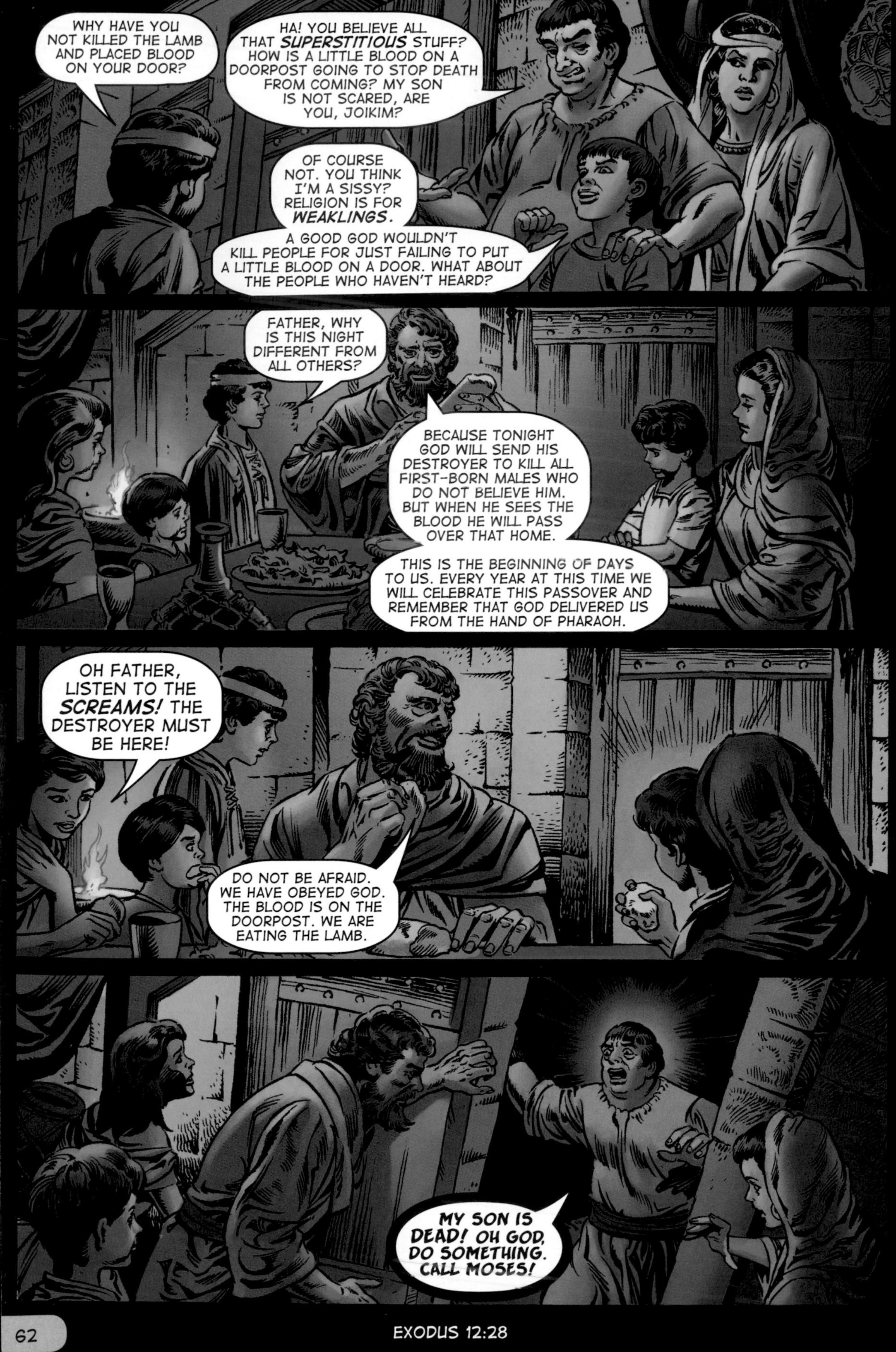
WHY HAVE YOU NOT KILLED THE LAMB AND PLACED BLOOD ON YOUR DOOR?
HA! YOU BELIEVE ALL THAT SUPERSTITIOUS STUFF? HOW IS A LITTLE BLOOD ON A DOORPOST GOING TO STOP DEATH FROM COMING? MY SON IS NOT SCARED, ARE YOU, JOIKIM?
OF COURSE NOT. YOU THINK I'M A SISSY? RELIGION IS FOR WEAKLINGS.
A GOOD GOD WOULDN'T KILL PEOPLE FOR JUST FAILING TO PUT A LITTLE BLOOD ON A DOOR. WHAT ABOUT THE PEOPLE WHO HAVEN'T HEARD?
FATHER, WHY IS THIS NIGHT DIFFERENT FROM ALL OTHERS?
BECAUSE TONIGHT GOD WILL SEND HIS DESTROYER TO KILL ALL FIRST-BORN MALES WHO DO NOT BELIEVE HIM. BUT WHEN HE SEES THE BLOOD HE WILL PASS OVER THAT HOME.
THIS IS THE BEGINNING OF DAYS TO US. EVERY YEAR AT THIS TIME WE WILL CELEBRATE THIS PASSOVER AND REMEMBER THAT GOD DELIVERED US FROM THE HAND OF PHARAOH.
OH FATHER, LISTEN TO THE SCREAMS! THE DESTROYER MUST BE HERE!
DO NOT BE AFRAID. WE HAVE OBEYED GOD. THE BLOOD IS ON THE DOORPOST. WE ARE EATING THE LAMB.
MY SON IS DEAD! OH GOD, DO SOMETHING. CALL MOSES!

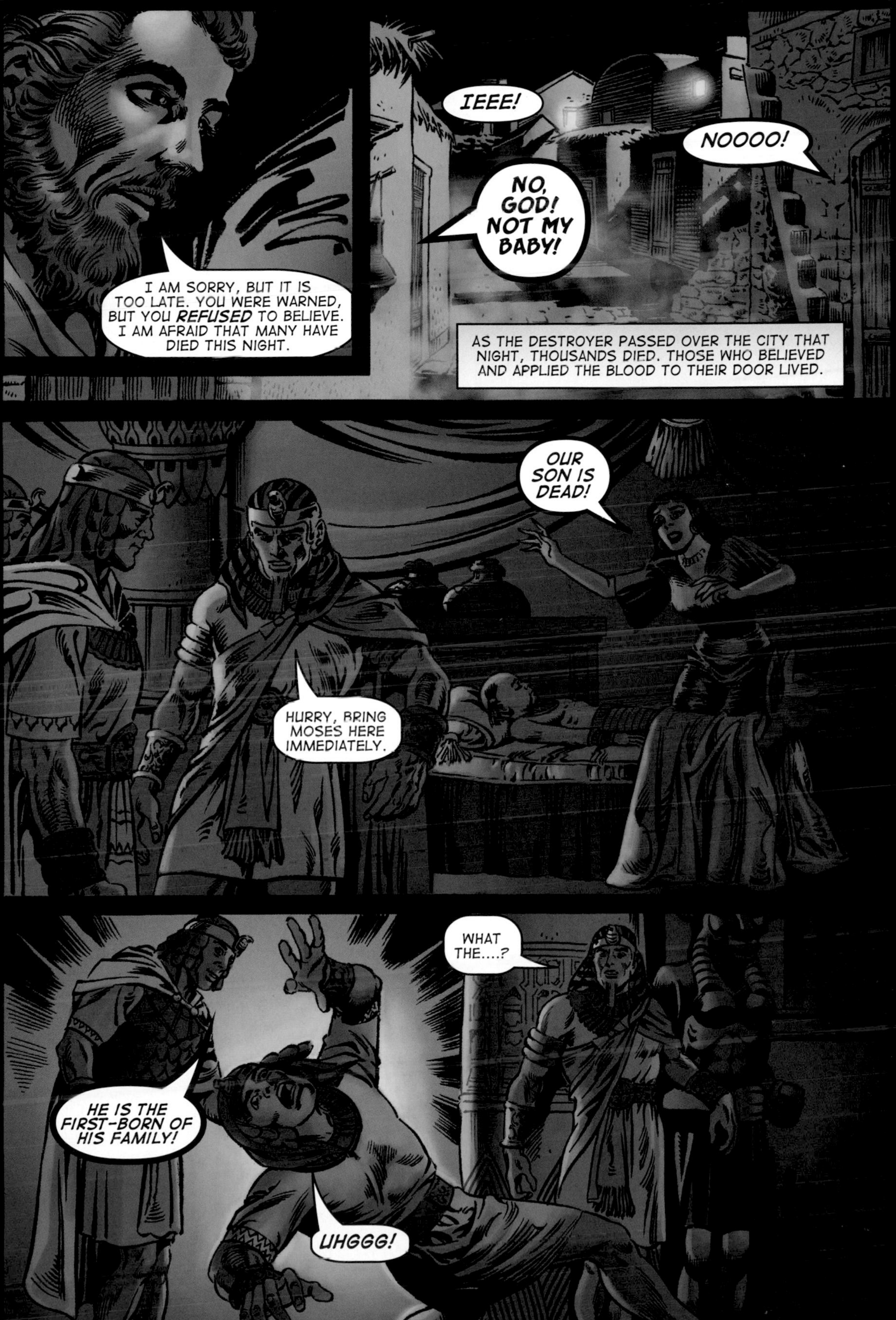
I AM SORRY, BUT IT IS TOO LATE. YOU WERE WARNED, BUT YOU REFUSED TO BELIEVE. I AM AFRAID THAT MANY HAVE DIED THIS NIGHT.
IEEE!
NO, GOD! NOT MY BABY!
NOOOO!
AS THE DESTROYER PASSED OVER THE CITY THAT NIGHT, THOUSANDS DIED. THOSE WHO BELIEVED AND APPLIED THE BLOOD TO THEIR DOOR LIVED.
OUR SON IS DEAD!
HURRY, BRING MOSES HERE IMMEDIATELY.
WHAT THE....?
HE IS THE FIRST-BORN OF HIS FAMILY!
UHGGG!

EXODUS 12:29-31

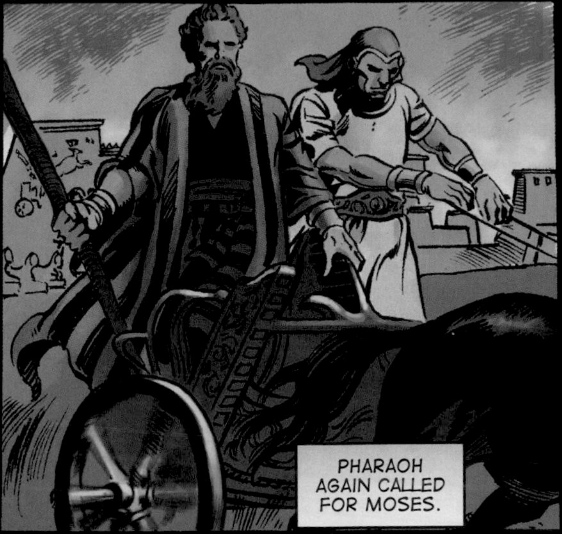
PHARAOH AGAIN CALLED FOR MOSES.

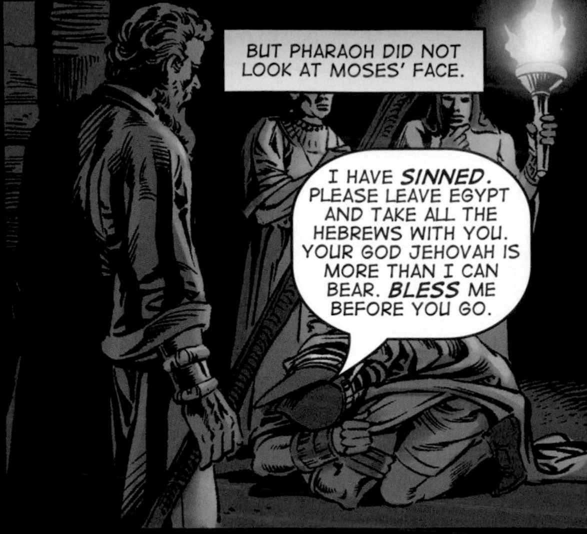
BUT PHARAOH DID NOT LOOK AT MOSES' FACE.
I HAVE SINNED. PLEASE LEAVE EGYPT AND TAKE ALL THE HEBREWS WITH YOU. YOUR GOD JEHOVAH IS MORE THAN I CAN BEAR. BLESS ME BEFORE YOU GO.

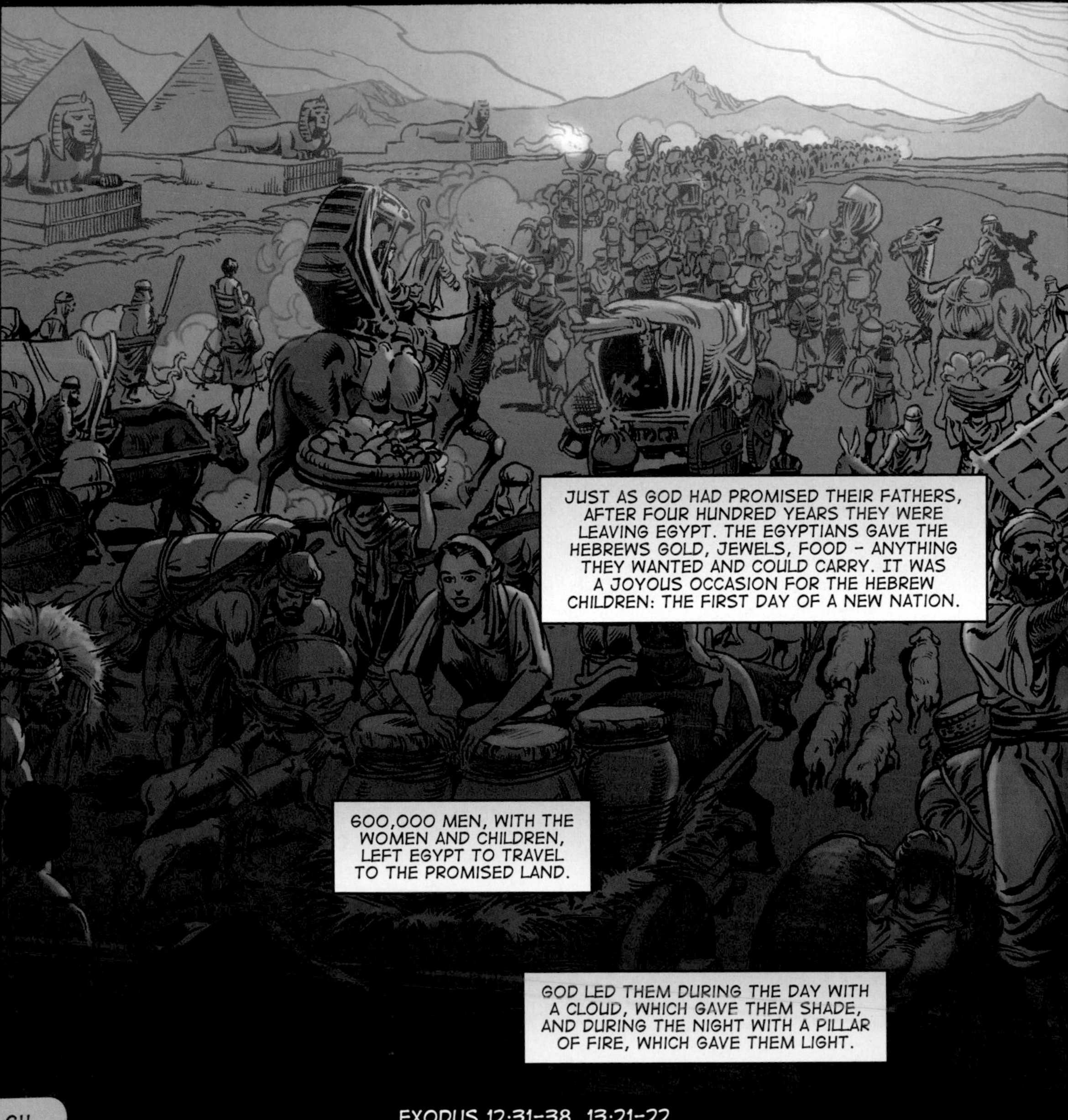
JUST AS GOD HAD PROMISED THEIR FATHERS, AFTER FOUR HUNDRED YEARS THEY WERE LEAVING EGYPT. THE EGYPTIANS GAVE THE HEBREWS GOLD, JEWELS, FOOD - ANYTHING THEY WANTED AND COULD CARRY. IT WAS A JOYOUS OCCASION FOR THE HEBREW CHILDREN: THE FIRST DAY OF A NEW NATION.
600,000 MEN, WITH THE WOMEN AND CHILDREN, LEFT EGYPT TO TRAVEL TO THE PROMISED LAND.
GOD LED THEM DURING THE DAY WITH A CLOUD, WHICH GAVE THEM SHADE, AND DURING THE NIGHT WITH A PILLAR OF FIRE, WHICH GAVE THEM LIGHT.

EXODUS 12:31-38, 13:21-22

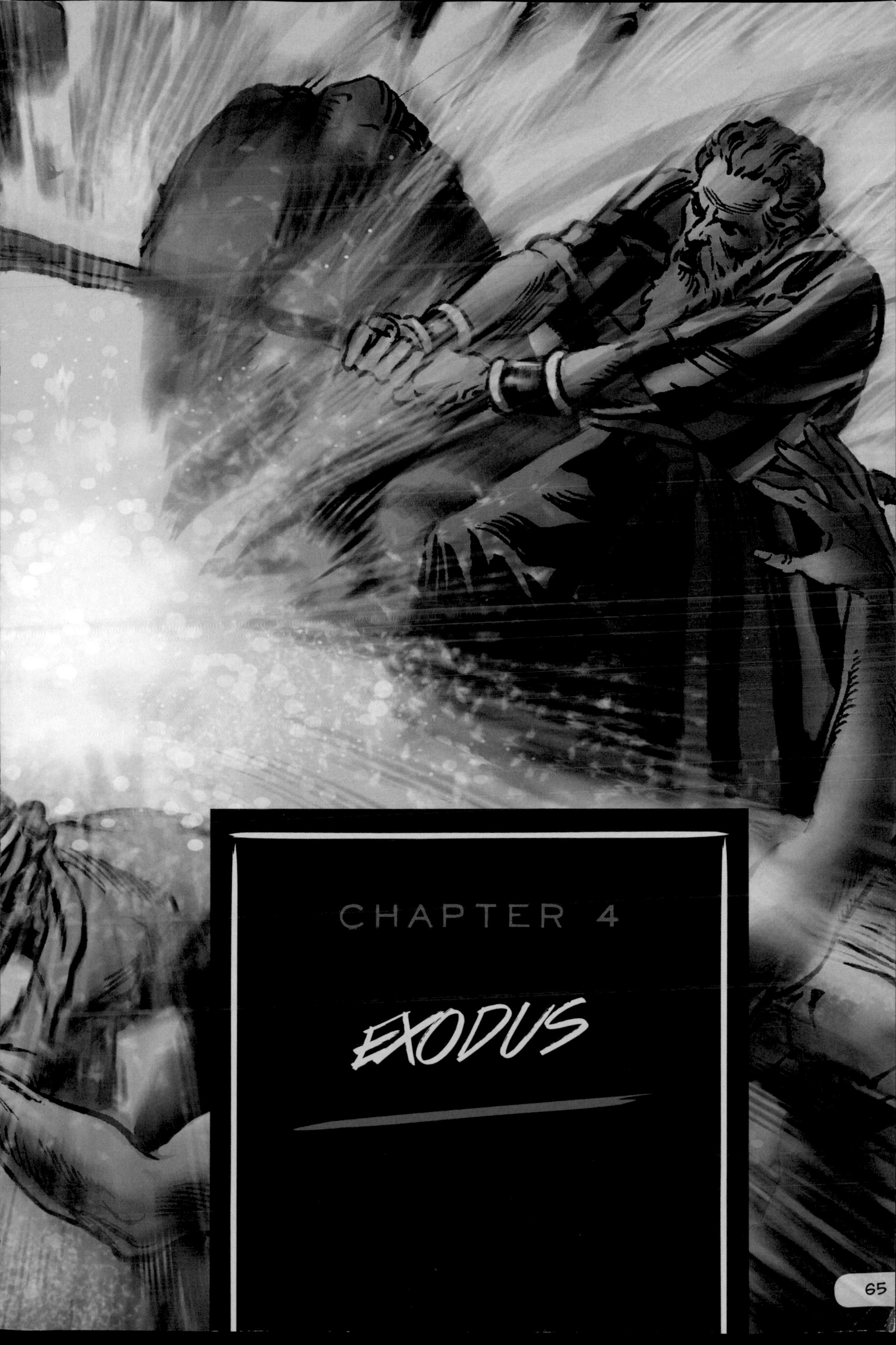

CHAPTER 4

EXODUS

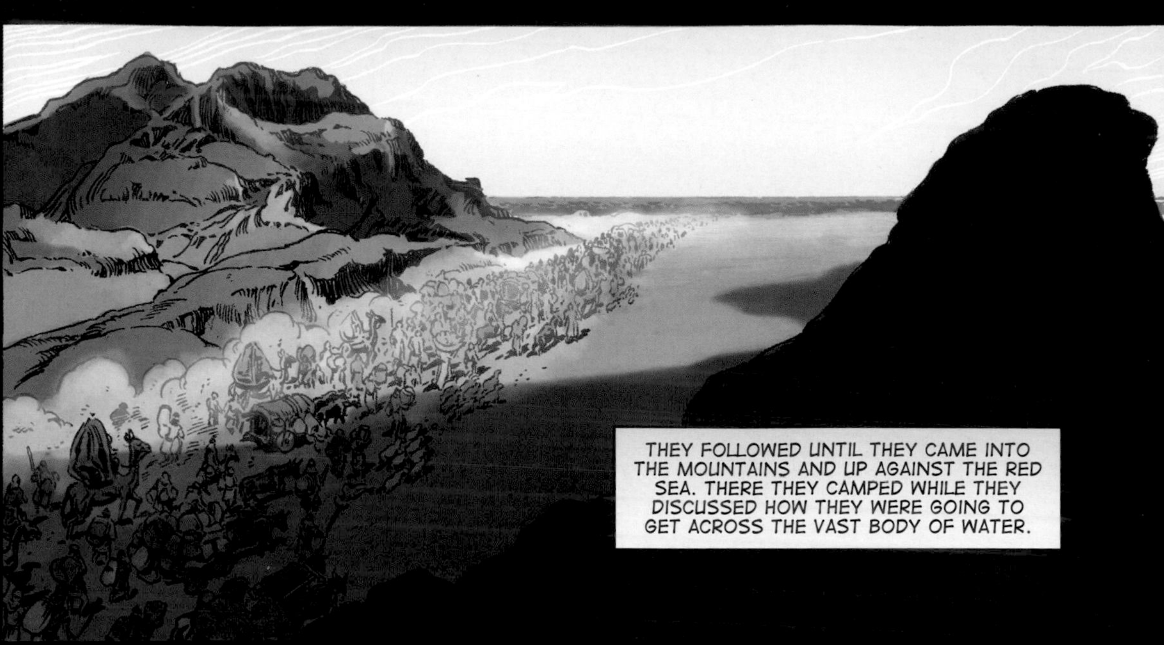
THEY FOLLOWED UNTIL THEY CAME INTO THE MOUNTAINS AND UP AGAINST THE RED SEA. THERE THEY CAMPED WHILE THEY DISCUSSED HOW THEY WERE GOING TO GET ACROSS THE VAST BODY OF WATER.

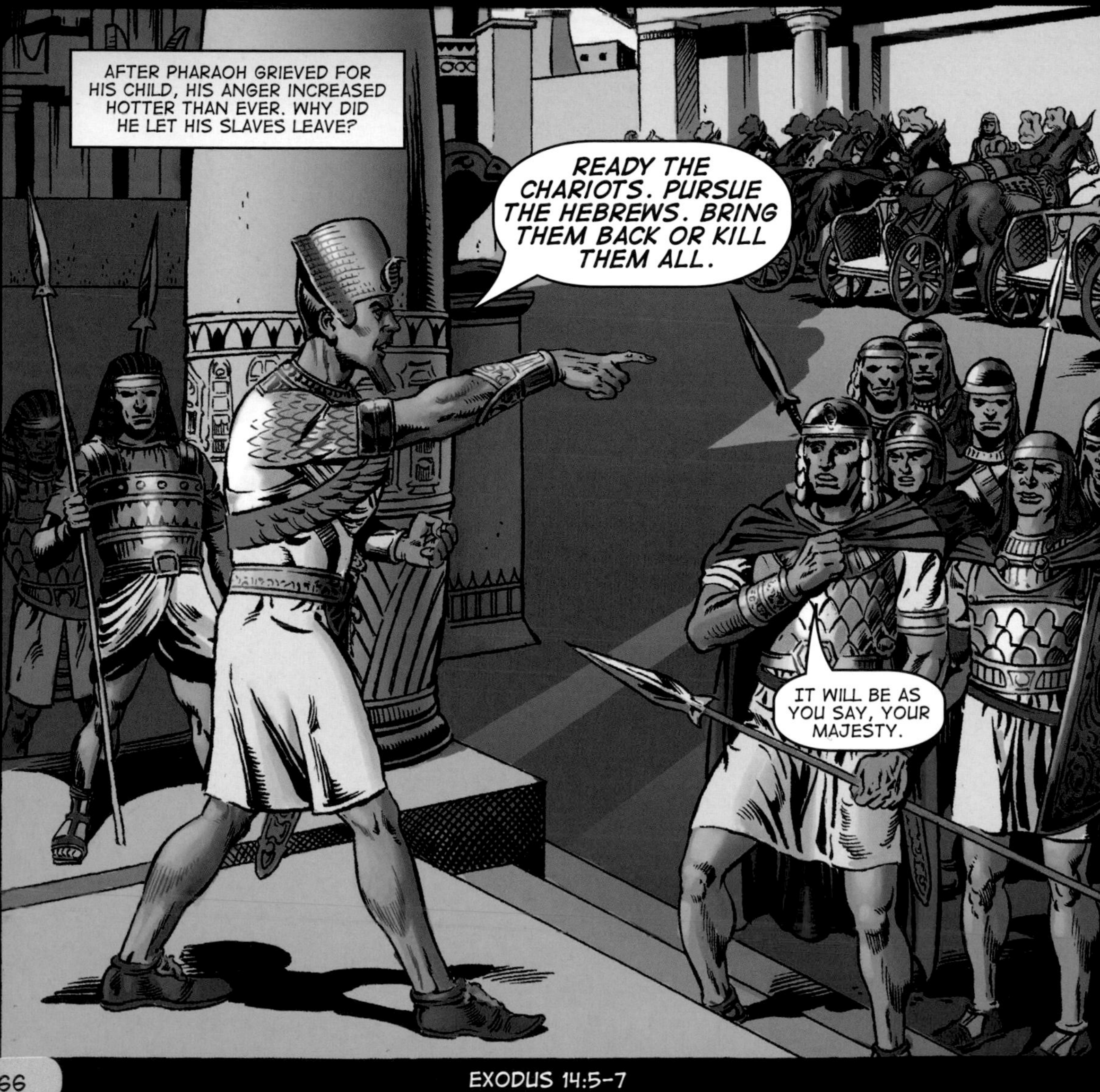
AFTER PHARAOH GRIEVED FOR HIS CHILD, HIS ANGER INCREASED HOTTER THAN EVER. WHY DID HE LET HIS SLAVES LEAVE?
READY THE CHARIOTS. PURSUE THE HEBREWS. BRING THEM BACK OR KILL THEM ALL.
IT WILL BE AS YOU SAY, YOUR MAJESTY.

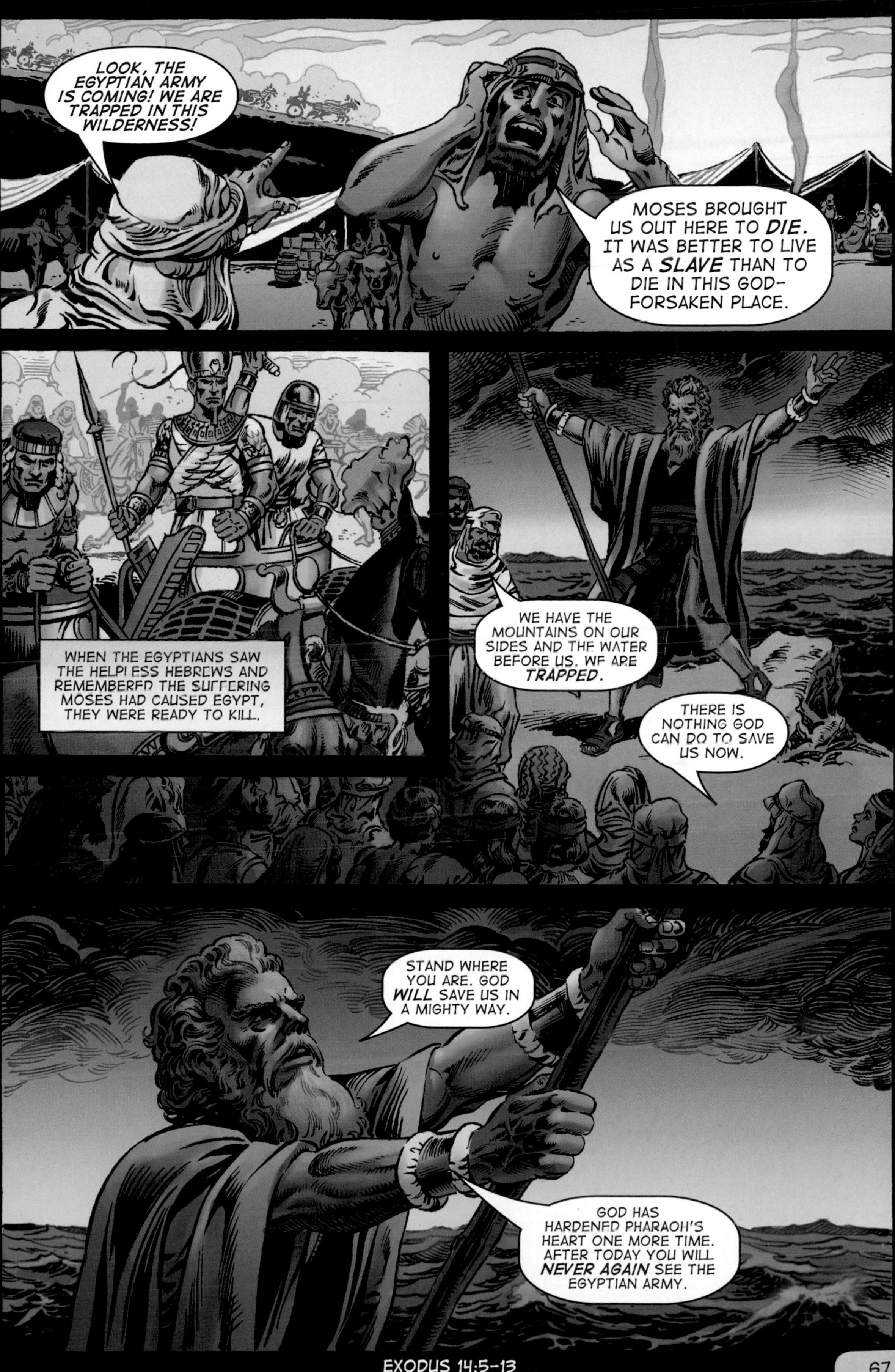
LOOK, THE EGYPTIAN ARMY IS COMING! WE ARE TRAPPED IN THIS WILDERNESS!
MOSES BROUGHT US OUT HERE TO DIE. IT WAS BETTER TO LIVE AS A SLAVE THAN TO DIE IN THIS GOD-FORSAKEN PLACE.
WHEN THE EGYPTIANS SAW THE HELPLESS HEBREWS AND REMEMBERED THE SUFFERING MOSES HAD CAUSED EGYPT, THEY WERE READY TO KILL.
WE HAVE THE MOUNTAINS ON OUR SIDES AND THE WATER BEFORE US. WE ARE TRAPPED.
THERE IS NOTHING GOD CAN DO TO SAVE US NOW.
STAND WHERE YOU ARE. GOD WILL SAVE US IN A MIGHTY WAY.
GOD HAS HARDENED PHARAOH'S HEART ONE MORE TIME. AFTER TODAY YOU WILL NEVER AGAIN SEE THE EGYPTIAN ARMY.

EXODUS 14:5-13

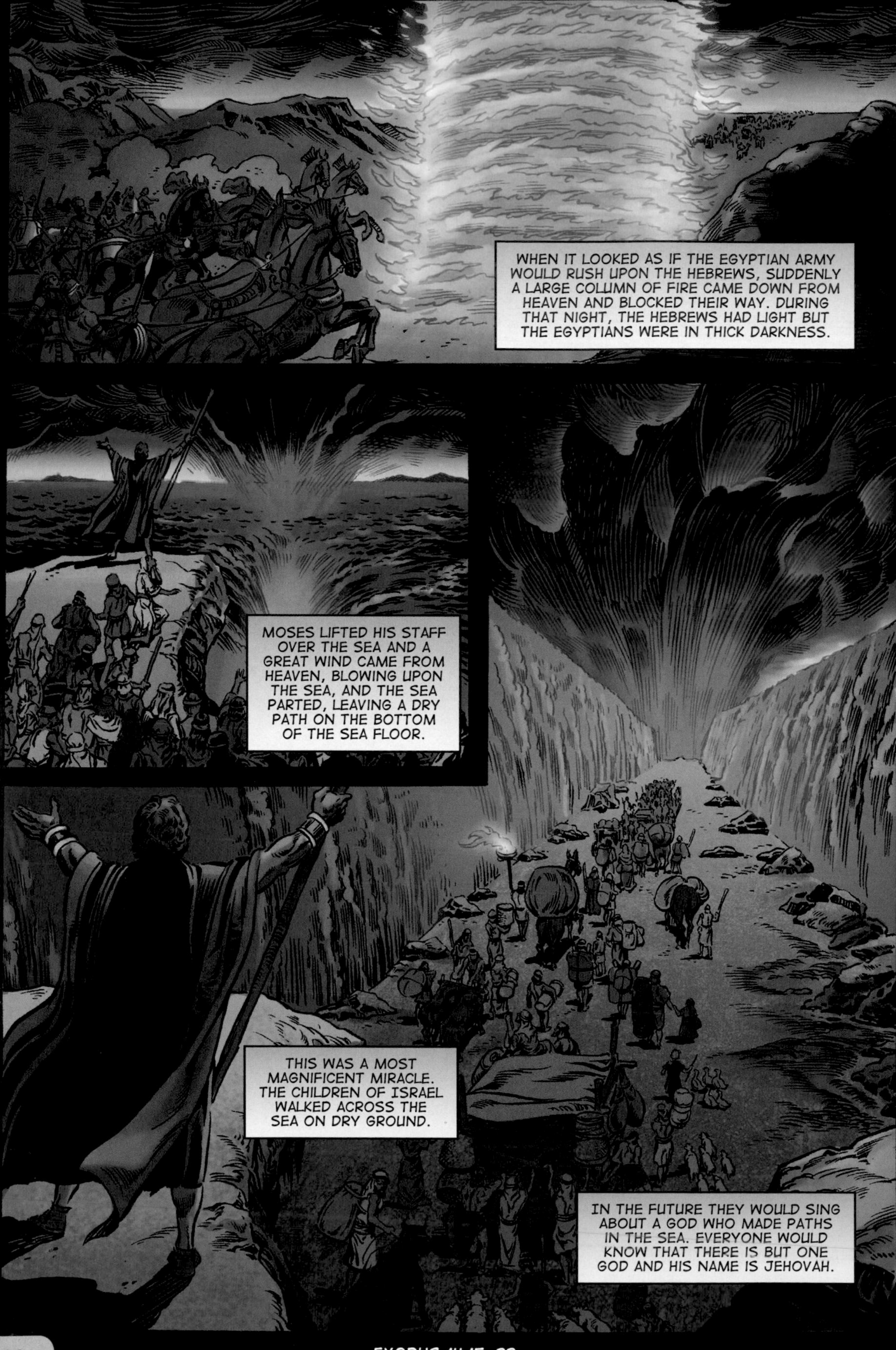

WHEN IT LOOKED AS IF THE EGYPTIAN ARMY WOULD RUSH UPON THE HEBREWS, SUDDENLY A LARGE COLUMN OF FIRE CAME DOWN FROM HEAVEN AND BLOCKED THEIR WAY. DURING THAT NIGHT, THE HEBREWS HAD LIGHT BUT THE EGYPTIANS WERE IN THICK DARKNESS.
MOSES LIFTED HIS STAFF OVER THE SEA AND A GREAT WIND CAME FROM HEAVEN, BLOWING UPON THE SEA, AND THE SEA PARTED, LEAVING A DRY PATH ON THE BOTTOM OF THE SEA FLOOR.
THIS WAS A MOST MAGNIFICENT MIRACLE. THE CHILDREN OF ISRAEL WALKED ACROSS THE SEA ON DRY GROUND.
IN THE FUTURE THEY WOULD SING ABOUT A GOD WHO MADE PATHS IN THE SEA. EVERYONE WOULD KNOW THAT THERE IS BUT ONE GOD AND HIS NAME IS JEHOVAH.

EXODUS 14:15-22

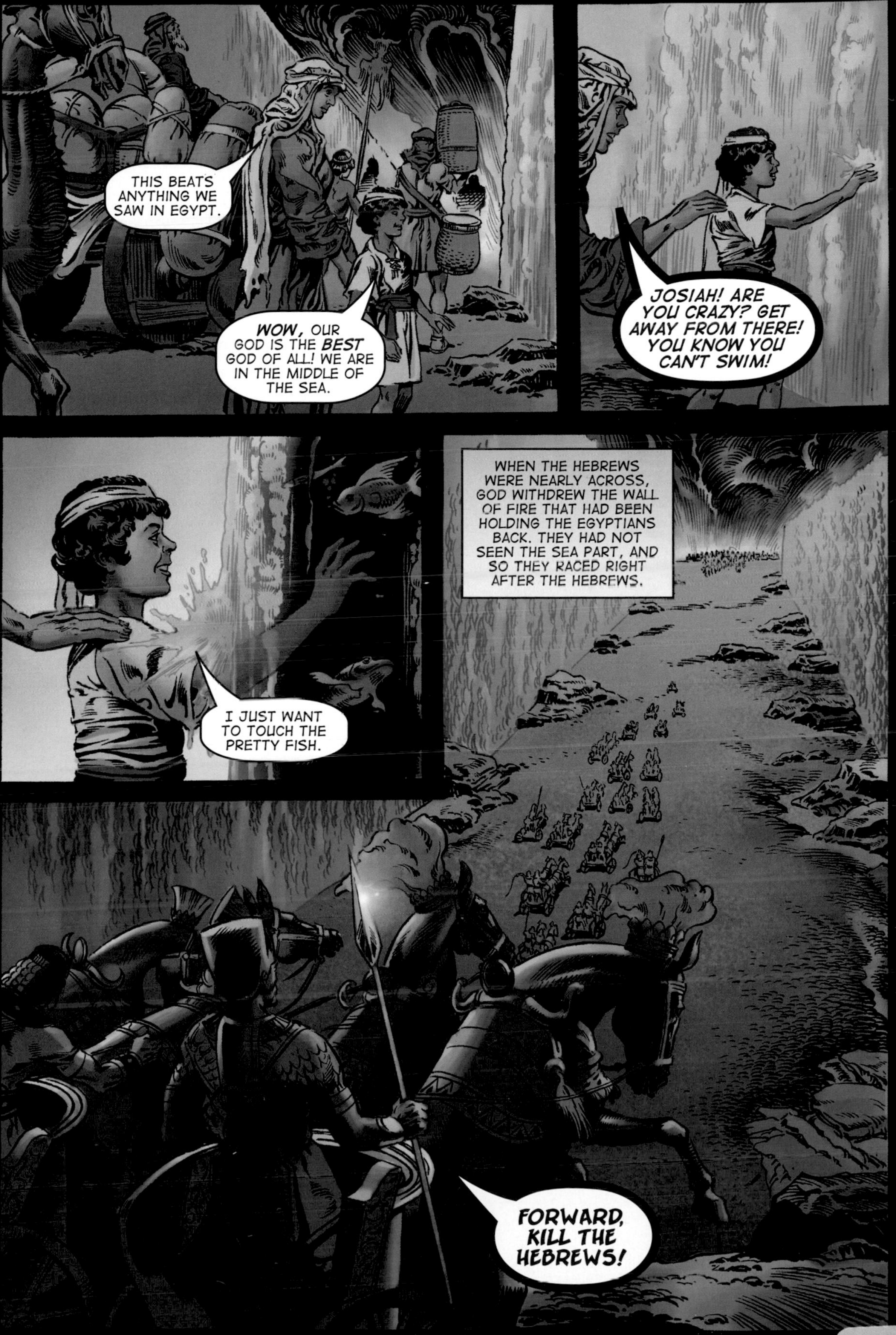
THIS BEATS ANYTHING WE SAW IN EGYPT.
WOW, OUR GOD IS THE BEST GOD OF ALL! WE ARE IN THE MIDDLE OF THE SEA.
JOSIAH! ARE YOU CRAZY? GET AWAY FROM THERE! YOU KNOW YOU CAN'T SWIM!
I JUST WANT TO TOUCH THE PRETTY FISH.
WHEN THE HEBREWS WERE NEARLY ACROSS, GOD WITHDREW THE WALL OF FIRE THAT HAD BEEN HOLDING THE EGYPTIANS BACK. THEY HAD NOT SEEN THE SEA PART, AND SO THEY RACED RIGHT AFTER THE HEBREWS.
FORWARD, KILL THE HEBREWS!

EXODUS 14:22-23

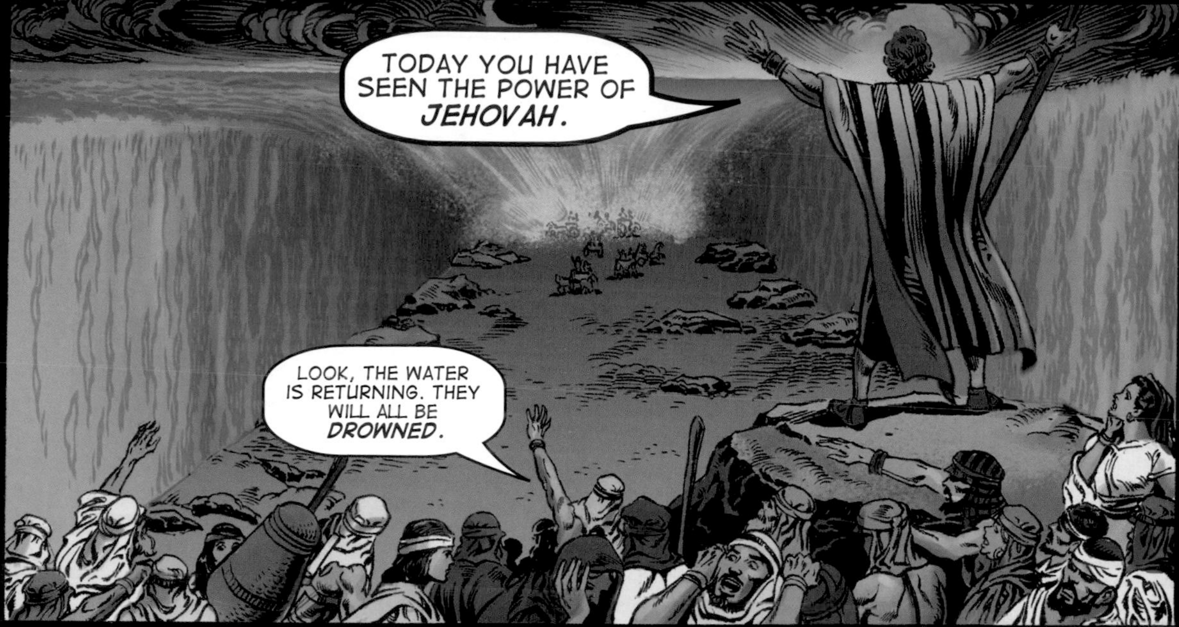
TODAY YOU HAVE SEEN THE POWER OF JEHOVAH.
LOOK, THE WATER IS RETURNING. THEY WILL ALL BE DROWNED.

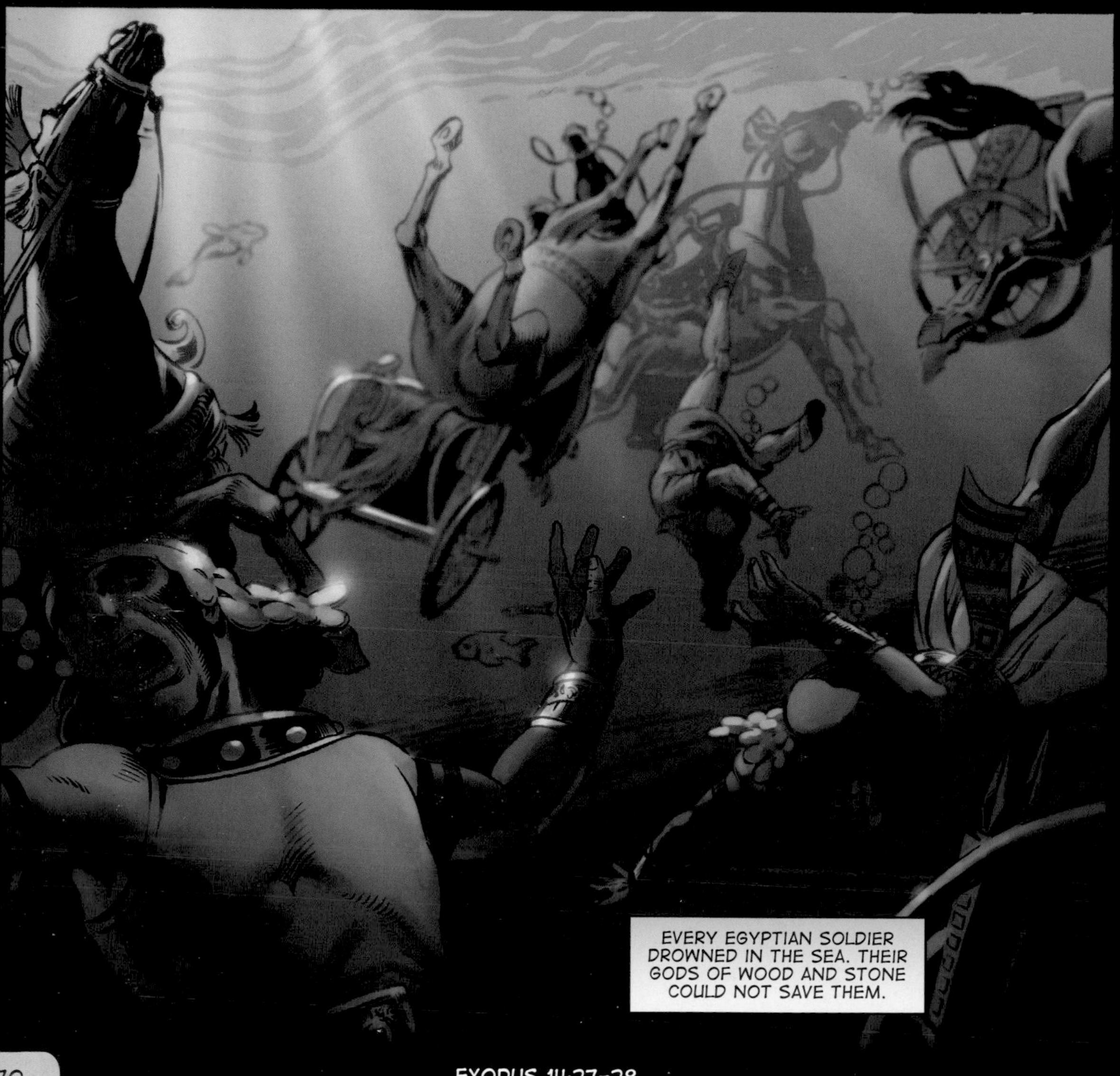
EVERY EGYPTIAN SOLDIER DROWNED IN THE SEA. THEIR GODS OF WOOD AND STONE COULD NOT SAVE THEM.

EXODUS 14:27-28

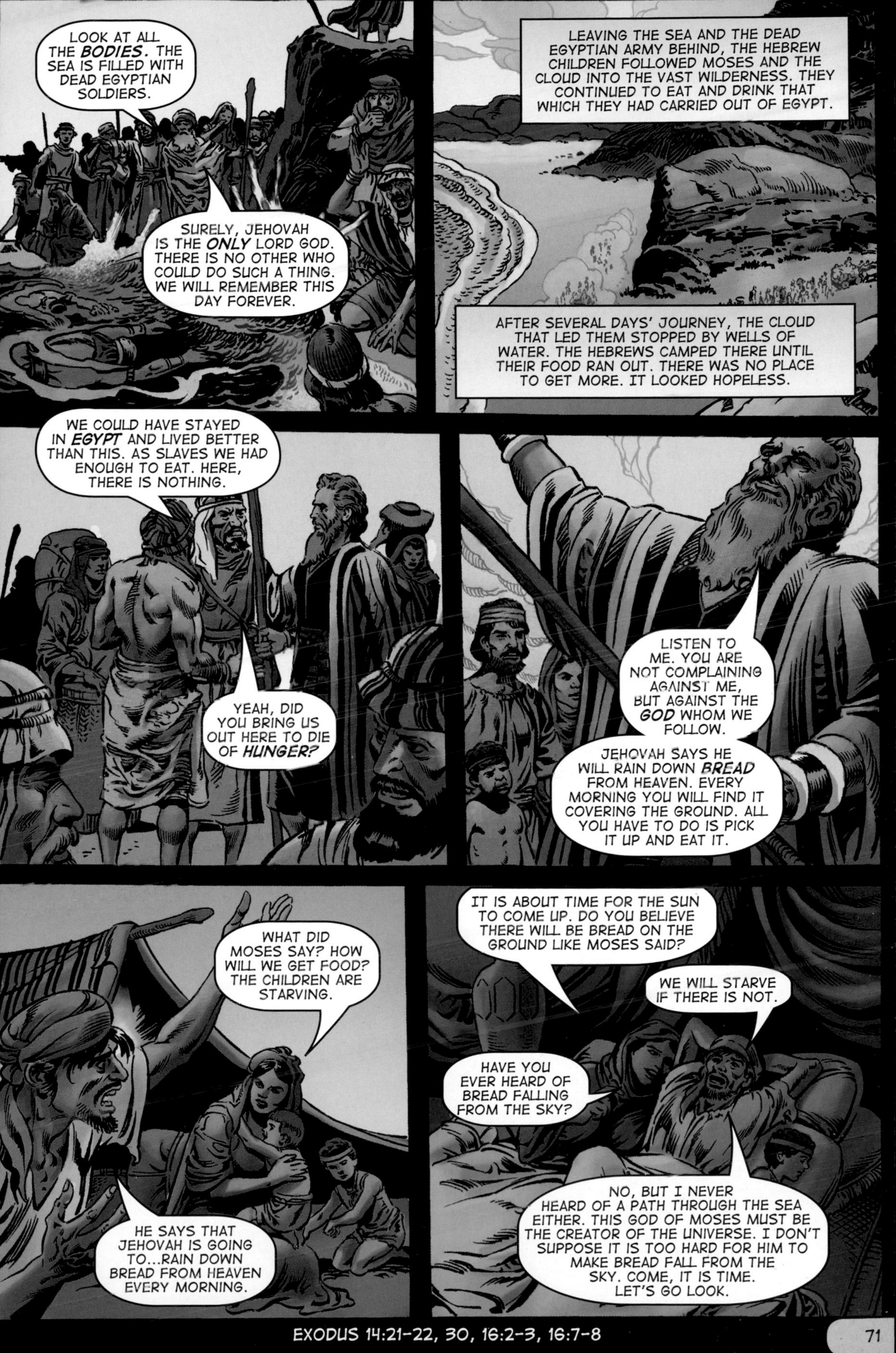
LOOK AT ALL THE BODIES. THE SEA IS FILLED WITH DEAD EGYPTIAN SOLDIERS.
SURELY, JEHOVAH IS THE ONLY LORD GOD. THERE IS NO OTHER WHO COULD DO SUCH A THING. WE WILL REMEMBER THIS DAY FOREVER.
LEAVING THE SEA AND THE DEAD EGYPTIAN ARMY BEHIND, THE HEBREW CHILDREN FOLLOWED MOSES AND THE CLOUD INTO THE VAST WILDERNESS. THEY CONTINUED TO EAT AND DRINK THAT WHICH THEY HAD CARRIED OUT OF EGYPT.
AFTER SEVERAL DAYS' JOURNEY, THE CLOUD THAT LED THEM STOPPED BY WELLS OF WATER. THE HEBREWS CAMPED THERE UNTIL THEIR FOOD RAN OUT. THERE WAS NO PLACE TO GET MORE. IT LOOKED HOPELESS.
WE COULD HAVE STAYED IN EGYPT AND LIVED BETTER THAN THIS. AS SLAVES WE HAD ENOUGH TO EAT. HERE, THERE IS NOTHING.
YEAH, DID YOU BRING US OUT HERE TO DIE OF HUNGER?
LISTEN TO ME. YOU ARE NOT COMPLAINING AGAINST ME, BUT AGAINST THE GOD WHOM WE FOLLOW.
JEHOVAH SAYS HE WILL RAIN DOWN BREAD FROM HEAVEN. EVERY MORNING YOU WILL FIND IT COVERING THE GROUND. ALL YOU HAVE TO DO IS PICK IT UP AND EAT IT.
WHAT DID MOSES SAY? HOW WILL WE GET FOOD? THE CHILDREN ARE STARVING.
HE SAYS THAT JEHOVAH IS GOING TO...RAIN DOWN BREAD FROM HEAVEN EVERY MORNING.
IT IS ABOUT TIME FOR THE SUN TO COME UP. DO YOU BELIEVE THERE WILL BE BREAD ON THE GROUND LIKE MOSES SAID?
WE WILL STARVE IF THERE IS NOT.
HAVE YOU EVER HEARD OF BREAD FALLING FROM THE SKY?
NO, BUT I NEVER HEARD OF A PATH THROUGH THE SEA EITHER. THIS GOD OF MOSES MUST BE THE CREATOR OF THE UNIVERSE. I DON'T SUPPOSE IT IS TOO HARD FOR HIM TO MAKE BREAD FALL FROM THE SKY. COME, IT IS TIME. LET'S GO LOOK.

EXODUS 14:21-22, 30, 16:2-3, 16:7-8

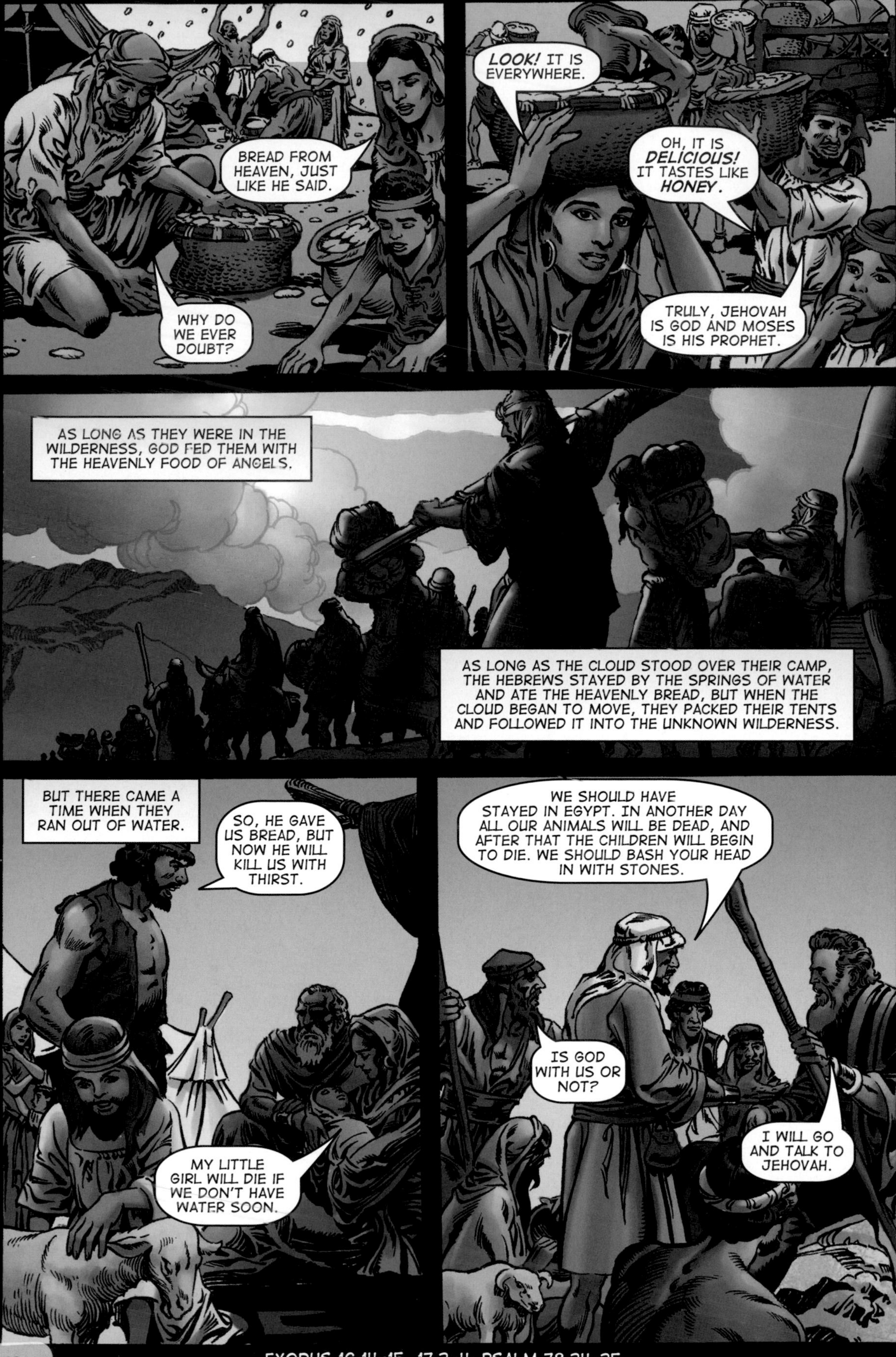
BREAD FROM HEAVEN, JUST LIKE HE SAID.
WHY DO WE EVER DOUBT?
LOOK! IT IS EVERYWHERE.
OH, IT IS DELICIOUS! IT TASTES LIKE HONEY.
TRULY, JEHOVAH IS GOD AND MOSES IS HIS PROPHET.
AS LONG AS THEY WERE IN THE WILDERNESS, GOD FED THEM WITH THE HEAVENLY FOOD OF ANGELS.
AS LONG AS THE CLOUD STOOD OVER THEIR CAMP, THE HEBREWS STAYED BY THE SPRINGS OF WATER AND ATE THE HEAVENLY BREAD, BUT WHEN THE CLOUD BEGAN TO MOVE, THEY PACKED THEIR TENTS AND FOLLOWED IT INTO THE UNKNOWN WILDERNESS.
BUT THERE CAME A TIME WHEN THEY RAN OUT OF WATER.
SO, HE GAVE US BREAD, BUT NOW HE WILL KILL US WITH THIRST.
MY LITTLE GIRL WILL DIE IF WE DON'T HAVE WATER SOON.
WE SHOULD HAVE STAYED IN EGYPT. IN ANOTHER DAY ALL OUR ANIMALS WILL BE DEAD, AND AFTER THAT THE CHILDREN WILL BEGIN TO DIE. WE SHOULD BASH YOUR HEAD IN WITH STONES.
IS GOD WITH US OR NOT?
I WILL GO AND TALK TO JEHOVAH.

EXODUS 16:14-15, 17:2-4; PSALM 78:24-25

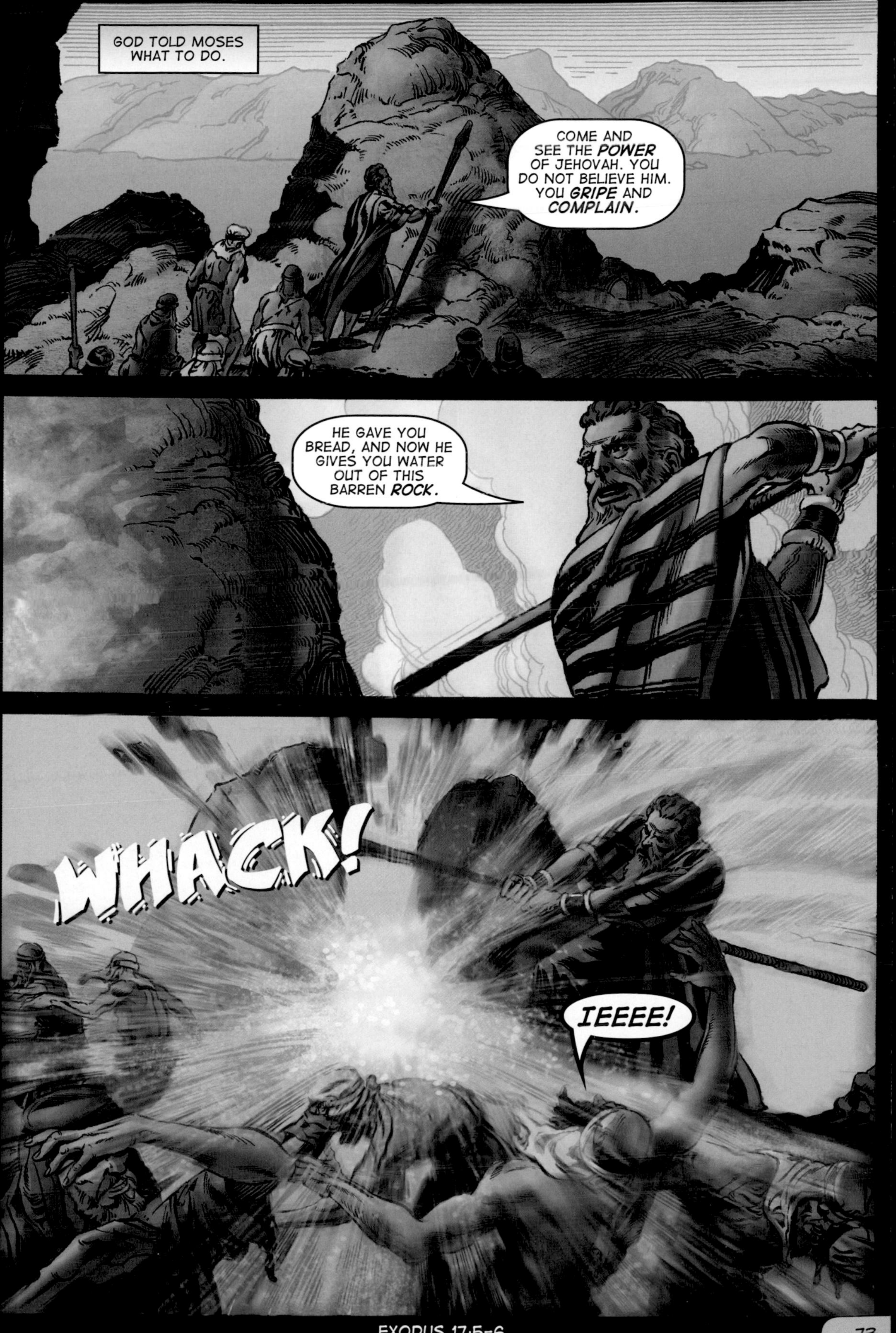
GOD TOLD MOSES WHAT TO DO.
COME AND SEE THE POWER OF JEHOVAH. YOU DO NOT BELIEVE HIM. YOU GRIPE AND COMPLAIN.
HE GAVE YOU BREAD, AND NOW HE GIVES YOU WATER OUT OF THIS BARREN ROCK.
WHACK!
IEEEE!

THE WATER FLOWED LIKE A RIVER.

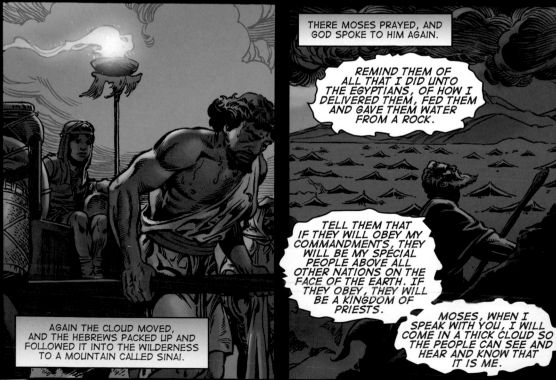

THERE MOSES PRAYED, AND GOD SPOKE TO HIM AGAIN.

REMIND THEM OF ALL THAT I DID UNTO THE EGYPTIANS, OF HOW I DELIVERED THEM, FED THEM AND GAVE THEM WATER FROM A ROCK.

TELL THEM THAT IF THEY WILL OBEY MY COMMANDMENTS, THEY WILL BE MY SPECIAL PEOPLE ABOVE ALL OTHER NATIONS ON THE FACE OF THE EARTH. IF THEY OBEY, THEY WILL BE A KINGDOM OF PRIESTS.

MOSES, WHEN I SPEAK WITH YOU, I WILL COME IN A THICK CLOUD SO THE PEOPLE CAN SEE AND HEAR AND KNOW THAT IT IS ME.

AGAIN THE CLOUD MOVED, AND THE HEBREWS PACKED UP AND FOLLOWED IT INTO THE WILDERNESS TO A MOUNTAIN CALLED SINAI.

EXODUS 17:6, 19:1-6, 9

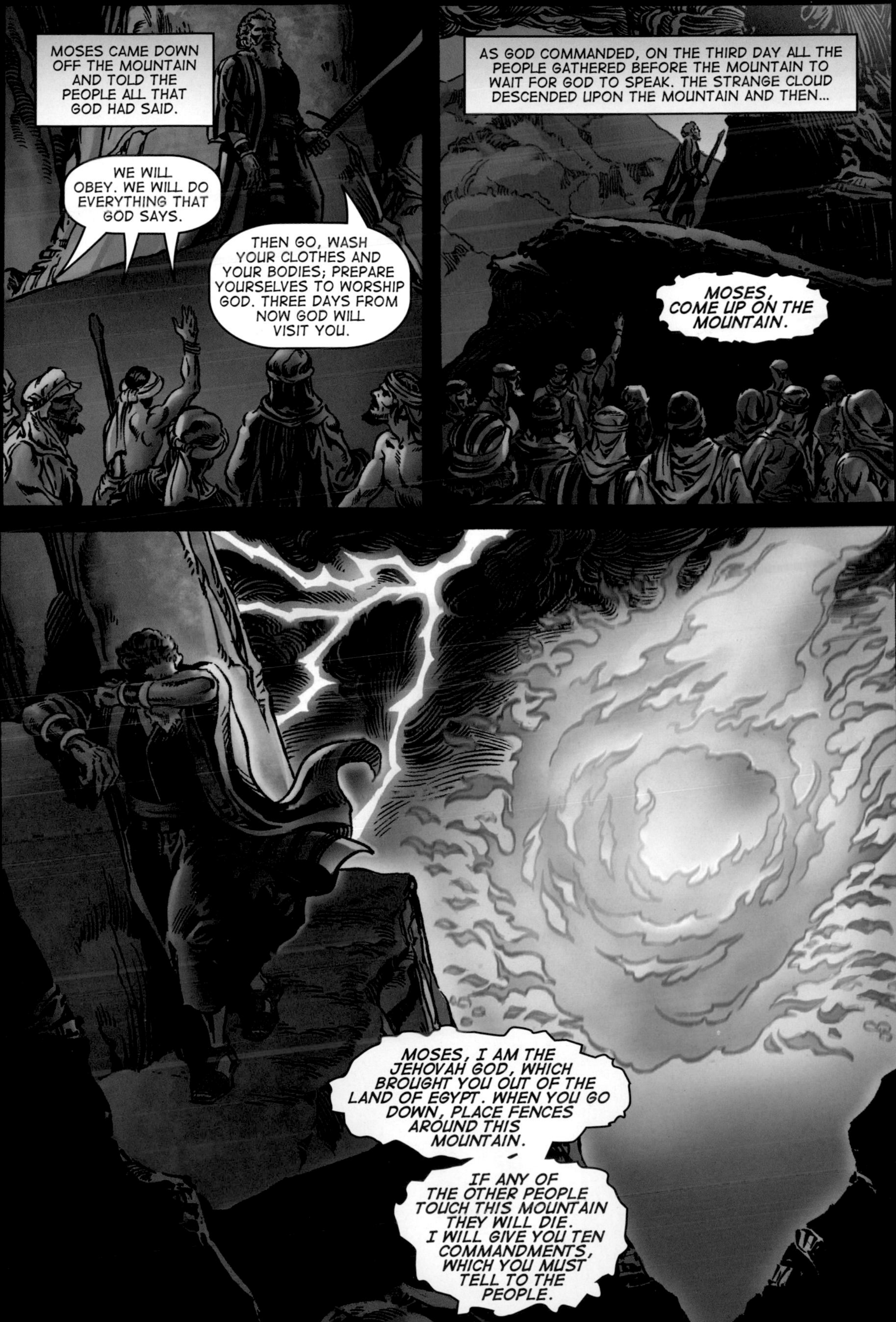

MOSES CAME DOWN OFF THE MOUNTAIN AND TOLD THE PEOPLE ALL THAT GOD HAD SAID.
WE WILL OBEY. WE WILL DO EVERYTHING THAT GOD SAYS.
THEN GO, WASH YOUR CLOTHES AND YOUR BODIES; PREPARE YOURSELVES TO WORSHIP GOD. THREE DAYS FROM NOW GOD WILL VISIT YOU.
AS GOD COMMANDED, ON THE THIRD DAY ALL THE PEOPLE GATHERED BEFORE THE MOUNTAIN TO WAIT FOR GOD TO SPEAK. THE STRANGE CLOUD DESCENDED UPON THE MOUNTAIN AND THEN...
MOSES, COME UP ON THE MOUNTAIN.
MOSES, I AM THE JEHOVAH GOD, WHICH BROUGHT YOU OUT OF THE LAND OF EGYPT. WHEN YOU GO DOWN, PLACE FENCES AROUND THIS MOUNTAIN.
IF ANY OF THE OTHER PEOPLE TOUCH THIS MOUNTAIN THEY WILL DIE. I WILL GIVE YOU TEN COMMANDMENTS, WHICH YOU MUST TELL TO THE PEOPLE.

EXODUS 19:7-25

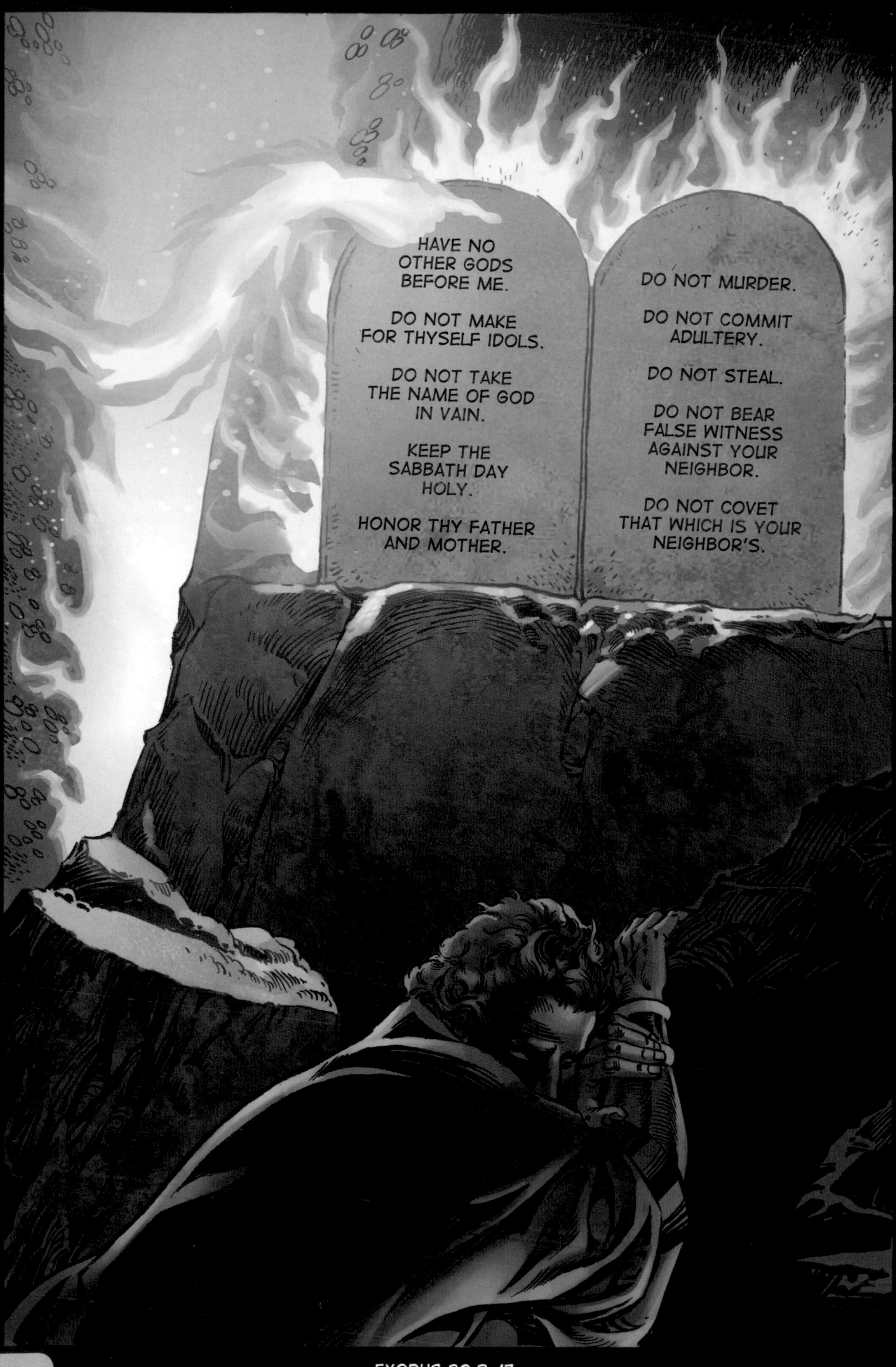
HAVE NO OTHER GODS BEFORE ME.
DO NOT MAKE FOR THYSELF IDOLS.
DO NOT TAKE THE NAME OF GOD IN VAIN.
KEEP THE SABBATH DAY HOLY.
HONOR THY FATHER AND MOTHER.
DO NOT MURDER.
DO NOT COMMIT ADULTERY.
DO NOT STEAL.
DO NOT BEAR FALSE WITNESS AGAINST YOUR NEIGHBOR.
DO NOT COVET THAT WHICH IS YOUR NEIGHBOR'S.

EXODUS 20:3-17

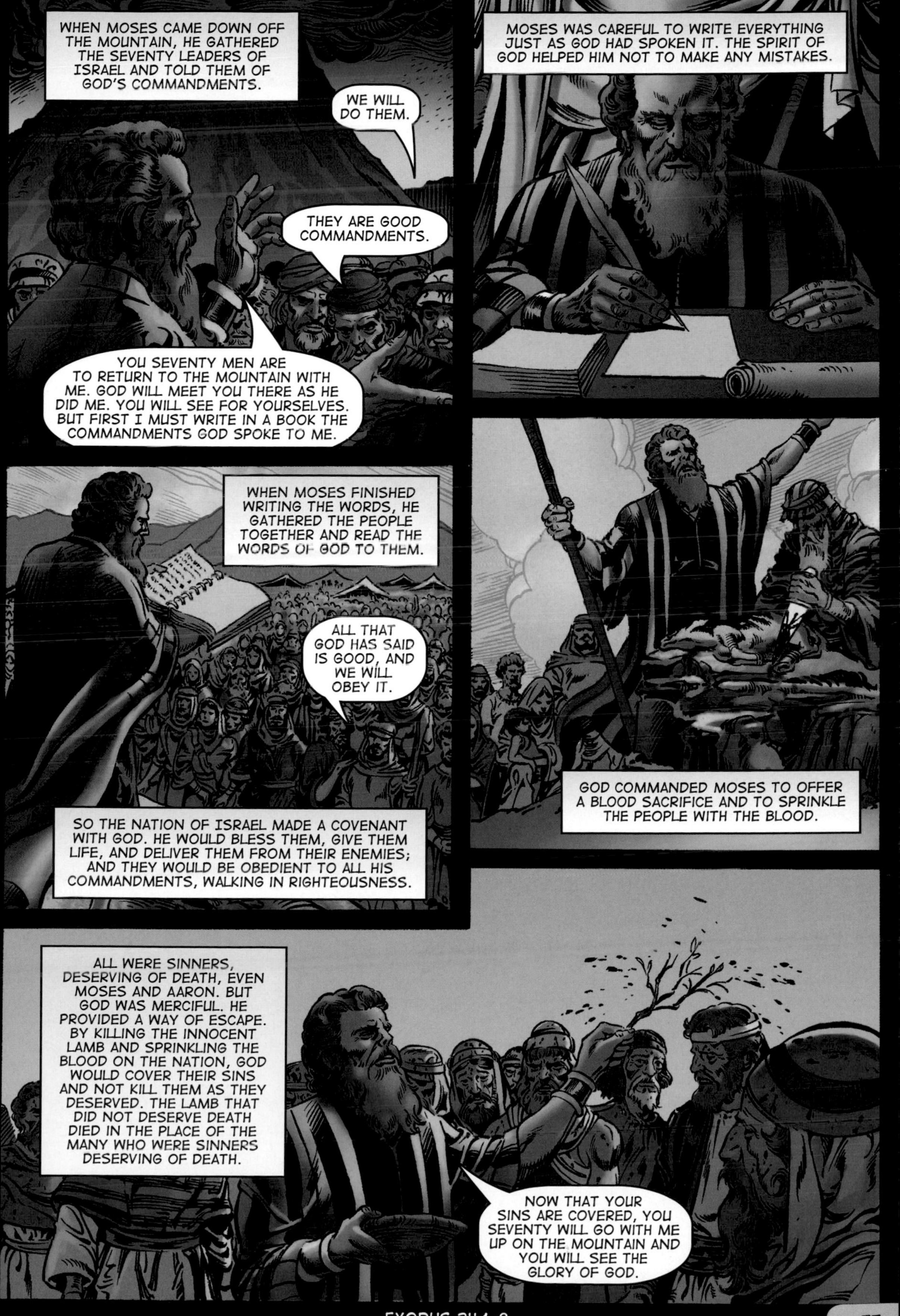
WHEN MOSES CAME DOWN OFF THE MOUNTAIN, HE GATHERED THE SEVENTY LEADERS OF ISRAEL AND TOLD THEM OF GOD'S COMMANDMENTS.
WE WILL DO THEM.
THEY ARE GOOD COMMANDMENTS.
YOU SEVENTY MEN ARE TO RETURN TO THE MOUNTAIN WITH ME. GOD WILL MEET YOU THERE AS HE DID ME. YOU WILL SEE FOR YOURSELVES. BUT FIRST I MUST WRITE IN A BOOK THE COMMANDMENTS GOD SPOKE TO ME.
MOSES WAS CAREFUL TO WRITE EVERYTHING JUST AS GOD HAD SPOKEN IT. THE SPIRIT OF GOD HELPED HIM NOT TO MAKE ANY MISTAKES.
WHEN MOSES FINISHED WRITING THE WORDS, HE GATHERED THE PEOPLE TOGETHER AND READ THE WORDS OF GOD TO THEM.
ALL THAT GOD HAS SAID IS GOOD, AND WE WILL OBEY IT.
SO THE NATION OF ISRAEL MADE A COVENANT WITH GOD. HE WOULD BLESS THEM, GIVE THEM LIFE, AND DELIVER THEM FROM THEIR ENEMIES; AND THEY WOULD BE OBEDIENT TO ALL HIS COMMANDMENTS, WALKING IN RIGHTEOUSNESS.
GOD COMMANDED MOSES TO OFFER A BLOOD SACRIFICE AND TO SPRINKLE THE PEOPLE WITH THE BLOOD.
ALL WERE SINNERS, DESERVING OF DEATH, EVEN MOSES AND AARON. BUT GOD WAS MERCIFUL. HE PROVIDED A WAY OF ESCAPE. BY KILLING THE INNOCENT LAMB AND SPRINKLING THE BLOOD ON THE NATION, GOD WOULD COVER THEIR SINS AND NOT KILL THEM AS THEY DESERVED. THE LAMB THAT DID NOT DESERVE DEATH DIED IN THE PLACE OF THE MANY WHO WERE SINNERS DESERVING OF DEATH.
NOW THAT YOUR SINS ARE COVERED, YOU SEVENTY WILL GO WITH ME UP ON THE MOUNTAIN AND YOU WILL SEE THE GLORY OF GOD.

EXODUS 24:1–8

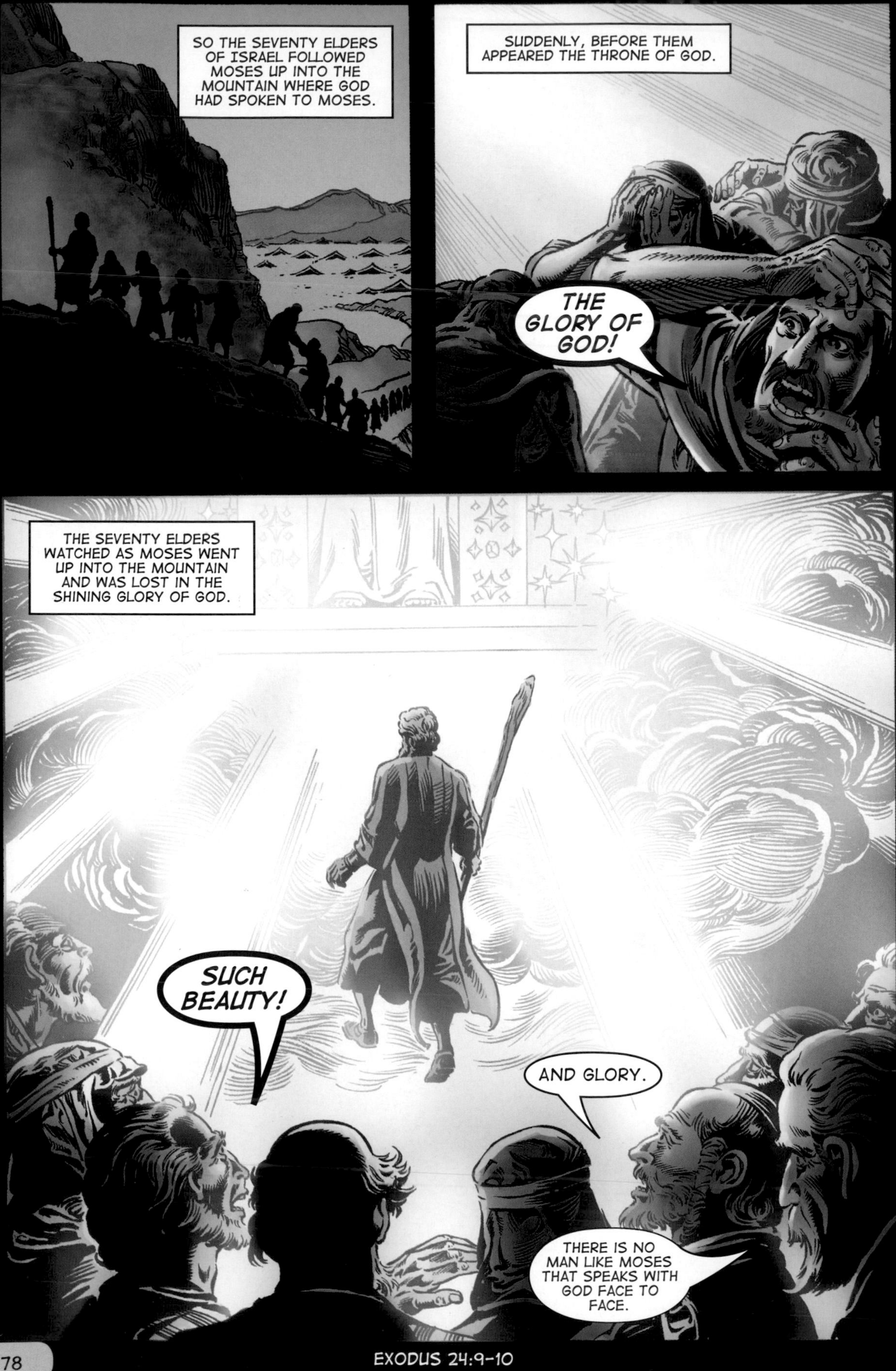
SO THE SEVENTY ELDERS OF ISRAEL FOLLOWED MOSES UP INTO THE MOUNTAIN WHERE GOD HAD SPOKEN TO MOSES.
SUDDENLY, BEFORE THEM APPEARED THE THRONE OF GOD.
THE GLORY OF GOD!
THE SEVENTY ELDERS WATCHED AS MOSES WENT UP INTO THE MOUNTAIN AND WAS LOST IN THE SHINING GLORY OF GOD.
SUCH BEAUTY!
AND GLORY.
THERE IS NO MAN LIKE MOSES THAT SPEAKS WITH GOD FACE TO FACE.

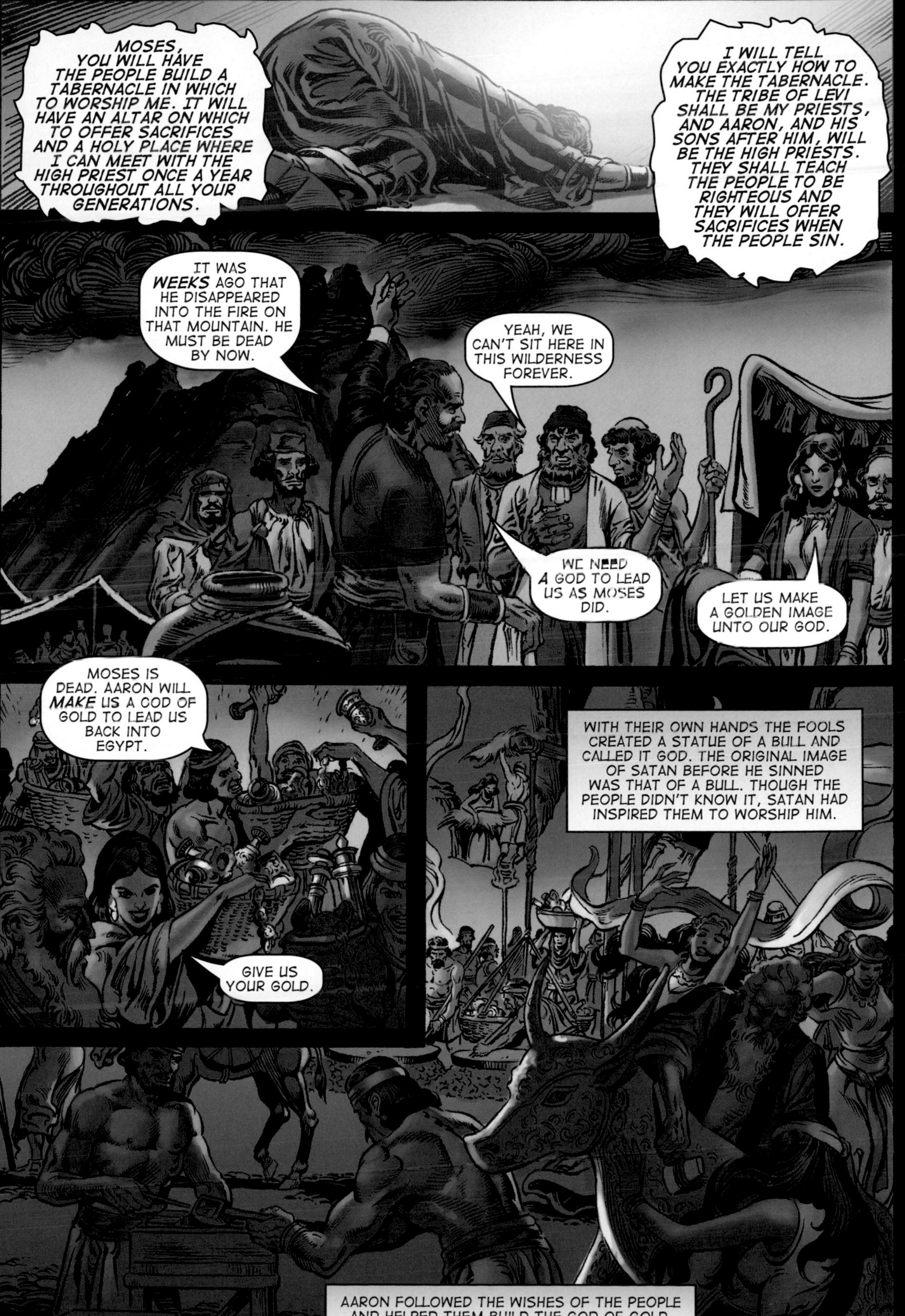
MOSES, YOU WILL HAVE THE PEOPLE BUILD A TABERNACLE IN WHICH TO WORSHIP ME. IT WILL HAVE AN ALTAR ON WHICH TO OFFER SACRIFICES AND A HOLY PLACE WHERE I CAN MEET WITH THE HIGH PRIEST ONCE A YEAR THROUGHOUT ALL YOUR GENERATIONS.
I WILL TELL YOU EXACTLY HOW TO MAKE THE TABERNACLE. THE TRIBE OF LEVI SHALL BE MY PRIESTS, AND AARON, AND HIS SONS AFTER HIM, WILL BE THE HIGH PRIESTS. THEY SHALL TEACH THE PEOPLE TO BE RIGHTEOUS AND THEY WILL OFFER SACRIFICES WHEN THE PEOPLE SIN.
IT WAS *WEEKS* AGO THAT HE DISAPPEARED INTO THE FIRE ON THAT MOUNTAIN. HE MUST BE DEAD BY NOW.
YEAH, WE CAN'T SIT HERE IN THIS WILDERNESS FOREVER.
WE NEED *A* GOD TO LEAD US AS MOSES DID.
LET US MAKE A GOLDEN IMAGE UNTO OUR GOD.
MOSES IS DEAD. AARON WILL *MAKE* US A COD OF GOLD TO LEAD US BACK INTO EGYPT.
GIVE US YOUR GOLD.
WITH THEIR OWN HANDS THE FOOLS CREATED A STATUE OF A BULL AND CALLED IT GOD. THE ORIGINAL IMAGE OF SATAN BEFORE HE SINNED WAS THAT OF A BULL. THOUGH THE PEOPLE DIDN'T KNOW IT, SATAN HAD INSPIRED THEM TO WORSHIP HIM.
AARON FOLLOWED THE WISHES OF THE PEOPLE AND HELPED THEM BUILD THE GOD OF GOLD.

EXODUS 20:4, 25:8-9, 28:1-3, 32:1-4; EZEKIEL 1:10, 10:11, 28:14

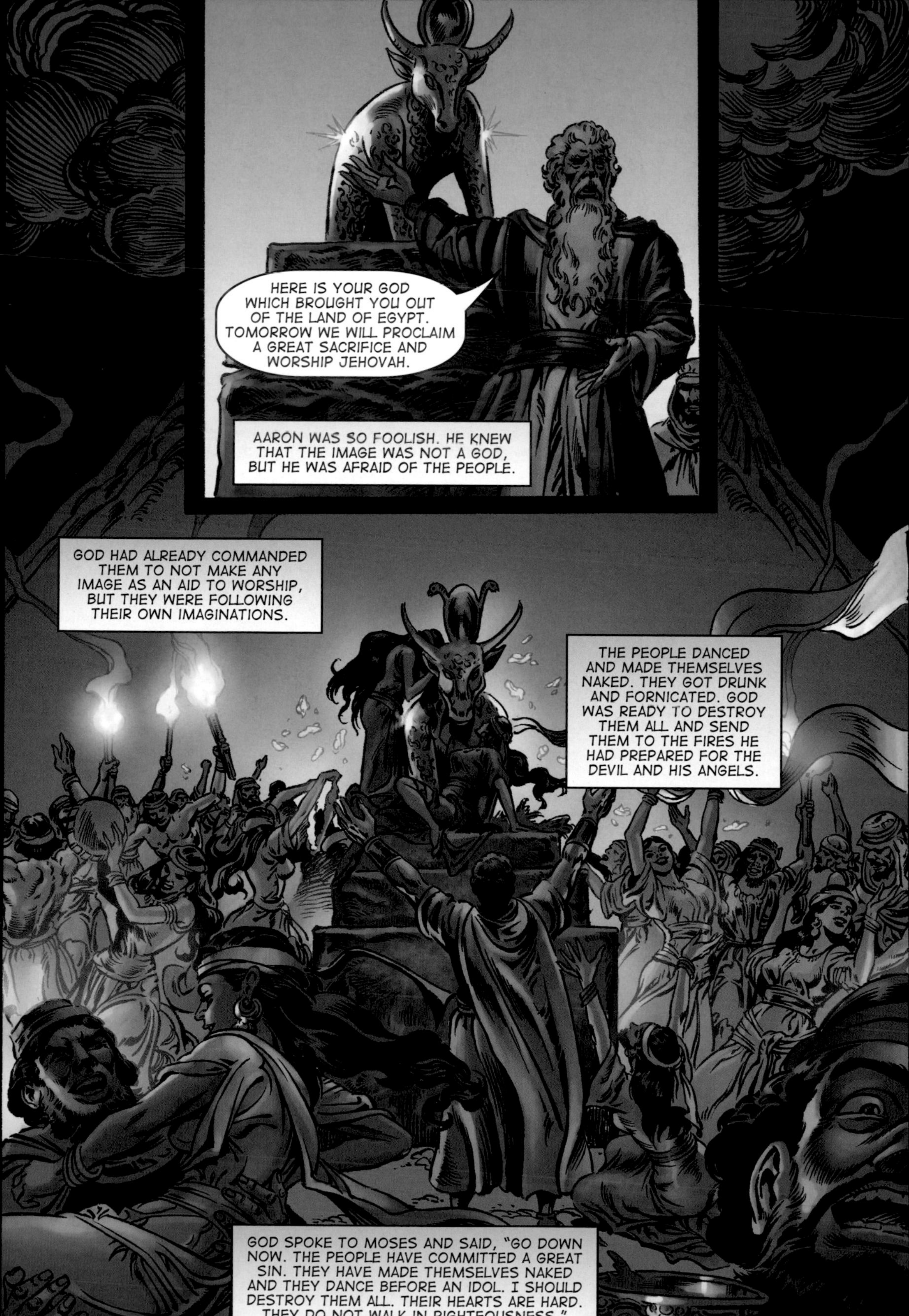
HERE IS YOUR GOD WHICH BROUGHT YOU OUT OF THE LAND OF EGYPT. TOMORROW WE WILL PROCLAIM A GREAT SACRIFICE AND WORSHIP JEHOVAH.
AARON WAS SO FOOLISH. HE KNEW THAT THE IMAGE WAS NOT A GOD, BUT HE WAS AFRAID OF THE PEOPLE.
GOD HAD ALREADY COMMANDED THEM TO NOT MAKE ANY IMAGE AS AN AID TO WORSHIP, BUT THEY WERE FOLLOWING THEIR OWN IMAGINATIONS.
THE PEOPLE DANCED AND MADE THEMSELVES NAKED. THEY GOT DRUNK AND FORNICATED. GOD WAS READY TO DESTROY THEM ALL AND SEND THEM TO THE FIRES HE HAD PREPARED FOR THE DEVIL AND HIS ANGELS.
GOD SPOKE TO MOSES AND SAID, "GO DOWN NOW. THE PEOPLE HAVE COMMITTED A GREAT SIN. THEY HAVE MADE THEMSELVES NAKED AND THEY DANCE BEFORE AN IDOL. I SHOULD DESTROY THEM ALL. THEIR HEARTS ARE HARD. THEY DO NOT WALK IN RIGHTEOUSNESS."

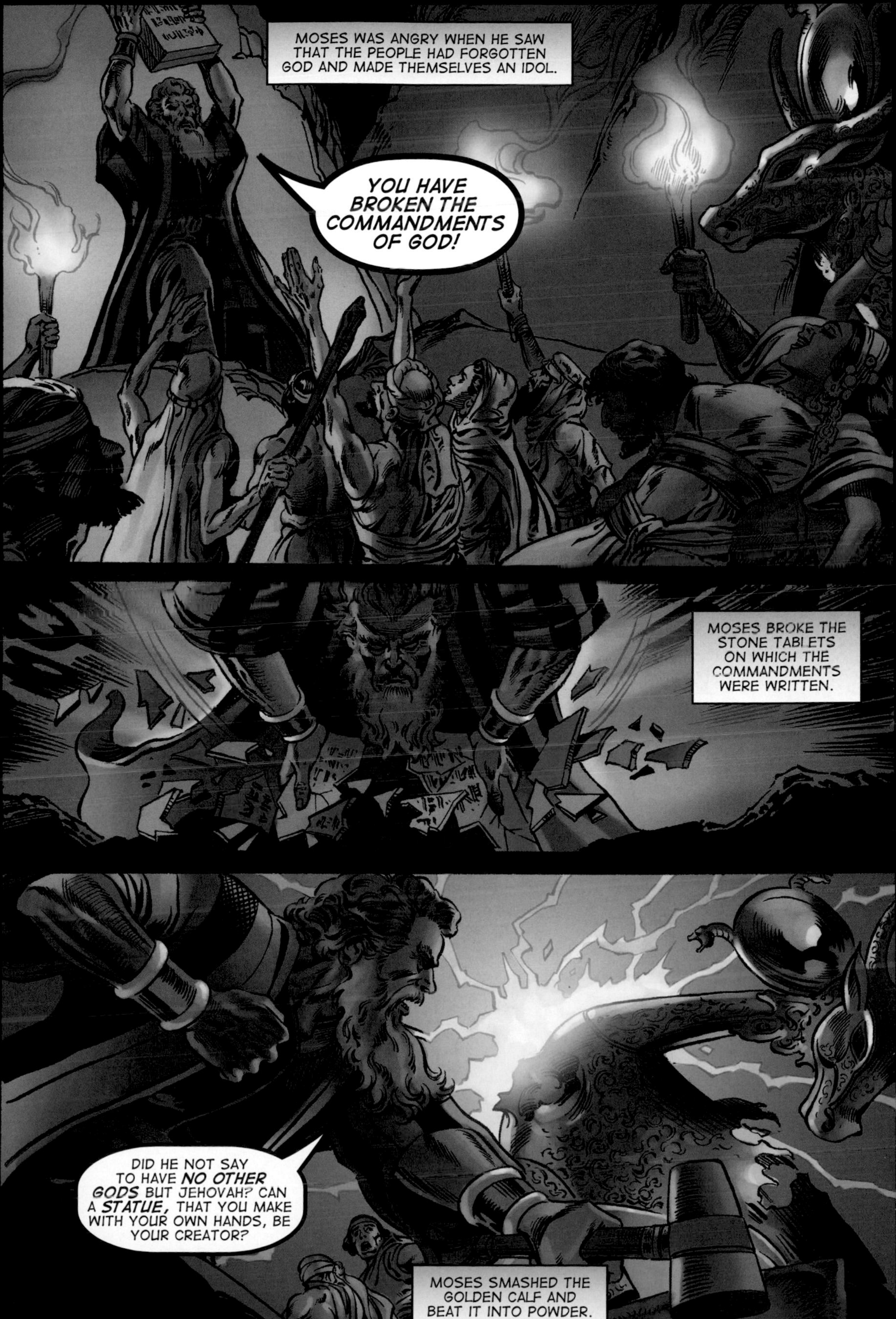
MOSES WAS ANGRY WHEN HE SAW THAT THE PEOPLE HAD FORGOTTEN GOD AND MADE THEMSELVES AN IDOL.
YOU HAVE BROKEN THE COMMANDMENTS OF GOD!
MOSES BROKE THE STONE TABLETS ON WHICH THE COMMANDMENTS WERE WRITTEN.
DID HE NOT SAY TO HAVE **NO OTHER GODS** BUT JEHOVAH? CAN A **STATUE,** THAT YOU MAKE WITH YOUR OWN HANDS, BE YOUR CREATOR?
MOSES SMASHED THE GOLDEN CALF AND BEAT IT INTO POWDER.

EXODUS 20:3-4, 32:15-20

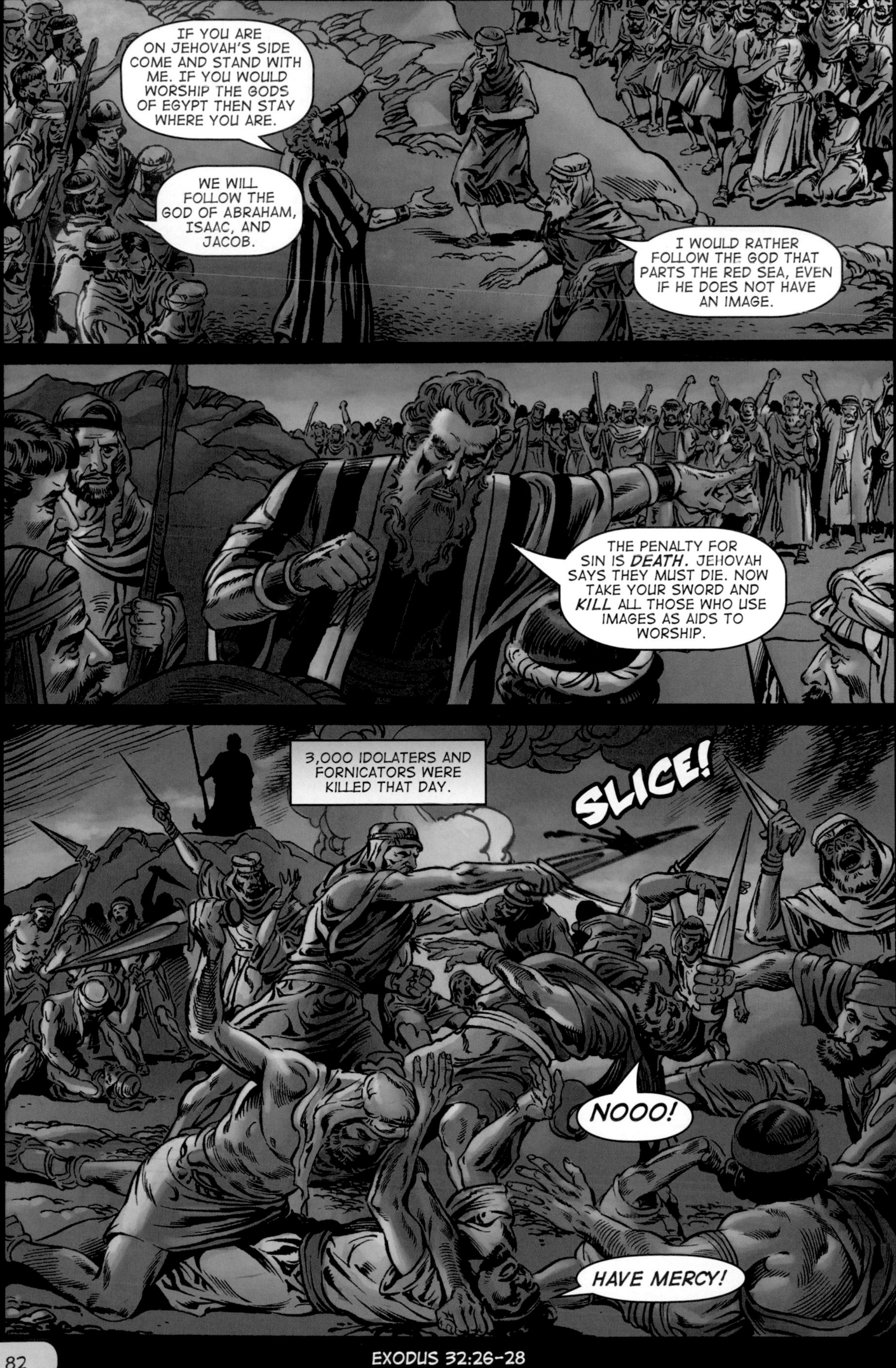
IF YOU ARE ON JEHOVAH'S SIDE COME AND STAND WITH ME. IF YOU WOULD WORSHIP THE GODS OF EGYPT THEN STAY WHERE YOU ARE.
WE WILL FOLLOW THE GOD OF ABRAHAM, ISAAC, AND JACOB.
I WOULD RATHER FOLLOW THE GOD THAT PARTS THE RED SEA, EVEN IF HE DOES NOT HAVE AN IMAGE.
THE PENALTY FOR SIN IS DEATH. JEHOVAH SAYS THEY MUST DIE. NOW TAKE YOUR SWORD AND KILL ALL THOSE WHO USE IMAGES AS AIDS TO WORSHIP.
3,000 IDOLATERS AND FORNICATORS WERE KILLED THAT DAY.
SLICE!
NOOO!
HAVE MERCY!

EXODUS 32:26-28

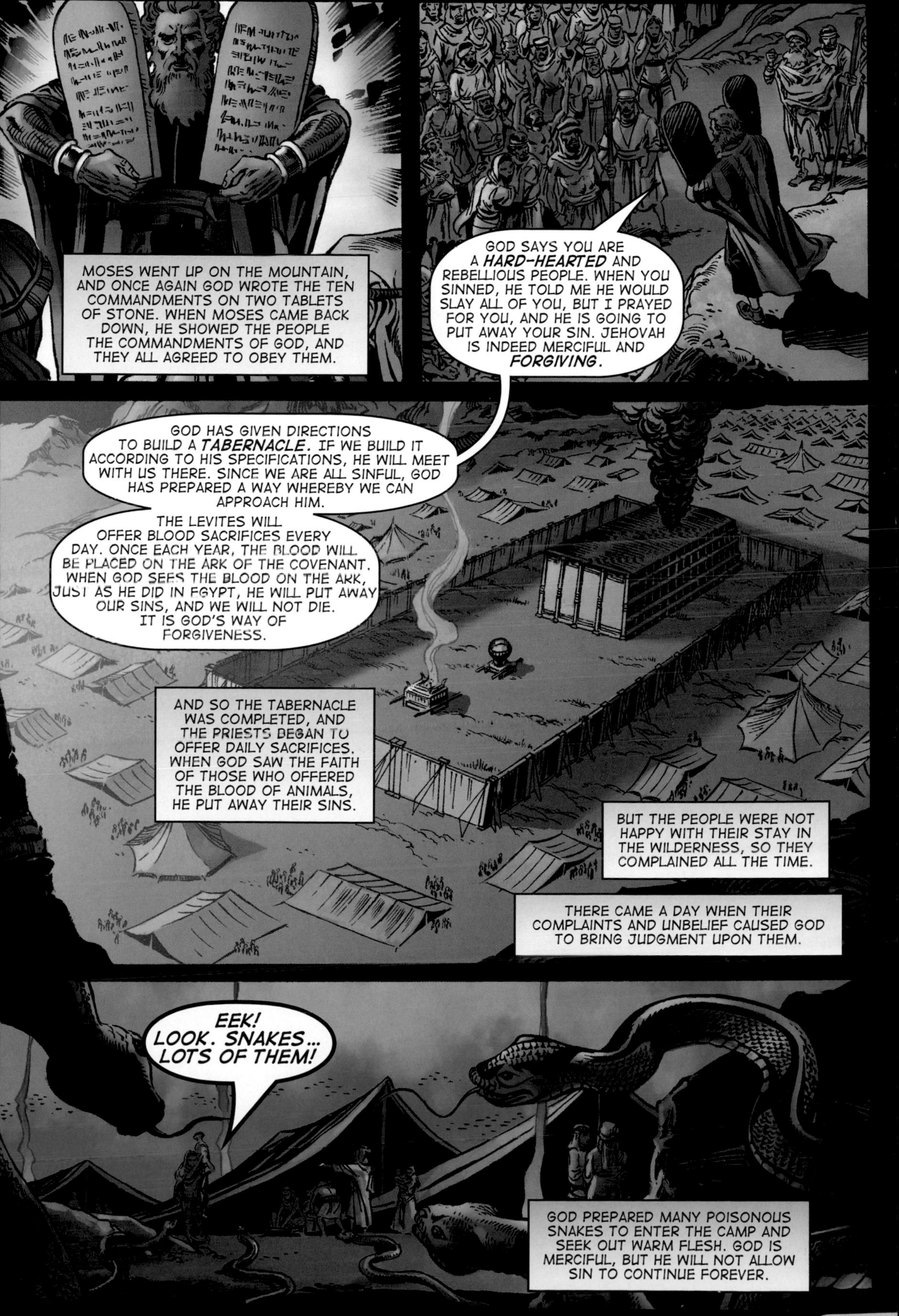
MOSES WENT UP ON THE MOUNTAIN, AND ONCE AGAIN GOD WROTE THE TEN COMMANDMENTS ON TWO TABLETS OF STONE. WHEN MOSES CAME BACK DOWN, HE SHOWED THE PEOPLE THE COMMANDMENTS OF GOD, AND THEY ALL AGREED TO OBEY THEM.
GOD SAYS YOU ARE A HARD-HEARTED AND REBELLIOUS PEOPLE. WHEN YOU SINNED, HE TOLD ME HE WOULD SLAY ALL OF YOU, BUT I PRAYED FOR YOU, AND HE IS GOING TO PUT AWAY YOUR SIN. JEHOVAH IS INDEED MERCIFUL AND FORGIVING.
GOD HAS GIVEN DIRECTIONS TO BUILD A TABERNACLE. IF WE BUILD IT ACCORDING TO HIS SPECIFICATIONS, HE WILL MEET WITH US THERE. SINCE WE ARE ALL SINFUL, GOD HAS PREPARED A WAY WHEREBY WE CAN APPROACH HIM.
THE LEVITES WILL OFFER BLOOD SACRIFICES EVERY DAY. ONCE EACH YEAR, THE BLOOD WILL BE PLACED ON THE ARK OF THE COVENANT. WHEN GOD SEES THE BLOOD ON THE ARK, JUST AS HE DID IN EGYPT, HE WILL PUT AWAY OUR SINS, AND WE WILL NOT DIE. IT IS GOD'S WAY OF FORGIVENESS.
AND SO THE TABERNACLE WAS COMPLETED, AND THE PRIESTS BEGAN TO OFFER DAILY SACRIFICES. WHEN GOD SAW THE FAITH OF THOSE WHO OFFERED THE BLOOD OF ANIMALS, HE PUT AWAY THEIR SINS.
BUT THE PEOPLE WERE NOT HAPPY WITH THEIR STAY IN THE WILDERNESS, SO THEY COMPLAINED ALL THE TIME.
THERE CAME A DAY WHEN THEIR COMPLAINTS AND UNBELIEF CAUSED GOD TO BRING JUDGMENT UPON THEM.
EEK! LOOK. SNAKES... LOTS OF THEM!
GOD PREPARED MANY POISONOUS SNAKES TO ENTER THE CAMP AND SEEK OUT WARM FLESH. GOD IS MERCIFUL, BUT HE WILL NOT ALLOW SIN TO CONTINUE FOREVER.

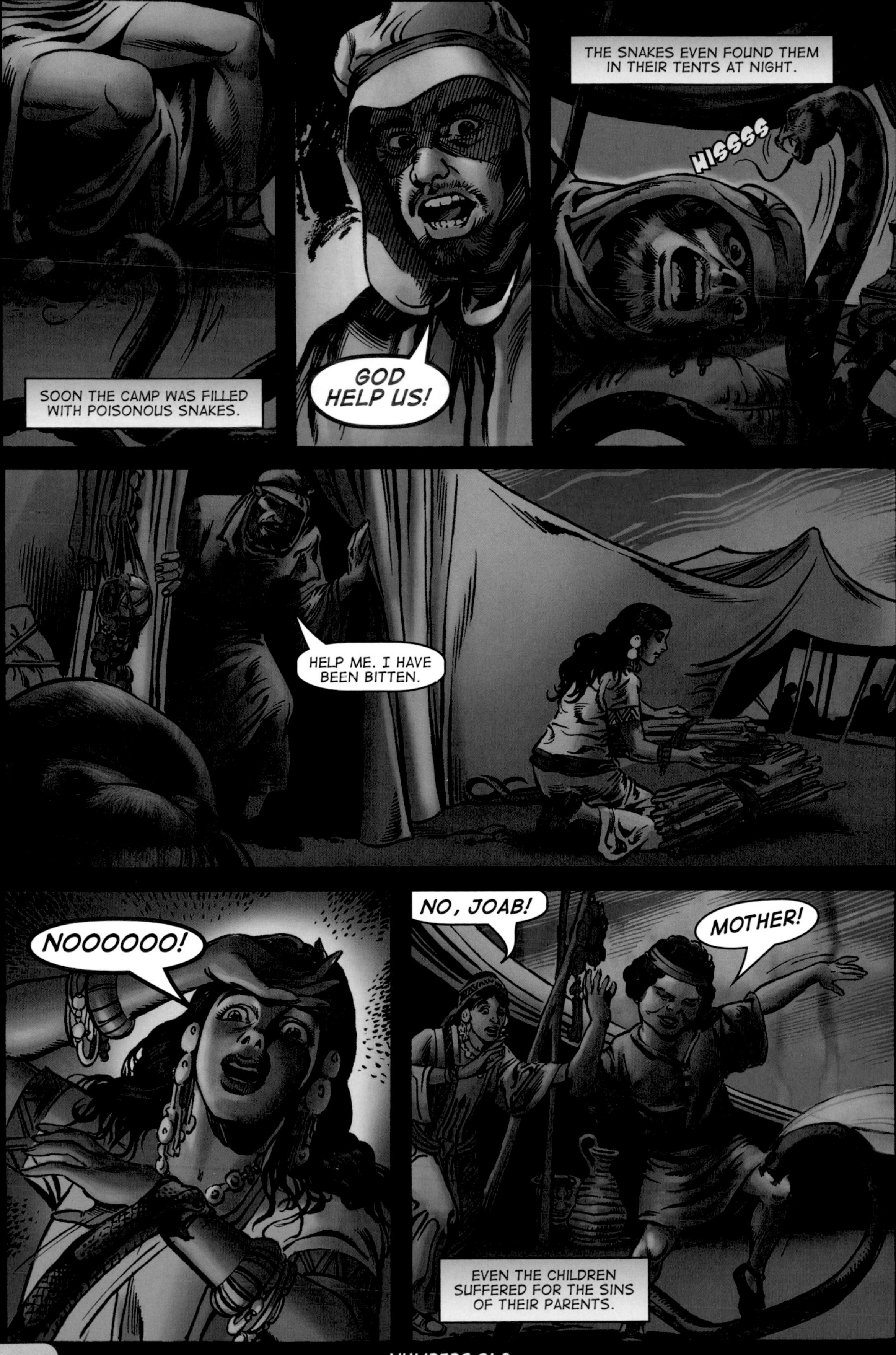
SOON THE CAMP WAS FILLED WITH POISONOUS SNAKES.
GOD HELP US!
THE SNAKES EVEN FOUND THEM IN THEIR TENTS AT NIGHT.
HISSSS
HELP ME. I HAVE BEEN BITTEN.
NOOOOOO!
NO, JOAB!
MOTHER!
EVEN THE CHILDREN SUFFERED FOR THE SINS OF THEIR PARENTS.

FROM ALL OVER THE CAMP CRIES OF THE SUFFERING AND GRIEVING COULD BE HEARD. THE WAGES OF SIN ARE TERRIBLE.

IT IS LIKE THIS ALL OVER THE CAMP AND GROWING WORSE BY THE MINUTE. MANY HAVE ALREADY *DIED*.

WE MUST FIND *MOSES*. SURELY THIS IS THE WORK OF GOD. HE IS ANGRY AT THE PEOPLE FOR THEIR SINS.

WHACK!

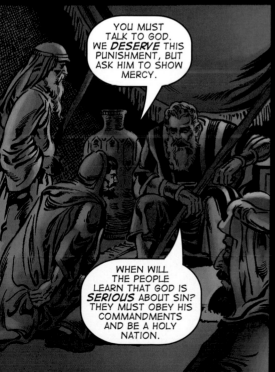

YOU MUST TALK TO GOD. WE *DESERVE* THIS PUNISHMENT, BUT ASK HIM TO SHOW MERCY.

WHEN WILL THE PEOPLE LEARN THAT GOD IS *SERIOUS* ABOUT SIN? THEY MUST OBEY HIS COMMANDMENTS AND BE A HOLY NATION.

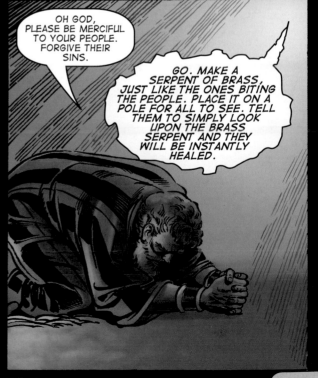

OH GOD, PLEASE BE MERCIFUL TO YOUR PEOPLE. FORGIVE THEIR SINS.

GO. MAKE A SERPENT OF BRASS, JUST LIKE THE ONES BITING THE PEOPLE. PLACE IT ON A POLE FOR ALL TO SEE. TELL THEM TO SIMPLY LOOK UPON THE BRASS SERPENT AND THEY WILL BE INSTANTLY HEALED.

NUMBERS 21:7-8

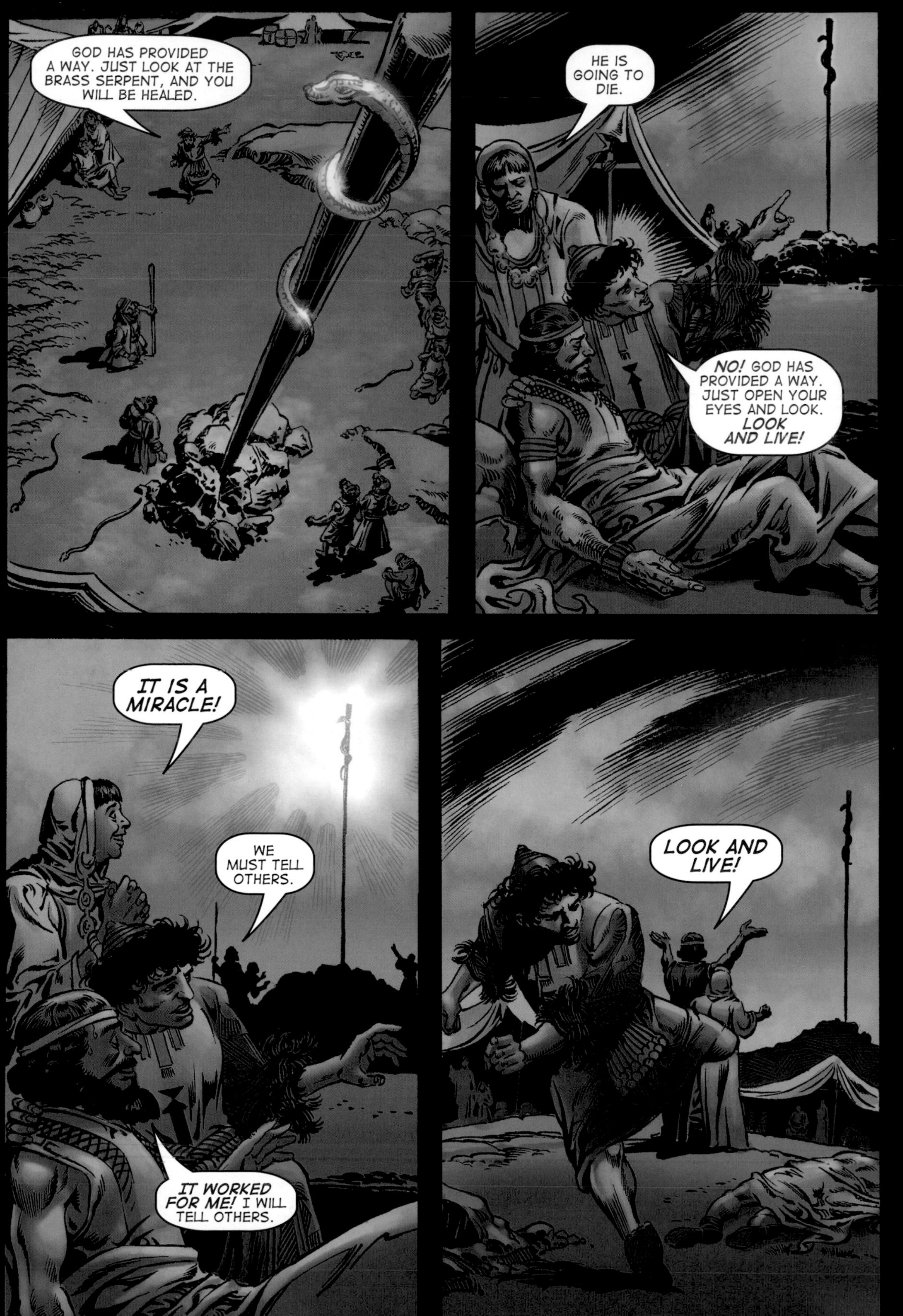
GOD HAS PROVIDED A WAY. JUST LOOK AT THE BRASS SERPENT, AND YOU WILL BE HEALED.
HE IS GOING TO DIE.
NO! GOD HAS PROVIDED A WAY. JUST OPEN YOUR EYES AND LOOK. LOOK AND LIVE!
IT IS A MIRACLE!
WE MUST TELL OTHERS.
IT WORKED FOR ME! I WILL TELL OTHERS.
LOOK AND LIVE!

NUMBERS 21:9

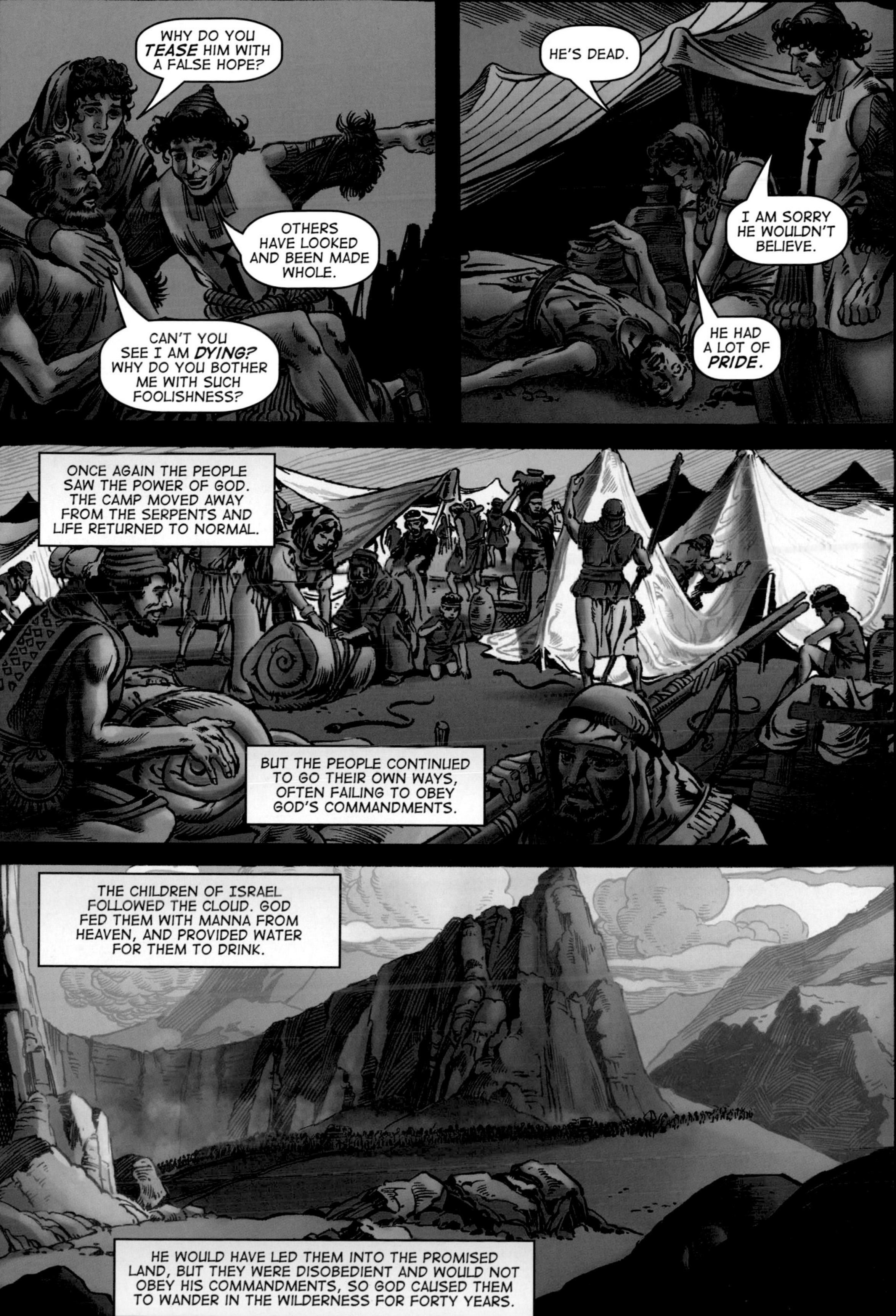
WHY DO YOU TEASE HIM WITH A FALSE HOPE?
OTHERS HAVE LOOKED AND BEEN MADE WHOLE.
CAN'T YOU SEE I AM DYING? WHY DO YOU BOTHER ME WITH SUCH FOOLISHNESS?
HE'S DEAD.
I AM SORRY HE WOULDN'T BELIEVE.
HE HAD A LOT OF PRIDE.
ONCE AGAIN THE PEOPLE SAW THE POWER OF GOD. THE CAMP MOVED AWAY FROM THE SERPENTS AND LIFE RETURNED TO NORMAL.
BUT THE PEOPLE CONTINUED TO GO THEIR OWN WAYS, OFTEN FAILING TO OBEY GOD'S COMMANDMENTS.
THE CHILDREN OF ISRAEL FOLLOWED THE CLOUD. GOD FED THEM WITH MANNA FROM HEAVEN, AND PROVIDED WATER FOR THEM TO DRINK.
HE WOULD HAVE LED THEM INTO THE PROMISED LAND, BUT THEY WERE DISOBEDIENT AND WOULD NOT OBEY HIS COMMANDMENTS, SO GOD CAUSED THEM TO WANDER IN THE WILDERNESS FOR FORTY YEARS.

NUMBERS 21:9, 32:13

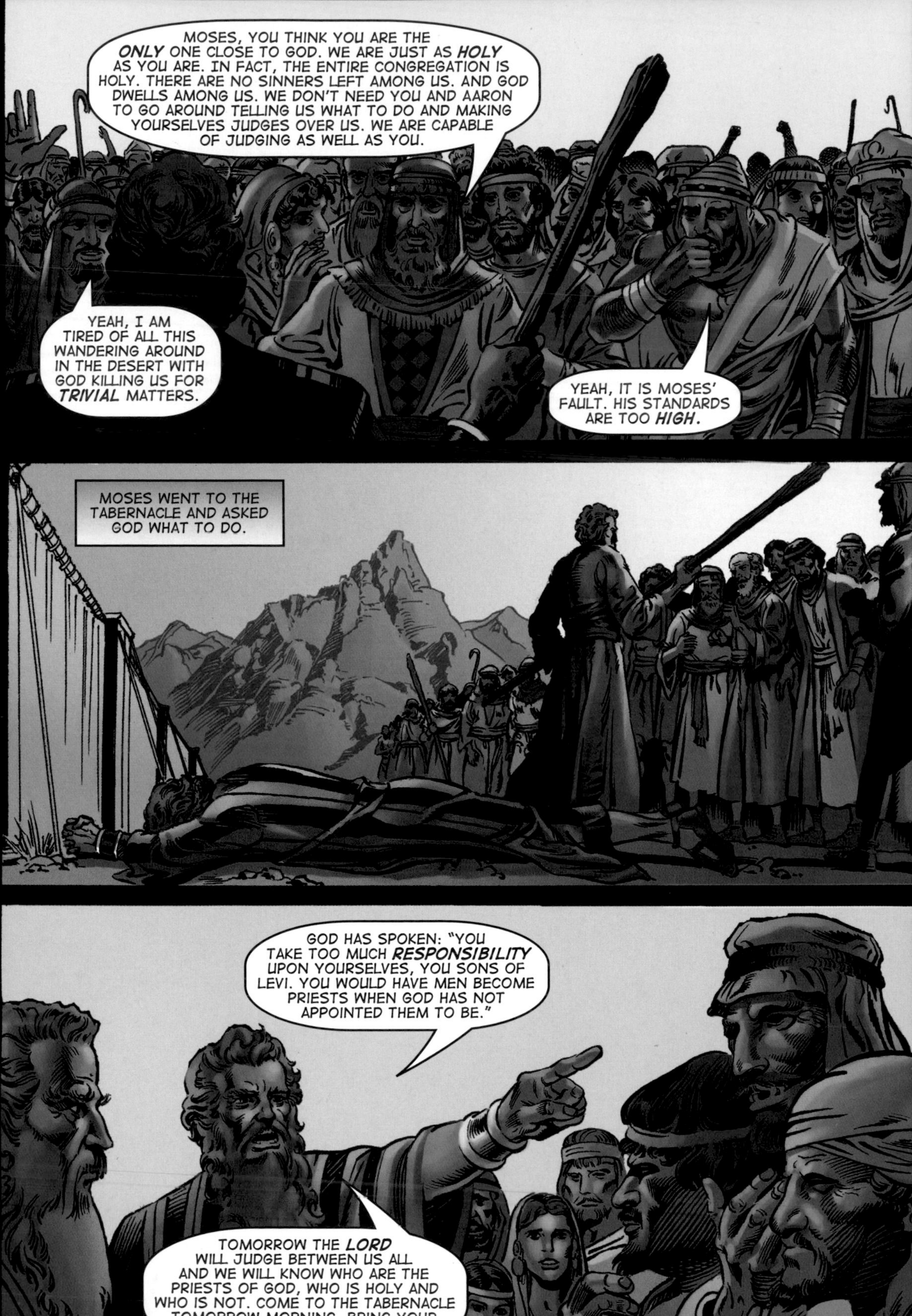
MOSES, YOU THINK YOU ARE THE ONLY ONE CLOSE TO GOD. WE ARE JUST AS HOLY AS YOU ARE. IN FACT, THE ENTIRE CONGREGATION IS HOLY. THERE ARE NO SINNERS LEFT AMONG US. AND GOD DWELLS AMONG US. WE DON'T NEED YOU AND AARON TO GO AROUND TELLING US WHAT TO DO AND MAKING YOURSELVES JUDGES OVER US. WE ARE CAPABLE OF JUDGING AS WELL AS YOU.
YEAH, I AM TIRED OF ALL THIS WANDERING AROUND IN THE DESERT WITH GOD KILLING US FOR TRIVIAL MATTERS.
YEAH, IT IS MOSES' FAULT. HIS STANDARDS ARE TOO HIGH.
MOSES WENT TO THE TABERNACLE AND ASKED GOD WHAT TO DO.
GOD HAS SPOKEN: "YOU TAKE TOO MUCH RESPONSIBILITY UPON YOURSELVES, YOU SONS OF LEVI. YOU WOULD HAVE MEN BECOME PRIESTS WHEN GOD HAS NOT APPOINTED THEM TO BE."
TOMORROW THE LORD WILL JUDGE BETWEEN US ALL AND WE WILL KNOW WHO ARE THE PRIESTS OF GOD, WHO IS HOLY AND WHO IS NOT. COME TO THE TABERNACLE TOMORROW MORNING. BRING YOUR CENSERS WITH FIRE IN THEM.

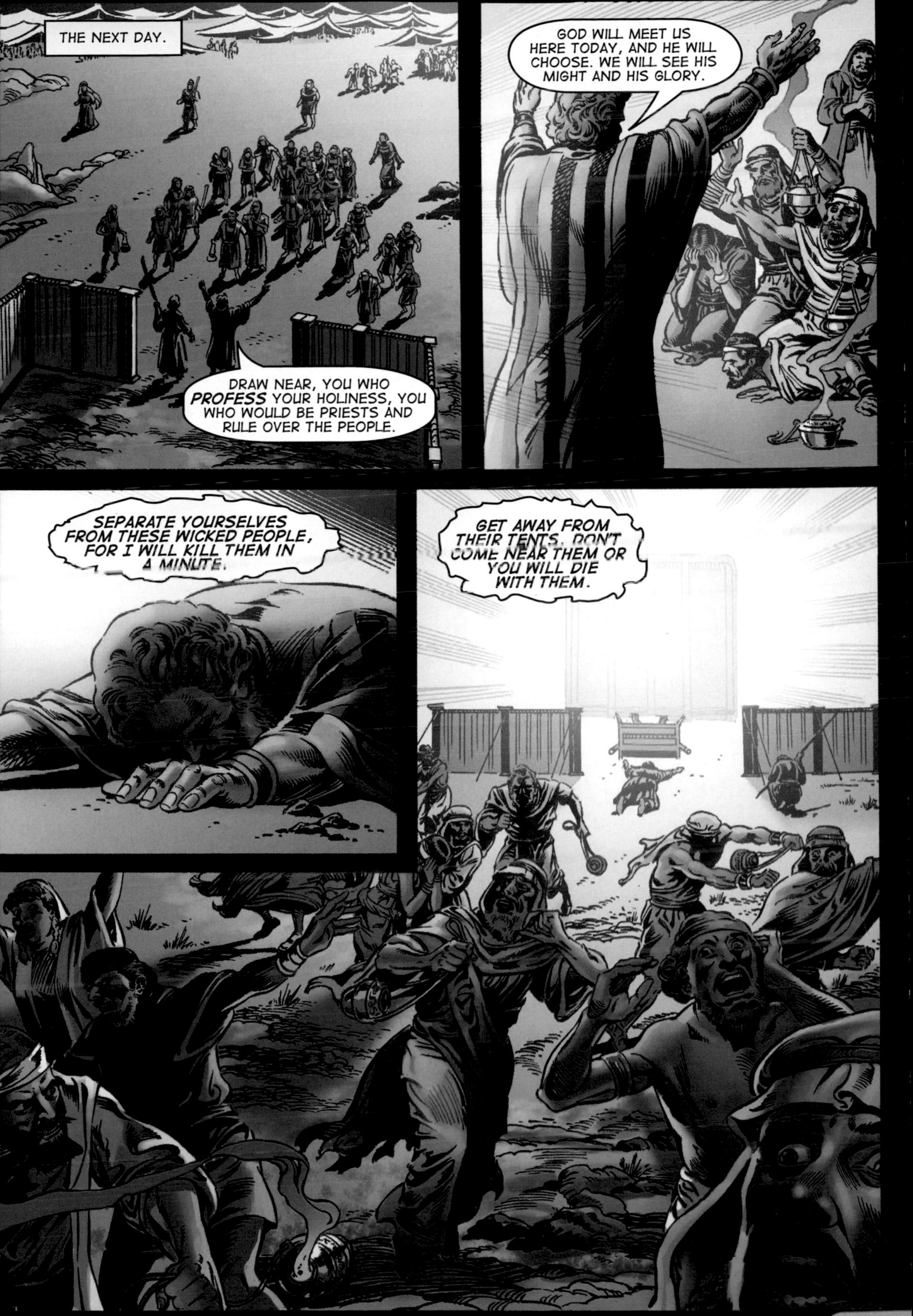
THE NEXT DAY.
DRAW NEAR, YOU WHO *PROFESS* YOUR HOLINESS, YOU WHO WOULD BE PRIESTS AND RULE OVER THE PEOPLE.
GOD WILL MEET US HERE TODAY, AND HE WILL CHOOSE. WE WILL SEE HIS MIGHT AND HIS GLORY.
SEPARATE YOURSELVES FROM THESE WICKED PEOPLE, FOR I WILL KILL THEM IN A MINUTE.
GET AWAY FROM THEIR TENTS. DON'T COME NEAR THEM OR YOU WILL DIE WITH THEM.

NUMBERS 16:19-24

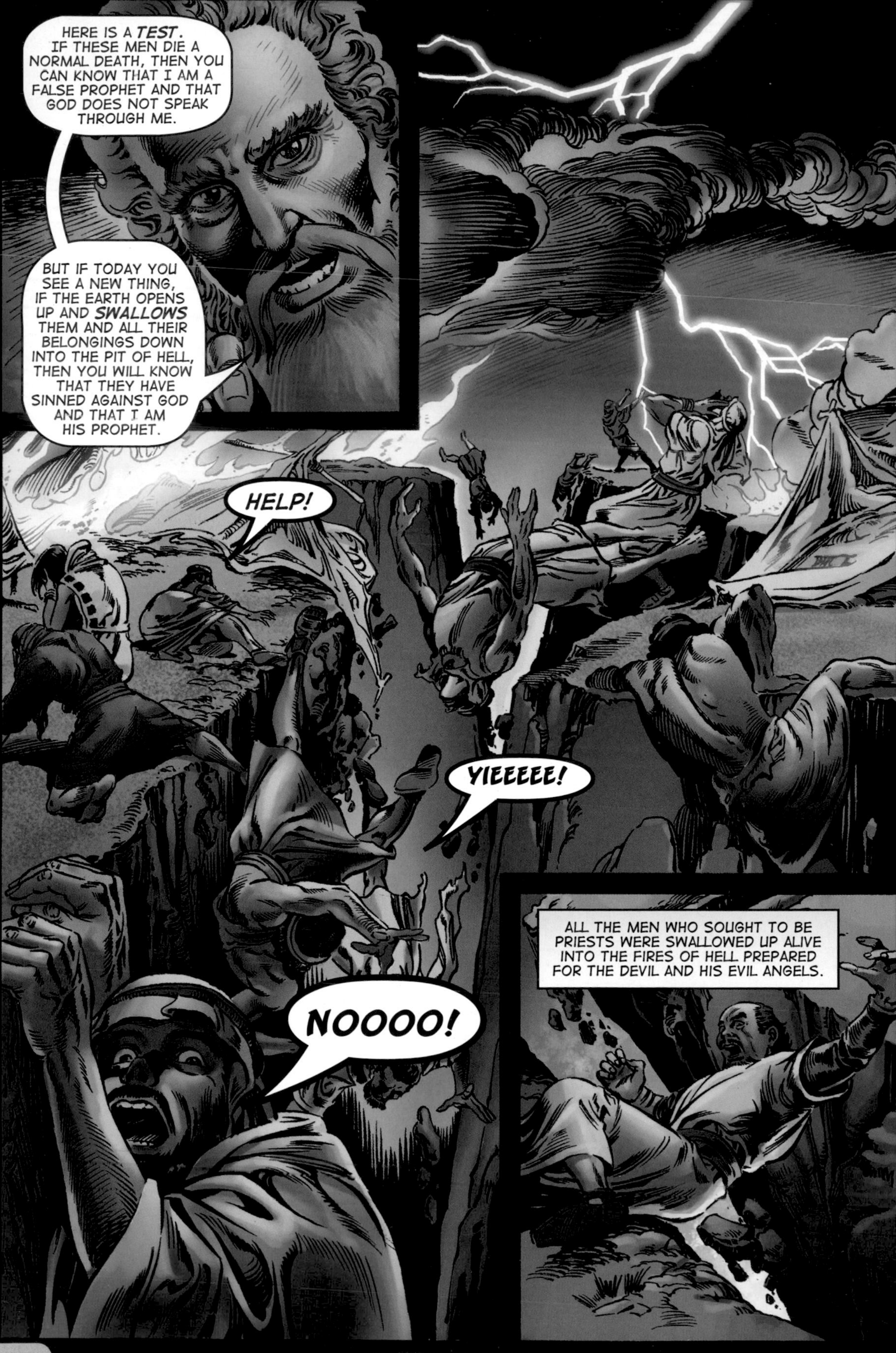
HERE IS A TEST. IF THESE MEN DIE A NORMAL DEATH, THEN YOU CAN KNOW THAT I AM A FALSE PROPHET AND THAT GOD DOES NOT SPEAK THROUGH ME.
BUT IF TODAY YOU SEE A NEW THING, IF THE EARTH OPENS UP AND SWALLOWS THEM AND ALL THEIR BELONGINGS DOWN INTO THE PIT OF HELL, THEN YOU WILL KNOW THAT THEY HAVE SINNED AGAINST GOD AND THAT I AM HIS PROPHET.
HELP!
YIEEEEE!
NOOOO!
ALL THE MEN WHO SOUGHT TO BE PRIESTS WERE SWALLOWED UP ALIVE INTO THE FIRES OF HELL PREPARED FOR THE DEVIL AND HIS EVIL ANGELS.

NUMBERS 16:28-33

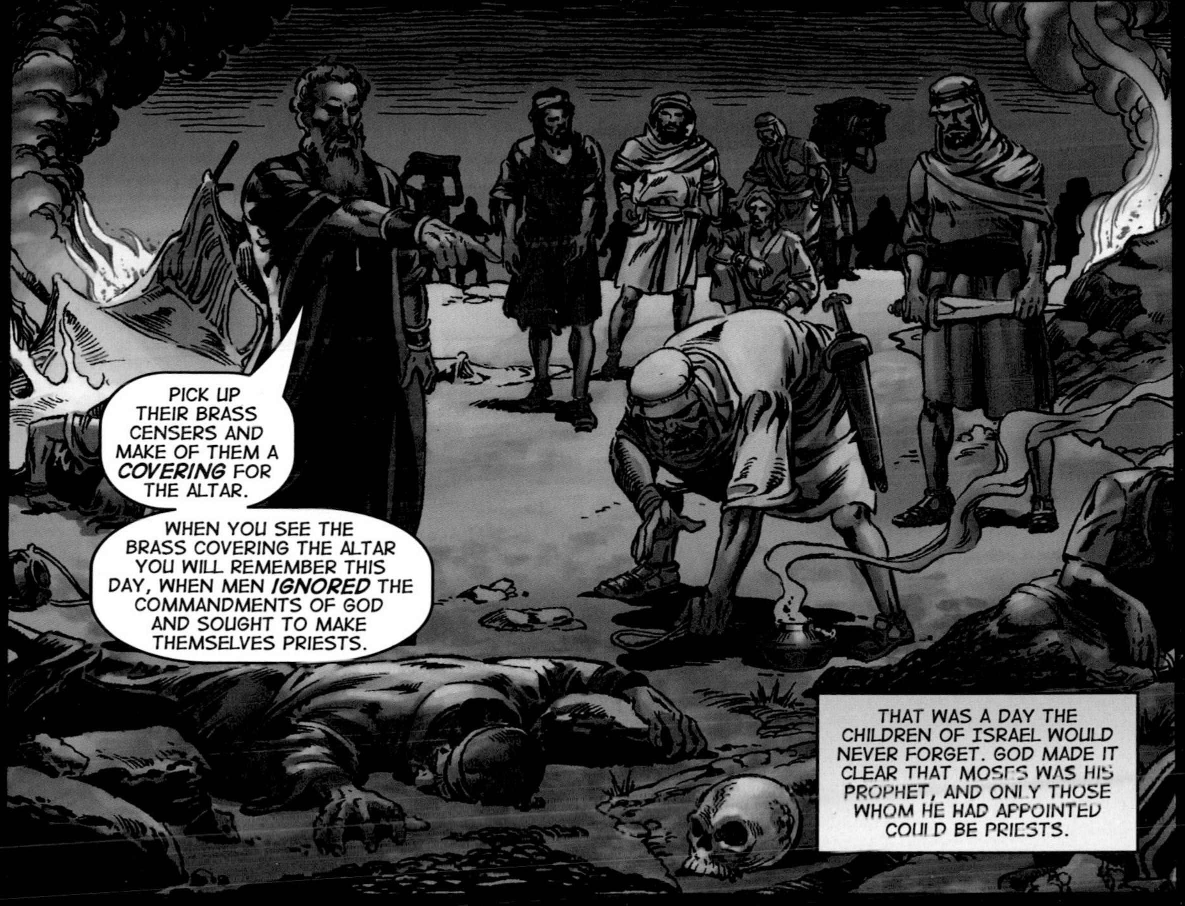
PICK UP THEIR BRASS CENSERS AND MAKE OF THEM A COVERING FOR THE ALTAR.
WHEN YOU SEE THE BRASS COVERING THE ALTAR YOU WILL REMEMBER THIS DAY, WHEN MEN IGNORED THE COMMANDMENTS OF GOD AND SOUGHT TO MAKE THEMSELVES PRIESTS.
THAT WAS A DAY THE CHILDREN OF ISRAEL WOULD NEVER FORGET. GOD MADE IT CLEAR THAT MOSES WAS HIS PROPHET, AND ONLY THOSE WHOM HE HAD APPOINTED COULD BE PRIESTS.

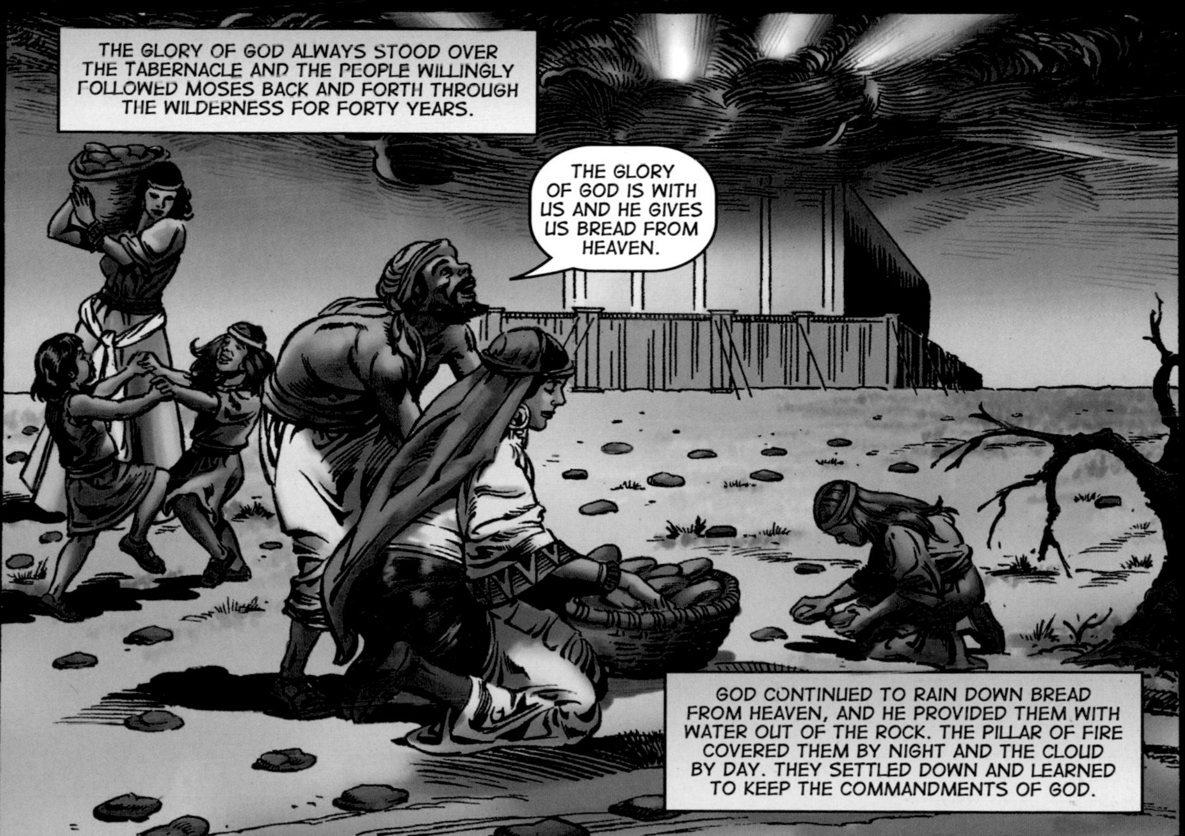
THE GLORY OF GOD ALWAYS STOOD OVER THE TABERNACLE AND THE PEOPLE WILLINGLY FOLLOWED MOSES BACK AND FORTH THROUGH THE WILDERNESS FOR FORTY YEARS.
THE GLORY OF GOD IS WITH US AND HE GIVES US BREAD FROM HEAVEN.
GOD CONTINUED TO RAIN DOWN BREAD FROM HEAVEN, AND HE PROVIDED THEM WITH WATER OUT OF THE ROCK. THE PILLAR OF FIRE COVERED THEM BY NIGHT AND THE CLOUD BY DAY. THEY SETTLED DOWN AND LEARNED TO KEEP THE COMMANDMENTS OF GOD.

NUMBERS 16:37-38

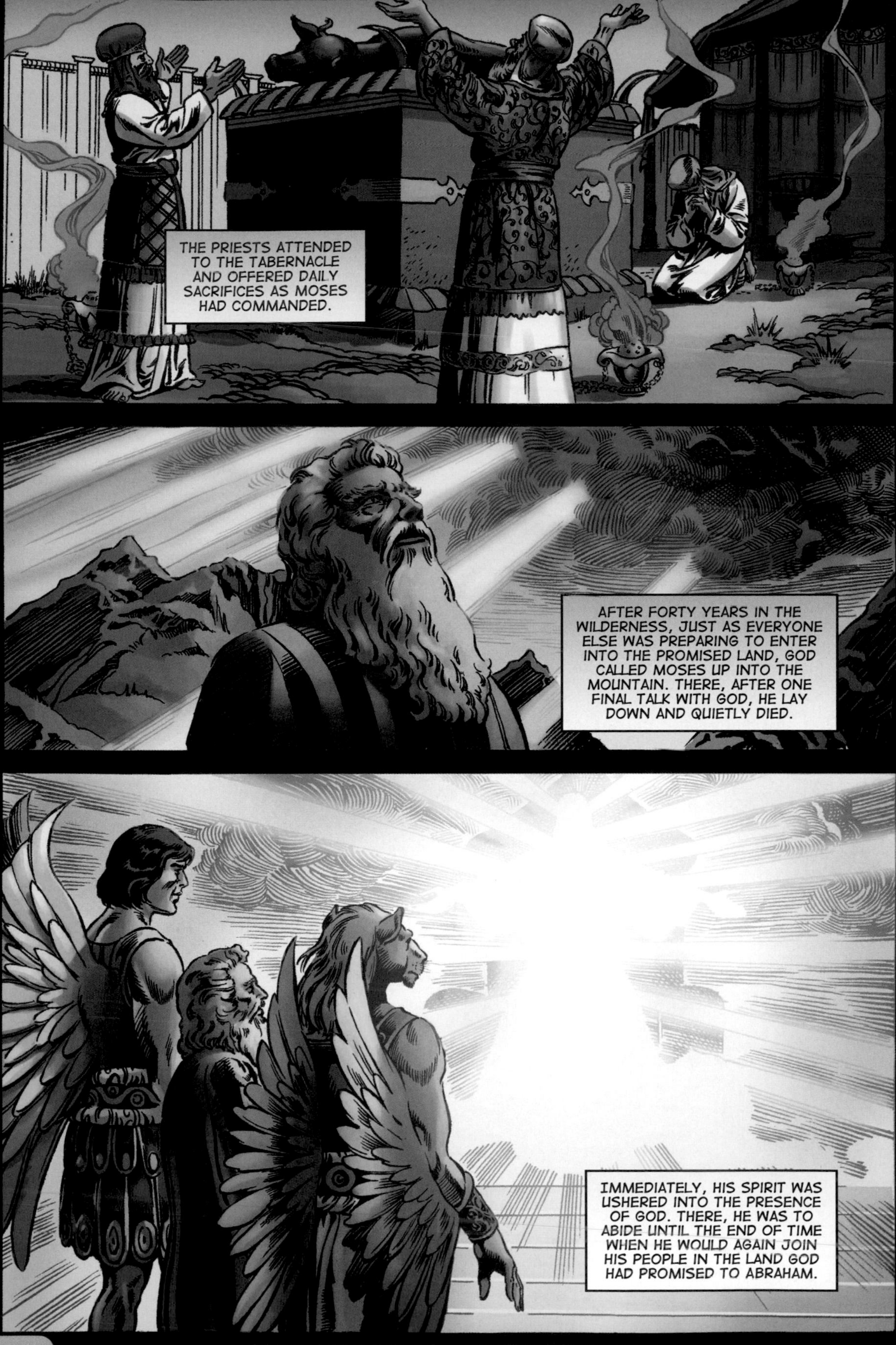
THE PRIESTS ATTENDED TO THE TABERNACLE AND OFFERED DAILY SACRIFICES AS MOSES HAD COMMANDED.
AFTER FORTY YEARS IN THE WILDERNESS, JUST AS EVERYONE ELSE WAS PREPARING TO ENTER INTO THE PROMISED LAND, GOD CALLED MOSES UP INTO THE MOUNTAIN. THERE, AFTER ONE FINAL TALK WITH GOD, HE LAY DOWN AND QUIETLY DIED.
IMMEDIATELY, HIS SPIRIT WAS USHERED INTO THE PRESENCE OF GOD. THERE, HE WAS TO ABIDE UNTIL THE END OF TIME WHEN HE WOULD AGAIN JOIN HIS PEOPLE IN THE LAND GOD HAD PROMISED TO ABRAHAM.

APPROXIMATELY 1451 B.C. - DEUTERONOMY 34:4-5

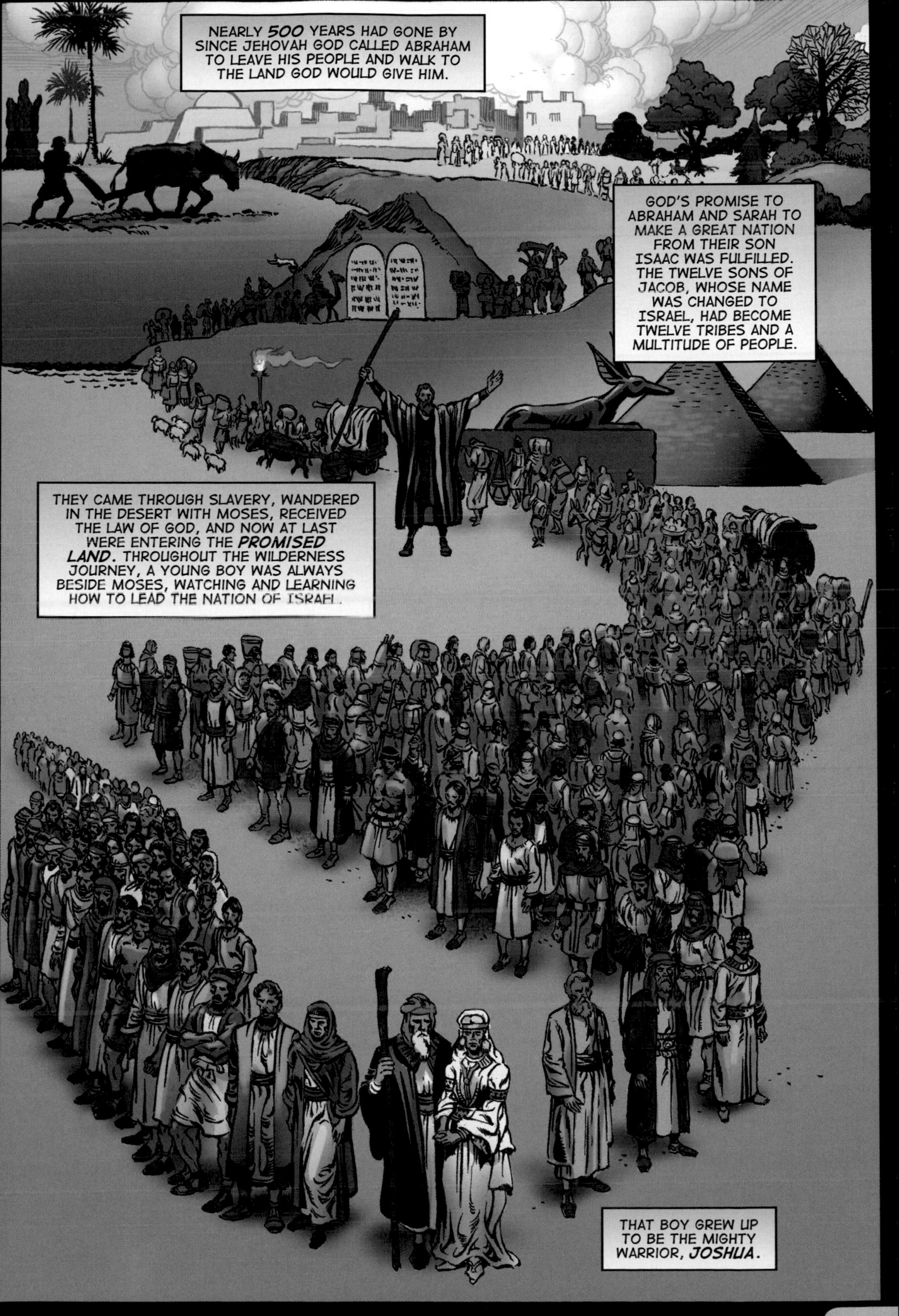
NEARLY 500 YEARS HAD GONE BY SINCE JEHOVAH GOD CALLED ABRAHAM TO LEAVE HIS PEOPLE AND WALK TO THE LAND GOD WOULD GIVE HIM.
GOD'S PROMISE TO ABRAHAM AND SARAH TO MAKE A GREAT NATION FROM THEIR SON ISAAC WAS FULFILLED. THE TWELVE SONS OF JACOB, WHOSE NAME WAS CHANGED TO ISRAEL, HAD BECOME TWELVE TRIBES AND A MULTITUDE OF PEOPLE.
THEY CAME THROUGH SLAVERY, WANDERED IN THE DESERT WITH MOSES, RECEIVED THE LAW OF GOD, AND NOW AT LAST WERE ENTERING THE PROMISED LAND. THROUGHOUT THE WILDERNESS JOURNEY, A YOUNG BOY WAS ALWAYS BESIDE MOSES, WATCHING AND LEARNING HOW TO LEAD THE NATION OF ISRAEL.
THAT BOY GREW UP TO BE THE MIGHTY WARRIOR, JOSHUA.

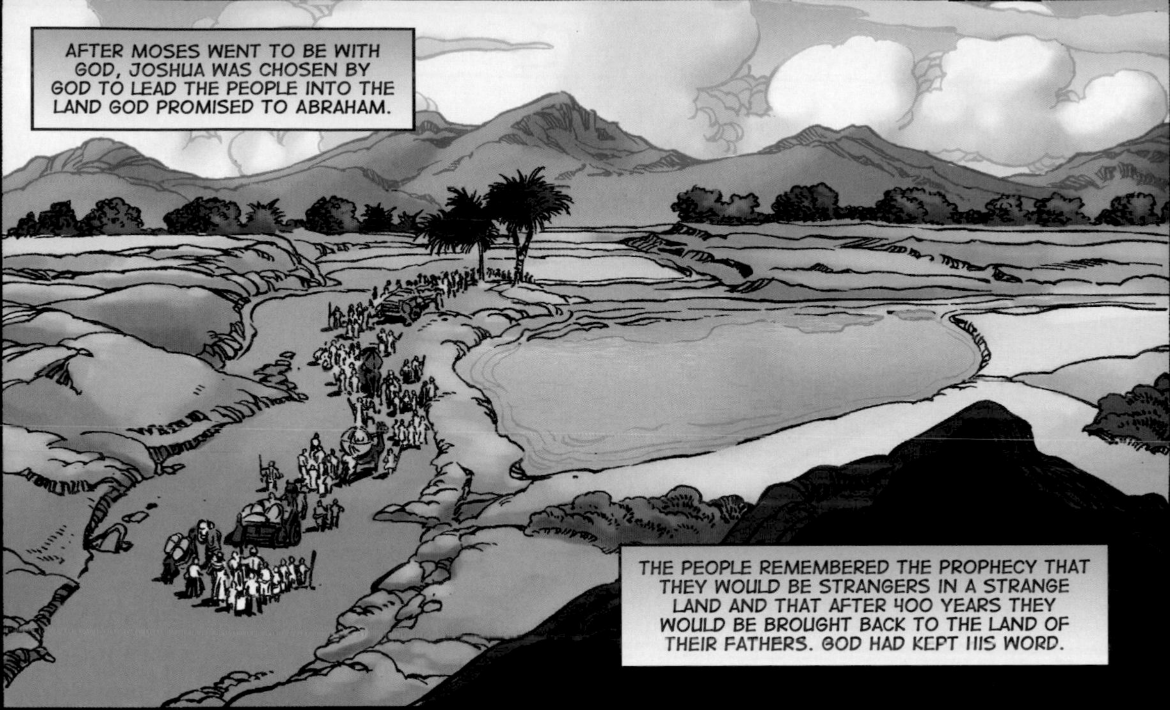
AFTER MOSES WENT TO BE WITH GOD, JOSHUA WAS CHOSEN BY GOD TO LEAD THE PEOPLE INTO THE LAND GOD PROMISED TO ABRAHAM.
THE PEOPLE REMEMBERED THE PROPHECY THAT THEY WOULD BE STRANGERS IN A STRANGE LAND AND THAT AFTER 400 YEARS THEY WOULD BE BROUGHT BACK TO THE LAND OF THEIR FATHERS. GOD HAD KEPT HIS WORD.

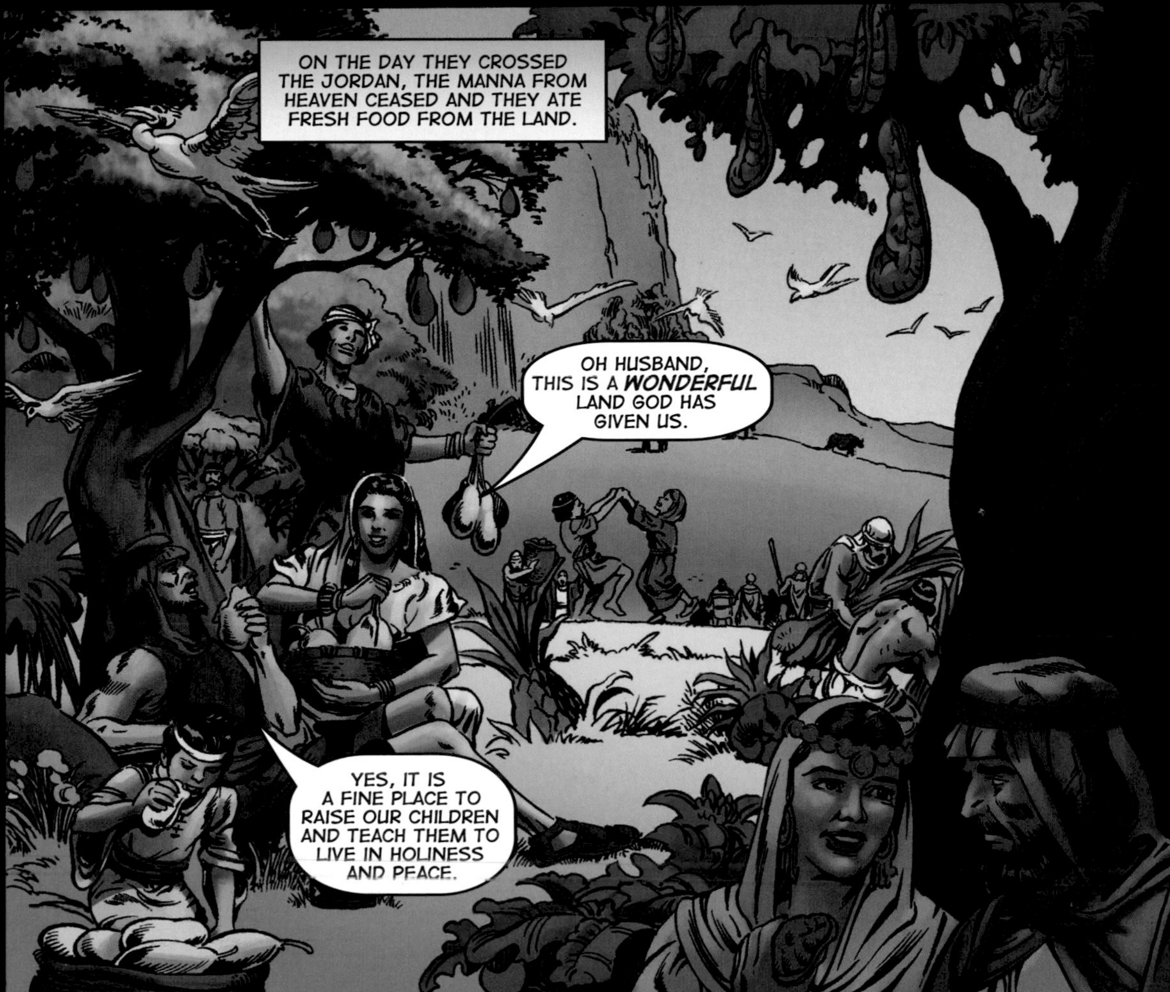
ON THE DAY THEY CROSSED THE JORDAN, THE MANNA FROM HEAVEN CEASED AND THEY ATE FRESH FOOD FROM THE LAND.
OH HUSBAND, THIS IS A ***WONDERFUL*** LAND GOD HAS GIVEN US.
YES, IT IS A FINE PLACE TO RAISE OUR CHILDREN AND TEACH THEM TO LIVE IN HOLINESS AND PEACE.

DEUTERONOMY 34:9; JOSHUA 5:12

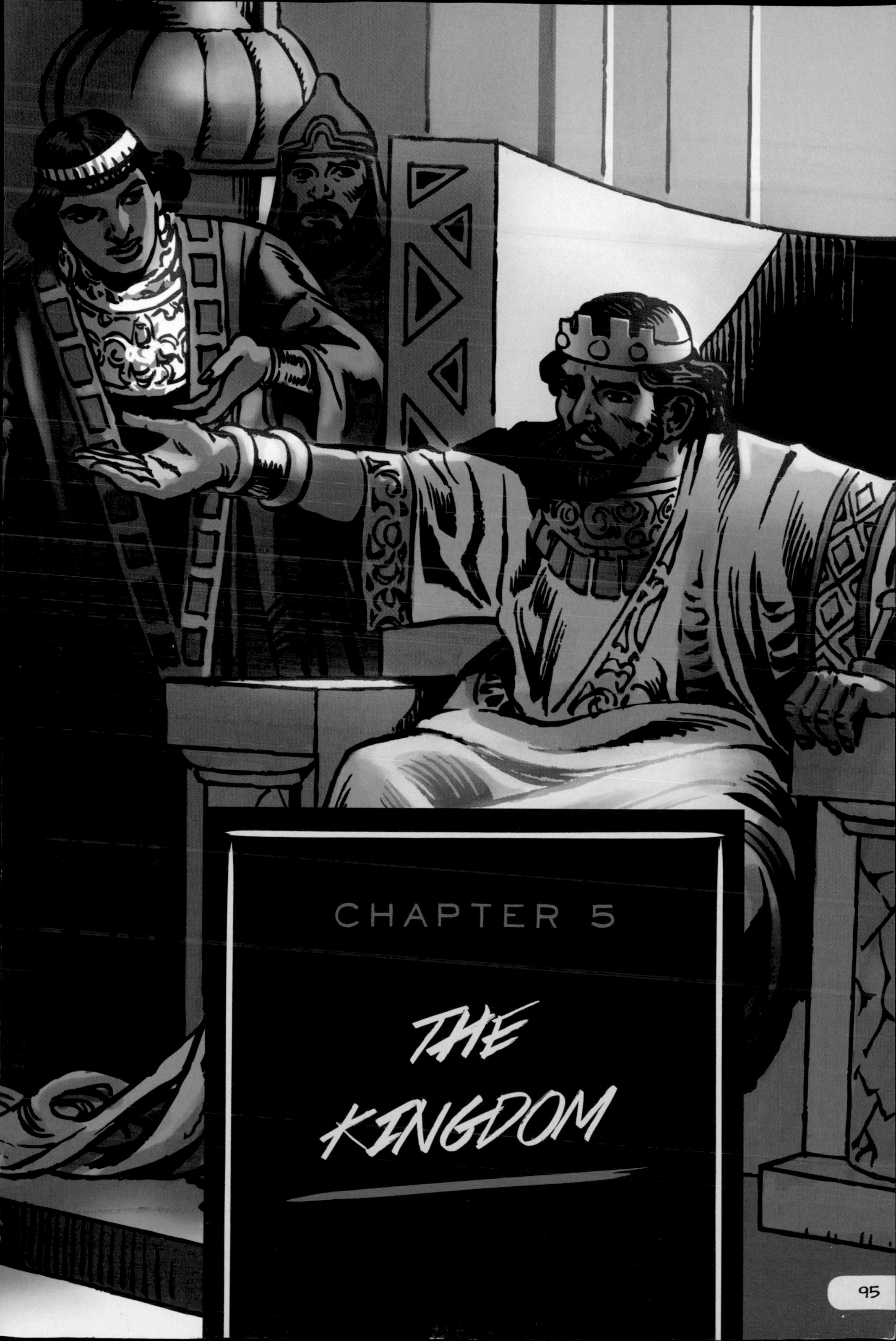

CHAPTER 5

THE KINGDOM

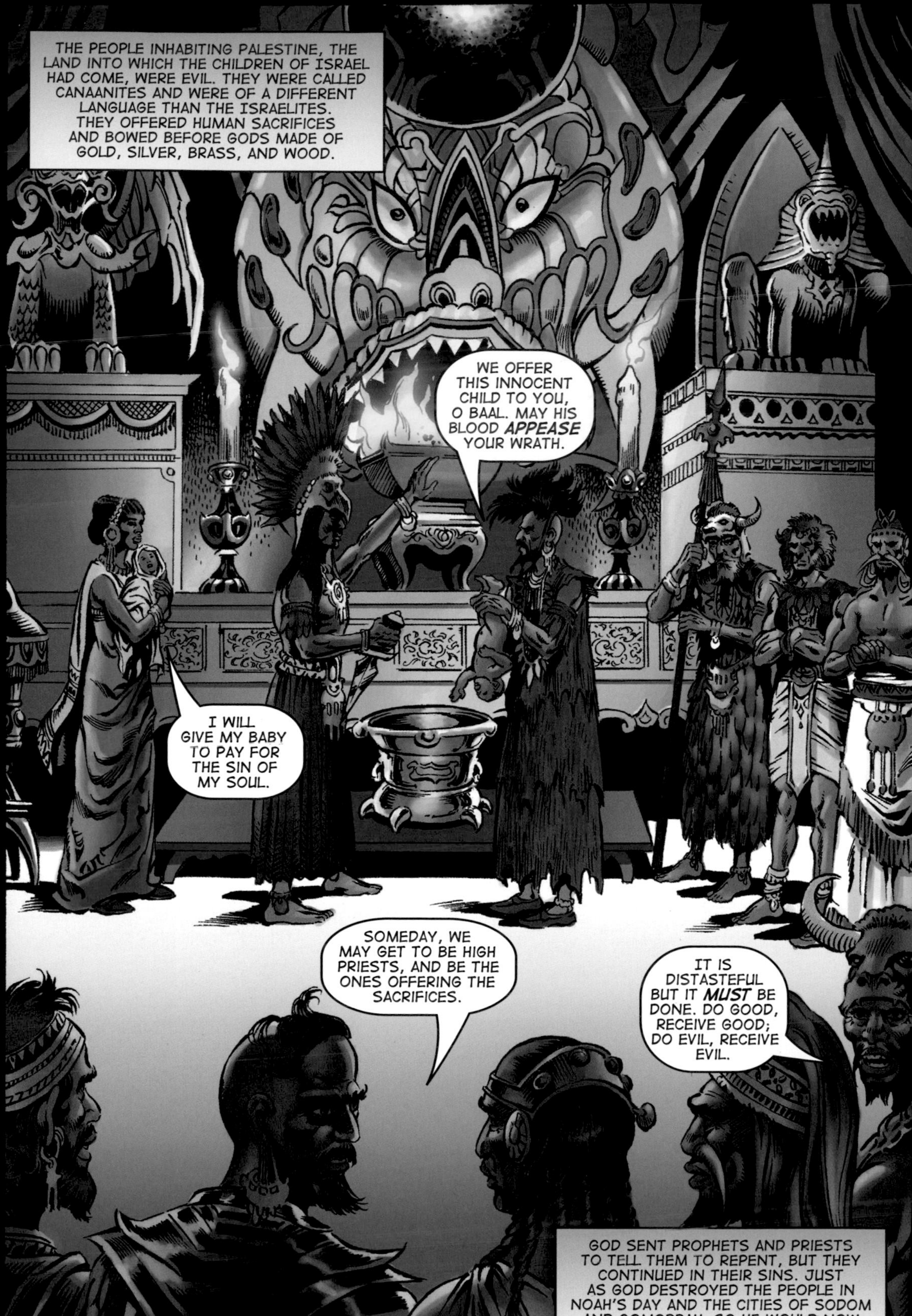
THE PEOPLE INHABITING PALESTINE, THE LAND INTO WHICH THE CHILDREN OF ISRAEL HAD COME, WERE EVIL. THEY WERE CALLED CANAANITES AND WERE OF A DIFFERENT LANGUAGE THAN THE ISRAELITES. THEY OFFERED HUMAN SACRIFICES AND BOWED BEFORE GODS MADE OF GOLD, SILVER, BRASS, AND WOOD.
WE OFFER THIS INNOCENT CHILD TO YOU, O BAAL. MAY HIS BLOOD *APPEASE* YOUR WRATH.
I WILL GIVE MY BABY TO PAY FOR THE SIN OF MY SOUL.
SOMEDAY, WE MAY GET TO BE HIGH PRIESTS, AND BE THE ONES OFFERING THE SACRIFICES.
IT IS DISTASTEFUL BUT IT *MUST* BE DONE. DO GOOD, RECEIVE GOOD; DO EVIL, RECEIVE EVIL.
GOD SENT PROPHETS AND PRIESTS TO TELL THEM TO REPENT, BUT THEY CONTINUED IN THEIR SINS. JUST AS GOD DESTROYED THE PEOPLE IN NOAH'S DAY AND THE CITIES OF SODOM AND GOMORRAH, SO HE WOULD NOW DESTROY THE PEOPLE OF CANAAN.

DEUTERONOMY 18:9-11

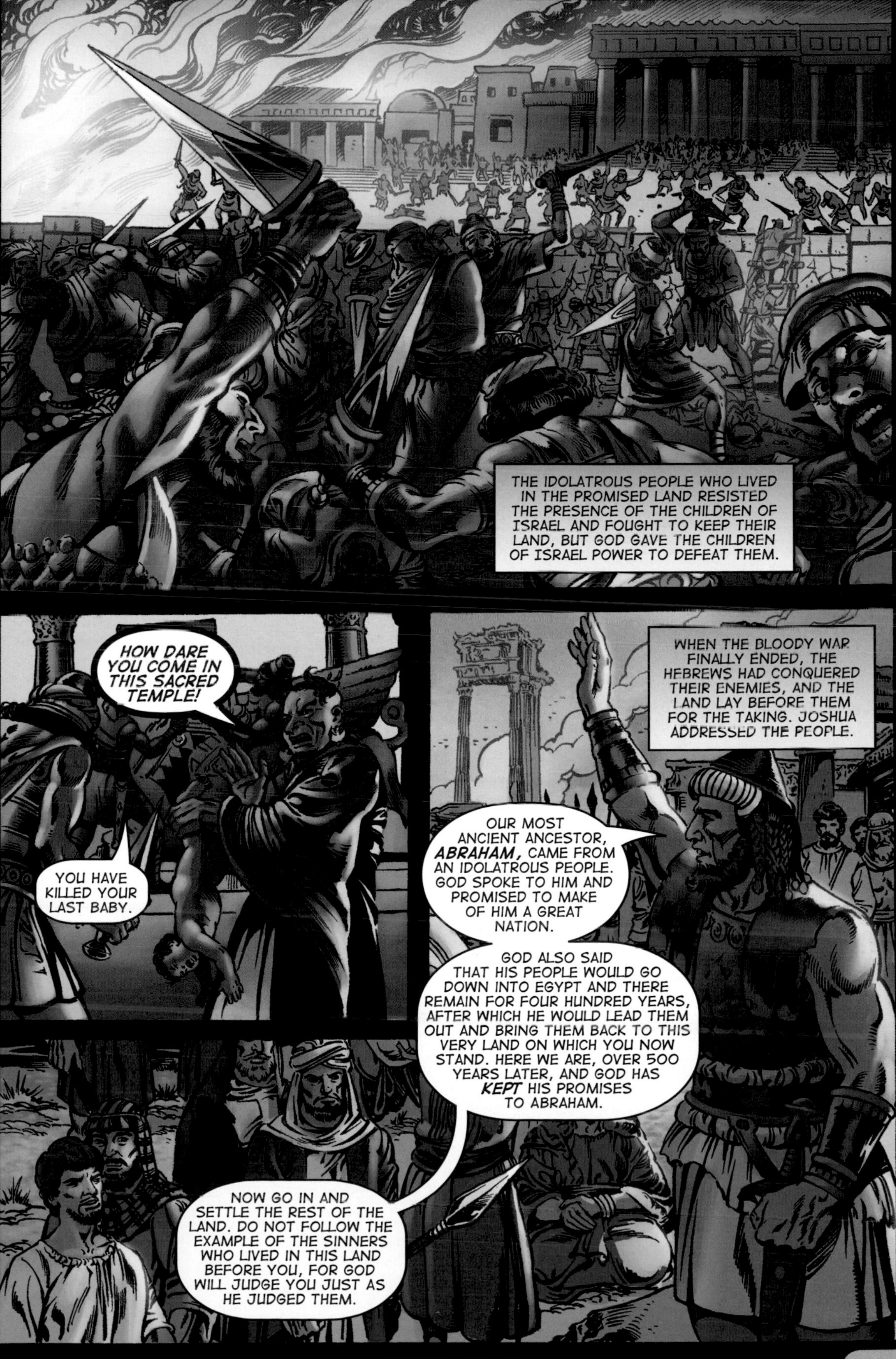

THE IDOLATROUS PEOPLE WHO LIVED IN THE PROMISED LAND RESISTED THE PRESENCE OF THE CHILDREN OF ISRAEL AND FOUGHT TO KEEP THEIR LAND, BUT GOD GAVE THE CHILDREN OF ISRAEL POWER TO DEFEAT THEM.
HOW DARE YOU COME IN THIS SACRED TEMPLE!
YOU HAVE KILLED YOUR LAST BABY.
WHEN THE BLOODY WAR FINALLY ENDED, THE HEBREWS HAD CONQUERED THEIR ENEMIES, AND THE LAND LAY BEFORE THEM FOR THE TAKING. JOSHUA ADDRESSED THE PEOPLE.
OUR MOST ANCIENT ANCESTOR, ABRAHAM, CAME FROM AN IDOLATROUS PEOPLE. GOD SPOKE TO HIM AND PROMISED TO MAKE OF HIM A GREAT NATION.
GOD ALSO SAID THAT HIS PEOPLE WOULD GO DOWN INTO EGYPT AND THERE REMAIN FOR FOUR HUNDRED YEARS, AFTER WHICH HE WOULD LEAD THEM OUT AND BRING THEM BACK TO THIS VERY LAND ON WHICH YOU NOW STAND. HERE WE ARE, OVER 500 YEARS LATER, AND GOD HAS KEPT HIS PROMISES TO ABRAHAM.
NOW GO IN AND SETTLE THE REST OF THE LAND. DO NOT FOLLOW THE EXAMPLE OF THE SINNERS WHO LIVED IN THIS LAND BEFORE YOU, FOR GOD WILL JUDGE YOU JUST AS HE JUDGED THEM.

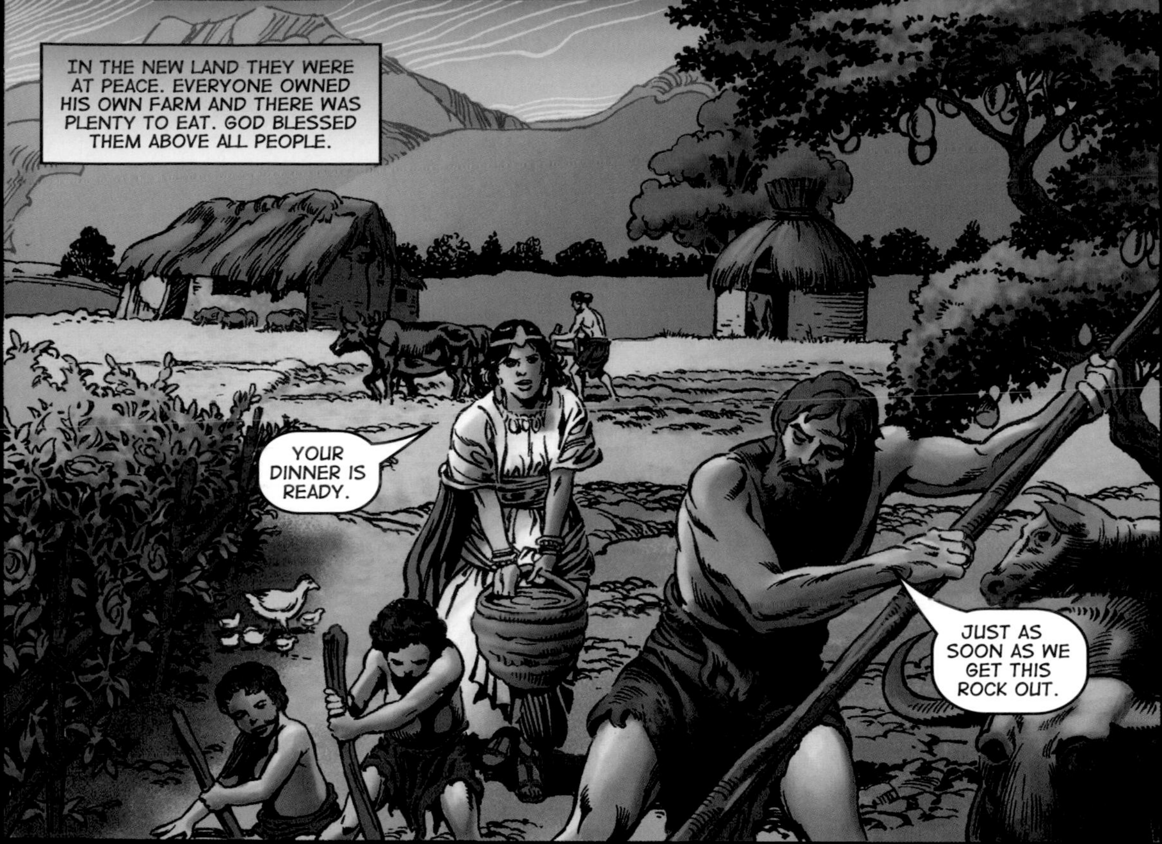
IN THE NEW LAND THEY WERE AT PEACE. EVERYONE OWNED HIS OWN FARM AND THERE WAS PLENTY TO EAT. GOD BLESSED THEM ABOVE ALL PEOPLE.
YOUR DINNER IS READY.
JUST AS SOON AS WE GET THIS ROCK OUT.

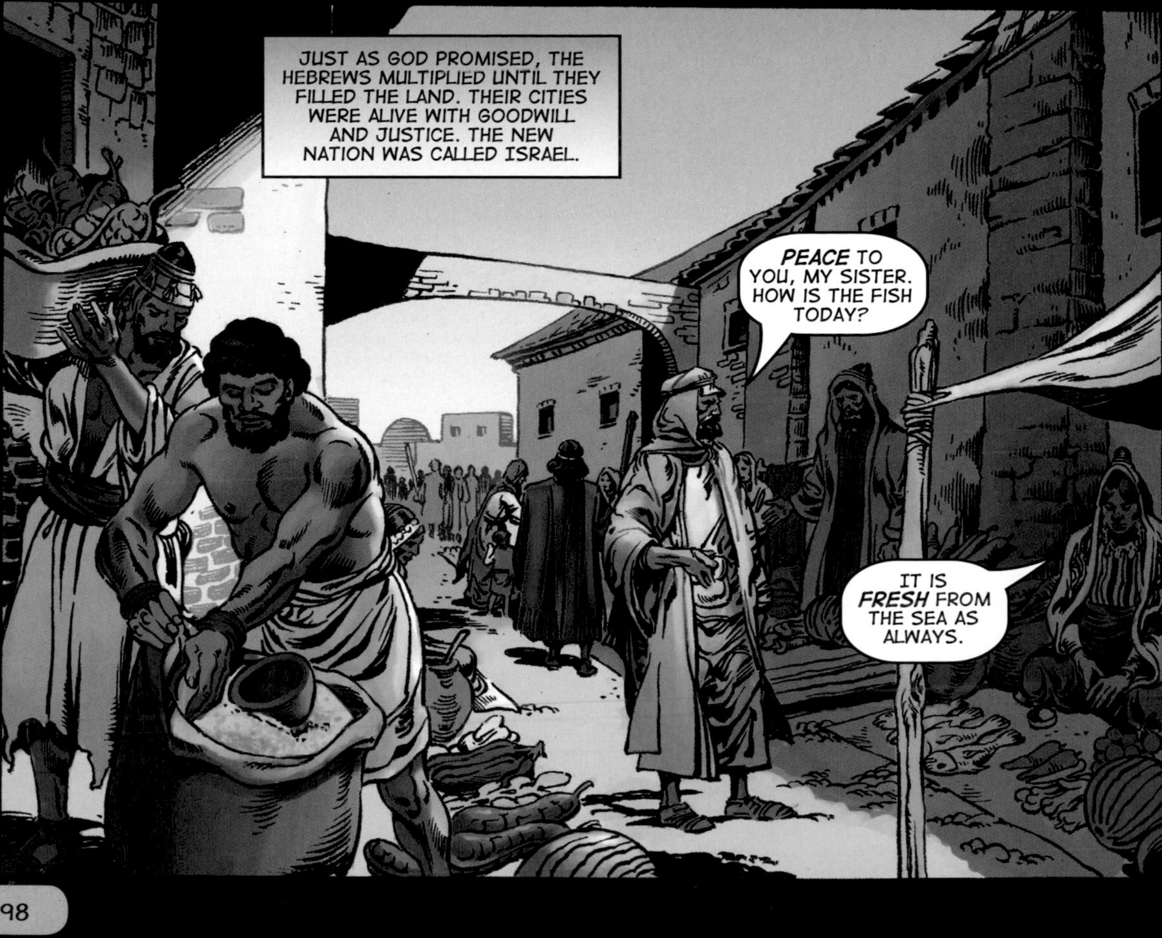
JUST AS GOD PROMISED, THE HEBREWS MULTIPLIED UNTIL THEY FILLED THE LAND. THEIR CITIES WERE ALIVE WITH GOODWILL AND JUSTICE. THE NEW NATION WAS CALLED ISRAEL.
PEACE TO YOU, MY SISTER. HOW IS THE FISH TODAY?
IT IS *FRESH* FROM THE SEA AS ALWAYS.

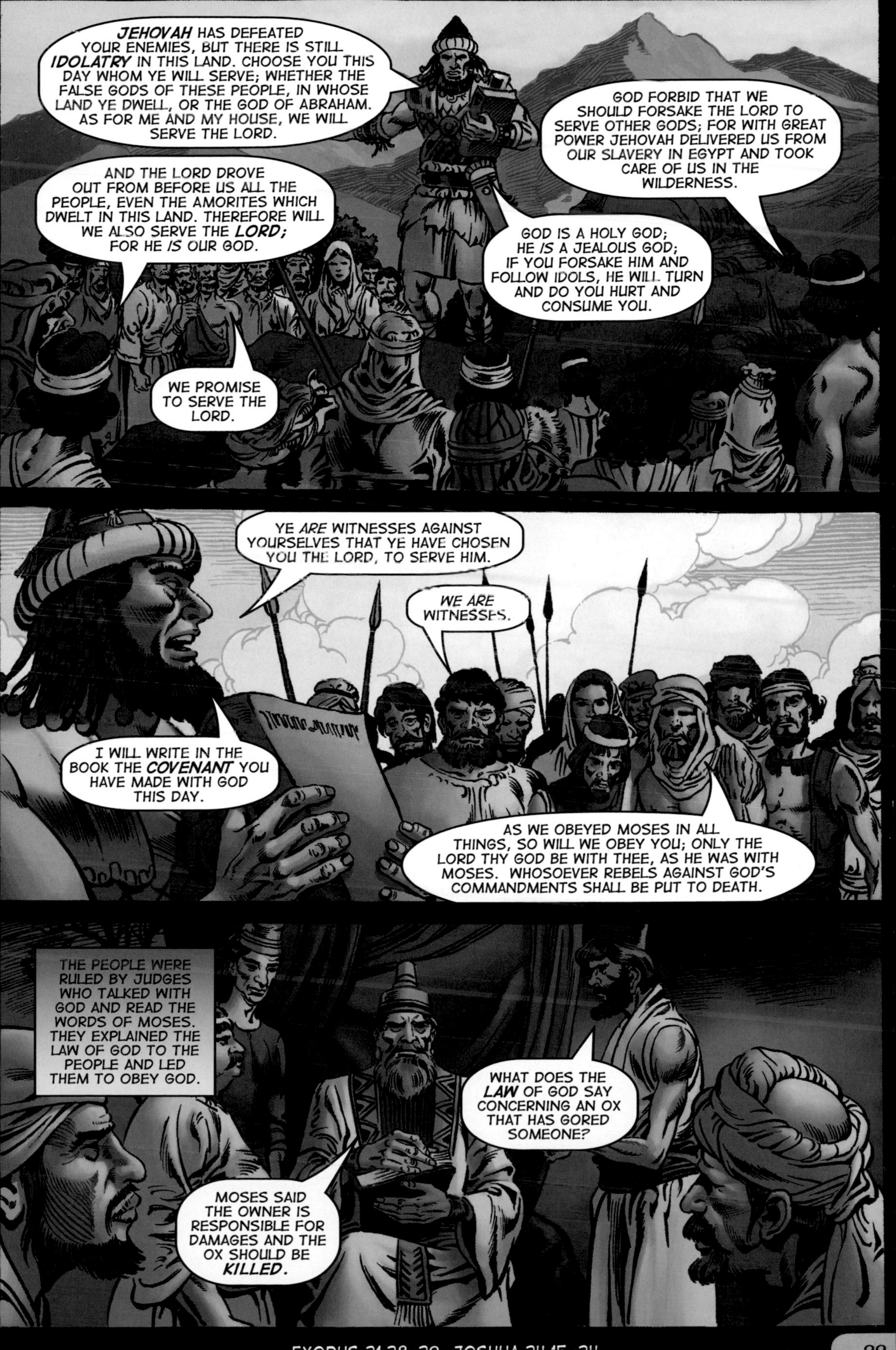
JEHOVAH HAS DEFEATED YOUR ENEMIES, BUT THERE IS STILL IDOLATRY IN THIS LAND. CHOOSE YOU THIS DAY WHOM YE WILL SERVE; WHETHER THE FALSE GODS OF THESE PEOPLE, IN WHOSE LAND YE DWELL, OR THE GOD OF ABRAHAM. AS FOR ME AND MY HOUSE, WE WILL SERVE THE LORD.
GOD FORBID THAT WE SHOULD FORSAKE THE LORD TO SERVE OTHER GODS; FOR WITH GREAT POWER JEHOVAH DELIVERED US FROM OUR SLAVERY IN EGYPT AND TOOK CARE OF US IN THE WILDERNESS.
AND THE LORD DROVE OUT FROM BEFORE US ALL THE PEOPLE, EVEN THE AMORITES WHICH DWELT IN THIS LAND. THEREFORE WILL WE ALSO SERVE THE LORD; FOR HE IS OUR GOD.
GOD IS A HOLY GOD; HE IS A JEALOUS GOD; IF YOU FORSAKE HIM AND FOLLOW IDOLS, HE WILL TURN AND DO YOU HURT AND CONSUME YOU.
WE PROMISE TO SERVE THE LORD.
YE ARE WITNESSES AGAINST YOURSELVES THAT YE HAVE CHOSEN YOU THE LORD, TO SERVE HIM.
WE ARE WITNESSES.
I WILL WRITE IN THE BOOK THE COVENANT YOU HAVE MADE WITH GOD THIS DAY.
AS WE OBEYED MOSES IN ALL THINGS, SO WILL WE OBEY YOU; ONLY THE LORD THY GOD BE WITH THEE, AS HE WAS WITH MOSES. WHOSOEVER REBELS AGAINST GOD'S COMMANDMENTS SHALL BE PUT TO DEATH.
THE PEOPLE WERE RULED BY JUDGES WHO TALKED WITH GOD AND READ THE WORDS OF MOSES. THEY EXPLAINED THE LAW OF GOD TO THE PEOPLE AND LED THEM TO OBEY GOD.
WHAT DOES THE LAW OF GOD SAY CONCERNING AN OX THAT HAS GORED SOMEONE?
MOSES SAID THE OWNER IS RESPONSIBLE FOR DAMAGES AND THE OX SHOULD BE KILLED.

EXODUS 21:28-29; JOSHUA 24:15-24

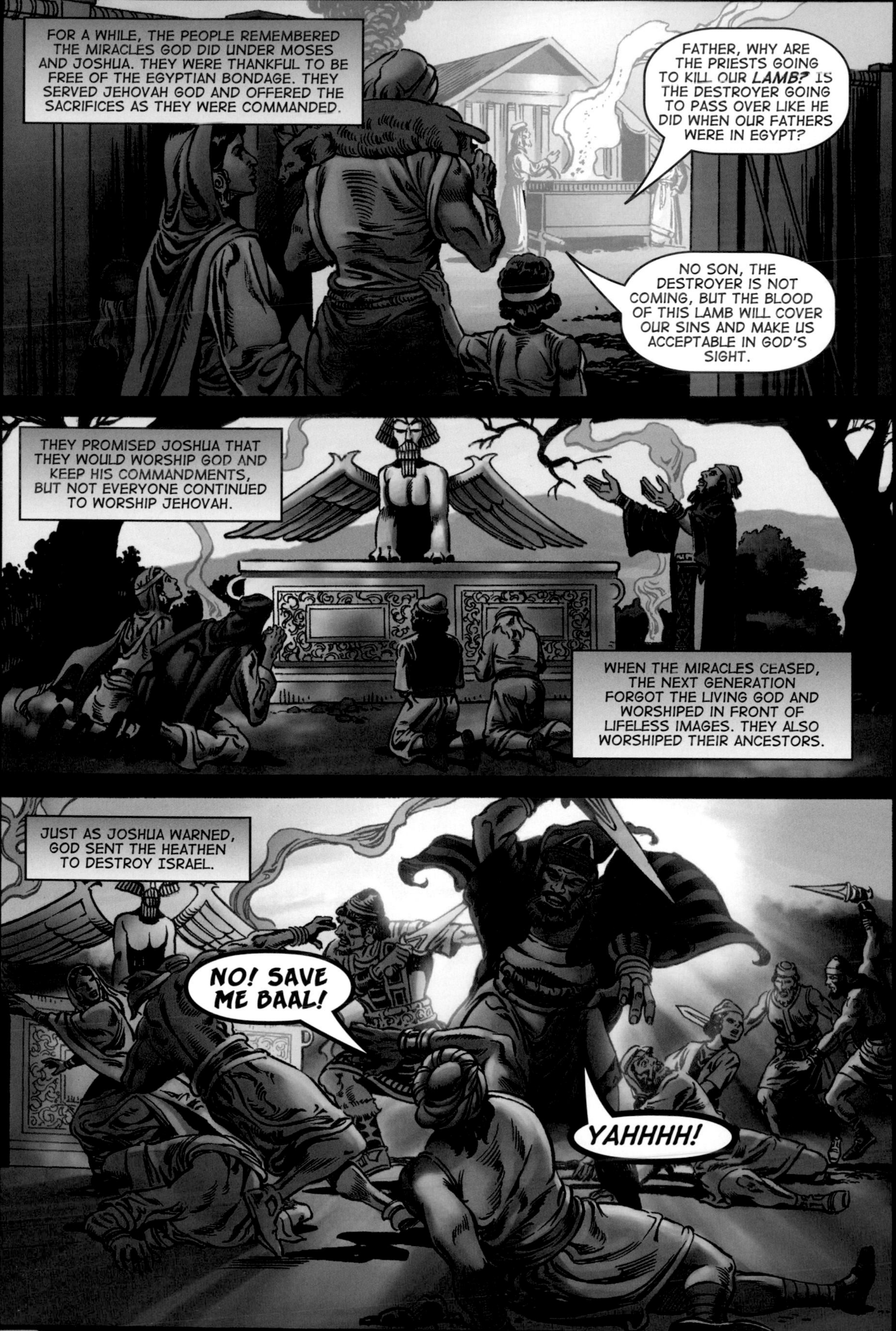
FOR A WHILE, THE PEOPLE REMEMBERED THE MIRACLES GOD DID UNDER MOSES AND JOSHUA. THEY WERE THANKFUL TO BE FREE OF THE EGYPTIAN BONDAGE. THEY SERVED JEHOVAH GOD AND OFFERED THE SACRIFICES AS THEY WERE COMMANDED.
FATHER, WHY ARE THE PRIESTS GOING TO KILL OUR LAMB? IS THE DESTROYER GOING TO PASS OVER LIKE HE DID WHEN OUR FATHERS WERE IN EGYPT?
NO SON, THE DESTROYER IS NOT COMING, BUT THE BLOOD OF THIS LAMB WILL COVER OUR SINS AND MAKE US ACCEPTABLE IN GOD'S SIGHT.
THEY PROMISED JOSHUA THAT THEY WOULD WORSHIP GOD AND KEEP HIS COMMANDMENTS, BUT NOT EVERYONE CONTINUED TO WORSHIP JEHOVAH.
WHEN THE MIRACLES CEASED, THE NEXT GENERATION FORGOT THE LIVING GOD AND WORSHIPED IN FRONT OF LIFELESS IMAGES. THEY ALSO WORSHIPED THEIR ANCESTORS.
JUST AS JOSHUA WARNED, GOD SENT THE HEATHEN TO DESTROY ISRAEL.
NO! SAVE ME BAAL!
YAHHHH!

JUDGES 3:7-8, 12-13, 4:1-2, 10:6-7

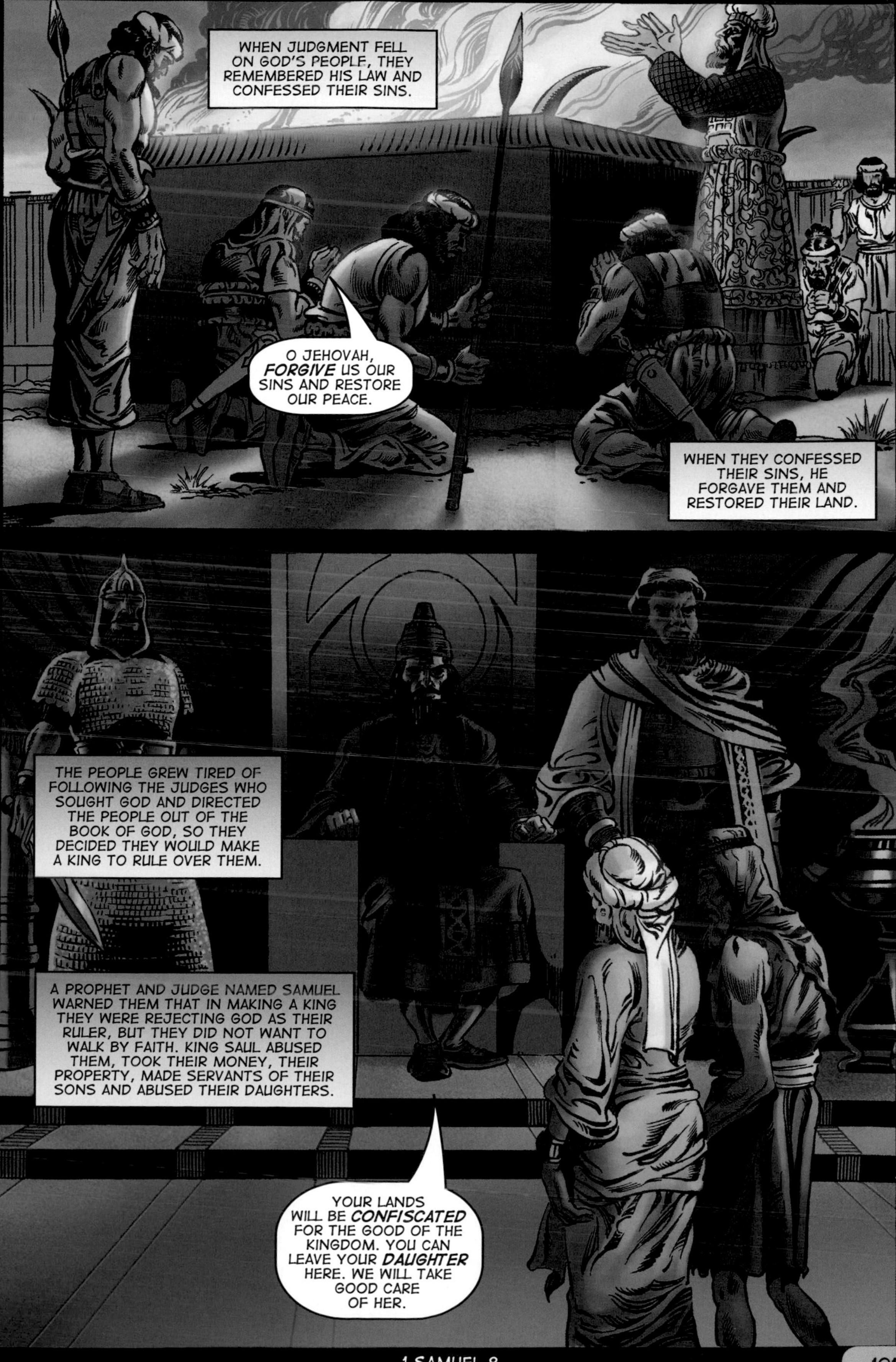
WHEN JUDGMENT FELL ON GOD'S PEOPLE, THEY REMEMBERED HIS LAW AND CONFESSED THEIR SINS.
O JEHOVAH, FORGIVE US OUR SINS AND RESTORE OUR PEACE.
WHEN THEY CONFESSED THEIR SINS, HE FORGAVE THEM AND RESTORED THEIR LAND.
THE PEOPLE GREW TIRED OF FOLLOWING THE JUDGES WHO SOUGHT GOD AND DIRECTED THE PEOPLE OUT OF THE BOOK OF GOD, SO THEY DECIDED THEY WOULD MAKE A KING TO RULE OVER THEM.
A PROPHET AND JUDGE NAMED SAMUEL WARNED THEM THAT IN MAKING A KING THEY WERE REJECTING GOD AS THEIR RULER, BUT THEY DID NOT WANT TO WALK BY FAITH. KING SAUL ABUSED THEM, TOOK THEIR MONEY, THEIR PROPERTY, MADE SERVANTS OF THEIR SONS AND ABUSED THEIR DAUGHTERS.
YOUR LANDS WILL BE CONFISCATED FOR THE GOOD OF THE KINGDOM. YOU CAN LEAVE YOUR DAUGHTER HERE. WE WILL TAKE GOOD CARE OF HER.

1 SAMUEL 8

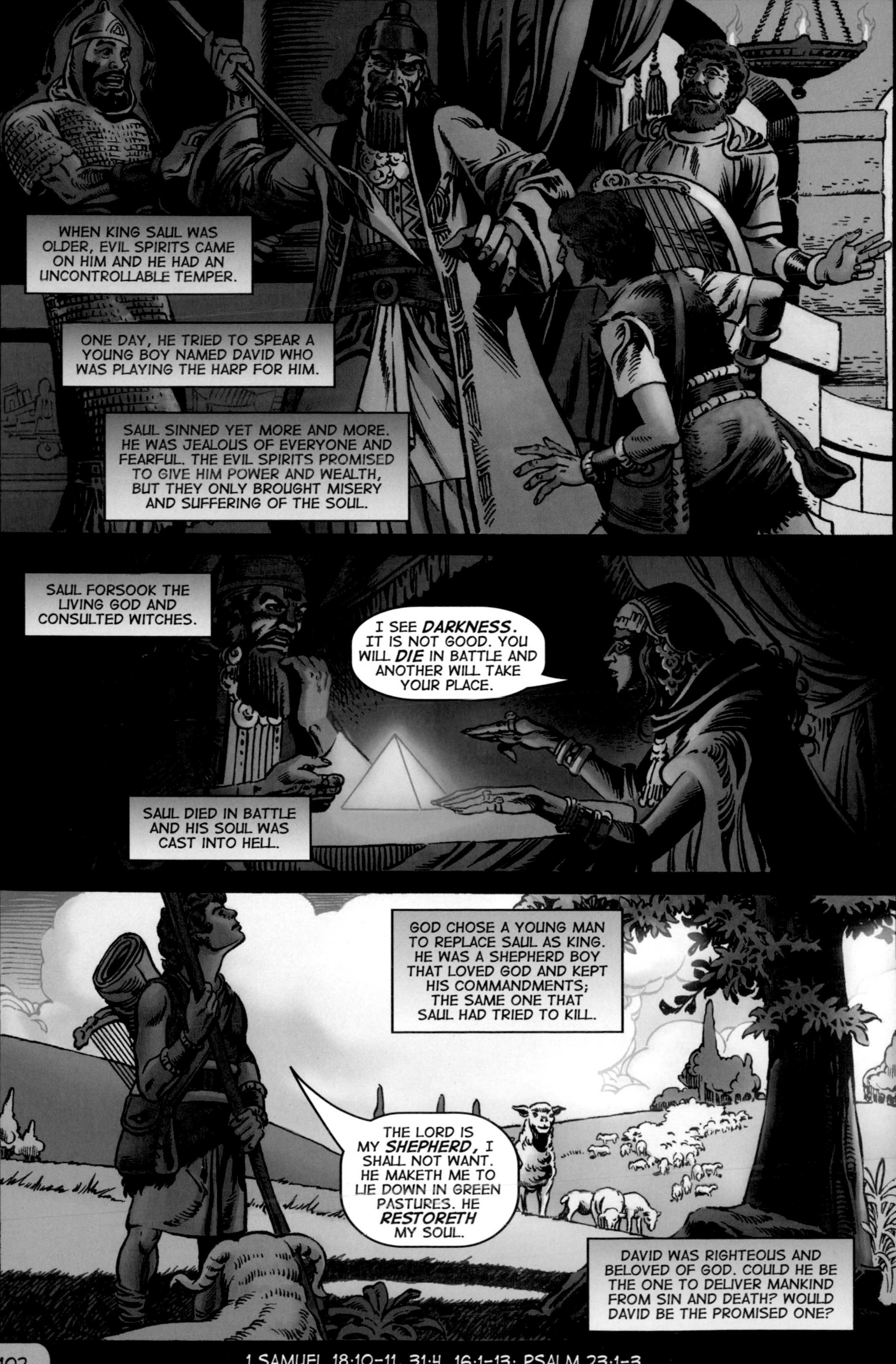
WHEN KING SAUL WAS OLDER, EVIL SPIRITS CAME ON HIM AND HE HAD AN UNCONTROLLABLE TEMPER.
ONE DAY, HE TRIED TO SPEAR A YOUNG BOY NAMED DAVID WHO WAS PLAYING THE HARP FOR HIM.
SAUL SINNED YET MORE AND MORE. HE WAS JEALOUS OF EVERYONE AND FEARFUL. THE EVIL SPIRITS PROMISED TO GIVE HIM POWER AND WEALTH, BUT THEY ONLY BROUGHT MISERY AND SUFFERING OF THE SOUL.
SAUL FORSOOK THE LIVING GOD AND CONSULTED WITCHES.
I SEE **DARKNESS.** IT IS NOT GOOD. YOU WILL **DIE** IN BATTLE AND ANOTHER WILL TAKE YOUR PLACE.
SAUL DIED IN BATTLE AND HIS SOUL WAS CAST INTO HELL.
GOD CHOSE A YOUNG MAN TO REPLACE SAUL AS KING. HE WAS A SHEPHERD BOY THAT LOVED GOD AND KEPT HIS COMMANDMENTS; THE SAME ONE THAT SAUL HAD TRIED TO KILL.
THE LORD IS MY **SHEPHERD,** I SHALL NOT WANT. HE MAKETH ME TO LIE DOWN IN GREEN PASTURES. HE **RESTORETH** MY SOUL.
DAVID WAS RIGHTEOUS AND BELOVED OF GOD. COULD HE BE THE ONE TO DELIVER MANKIND FROM SIN AND DEATH? WOULD DAVID BE THE PROMISED ONE?

1 SAMUEL 18:10-11, 31:4, 16:1-13; PSALM 23:1-3

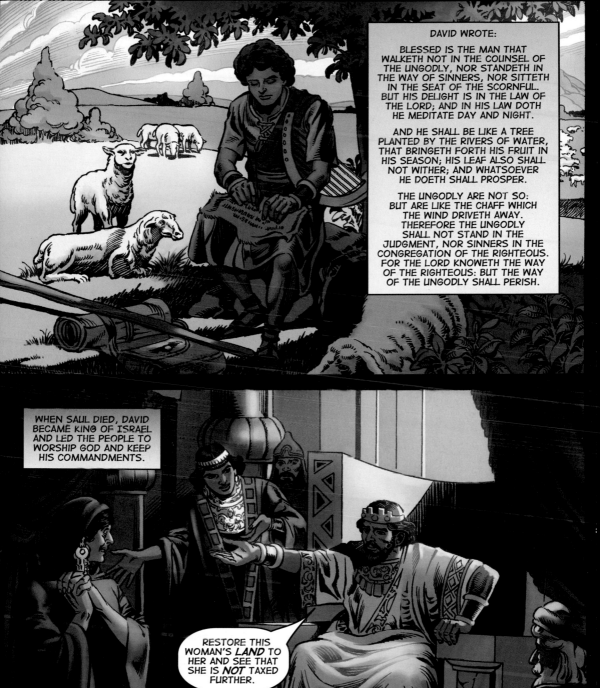

DAVID WROTE:

BLESSED IS THE MAN THAT WALKETH NOT IN THE COUNSEL OF THE UNGODLY, NOR STANDETH IN THE WAY OF SINNERS, NOR SITTETH IN THE SEAT OF THE SCORNFUL. BUT HIS DELIGHT IS IN THE LAW OF THE LORD; AND IN HIS LAW DOTH HE MEDITATE DAY AND NIGHT.

AND HE SHALL BE LIKE A TREE PLANTED BY THE RIVERS OF WATER, THAT BRINGETH FORTH HIS FRUIT IN HIS SEASON; HIS LEAF ALSO SHALL NOT WITHER; AND WHATSOEVER HE DOETH SHALL PROSPER.

THE UNGODLY ARE NOT SO: BUT ARE LIKE THE CHAFF WHICH THE WIND DRIVETH AWAY. THEREFORE THE UNGODLY SHALL NOT STAND IN THE JUDGMENT, NOR SINNERS IN THE CONGREGATION OF THE RIGHTEOUS. FOR THE LORD KNOWETH THE WAY OF THE RIGHTEOUS: BUT THE WAY OF THE UNGODLY SHALL PERISH.

WHEN SAUL DIED, DAVID BECAME KING OF ISRAEL AND LED THE PEOPLE TO WORSHIP GOD AND KEEP HIS COMMANDMENTS.

RESTORE THIS WOMAN'S *LAND* TO HER AND SEE THAT SHE IS *NOT* TAXED FURTHER.

UNDER DAVID'S REIGN THE NATION PROSPERED AND LIVED UPRIGHTLY.

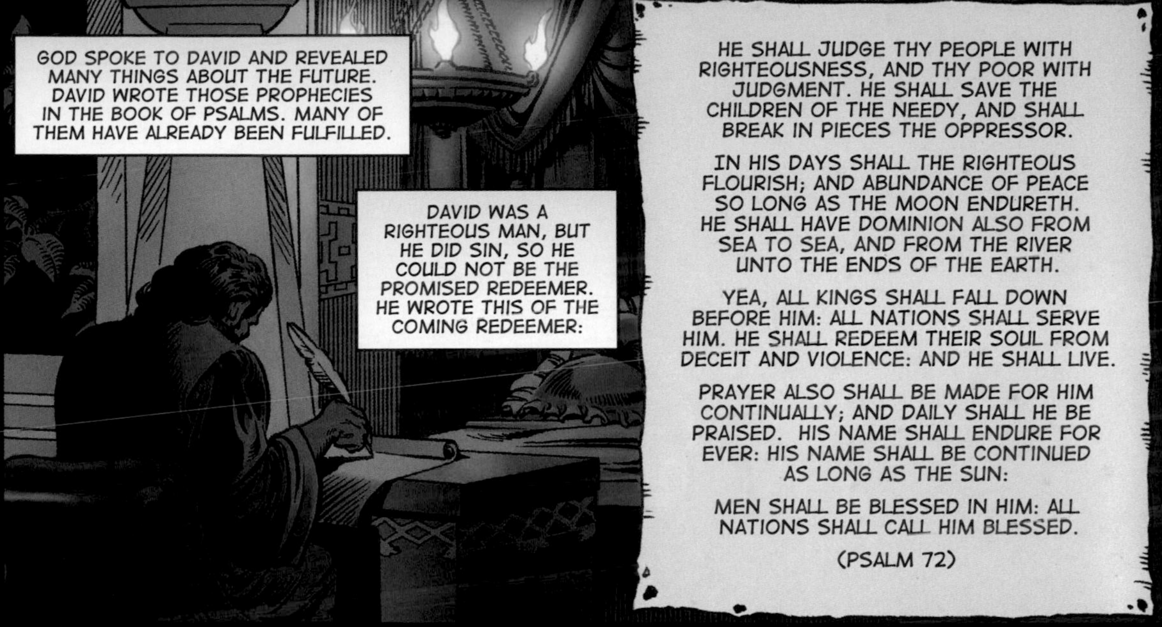
GOD SPOKE TO DAVID AND REVEALED MANY THINGS ABOUT THE FUTURE. DAVID WROTE THOSE PROPHECIES IN THE BOOK OF PSALMS. MANY OF THEM HAVE ALREADY BEEN FULFILLED.
DAVID WAS A RIGHTEOUS MAN, BUT HE DID SIN, SO HE COULD NOT BE THE PROMISED REDEEMER. HE WROTE THIS OF THE COMING REDEEMER:
HE SHALL JUDGE THY PEOPLE WITH RIGHTEOUSNESS, AND THY POOR WITH JUDGMENT. HE SHALL SAVE THE CHILDREN OF THE NEEDY, AND SHALL BREAK IN PIECES THE OPPRESSOR.
IN HIS DAYS SHALL THE RIGHTEOUS FLOURISH; AND ABUNDANCE OF PEACE SO LONG AS THE MOON ENDURETH. HE SHALL HAVE DOMINION ALSO FROM SEA TO SEA, AND FROM THE RIVER UNTO THE ENDS OF THE EARTH.
YEA, ALL KINGS SHALL FALL DOWN BEFORE HIM: ALL NATIONS SHALL SERVE HIM. HE SHALL REDEEM THEIR SOUL FROM DECEIT AND VIOLENCE: AND HE SHALL LIVE.
PRAYER ALSO SHALL BE MADE FOR HIM CONTINUALLY; AND DAILY SHALL HE BE PRAISED. HIS NAME SHALL ENDURE FOR EVER: HIS NAME SHALL BE CONTINUED AS LONG AS THE SUN:
MEN SHALL BE BLESSED IN HIM: ALL NATIONS SHALL CALL HIM BLESSED.
(PSALM 72)

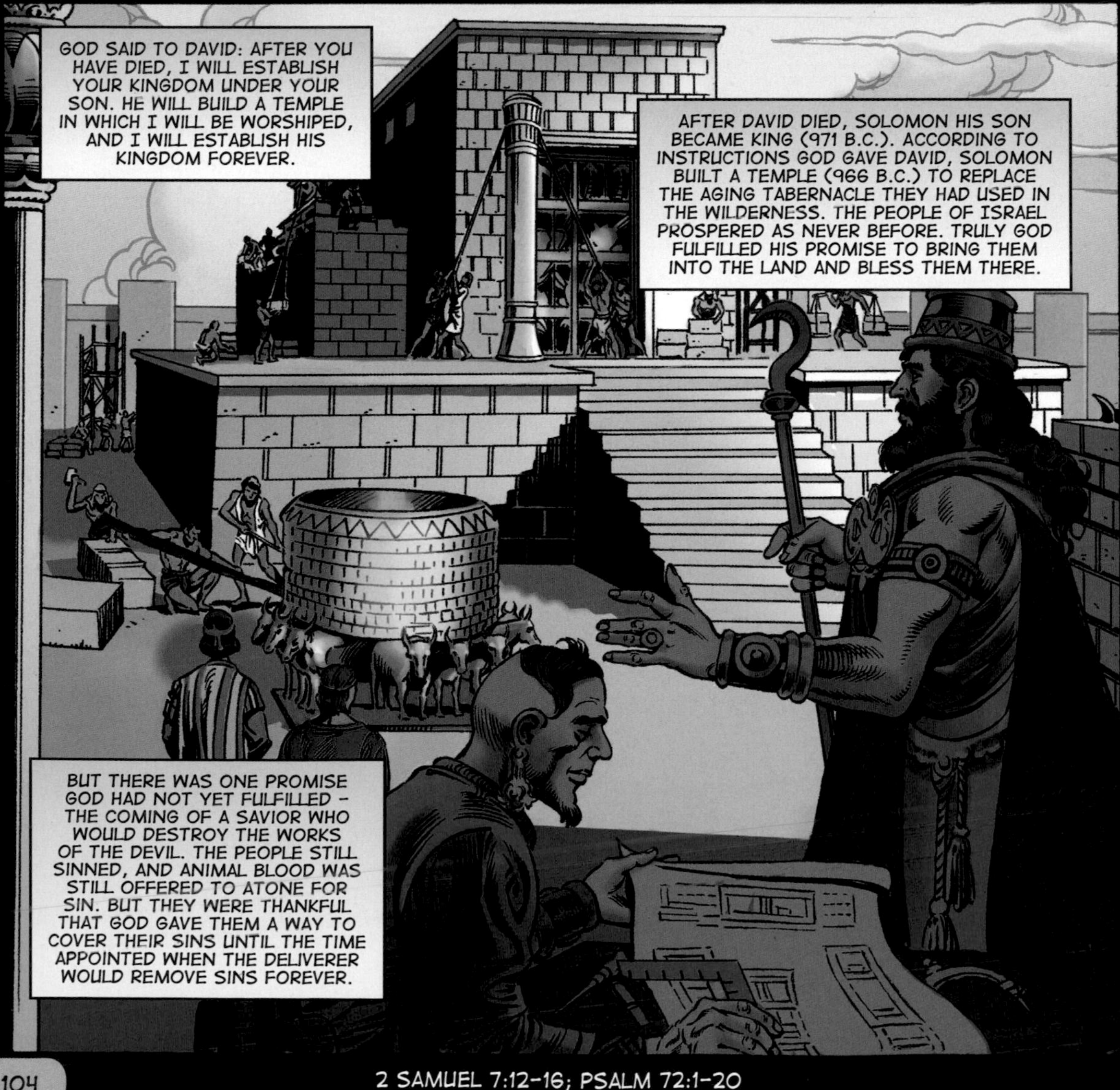
GOD SAID TO DAVID: AFTER YOU HAVE DIED, I WILL ESTABLISH YOUR KINGDOM UNDER YOUR SON. HE WILL BUILD A TEMPLE IN WHICH I WILL BE WORSHIPED, AND I WILL ESTABLISH HIS KINGDOM FOREVER.
AFTER DAVID DIED, SOLOMON HIS SON BECAME KING (971 B.C.). ACCORDING TO INSTRUCTIONS GOD GAVE DAVID, SOLOMON BUILT A TEMPLE (966 B.C.) TO REPLACE THE AGING TABERNACLE THEY HAD USED IN THE WILDERNESS. THE PEOPLE OF ISRAEL PROSPERED AS NEVER BEFORE. TRULY GOD FULFILLED HIS PROMISE TO BRING THEM INTO THE LAND AND BLESS THEM THERE.
BUT THERE WAS ONE PROMISE GOD HAD NOT YET FULFILLED - THE COMING OF A SAVIOR WHO WOULD DESTROY THE WORKS OF THE DEVIL. THE PEOPLE STILL SINNED, AND ANIMAL BLOOD WAS STILL OFFERED TO ATONE FOR SIN. BUT THEY WERE THANKFUL THAT GOD GAVE THEM A WAY TO COVER THEIR SINS UNTIL THE TIME APPOINTED WHEN THE DELIVERER WOULD REMOVE SINS FOREVER.

2 SAMUEL 7:12-16; PSALM 72:1-20

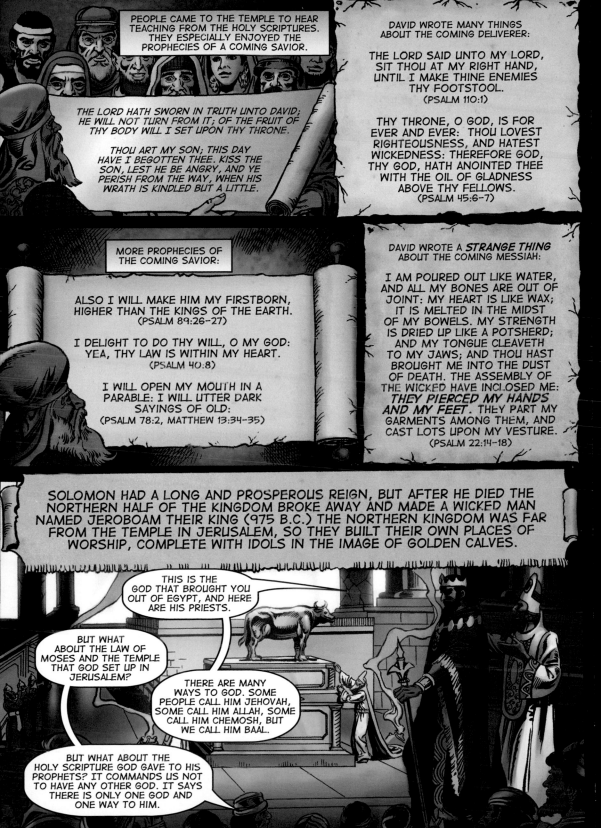

PEOPLE CAME TO THE TEMPLE TO HEAR TEACHING FROM THE HOLY SCRIPTURES. THEY ESPECIALLY ENJOYED THE PROPHECIES OF A COMING SAVIOR.

THE LORD HATH SWORN IN TRUTH UNTO DAVID; HE WILL NOT TURN FROM IT; OF THE FRUIT OF THY BODY WILL I SET UPON THY THRONE.

THOU ART MY SON; THIS DAY HAVE I BEGOTTEN THEE. KISS THE SON, LEST HE BE ANGRY, AND YE PERISH FROM THE WAY, WHEN HIS WRATH IS KINDLED BUT A LITTLE.

DAVID WROTE MANY THINGS ABOUT THE COMING DELIVERER:

THE LORD SAID UNTO MY LORD, SIT THOU AT MY RIGHT HAND, UNTIL I MAKE THINE ENEMIES THY FOOTSTOOL.
(PSALM 110:1)

THY THRONE, O GOD, IS FOR EVER AND EVER: THOU LOVEST RIGHTEOUSNESS, AND HATEST WICKEDNESS: THEREFORE GOD, THY GOD, HATH ANOINTED THEE WITH THE OIL OF GLADNESS ABOVE THY FELLOWS.
(PSALM 45:6-7)

MORE PROPHECIES OF THE COMING SAVIOR:

ALSO I WILL MAKE HIM MY FIRSTBORN, HIGHER THAN THE KINGS OF THE EARTH.
(PSALM 89:26-27)

I DELIGHT TO DO THY WILL, O MY GOD: YEA, THY LAW IS WITHIN MY HEART.
(PSALM 40:8)

I WILL OPEN MY MOUTH IN A PARABLE: I WILL UTTER DARK SAYINGS OF OLD:
(PSALM 78:2, MATTHEW 13:34-35)

DAVID WROTE A *STRANGE THING* ABOUT THE COMING MESSIAH:

I AM POURED OUT LIKE WATER, AND ALL MY BONES ARE OUT OF JOINT: MY HEART IS LIKE WAX; IT IS MELTED IN THE MIDST OF MY BOWELS. MY STRENGTH IS DRIED UP LIKE A POTSHERD; AND MY TONGUE CLEAVETH TO MY JAWS; AND THOU HAST BROUGHT ME INTO THE DUST OF DEATH. THE ASSEMBLY OF THE WICKED HAVE INCLOSED ME: *THEY PIERCED MY HANDS AND MY FEET.* THEY PART MY GARMENTS AMONG THEM, AND CAST LOTS UPON MY VESTURE.
(PSALM 22:14-18)

SOLOMON HAD A LONG AND PROSPEROUS REIGN, BUT AFTER HE DIED THE NORTHERN HALF OF THE KINGDOM BROKE AWAY AND MADE A WICKED MAN NAMED JEROBOAM THEIR KING (975 B.C.) THE NORTHERN KINGDOM WAS FAR FROM THE TEMPLE IN JERUSALEM, SO THEY BUILT THEIR OWN PLACES OF WORSHIP, COMPLETE WITH IDOLS IN THE IMAGE OF GOLDEN CALVES.

THIS IS THE GOD THAT BROUGHT YOU OUT OF EGYPT, AND HERE ARE HIS PRIESTS.

BUT WHAT ABOUT THE LAW OF MOSES AND THE TEMPLE THAT GOD SET UP IN JERUSALEM?

THERE ARE MANY WAYS TO GOD. SOME PEOPLE CALL HIM JEHOVAH, SOME CALL HIM ALLAH, SOME CALL HIM CHEMOSH, BUT WE CALL HIM BAAL.

BUT WHAT ABOUT THE HOLY SCRIPTURE GOD GAVE TO HIS PROPHETS? IT COMMANDS US NOT TO HAVE ANY OTHER GOD. IT SAYS THERE IS ONLY ONE GOD AND ONE WAY TO HIM.

1 KINGS 12:20, 28-29; PSALM 2:7,12, 22:6, 14-18, 40:8, 78:2, 45:6-7, 89:26-27, 110:1, 4, 132:11

DO YOU THINK GOD IS SO NARROW-MINDED?
I WILL HEAR NO MORE OF THIS! BAAL WORSHIP IS NOW THE OFFICIAL RELIGION OF THE LAND. INFIDELS WILL BE PUT TO DEATH!
WHEN THE PRIESTS SELECTED THE BULL AS THE IMAGE TO WORSHIP THEY UNKNOWINGLY SELECTED THE VERY IMAGE OF LUCIFER, THE SINFUL CHERUB. THEY WERE WORSHIPING THE DEVIL, AND HE WAS DELIGHTED; FOR HE WAS TURNING THE PEOPLE AWAY FROM THE PROMISE OF GOD CONCERNING A COMING REDEEMER.
O BAAL, RECEIVE THIS SACRIFICE FROM OUR HUMBLE HANDS.
BLESSED ART THOU, QUEEN OF HEAVEN, MOTHER OF GOD. HEAR OUR PRAYERS AND FORGIVE US OUR SINS.
WHAT ARE YOU DOING ON THIS SACRED GROUND?
IN THE NAME OF JEHOVAH, FROM WHOM YOU HAVE DEPARTED, HEAR THE WORD OF THE LORD. A CHILD SHALL BE BORN OF THE SEED OF DAVID. FROM HIS LINEAGE WILL COME THE DELIVERER. HIS NAME WILL BE JOSIAH, AND UPON THIS ALTAR HE WILL BURN THE PRIESTS OF BAAL.

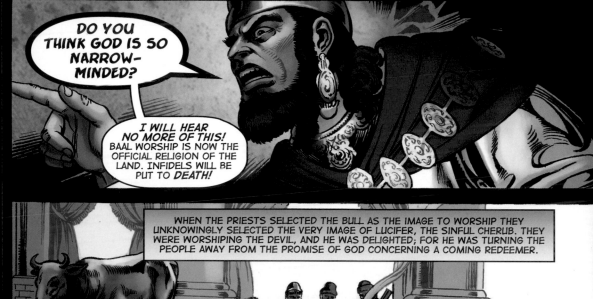

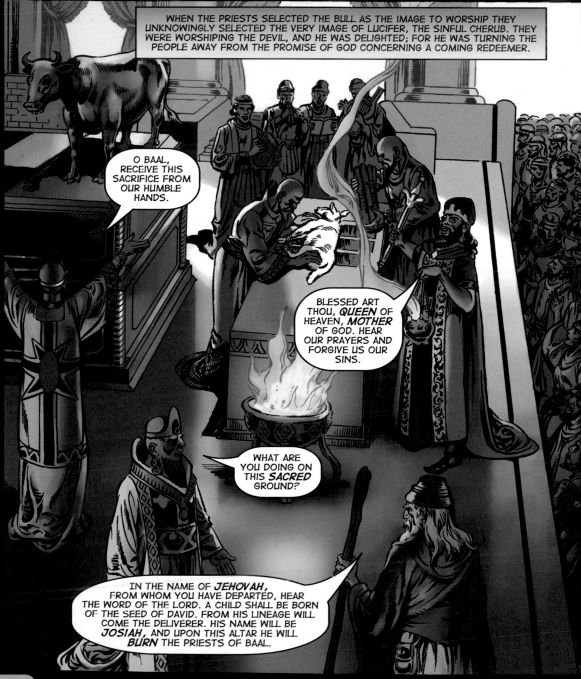

1 KINGS 12:28, 13:1-2; JEREMIAH 44:17-25

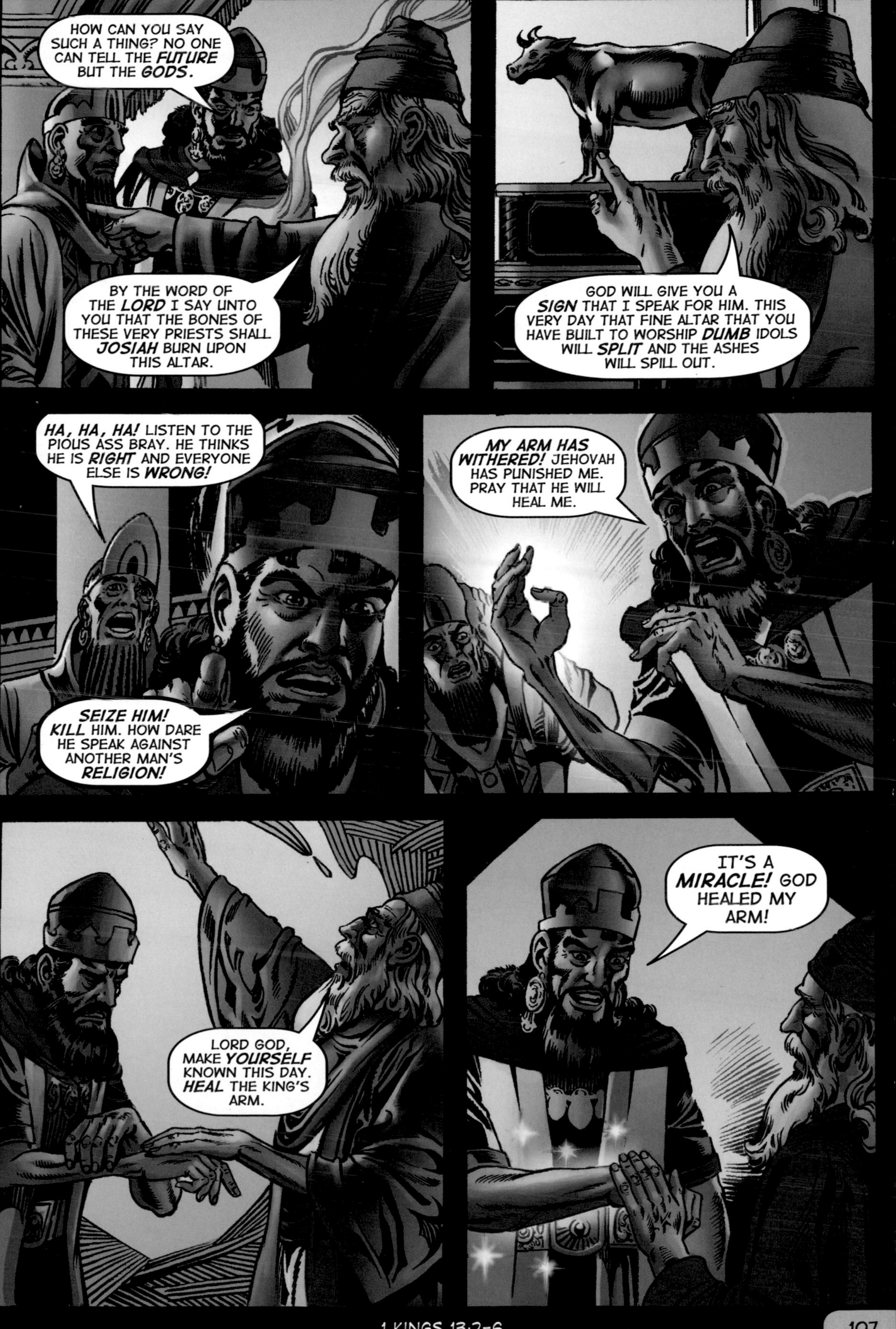
HOW CAN YOU SAY SUCH A THING? NO ONE CAN TELL THE FUTURE BUT THE GODS.
BY THE WORD OF THE LORD I SAY UNTO YOU THAT THE BONES OF THESE VERY PRIESTS SHALL JOSIAH BURN UPON THIS ALTAR.
GOD WILL GIVE YOU A SIGN THAT I SPEAK FOR HIM. THIS VERY DAY THAT FINE ALTAR THAT YOU HAVE BUILT TO WORSHIP DUMB IDOLS WILL SPLIT AND THE ASHES WILL SPILL OUT.
HA, HA, HA! LISTEN TO THE PIOUS ASS BRAY. HE THINKS HE IS RIGHT AND EVERYONE ELSE IS WRONG!
SEIZE HIM! KILL HIM. HOW DARE HE SPEAK AGAINST ANOTHER MAN'S RELIGION!
MY ARM HAS WITHERED! JEHOVAH HAS PUNISHED ME. PRAY THAT HE WILL HEAL ME.
LORD GOD, MAKE YOURSELF KNOWN THIS DAY. HEAL THE KING'S ARM.
IT'S A MIRACLE! GOD HEALED MY ARM!

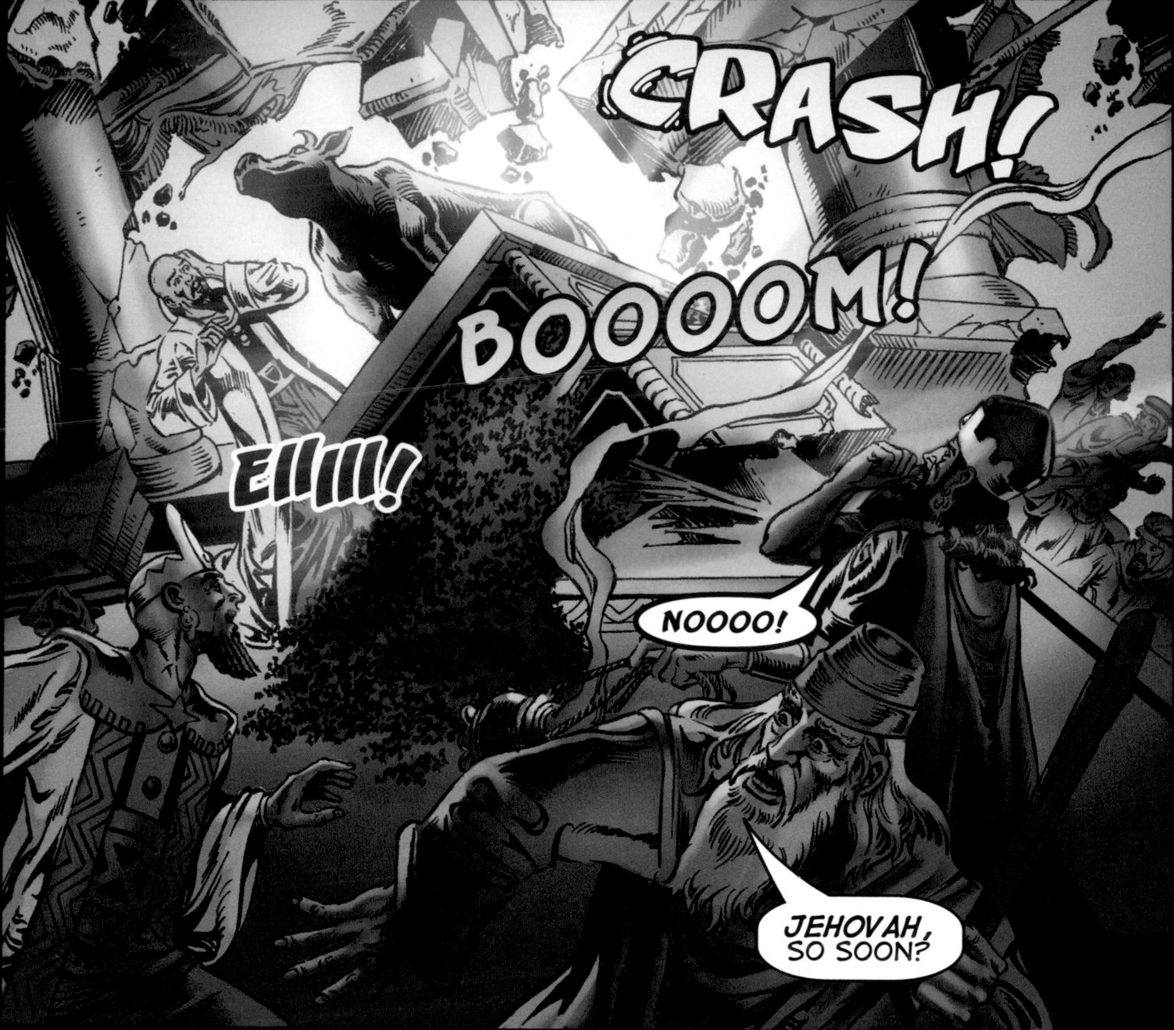
CRASH!
BOOOOM!
EIIIII!
NOOOO!
JEHOVAH, SO SOON?

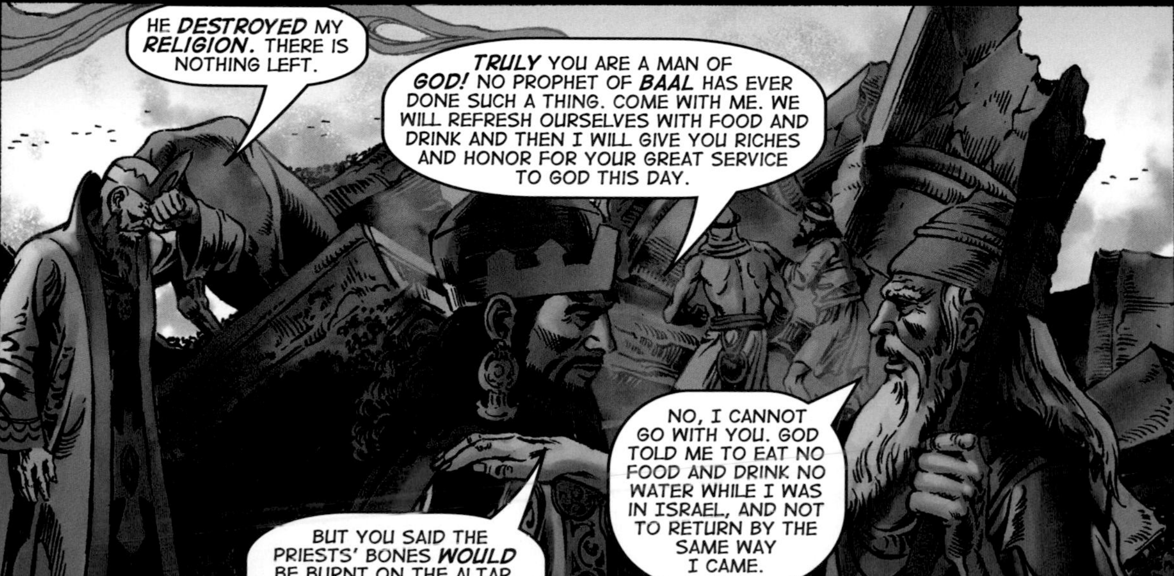
HE DESTROYED MY RELIGION. THERE IS NOTHING LEFT.
TRULY YOU ARE A MAN OF GOD! NO PROPHET OF BAAL HAS EVER DONE SUCH A THING. COME WITH ME. WE WILL REFRESH OURSELVES WITH FOOD AND DRINK AND THEN I WILL GIVE YOU RICHES AND HONOR FOR YOUR GREAT SERVICE TO GOD THIS DAY.
NO, I CANNOT GO WITH YOU. GOD TOLD ME TO EAT NO FOOD AND DRINK NO WATER WHILE I WAS IN ISRAEL, AND NOT TO RETURN BY THE SAME WAY I CAME.
THEY WERE GOD'S WORDS, NOT MINE.
BUT YOU SAID THE PRIESTS' BONES WOULD BE BURNT ON THE ALTAR. THE ALTAR IS GONE AND NO ONE DIED.

1 KINGS 13:5, 7–9

FATHER, I WOULD NOT HAVE BELIEVED IT IF I HADN'T SEEN IT. *IT WAS JUST LIKE THE OLD PROPHETS OF ISRAEL!*

FATHER, DO YOU THINK WHAT HE SAID IS *TRUE?* IS JEHOVAH THE *ONLY* LIVING GOD? ARE OUR IDOLS NOTHING BUT WOOD AND GOLD?

QUICK! SADDLE THE ASS! I MUST FIND HIM!

SO AS GOD COMMANDED, THE PROPHET OF GOD RETURNED BY A DIFFERENT ROUTE. HE HAD BEEN WITHOUT FOOD OR WATER FOR TWO DAYS AND HE WAS TERRIBLY THIRSTY AND HUNGRY. TWO YOUNG MEN, WHO WERE WORSHIPING THE GOLDEN CALF THAT DAY, FOLLOWED HIM TO SEE WHICH WAY HE WOULD GO.

YOU MUST BE THE MAN OF GOD FROM JUDAH. YOU LOOK *TIRED.* COME HOME WITH ME AND I WILL SERVE YOU *FOOD* AND *DRINK.*

I CANNOT, GOD TOLD ME NOT TO *EAT* OR *DRINK* IN THIS PLACE.

BUT YOU SEE, I AM A *PROPHET* JUST LIKE YOU, AND THIS VERY MORNING AN *ANGEL* OF JEHOVAH SPOKE TO ME AND TOLD ME TO BRING YOU TO MY HOUSE TO EAT AND DRINK.

THANK GOD, I AM SO THIRSTY.

HE FOUND THE PROPHET OF JEHOVAH SITTING UNDER A TREE. HE WANTED TO BE CLOSE TO THIS MAN WITH SUCH POWER. HE WAS ONCE A PROPHET OF JEHOVAH, BUT WHEN THE KINGDOMS DIVIDED HE FOLLOWED THE IDOLATRY OF HIS COUNTRYMEN. HE HAD REASONED, "WEREN'T ALL RELIGIONS THE SAME?"

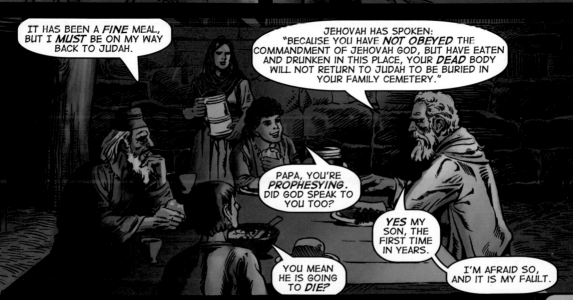

IT HAS BEEN A *FINE* MEAL, BUT I *MUST* BE ON MY WAY BACK TO JUDAH.

JEHOVAH HAS SPOKEN: "BECAUSE YOU HAVE *NOT OBEYED* THE COMMANDMENT OF JEHOVAH GOD, BUT HAVE EATEN AND DRUNKEN IN THIS PLACE, YOUR *DEAD* BODY WILL NOT RETURN TO JUDAH TO BE BURIED IN YOUR FAMILY CEMETERY."

PAPA, YOU'RE *PROPHESYING.* DID GOD SPEAK TO YOU TOO?

YES MY SON, THE FIRST TIME IN YEARS.

YOU MEAN HE IS GOING TO *DIE?*

I'M AFRAID SO, AND IT IS MY FAULT.

1 KINGS 13:10-22

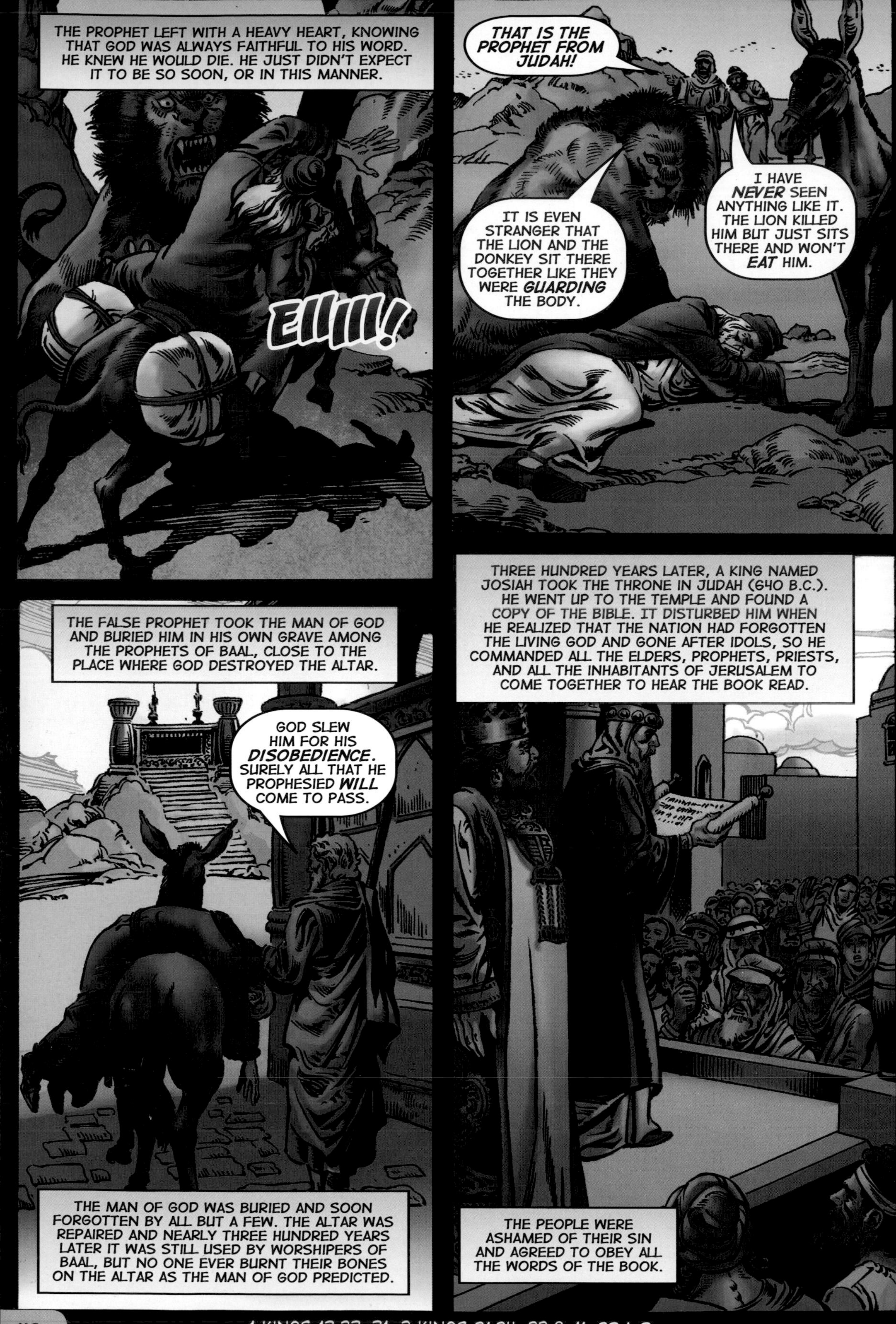
THE PROPHET LEFT WITH A HEAVY HEART, KNOWING THAT GOD WAS ALWAYS FAITHFUL TO HIS WORD. HE KNEW HE WOULD DIE. HE JUST DIDN'T EXPECT IT TO BE SO SOON, OR IN THIS MANNER.
EIIIII!
THAT IS THE PROPHET FROM JUDAH!
IT IS EVEN STRANGER THAT THE LION AND THE DONKEY SIT THERE TOGETHER LIKE THEY WERE GUARDING THE BODY.
I HAVE NEVER SEEN ANYTHING LIKE IT. THE LION KILLED HIM BUT JUST SITS THERE AND WON'T EAT HIM.
THE FALSE PROPHET TOOK THE MAN OF GOD AND BURIED HIM IN HIS OWN GRAVE AMONG THE PROPHETS OF BAAL, CLOSE TO THE PLACE WHERE GOD DESTROYED THE ALTAR.
GOD SLEW HIM FOR HIS DISOBEDIENCE. SURELY ALL THAT HE PROPHESIED WILL COME TO PASS.
THE MAN OF GOD WAS BURIED AND SOON FORGOTTEN BY ALL BUT A FEW. THE ALTAR WAS REPAIRED AND NEARLY THREE HUNDRED YEARS LATER IT WAS STILL USED BY WORSHIPERS OF BAAL, BUT NO ONE EVER BURNT THEIR BONES ON THE ALTAR AS THE MAN OF GOD PREDICTED.
THREE HUNDRED YEARS LATER, A KING NAMED JOSIAH TOOK THE THRONE IN JUDAH (640 B.C.). HE WENT UP TO THE TEMPLE AND FOUND A COPY OF THE BIBLE. IT DISTURBED HIM WHEN HE REALIZED THAT THE NATION HAD FORGOTTEN THE LIVING GOD AND GONE AFTER IDOLS, SO HE COMMANDED ALL THE ELDERS, PROPHETS, PRIESTS, AND ALL THE INHABITANTS OF JERUSALEM TO COME TOGETHER TO HEAR THE BOOK READ.
THE PEOPLE WERE ASHAMED OF THEIR SIN AND AGREED TO OBEY ALL THE WORDS OF THE BOOK.

1 KINGS 13:23-31; 2 KINGS 21:24, 22:8-11, 23:1-3

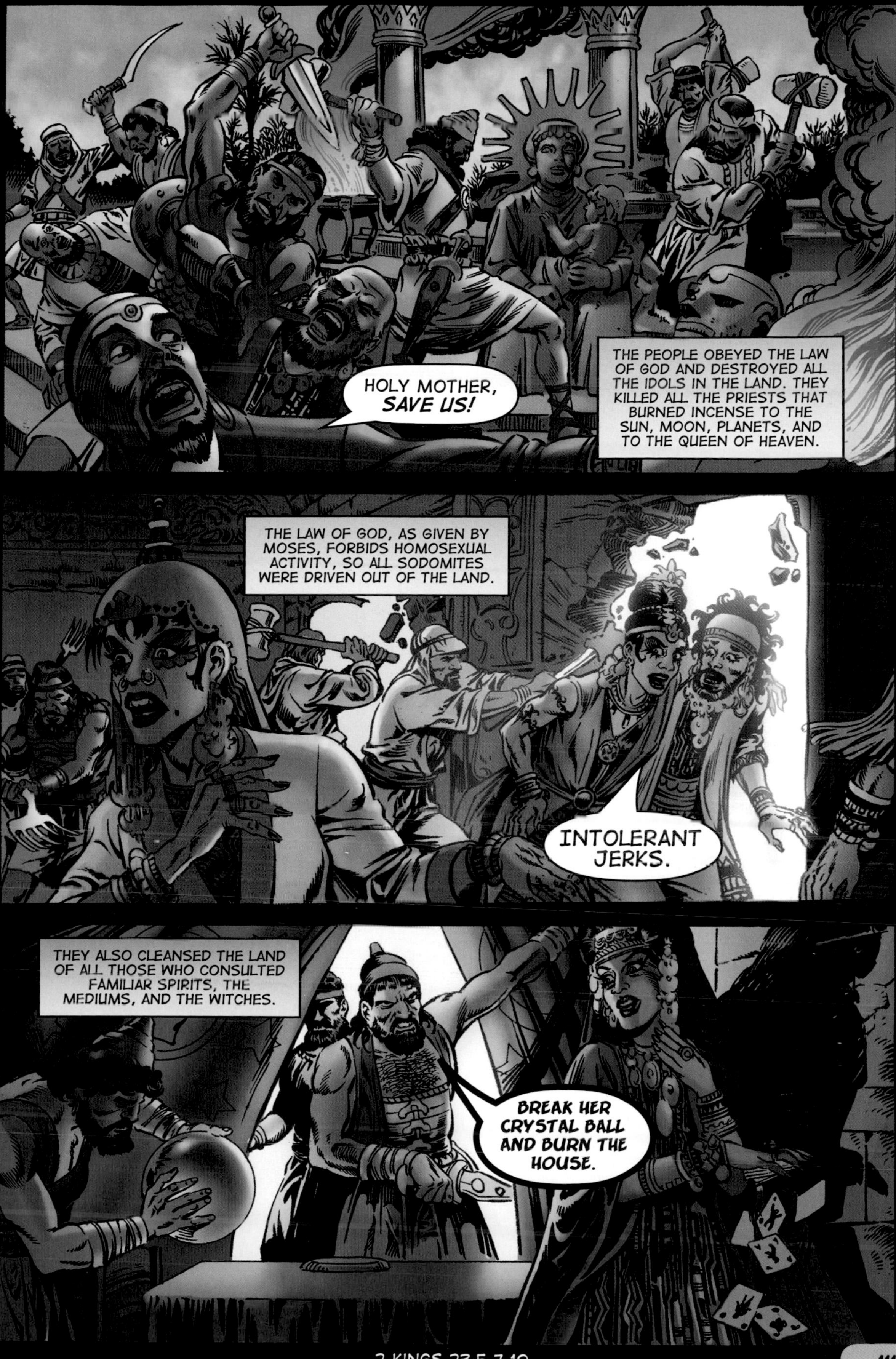
HOLY MOTHER, *SAVE US!*
THE PEOPLE OBEYED THE LAW OF GOD AND DESTROYED ALL THE IDOLS IN THE LAND. THEY KILLED ALL THE PRIESTS THAT BURNED INCENSE TO THE SUN, MOON, PLANETS, AND TO THE QUEEN OF HEAVEN.
THE LAW OF GOD, AS GIVEN BY MOSES, FORBIDS HOMOSEXUAL ACTIVITY, SO ALL SODOMITES WERE DRIVEN OUT OF THE LAND.
INTOLERANT JERKS.
THEY ALSO CLEANSED THE LAND OF ALL THOSE WHO CONSULTED FAMILIAR SPIRITS, THE MEDIUMS, AND THE WITCHES.
BREAK HER CRYSTAL BALL AND BURN THE HOUSE.

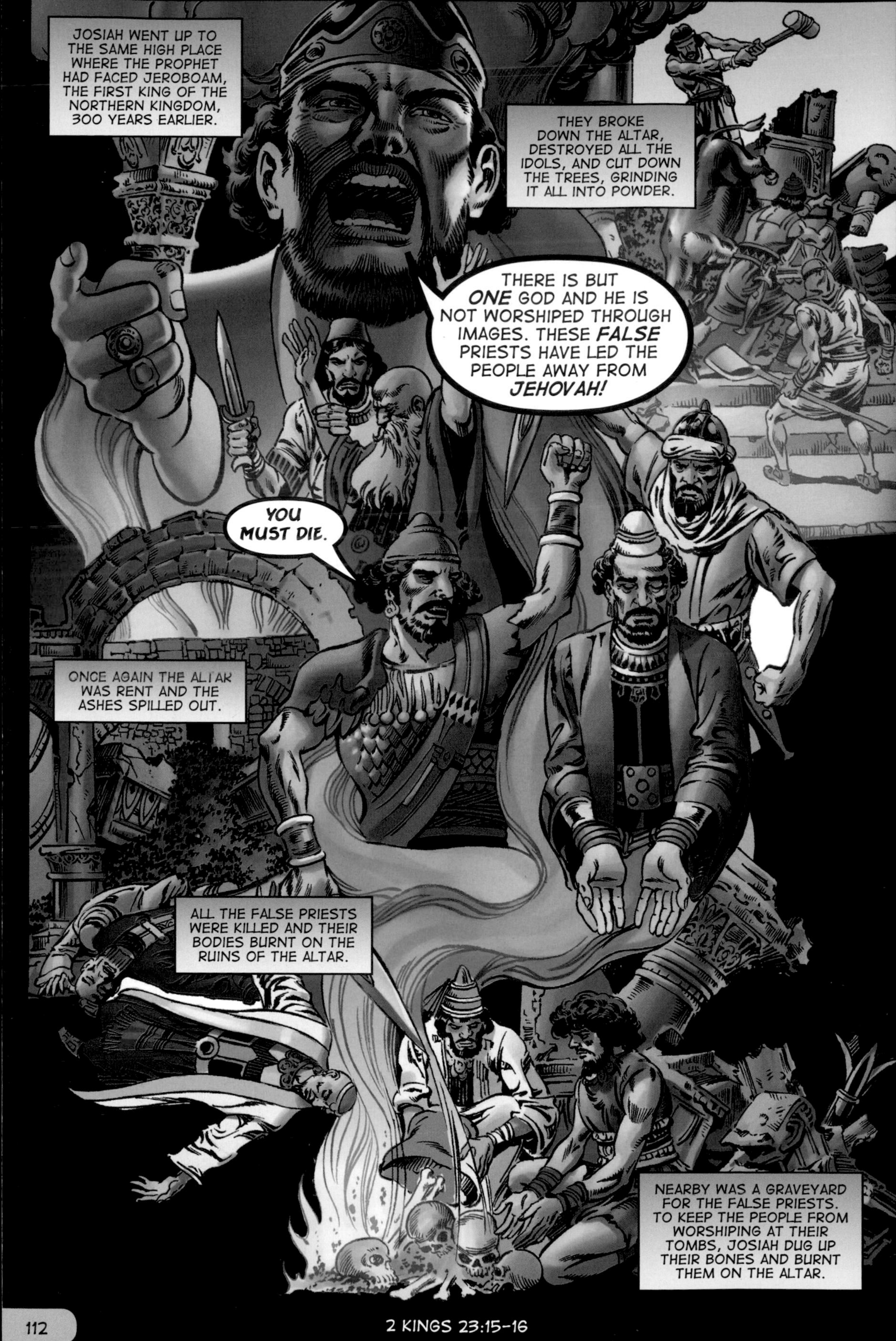
JOSIAH WENT UP TO THE SAME HIGH PLACE WHERE THE PROPHET HAD FACED JEROBOAM, THE FIRST KING OF THE NORTHERN KINGDOM, 300 YEARS EARLIER.
THEY BROKE DOWN THE ALTAR, DESTROYED ALL THE IDOLS, AND CUT DOWN THE TREES, GRINDING IT ALL INTO POWDER.
THERE IS BUT *ONE* GOD AND HE IS NOT WORSHIPED THROUGH IMAGES. THESE *FALSE* PRIESTS HAVE LED THE PEOPLE AWAY FROM *JEHOVAH!*
YOU MUST DIE.
ONCE AGAIN THE ALTAR WAS RENT AND THE ASHES SPILLED OUT.
ALL THE FALSE PRIESTS WERE KILLED AND THEIR BODIES BURNT ON THE RUINS OF THE ALTAR.
NEARBY WAS A GRAVEYARD FOR THE FALSE PRIESTS. TO KEEP THE PEOPLE FROM WORSHIPING AT THEIR TOMBS, JOSIAH DUG UP THEIR BONES AND BURNT THEM ON THE ALTAR.

2 KINGS 23:15-16

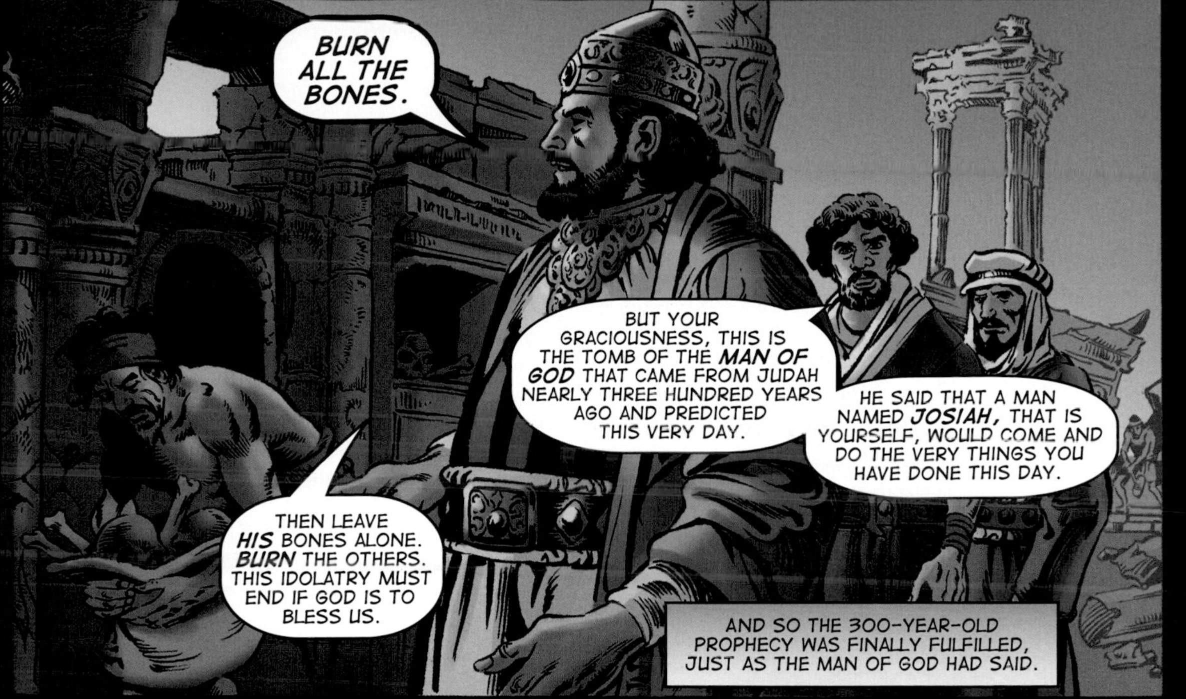
BURN ALL THE BONES.
BUT YOUR GRACIOUSNESS, THIS IS THE TOMB OF THE MAN OF GOD THAT CAME FROM JUDAH NEARLY THREE HUNDRED YEARS AGO AND PREDICTED THIS VERY DAY.
HE SAID THAT A MAN NAMED JOSIAH, THAT IS YOURSELF, WOULD COME AND DO THE VERY THINGS YOU HAVE DONE THIS DAY.
THEN LEAVE HIS BONES ALONE. BURN THE OTHERS. THIS IDOLATRY MUST END IF GOD IS TO BLESS US.
AND SO THE 300-YEAR-OLD PROPHECY WAS FINALLY FULFILLED, JUST AS THE MAN OF GOD HAD SAID.

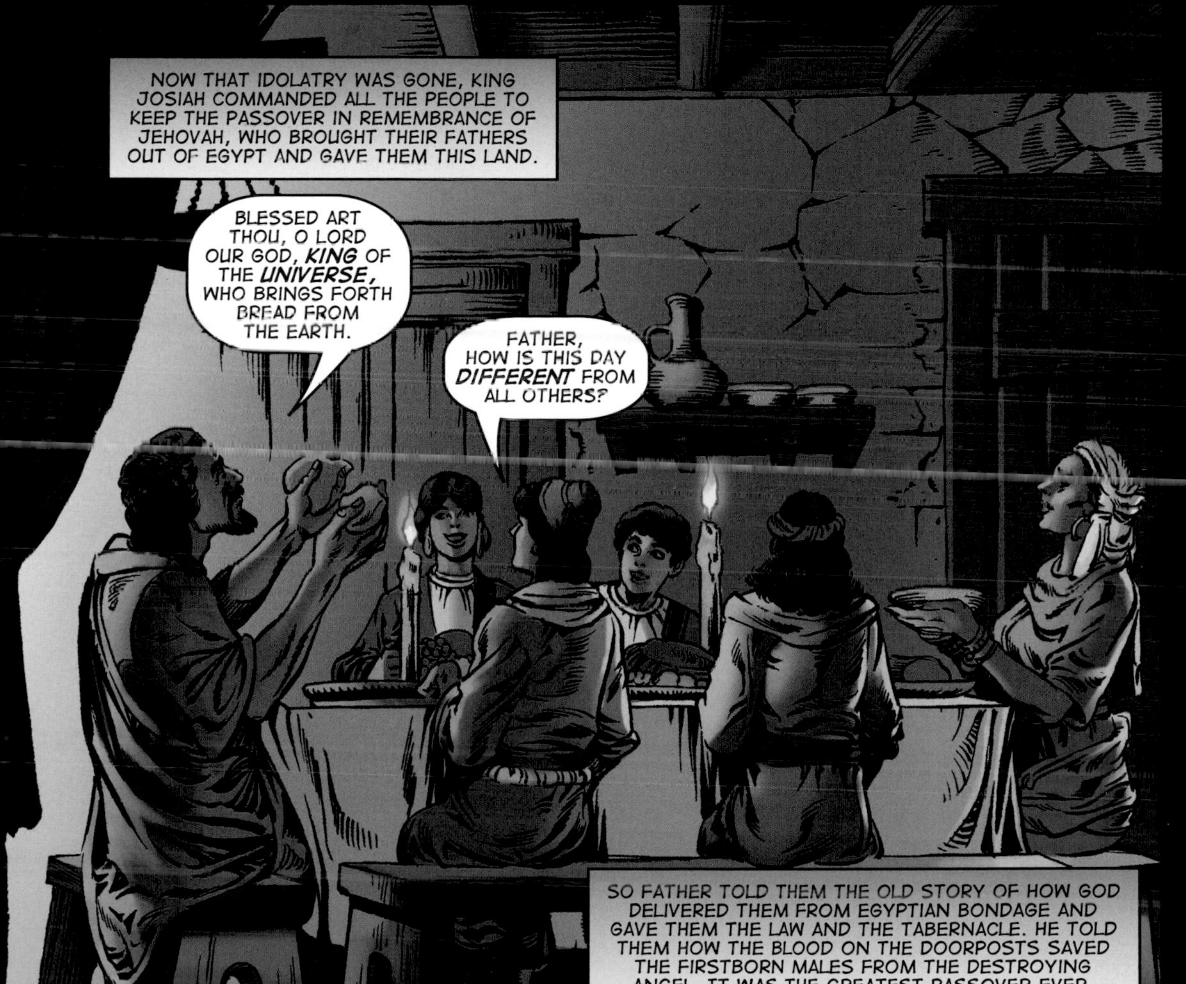
NOW THAT IDOLATRY WAS GONE, KING JOSIAH COMMANDED ALL THE PEOPLE TO KEEP THE PASSOVER IN REMEMBRANCE OF JEHOVAH, WHO BROUGHT THEIR FATHERS OUT OF EGYPT AND GAVE THEM THIS LAND.
BLESSED ART THOU, O LORD OUR GOD, KING OF THE UNIVERSE, WHO BRINGS FORTH BREAD FROM THE EARTH.
FATHER, HOW IS THIS DAY DIFFERENT FROM ALL OTHERS?
SO FATHER TOLD THEM THE OLD STORY OF HOW GOD DELIVERED THEM FROM EGYPTIAN BONDAGE AND GAVE THEM THE LAW AND THE TABERNACLE. HE TOLD THEM HOW THE BLOOD ON THE DOORPOSTS SAVED THE FIRSTBORN MALES FROM THE DESTROYING ANGEL. IT WAS THE GREATEST PASSOVER EVER.

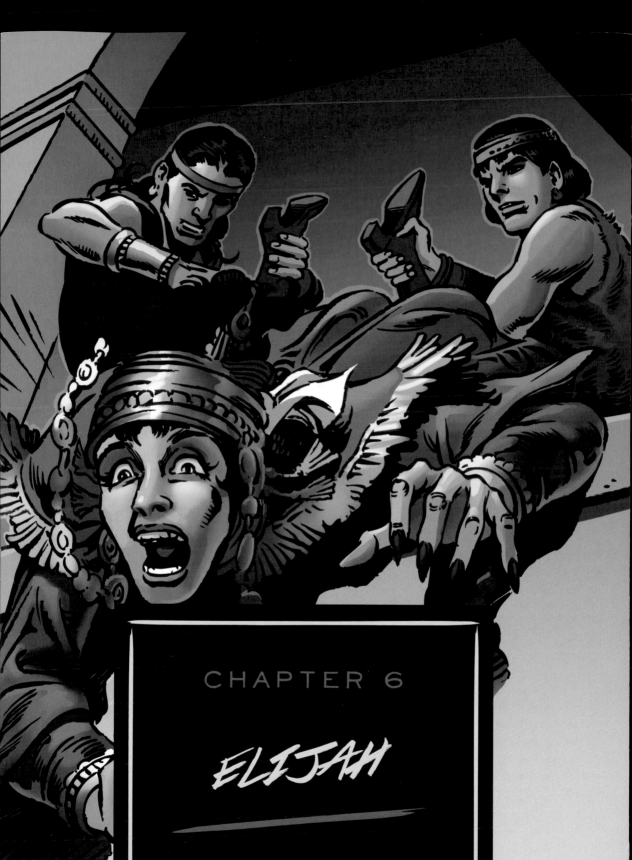

CHAPTER 6

ELIJAH

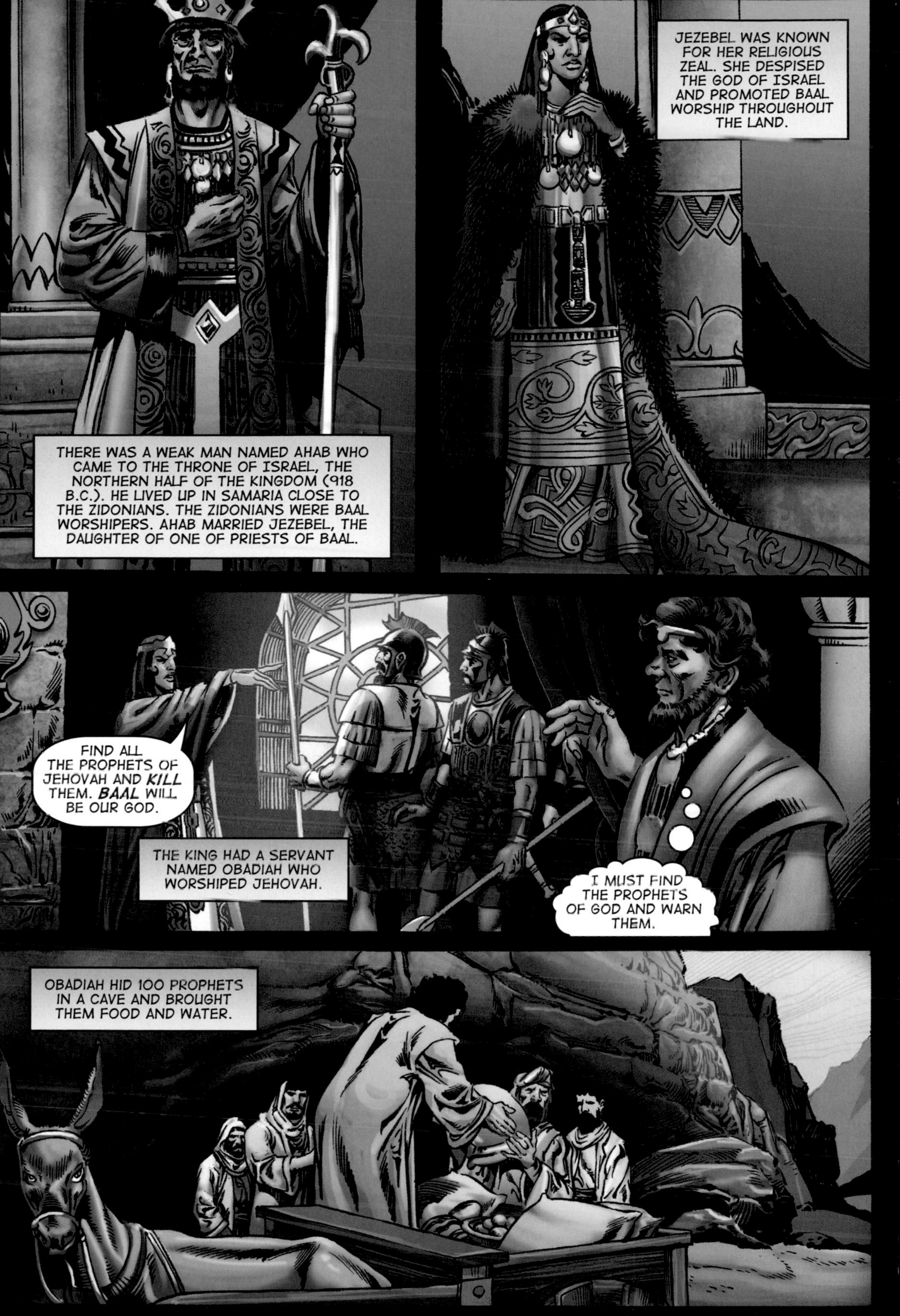

THERE WAS A WEAK MAN NAMED AHAB WHO CAME TO THE THRONE OF ISRAEL, THE NORTHERN HALF OF THE KINGDOM (918 B.C.). HE LIVED UP IN SAMARIA CLOSE TO THE ZIDONIANS. THE ZIDONIANS WERE BAAL WORSHIPERS. AHAB MARRIED JEZEBEL, THE DAUGHTER OF ONE OF PRIESTS OF BAAL.
JEZEBEL WAS KNOWN FOR HER RELIGIOUS ZEAL. SHE DESPISED THE GOD OF ISRAEL AND PROMOTED BAAL WORSHIP THROUGHOUT THE LAND.
FIND ALL THE PROPHETS OF JEHOVAH AND ***KILL*** THEM. ***BAAL*** WILL BE OUR GOD.
THE KING HAD A SERVANT NAMED OBADIAH WHO WORSHIPED JEHOVAH.
I MUST FIND THE PROPHETS OF GOD AND WARN THEM.
OBADIAH HID 100 PROPHETS IN A CAVE AND BROUGHT THEM FOOD AND WATER.

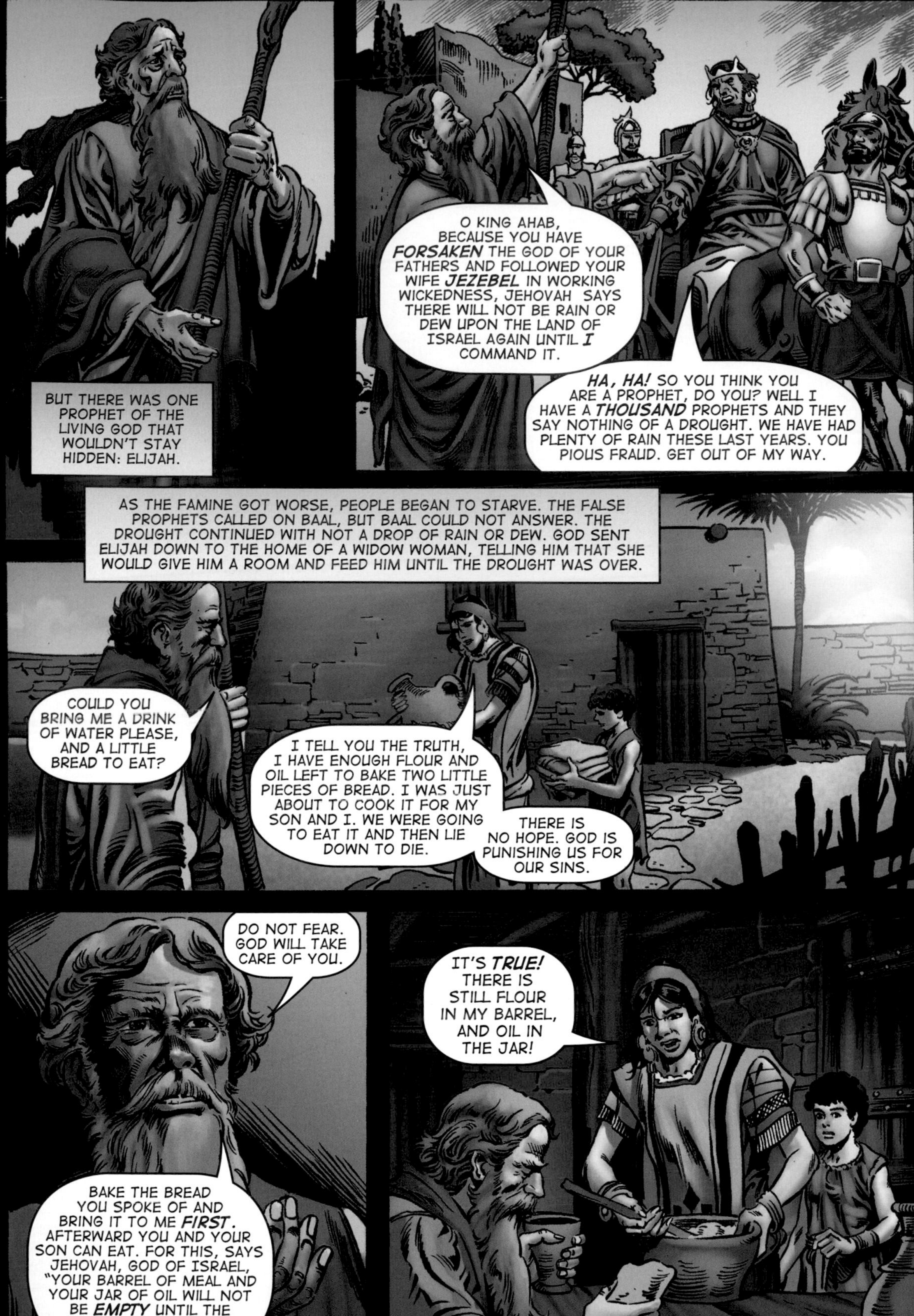
BUT THERE WAS ONE PROPHET OF THE LIVING GOD THAT WOULDN'T STAY HIDDEN: ELIJAH.
O KING AHAB, BECAUSE YOU HAVE **FORSAKEN** THE GOD OF YOUR FATHERS AND FOLLOWED YOUR WIFE **JEZEBEL** IN WORKING WICKEDNESS, JEHOVAH SAYS THERE WILL NOT BE RAIN OR DEW UPON THE LAND OF ISRAEL AGAIN UNTIL *I* COMMAND IT.
HA, HA! SO YOU THINK YOU ARE A PROPHET, DO YOU? WELL I HAVE A **THOUSAND** PROPHETS AND THEY SAY NOTHING OF A DROUGHT. WE HAVE HAD PLENTY OF RAIN THESE LAST YEARS. YOU PIOUS FRAUD. GET OUT OF MY WAY.
AS THE FAMINE GOT WORSE, PEOPLE BEGAN TO STARVE. THE FALSE PROPHETS CALLED ON BAAL, BUT BAAL COULD NOT ANSWER. THE DROUGHT CONTINUED WITH NOT A DROP OF RAIN OR DEW. GOD SENT ELIJAH DOWN TO THE HOME OF A WIDOW WOMAN, TELLING HIM THAT SHE WOULD GIVE HIM A ROOM AND FEED HIM UNTIL THE DROUGHT WAS OVER.
COULD YOU BRING ME A DRINK OF WATER PLEASE, AND A LITTLE BREAD TO EAT?
I TELL YOU THE TRUTH, I HAVE ENOUGH FLOUR AND OIL LEFT TO BAKE TWO LITTLE PIECES OF BREAD. I WAS JUST ABOUT TO COOK IT FOR MY SON AND I. WE WERE GOING TO EAT IT AND THEN LIE DOWN TO DIE.
THERE IS NO HOPE. GOD IS PUNISHING US FOR OUR SINS.
DO NOT FEAR. GOD WILL TAKE CARE OF YOU.
BAKE THE BREAD YOU SPOKE OF AND BRING IT TO ME **FIRST**. AFTERWARD YOU AND YOUR SON CAN EAT. FOR THIS, SAYS JEHOVAH, GOD OF ISRAEL, "YOUR BARREL OF MEAL AND YOUR JAR OF OIL WILL NOT BE **EMPTY** UNTIL THE DAY GOD SENDS RAIN UPON ISRAEL."
IT'S **TRUE!** THERE IS STILL FLOUR IN MY BARREL, AND OIL IN THE JAR!

1 KINGS 17:1, 10–16

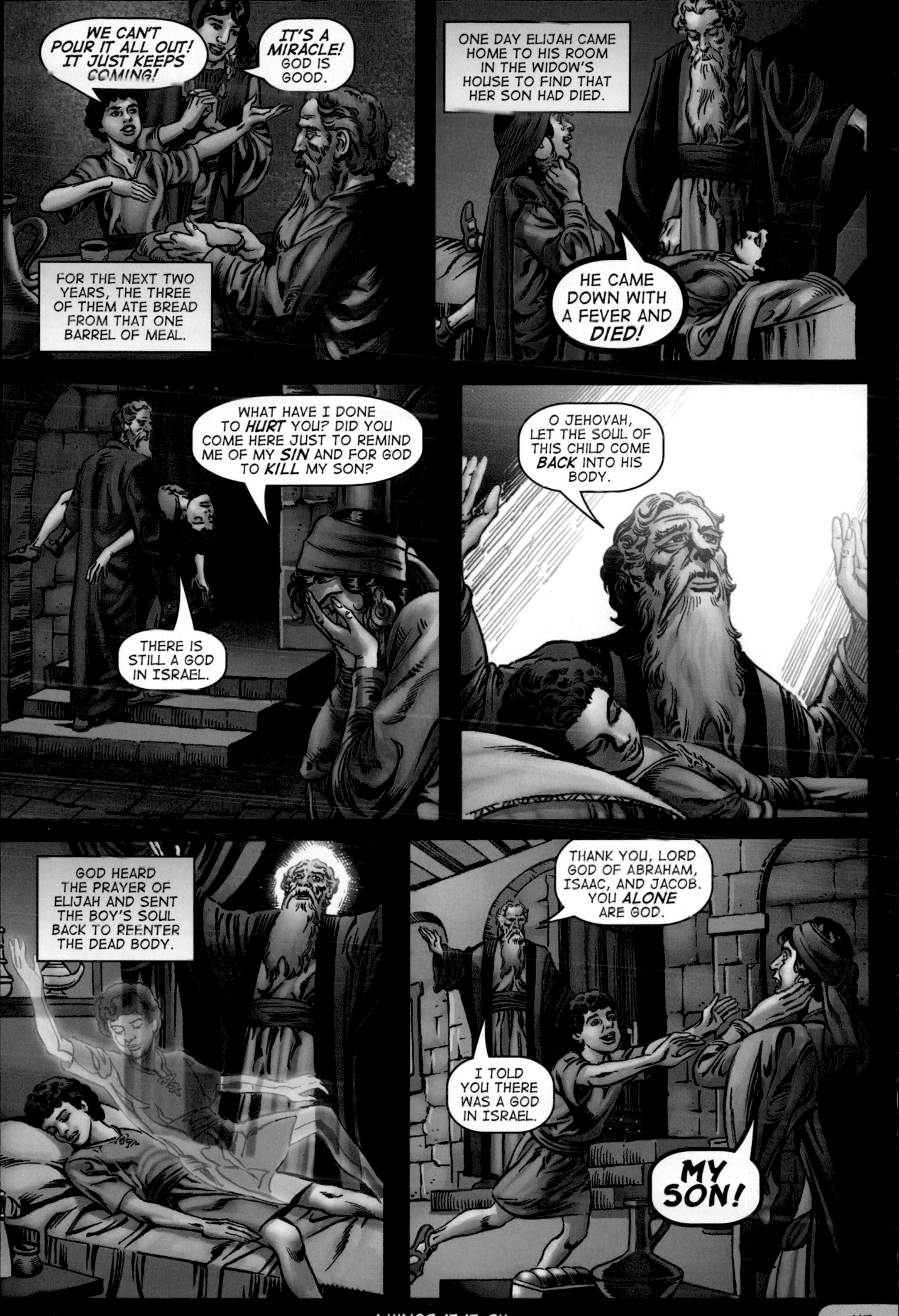
WE CAN'T POUR IT ALL OUT! IT JUST KEEPS COMING!
IT'S A MIRACLE! GOD IS GOOD.
FOR THE NEXT TWO YEARS, THE THREE OF THEM ATE BREAD FROM THAT ONE BARREL OF MEAL.
ONE DAY ELIJAH CAME HOME TO HIS ROOM IN THE WIDOW'S HOUSE TO FIND THAT HER SON HAD DIED.
HE CAME DOWN WITH A FEVER AND DIED!
WHAT HAVE I DONE TO HURT YOU? DID YOU COME HERE JUST TO REMIND ME OF MY SIN AND FOR GOD TO KILL MY SON?
THERE IS STILL A GOD IN ISRAEL.
O JEHOVAH, LET THE SOUL OF THIS CHILD COME BACK INTO HIS BODY.
GOD HEARD THE PRAYER OF ELIJAH AND SENT THE BOY'S SOUL BACK TO REENTER THE DEAD BODY.
THANK YOU, LORD GOD OF ABRAHAM, ISAAC, AND JACOB. YOU ALONE ARE GOD.
I TOLD YOU THERE WAS A GOD IN ISRAEL.
MY SON!

1 KINGS 17:17-24

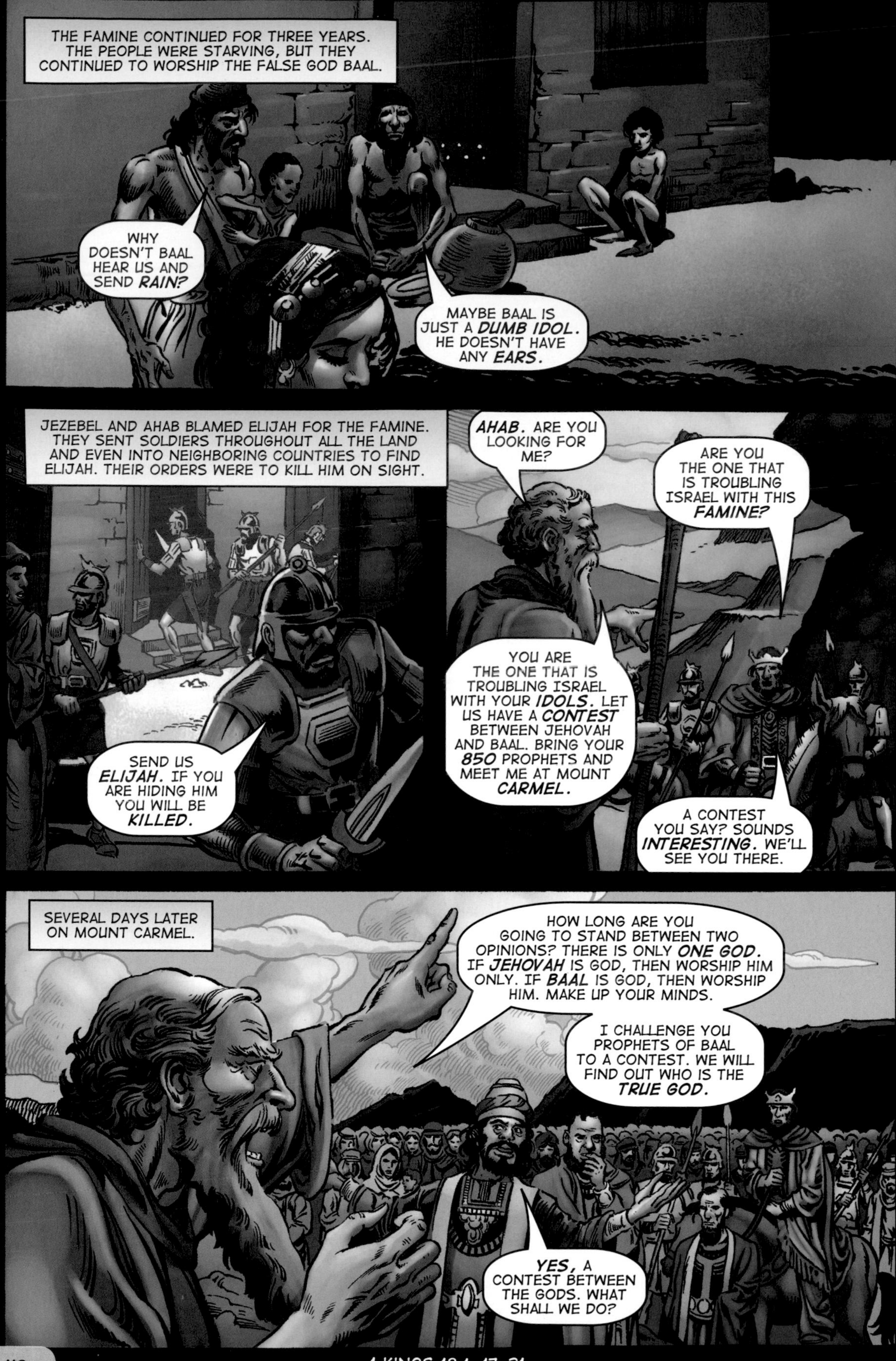
THE FAMINE CONTINUED FOR THREE YEARS. THE PEOPLE WERE STARVING, BUT THEY CONTINUED TO WORSHIP THE FALSE GOD BAAL.
WHY DOESN'T BAAL HEAR US AND SEND *RAIN?*
MAYBE BAAL IS JUST A *DUMB IDOL*. HE DOESN'T HAVE ANY *EARS*.
JEZEBEL AND AHAB BLAMED ELIJAH FOR THE FAMINE. THEY SENT SOLDIERS THROUGHOUT ALL THE LAND AND EVEN INTO NEIGHBORING COUNTRIES TO FIND ELIJAH. THEIR ORDERS WERE TO KILL HIM ON SIGHT.
SEND US *ELIJAH*. IF YOU ARE HIDING HIM YOU WILL BE *KILLED*.
AHAB. ARE YOU LOOKING FOR ME?
ARE YOU THE ONE THAT IS TROUBLING ISRAEL WITH THIS *FAMINE?*
YOU ARE THE ONE THAT IS TROUBLING ISRAEL WITH YOUR *IDOLS*. LET US HAVE A *CONTEST* BETWEEN JEHOVAH AND BAAL. BRING YOUR *850* PROPHETS AND MEET ME AT MOUNT *CARMEL*.
A CONTEST YOU SAY? SOUNDS *INTERESTING*. WE'LL SEE YOU THERE.
SEVERAL DAYS LATER ON MOUNT CARMEL.
HOW LONG ARE YOU GOING TO STAND BETWEEN TWO OPINIONS? THERE IS ONLY *ONE GOD*. IF *JEHOVAH* IS GOD, THEN WORSHIP HIM ONLY. IF *BAAL* IS GOD, THEN WORSHIP HIM. MAKE UP YOUR MINDS.
I CHALLENGE YOU PROPHETS OF BAAL TO A CONTEST. WE WILL FIND OUT WHO IS THE *TRUE GOD*.
YES, A CONTEST BETWEEN THE GODS. WHAT SHALL WE DO?

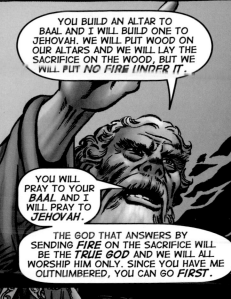

YOU BUILD AN ALTAR TO BAAL AND I WILL BUILD ONE TO JEHOVAH. WE WILL PUT WOOD ON OUR ALTARS AND WE WILL LAY THE SACRIFICE ON THE WOOD, BUT WE WILL PUT *NO FIRE UNDER IT*.

O *BAAL*, HEAR US THIS DAY. WE DEDICATE THIS SACRIFICE TO YOUR GREAT NAME.

YOU WILL PRAY TO YOUR *BAAL* AND I WILL PRAY TO *JEHOVAH*.

THE GOD THAT ANSWERS BY SENDING *FIRE* ON THE SACRIFICE WILL BE THE *TRUE GOD* AND WE WILL ALL WORSHIP HIM ONLY. SINCE YOU HAVE ME OUTNUMBERED, YOU CAN GO *FIRST*.

O BAAL, THE *GREAT* AND *MIGHTY*.

O *QUEEN* OF HEAVEN, COME AND *HELP* BAAL THIS DAY.

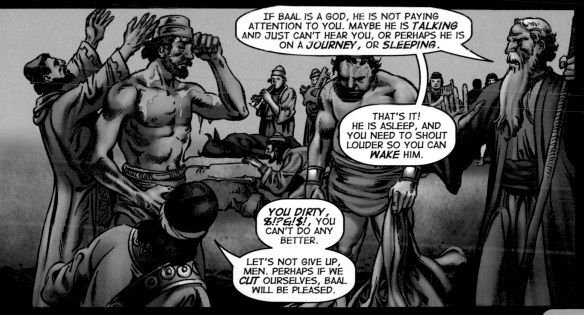

IF BAAL IS A GOD, HE IS NOT PAYING ATTENTION TO YOU. MAYBE HE IS *TALKING* AND JUST CAN'T HEAR YOU, OR PERHAPS HE IS ON A *JOURNEY*, OR *SLEEPING*.

THAT'S IT! HE IS ASLEEP, AND YOU NEED TO SHOUT LOUDER SO YOU CAN *WAKE* HIM.

YOU DIRTY, %!?&!$!, YOU CAN'T DO ANY BETTER.

LET'S NOT GIVE UP, MEN. PERHAPS IF WE *CUT* OURSELVES, BAAL WILL BE PLEASED.

1 KINGS 18:22-27

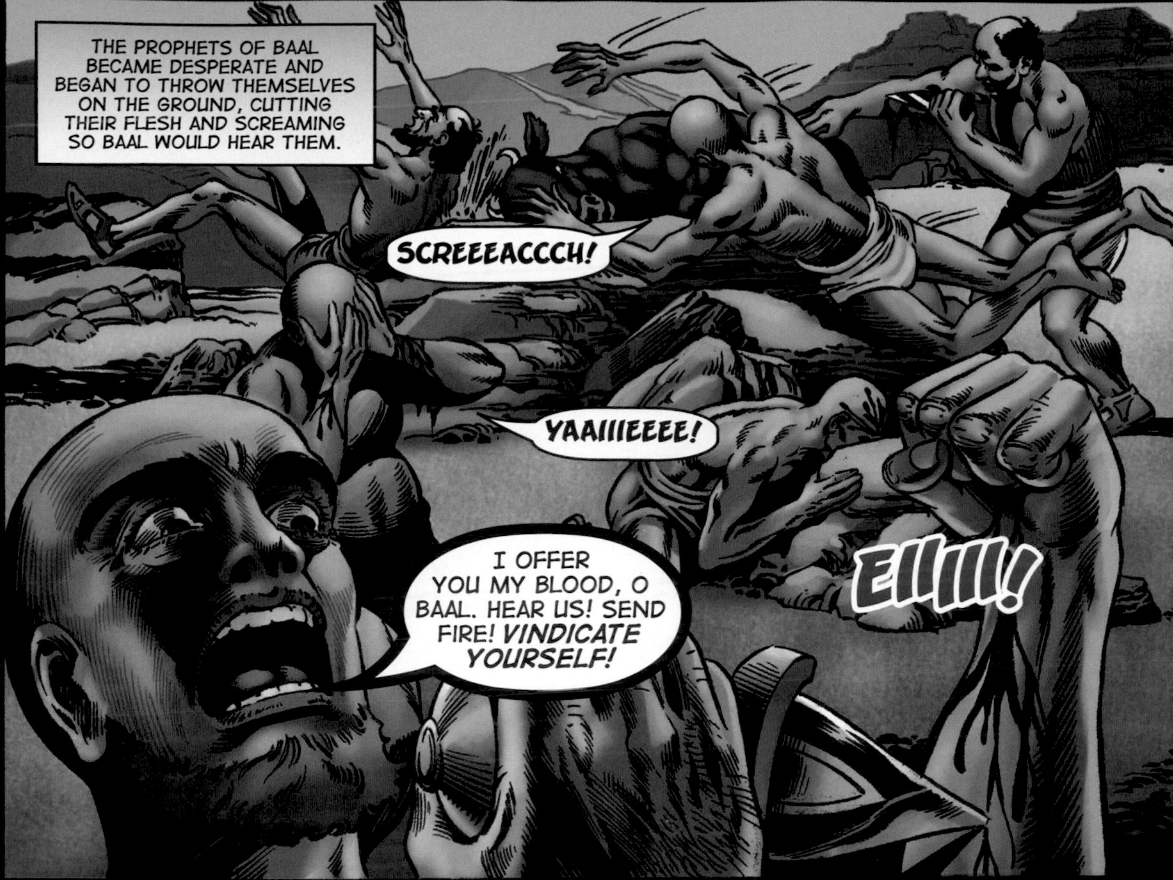
THE PROPHETS OF BAAL BECAME DESPERATE AND BEGAN TO THROW THEMSELVES ON THE GROUND, CUTTING THEIR FLESH AND SCREAMING SO BAAL WOULD HEAR THEM.
SCREEEACCCH!
YAAIIIEEEE!
I OFFER YOU MY BLOOD, O BAAL. HEAR US! SEND FIRE! VINDICATE YOURSELF!
EIIIII!

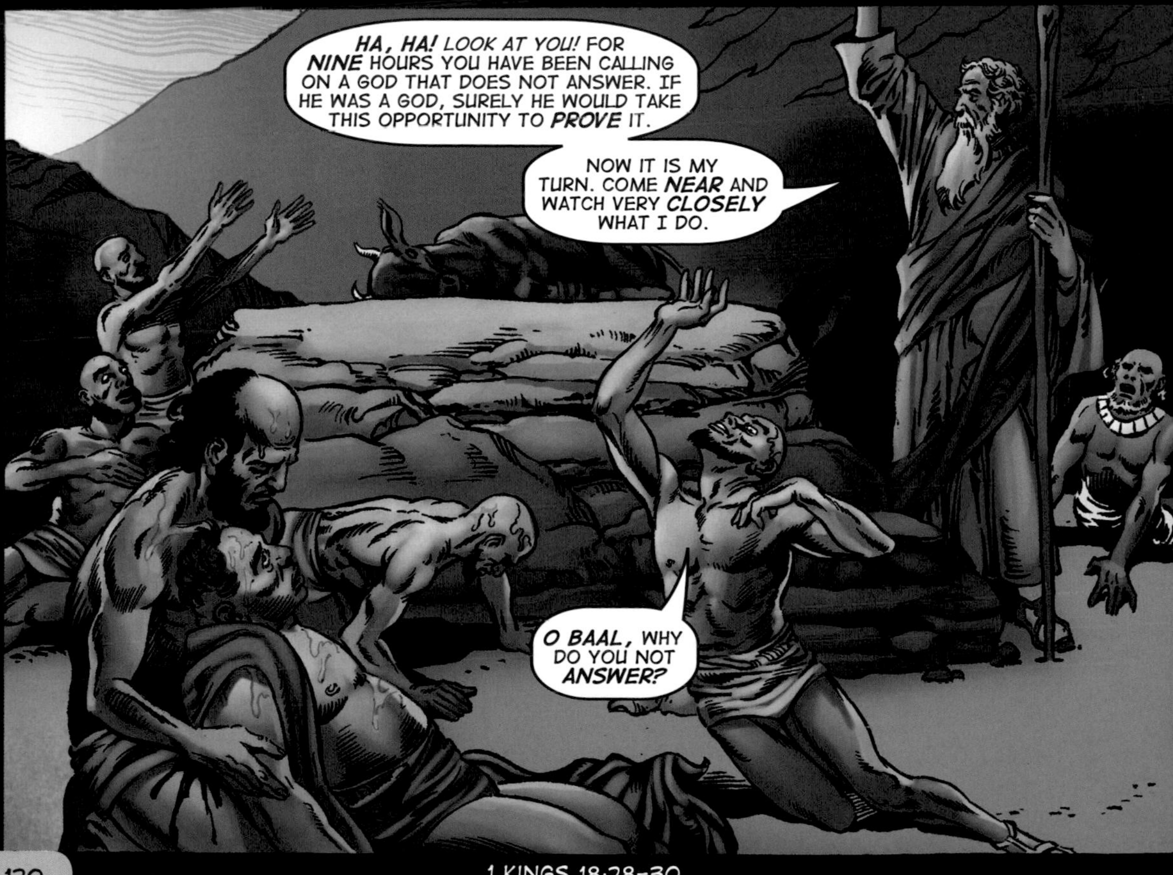
HA, HA! LOOK AT YOU! FOR NINE HOURS YOU HAVE BEEN CALLING ON A GOD THAT DOES NOT ANSWER. IF HE WAS A GOD, SURELY HE WOULD TAKE THIS OPPORTUNITY TO PROVE IT.
NOW IT IS MY TURN. COME NEAR AND WATCH VERY CLOSELY WHAT I DO.
O BAAL, WHY DO YOU NOT ANSWER?

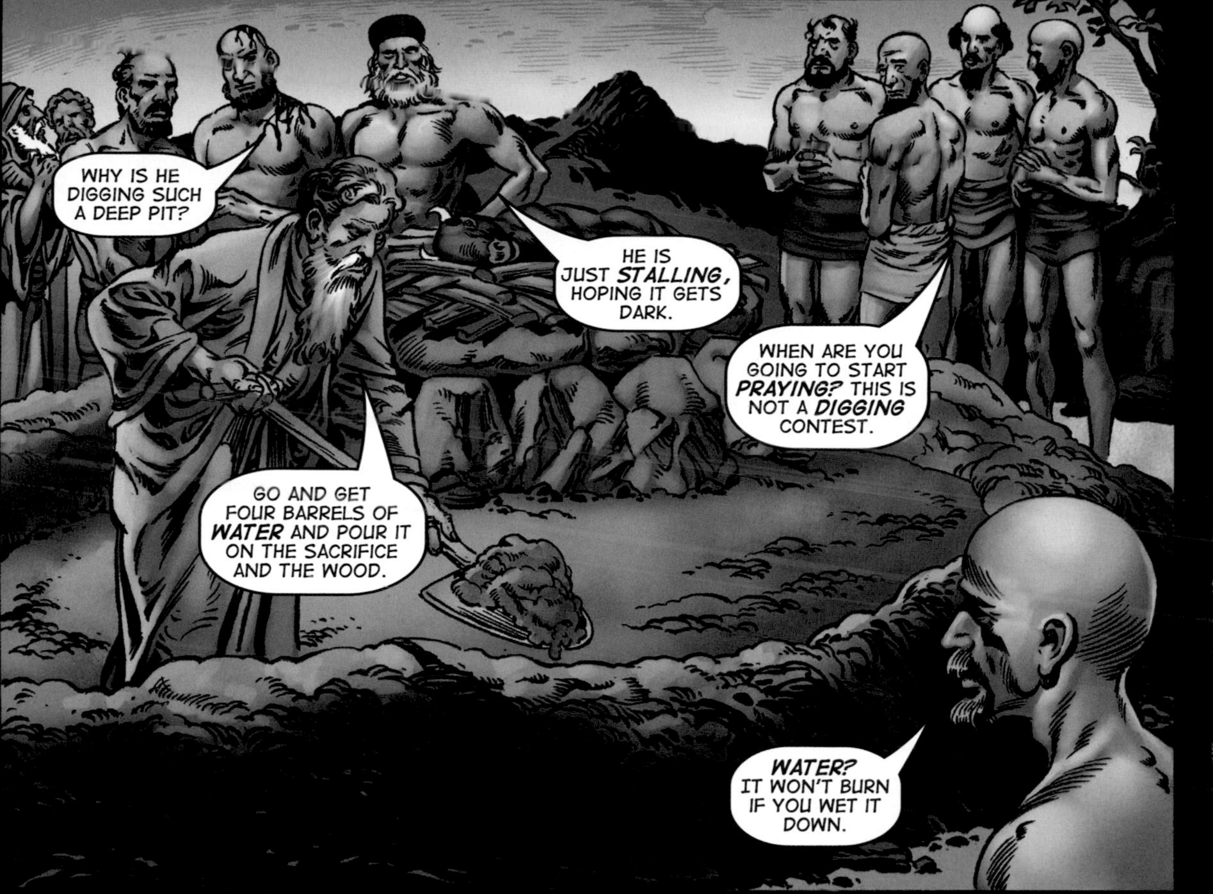
WHY IS HE DIGGING SUCH A DEEP PIT?
HE IS JUST STALLING, HOPING IT GETS DARK.
WHEN ARE YOU GOING TO START PRAYING? THIS IS NOT A DIGGING CONTEST.
GO AND GET FOUR BARRELS OF WATER AND POUR IT ON THE SACRIFICE AND THE WOOD.
WATER? IT WON'T BURN IF YOU WET IT DOWN.

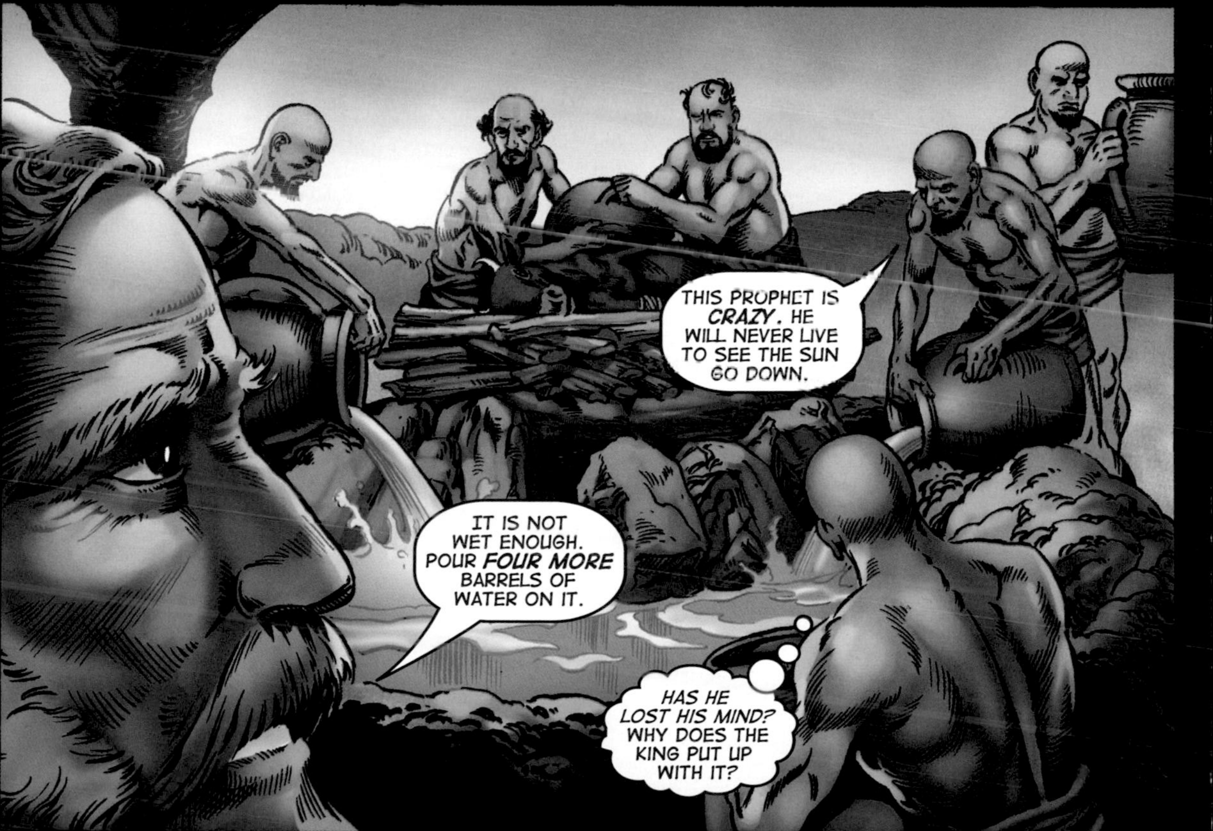
THIS PROPHET IS CRAZY. HE WILL NEVER LIVE TO SEE THE SUN GO DOWN.
IT IS NOT WET ENOUGH. POUR FOUR MORE BARRELS OF WATER ON IT.
HAS HE LOST HIS MIND? WHY DOES THE KING PUT UP WITH IT?

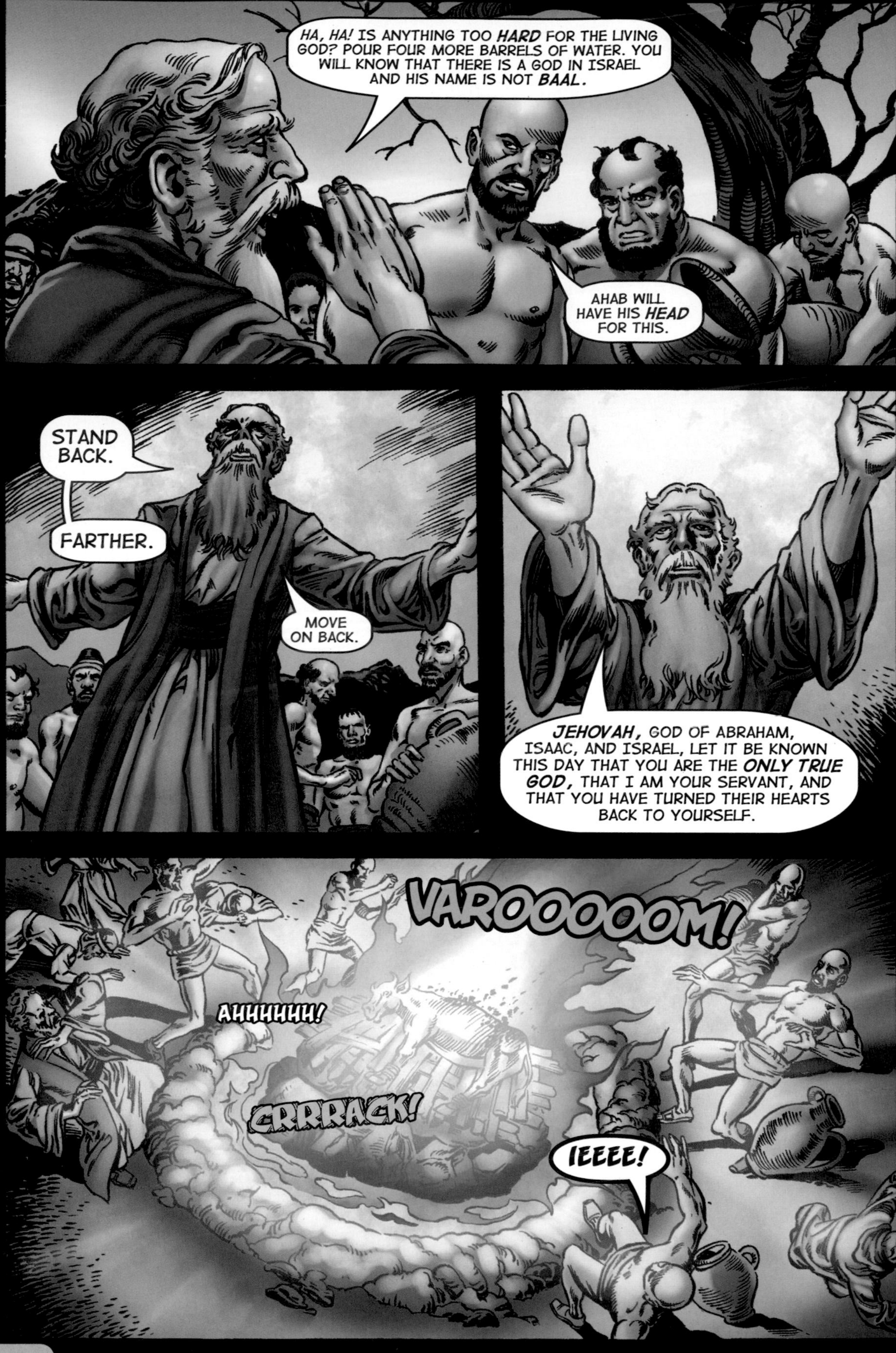
HA, HA! IS ANYTHING TOO HARD FOR THE LIVING GOD? POUR FOUR MORE BARRELS OF WATER. YOU WILL KNOW THAT THERE IS A GOD IN ISRAEL AND HIS NAME IS NOT BAAL.
AHAB WILL HAVE HIS HEAD FOR THIS.
STAND BACK.
FARTHER.
MOVE ON BACK.
JEHOVAH, GOD OF ABRAHAM, ISAAC, AND ISRAEL, LET IT BE KNOWN THIS DAY THAT YOU ARE THE ONLY TRUE GOD, THAT I AM YOUR SERVANT, AND THAT YOU HAVE TURNED THEIR HEARTS BACK TO YOURSELF.
VAROOOOOOM!
AHHHHHH!
CRRRACK!
IEEEE!

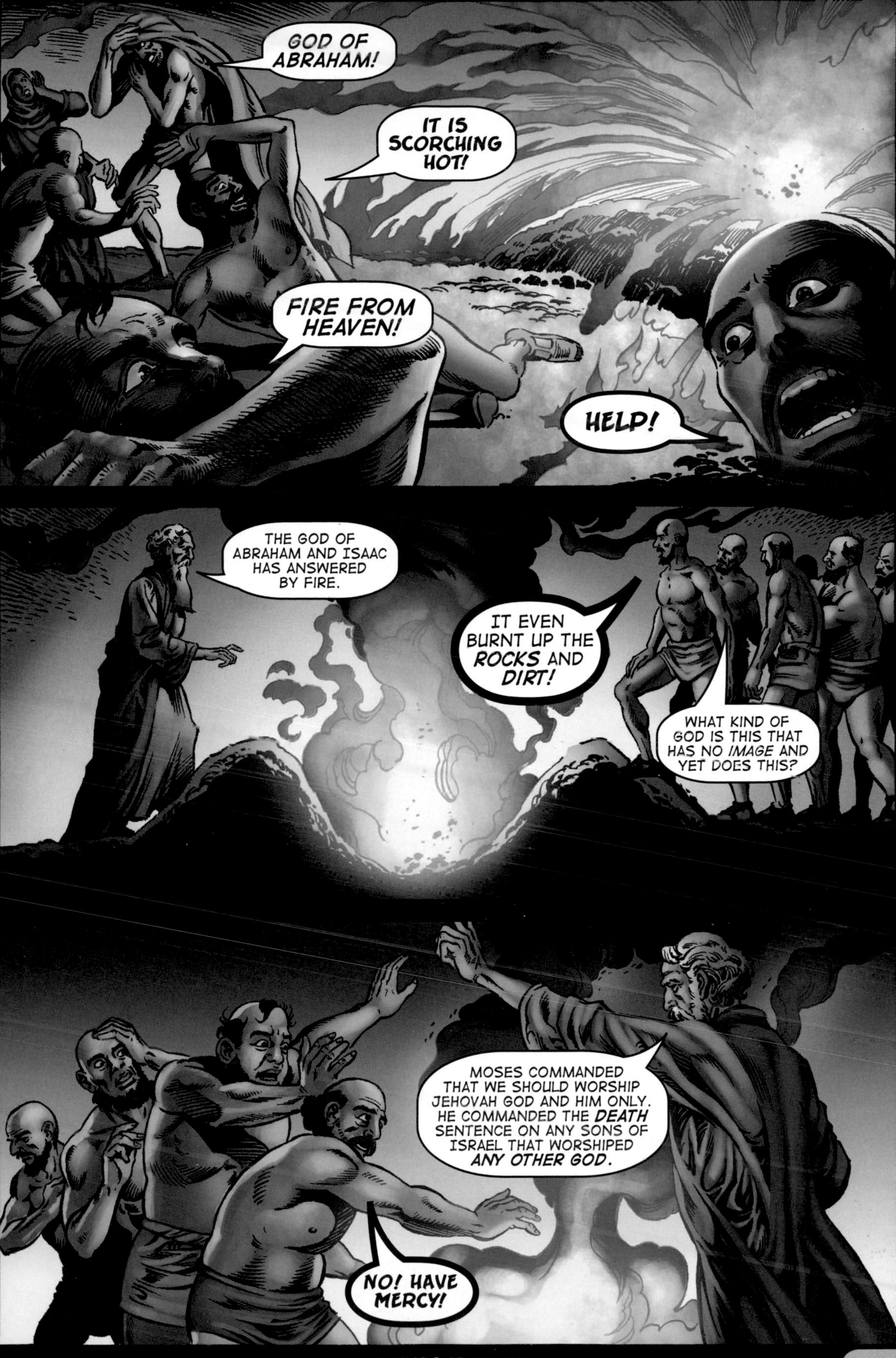
GOD OF ABRAHAM!
IT IS SCORCHING HOT!
FIRE FROM HEAVEN!
HELP!
THE GOD OF ABRAHAM AND ISAAC HAS ANSWERED BY FIRE.
IT EVEN BURNT UP THE ROCKS AND DIRT!
WHAT KIND OF GOD IS THIS THAT HAS NO IMAGE AND YET DOES THIS?
MOSES COMMANDED THAT WE SHOULD WORSHIP JEHOVAH GOD AND HIM ONLY. HE COMMANDED THE DEATH SENTENCE ON ANY SONS OF ISRAEL THAT WORSHIPED ANY OTHER GOD.
NO! HAVE MERCY!

1 KINGS 18:38-40

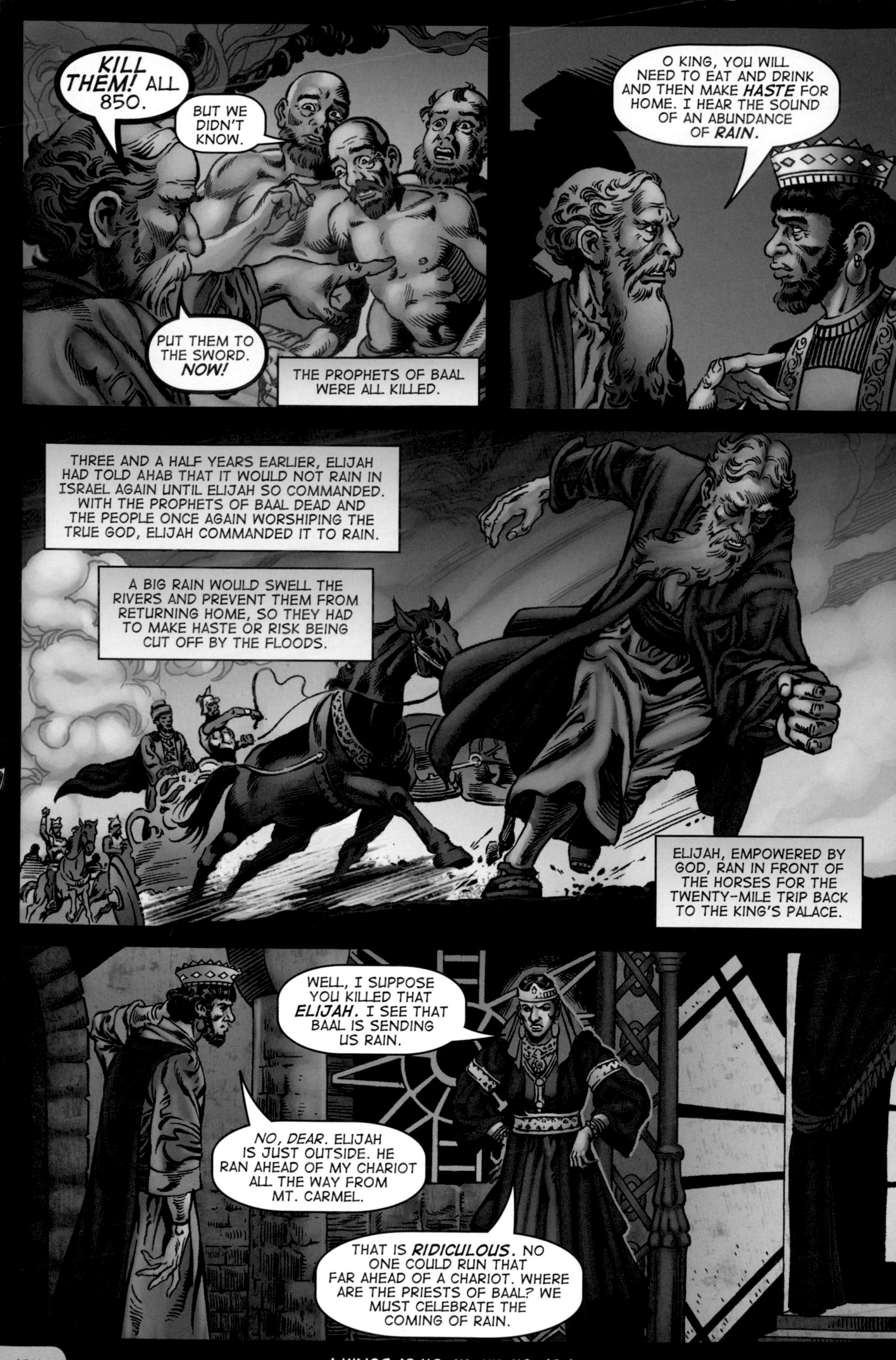
KILL THEM! ALL 850.
BUT WE DIDN'T KNOW.
PUT THEM TO THE SWORD. NOW!
THE PROPHETS OF BAAL WERE ALL KILLED.
O KING, YOU WILL NEED TO EAT AND DRINK AND THEN MAKE HASTE FOR HOME. I HEAR THE SOUND OF AN ABUNDANCE OF RAIN.
THREE AND A HALF YEARS EARLIER, ELIJAH HAD TOLD AHAB THAT IT WOULD NOT RAIN IN ISRAEL AGAIN UNTIL ELIJAH SO COMMANDED. WITH THE PROPHETS OF BAAL DEAD AND THE PEOPLE ONCE AGAIN WORSHIPING THE TRUE GOD, ELIJAH COMMANDED IT TO RAIN.
A BIG RAIN WOULD SWELL THE RIVERS AND PREVENT THEM FROM RETURNING HOME, SO THEY HAD TO MAKE HASTE OR RISK BEING CUT OFF BY THE FLOODS.
ELIJAH, EMPOWERED BY GOD, RAN IN FRONT OF THE HORSES FOR THE TWENTY-MILE TRIP BACK TO THE KING'S PALACE.
WELL, I SUPPOSE YOU KILLED THAT ELIJAH. I SEE THAT BAAL IS SENDING US RAIN.
NO, DEAR. ELIJAH IS JUST OUTSIDE. HE RAN AHEAD OF MY CHARIOT ALL THE WAY FROM MT. CARMEL.
THAT IS RIDICULOUS. NO ONE COULD RUN THAT FAR AHEAD OF A CHARIOT. WHERE ARE THE PRIESTS OF BAAL? WE MUST CELEBRATE THE COMING OF RAIN.

1 KINGS 18:40-41, 44-46, 19:1

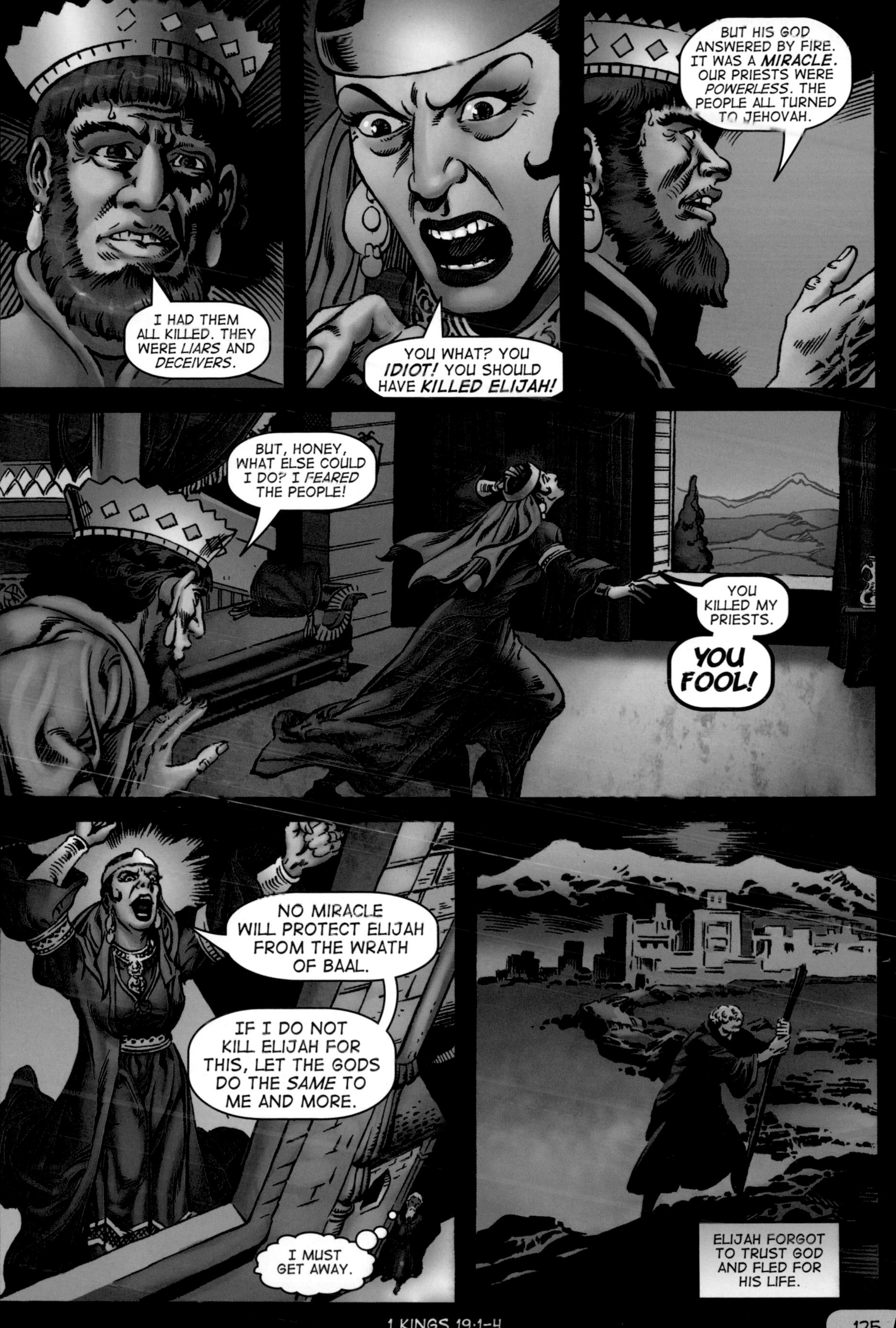
I HAD THEM ALL KILLED. THEY WERE *LIARS* AND *DECEIVERS*.
YOU WHAT? YOU ***IDIOT!*** YOU SHOULD HAVE ***KILLED ELIJAH!***
BUT HIS GOD ANSWERED BY FIRE. IT WAS A ***MIRACLE.*** OUR PRIESTS WERE *POWERLESS*. THE PEOPLE ALL TURNED TO JEHOVAH.
BUT, HONEY, WHAT ELSE COULD I DO? I *FEARED* THE PEOPLE!
YOU KILLED MY PRIESTS.
YOU FOOL!
NO MIRACLE WILL PROTECT ELIJAH FROM THE WRATH OF BAAL.
IF I DO NOT KILL ELIJAH FOR THIS, LET THE GODS DO THE *SAME* TO ME AND MORE.
I MUST GET AWAY.
ELIJAH FORGOT TO TRUST GOD AND FLED FOR HIS LIFE.

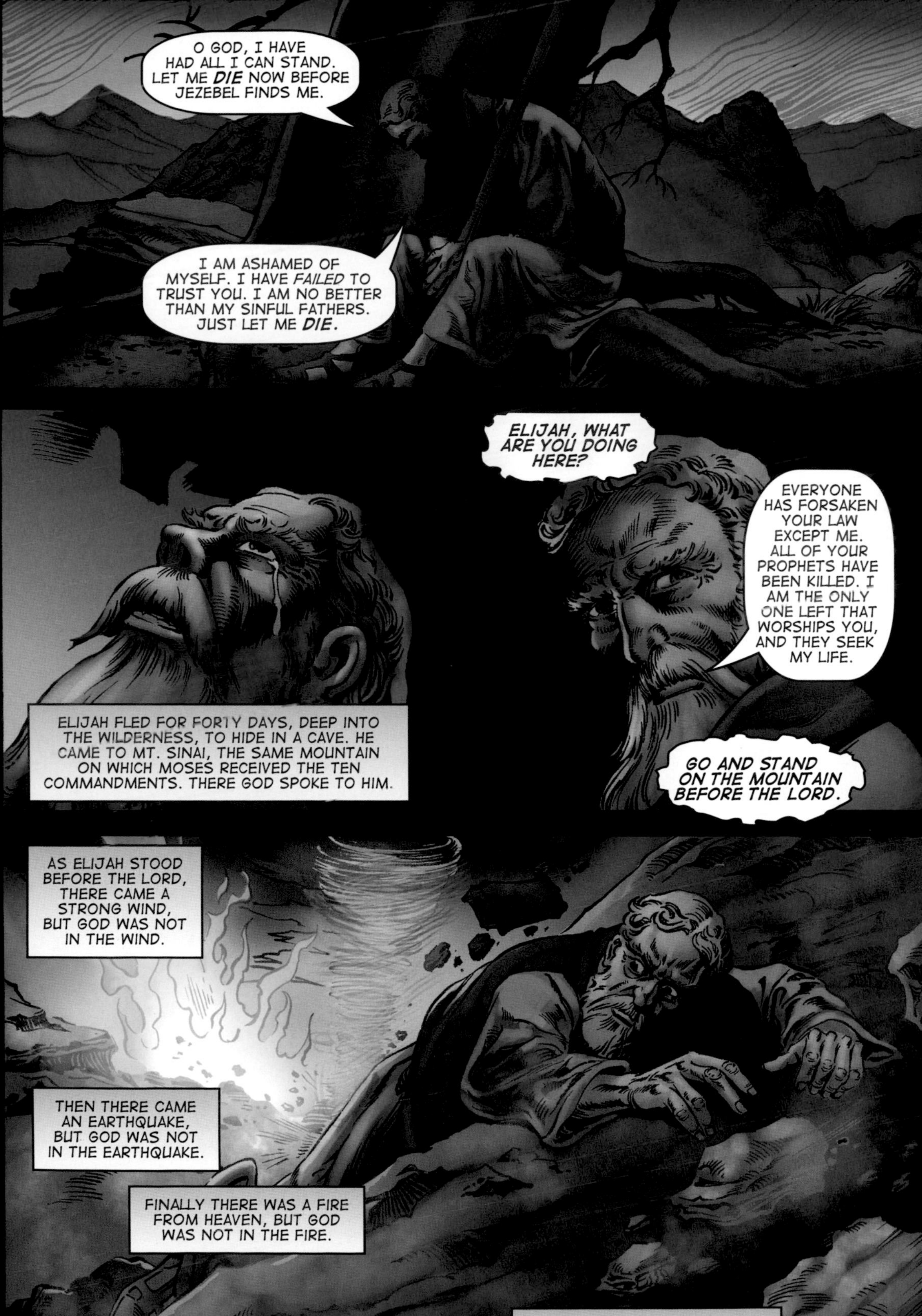

O GOD, I HAVE HAD ALL I CAN STAND. LET ME DIE NOW BEFORE JEZEBEL FINDS ME.
I AM ASHAMED OF MYSELF. I HAVE FAILED TO TRUST YOU. I AM NO BETTER THAN MY SINFUL FATHERS. JUST LET ME DIE.
ELIJAH FLED FOR FORTY DAYS, DEEP INTO THE WILDERNESS, TO HIDE IN A CAVE. HE CAME TO MT. SINAI, THE SAME MOUNTAIN ON WHICH MOSES RECEIVED THE TEN COMMANDMENTS. THERE GOD SPOKE TO HIM.
ELIJAH, WHAT ARE YOU DOING HERE?
EVERYONE HAS FORSAKEN YOUR LAW EXCEPT ME. ALL OF YOUR PROPHETS HAVE BEEN KILLED. I AM THE ONLY ONE LEFT THAT WORSHIPS YOU, AND THEY SEEK MY LIFE.
GO AND STAND ON THE MOUNTAIN BEFORE THE LORD.
AS ELIJAH STOOD BEFORE THE LORD, THERE CAME A STRONG WIND, BUT GOD WAS NOT IN THE WIND.
THEN THERE CAME AN EARTHQUAKE, BUT GOD WAS NOT IN THE EARTHQUAKE.
FINALLY THERE WAS A FIRE FROM HEAVEN, BUT GOD WAS NOT IN THE FIRE.
GOD WAS TRYING TO SHOW ELIJAH THAT HE WAS FAR MORE TERRIBLE THAN JEZEBEL.

1 KINGS 19:4, 8–12

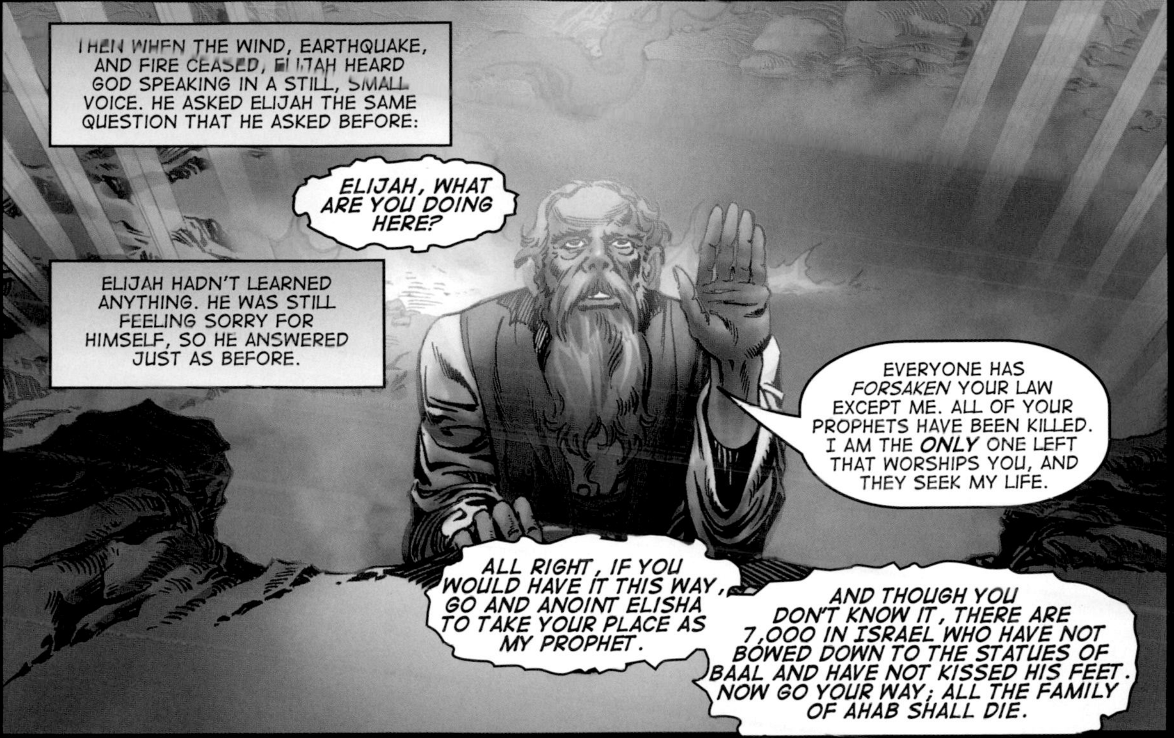
THEN WHEN THE WIND, EARTHQUAKE, AND FIRE CEASED, ELIJAH HEARD GOD SPEAKING IN A STILL, SMALL VOICE. HE ASKED ELIJAH THE SAME QUESTION THAT HE ASKED BEFORE:
ELIJAH, WHAT ARE YOU DOING HERE?
ELIJAH HADN'T LEARNED ANYTHING. HE WAS STILL FEELING SORRY FOR HIMSELF, SO HE ANSWERED JUST AS BEFORE.
EVERYONE HAS FORSAKEN YOUR LAW EXCEPT ME. ALL OF YOUR PROPHETS HAVE BEEN KILLED. I AM THE ONLY ONE LEFT THAT WORSHIPS YOU, AND THEY SEEK MY LIFE.
ALL RIGHT, IF YOU WOULD HAVE IT THIS WAY, GO AND ANOINT ELISHA TO TAKE YOUR PLACE AS MY PROPHET.
AND THOUGH YOU DON'T KNOW IT, THERE ARE 7,000 IN ISRAEL WHO HAVE NOT BOWED DOWN TO THE STATUES OF BAAL AND HAVE NOT KISSED HIS FEET. NOW GO YOUR WAY; ALL THE FAMILY OF AHAB SHALL DIE.

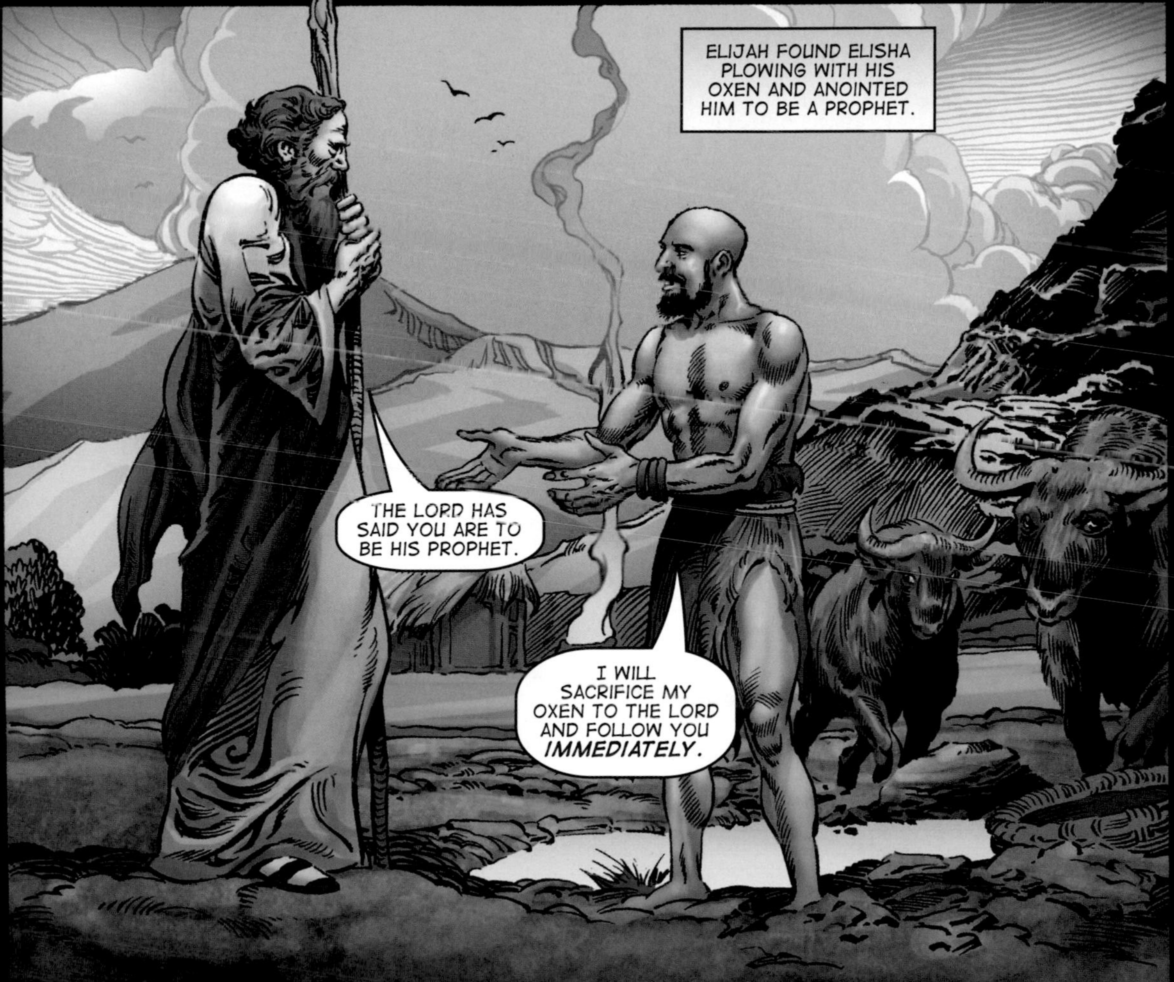
ELIJAH FOUND ELISHA PLOWING WITH HIS OXEN AND ANOINTED HIM TO BE A PROPHET.
THE LORD HAS SAID YOU ARE TO BE HIS PROPHET.
I WILL SACRIFICE MY OXEN TO THE LORD AND FOLLOW YOU IMMEDIATELY.

RIGHT NEXT TO AHAB'S PALACE WAS A VINEYARD OWNED BY NABOTH. AHAB OFTEN LOOKED OUT THE WINDOW AND ADMIRED ITS BEAUTY, WISHING IT WAS HIS. THE MORE HE THOUGHT ABOUT IT THE MORE HE WANTED HIS NEIGHBOR'S PROPERTY. THE COMMANDMENT SAYS, "THOU SHALT NOT COVET," BUT AHAB DID NOT REGARD JEHOVAH.

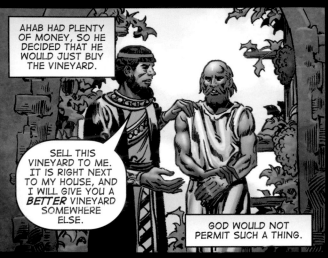

AHAB HAD PLENTY OF MONEY, SO HE DECIDED THAT HE WOULD JUST BUY THE VINEYARD.

SELL THIS VINEYARD TO ME. IT IS RIGHT NEXT TO MY HOUSE, AND I WILL GIVE YOU A *BETTER* VINEYARD SOMEWHERE ELSE.

GOD WOULD NOT PERMIT SUCH A THING.

THIS PROPERTY HAS BEEN IN MY FAMILY FOR OVER *500* YEARS. THE LAW COMMANDS US NOT TO SELL OUR LAND OUTSIDE THE FAMILY.

TELL ME, MY DEAR, WHY DO YOU NOT *EAT?* WHY ARE YOU SO *SAD?*

BECAUSE *NABOTH* WILL NOT SELL HIS VINEYARD TO ME.

YOU ARE THE KING. YOU HAVE THE POWER TO DO *ANYTHING YOU PLEASE.* DON'T LET ONE LOWLY PEASANT STAND IN THE WAY OF YOUR *HAPPINESS.* I WILL GET THE VINEYARD FOR YOU.

EXODUS 20:17; 1 KINGS 21:1-7

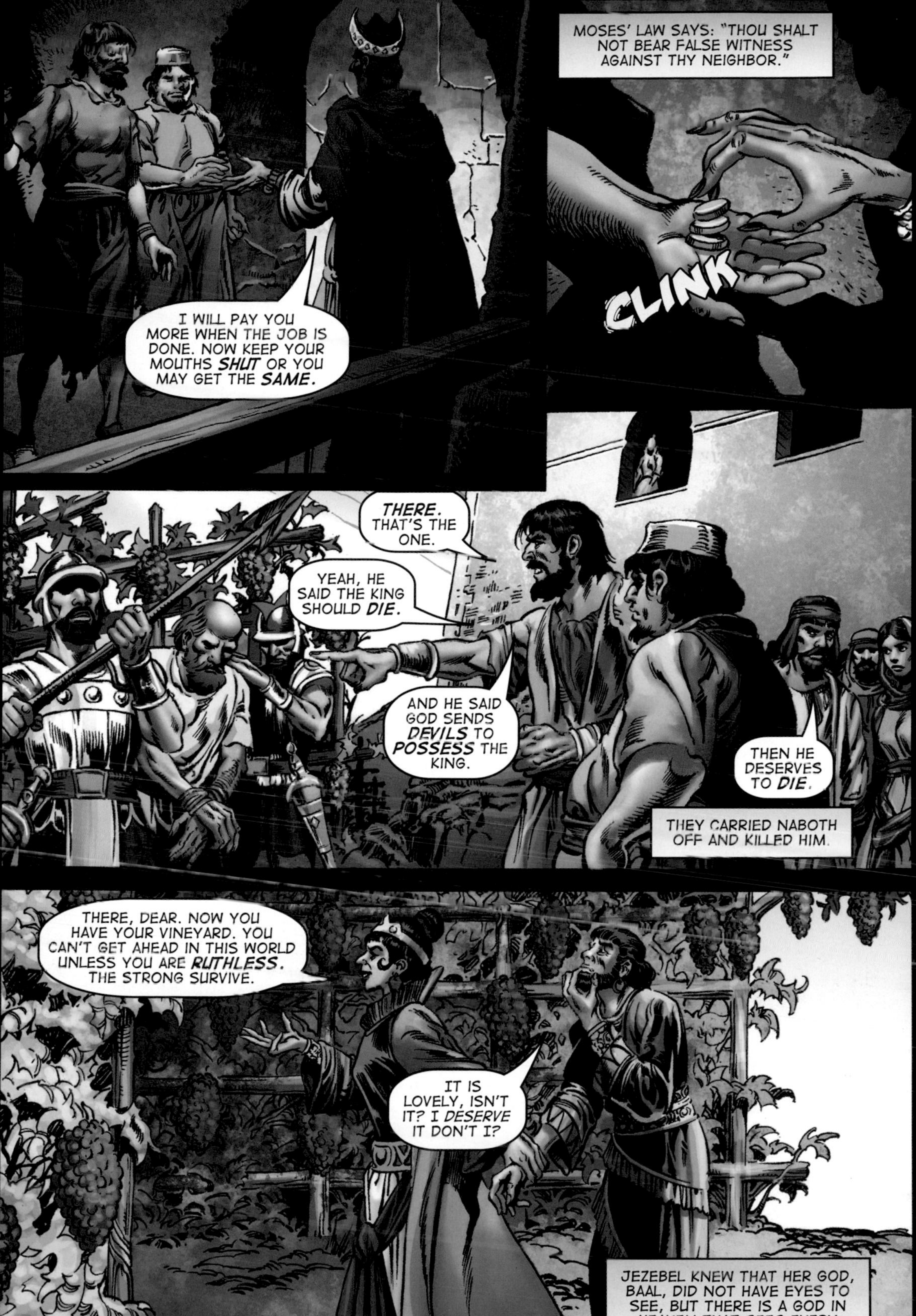
MOSES' LAW SAYS: "THOU SHALT NOT BEAR FALSE WITNESS AGAINST THY NEIGHBOR."
I WILL PAY YOU MORE WHEN THE JOB IS DONE. NOW KEEP YOUR MOUTHS *SHUT* OR YOU MAY GET THE *SAME*.
CLINK
THERE. THAT'S THE ONE.
YEAH, HE SAID THE KING SHOULD *DIE*.
AND HE SAID GOD SENDS *DEVILS* TO *POSSESS* THE KING.
THEN HE DESERVES TO *DIE*.
THEY CARRIED NABOTH OFF AND KILLED HIM.
THERE, DEAR. NOW YOU HAVE YOUR VINEYARD. YOU CAN'T GET AHEAD IN THIS WORLD UNLESS YOU ARE *RUTHLESS*. THE STRONG SURVIVE.
IT IS LOVELY, ISN'T IT? I *DESERVE* IT DON'T I?
JEZEBEL KNEW THAT HER GOD, BAAL, DID NOT HAVE EYES TO SEE, BUT THERE IS A GOD IN HEAVEN THAT SEES EVERY ACT AND NEVER FORGETS.

EXODUS 20:16; 1 KINGS 21:10-16

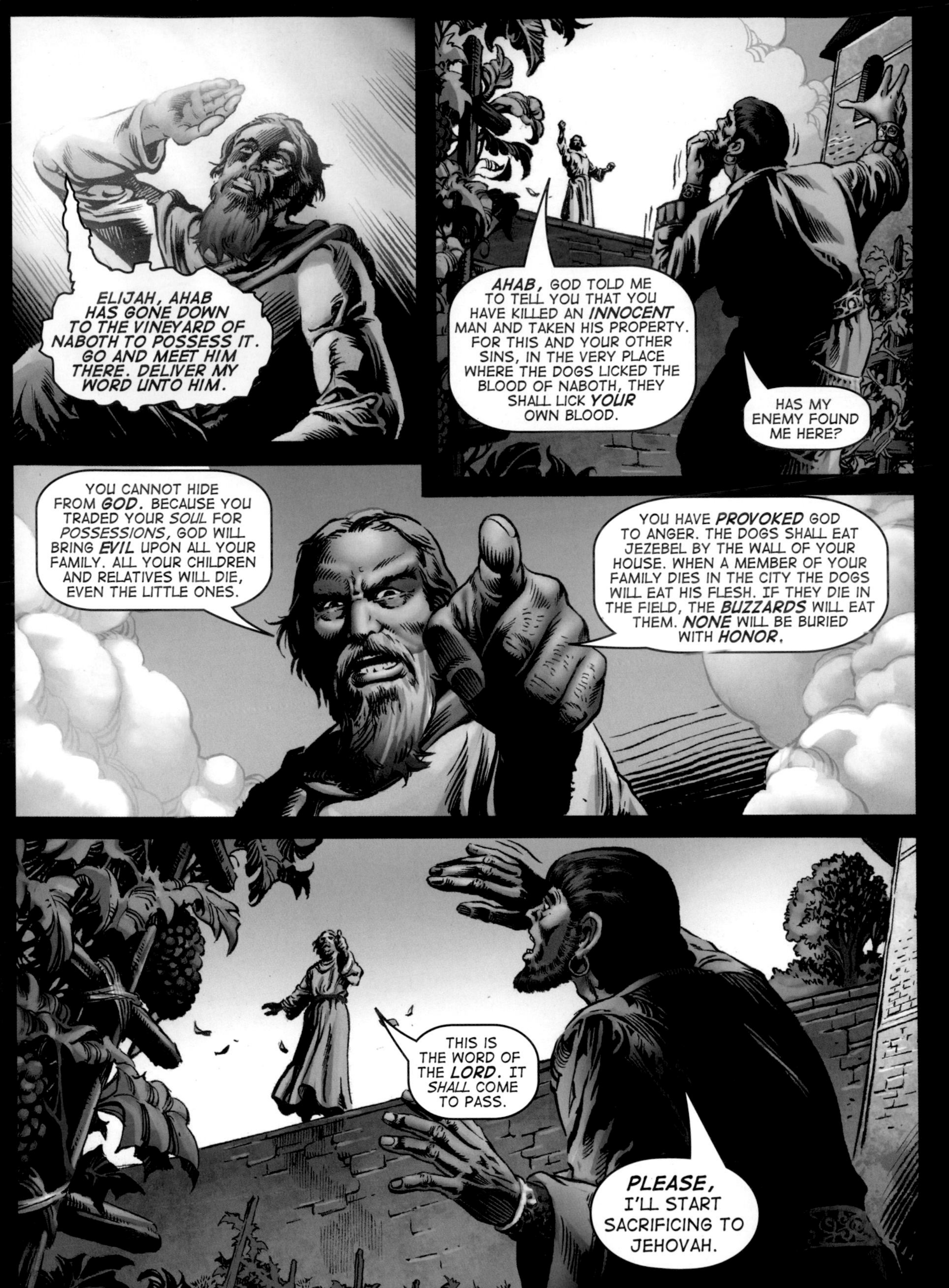
ELIJAH, AHAB HAS GONE DOWN TO THE VINEYARD OF NABOTH TO POSSESS IT. GO AND MEET HIM THERE. DELIVER MY WORD UNTO HIM.
AHAB, GOD TOLD ME TO TELL YOU THAT YOU HAVE KILLED AN INNOCENT MAN AND TAKEN HIS PROPERTY. FOR THIS AND YOUR OTHER SINS, IN THE VERY PLACE WHERE THE DOGS LICKED THE BLOOD OF NABOTH, THEY SHALL LICK YOUR OWN BLOOD.
HAS MY ENEMY FOUND ME HERE?
YOU CANNOT HIDE FROM GOD. BECAUSE YOU TRADED YOUR SOUL FOR POSSESSIONS, GOD WILL BRING EVIL UPON ALL YOUR FAMILY. ALL YOUR CHILDREN AND RELATIVES WILL DIE, EVEN THE LITTLE ONES.
YOU HAVE PROVOKED GOD TO ANGER. THE DOGS SHALL EAT JEZEBEL BY THE WALL OF YOUR HOUSE. WHEN A MEMBER OF YOUR FAMILY DIES IN THE CITY THE DOGS WILL EAT HIS FLESH. IF THEY DIE IN THE FIELD, THE BUZZARDS WILL EAT THEM. NONE WILL BE BURIED WITH HONOR.
THIS IS THE WORD OF THE LORD. IT SHALL COME TO PASS.
PLEASE, I'LL START SACRIFICING TO JEHOVAH.

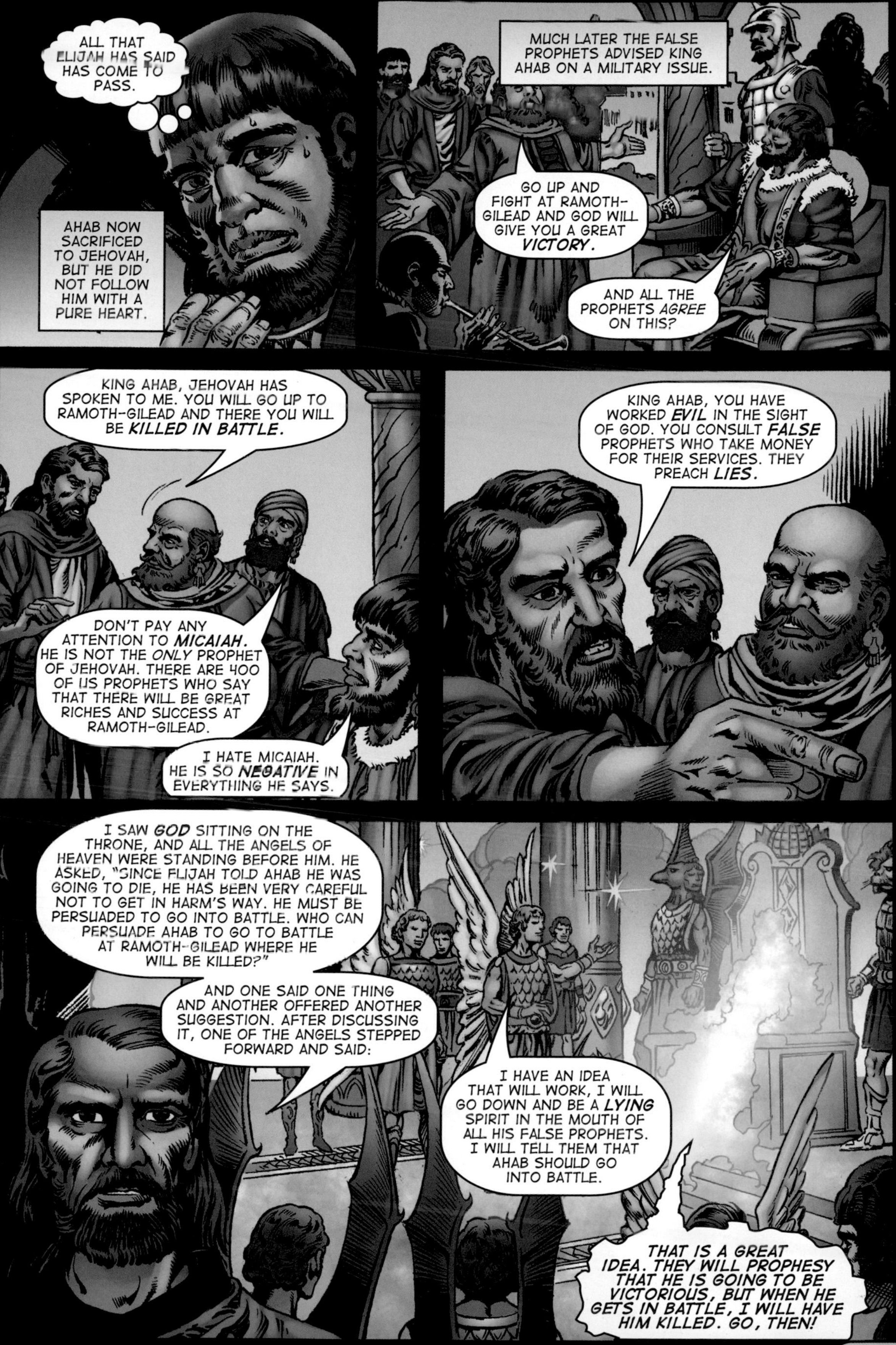
ALL THAT ELIJAH HAS SAID HAS COME TO PASS.
AHAB NOW SACRIFICED TO JEHOVAH, BUT HE DID NOT FOLLOW HIM WITH A PURE HEART.
MUCH LATER THE FALSE PROPHETS ADVISED KING AHAB ON A MILITARY ISSUE.
GO UP AND FIGHT AT RAMOTH-GILEAD AND GOD WILL GIVE YOU A GREAT VICTORY.
AND ALL THE PROPHETS AGREE ON THIS?
KING AHAB, JEHOVAH HAS SPOKEN TO ME. YOU WILL GO UP TO RAMOTH-GILEAD AND THERE YOU WILL BE KILLED IN BATTLE.
DON'T PAY ANY ATTENTION TO MICAIAH. HE IS NOT THE ONLY PROPHET OF JEHOVAH. THERE ARE 400 OF US PROPHETS WHO SAY THAT THERE WILL BE GREAT RICHES AND SUCCESS AT RAMOTH-GILEAD.
I HATE MICAIAH. HE IS SO NEGATIVE IN EVERYTHING HE SAYS.
KING AHAB, YOU HAVE WORKED EVIL IN THE SIGHT OF GOD. YOU CONSULT FALSE PROPHETS WHO TAKE MONEY FOR THEIR SERVICES. THEY PREACH LIES.
I SAW GOD SITTING ON THE THRONE, AND ALL THE ANGELS OF HEAVEN WERE STANDING BEFORE HIM. HE ASKED, "SINCE ELIJAH TOLD AHAB HE WAS GOING TO DIE, HE HAS BEEN VERY CAREFUL NOT TO GET IN HARM'S WAY. HE MUST BE PERSUADED TO GO INTO BATTLE. WHO CAN PERSUADE AHAB TO GO TO BATTLE AT RAMOTH-GILEAD WHERE HE WILL BE KILLED?"
AND ONE SAID ONE THING AND ANOTHER OFFERED ANOTHER SUGGESTION. AFTER DISCUSSING IT, ONE OF THE ANGELS STEPPED FORWARD AND SAID:
I HAVE AN IDEA THAT WILL WORK, I WILL GO DOWN AND BE A LYING SPIRIT IN THE MOUTH OF ALL HIS FALSE PROPHETS. I WILL TELL THEM THAT AHAB SHOULD GO INTO BATTLE.
THAT IS A GREAT IDEA. THEY WILL PROPHESY THAT HE IS GOING TO BE VICTORIOUS, BUT WHEN HE GETS IN BATTLE, I WILL HAVE HIM KILLED. GO, THEN!

1 KINGS 21:27, 22:6-22

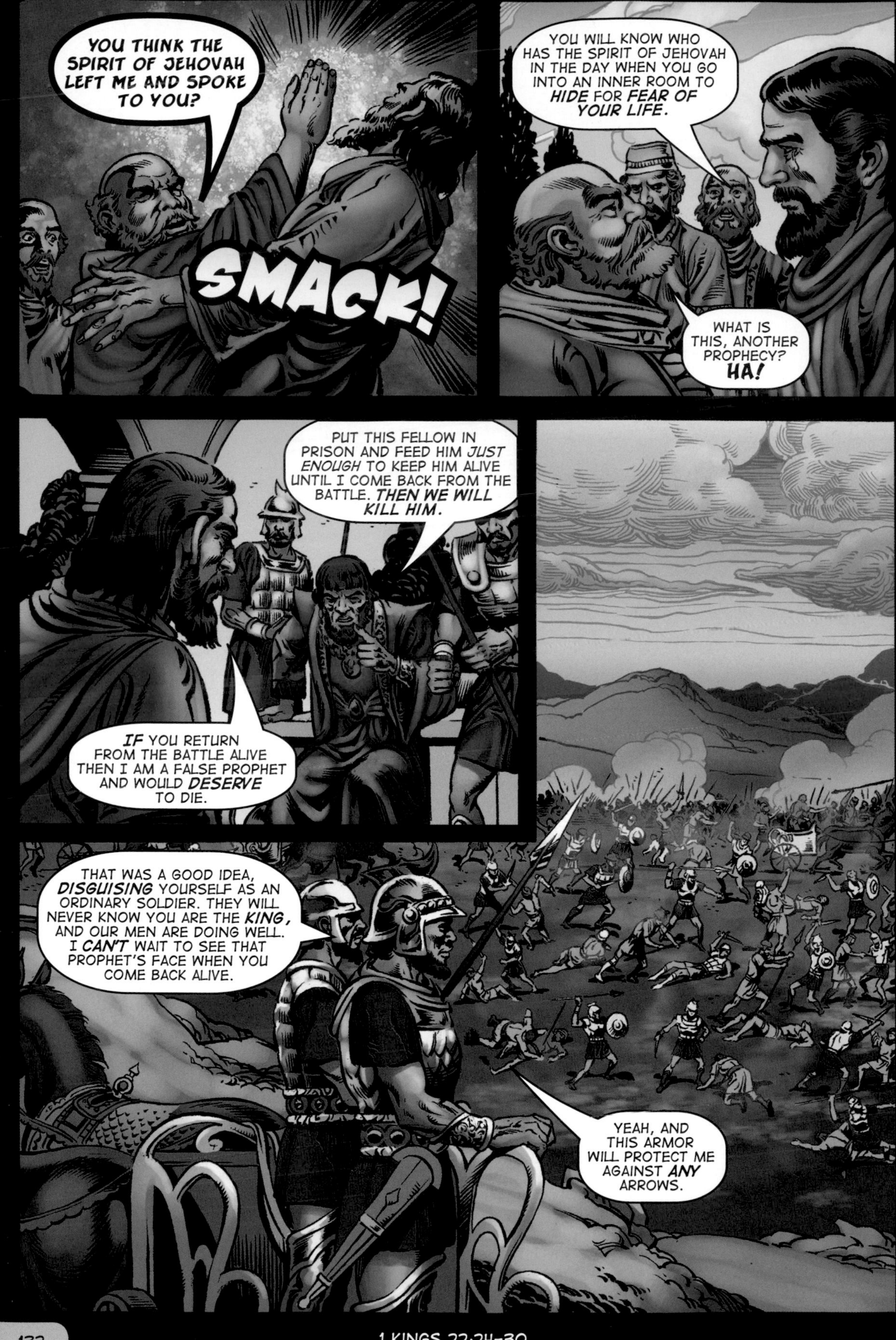
YOU THINK THE SPIRIT OF JEHOVAH LEFT ME AND SPOKE TO YOU?
SMACK!
YOU WILL KNOW WHO HAS THE SPIRIT OF JEHOVAH IN THE DAY WHEN YOU GO INTO AN INNER ROOM TO *HIDE* FOR *FEAR OF YOUR LIFE*.
WHAT IS THIS, ANOTHER PROPHECY? **HA!**
PUT THIS FELLOW IN PRISON AND FEED HIM *JUST ENOUGH* TO KEEP HIM ALIVE UNTIL I COME BACK FROM THE BATTLE. *THEN WE WILL KILL HIM*.
IF YOU RETURN FROM THE BATTLE ALIVE THEN I AM A FALSE PROPHET AND WOULD *DESERVE* TO DIE.
THAT WAS A GOOD IDEA, *DISGUISING* YOURSELF AS AN ORDINARY SOLDIER. THEY WILL NEVER KNOW YOU ARE THE *KING*, AND OUR MEN ARE DOING WELL. I *CAN'T* WAIT TO SEE THAT PROPHET'S FACE WHEN YOU COME BACK ALIVE.
YEAH, AND THIS ARMOR WILL PROTECT ME AGAINST *ANY* ARROWS.

1 KINGS 22:24-30

A SOLDIER SHOT AN ARROW HIGH IN THE AIR, NOT AIMING AT ANYONE IN PARTICULAR, JUST HOPING TO HIT ONE OF HIS ENEMIES.

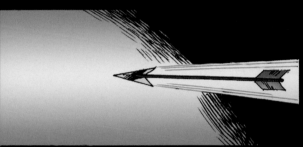

THUD!

UGGGHH!

WHAT?

HURRY, IT IS BLEEDING BADLY.

HANG ON!

I AM AFRAID HE IS DEAD.

THE ARROW FOUND THE *ONE SPOT* THAT WAS NOT PROTECTED BY ARMOR. I GUESS IT WAS JUST HIS TIME TO DIE.

OH GOD, NO!

PUT HIS BODY IN NABOTH'S VINEYARD UNTIL WE HAVE TIME TO DEAL WITH IT PROPERLY.

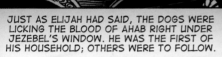

JUST AS ELIJAH HAD SAID, THE DOGS WERE LICKING THE BLOOD OF AHAB RIGHT UNDER JEZEBEL'S WINDOW. HE WAS THE FIRST OF HIS HOUSEHOLD; OTHERS WERE TO FOLLOW.

AFTER WASHING THE BLOOD FROM AHAB'S CHARIOT THE SOLDIER RETURNED TO THE PALACE.

WHERE IS KING AHAB? IS HE CELEBRATING HIS VICTORY?

1 KINGS 22:37-38; 2 KINGS 9:8-10

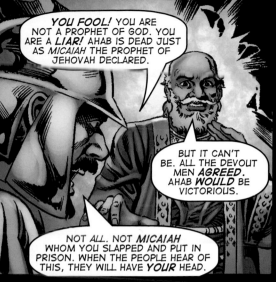

YOU FOOL! YOU ARE NOT A PROPHET OF GOD. YOU ARE A LIAR! AHAB IS DEAD JUST AS MICAIAH THE PROPHET OF JEHOVAH DECLARED.

BUT IT CAN'T BE. ALL THE DEVOUT MEN AGREED. AHAB WOULD BE VICTORIOUS.

NOT ALL. NOT MICAIAH WHOM YOU SLAPPED AND PUT IN PRISON. WHEN THE PEOPLE HEAR OF THIS, THEY WILL HAVE YOUR HEAD.

YOU ARE FREE TO GO. AHAB IS DEAD.

YES I KNOW, AND NO DOUBT THE DOGS HAVE LICKED HIS BLOOD AS GOD SAID. JEZEBEL WILL BE NEXT AND ALL THAT ARE RELATED TO AHAB. GOD HAS SPOKEN.

I MUST HIDE.

OH NO! MICAIAH SAID I WOULD KNOW WHO HAD THE SPIRIT OF GOD ON THE DAY I HID IN A SMALL ROOM INSIDE OF A ROOM.

AHAB'S SONS WOULD REIGN IN HIS PLACE, AND TWELVE YEARS WOULD PASS WITH JEZEBEL STILL LIVING AS QUEEN. ISRAEL WOULD CONTINUE TO WORSHIP FALSE GODS AND BREAK THE COMMANDMENTS OF GOD.

12 YEARS LATER.

I MUST PAINT MY FACE, SO I WILL BE ATTRACTIVE TO GENERAL JEHU WHEN HE RETURNS FROM BATTLE.

GOD SPOKE AGAINST THE HOUSE OF AHAB, SAYING, "THE TIME HAS COME. ALL OF AHAB'S FAMILY WILL PERISH, EVEN THE LITTLE CHILDREN. NONE WILL BE LEFT ALIVE. JEZEBEL WILL BE EATEN BY THE DOGS, AND THERE WILL BE NO ONE TO MOURN HER OR BURY HER."

2 KINGS 9:30

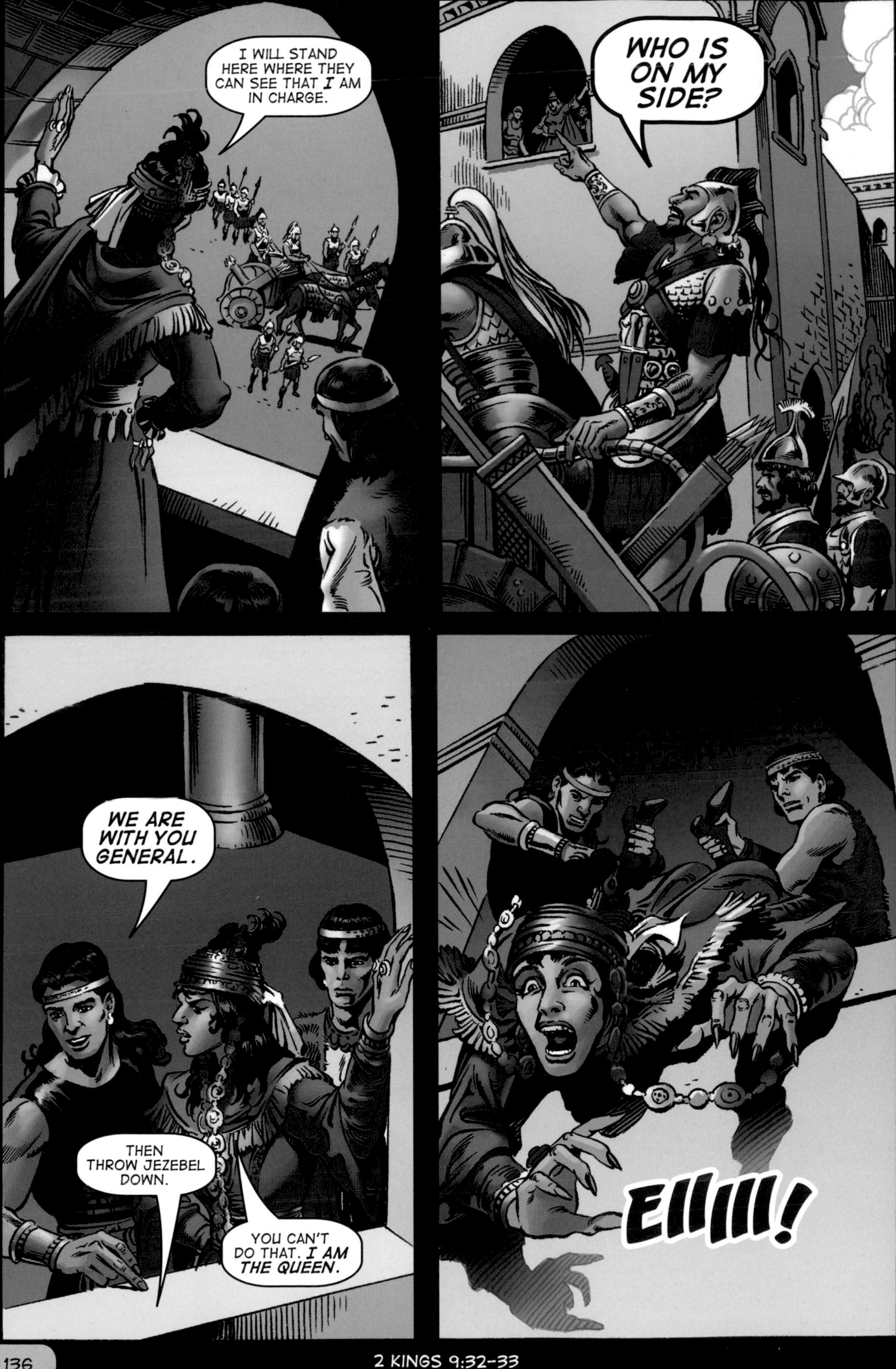
I WILL STAND HERE WHERE THEY CAN SEE THAT *I* AM IN CHARGE.
WHO IS ON MY SIDE?
WE ARE WITH YOU GENERAL.
THEN THROW JEZEBEL DOWN.
YOU CAN'T DO THAT. *I AM THE QUEEN.*
EIIIII!

2 KINGS 9:32-33

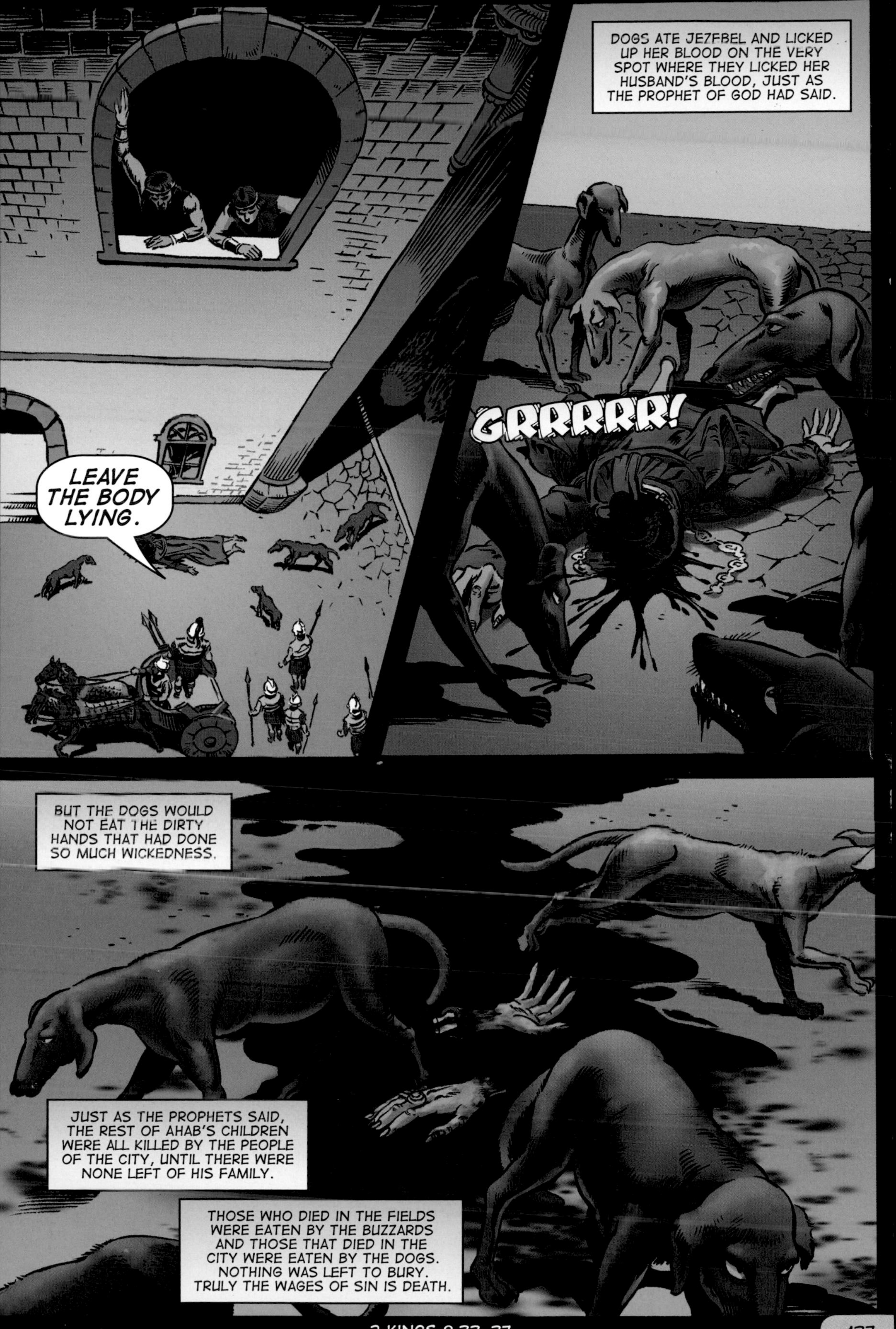
DOGS ATE JEZEBEL AND LICKED UP HER BLOOD ON THE VERY SPOT WHERE THEY LICKED HER HUSBAND'S BLOOD, JUST AS THE PROPHET OF GOD HAD SAID.
LEAVE THE BODY LYING.
GRRRRR!
BUT THE DOGS WOULD NOT EAT THE DIRTY HANDS THAT HAD DONE SO MUCH WICKEDNESS.
JUST AS THE PROPHETS SAID, THE REST OF AHAB'S CHILDREN WERE ALL KILLED BY THE PEOPLE OF THE CITY, UNTIL THERE WERE NONE LEFT OF HIS FAMILY.
THOSE WHO DIED IN THE FIELDS WERE EATEN BY THE BUZZARDS AND THOSE THAT DIED IN THE CITY WERE EATEN BY THE DOGS. NOTHING WAS LEFT TO BURY. TRULY THE WAGES OF SIN IS DEATH.

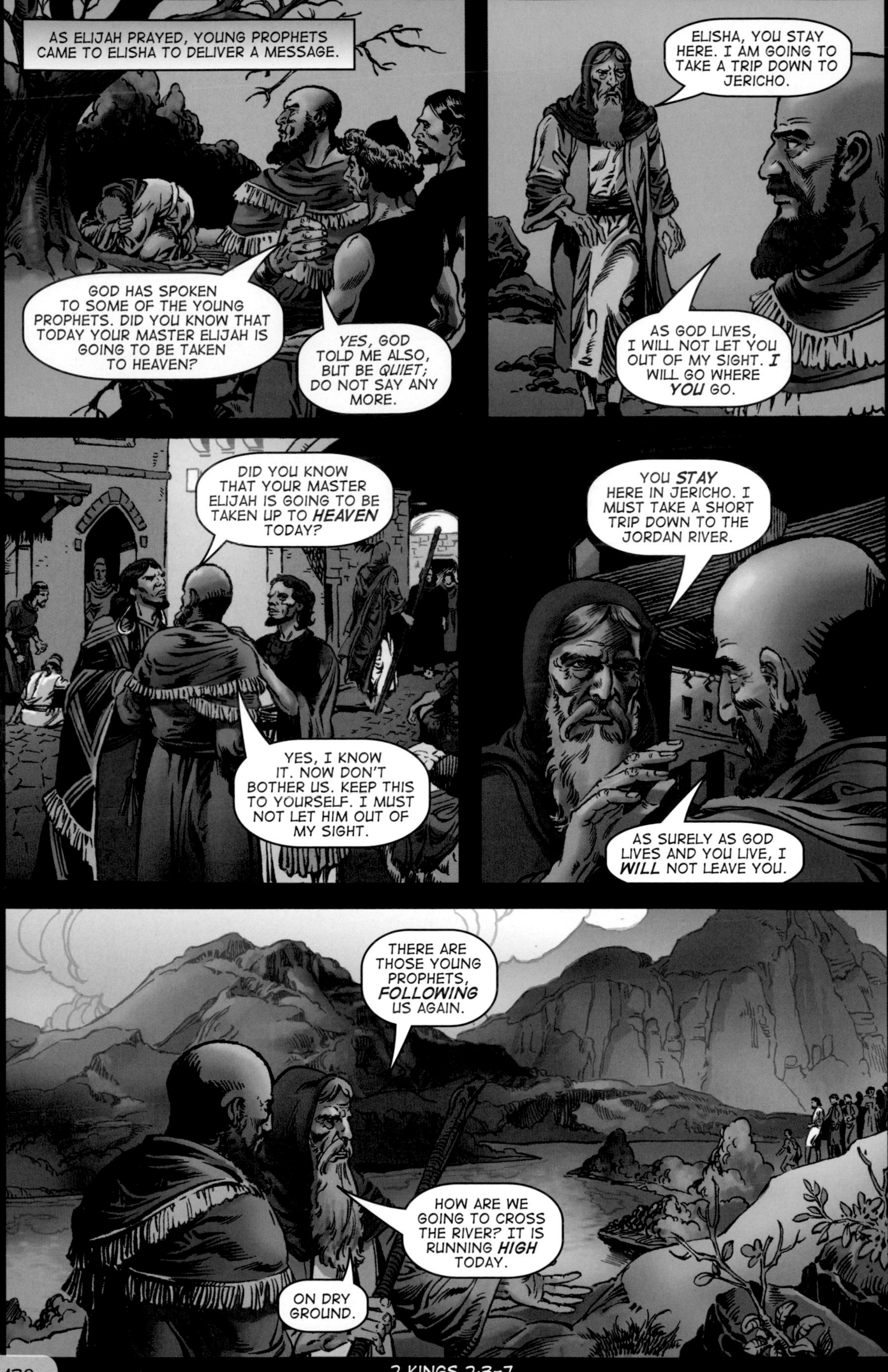
AS ELIJAH PRAYED, YOUNG PROPHETS CAME TO ELISHA TO DELIVER A MESSAGE.
GOD HAS SPOKEN TO SOME OF THE YOUNG PROPHETS. DID YOU KNOW THAT TODAY YOUR MASTER ELIJAH IS GOING TO BE TAKEN TO HEAVEN?
YES, GOD TOLD ME ALSO, BUT BE *QUIET*; DO NOT SAY ANY MORE.
ELISHA, YOU STAY HERE. I AM GOING TO TAKE A TRIP DOWN TO JERICHO.
AS GOD LIVES, I WILL NOT LET YOU OUT OF MY SIGHT. ***I*** WILL GO WHERE ***YOU*** GO.
DID YOU KNOW THAT YOUR MASTER ELIJAH IS GOING TO BE TAKEN UP TO ***HEAVEN*** TODAY?
YES, I KNOW IT. NOW DON'T BOTHER US. KEEP THIS TO YOURSELF. I MUST NOT LET HIM OUT OF MY SIGHT.
YOU ***STAY*** HERE IN JERICHO. I MUST TAKE A SHORT TRIP DOWN TO THE JORDAN RIVER.
AS SURELY AS GOD LIVES AND YOU LIVE, I ***WILL*** NOT LEAVE YOU.
THERE ARE THOSE YOUNG PROPHETS, ***FOLLOWING*** US AGAIN.
HOW ARE WE GOING TO CROSS THE RIVER? IT IS RUNNING ***HIGH*** TODAY.
ON DRY GROUND.

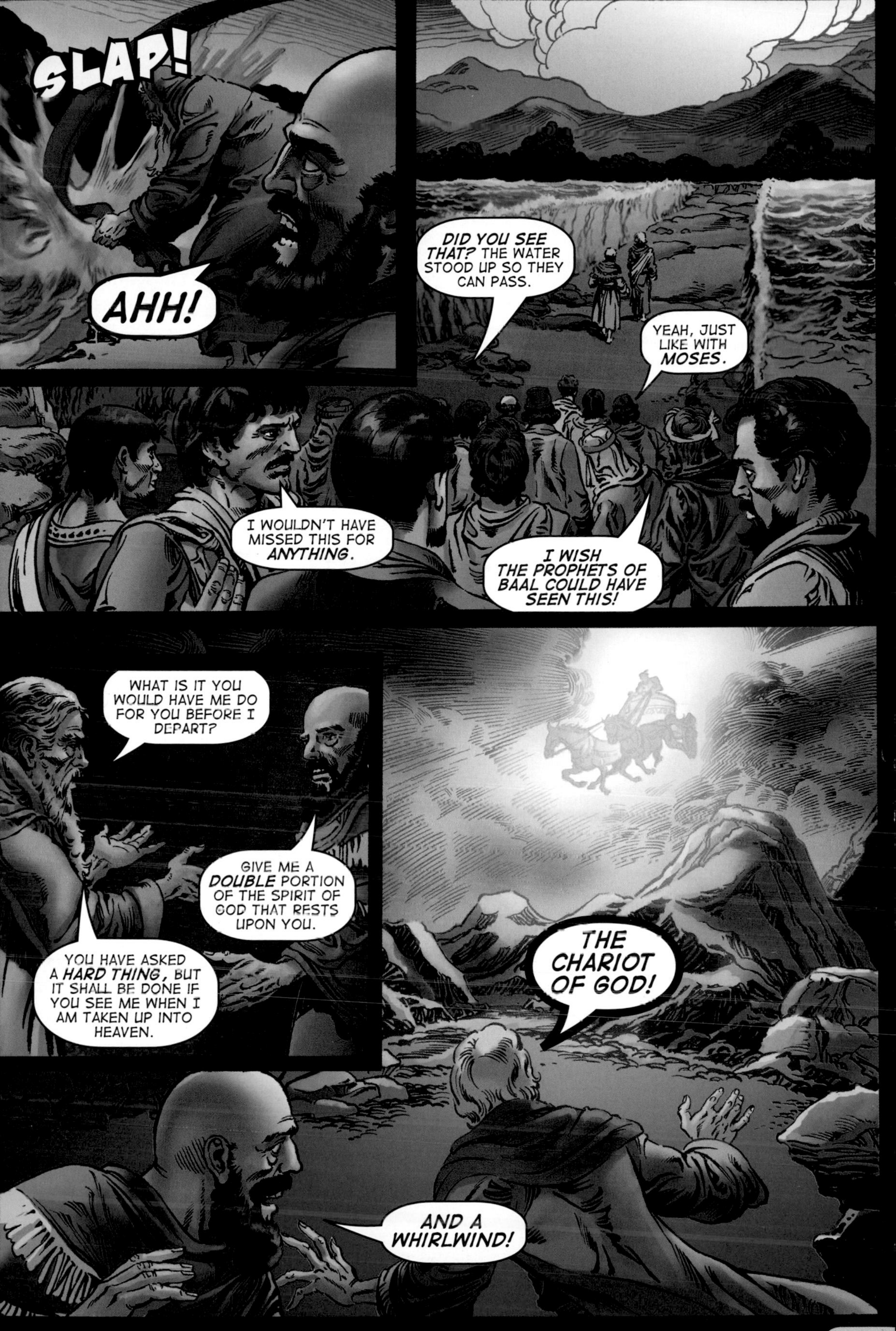

SLAP!
AHH!
DID YOU SEE THAT? THE WATER STOOD UP SO THEY CAN PASS.
YEAH, JUST LIKE WITH MOSES.
I WOULDN'T HAVE MISSED THIS FOR ANYTHING.
I WISH THE PROPHETS OF BAAL COULD HAVE SEEN THIS!
WHAT IS IT YOU WOULD HAVE ME DO FOR YOU BEFORE I DEPART?
GIVE ME A DOUBLE PORTION OF THE SPIRIT OF GOD THAT RESTS UPON YOU.
YOU HAVE ASKED A HARD THING, BUT IT SHALL BE DONE IF YOU SEE ME WHEN I AM TAKEN UP INTO HEAVEN.
THE CHARIOT OF GOD!
AND A WHIRLWIND!

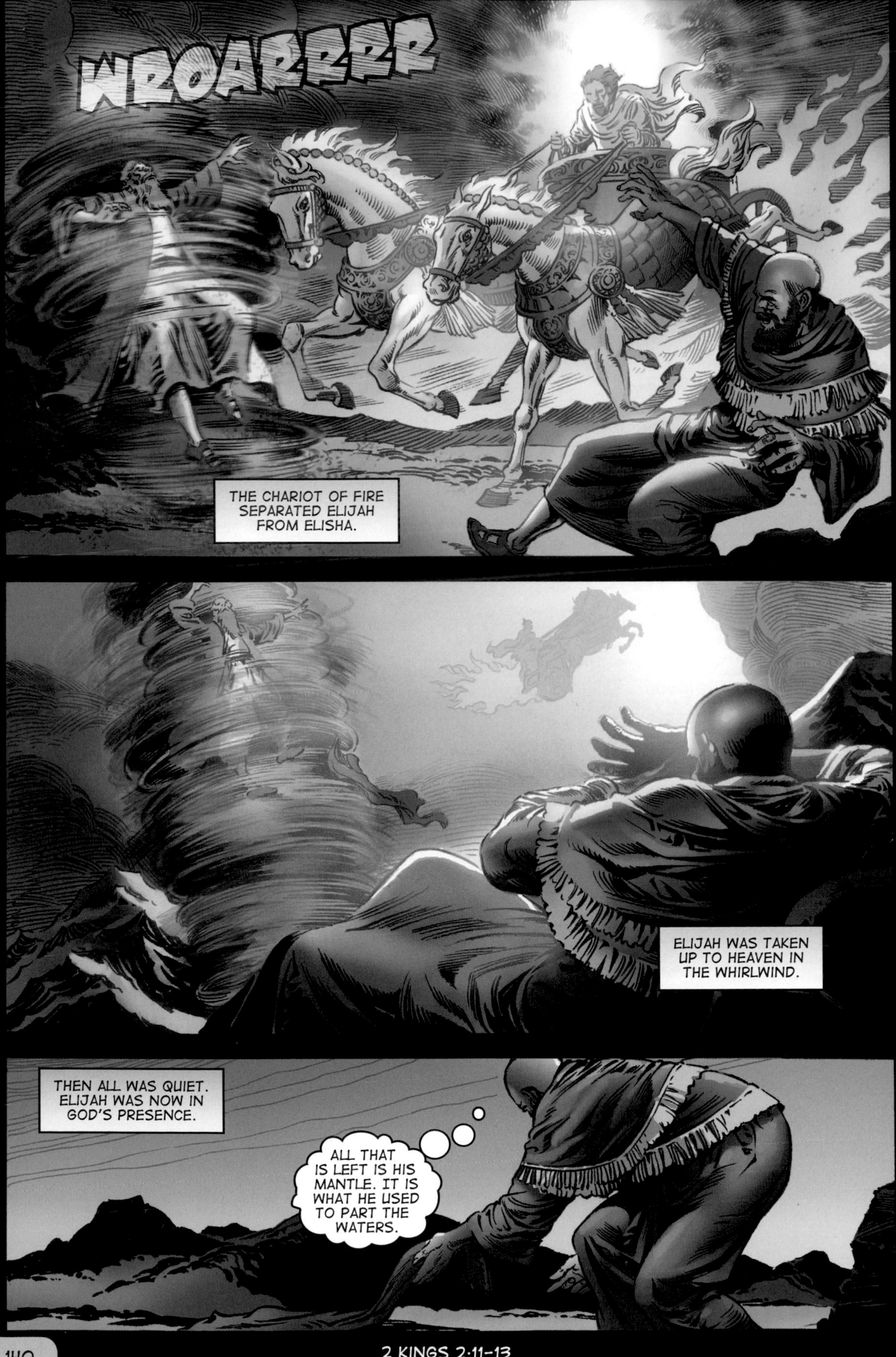
WROARRRR
THE CHARIOT OF FIRE SEPARATED ELIJAH FROM ELISHA.
ELIJAH WAS TAKEN UP TO HEAVEN IN THE WHIRLWIND.
THEN ALL WAS QUIET. ELIJAH WAS NOW IN GOD'S PRESENCE.
ALL THAT IS LEFT IS HIS MANTLE. IT IS WHAT HE USED TO PART THE WATERS.

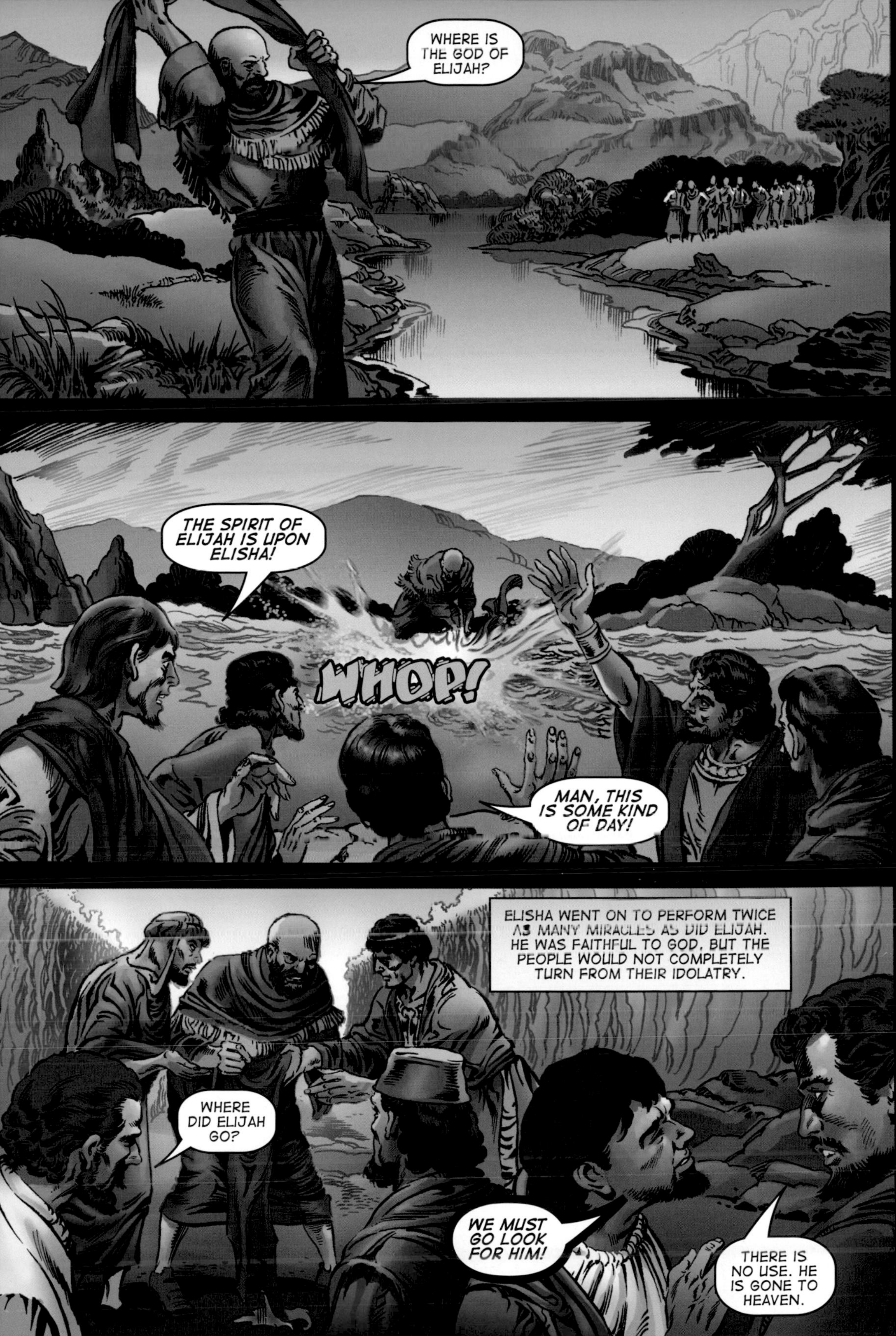
WHERE IS THE GOD OF ELIJAH?
THE SPIRIT OF ELIJAH IS UPON ELISHA!
WHOP!
MAN, THIS IS SOME KIND OF DAY!
ELISHA WENT ON TO PERFORM TWICE AS MANY MIRACLES AS DID ELIJAH. HE WAS FAITHFUL TO GOD, BUT THE PEOPLE WOULD NOT COMPLETELY TURN FROM THEIR IDOLATRY.
WHERE DID ELIJAH GO?
WE MUST GO LOOK FOR HIM!
THERE IS NO USE. HE IS GONE TO HEAVEN.

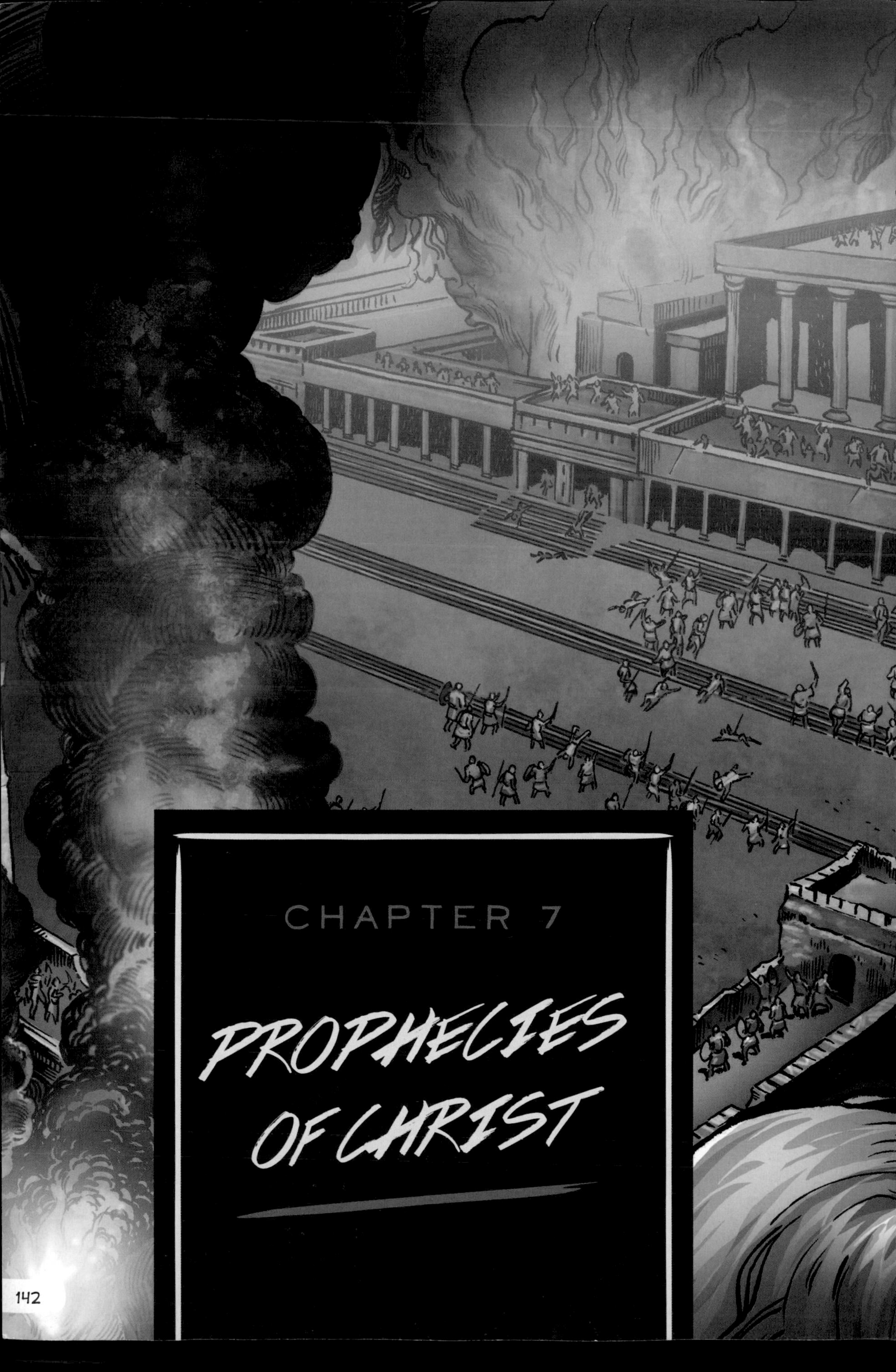

CHAPTER 7

PROPHECIES OF CHRIST

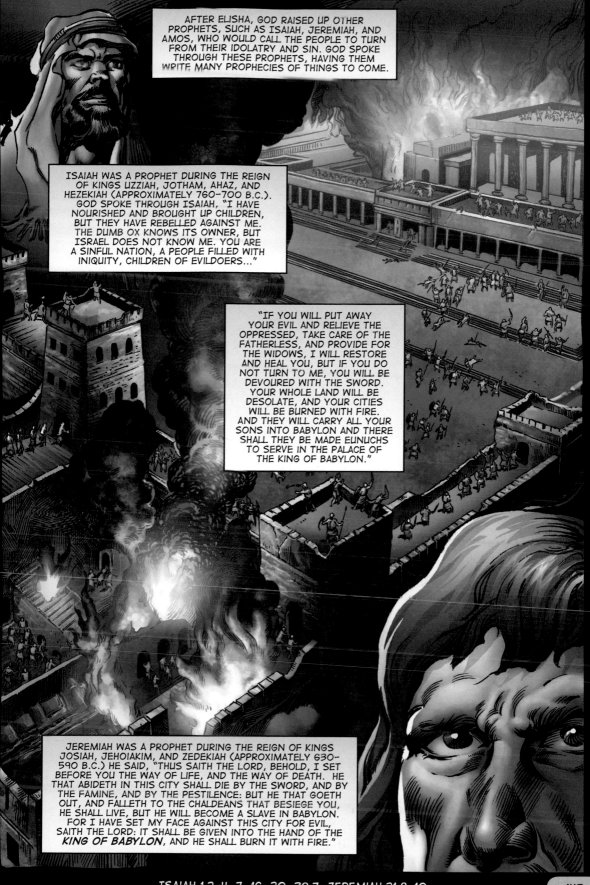

AFTER ELISHA, GOD RAISED UP OTHER PROPHETS, SUCH AS ISAIAH, JEREMIAH, AND AMOS, WHO WOULD CALL THE PEOPLE TO TURN FROM THEIR IDOLATRY AND SIN. GOD SPOKE THROUGH THESE PROPHETS, HAVING THEM WRITE MANY PROPHECIES OF THINGS TO COME.

ISAIAH WAS A PROPHET DURING THE REIGN OF KINGS UZZIAH, JOTHAM, AHAZ, AND HEZEKIAH (APPROXIMATELY 760-700 B.C.). GOD SPOKE THROUGH ISAIAH, "I HAVE NOURISHED AND BROUGHT UP CHILDREN, BUT THEY HAVE REBELLED AGAINST ME. THE DUMB OX KNOWS ITS OWNER, BUT ISRAEL DOES NOT KNOW ME. YOU ARE A SINFUL NATION, A PEOPLE FILLED WITH INIQUITY, CHILDREN OF EVILDOERS..."

"IF YOU WILL PUT AWAY YOUR EVIL AND RELIEVE THE OPPRESSED, TAKE CARE OF THE FATHERLESS, AND PROVIDE FOR THE WIDOWS, I WILL RESTORE AND HEAL YOU, BUT IF YOU DO NOT TURN TO ME, YOU WILL BE DEVOURED WITH THE SWORD. YOUR WHOLE LAND WILL BE DESOLATE, AND YOUR CITIES WILL BE BURNED WITH FIRE. AND THEY WILL CARRY ALL YOUR SONS INTO BABYLON AND THERE SHALL THEY BE MADE EUNUCHS TO SERVE IN THE PALACE OF THE KING OF BABYLON."

JEREMIAH WAS A PROPHET DURING THE REIGN OF KINGS JOSIAH, JEHOIAKIM, AND ZEDEKIAH (APPROXIMATELY 630-590 B.C.) HE SAID, "THUS SAITH THE LORD, BEHOLD, I SET BEFORE YOU THE WAY OF LIFE, AND THE WAY OF DEATH. HE THAT ABIDETH IN THIS CITY SHALL DIE BY THE SWORD, AND BY THE FAMINE, AND BY THE PESTILENCE: BUT HE THAT GOETH OUT, AND FALLETH TO THE CHALDEANS THAT BESIEGE YOU, HE SHALL LIVE, BUT HE WILL BECOME A SLAVE IN BABYLON. FOR I HAVE SET MY FACE AGAINST THIS CITY FOR EVIL, SAITH THE LORD: IT SHALL BE GIVEN INTO THE HAND OF THE KING OF BABYLON, AND HE SHALL BURN IT WITH FIRE."

ISAIAH 1:2-4, 7, 16, 20, 39:7; JEREMIAH 21:8-10

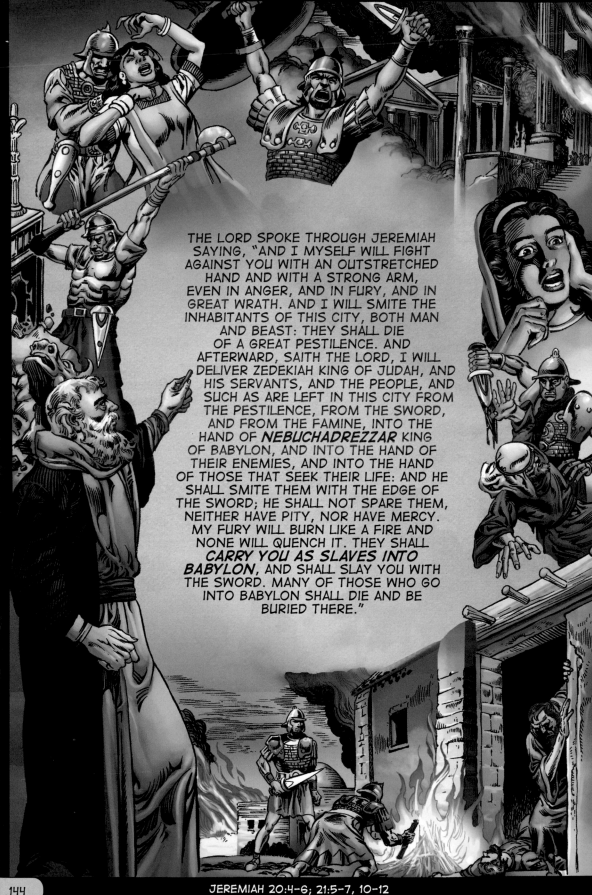

THE LORD SPOKE THROUGH JEREMIAH SAYING, "AND I MYSELF WILL FIGHT AGAINST YOU WITH AN OUTSTRETCHED HAND AND WITH A STRONG ARM, EVEN IN ANGER, AND IN FURY, AND IN GREAT WRATH. AND I WILL SMITE THE INHABITANTS OF THIS CITY, BOTH MAN AND BEAST: THEY SHALL DIE OF A GREAT PESTILENCE. AND AFTERWARD, SAITH THE LORD, I WILL DELIVER ZEDEKIAH KING OF JUDAH, AND HIS SERVANTS, AND THE PEOPLE, AND SUCH AS ARE LEFT IN THIS CITY FROM THE PESTILENCE, FROM THE SWORD, AND FROM THE FAMINE, INTO THE HAND OF *NEBUCHADREZZAR* KING OF BABYLON, AND INTO THE HAND OF THEIR ENEMIES, AND INTO THE HAND OF THOSE THAT SEEK THEIR LIFE: AND HE SHALL SMITE THEM WITH THE EDGE OF THE SWORD; HE SHALL NOT SPARE THEM, NEITHER HAVE PITY, NOR HAVE MERCY. MY FURY WILL BURN LIKE A FIRE AND NONE WILL QUENCH IT. THEY SHALL *CARRY YOU AS SLAVES INTO BABYLON*, AND SHALL SLAY YOU WITH THE SWORD. MANY OF THOSE WHO GO INTO BABYLON SHALL DIE AND BE BURIED THERE."

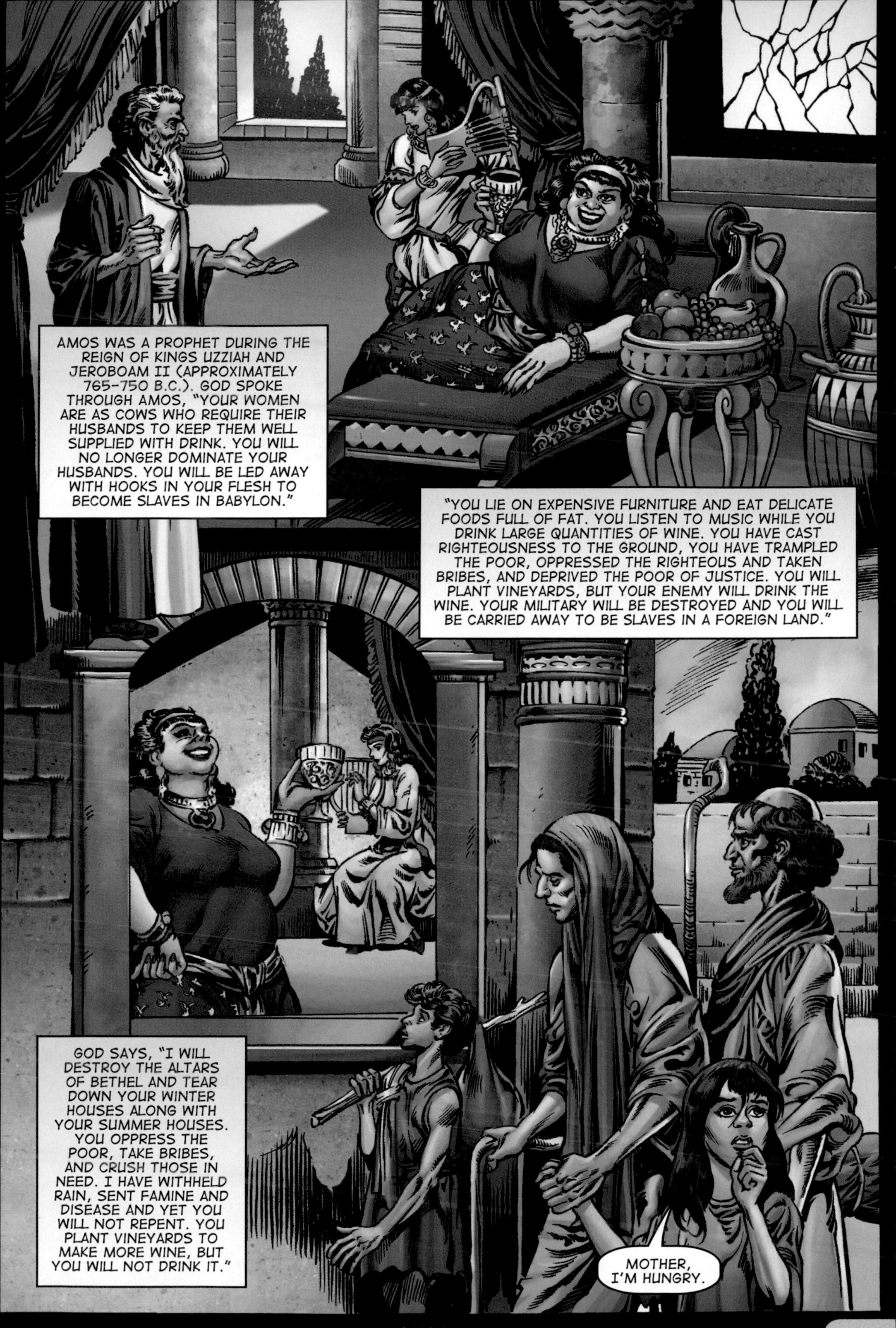
AMOS WAS A PROPHET DURING THE REIGN OF KINGS UZZIAH AND JEROBOAM II (APPROXIMATELY 765-750 B.C.). GOD SPOKE THROUGH AMOS, "YOUR WOMEN ARE AS COWS WHO REQUIRE THEIR HUSBANDS TO KEEP THEM WELL SUPPLIED WITH DRINK. YOU WILL NO LONGER DOMINATE YOUR HUSBANDS. YOU WILL BE LED AWAY WITH HOOKS IN YOUR FLESH TO BECOME SLAVES IN BABYLON."
"YOU LIE ON EXPENSIVE FURNITURE AND EAT DELICATE FOODS FULL OF FAT. YOU LISTEN TO MUSIC WHILE YOU DRINK LARGE QUANTITIES OF WINE. YOU HAVE CAST RIGHTEOUSNESS TO THE GROUND, YOU HAVE TRAMPLED THE POOR, OPPRESSED THE RIGHTEOUS AND TAKEN BRIBES, AND DEPRIVED THE POOR OF JUSTICE. YOU WILL PLANT VINEYARDS, BUT YOUR ENEMY WILL DRINK THE WINE. YOUR MILITARY WILL BE DESTROYED AND YOU WILL BE CARRIED AWAY TO BE SLAVES IN A FOREIGN LAND."
GOD SAYS, "I WILL DESTROY THE ALTARS OF BETHEL AND TEAR DOWN YOUR WINTER HOUSES ALONG WITH YOUR SUMMER HOUSES. YOU OPPRESS THE POOR, TAKE BRIBES, AND CRUSH THOSE IN NEED. I HAVE WITHHELD RAIN, SENT FAMINE AND DISEASE AND YET YOU WILL NOT REPENT. YOU PLANT VINEYARDS TO MAKE MORE WINE, BUT YOU WILL NOT DRINK IT."
MOTHER, I'M HUNGRY.

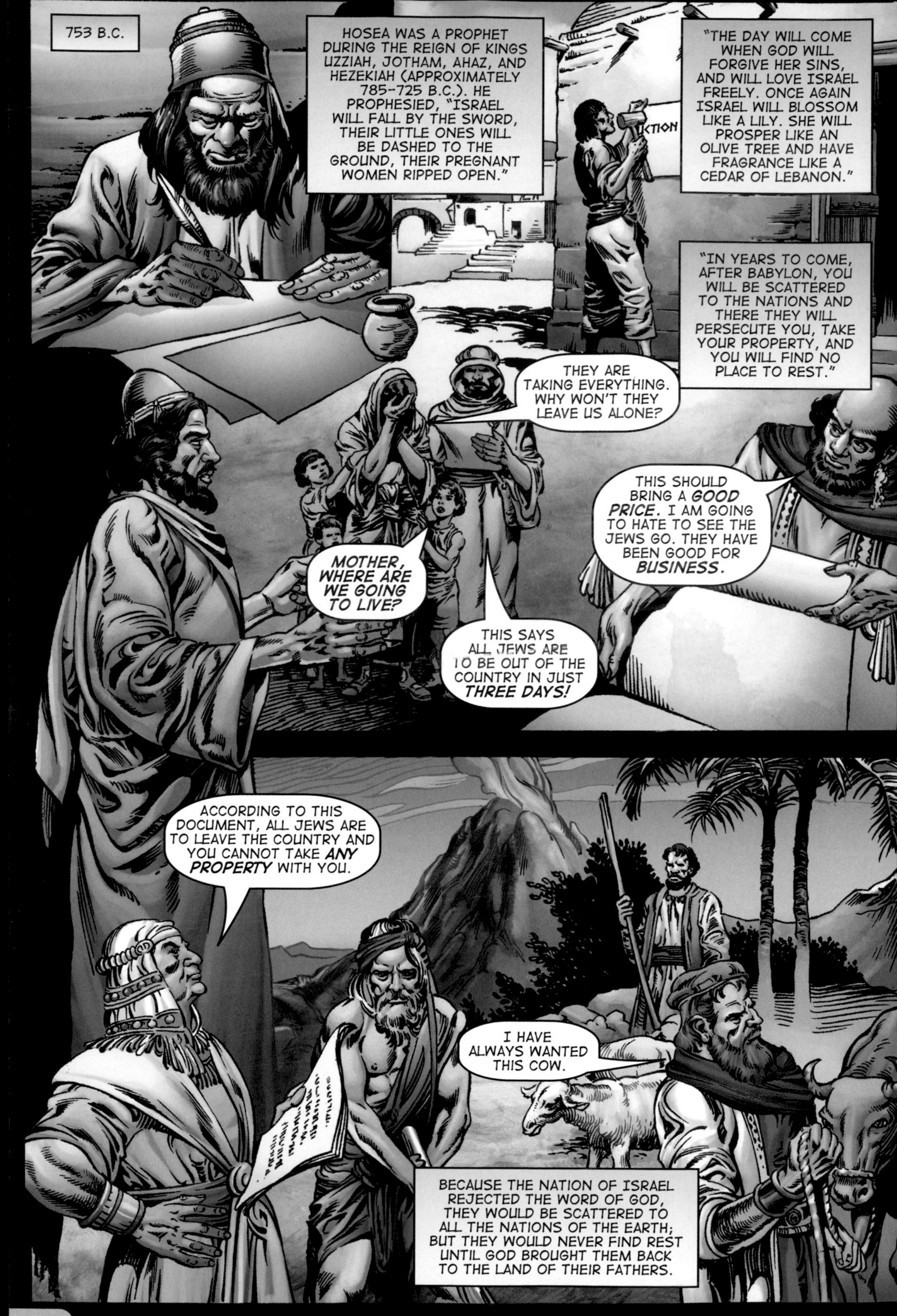
753 B.C.
HOSEA WAS A PROPHET DURING THE REIGN OF KINGS UZZIAH, JOTHAM, AHAZ, AND HEZEKIAH (APPROXIMATELY 785-725 B.C.). HE PROPHESIED, "ISRAEL WILL FALL BY THE SWORD, THEIR LITTLE ONES WILL BE DASHED TO THE GROUND, THEIR PREGNANT WOMEN RIPPED OPEN."
"THE DAY WILL COME WHEN GOD WILL FORGIVE HER SINS, AND WILL LOVE ISRAEL FREELY. ONCE AGAIN ISRAEL WILL BLOSSOM LIKE A LILY. SHE WILL PROSPER LIKE AN OLIVE TREE AND HAVE FRAGRANCE LIKE A CEDAR OF LEBANON."
"IN YEARS TO COME, AFTER BABYLON, YOU WILL BE SCATTERED TO THE NATIONS AND THERE THEY WILL PERSECUTE YOU, TAKE YOUR PROPERTY, AND YOU WILL FIND NO PLACE TO REST."
THEY ARE TAKING EVERYTHING. WHY WON'T THEY LEAVE US ALONE?
MOTHER, WHERE ARE WE GOING TO LIVE?
THIS SHOULD BRING A GOOD PRICE. I AM GOING TO HATE TO SEE THE JEWS GO. THEY HAVE BEEN GOOD FOR BUSINESS.
THIS SAYS ALL JEWS ARE TO BE OUT OF THE COUNTRY IN JUST THREE DAYS!
ACCORDING TO THIS DOCUMENT, ALL JEWS ARE TO LEAVE THE COUNTRY AND YOU CANNOT TAKE ANY PROPERTY WITH YOU.
I HAVE ALWAYS WANTED THIS COW.
BECAUSE THE NATION OF ISRAEL REJECTED THE WORD OF GOD, THEY WOULD BE SCATTERED TO ALL THE NATIONS OF THE EARTH; BUT THEY WOULD NEVER FIND REST UNTIL GOD BROUGHT THEM BACK TO THE LAND OF THEIR FATHERS.

ISAIAH 10:21, CHAPTER 35, 51:11, JEREMIAH 30:11; EZEKIEL 17:21; JOEL 3:2; HOSEA 13:16, 14:1-6

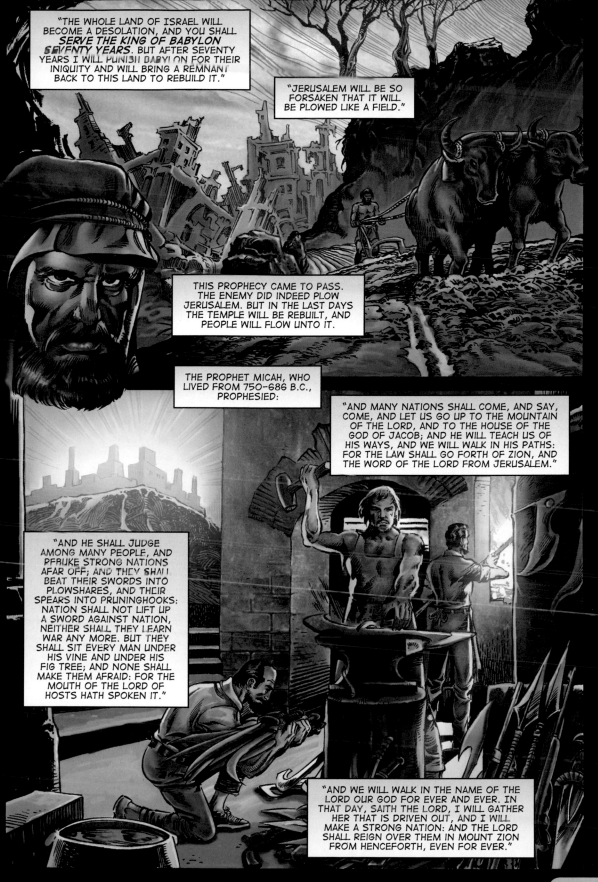

"THE WHOLE LAND OF ISRAEL WILL BECOME A DESOLATION, AND YOU SHALL *SERVE THE KING OF BABYLON SEVENTY YEARS*. BUT AFTER SEVENTY YEARS I WILL PUNISH BABYLON FOR THEIR INIQUITY AND WILL BRING A REMNANT BACK TO THIS LAND TO REBUILD IT."

"JERUSALEM WILL BE SO FORSAKEN THAT IT WILL BE PLOWED LIKE A FIELD."

THIS PROPHECY CAME TO PASS. THE ENEMY DID INDEED PLOW JERUSALEM. BUT IN THE LAST DAYS THE TEMPLE WILL BE REBUILT, AND PEOPLE WILL FLOW UNTO IT.

THE PROPHET MICAH, WHO LIVED FROM 750-686 B.C., PROPHESIED:

"AND MANY NATIONS SHALL COME, AND SAY, COME, AND LET US GO UP TO THE MOUNTAIN OF THE LORD, AND TO THE HOUSE OF THE GOD OF JACOB; AND HE WILL TEACH US OF HIS WAYS, AND WE WILL WALK IN HIS PATHS: FOR THE LAW SHALL GO FORTH OF ZION, AND THE WORD OF THE LORD FROM JERUSALEM."

"AND HE SHALL JUDGE AMONG MANY PEOPLE, AND REBUKE STRONG NATIONS AFAR OFF; AND THEY SHALL BEAT THEIR SWORDS INTO PLOWSHARES, AND THEIR SPEARS INTO PRUNINGHOOKS: NATION SHALL NOT LIFT UP A SWORD AGAINST NATION, NEITHER SHALL THEY LEARN WAR ANY MORE. BUT THEY SHALL SIT EVERY MAN UNDER HIS VINE AND UNDER HIS FIG TREE; AND NONE SHALL MAKE THEM AFRAID: FOR THE MOUTH OF THE LORD OF HOSTS HATH SPOKEN IT."

"AND WE WILL WALK IN THE NAME OF THE LORD OUR GOD FOR EVER AND EVER. IN THAT DAY, SAITH THE LORD, I WILL GATHER HER THAT IS DRIVEN OUT, AND I WILL MAKE A STRONG NATION: AND THE LORD SHALL REIGN OVER THEM IN MOUNT ZION FROM HENCEFORTH, EVEN FOR EVER."

JEREMIAH 25:11-12; MICAH 3:12, 4:1-7

147

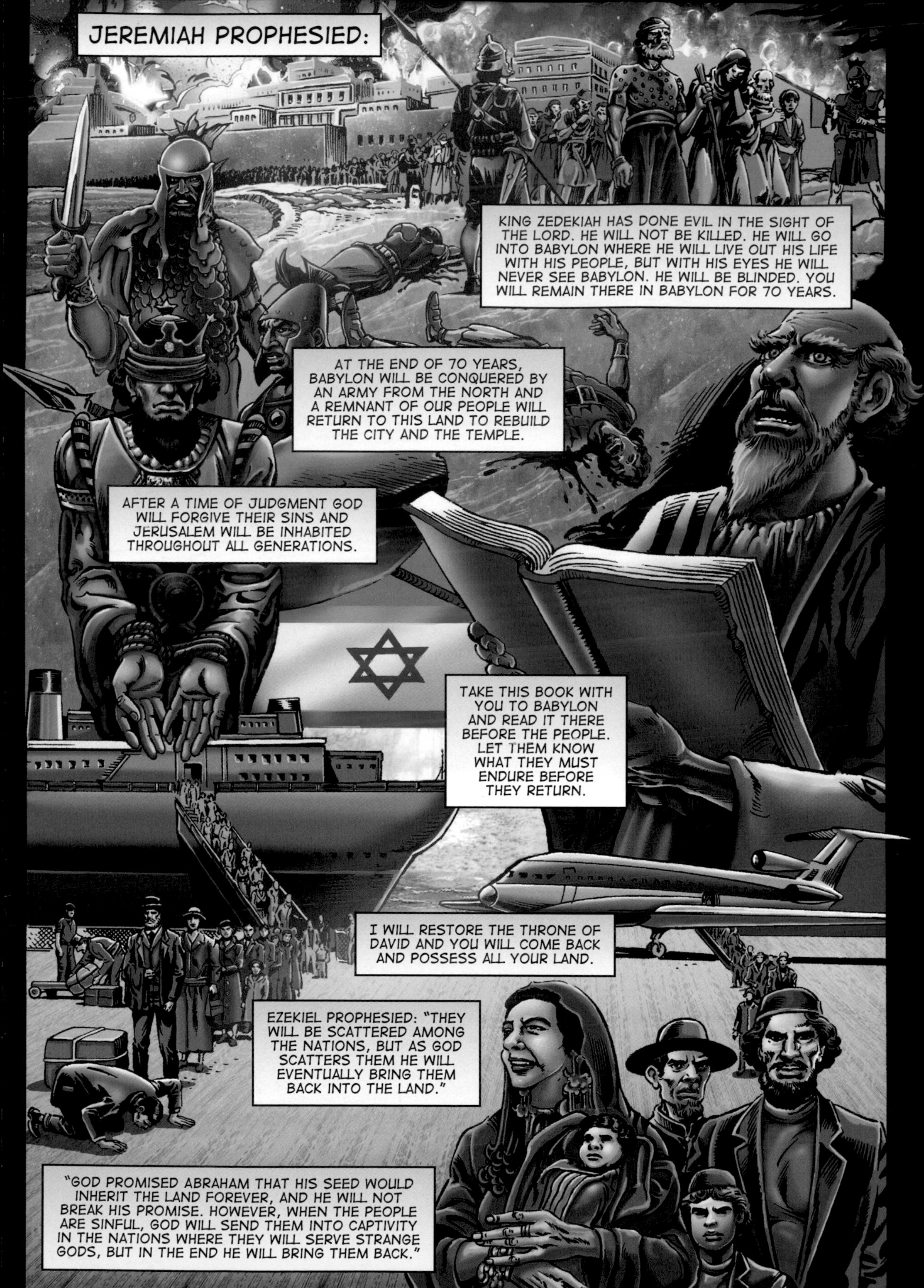
JEREMIAH PROPHESIED:
KING ZEDEKIAH HAS DONE EVIL IN THE SIGHT OF THE LORD. HE WILL NOT BE KILLED. HE WILL GO INTO BABYLON WHERE HE WILL LIVE OUT HIS LIFE WITH HIS PEOPLE, BUT WITH HIS EYES HE WILL NEVER SEE BABYLON. HE WILL BE BLINDED. YOU WILL REMAIN THERE IN BABYLON FOR 70 YEARS.
AT THE END OF 70 YEARS, BABYLON WILL BE CONQUERED BY AN ARMY FROM THE NORTH AND A REMNANT OF OUR PEOPLE WILL RETURN TO THIS LAND TO REBUILD THE CITY AND THE TEMPLE.
AFTER A TIME OF JUDGMENT GOD WILL FORGIVE THEIR SINS AND JERUSALEM WILL BE INHABITED THROUGHOUT ALL GENERATIONS.
TAKE THIS BOOK WITH YOU TO BABYLON AND READ IT THERE BEFORE THE PEOPLE. LET THEM KNOW WHAT THEY MUST ENDURE BEFORE THEY RETURN.
I WILL RESTORE THE THRONE OF DAVID AND YOU WILL COME BACK AND POSSESS ALL YOUR LAND.
EZEKIEL PROPHESIED: "THEY WILL BE SCATTERED AMONG THE NATIONS, BUT AS GOD SCATTERS THEM HE WILL EVENTUALLY BRING THEM BACK INTO THE LAND."
"GOD PROMISED ABRAHAM THAT HIS SEED WOULD INHERIT THE LAND FOREVER, AND HE WILL NOT BREAK HIS PROMISE. HOWEVER, WHEN THE PEOPLE ARE SINFUL, GOD WILL SEND THEM INTO CAPTIVITY IN THE NATIONS WHERE THEY WILL SERVE STRANGE GODS, BUT IN THE END HE WILL BRING THEM BACK."

JEREMIAH 34:3, 39:7, 51:60-61, 52:11 (627-586 B.C.); JOEL 3:20-21; AMOS 9:11-15; EZEKIEL 12:15-16

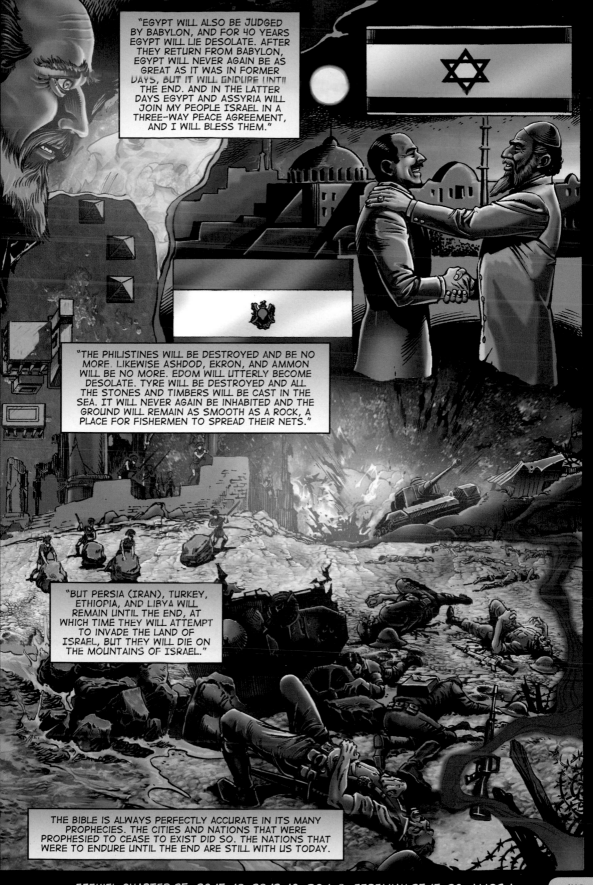

"EGYPT WILL ALSO BE JUDGED BY BABYLON, AND FOR 40 YEARS EGYPT WILL LIE DESOLATE. AFTER THEY RETURN FROM BABYLON, EGYPT WILL NEVER AGAIN BE AS GREAT AS IT WAS IN FORMER DAYS, BUT IT WILL ENDURE UNTIL THE END. AND IN THE LATTER DAYS EGYPT AND ASSYRIA WILL JOIN MY PEOPLE ISRAEL IN A THREE-WAY PEACE AGREEMENT, AND I WILL BLESS THEM."

"THE PHILISTINES WILL BE DESTROYED AND BE NO MORE. LIKEWISE ASHDOD, EKRON, AND AMMON WILL BE NO MORE. EDOM WILL UTTERLY BECOME DESOLATE. TYRE WILL BE DESTROYED AND ALL THE STONES AND TIMBERS WILL BE CAST IN THE SEA. IT WILL NEVER AGAIN BE INHABITED AND THE GROUND WILL REMAIN AS SMOOTH AS A ROCK, A PLACE FOR FISHERMEN TO SPREAD THEIR NETS."

"BUT PERSIA (IRAN), TURKEY, ETHIOPIA, AND LIBYA WILL REMAIN UNTIL THE END, AT WHICH TIME THEY WILL ATTEMPT TO INVADE THE LAND OF ISRAEL, BUT THEY WILL DIE ON THE MOUNTAINS OF ISRAEL."

THE BIBLE IS ALWAYS PERFECTLY ACCURATE IN ITS MANY PROPHECIES. THE CITIES AND NATIONS THAT WERE PROPHESIED TO CEASE TO EXIST DID SO. THE NATIONS THAT WERE TO ENDURE UNTIL THE END ARE STILL WITH US TODAY.

EZEKIEL CHAPTER 25, 26:15-19, 29:12-16, 30:1-8; JEREMIAH 25:15-26; AMOS 1

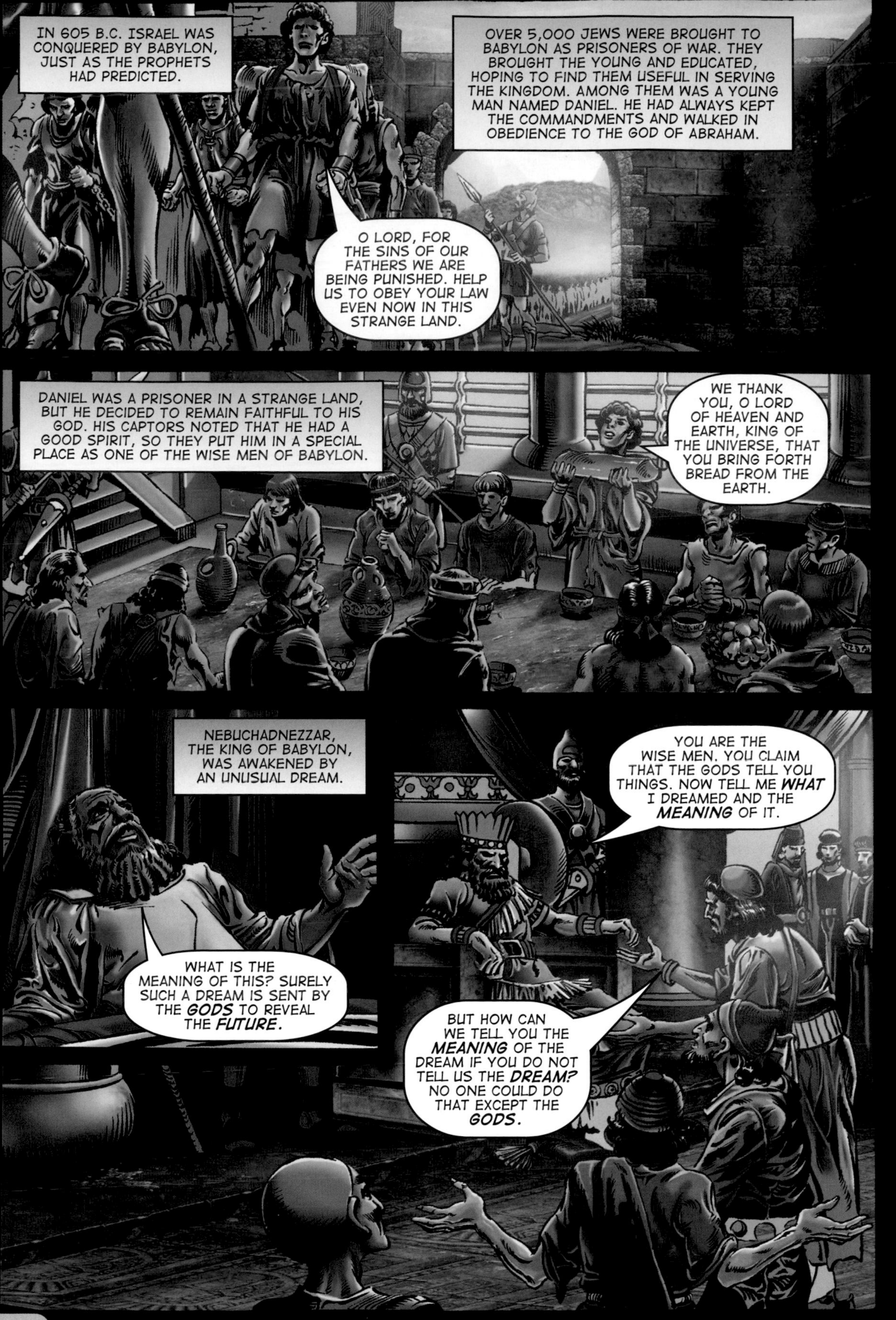

IN 605 B.C. ISRAEL WAS CONQUERED BY BABYLON, JUST AS THE PROPHETS HAD PREDICTED.
OVER 5,000 JEWS WERE BROUGHT TO BABYLON AS PRISONERS OF WAR. THEY BROUGHT THE YOUNG AND EDUCATED, HOPING TO FIND THEM USEFUL IN SERVING THE KINGDOM. AMONG THEM WAS A YOUNG MAN NAMED DANIEL. HE HAD ALWAYS KEPT THE COMMANDMENTS AND WALKED IN OBEDIENCE TO THE GOD OF ABRAHAM.
O LORD, FOR THE SINS OF OUR FATHERS WE ARE BEING PUNISHED. HELP US TO OBEY YOUR LAW EVEN NOW IN THIS STRANGE LAND.
DANIEL WAS A PRISONER IN A STRANGE LAND, BUT HE DECIDED TO REMAIN FAITHFUL TO HIS GOD. HIS CAPTORS NOTED THAT HE HAD A GOOD SPIRIT, SO THEY PUT HIM IN A SPECIAL PLACE AS ONE OF THE WISE MEN OF BABYLON.
WE THANK YOU, O LORD OF HEAVEN AND EARTH, KING OF THE UNIVERSE, THAT YOU BRING FORTH BREAD FROM THE EARTH.
NEBUCHADNEZZAR, THE KING OF BABYLON, WAS AWAKENED BY AN UNUSUAL DREAM.
WHAT IS THE MEANING OF THIS? SURELY SUCH A DREAM IS SENT BY THE **GODS** TO REVEAL THE **FUTURE**.
YOU ARE THE WISE MEN. YOU CLAIM THAT THE GODS TELL YOU THINGS. NOW TELL ME **WHAT** I DREAMED AND THE **MEANING** OF IT.
BUT HOW CAN WE TELL YOU THE **MEANING** OF THE DREAM IF YOU DO NOT TELL US THE **DREAM?** NO ONE COULD DO THAT EXCEPT THE **GODS**.

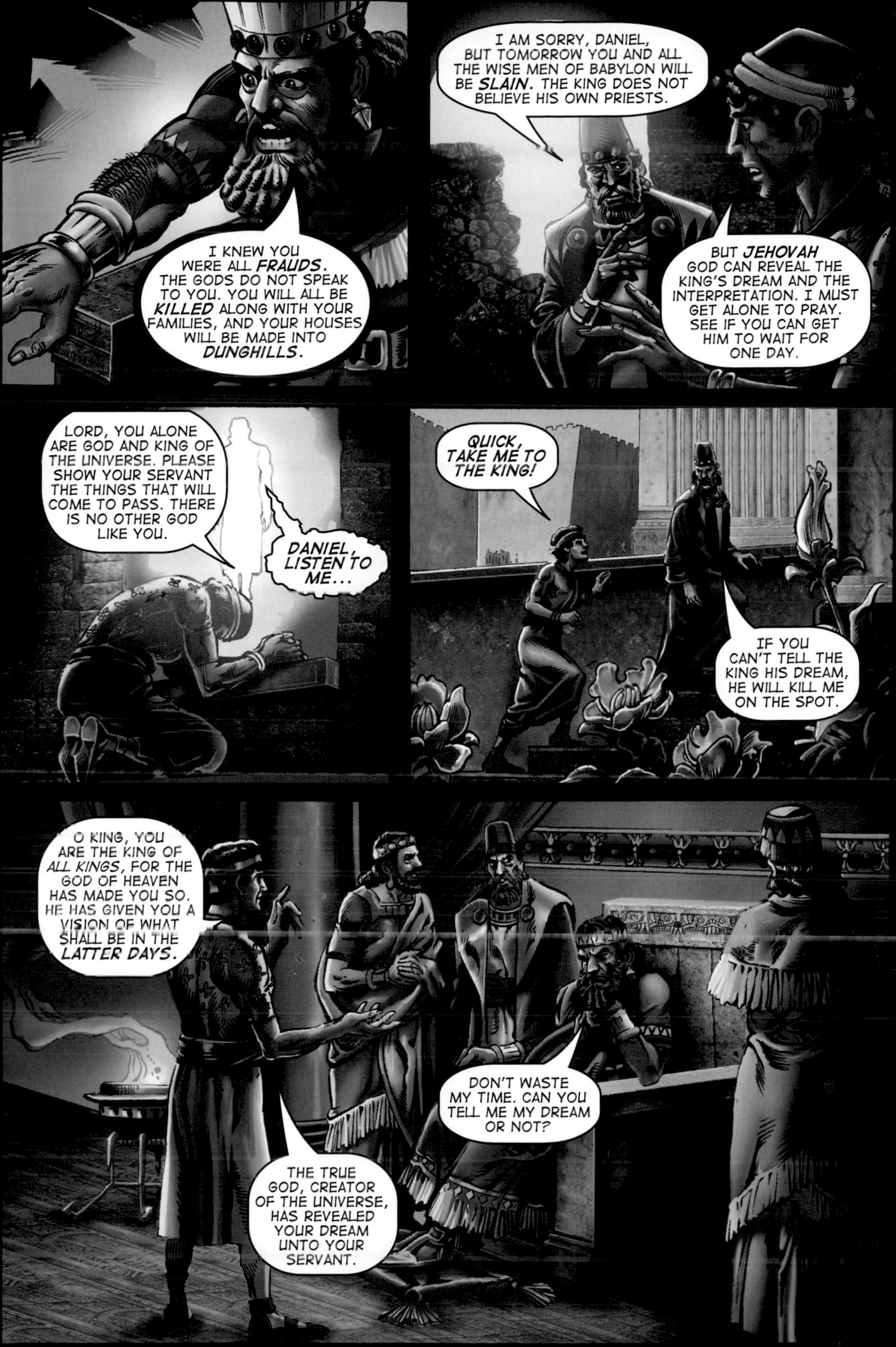
I KNEW YOU WERE ALL FRAUDS. THE GODS DO NOT SPEAK TO YOU. YOU WILL ALL BE KILLED ALONG WITH YOUR FAMILIES, AND YOUR HOUSES WILL BE MADE INTO DUNGHILLS.
I AM SORRY, DANIEL, BUT TOMORROW YOU AND ALL THE WISE MEN OF BABYLON WILL BE SLAIN. THE KING DOES NOT BELIEVE HIS OWN PRIESTS.
BUT JEHOVAH GOD CAN REVEAL THE KING'S DREAM AND THE INTERPRETATION. I MUST GET ALONE TO PRAY. SEE IF YOU CAN GET HIM TO WAIT FOR ONE DAY.
LORD, YOU ALONE ARE GOD AND KING OF THE UNIVERSE. PLEASE SHOW YOUR SERVANT THE THINGS THAT WILL COME TO PASS. THERE IS NO OTHER GOD LIKE YOU.
DANIEL, LISTEN TO ME...
QUICK, TAKE ME TO THE KING!
IF YOU CAN'T TELL THE KING HIS DREAM, HE WILL KILL ME ON THE SPOT.
O KING, YOU ARE THE KING OF ALL KINGS, FOR THE GOD OF HEAVEN HAS MADE YOU SO. HE HAS GIVEN YOU A VISION OF WHAT SHALL BE IN THE LATTER DAYS.
DON'T WASTE MY TIME. CAN YOU TELL ME MY DREAM OR NOT?
THE TRUE GOD, CREATOR OF THE UNIVERSE, HAS REVEALED YOUR DREAM UNTO YOUR SERVANT.

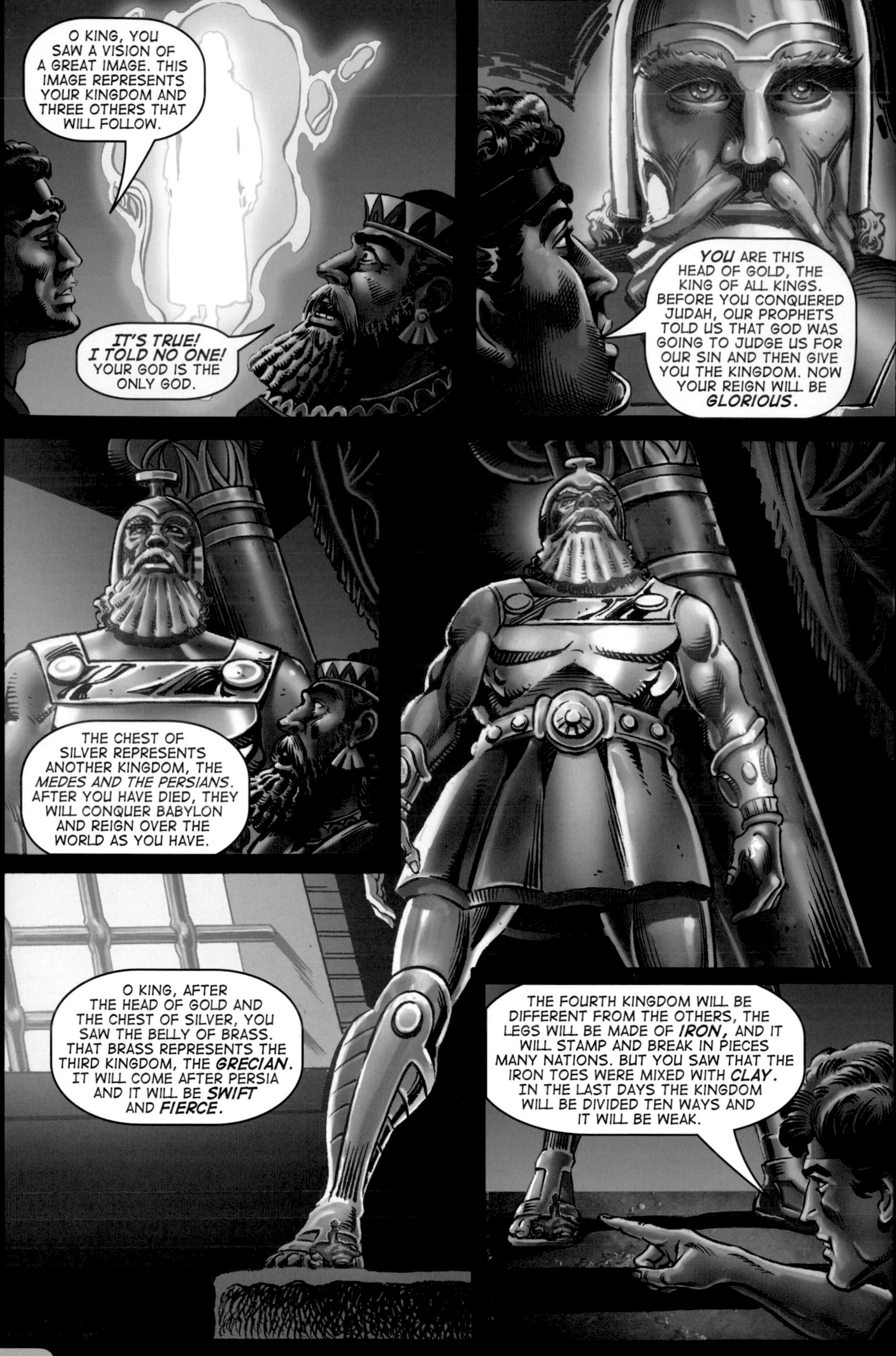
O KING, YOU SAW A VISION OF A GREAT IMAGE. THIS IMAGE REPRESENTS YOUR KINGDOM AND THREE OTHERS THAT WILL FOLLOW.
IT'S TRUE! I TOLD NO ONE! YOUR GOD IS THE ONLY GOD.
YOU ARE THIS HEAD OF GOLD, THE KING OF ALL KINGS. BEFORE YOU CONQUERED JUDAH, OUR PROPHETS TOLD US THAT GOD WAS GOING TO JUDGE US FOR OUR SIN AND THEN GIVE YOU THE KINGDOM. NOW YOUR REIGN WILL BE **GLORIOUS**.
THE CHEST OF SILVER REPRESENTS ANOTHER KINGDOM, THE *MEDES AND THE PERSIANS*. AFTER YOU HAVE DIED, THEY WILL CONQUER BABYLON AND REIGN OVER THE WORLD AS YOU HAVE.
O KING, AFTER THE HEAD OF GOLD AND THE CHEST OF SILVER, YOU SAW THE BELLY OF BRASS. THAT BRASS REPRESENTS THE THIRD KINGDOM, THE **GRECIAN**. IT WILL COME AFTER PERSIA AND IT WILL BE **SWIFT** AND **FIERCE**.
THE FOURTH KINGDOM WILL BE DIFFERENT FROM THE OTHERS, THE LEGS WILL BE MADE OF **IRON**, AND IT WILL STAMP AND BREAK IN PIECES MANY NATIONS. BUT YOU SAW THAT THE IRON TOES WERE MIXED WITH **CLAY**. IN THE LAST DAYS THE KINGDOM WILL BE DIVIDED TEN WAYS AND IT WILL BE WEAK.

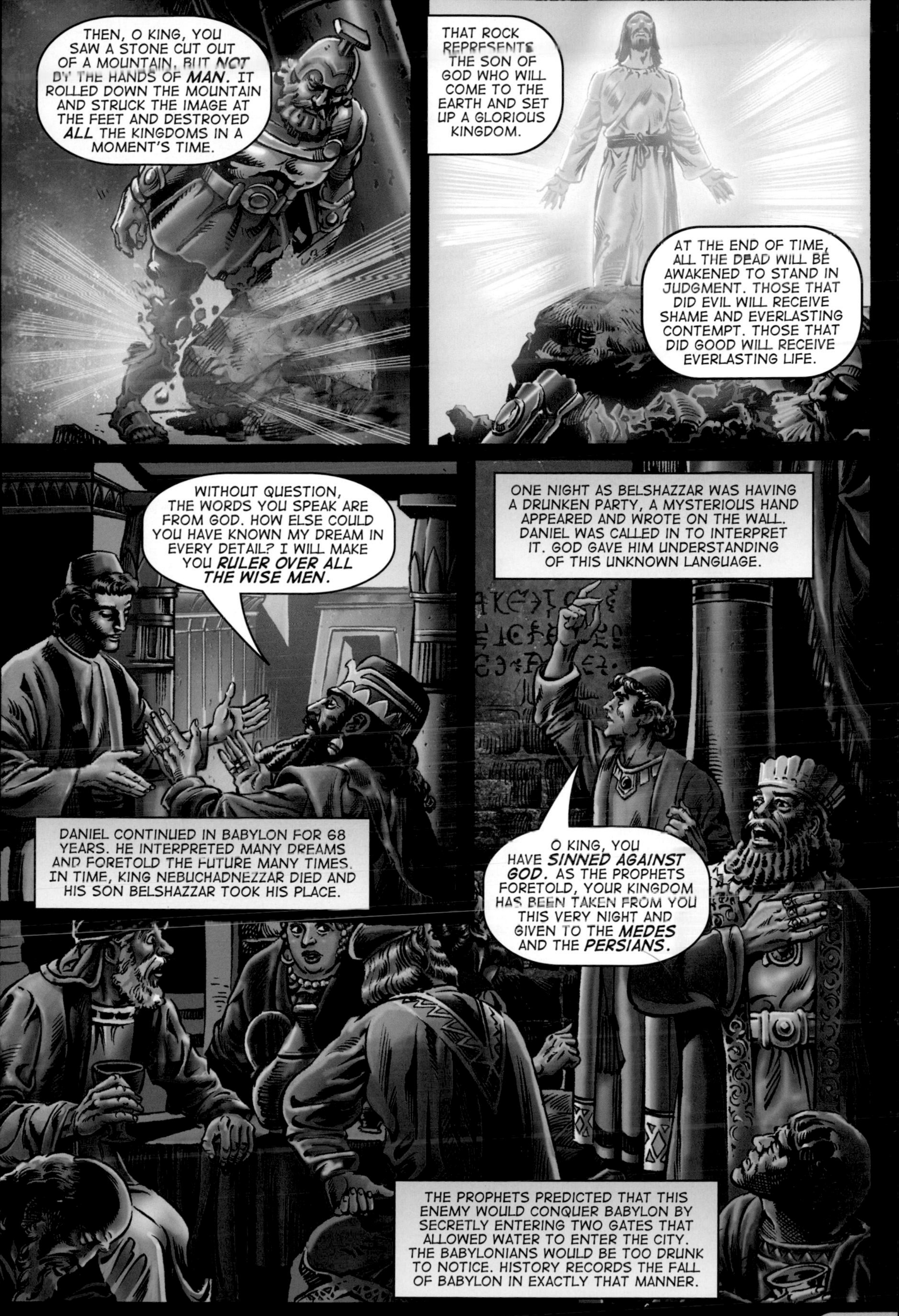

THEN, O KING, YOU SAW A STONE CUT OUT OF A MOUNTAIN, BUT *NOT* BY THE HANDS OF *MAN*. IT ROLLED DOWN THE MOUNTAIN AND STRUCK THE IMAGE AT THE FEET AND DESTROYED *ALL* THE KINGDOMS IN A MOMENT'S TIME.
THAT ROCK REPRESENTS THE SON OF GOD WHO WILL COME TO THE EARTH AND SET UP A GLORIOUS KINGDOM.
AT THE END OF TIME, ALL THE DEAD WILL BE AWAKENED TO STAND IN JUDGMENT. THOSE THAT DID EVIL WILL RECEIVE SHAME AND EVERLASTING CONTEMPT. THOSE THAT DID GOOD WILL RECEIVE EVERLASTING LIFE.
WITHOUT QUESTION, THE WORDS YOU SPEAK ARE FROM GOD. HOW ELSE COULD YOU HAVE KNOWN MY DREAM IN EVERY DETAIL? I WILL MAKE YOU *RULER OVER ALL THE WISE MEN*.
DANIEL CONTINUED IN BABYLON FOR 68 YEARS. HE INTERPRETED MANY DREAMS AND FORETOLD THE FUTURE MANY TIMES. IN TIME, KING NEBUCHADNEZZAR DIED AND HIS SON BELSHAZZAR TOOK HIS PLACE.
ONE NIGHT AS BELSHAZZAR WAS HAVING A DRUNKEN PARTY, A MYSTERIOUS HAND APPEARED AND WROTE ON THE WALL. DANIEL WAS CALLED IN TO INTERPRET IT. GOD GAVE HIM UNDERSTANDING OF THIS UNKNOWN LANGUAGE.
O KING, YOU HAVE *SINNED AGAINST GOD*. AS THE PROPHETS FORETOLD, YOUR KINGDOM HAS BEEN TAKEN FROM YOU THIS VERY NIGHT AND GIVEN TO THE *MEDES* AND THE *PERSIANS*.
THE PROPHETS PREDICTED THAT THIS ENEMY WOULD CONQUER BABYLON BY SECRETLY ENTERING TWO GATES THAT ALLOWED WATER TO ENTER THE CITY. THE BABYLONIANS WOULD BE TOO DRUNK TO NOTICE. HISTORY RECORDS THE FALL OF BABYLON IN EXACTLY THAT MANNER.

ECCLESIASTES 12:13-14; ISAIAH 9:6-7, 45:1; DANIEL 2:34-35, 44-48, 5:1-29; REVELATION 20:11-21:5

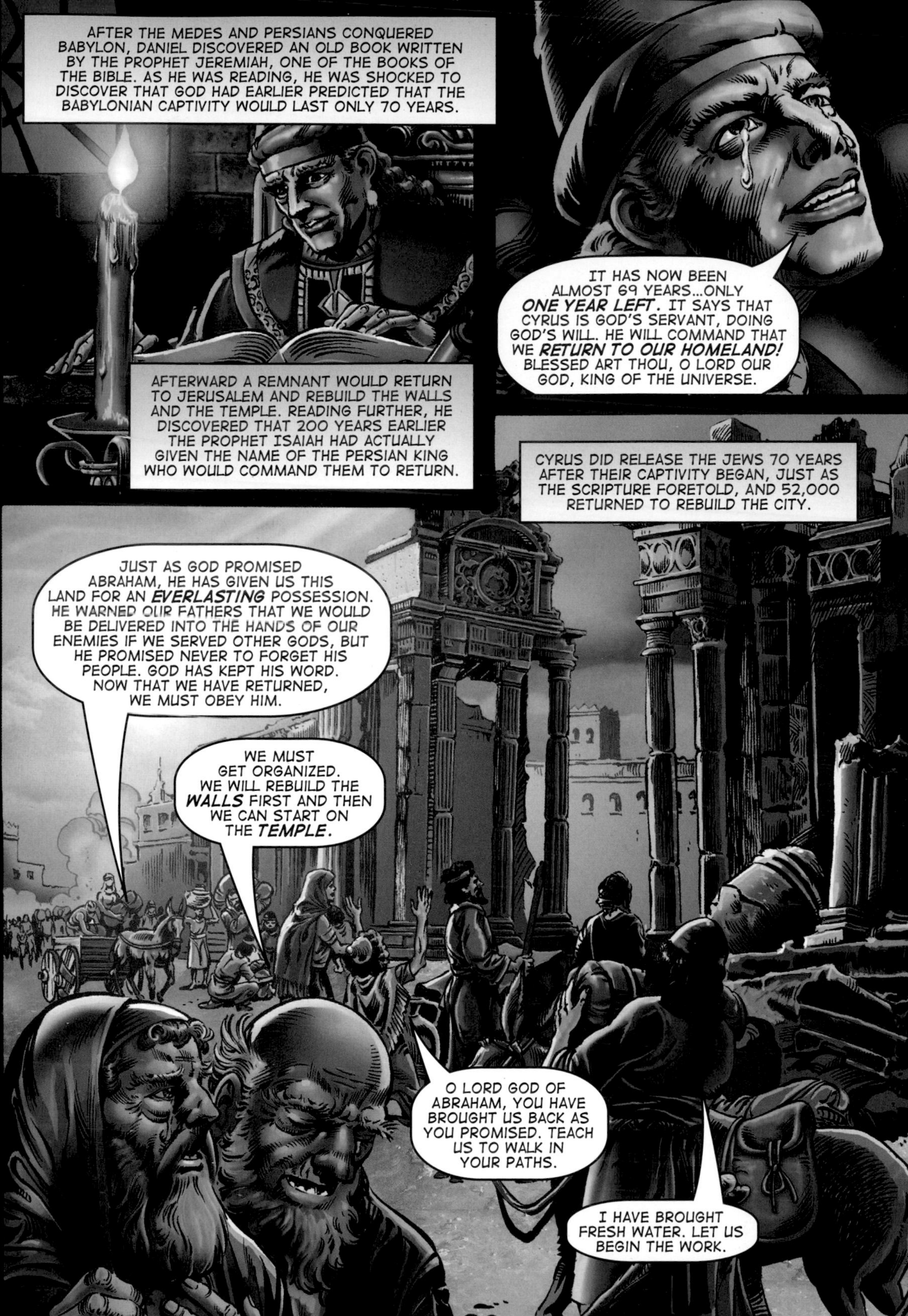
AFTER THE MEDES AND PERSIANS CONQUERED BABYLON, DANIEL DISCOVERED AN OLD BOOK WRITTEN BY THE PROPHET JEREMIAH, ONE OF THE BOOKS OF THE BIBLE. AS HE WAS READING, HE WAS SHOCKED TO DISCOVER THAT GOD HAD EARLIER PREDICTED THAT THE BABYLONIAN CAPTIVITY WOULD LAST ONLY 70 YEARS.
AFTERWARD A REMNANT WOULD RETURN TO JERUSALEM AND REBUILD THE WALLS AND THE TEMPLE. READING FURTHER, HE DISCOVERED THAT 200 YEARS EARLIER THE PROPHET ISAIAH HAD ACTUALLY GIVEN THE NAME OF THE PERSIAN KING WHO WOULD COMMAND THEM TO RETURN.
IT HAS NOW BEEN ALMOST 69 YEARS...ONLY ***ONE YEAR LEFT***. IT SAYS THAT CYRUS IS GOD'S SERVANT, DOING GOD'S WILL. HE WILL COMMAND THAT WE ***RETURN TO OUR HOMELAND!*** BLESSED ART THOU, O LORD OUR GOD, KING OF THE UNIVERSE.
CYRUS DID RELEASE THE JEWS 70 YEARS AFTER THEIR CAPTIVITY BEGAN, JUST AS THE SCRIPTURE FORETOLD, AND 52,000 RETURNED TO REBUILD THE CITY.
JUST AS GOD PROMISED ABRAHAM, HE HAS GIVEN US THIS LAND FOR AN ***EVERLASTING*** POSSESSION. HE WARNED OUR FATHERS THAT WE WOULD BE DELIVERED INTO THE HANDS OF OUR ENEMIES IF WE SERVED OTHER GODS, BUT HE PROMISED NEVER TO FORGET HIS PEOPLE. GOD HAS KEPT HIS WORD. NOW THAT WE HAVE RETURNED, WE MUST OBEY HIM.
WE MUST GET ORGANIZED. WE WILL REBUILD THE ***WALLS*** FIRST AND THEN WE CAN START ON THE ***TEMPLE***.
O LORD GOD OF ABRAHAM, YOU HAVE BROUGHT US BACK AS YOU PROMISED. TEACH US TO WALK IN YOUR PATHS.
I HAVE BROUGHT FRESH WATER. LET US BEGIN THE WORK.

ISAIAH 44:28; JEREMIAH 25:11-12, 29:10; DANIEL 9:1-2

DANIEL WAS VERY OLD, SO HE DID NOT GO BACK WITH THE OTHERS. HE STILL PLAYED AN IMPORTANT ROLE AS HE ADVISED THE KINGS OF THE MEDO-PERSIAN EMPIRE, NOW LOCATED IN THE CITY OF BABYLON. GOD GAVE HIM SEVERAL MORE VISIONS CONCERNING THE FUTURE, EVEN TO THE END OF DAYS. IN ONE DREAM HE SAW A METALLIC BEAST. AN ANGEL TOLD HIM WHAT IT MEANT.

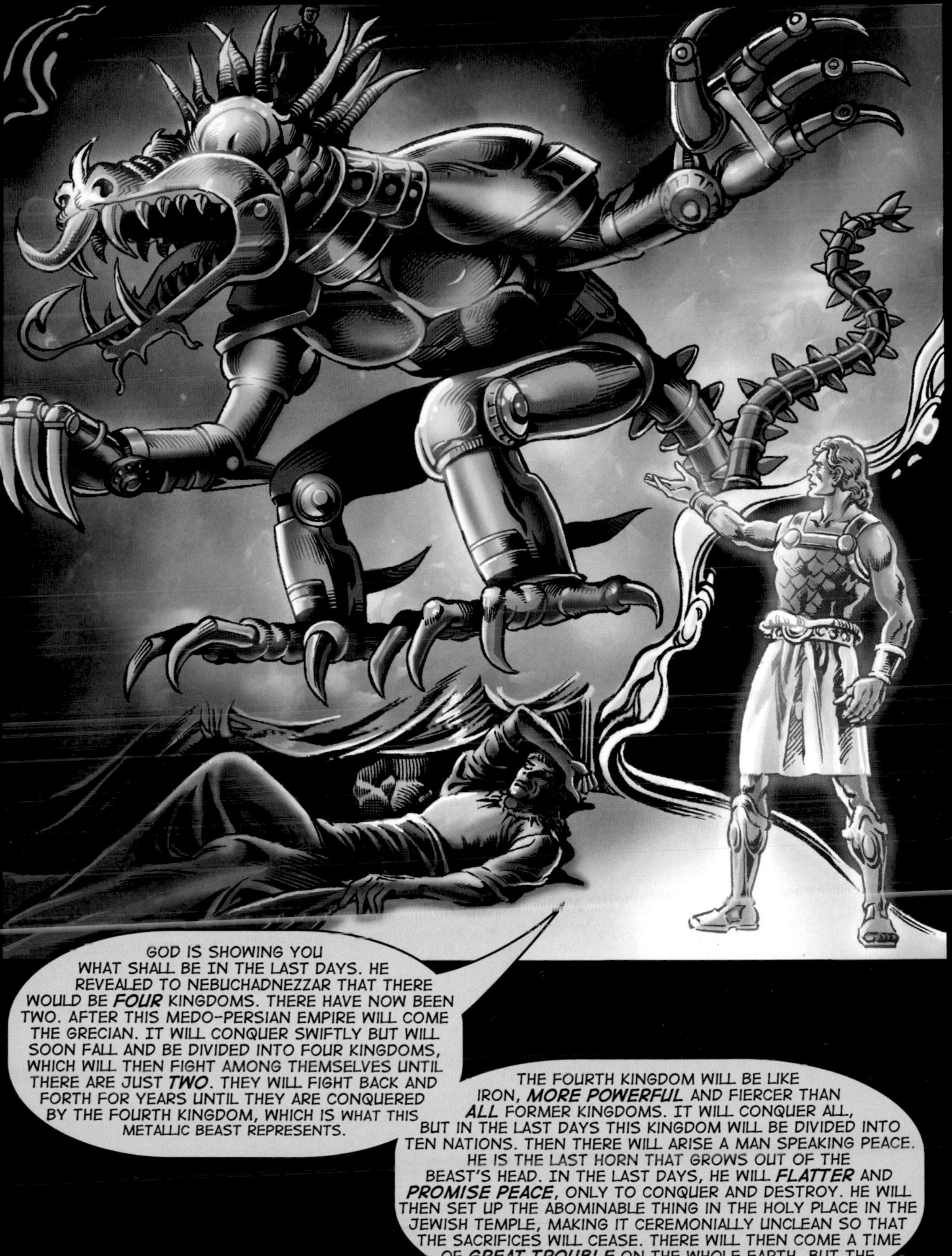
GOD IS SHOWING YOU WHAT SHALL BE IN THE LAST DAYS. HE REVEALED TO NEBUCHADNEZZAR THAT THERE WOULD BE **FOUR** KINGDOMS. THERE HAVE NOW BEEN TWO. AFTER THIS MEDO-PERSIAN EMPIRE WILL COME THE GRECIAN. IT WILL CONQUER SWIFTLY BUT WILL SOON FALL AND BE DIVIDED INTO FOUR KINGDOMS, WHICH WILL THEN FIGHT AMONG THEMSELVES UNTIL THERE ARE JUST **TWO**. THEY WILL FIGHT BACK AND FORTH FOR YEARS UNTIL THEY ARE CONQUERED BY THE FOURTH KINGDOM, WHICH IS WHAT THIS METALLIC BEAST REPRESENTS.
THE FOURTH KINGDOM WILL BE LIKE IRON, **MORE POWERFUL** AND FIERCER THAN **ALL** FORMER KINGDOMS. IT WILL CONQUER ALL, BUT IN THE LAST DAYS THIS KINGDOM WILL BE DIVIDED INTO TEN NATIONS. THEN THERE WILL ARISE A MAN SPEAKING PEACE. HE IS THE LAST HORN THAT GROWS OUT OF THE BEAST'S HEAD. IN THE LAST DAYS, HE WILL **FLATTER** AND **PROMISE PEACE**, ONLY TO CONQUER AND DESTROY. HE WILL THEN SET UP THE ABOMINABLE THING IN THE HOLY PLACE IN THE JEWISH TEMPLE, MAKING IT CEREMONIALLY UNCLEAN SO THAT THE SACRIFICES WILL CEASE. THERE WILL THEN COME A TIME OF **GREAT TROUBLE** ON THE WHOLE EARTH, BUT THE RIGHTEOUS WILL BE DELIVERED.

DANIEL 7:17–28; MATTHEW 24:4–25

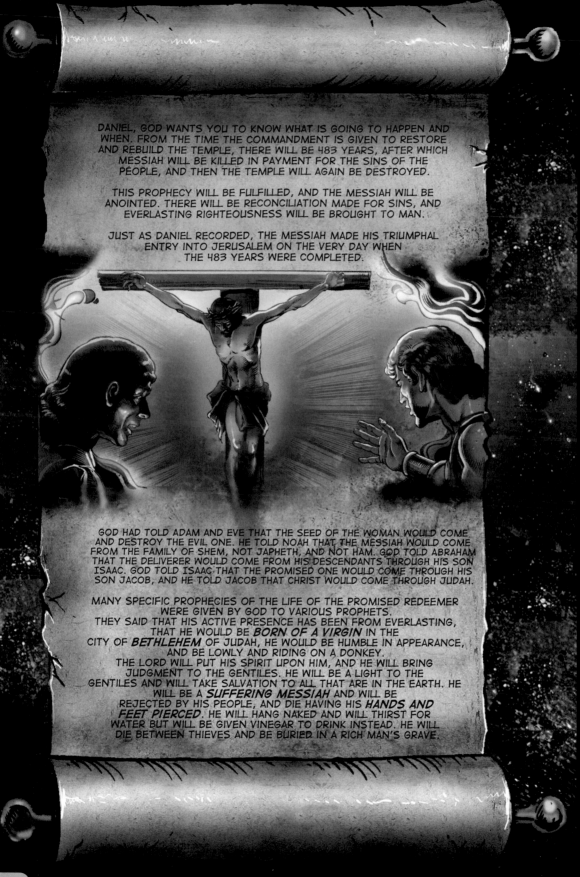

DANIEL, GOD WANTS YOU TO KNOW WHAT IS GOING TO HAPPEN AND WHEN. FROM THE TIME THE COMMANDMENT IS GIVEN TO RESTORE AND REBUILD THE TEMPLE, THERE WILL BE 483 YEARS, AFTER WHICH MESSIAH WILL BE KILLED IN PAYMENT FOR THE SINS OF THE PEOPLE, AND THEN THE TEMPLE WILL AGAIN BE DESTROYED.

THIS PROPHECY WILL BE FULFILLED, AND THE MESSIAH WILL BE ANOINTED. THERE WILL BE RECONCILIATION MADE FOR SINS, AND EVERLASTING RIGHTEOUSNESS WILL BE BROUGHT TO MAN.

JUST AS DANIEL RECORDED, THE MESSIAH MADE HIS TRIUMPHAL ENTRY INTO JERUSALEM ON THE VERY DAY WHEN THE 483 YEARS WERE COMPLETED.

GOD HAD TOLD ADAM AND EVE THAT THE SEED OF THE WOMAN WOULD COME AND DESTROY THE EVIL ONE. HE TOLD NOAH THAT THE MESSIAH WOULD COME FROM THE FAMILY OF SHEM, NOT JAPHETH, AND NOT HAM. GOD TOLD ABRAHAM THAT THE DELIVERER WOULD COME FROM HIS DESCENDANTS THROUGH HIS SON ISAAC. GOD TOLD ISAAC THAT THE PROMISED ONE WOULD COME THROUGH HIS SON JACOB, AND HE TOLD JACOB THAT CHRIST WOULD COME THROUGH JUDAH.

MANY SPECIFIC PROPHECIES OF THE LIFE OF THE PROMISED REDEEMER WERE GIVEN BY GOD TO VARIOUS PROPHETS. THEY SAID THAT HIS ACTIVE PRESENCE HAS BEEN FROM EVERLASTING, THAT HE WOULD BE *BORN OF A VIRGIN* IN THE CITY OF *BETHLEHEM* OF JUDAH, HE WOULD BE HUMBLE IN APPEARANCE, AND BE LOWLY AND RIDING ON A DONKEY. THE LORD WILL PUT HIS SPIRIT UPON HIM, AND HE WILL BRING JUDGMENT TO THE GENTILES. HE WILL BE A LIGHT TO THE GENTILES AND WILL TAKE SALVATION TO ALL THAT ARE IN THE EARTH. HE WILL BE A *SUFFERING MESSIAH* AND WILL BE REJECTED BY HIS PEOPLE, AND DIE HAVING HIS *HANDS AND FEET PIERCED*. HE WILL HANG NAKED AND WILL THIRST FOR WATER BUT WILL BE GIVEN VINEGAR TO DRINK INSTEAD. HE WILL DIE BETWEEN THIEVES AND BE BURIED IN A RICH MAN'S GRAVE.

GENESIS 49:9-10; PSALM 22, 53; ISAIAH 7, 9:1-2, 42:1, 49:6, 53; DANIEL 9:25-26; MICAH 5:2; ZECHARIAH 9:9; MATTHEW 24:1-2; HEBREWS 2:9

THE PROPHECIES OF DANIEL CONCERNING THE FOUR KINGDOMS WERE FULFILLED EXACTLY AS HE PREDICTED. IN 330 B.C., ALEXANDER THE GREAT, FROM GREECE, BEGAN A CAMPAIGN WHICH LASTED SEVEN YEARS, IN WHICH HE CONQUERED THE KNOWN WORLD, INCLUDING THE VAST MEDO-PERSIAN EMPIRE. GREECE HELD POWER UNTIL ABOUT 167 B.C. WHEN THE FOURTH WORLD KINGDOM, ROME, BEGAN TO CONQUER.

ROME, REPRESENTED IN NEBUCHADNEZZAR'S DREAM AS THE FEET AND LEGS OF IRON, AND IN DANIEL'S VISION AS THE METALLIC BEAST, INCREASED ITS POWER AND TERRITORY, JUST AS THE PROPHETS PREDICTED. BY 5 B.C., IT RULED ISRAEL WITH AN IRON HAND.

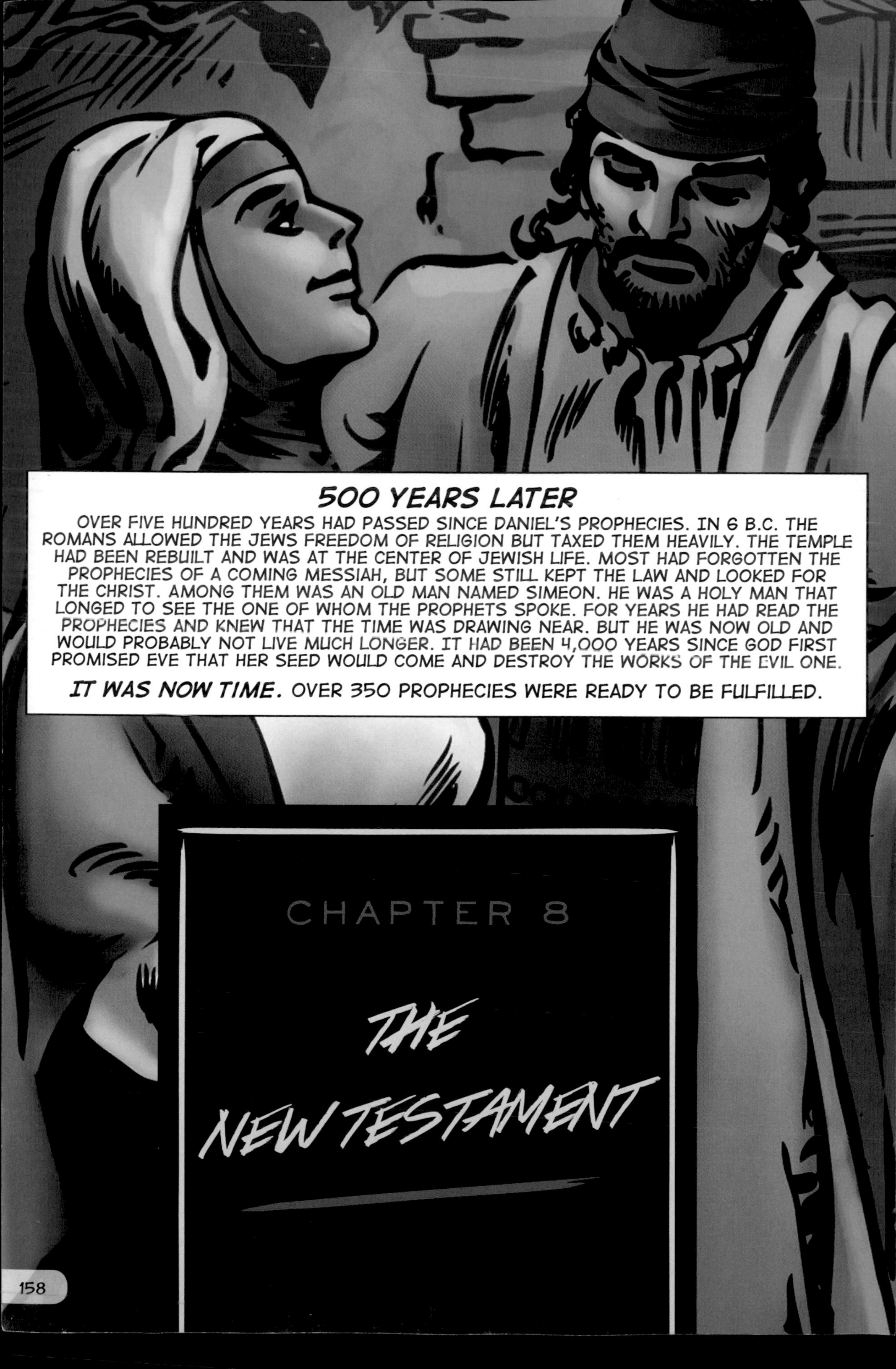
500 YEARS LATER
OVER FIVE HUNDRED YEARS HAD PASSED SINCE DANIEL'S PROPHECIES. IN 6 B.C. THE ROMANS ALLOWED THE JEWS FREEDOM OF RELIGION BUT TAXED THEM HEAVILY. THE TEMPLE HAD BEEN REBUILT AND WAS AT THE CENTER OF JEWISH LIFE. MOST HAD FORGOTTEN THE PROPHECIES OF A COMING MESSIAH, BUT SOME STILL KEPT THE LAW AND LOOKED FOR THE CHRIST. AMONG THEM WAS AN OLD MAN NAMED SIMEON. HE WAS A HOLY MAN THAT LONGED TO SEE THE ONE OF WHOM THE PROPHETS SPOKE. FOR YEARS HE HAD READ THE PROPHECIES AND KNEW THAT THE TIME WAS DRAWING NEAR. BUT HE WAS NOW OLD AND WOULD PROBABLY NOT LIVE MUCH LONGER. IT HAD BEEN 4,000 YEARS SINCE GOD FIRST PROMISED EVE THAT HER SEED WOULD COME AND DESTROY THE WORKS OF THE EVIL ONE.
IT WAS NOW TIME. OVER 350 PROPHECIES WERE READY TO BE FULFILLED.
CHAPTER 8
THE NEW TESTAMENT

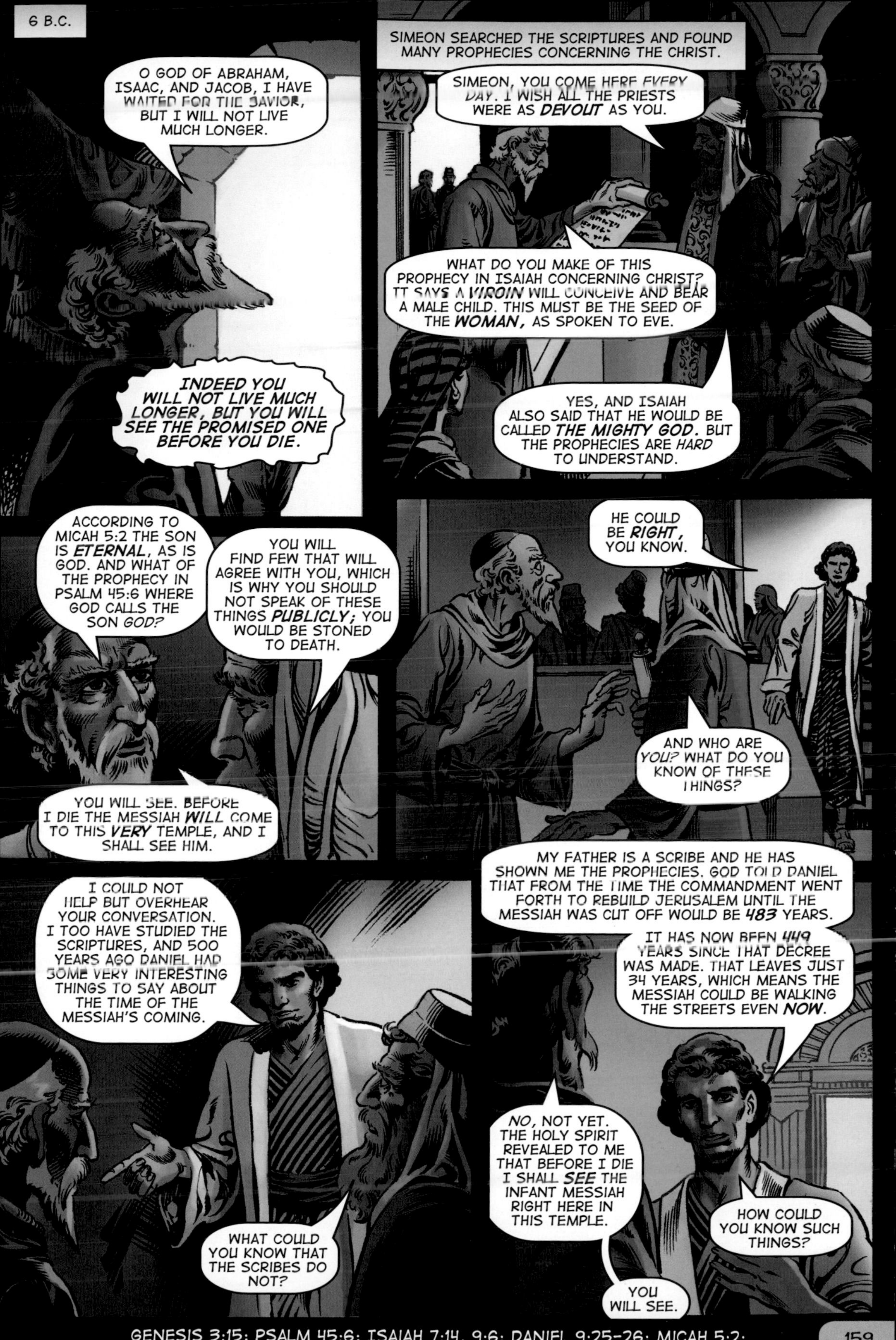
6 B.C.
O GOD OF ABRAHAM, ISAAC, AND JACOB, I HAVE WAITED FOR THE SAVIOR, BUT I WILL NOT LIVE MUCH LONGER.
INDEED YOU WILL NOT LIVE MUCH LONGER, BUT YOU WILL SEE THE PROMISED ONE BEFORE YOU DIE.
SIMEON SEARCHED THE SCRIPTURES AND FOUND MANY PROPHECIES CONCERNING THE CHRIST.
SIMEON, YOU COME HERE EVERY DAY. I WISH ALL THE PRIESTS WERE AS DEVOUT AS YOU.
WHAT DO YOU MAKE OF THIS PROPHECY IN ISAIAH CONCERNING CHRIST? IT SAYS A VIRGIN WILL CONCEIVE AND BEAR A MALE CHILD. THIS MUST BE THE SEED OF THE WOMAN, AS SPOKEN TO EVE.
YES, AND ISAIAH ALSO SAID THAT HE WOULD BE CALLED THE MIGHTY GOD. BUT THE PROPHECIES ARE HARD TO UNDERSTAND.
ACCORDING TO MICAH 5:2 THE SON IS ETERNAL, AS IS GOD. AND WHAT OF THE PROPHECY IN PSALM 45:6 WHERE GOD CALLS THE SON GOD?
YOU WILL FIND FEW THAT WILL AGREE WITH YOU, WHICH IS WHY YOU SHOULD NOT SPEAK OF THESE THINGS PUBLICLY; YOU WOULD BE STONED TO DEATH.
YOU WILL SEE. BEFORE I DIE THE MESSIAH WILL COME TO THIS VERY TEMPLE, AND I SHALL SEE HIM.
HE COULD BE RIGHT, YOU KNOW.
AND WHO ARE YOU? WHAT DO YOU KNOW OF THESE THINGS?
I COULD NOT HELP BUT OVERHEAR YOUR CONVERSATION. I TOO HAVE STUDIED THE SCRIPTURES, AND 500 YEARS AGO DANIEL HAD SOME VERY INTERESTING THINGS TO SAY ABOUT THE TIME OF THE MESSIAH'S COMING.
WHAT COULD YOU KNOW THAT THE SCRIBES DO NOT?
MY FATHER IS A SCRIBE AND HE HAS SHOWN ME THE PROPHECIES. GOD TOLD DANIEL THAT FROM THE TIME THE COMMANDMENT WENT FORTH TO REBUILD JERUSALEM UNTIL THE MESSIAH WAS CUT OFF WOULD BE 483 YEARS.
IT HAS NOW BEEN 449 YEARS SINCE THAT DECREE WAS MADE. THAT LEAVES JUST 34 YEARS, WHICH MEANS THE MESSIAH COULD BE WALKING THE STREETS EVEN NOW.
NO, NOT YET. THE HOLY SPIRIT REVEALED TO ME THAT BEFORE I DIE I SHALL SEE THE INFANT MESSIAH RIGHT HERE IN THIS TEMPLE.
HOW COULD YOU KNOW SUCH THINGS?
YOU WILL SEE.

GENESIS 3:15; PSALM 45:6; ISAIAH 7:14, 9:6; DANIEL 9:25-26; MICAH 5:2; LUKE 2:25-26

AS SIMEON GREW OLDER AND WAITED AT THE TEMPLE, LOOKING FOR THE PROMISED CHRIST, A PRIEST BY THE NAME OF ZACHARIAS WENT INTO THE TEMPLE TO PRAY. HE AND HIS WIFE WERE OLD, BUT THEY HAD NEVER HAD ANY CHILDREN.

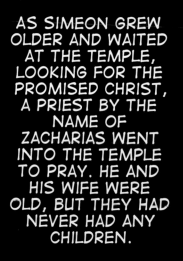

SUDDENLY AN ANGEL APPEARED ON THE RIGHT SIDE OF THE ALTAR!

DO NOT BE AFRAID. YOUR PRAYER HAS BEEN HEARD AND YOUR WIFE ELIZABETH WILL BEAR A SON, AND YOU WILL NAME HIM *JOHN*.

MANY WILL REJOICE WHEN HE IS BORN, BECAUSE HE IS THE ONE THAT WILL PREPARE THE PEOPLE FOR THE COMING OF THE *MESSIAH*. HE WILL NOT DRINK WINE OR STRONG DRINK AND HE WILL RECEIVE THE SPIRIT AND POWER OF *ELIJAH*.

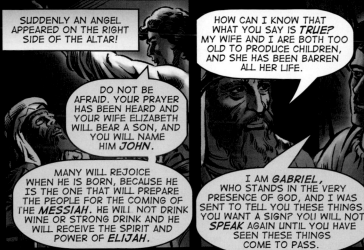

HOW CAN I KNOW THAT WHAT YOU SAY IS *TRUE*? MY WIFE AND I ARE BOTH TOO OLD TO PRODUCE CHILDREN, AND SHE HAS BEEN BARREN ALL HER LIFE.

I AM *GABRIEL*, WHO STANDS IN THE VERY PRESENCE OF GOD, AND I WAS SENT TO TELL YOU THESE THINGS. YOU WANT A SIGN? YOU WILL NOT *SPEAK* AGAIN UNTIL YOU HAVE SEEN THESE THINGS COME TO PASS.

I WILL BE GLAD WHEN WE CAN TALK ABOUT IT. THIS HOUSE IS *SO QUIET*. YOU SHOULD NOT TALK BACK TO *ANGELS*, YOU KNOW.

ZACHARIAS, IT IS STILL HARD TO BELIEVE. JUST LIKE SARAH, THE MOTHER OF OUR NATION, GOD HEARD OUR PRAYERS, AND NOW I AM TO BE THE MOTHER OF A *GREAT PROPHET*.

FOR 4,000 YEARS, THE PROPHETS FORETOLD THE COMING OF MESSIAH. 700 YEARS EARLIER, THE PROPHET ISAIAH SAID: "BEHOLD, A VIRGIN SHALL CONCEIVE, AND BEAR A SON, AND HE SHALL BE CALLED EMMANUEL, GOD WITH US."

MARY WAS ENGAGED TO BE MARRIED TO JOSEPH. SHE HAD NEVER HAD INTIMATE RELATIONSHIPS WITH ANYONE. SHE WAS OBEDIENT TO ALL THE LAWS OF MOSES.

SUDDENLY, AN ANGEL APPEARED UNTO MARY!

MARY, YOU HAVE FOUND *GREAT FAVOR* IN THE SIGHT OF GOD. YOU WILL CONCEIVE IN YOUR WOMB AND BRING FORTH THE SON OF GOD.

HOW COULD SUCH A THING HAPPEN SINCE I HAVE NEVER HAD RELATIONS WITH ANY MAN?

THE HOLY SPIRIT OF GOD WILL COVER YOU. THE HOLY FETUS THAT WILL BE CONCEIVED IN YOUR WOMB WILL BE THE *SON OF GOD*. YOUR COUSIN ELIZABETH, WHO WAS CALLED BARREN, IS NOW WITH CHILD. THIS IS HER SIXTH MONTH.

I AM THE *LORD'S* MAIDSERVANT. MAY IT BE UNTO ME AS HE WILLS.

I AM GOING TO BE THE *MOTHER* OF THE SON OF GOD. WILL JOSEPH BELIEVE ME? WILL HE UNDERSTAND? WHAT WILL EVERYONE THINK WHEN THEY REALIZE I AM *PREGNANT*? I KNOW; I WILL GO TO STAY WITH ELIZABETH.

ISAIAH 7:14; LUKE 1:5-20, 26-40

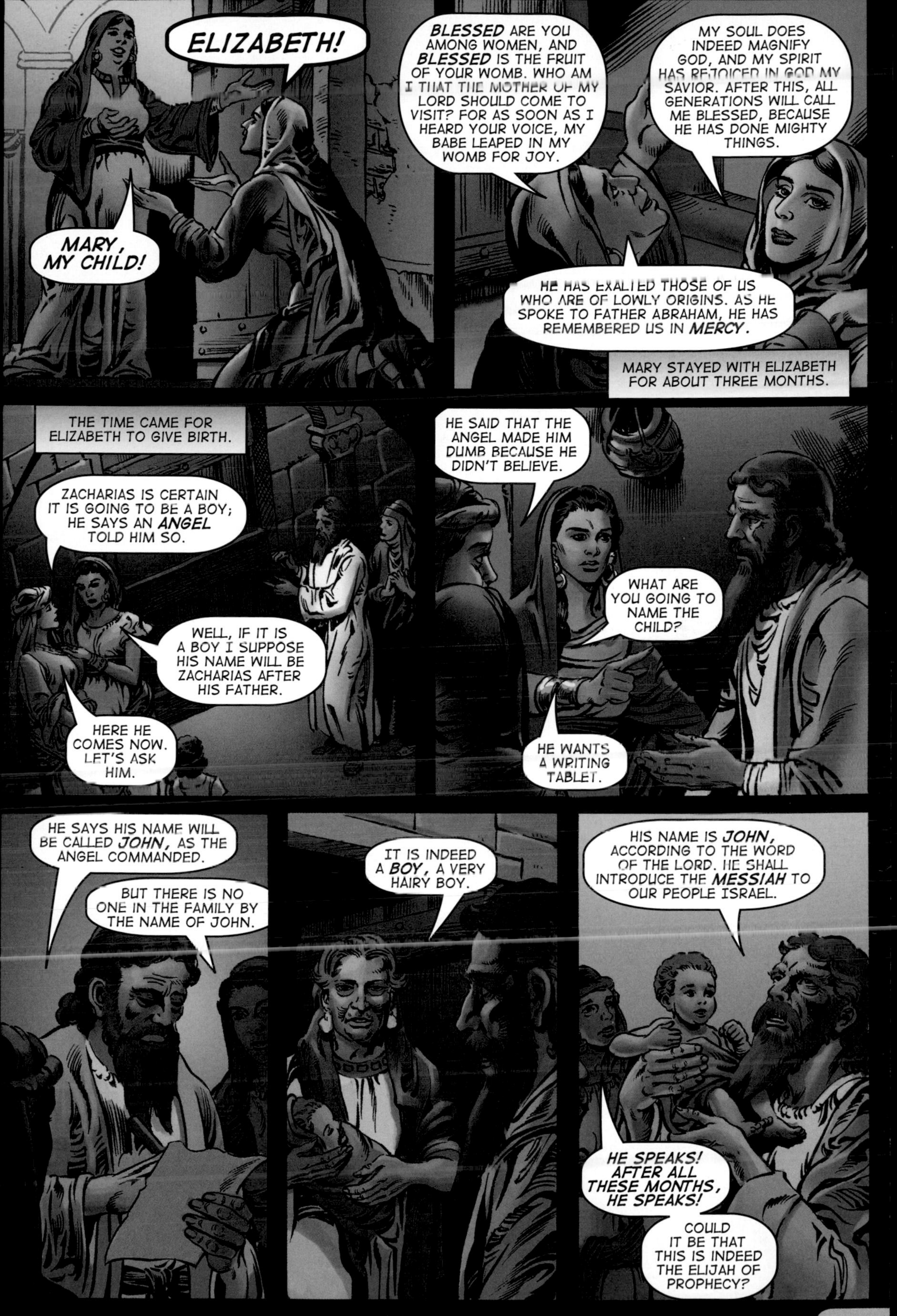
ELIZABETH!
MARY, MY CHILD!
BLESSED ARE YOU AMONG WOMEN, AND BLESSED IS THE FRUIT OF YOUR WOMB. WHO AM I THAT THE MOTHER OF MY LORD SHOULD COME TO VISIT? FOR AS SOON AS I HEARD YOUR VOICE, MY BABE LEAPED IN MY WOMB FOR JOY.
MY SOUL DOES INDEED MAGNIFY GOD, AND MY SPIRIT HAS REJOICED IN GOD MY SAVIOR. AFTER THIS, ALL GENERATIONS WILL CALL ME BLESSED, BECAUSE HE HAS DONE MIGHTY THINGS.
HE HAS EXALTED THOSE OF US WHO ARE OF LOWLY ORIGINS. AS HE SPOKE TO FATHER ABRAHAM, HE HAS REMEMBERED US IN MERCY.
MARY STAYED WITH ELIZABETH FOR ABOUT THREE MONTHS.
THE TIME CAME FOR ELIZABETH TO GIVE BIRTH.
ZACHARIAS IS CERTAIN IT IS GOING TO BE A BOY; HE SAYS AN ANGEL TOLD HIM SO.
WELL, IF IT IS A BOY I SUPPOSE HIS NAME WILL BE ZACHARIAS AFTER HIS FATHER.
HERE HE COMES NOW. LET'S ASK HIM.
HE SAID THAT THE ANGEL MADE HIM DUMB BECAUSE HE DIDN'T BELIEVE.
WHAT ARE YOU GOING TO NAME THE CHILD?
HE WANTS A WRITING TABLET.
HE SAYS HIS NAME WILL BE CALLED JOHN, AS THE ANGEL COMMANDED.
BUT THERE IS NO ONE IN THE FAMILY BY THE NAME OF JOHN.
IT IS INDEED A BOY, A VERY HAIRY BOY.
HIS NAME IS JOHN, ACCORDING TO THE WORD OF THE LORD. HE SHALL INTRODUCE THE MESSIAH TO OUR PEOPLE ISRAEL.
HE SPEAKS! AFTER ALL THESE MONTHS, HE SPEAKS!
COULD IT BE THAT THIS IS INDEED THE ELIJAH OF PROPHECY?

LUKE 1:41-64

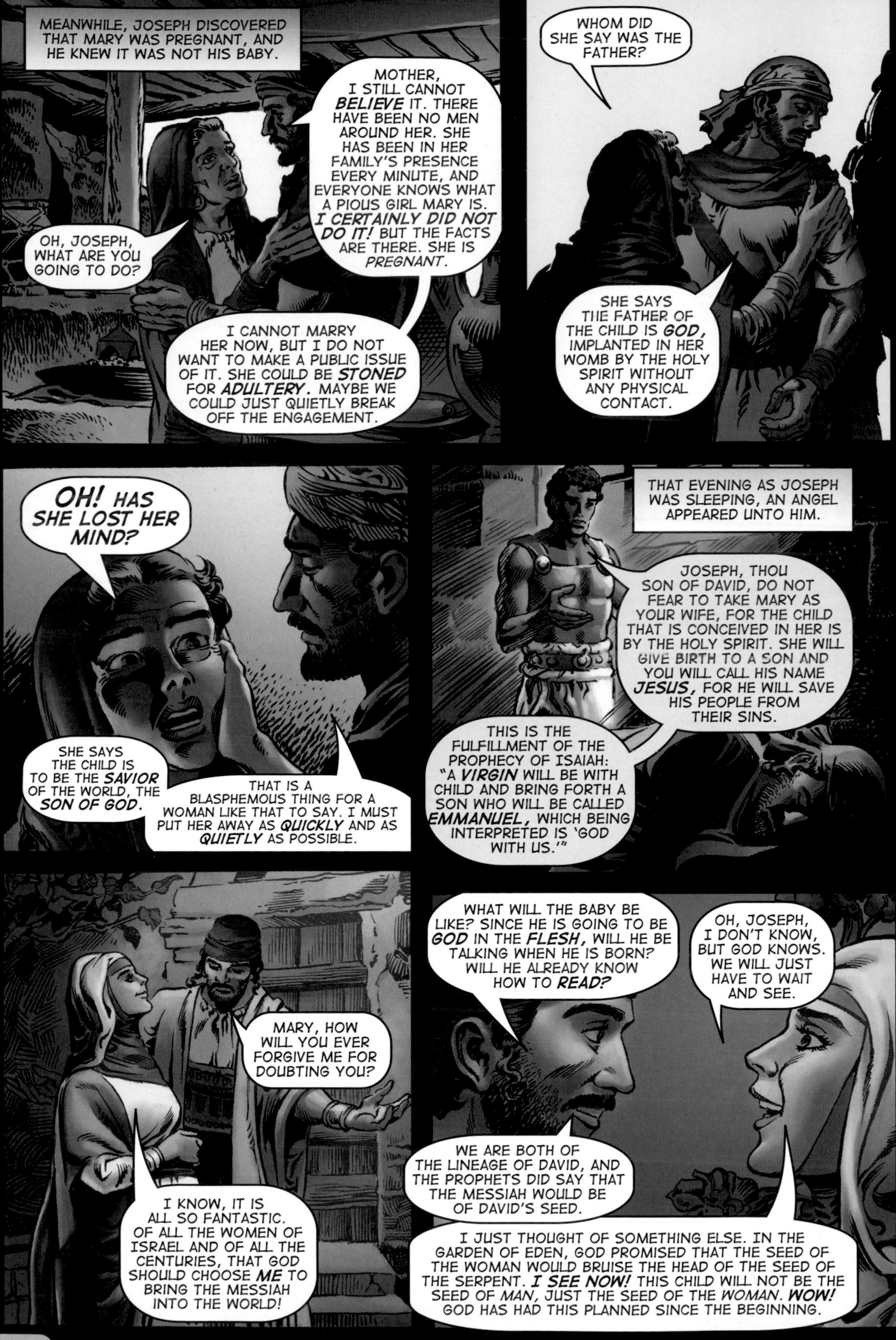
MEANWHILE, JOSEPH DISCOVERED THAT MARY WAS PREGNANT, AND HE KNEW IT WAS NOT HIS BABY.
MOTHER, I STILL CANNOT **BELIEVE** IT. THERE HAVE BEEN NO MEN AROUND HER. SHE HAS BEEN IN HER FAMILY'S PRESENCE EVERY MINUTE, AND EVERYONE KNOWS WHAT A PIOUS GIRL MARY IS. ***I CERTAINLY DID NOT DO IT!*** BUT THE FACTS ARE THERE. SHE IS *PREGNANT*.
OH, JOSEPH, WHAT ARE YOU GOING TO DO?
I CANNOT MARRY HER NOW, BUT I DO NOT WANT TO MAKE A PUBLIC ISSUE OF IT. SHE COULD BE ***STONED*** FOR ***ADULTERY***. MAYBE WE COULD JUST QUIETLY BREAK OFF THE ENGAGEMENT.
WHOM DID SHE SAY WAS THE FATHER?
SHE SAYS THE FATHER OF THE CHILD IS ***GOD***, IMPLANTED IN HER WOMB BY THE HOLY SPIRIT WITHOUT ANY PHYSICAL CONTACT.
OH! HAS SHE LOST HER MIND?
SHE SAYS THE CHILD IS TO BE THE ***SAVIOR*** OF THE WORLD, THE ***SON OF GOD***.
THAT IS A BLASPHEMOUS THING FOR A WOMAN LIKE THAT TO SAY. I MUST PUT HER AWAY AS ***QUICKLY*** AND AS ***QUIETLY*** AS POSSIBLE.
THAT EVENING AS JOSEPH WAS SLEEPING, AN ANGEL APPEARED UNTO HIM.
JOSEPH, THOU SON OF DAVID, DO NOT FEAR TO TAKE MARY AS YOUR WIFE, FOR THE CHILD THAT IS CONCEIVED IN HER IS BY THE HOLY SPIRIT. SHE WILL GIVE BIRTH TO A SON AND YOU WILL CALL HIS NAME ***JESUS***, FOR HE WILL SAVE HIS PEOPLE FROM THEIR SINS.
THIS IS THE FULFILLMENT OF THE PROPHECY OF ISAIAH: "A ***VIRGIN*** WILL BE WITH CHILD AND BRING FORTH A SON WHO WILL BE CALLED ***EMMANUEL***, WHICH BEING INTERPRETED IS 'GOD WITH US.'"
MARY, HOW WILL YOU EVER FORGIVE ME FOR DOUBTING YOU?
I KNOW, IT IS ALL SO FANTASTIC. OF ALL THE WOMEN OF ISRAEL AND OF ALL THE CENTURIES, THAT GOD SHOULD CHOOSE ***ME*** TO BRING THE MESSIAH INTO THE WORLD!
WHAT WILL THE BABY BE LIKE? SINCE HE IS GOING TO BE ***GOD*** IN THE ***FLESH***, WILL HE BE TALKING WHEN HE IS BORN? WILL HE ALREADY KNOW HOW TO ***READ?***
OH, JOSEPH, I DON'T KNOW, BUT GOD KNOWS. WE WILL JUST HAVE TO WAIT AND SEE.
WE ARE BOTH OF THE LINEAGE OF DAVID, AND THE PROPHETS DID SAY THAT THE MESSIAH WOULD BE OF DAVID'S SEED.
I JUST THOUGHT OF SOMETHING ELSE. IN THE GARDEN OF EDEN, GOD PROMISED THAT THE SEED OF THE WOMAN WOULD BRUISE THE HEAD OF THE SEED OF THE SERPENT. ***I SEE NOW!*** THIS CHILD WILL NOT BE THE SEED OF *MAN*, JUST THE SEED OF THE *WOMAN*. ***WOW!*** GOD HAS HAD THIS PLANNED SINCE THE BEGINNING.

GENESIS 3:15; ISAIAH 7:14, 9:7; MATTHEW 1:18-23; LUKE 1:32-33

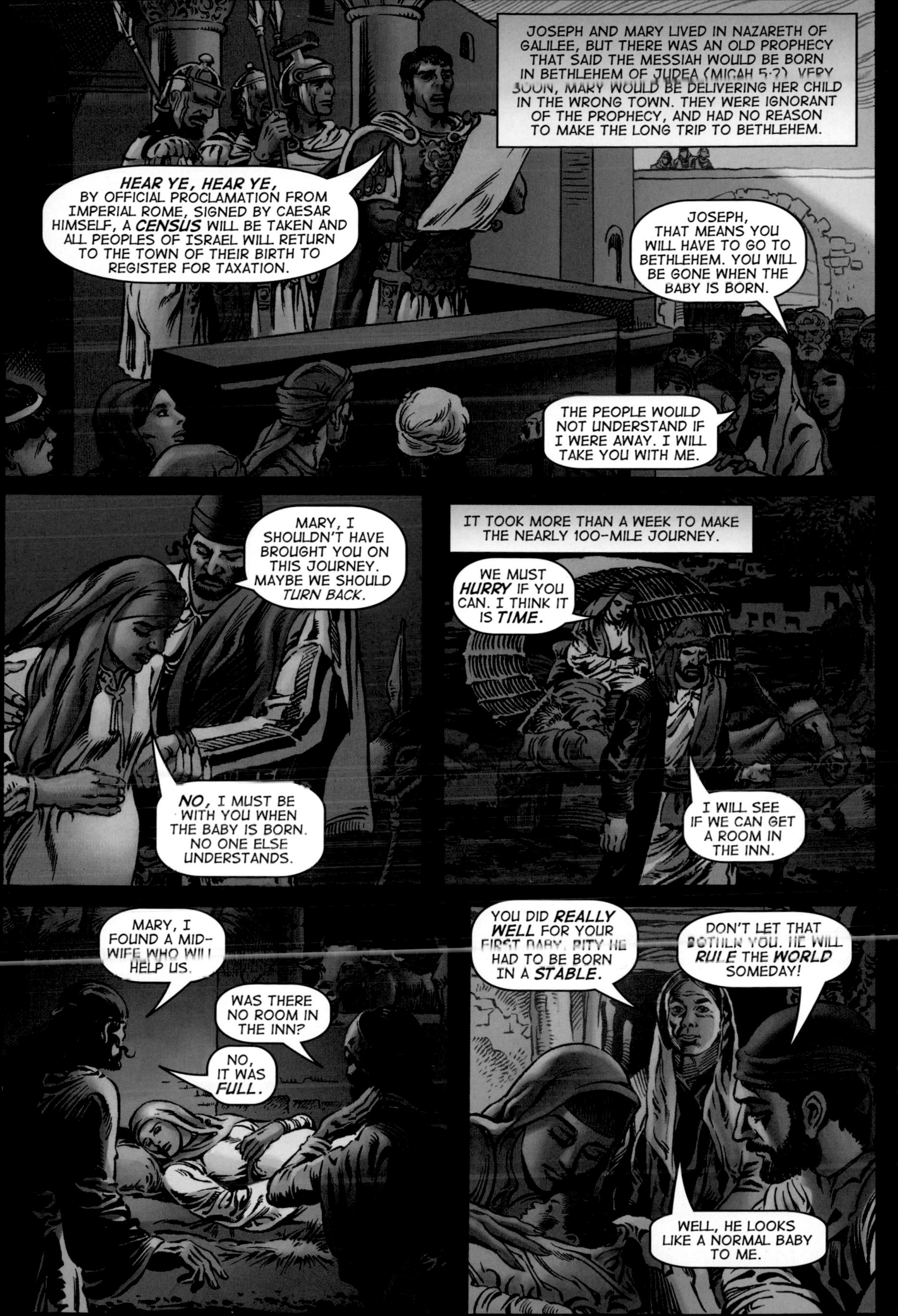

JOSEPH AND MARY LIVED IN NAZARETH OF GALILEE, BUT THERE WAS AN OLD PROPHECY THAT SAID THE MESSIAH WOULD BE BORN IN BETHLEHEM OF JUDEA (MICAH 5:2). VERY SOON, MARY WOULD BE DELIVERING HER CHILD IN THE WRONG TOWN. THEY WERE IGNORANT OF THE PROPHECY, AND HAD NO REASON TO MAKE THE LONG TRIP TO BETHLEHEM.
HEAR YE, HEAR YE, BY OFFICIAL PROCLAMATION FROM IMPERIAL ROME, SIGNED BY CAESAR HIMSELF, A CENSUS WILL BE TAKEN AND ALL PEOPLES OF ISRAEL WILL RETURN TO THE TOWN OF THEIR BIRTH TO REGISTER FOR TAXATION.
JOSEPH, THAT MEANS YOU WILL HAVE TO GO TO BETHLEHEM. YOU WILL BE GONE WHEN THE BABY IS BORN.
THE PEOPLE WOULD NOT UNDERSTAND IF I WERE AWAY. I WILL TAKE YOU WITH ME.
MARY, I SHOULDN'T HAVE BROUGHT YOU ON THIS JOURNEY. MAYBE WE SHOULD TURN BACK.
NO, I MUST BE WITH YOU WHEN THE BABY IS BORN. NO ONE ELSE UNDERSTANDS.
IT TOOK MORE THAN A WEEK TO MAKE THE NEARLY 100-MILE JOURNEY.
WE MUST HURRY IF YOU CAN. I THINK IT IS TIME.
I WILL SEE IF WE CAN GET A ROOM IN THE INN.
MARY, I FOUND A MID-WIFE WHO WILL HELP US.
WAS THERE NO ROOM IN THE INN?
NO, IT WAS FULL.
YOU DID REALLY WELL FOR YOUR FIRST BABY. PITY HE HAD TO BE BORN IN A STABLE.
DON'T LET THAT BOTHER YOU. HE WILL RULE THE WORLD SOMEDAY!
WELL, HE LOOKS LIKE A NORMAL BABY TO ME.

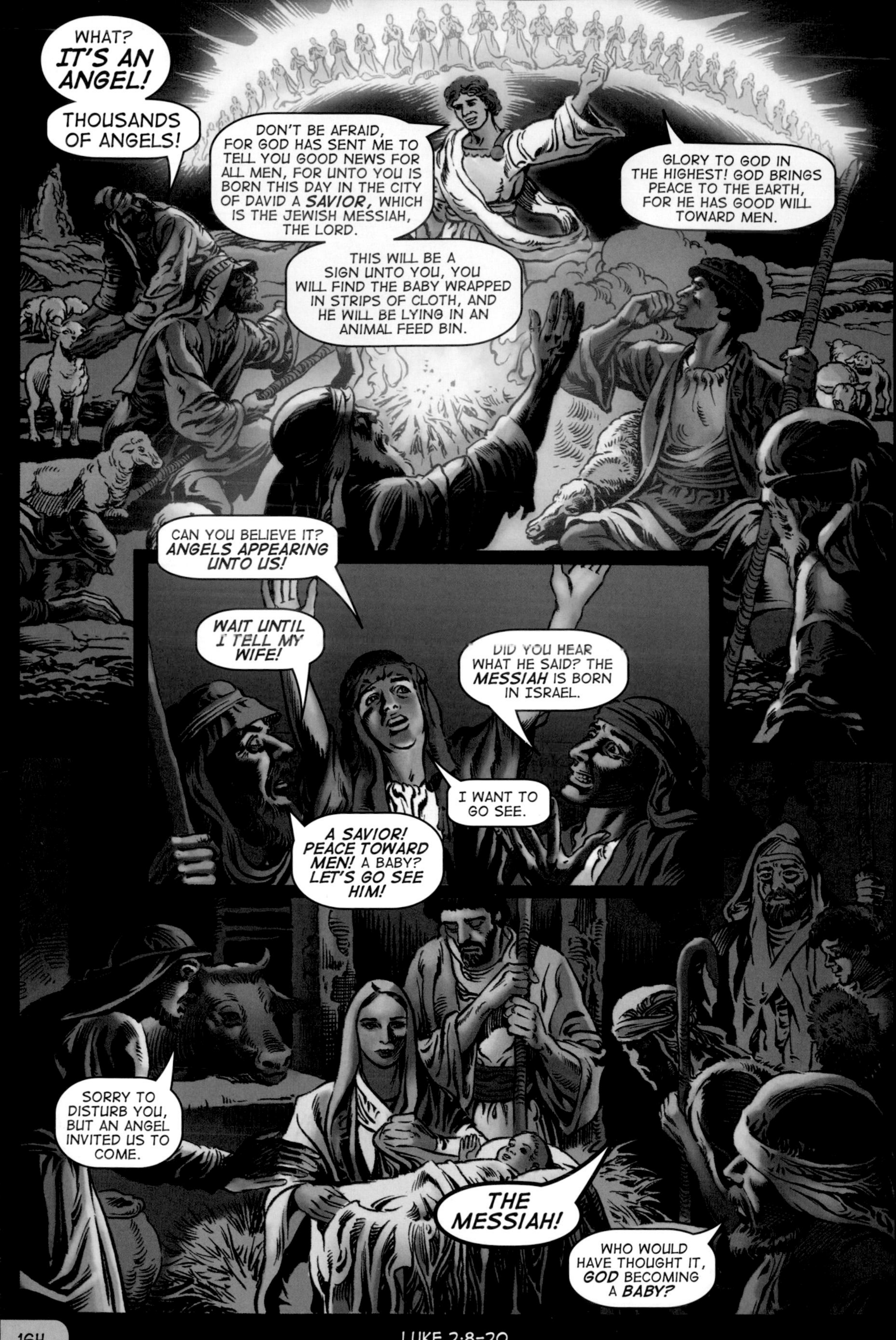
WHAT? IT'S AN ANGEL!
THOUSANDS OF ANGELS!
DON'T BE AFRAID, FOR GOD HAS SENT ME TO TELL YOU GOOD NEWS FOR ALL MEN, FOR UNTO YOU IS BORN THIS DAY IN THE CITY OF DAVID A SAVIOR, WHICH IS THE JEWISH MESSIAH, THE LORD.
THIS WILL BE A SIGN UNTO YOU, YOU WILL FIND THE BABY WRAPPED IN STRIPS OF CLOTH, AND HE WILL BE LYING IN AN ANIMAL FEED BIN.
GLORY TO GOD IN THE HIGHEST! GOD BRINGS PEACE TO THE EARTH, FOR HE HAS GOOD WILL TOWARD MEN.
CAN YOU BELIEVE IT? ANGELS APPEARING UNTO US!
WAIT UNTIL I TELL MY WIFE!
DID YOU HEAR WHAT HE SAID? THE MESSIAH IS BORN IN ISRAEL.
I WANT TO GO SEE.
A SAVIOR! PEACE TOWARD MEN! A BABY? LET'S GO SEE HIM!
SORRY TO DISTURB YOU, BUT AN ANGEL INVITED US TO COME.
THE MESSIAH!
WHO WOULD HAVE THOUGHT IT, GOD BECOMING A BABY?

LUKE 2:8–20

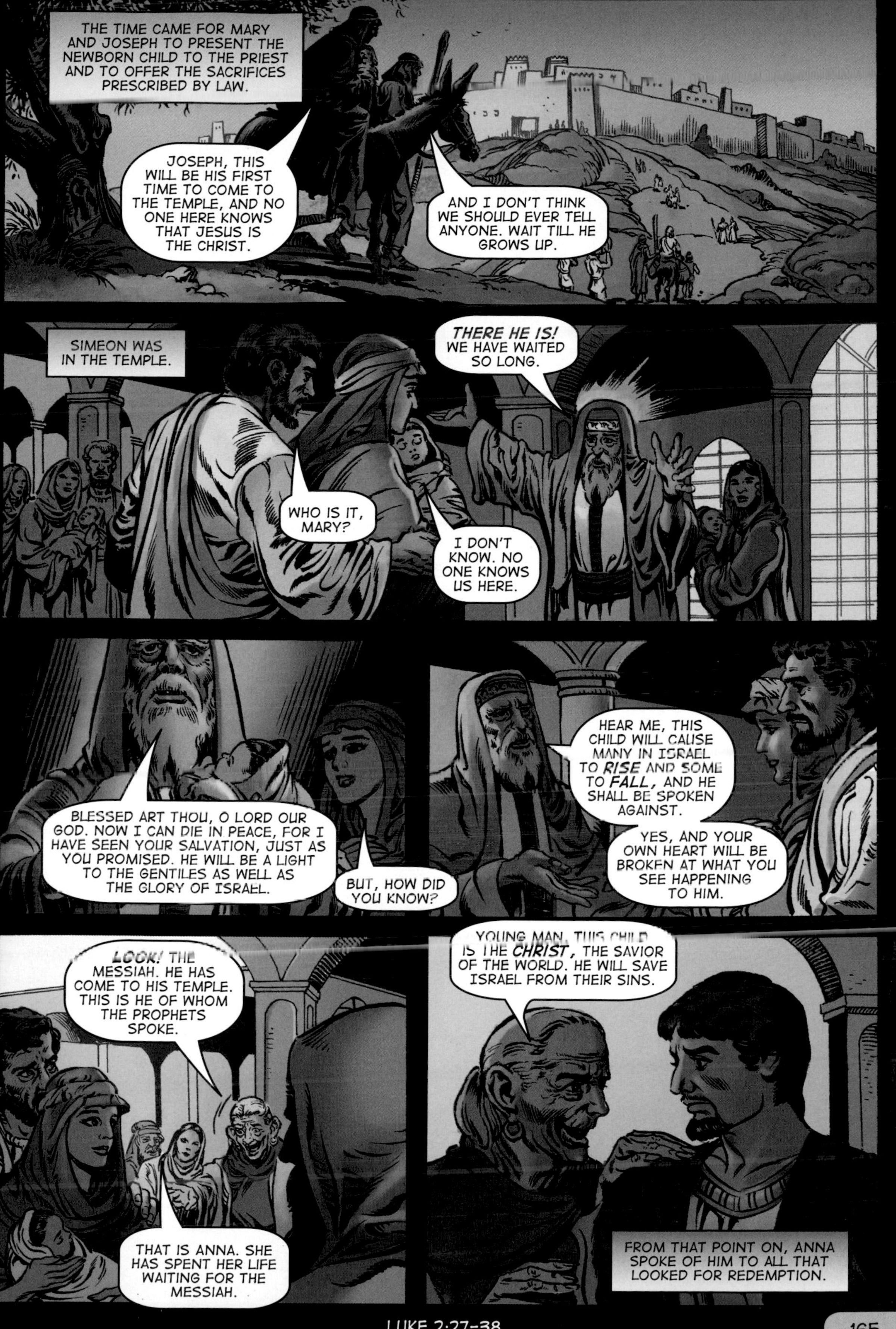
THE TIME CAME FOR MARY AND JOSEPH TO PRESENT THE NEWBORN CHILD TO THE PRIEST AND TO OFFER THE SACRIFICES PRESCRIBED BY LAW.
JOSEPH, THIS WILL BE HIS FIRST TIME TO COME TO THE TEMPLE, AND NO ONE HERE KNOWS THAT JESUS IS THE CHRIST.
AND I DON'T THINK WE SHOULD EVER TELL ANYONE. WAIT TILL HE GROWS UP.
SIMEON WAS IN THE TEMPLE.
THERE HE IS! WE HAVE WAITED SO LONG.
WHO IS IT, MARY?
I DON'T KNOW. NO ONE KNOWS US HERE.
BLESSED ART THOU, O LORD OUR GOD. NOW I CAN DIE IN PEACE, FOR I HAVE SEEN YOUR SALVATION, JUST AS YOU PROMISED. HE WILL BE A LIGHT TO THE GENTILES AS WELL AS THE GLORY OF ISRAEL.
BUT, HOW DID YOU KNOW?
HEAR ME, THIS CHILD WILL CAUSE MANY IN ISRAEL TO RISE AND SOME TO FALL, AND HE SHALL BE SPOKEN AGAINST.
YES, AND YOUR OWN HEART WILL BE BROKEN AT WHAT YOU SEE HAPPENING TO HIM.
LOOK! THE MESSIAH. HE HAS COME TO HIS TEMPLE. THIS IS HE OF WHOM THE PROPHETS SPOKE.
THAT IS ANNA. SHE HAS SPENT HER LIFE WAITING FOR THE MESSIAH.
YOUNG MAN, THIS CHILD IS THE CHRIST, THE SAVIOR OF THE WORLD. HE WILL SAVE ISRAEL FROM THEIR SINS.
FROM THAT POINT ON, ANNA SPOKE OF HIM TO ALL THAT LOOKED FOR REDEMPTION.

LUKE 2:27-38

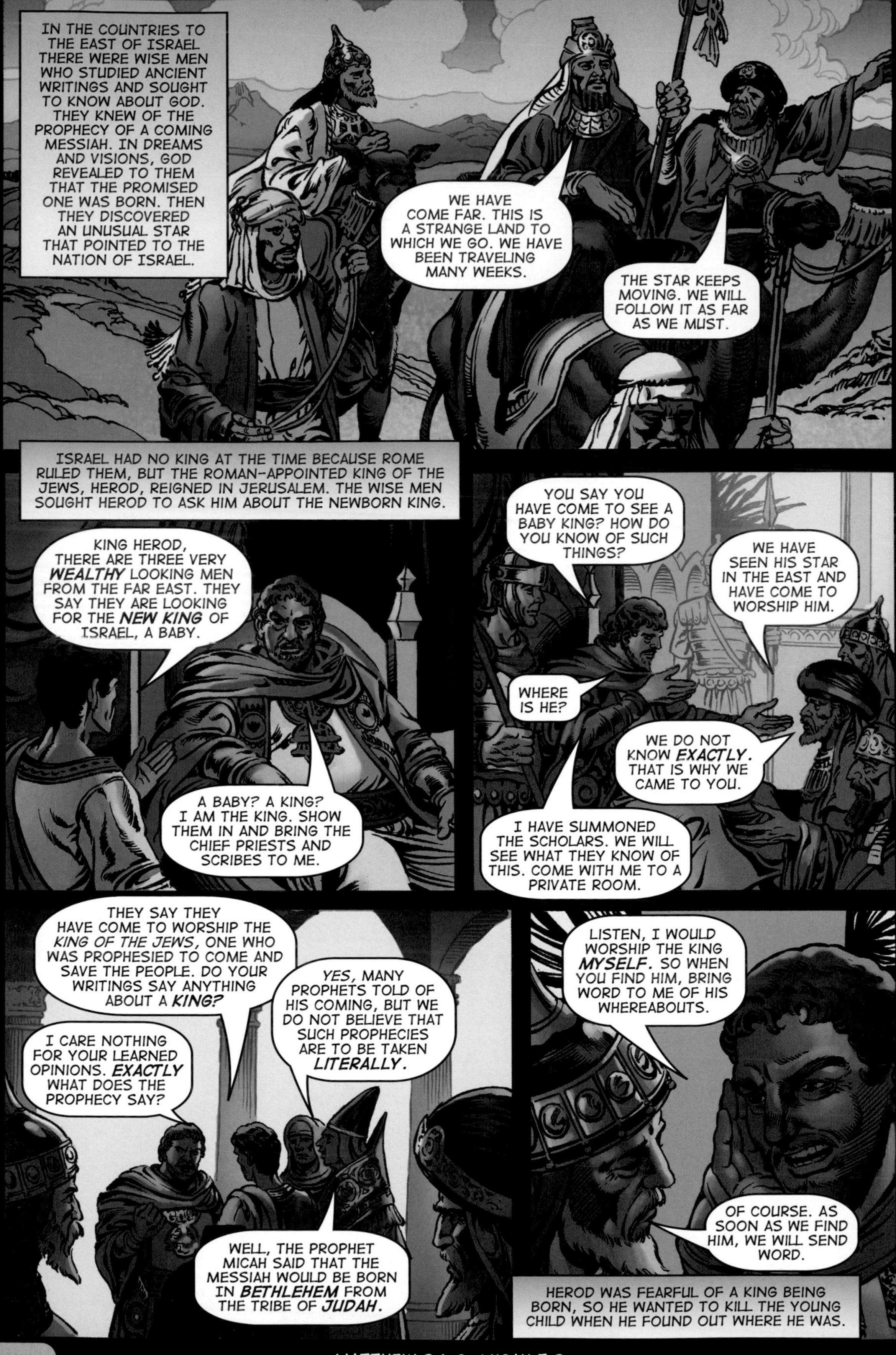

IN THE COUNTRIES TO THE EAST OF ISRAEL THERE WERE WISE MEN WHO STUDIED ANCIENT WRITINGS AND SOUGHT TO KNOW ABOUT GOD. THEY KNEW OF THE PROPHECY OF A COMING MESSIAH. IN DREAMS AND VISIONS, GOD REVEALED TO THEM THAT THE PROMISED ONE WAS BORN. THEN THEY DISCOVERED AN UNUSUAL STAR THAT POINTED TO THE NATION OF ISRAEL.
WE HAVE COME FAR. THIS IS A STRANGE LAND TO WHICH WE GO. WE HAVE BEEN TRAVELING MANY WEEKS.
THE STAR KEEPS MOVING. WE WILL FOLLOW IT AS FAR AS WE MUST.
ISRAEL HAD NO KING AT THE TIME BECAUSE ROME RULED THEM, BUT THE ROMAN-APPOINTED KING OF THE JEWS, HEROD, REIGNED IN JERUSALEM. THE WISE MEN SOUGHT HEROD TO ASK HIM ABOUT THE NEWBORN KING.
KING HEROD, THERE ARE THREE VERY **WEALTHY** LOOKING MEN FROM THE FAR EAST. THEY SAY THEY ARE LOOKING FOR THE ***NEW KING*** OF ISRAEL, A BABY.
A BABY? A KING? I AM THE KING. SHOW THEM IN AND BRING THE CHIEF PRIESTS AND SCRIBES TO ME.
YOU SAY YOU HAVE COME TO SEE A BABY KING? HOW DO YOU KNOW OF SUCH THINGS?
WE HAVE SEEN HIS STAR IN THE EAST AND HAVE COME TO WORSHIP HIM.
WHERE IS HE?
WE DO NOT KNOW ***EXACTLY.*** THAT IS WHY WE CAME TO YOU.
I HAVE SUMMONED THE SCHOLARS. WE WILL SEE WHAT THEY KNOW OF THIS. COME WITH ME TO A PRIVATE ROOM.
THEY SAY THEY HAVE COME TO WORSHIP THE *KING OF THE JEWS,* ONE WHO WAS PROPHESIED TO COME AND SAVE THE PEOPLE. DO YOUR WRITINGS SAY ANYTHING ABOUT A ***KING?***
YES, MANY PROPHETS TOLD OF HIS COMING, BUT WE DO NOT BELIEVE THAT SUCH PROPHECIES ARE TO BE TAKEN ***LITERALLY.***
I CARE NOTHING FOR YOUR LEARNED OPINIONS. ***EXACTLY*** WHAT DOES THE PROPHECY SAY?
WELL, THE PROPHET MICAH SAID THAT THE MESSIAH WOULD BE BORN IN ***BETHLEHEM*** FROM THE TRIBE OF ***JUDAH.***
LISTEN, I WOULD WORSHIP THE KING ***MYSELF.*** SO WHEN YOU FIND HIM, BRING WORD TO ME OF HIS WHEREABOUTS.
OF COURSE. AS SOON AS WE FIND HIM, WE WILL SEND WORD.
HEROD WAS FEARFUL OF A KING BEING BORN, SO HE WANTED TO KILL THE YOUNG CHILD WHEN HE FOUND OUT WHERE HE WAS.

MATTHEW 2:1–8; MICAH 5:2

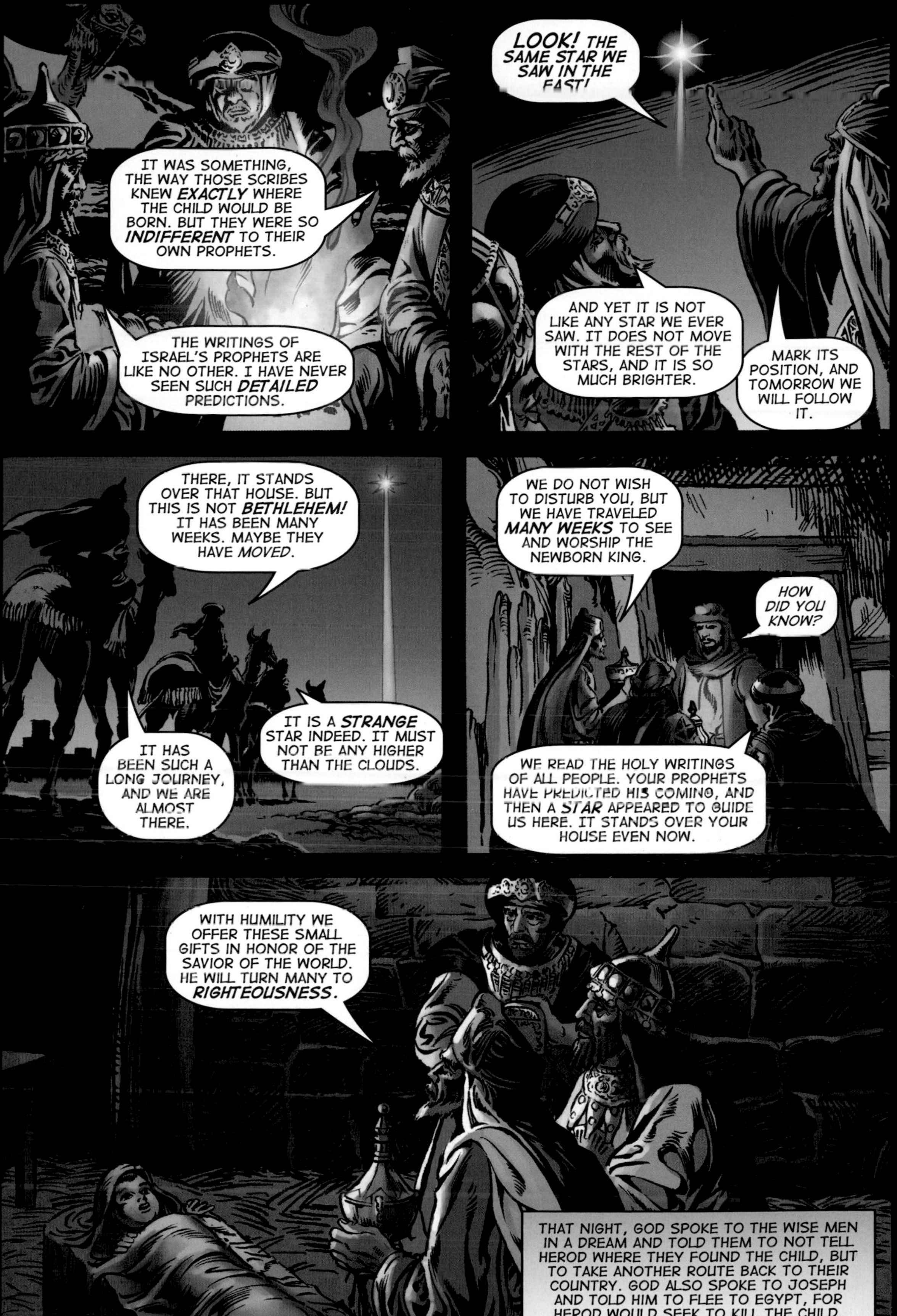
IT WAS SOMETHING, THE WAY THOSE SCRIBES KNEW EXACTLY WHERE THE CHILD WOULD BE BORN. BUT THEY WERE SO INDIFFERENT TO THEIR OWN PROPHETS.
THE WRITINGS OF ISRAEL'S PROPHETS ARE LIKE NO OTHER. I HAVE NEVER SEEN SUCH DETAILED PREDICTIONS.
LOOK! THE SAME STAR WE SAW IN THE EAST!
AND YET IT IS NOT LIKE ANY STAR WE EVER SAW. IT DOES NOT MOVE WITH THE REST OF THE STARS, AND IT IS SO MUCH BRIGHTER.
MARK ITS POSITION, AND TOMORROW WE WILL FOLLOW IT.
THERE, IT STANDS OVER THAT HOUSE. BUT THIS IS NOT BETHLEHEM! IT HAS BEEN MANY WEEKS. MAYBE THEY HAVE MOVED.
IT HAS BEEN SUCH A LONG JOURNEY, AND WE ARE ALMOST THERE.
IT IS A STRANGE STAR INDEED. IT MUST NOT BE ANY HIGHER THAN THE CLOUDS.
WE DO NOT WISH TO DISTURB YOU, BUT WE HAVE TRAVELED MANY WEEKS TO SEE AND WORSHIP THE NEWBORN KING.
HOW DID YOU KNOW?
WE READ THE HOLY WRITINGS OF ALL PEOPLE. YOUR PROPHETS HAVE PREDICTED HIS COMING, AND THEN A STAR APPEARED TO GUIDE US HERE. IT STANDS OVER YOUR HOUSE EVEN NOW.
WITH HUMILITY WE OFFER THESE SMALL GIFTS IN HONOR OF THE SAVIOR OF THE WORLD. HE WILL TURN MANY TO RIGHTEOUSNESS.
THAT NIGHT, GOD SPOKE TO THE WISE MEN IN A DREAM AND TOLD THEM TO NOT TELL HEROD WHERE THEY FOUND THE CHILD, BUT TO TAKE ANOTHER ROUTE BACK TO THEIR COUNTRY. GOD ALSO SPOKE TO JOSEPH AND TOLD HIM TO FLEE TO EGYPT, FOR HEROD WOULD SEEK TO KILL THE CHILD.

MATTHEW 2:9-12

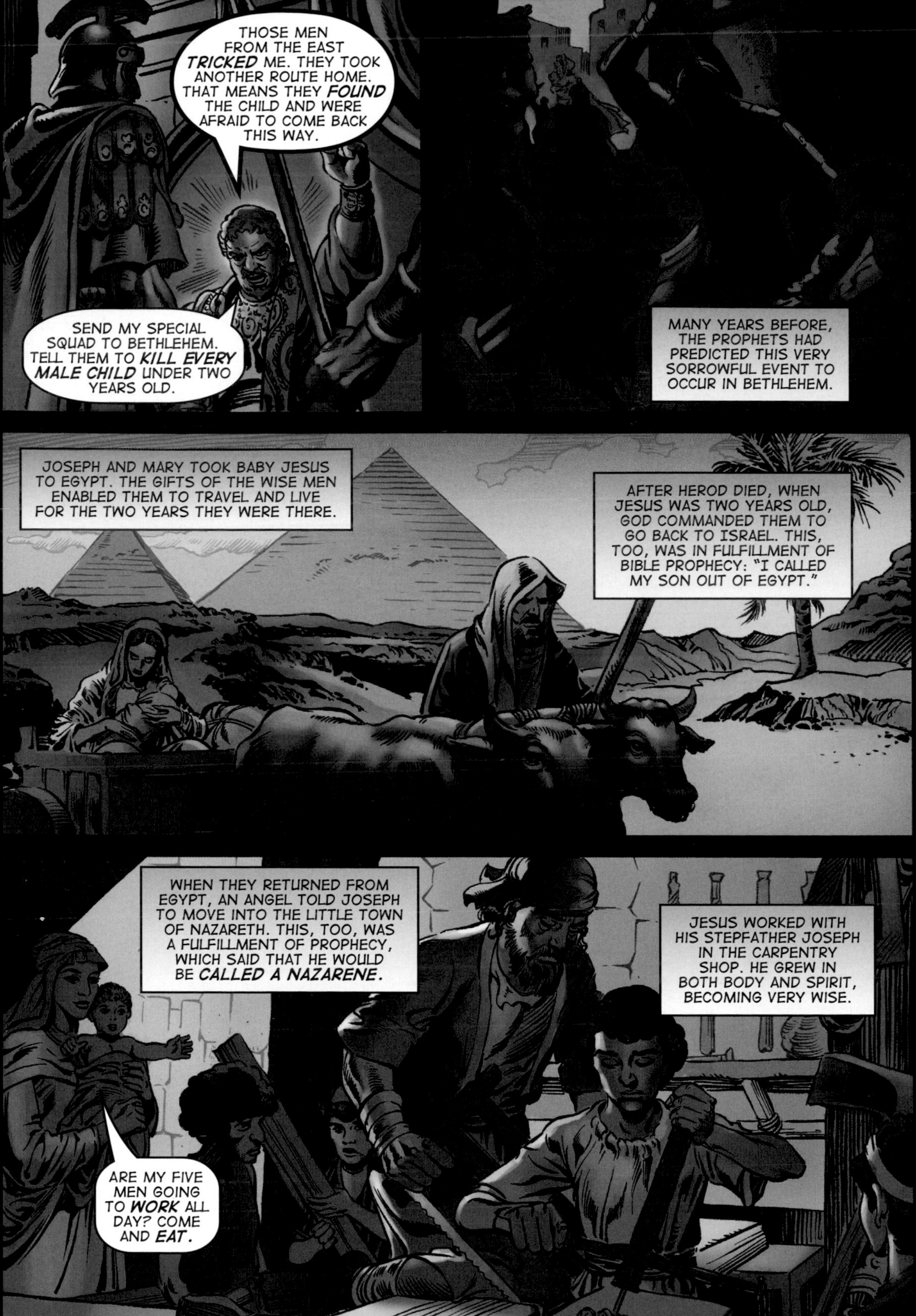
THOSE MEN FROM THE EAST TRICKED ME. THEY TOOK ANOTHER ROUTE HOME. THAT MEANS THEY FOUND THE CHILD AND WERE AFRAID TO COME BACK THIS WAY.
SEND MY SPECIAL SQUAD TO BETHLEHEM. TELL THEM TO KILL EVERY MALE CHILD UNDER TWO YEARS OLD.
MANY YEARS BEFORE, THE PROPHETS HAD PREDICTED THIS VERY SORROWFUL EVENT TO OCCUR IN BETHLEHEM.
JOSEPH AND MARY TOOK BABY JESUS TO EGYPT. THE GIFTS OF THE WISE MEN ENABLED THEM TO TRAVEL AND LIVE FOR THE TWO YEARS THEY WERE THERE.
AFTER HEROD DIED, WHEN JESUS WAS TWO YEARS OLD, GOD COMMANDED THEM TO GO BACK TO ISRAEL. THIS, TOO, WAS IN FULFILLMENT OF BIBLE PROPHECY: "I CALLED MY SON OUT OF EGYPT."
WHEN THEY RETURNED FROM EGYPT, AN ANGEL TOLD JOSEPH TO MOVE INTO THE LITTLE TOWN OF NAZARETH. THIS, TOO, WAS A FULFILLMENT OF PROPHECY, WHICH SAID THAT HE WOULD BE CALLED A NAZARENE.
JESUS WORKED WITH HIS STEPFATHER JOSEPH IN THE CARPENTRY SHOP. HE GREW IN BOTH BODY AND SPIRIT, BECOMING VERY WISE.
ARE MY FIVE MEN GOING TO WORK ALL DAY? COME AND EAT.

JEREMIAH 31:15; HOSEA 11:1; MATTHEW 2:13-23

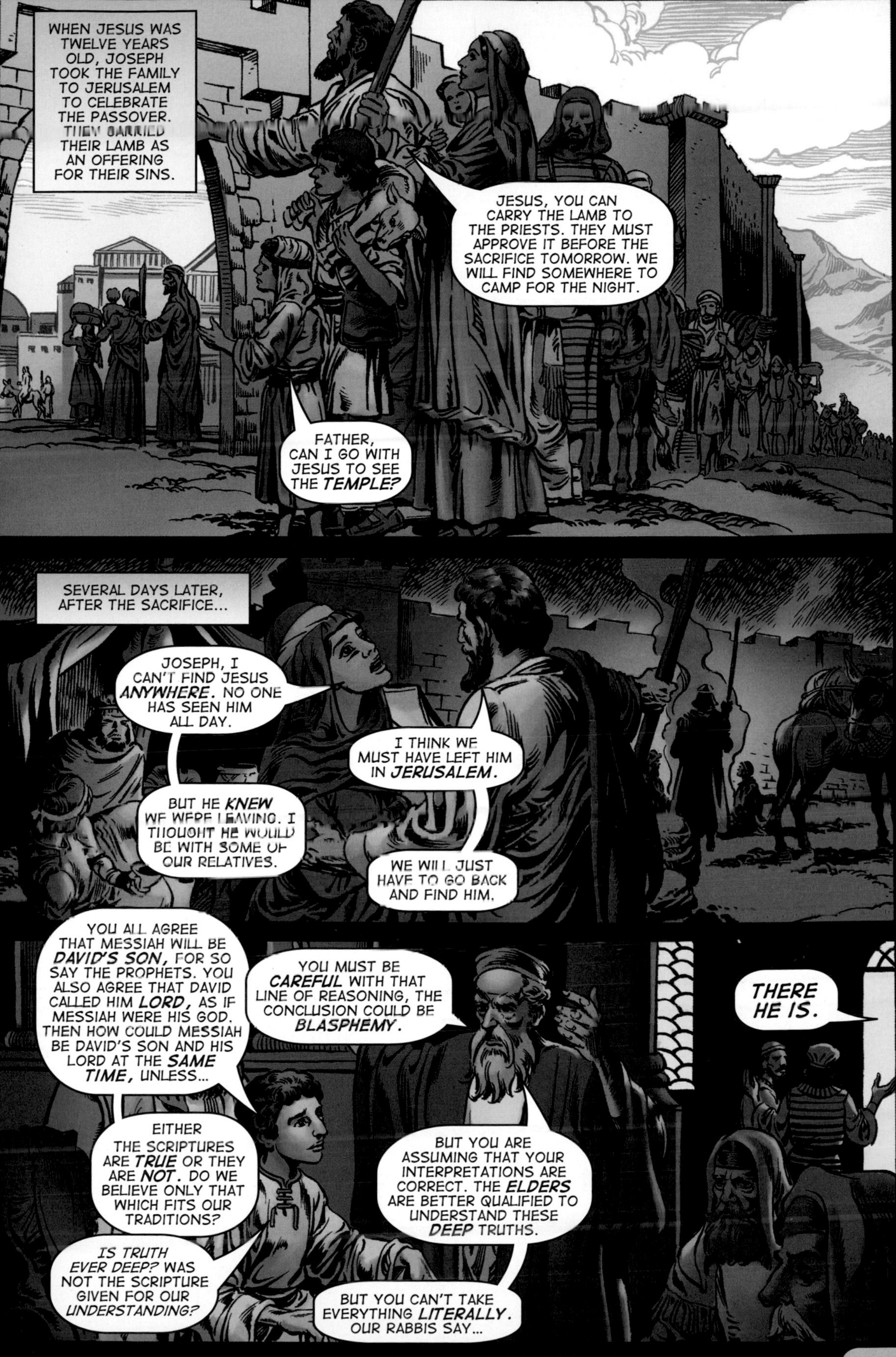
WHEN JESUS WAS TWELVE YEARS OLD, JOSEPH TOOK THE FAMILY TO JERUSALEM TO CELEBRATE THE PASSOVER. THEY CARRIED THEIR LAMB AS AN OFFERING FOR THEIR SINS.
JESUS, YOU CAN CARRY THE LAMB TO THE PRIESTS. THEY MUST APPROVE IT BEFORE THE SACRIFICE TOMORROW. WE WILL FIND SOMEWHERE TO CAMP FOR THE NIGHT.
FATHER, CAN I GO WITH JESUS TO SEE THE *TEMPLE?*
SEVERAL DAYS LATER, AFTER THE SACRIFICE...
JOSEPH, I CAN'T FIND JESUS *ANYWHERE*. NO ONE HAS SEEN HIM ALL DAY.
I THINK WE MUST HAVE LEFT HIM IN *JERUSALEM*.
BUT HE *KNEW* WE WERE LEAVING. I THOUGHT HE WOULD BE WITH SOME OF OUR RELATIVES.
WE WILL JUST HAVE TO GO BACK AND FIND HIM.
YOU ALL AGREE THAT MESSIAH WILL BE *DAVID'S SON*, FOR SO SAY THE PROPHETS. YOU ALSO AGREE THAT DAVID CALLED HIM *LORD*, AS IF MESSIAH WERE HIS GOD. THEN HOW COULD MESSIAH BE DAVID'S SON AND HIS LORD AT THE *SAME TIME*, UNLESS...
YOU MUST BE *CAREFUL* WITH THAT LINE OF REASONING, THE CONCLUSION COULD BE *BLASPHEMY*.
THERE HE IS.
EITHER THE SCRIPTURES ARE *TRUE* OR THEY ARE *NOT*. DO WE BELIEVE ONLY THAT WHICH FITS OUR TRADITIONS?
BUT YOU ARE ASSUMING THAT YOUR INTERPRETATIONS ARE CORRECT. THE *ELDERS* ARE BETTER QUALIFIED TO UNDERSTAND THESE *DEEP* TRUTHS.
IS TRUTH EVER DEEP? WAS NOT THE SCRIPTURE GIVEN FOR OUR *UNDERSTANDING?*
BUT YOU CAN'T TAKE EVERYTHING *LITERALLY*. OUR RABBIS SAY...

ISAIAH 9:7; LUKE 2:42-46; 2 TIMOTHY 3:16-17

JESUS, WE HAVE LOOKED *EVERYWHERE* FOR YOU. *WHY HAVE YOU DONE THIS TO US?*

HE HAS BEEN WITH US FOR TWO DAYS. YOU HAVE A MOST *UNUSUAL* SON.

WHY DID YOU LOOK *EVERYWHERE?* DID YOU NOT KNOW THAT I MUST BE DOING MY FATHER'S BUSINESS?

I HAVE *NEVER* SEEN A YOUNG MAN WHO KNEW SO MUCH *SCRIPTURE.*

WHAT DID HE MEAN, HE "*MUST BE ABOUT HIS FATHER'S BUSINESS?*" WAS NOT THAT HIS *FATHER* WHO WAS LOOKING FOR HIM?

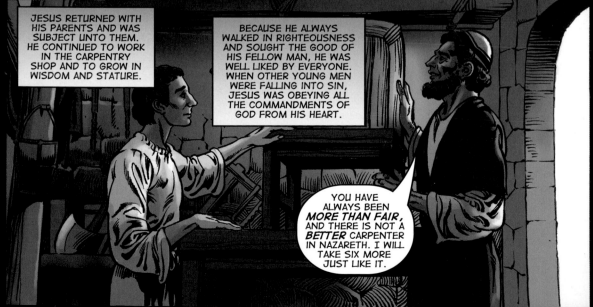

JESUS RETURNED WITH HIS PARENTS AND WAS SUBJECT UNTO THEM. HE CONTINUED TO WORK IN THE CARPENTRY SHOP AND TO GROW IN WISDOM AND STATURE.

BECAUSE HE ALWAYS WALKED IN RIGHTEOUSNESS AND SOUGHT THE GOOD OF HIS FELLOW MAN, HE WAS WELL LIKED BY EVERYONE. WHEN OTHER YOUNG MEN WERE FALLING INTO SIN, JESUS WAS OBEYING ALL THE COMMANDMENTS OF GOD FROM HIS HEART.

YOU HAVE ALWAYS BEEN *MORE THAN FAIR,* AND THERE IS NOT A *BETTER* CARPENTER IN NAZARETH. I WILL TAKE SIX MORE JUST LIKE IT.

REMEMBER THAT ELIZABETH HAD GIVEN BIRTH TO A SON SIX MONTHS BEFORE MARY. THE ANGEL TOLD ZACHARIAS TO NAME HIM JOHN, AND THAT HE WOULD PREPARE THE HEARTS OF THE PEOPLE FOR THE COMING OF MESSIAH. THIS WAS ALSO PREDICTED FIVE HUNDRED YEARS EARLIER BY SEVERAL OF THE PROPHETS.

YOU MUST TURN FROM YOUR *EVIL WAYS* AND *OBEY GOD,* FOR THE KINGDOM OF HEAVEN IS ABOUT TO BE INSTITUTED. IF YOU WILL PREPARE YOUR HEARTS TO RECEIVE THE MESSIAH, I WILL BAPTIZE YOU IN WATER.

BUT THERE IS ONE COMING AFTER ME WHO IS PREFERRED BEFORE ME, FOR HE EXISTED BEFORE I DID. HE WILL BAPTIZE YOU, NOT INTO WATER, BUT INTO THE HOLY SPIRIT OF GOD HIMSELF. TURN FROM YOUR SINS BEFORE IT IS TOO LATE.

WHAT SHOULD WE DO, JOHN? WHAT DOES GOD REQUIRE FOR US TO BE *RIGHTEOUS?*

JOHN, WHAT MUST WE WHO WORK IN THE GOVERNMENT DO TO PLEASE GOD? I AM A TAX COLLECTOR AND NABAL HERE IS A CUSTOMS WORKER.

IF YOU HAVE *TWO COATS* AND YOU MEET A MAN WHO HAS NONE, *GIVE* HIM ONE OF YOUR COATS. IF YOU HAVE FOOD AND SOMEONE IS *HUNGRY,* THEN *FEED* HIM.

SEEK *JUSTICE* FOR ALL MEN.

DO NOT TAKE *BRIBES.* DO NOT USE YOUR OFFICE TO EXACT MONEY FROM ANYONE. BE *FAIR* AND *JUST* IN ALL YOUR DEALINGS.

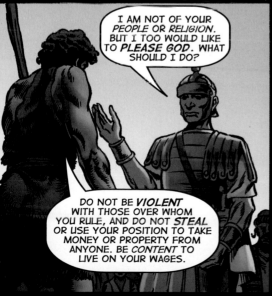

I AM NOT OF YOUR *PEOPLE* OR *RELIGION.* BUT I TOO WOULD LIKE TO *PLEASE GOD.* WHAT SHOULD I DO?

DO NOT BE *VIOLENT* WITH THOSE OVER WHOM YOU RULE, AND DO NOT *STEAL* OR USE YOUR POSITION TO TAKE MONEY OR PROPERTY FROM ANYONE. BE *CONTENT* TO LIVE ON YOUR WAGES.

HE THAT COMES AFTER ME IS *MIGHTIER* THAN I AM, AND I AM NOT WORTHY TO *UNTIE HIS SHOES.* IF YOU REPENT AND BELIEVE, HE WILL BAPTIZE YOU WITH THE HOLY SPIRIT.

IF YOU *REJECT* HIM AND CONTINUE IN YOUR SIN, HE WILL PLUNGE YOU INTO THE FIRES OF *ETERNAL DAMNATION.* STOP YOUR SINNING NOW.

MALACHI 3:1; LUKE 3:2-18, 7:24, 27

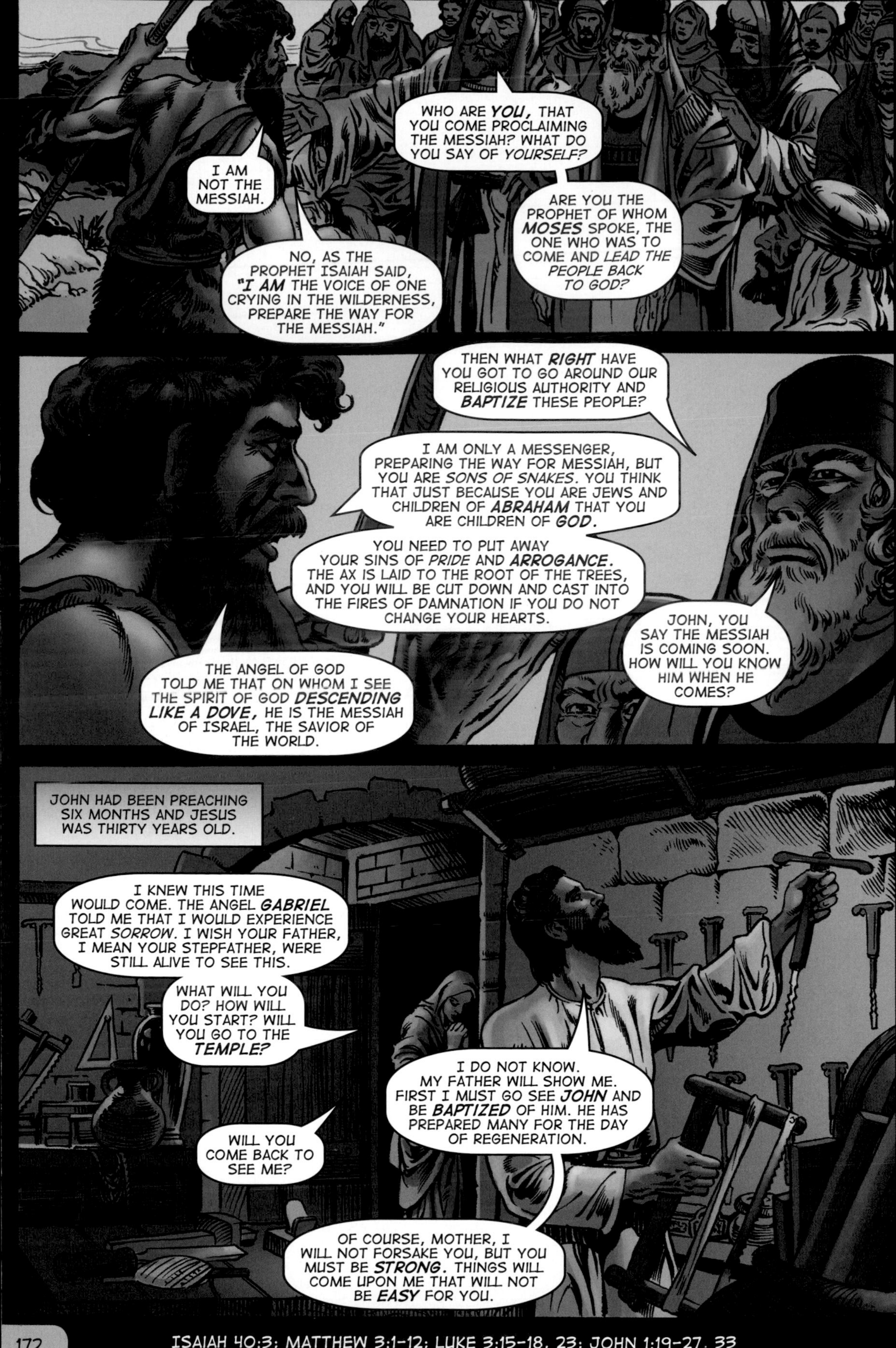
WHO ARE YOU, THAT YOU COME PROCLAIMING THE MESSIAH? WHAT DO YOU SAY OF YOURSELF?
I AM NOT THE MESSIAH.
ARE YOU THE PROPHET OF WHOM MOSES SPOKE, THE ONE WHO WAS TO COME AND LEAD THE PEOPLE BACK TO GOD?
NO, AS THE PROPHET ISAIAH SAID, "I AM THE VOICE OF ONE CRYING IN THE WILDERNESS, PREPARE THE WAY FOR THE MESSIAH."
THEN WHAT RIGHT HAVE YOU GOT TO GO AROUND OUR RELIGIOUS AUTHORITY AND BAPTIZE THESE PEOPLE?
I AM ONLY A MESSENGER, PREPARING THE WAY FOR MESSIAH, BUT YOU ARE SONS OF SNAKES. YOU THINK THAT JUST BECAUSE YOU ARE JEWS AND CHILDREN OF ABRAHAM THAT YOU ARE CHILDREN OF GOD.
YOU NEED TO PUT AWAY YOUR SINS OF PRIDE AND ARROGANCE. THE AX IS LAID TO THE ROOT OF THE TREES, AND YOU WILL BE CUT DOWN AND CAST INTO THE FIRES OF DAMNATION IF YOU DO NOT CHANGE YOUR HEARTS.
JOHN, YOU SAY THE MESSIAH IS COMING SOON. HOW WILL YOU KNOW HIM WHEN HE COMES?
THE ANGEL OF GOD TOLD ME THAT ON WHOM I SEE THE SPIRIT OF GOD DESCENDING LIKE A DOVE, HE IS THE MESSIAH OF ISRAEL, THE SAVIOR OF THE WORLD.
JOHN HAD BEEN PREACHING SIX MONTHS AND JESUS WAS THIRTY YEARS OLD.
I KNEW THIS TIME WOULD COME. THE ANGEL GABRIEL TOLD ME THAT I WOULD EXPERIENCE GREAT SORROW. I WISH YOUR FATHER, I MEAN YOUR STEPFATHER, WERE STILL ALIVE TO SEE THIS.
WHAT WILL YOU DO? HOW WILL YOU START? WILL YOU GO TO THE TEMPLE?
I DO NOT KNOW. MY FATHER WILL SHOW ME. FIRST I MUST GO SEE JOHN AND BE BAPTIZED OF HIM. HE HAS PREPARED MANY FOR THE DAY OF REGENERATION.
WILL YOU COME BACK TO SEE ME?
OF COURSE, MOTHER, I WILL NOT FORSAKE YOU, BUT YOU MUST BE STRONG. THINGS WILL COME UPON ME THAT WILL NOT BE EASY FOR YOU.

ISAIAH 40:3; MATTHEW 3:1-12; LUKE 3:15-18, 23; JOHN 1:19-27, 33

PREPARE FOR THE COMING OF THE **MESSIAH.** YOU FATHERS MUST TURN YOUR HEARTS TO YOUR **CHILDREN.** YOU MUST BECOME **WISE** AND DEDICATE YOUR TIME AND ENERGIES TO TEACHING THEM THE *LAWS OF GOD*. IF YOUR DISOBEDIENT CHILDREN SEE YOUR SINCERITY, IT WILL TURN THEIR HEARTS TO THEIR FATHERS AND YOUR FAMILIES **WILL BE HEALED.**
IF THIS IS YOUR HEART, AND YOU ARE WILLING TO FOLLOW THE MESSIAH WHEN HE COMES, THEN COME DOWN INTO THE WATER AND I WILL BAPTIZE YOU WITH THE BAPTISM OF REPENTANCE, AND WHEN MESSIAH COMES HE WILL ***FORGIVE YOUR SINS.***
JOHN, WILL YOU BAPTIZE ME?
IT WOULD BE MORE APPROPRIATE IF ***YOU*** WOULD BAPTIZE ***ME.*** YOU ARE INDEED A ***RIGHTEOUS*** MAN.
JOHN, I MUST OBEY ALL THE LAWS OF GOD. I WILL DO AS MY FATHER HAS COMMANDED HIS PEOPLE.
THE DOVE! I SEE THE DOVE!

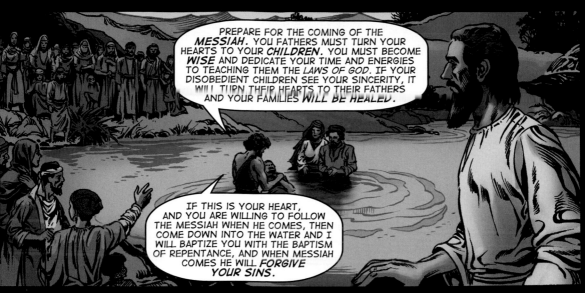

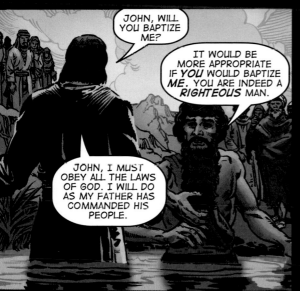

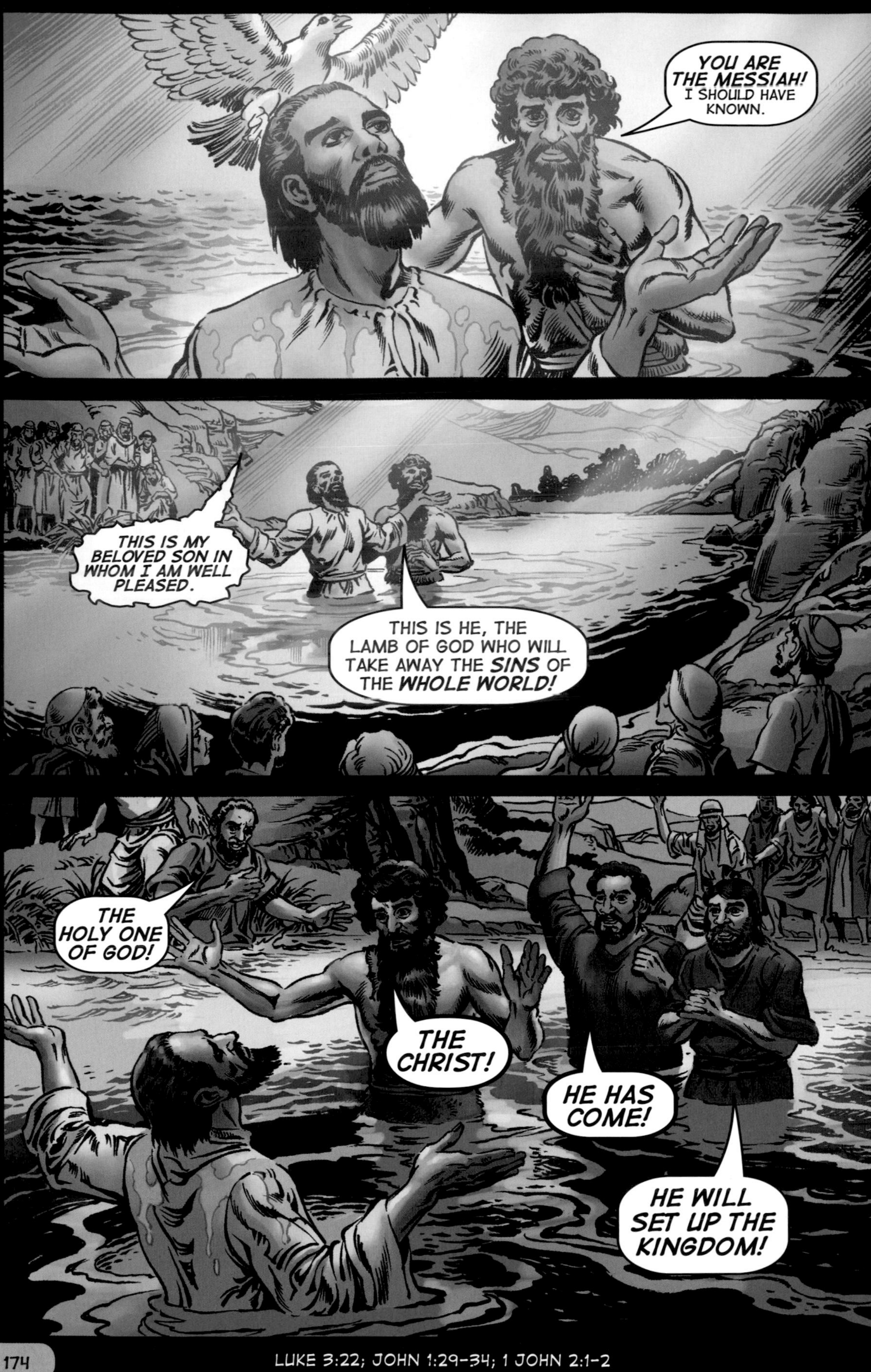
YOU ARE THE MESSIAH! I SHOULD HAVE KNOWN.
THIS IS MY BELOVED SON IN WHOM I AM WELL PLEASED.
THIS IS HE, THE LAMB OF GOD WHO WILL TAKE AWAY THE SINS OF THE WHOLE WORLD!
THE HOLY ONE OF GOD!
THE CHRIST!
HE HAS COME!
HE WILL SET UP THE KINGDOM!

LUKE 3:22; JOHN 1:29-34; 1 JOHN 2:1-2

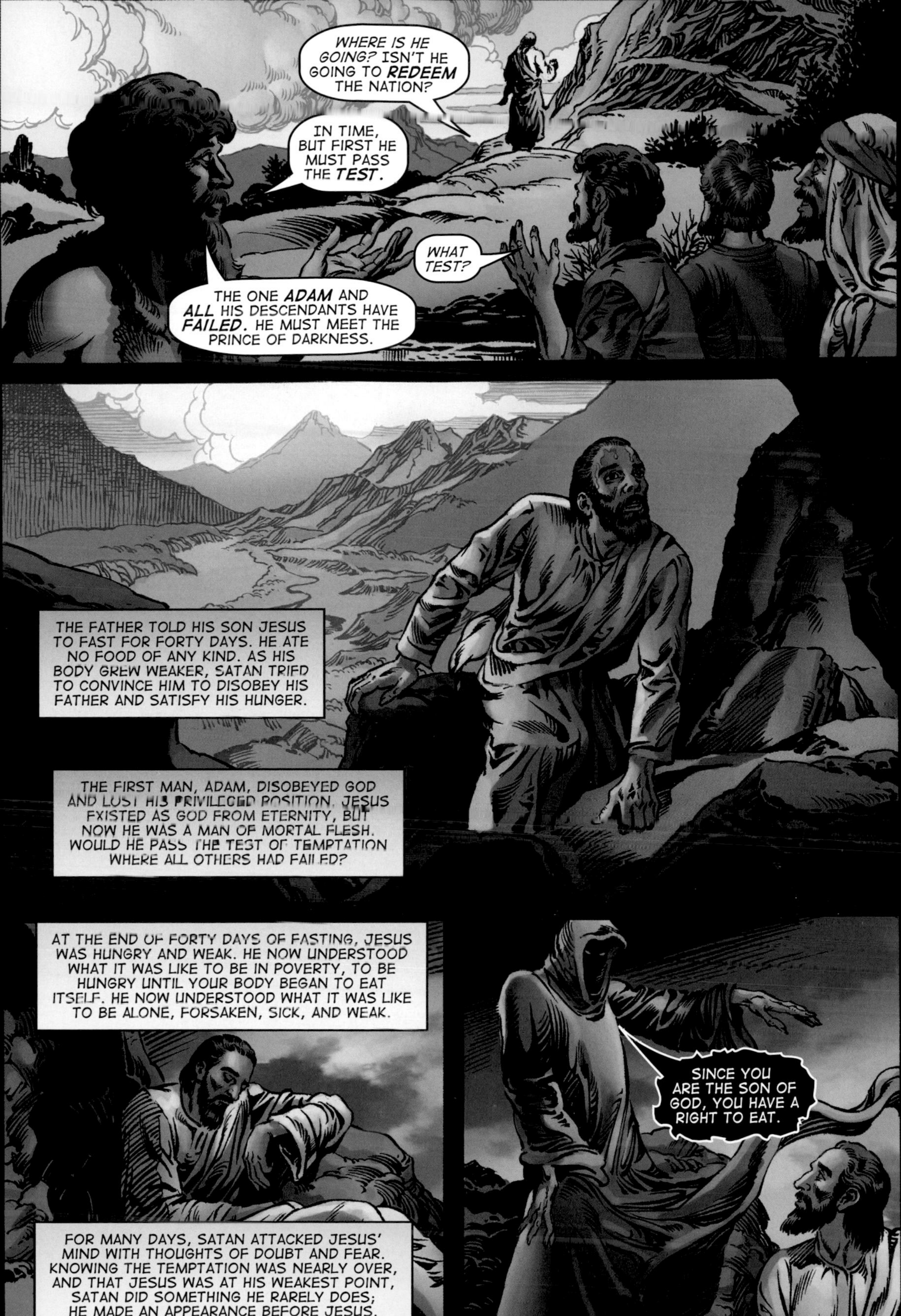

WHERE IS HE GOING? ISN'T HE GOING TO REDEEM THE NATION?
IN TIME, BUT FIRST HE MUST PASS THE TEST.
WHAT TEST?
THE ONE ADAM AND ALL HIS DESCENDANTS HAVE FAILED. HE MUST MEET THE PRINCE OF DARKNESS.
THE FATHER TOLD HIS SON JESUS TO FAST FOR FORTY DAYS. HE ATE NO FOOD OF ANY KIND. AS HIS BODY GREW WEAKER, SATAN TRIED TO CONVINCE HIM TO DISOBEY HIS FATHER AND SATISFY HIS HUNGER.
THE FIRST MAN, ADAM, DISOBEYED GOD AND LOST HIS PRIVILEGED POSITION. JESUS EXISTED AS GOD FROM ETERNITY, BUT NOW HE WAS A MAN OF MORTAL FLESH. WOULD HE PASS THE TEST OF TEMPTATION WHERE ALL OTHERS HAD FAILED?
AT THE END OF FORTY DAYS OF FASTING, JESUS WAS HUNGRY AND WEAK. HE NOW UNDERSTOOD WHAT IT WAS LIKE TO BE IN POVERTY, TO BE HUNGRY UNTIL YOUR BODY BEGAN TO EAT ITSELF. HE NOW UNDERSTOOD WHAT IT WAS LIKE TO BE ALONE, FORSAKEN, SICK, AND WEAK.
FOR MANY DAYS, SATAN ATTACKED JESUS' MIND WITH THOUGHTS OF DOUBT AND FEAR. KNOWING THE TEMPTATION WAS NEARLY OVER, AND THAT JESUS WAS AT HIS WEAKEST POINT, SATAN DID SOMETHING HE RARELY DOES; HE MADE AN APPEARANCE BEFORE JESUS.
SINCE YOU ARE THE SON OF GOD, YOU HAVE A RIGHT TO EAT.

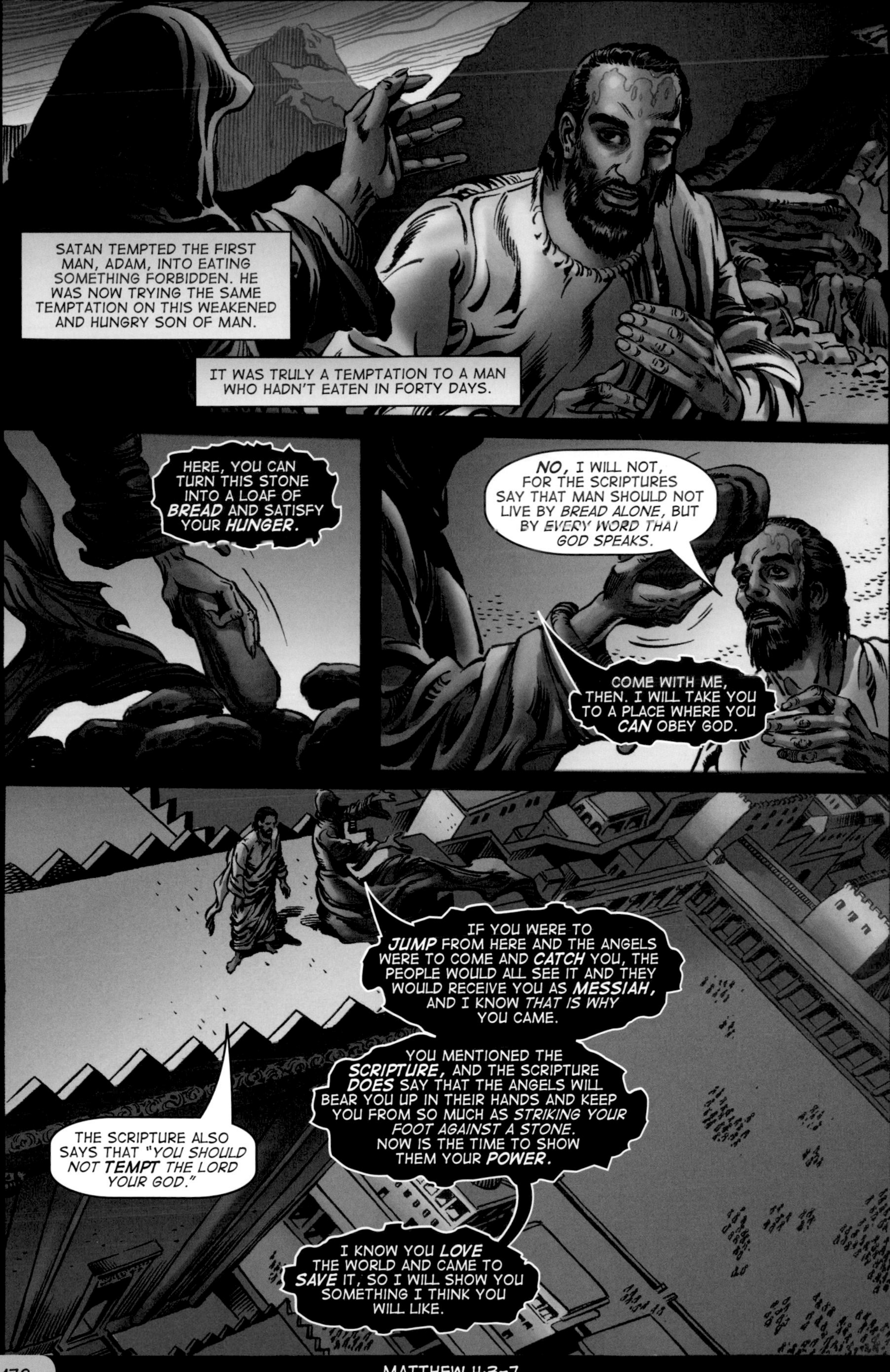
SATAN TEMPTED THE FIRST MAN, ADAM, INTO EATING SOMETHING FORBIDDEN. HE WAS NOW TRYING THE SAME TEMPTATION ON THIS WEAKENED AND HUNGRY SON OF MAN.
IT WAS TRULY A TEMPTATION TO A MAN WHO HADN'T EATEN IN FORTY DAYS.
HERE, YOU CAN TURN THIS STONE INTO A LOAF OF BREAD AND SATISFY YOUR HUNGER.
NO, I WILL NOT, FOR THE SCRIPTURES SAY THAT MAN SHOULD NOT LIVE BY BREAD ALONE, BUT BY EVERY WORD THAT GOD SPEAKS.
COME WITH ME, THEN. I WILL TAKE YOU TO A PLACE WHERE YOU CAN OBEY GOD.
IF YOU WERE TO JUMP FROM HERE AND THE ANGELS WERE TO COME AND CATCH YOU, THE PEOPLE WOULD ALL SEE IT AND THEY WOULD RECEIVE YOU AS MESSIAH, AND I KNOW THAT IS WHY YOU CAME.
YOU MENTIONED THE SCRIPTURE, AND THE SCRIPTURE DOES SAY THAT THE ANGELS WILL BEAR YOU UP IN THEIR HANDS AND KEEP YOU FROM SO MUCH AS STRIKING YOUR FOOT AGAINST A STONE. NOW IS THE TIME TO SHOW THEM YOUR POWER.
THE SCRIPTURE ALSO SAYS THAT "YOU SHOULD NOT TEMPT THE LORD YOUR GOD."
I KNOW YOU LOVE THE WORLD AND CAME TO SAVE IT, SO I WILL SHOW YOU SOMETHING I THINK YOU WILL LIKE.

THERE NOW, FROM HERE WE CAN SEE MOST OF THE WORLD'S LEADING KINGDOMS. AREN'T THEY JUST *ABSOLUTELY GLORIOUS?* EVER SINCE ADAM TURNED HIS BACK ON YOUR RULE, I HAVE OWNED THIS WORLD. MEN *GIVE IT* TO ME OVER AND OVER AGAIN. IT IS *ALL MINE.* I AM THE GOD OF THIS WORLD, NOT *YOU.*

BUT I WOULD GIVE IT ALL TO YOU...ON JUST *ONE* CONDITION. IF YOU WILL JUST KNEEL DOWN THIS ONCE AND *WORSHIP* ME, I WILL GIVE UP MY CONTROL OF THE WORLD, AND YOU CAN HAVE IT AND EVERYBODY IN IT. WHAT DO YOU SAY?

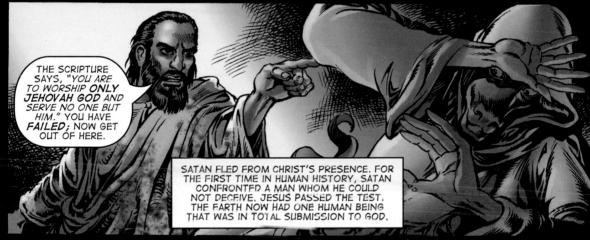

THE SCRIPTURE SAYS, "YOU ARE TO WORSHIP *ONLY* JEHOVAH GOD AND SERVE NO ONE BUT HIM." YOU HAVE *FAILED;* NOW GET OUT OF HERE.

SATAN FLED FROM CHRIST'S PRESENCE. FOR THE FIRST TIME IN HUMAN HISTORY, SATAN CONFRONTED A MAN WHOM HE COULD NOT DECEIVE. JESUS PASSED THE TEST. THE EARTH NOW HAD ONE HUMAN BEING THAT WAS IN TOTAL SUBMISSION TO GOD,

THE FORTY-DAY TRIAL WAS OVER, BUT JESUS WAS TOO WEAK TO GO ON.

ANGELS CAME WITH FOOD AND WATER AND MINISTERED UNTO HIM. WHEN HIS BODY WAS STRENGTHENED, HE RETURNED TO WHERE JOHN WAS PREACHING.

MATTHEW 4:8-11; LUKE 4:14

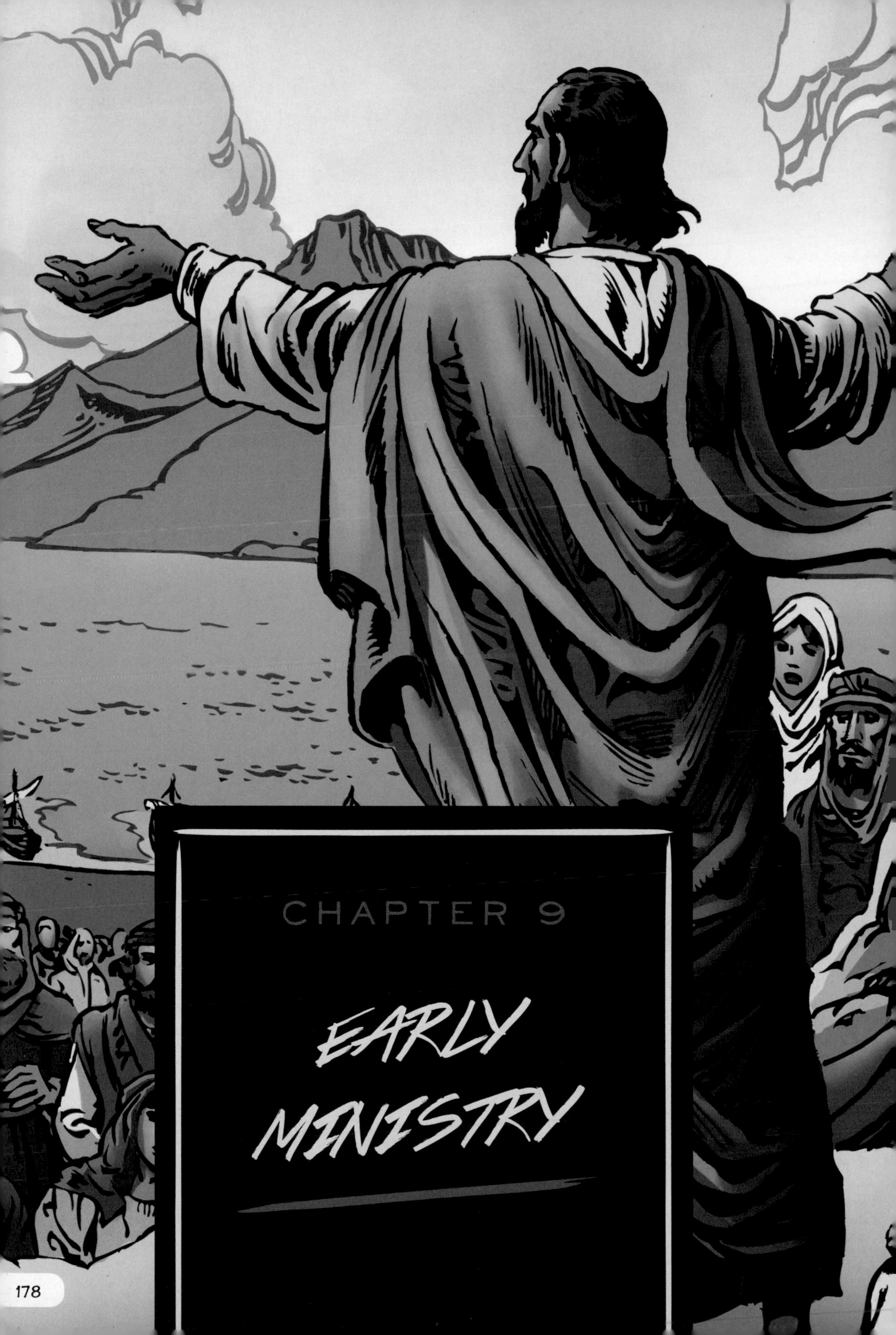

CHAPTER 9

EARLY MINISTRY

LOOK, HERE COMES THE *LAMB OF GOD* WHO WILL TAKE AWAY THE SINS OF THE ENTIRE WORLD.

THIS IS THE MESSIAH!

HE OF WHOM THE PROPHETS SPOKE.

WHAT WILL HE DO?

FOLLOW JESUS.

BUT I CANNOT LEAVE YOU, MASTER.

I AM NOT YOUR MASTER. I MUST *DECREASE* TO NOTHING AND HE MUST *INCREASE* UNTIL HE IS *ALL*. HE IS TRULY THE MESSIAH, THE SAVIOR OF THE WORLD. *FOLLOW HIM.*

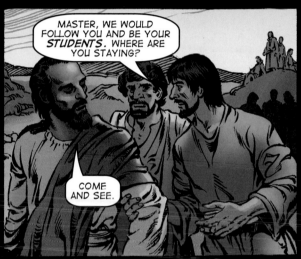

MASTER, WE WOULD FOLLOW YOU AND BE YOUR *STUDENTS*. WHERE ARE YOU STAYING?

COME AND SEE.

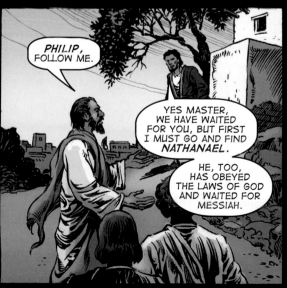

PHILIP, FOLLOW ME.

YES MASTER, WE HAVE WAITED FOR YOU, BUT FIRST I MUST GO AND FIND *NATHANAEL.*

HE, TOO, HAS OBEYED THE LAWS OF GOD AND WAITED FOR MESSIAH.

WHERE IS *NATHANAEL?*

HE IS IN THE ORCHARD. IS ANYTHING WRONG?

NO, EVERYTHING IS *RIGHT.*

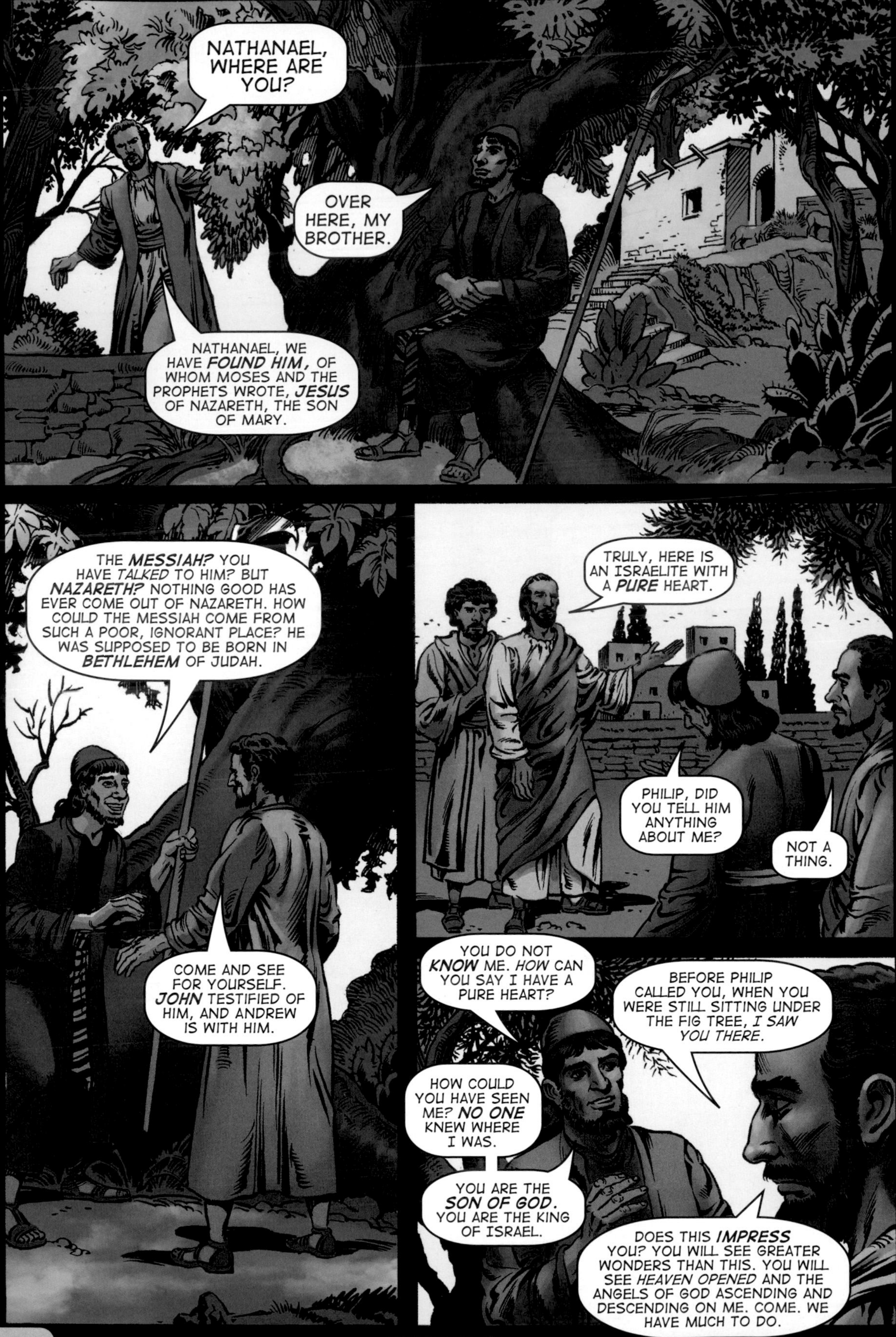
NATHANAEL, WHERE ARE YOU?
OVER HERE, MY BROTHER.
NATHANAEL, WE HAVE FOUND HIM, OF WHOM MOSES AND THE PROPHETS WROTE, JESUS OF NAZARETH, THE SON OF MARY.
THE MESSIAH? YOU HAVE TALKED TO HIM? BUT NAZARETH? NOTHING GOOD HAS EVER COME OUT OF NAZARETH. HOW COULD THE MESSIAH COME FROM SUCH A POOR, IGNORANT PLACE? HE WAS SUPPOSED TO BE BORN IN BETHLEHEM OF JUDAH.
COME AND SEE FOR YOURSELF. JOHN TESTIFIED OF HIM, AND ANDREW IS WITH HIM.
TRULY, HERE IS AN ISRAELITE WITH A PURE HEART.
PHILIP, DID YOU TELL HIM ANYTHING ABOUT ME?
NOT A THING.
YOU DO NOT KNOW ME. HOW CAN YOU SAY I HAVE A PURE HEART?
BEFORE PHILIP CALLED YOU, WHEN YOU WERE STILL SITTING UNDER THE FIG TREE, I SAW YOU THERE.
HOW COULD YOU HAVE SEEN ME? NO ONE KNEW WHERE I WAS.
YOU ARE THE SON OF GOD. YOU ARE THE KING OF ISRAEL.
DOES THIS IMPRESS YOU? YOU WILL SEE GREATER WONDERS THAN THIS. YOU WILL SEE HEAVEN OPENED AND THE ANGELS OF GOD ASCENDING AND DESCENDING ON ME. COME. WE HAVE MUCH TO DO.

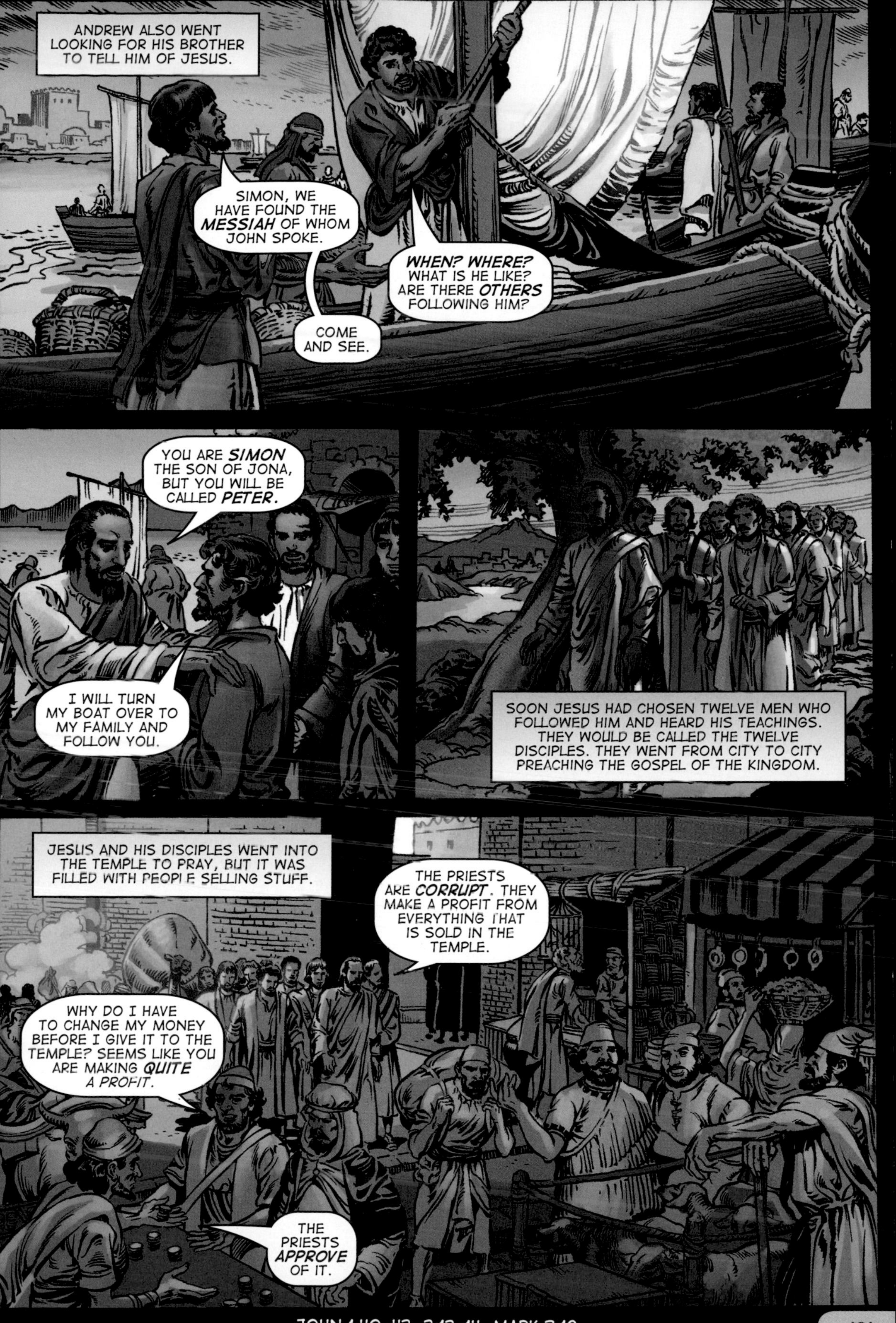
ANDREW ALSO WENT LOOKING FOR HIS BROTHER TO TELL HIM OF JESUS.
SIMON, WE HAVE FOUND THE MESSIAH OF WHOM JOHN SPOKE.
WHEN? WHERE? WHAT IS HE LIKE? ARE THERE OTHERS FOLLOWING HIM?
COME AND SEE.
YOU ARE SIMON THE SON OF JONA, BUT YOU WILL BE CALLED PETER.
I WILL TURN MY BOAT OVER TO MY FAMILY AND FOLLOW YOU.
SOON JESUS HAD CHOSEN TWELVE MEN WHO FOLLOWED HIM AND HEARD HIS TEACHINGS. THEY WOULD BE CALLED THE TWELVE DISCIPLES. THEY WENT FROM CITY TO CITY PREACHING THE GOSPEL OF THE KINGDOM.
JESUS AND HIS DISCIPLES WENT INTO THE TEMPLE TO PRAY, BUT IT WAS FILLED WITH PEOPLE SELLING STUFF.
THE PRIESTS ARE CORRUPT. THEY MAKE A PROFIT FROM EVERYTHING THAT IS SOLD IN THE TEMPLE.
WHY DO I HAVE TO CHANGE MY MONEY BEFORE I GIVE IT TO THE TEMPLE? SEEMS LIKE YOU ARE MAKING QUITE A PROFIT.
THE PRIESTS APPROVE OF IT.

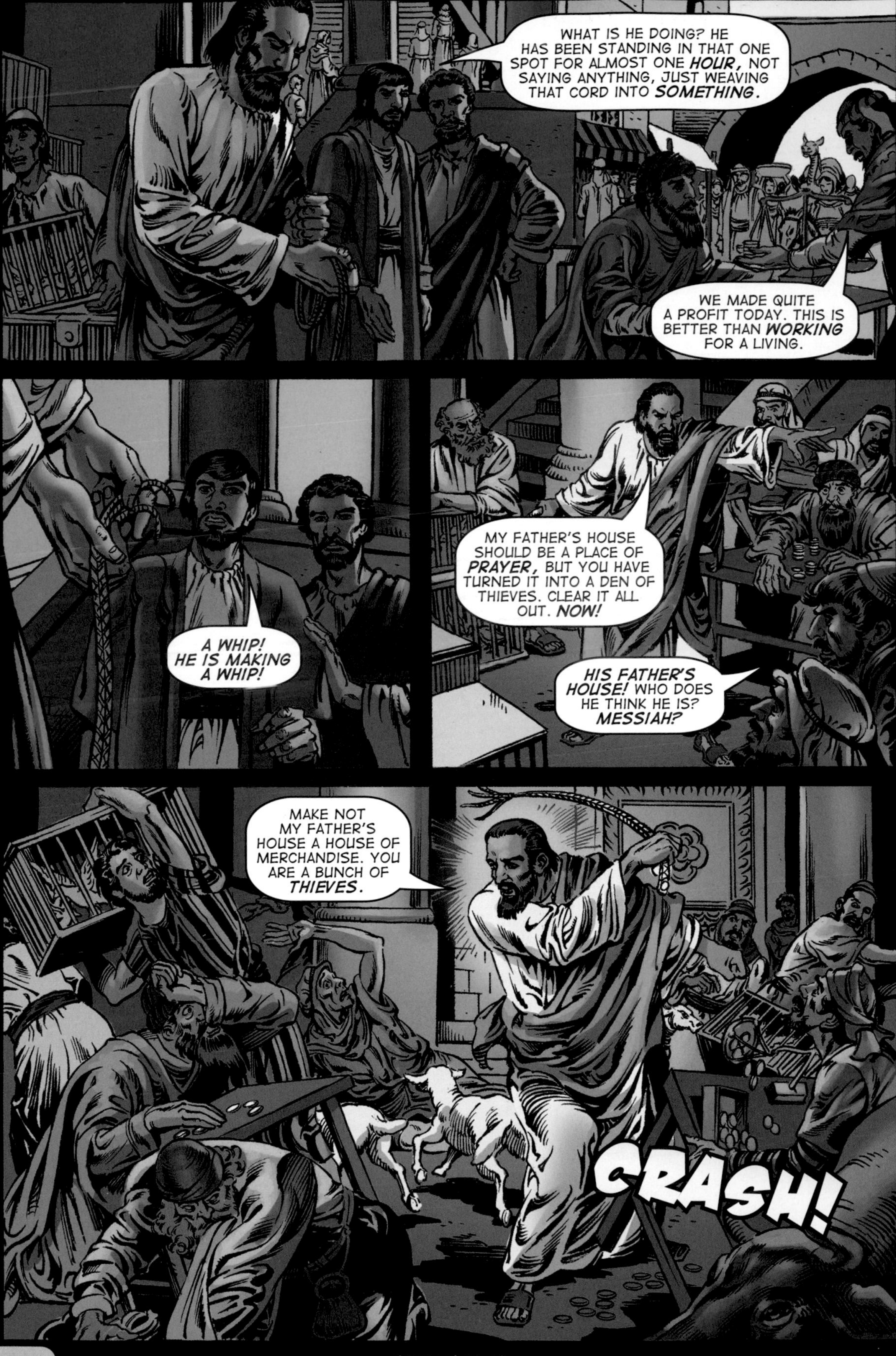
WHAT IS HE DOING? HE HAS BEEN STANDING IN THAT ONE SPOT FOR ALMOST ONE HOUR, NOT SAYING ANYTHING, JUST WEAVING THAT CORD INTO SOMETHING.
WE MADE QUITE A PROFIT TODAY. THIS IS BETTER THAN WORKING FOR A LIVING.
A WHIP! HE IS MAKING A WHIP!
MY FATHER'S HOUSE SHOULD BE A PLACE OF PRAYER, BUT YOU HAVE TURNED IT INTO A DEN OF THIEVES. CLEAR IT ALL OUT. NOW!
HIS FATHER'S HOUSE! WHO DOES HE THINK HE IS? MESSIAH?
MAKE NOT MY FATHER'S HOUSE A HOUSE OF MERCHANDISE. YOU ARE A BUNCH OF THIEVES.
CRASH!

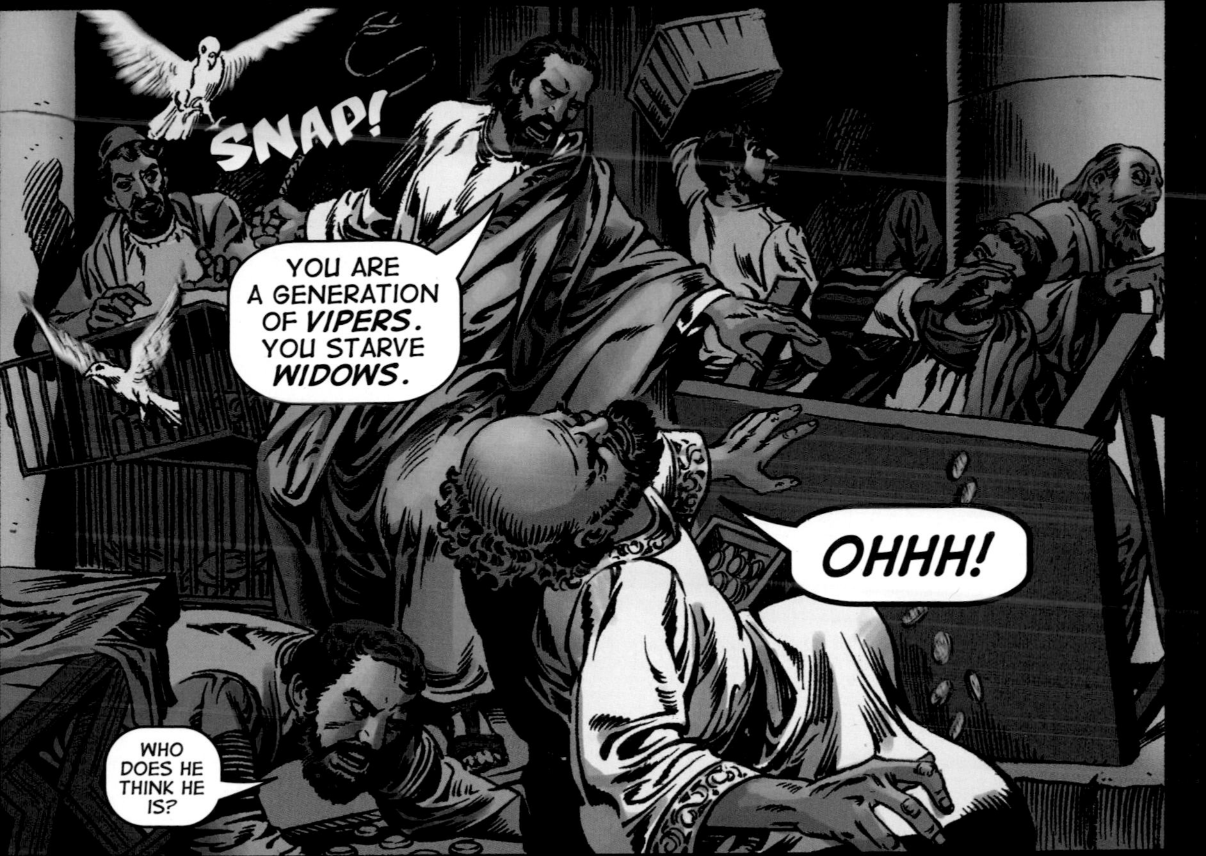
SNAP!
YOU ARE A GENERATION OF VIPERS. YOU STARVE WIDOWS.
OHHH!
WHO DOES HE THINK HE IS?

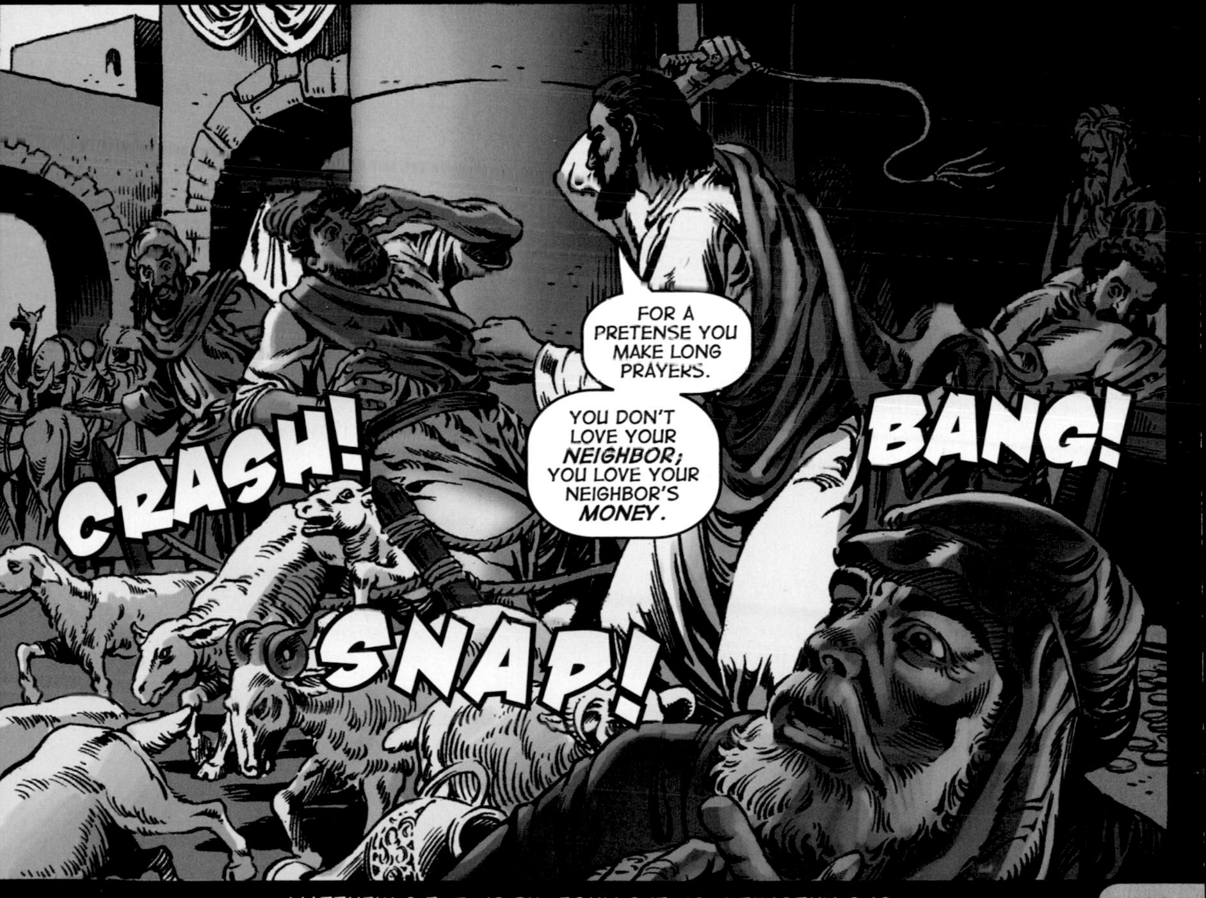
FOR A PRETENSE YOU MAKE LONG PRAYERS.
YOU DON'T LOVE YOUR NEIGHBOR; YOU LOVE YOUR NEIGHBOR'S MONEY.
CRASH!
BANG!
SNAP!

MATTHEW 6:5-7, 12:34; JOHN 2:15-16; 1 TIMOTHY 6:10

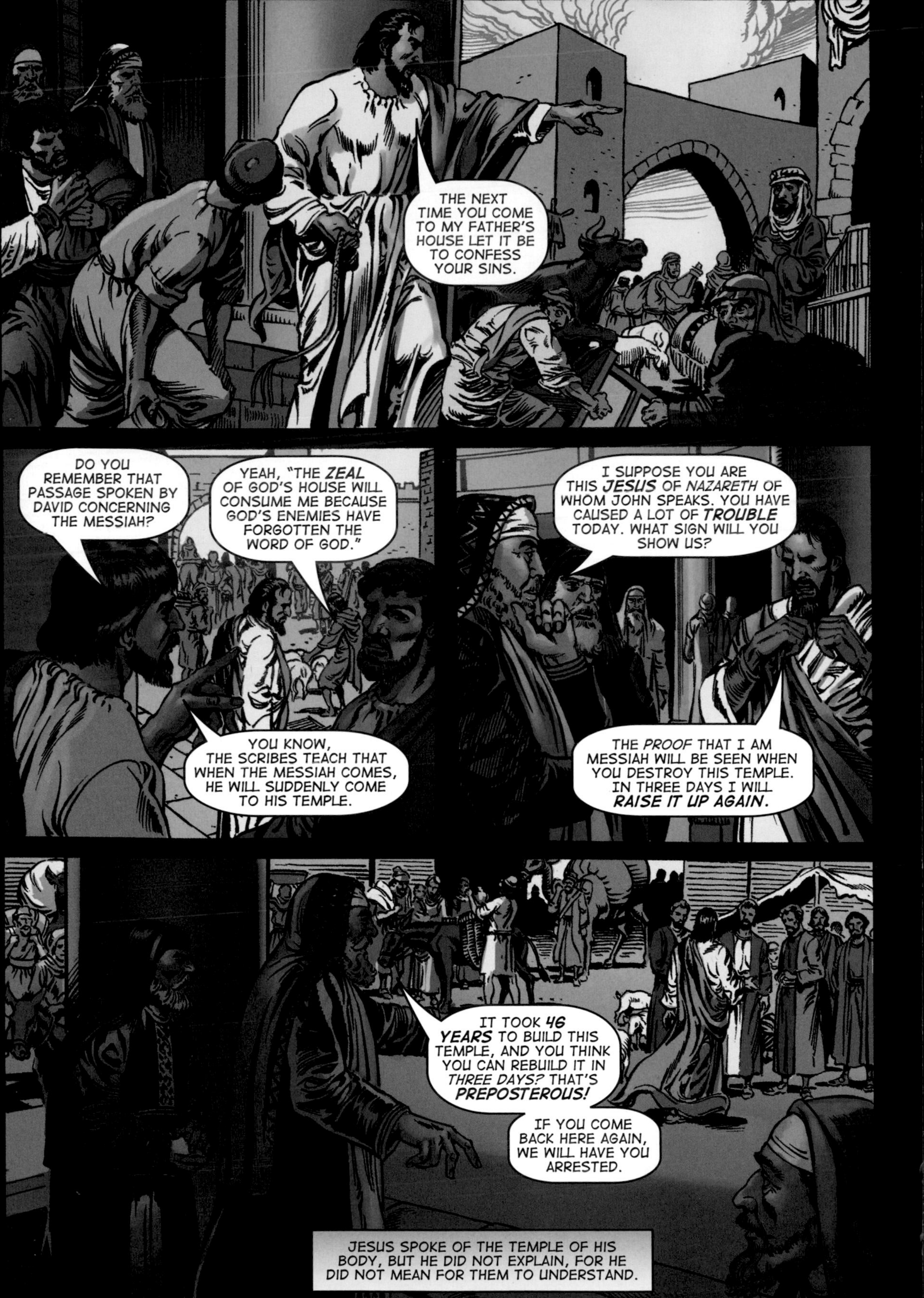
THE NEXT TIME YOU COME TO MY FATHER'S HOUSE LET IT BE TO CONFESS YOUR SINS.
DO YOU REMEMBER THAT PASSAGE SPOKEN BY DAVID CONCERNING THE MESSIAH?
YEAH, "THE *ZEAL* OF GOD'S HOUSE WILL CONSUME ME BECAUSE GOD'S ENEMIES HAVE FORGOTTEN THE WORD OF GOD."
YOU KNOW, THE SCRIBES TEACH THAT WHEN THE MESSIAH COMES, HE WILL SUDDENLY COME TO HIS TEMPLE.
I SUPPOSE YOU ARE THIS ***JESUS*** OF *NAZARETH* OF WHOM JOHN SPEAKS. YOU HAVE CAUSED A LOT OF ***TROUBLE*** TODAY. WHAT SIGN WILL YOU SHOW US?
THE *PROOF* THAT I AM MESSIAH WILL BE SEEN WHEN YOU DESTROY THIS TEMPLE. IN THREE DAYS I WILL ***RAISE IT UP AGAIN.***
IT TOOK ***46 YEARS*** TO BUILD THIS TEMPLE, AND YOU THINK YOU CAN REBUILD IT IN *THREE DAYS?* THAT'S ***PREPOSTEROUS!***
IF YOU COME BACK HERE AGAIN, WE WILL HAVE YOU ARRESTED.
JESUS SPOKE OF THE TEMPLE OF HIS BODY, BUT HE DID NOT EXPLAIN, FOR HE DID NOT MEAN FOR THEM TO UNDERSTAND.

PSALM 69:9, 119:139; JOHN 2:17–22

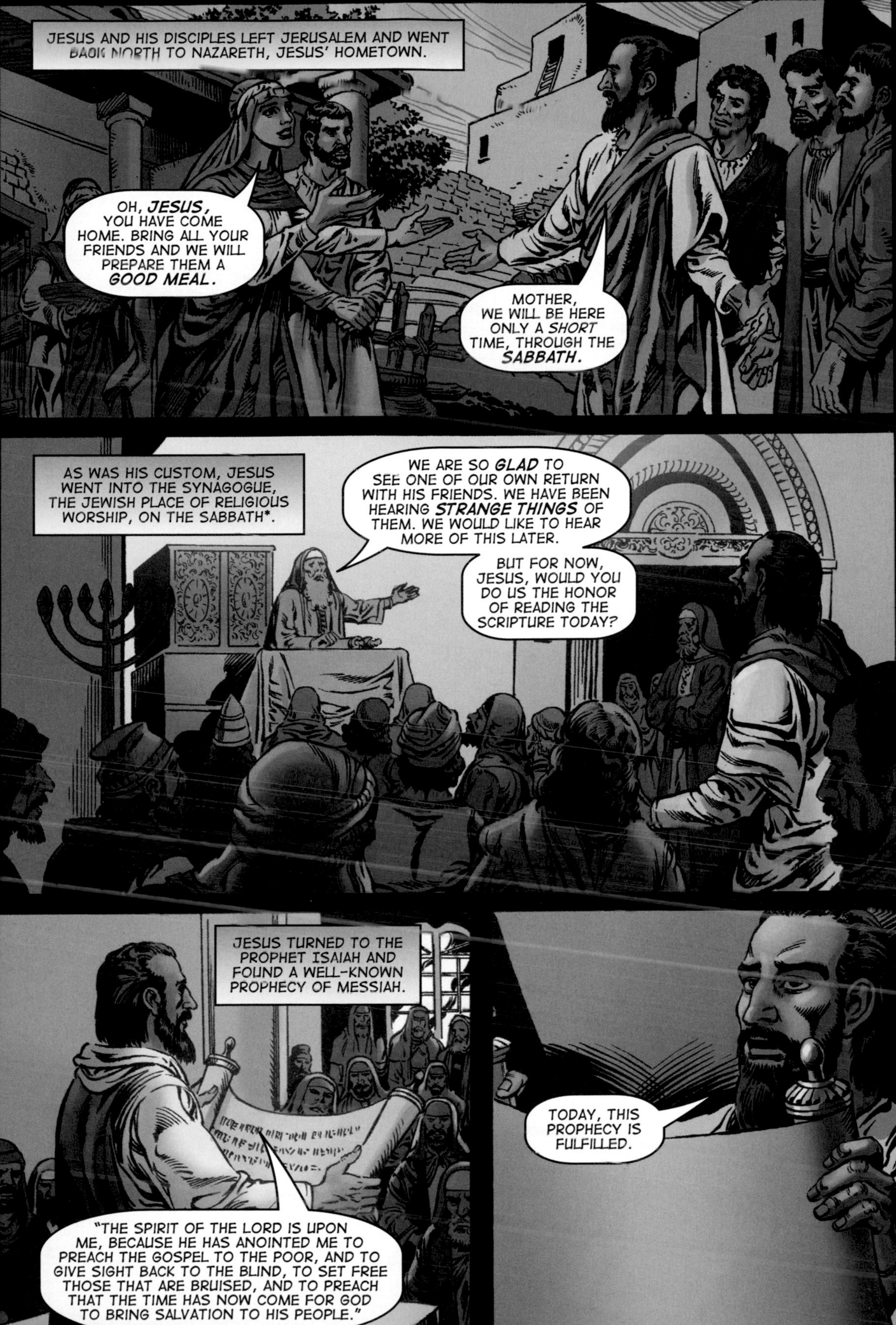
JESUS AND HIS DISCIPLES LEFT JERUSALEM AND WENT BACK NORTH TO NAZARETH, JESUS' HOMETOWN.
OH, JESUS, YOU HAVE COME HOME. BRING ALL YOUR FRIENDS AND WE WILL PREPARE THEM A GOOD MEAL.
MOTHER, WE WILL BE HERE ONLY A SHORT TIME, THROUGH THE SABBATH.
AS WAS HIS CUSTOM, JESUS WENT INTO THE SYNAGOGUE, THE JEWISH PLACE OF RELIGIOUS WORSHIP, ON THE SABBATH*.
WE ARE SO GLAD TO SEE ONE OF OUR OWN RETURN WITH HIS FRIENDS. WE HAVE BEEN HEARING STRANGE THINGS OF THEM. WE WOULD LIKE TO HEAR MORE OF THIS LATER.
BUT FOR NOW, JESUS, WOULD YOU DO US THE HONOR OF READING THE SCRIPTURE TODAY?
JESUS TURNED TO THE PROPHET ISAIAH AND FOUND A WELL-KNOWN PROPHECY OF MESSIAH.
"THE SPIRIT OF THE LORD IS UPON ME, BECAUSE HE HAS ANOINTED ME TO PREACH THE GOSPEL TO THE POOR, AND TO GIVE SIGHT BACK TO THE BLIND, TO SET FREE THOSE THAT ARE BRUISED, AND TO PREACH THAT THE TIME HAS NOW COME FOR GOD TO BRING SALVATION TO HIS PEOPLE."
TODAY, THIS PROPHECY IS FULFILLED.

*THE SABBATH IS A WEEKLY RELIGIOUS DAY OF REST ESTABLISHED BY GOD ON THE SEVENTH DAY AND ORDAINED AS ONE OF THE TEN COMMANDMENTS TO THE JEWS (GENESIS 2:2-3; EXODUS 20:10). LUKE 4:16-21

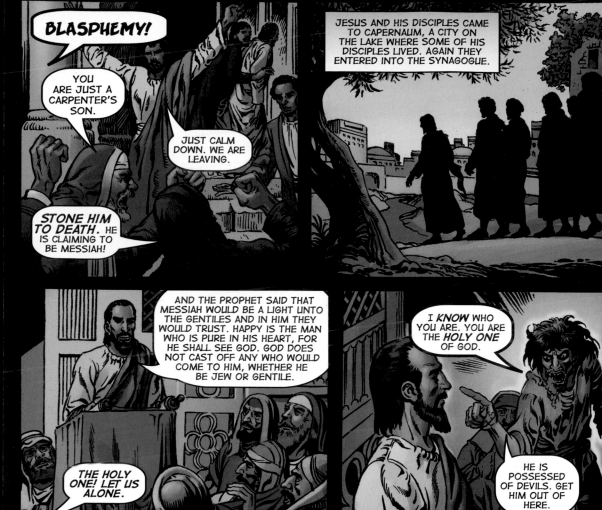

BLASPHEMY!

YOU ARE JUST A CARPENTER'S SON.

JUST CALM DOWN. WE ARE LEAVING.

STONE HIM TO DEATH. HE IS CLAIMING TO BE MESSIAH!

JESUS AND HIS DISCIPLES CAME TO CAPERNAUM, A CITY ON THE LAKE WHERE SOME OF HIS DISCIPLES LIVED. AGAIN THEY ENTERED INTO THE SYNAGOGUE.

AND THE PROPHET SAID THAT MESSIAH WOULD BE A LIGHT UNTO THE GENTILES AND IN HIM THEY WOULD TRUST. HAPPY IS THE MAN WHO IS PURE IN HIS HEART, FOR HE SHALL SEE GOD. GOD DOES NOT CAST OFF ANY WHO WOULD COME TO HIM, WHETHER HE BE JEW OR GENTILE.

THE HOLY ONE! LET US ALONE.

I *KNOW* WHO YOU ARE. YOU ARE THE *HOLY ONE* OF GOD.

HE IS POSSESSED OF DEVILS. GET HIM OUT OF HERE.

HAVE YOU COME TO DESTROY US DEVILS *BEFORE OUR TIME?* LET US ALONE. WHAT HAVE *WE* GOT TO DO WITH *YOU?*

WHO LET HIM IN HERE? *LOOK OUT!* HE IS *DANGEROUS.*

DEVILS, I *COMMAND* YOU TO COME OUT OF THIS MAN AND TORMENT HIM NO MORE!

BE GONE!

EEAAHHH!

WHAT DID YOU *DO* TO HIM?

IS HE *DEAD?*

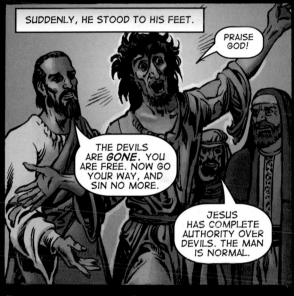

SUDDENLY, HE STOOD TO HIS FEET.

PRAISE GOD!

THE DEVILS ARE *GONE.* YOU ARE FREE. NOW GO YOUR WAY, AND SIN NO MORE.

JESUS HAS COMPLETE AUTHORITY OVER DEVILS. THE MAN IS NORMAL.

PETER, YOUR WIFE SAYS YOU SHOULD COME HOME. HER MOTHER IS *VERY SICK* WITH A HIGH FEVER.

WE WILL COME.

OH, *PETER,* MY HUSBAND, I AM SO AFRAID. THE FEVER GROWS WORSE.

DON'T BE *AFRAID.* THE MASTER IS HERE.

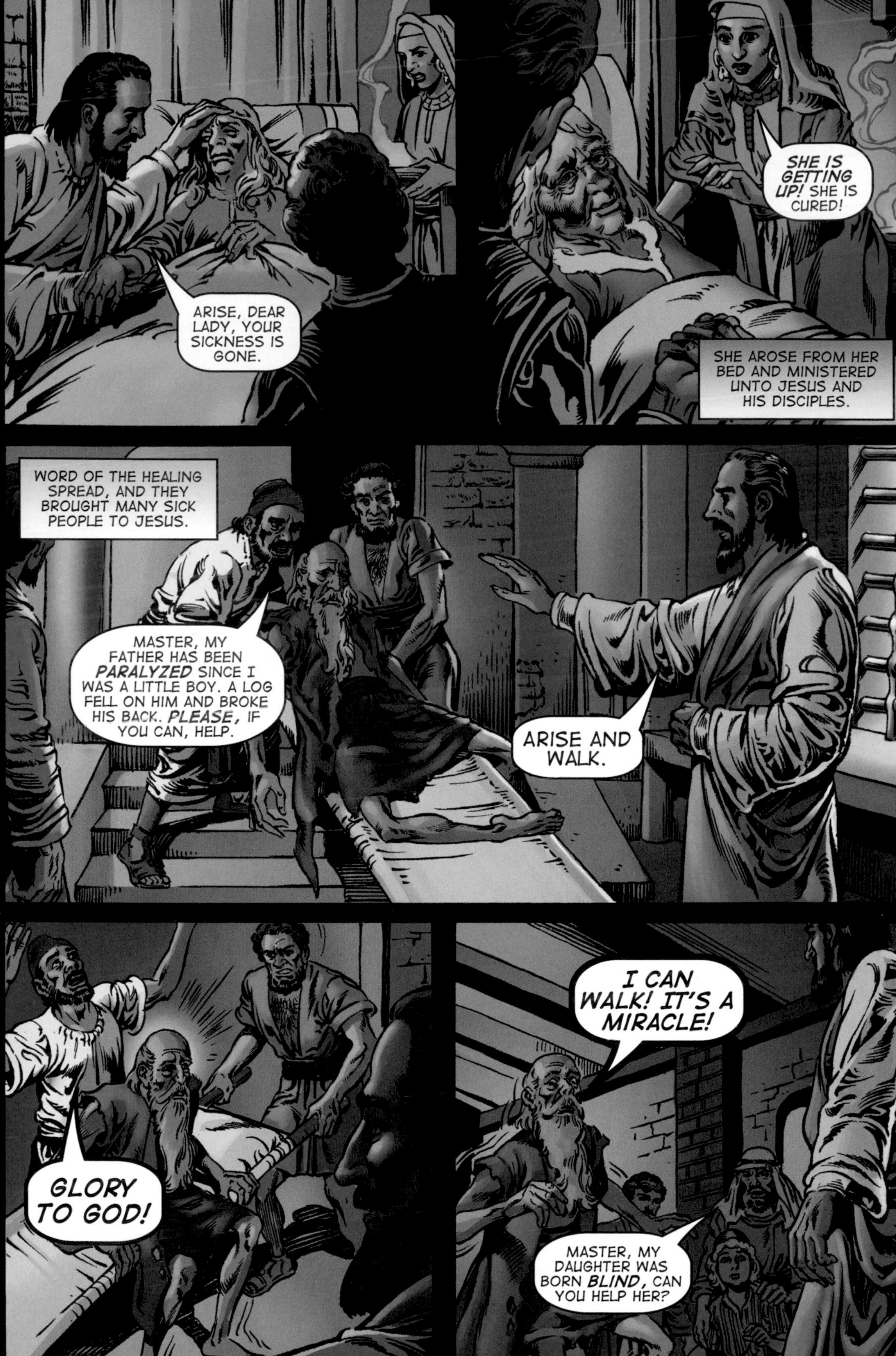
ARISE, DEAR LADY, YOUR SICKNESS IS GONE.
SHE IS GETTING UP! SHE IS CURED!
SHE AROSE FROM HER BED AND MINISTERED UNTO JESUS AND HIS DISCIPLES.
WORD OF THE HEALING SPREAD, AND THEY BROUGHT MANY SICK PEOPLE TO JESUS.
MASTER, MY FATHER HAS BEEN PARALYZED SINCE I WAS A LITTLE BOY. A LOG FELL ON HIM AND BROKE HIS BACK. PLEASE, IF YOU CAN, HELP.
ARISE AND WALK.
GLORY TO GOD!
I CAN WALK! IT'S A MIRACLE!
MASTER, MY DAUGHTER WAS BORN BLIND, CAN YOU HELP HER?

MARK 1:30-34; LUKE 4:38-40

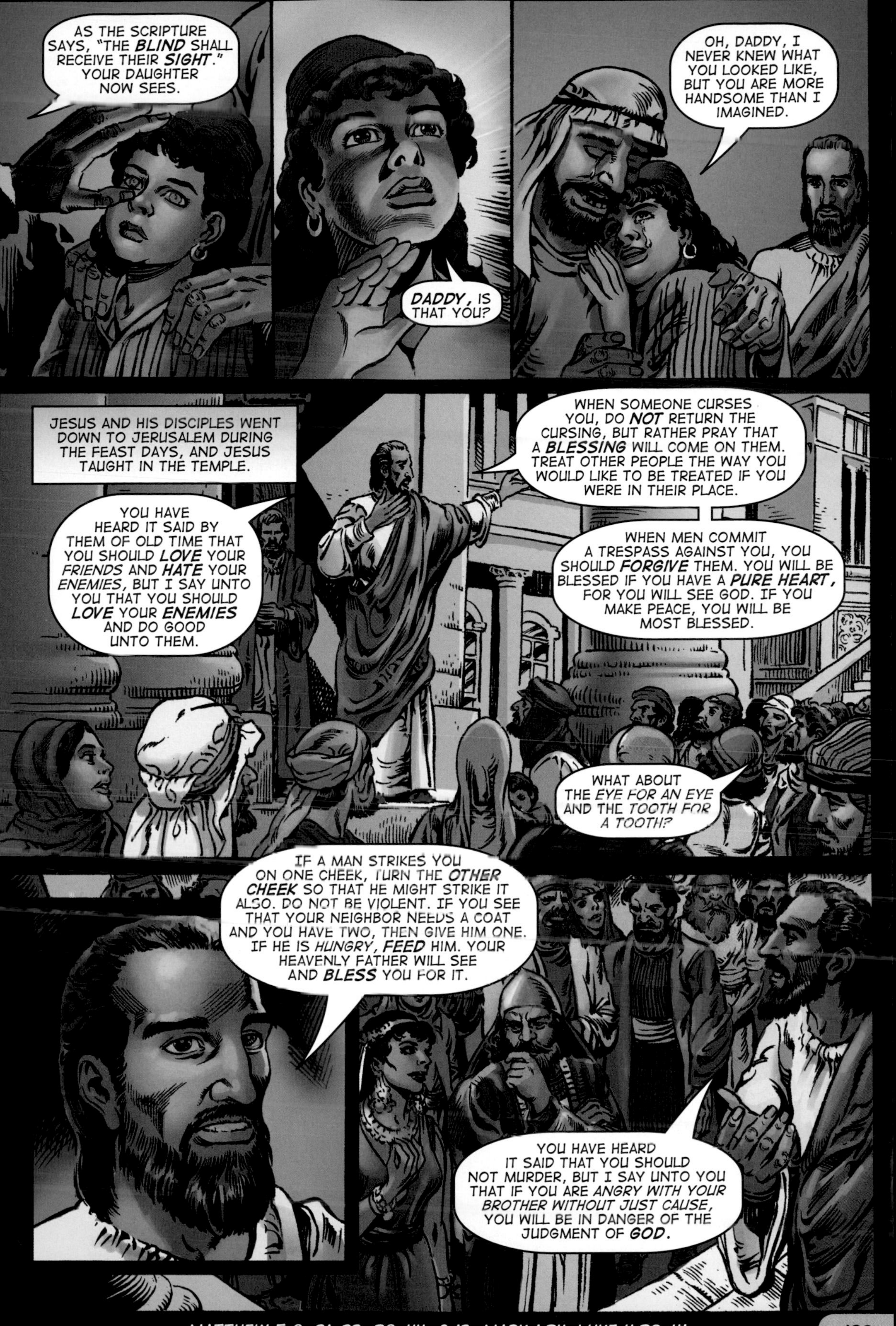
AS THE SCRIPTURE SAYS, "THE BLIND SHALL RECEIVE THEIR SIGHT." YOUR DAUGHTER NOW SEES.
DADDY, IS THAT YOU?
OH, DADDY, I NEVER KNEW WHAT YOU LOOKED LIKE, BUT YOU ARE MORE HANDSOME THAN I IMAGINED.
JESUS AND HIS DISCIPLES WENT DOWN TO JERUSALEM DURING THE FEAST DAYS, AND JESUS TAUGHT IN THE TEMPLE.
YOU HAVE HEARD IT SAID BY THEM OF OLD TIME THAT YOU SHOULD LOVE YOUR FRIENDS AND HATE YOUR ENEMIES, BUT I SAY UNTO YOU THAT YOU SHOULD LOVE YOUR ENEMIES AND DO GOOD UNTO THEM.
WHEN SOMEONE CURSES YOU, DO NOT RETURN THE CURSING, BUT RATHER PRAY THAT A BLESSING WILL COME ON THEM. TREAT OTHER PEOPLE THE WAY YOU WOULD LIKE TO BE TREATED IF YOU WERE IN THEIR PLACE.
WHEN MEN COMMIT A TRESPASS AGAINST YOU, YOU SHOULD FORGIVE THEM. YOU WILL BE BLESSED IF YOU HAVE A PURE HEART, FOR YOU WILL SEE GOD. IF YOU MAKE PEACE, YOU WILL BE MOST BLESSED.
WHAT ABOUT THE EYE FOR AN EYE AND THE TOOTH FOR A TOOTH?
IF A MAN STRIKES YOU ON ONE CHEEK, TURN THE OTHER CHEEK SO THAT HE MIGHT STRIKE IT ALSO. DO NOT BE VIOLENT. IF YOU SEE THAT YOUR NEIGHBOR NEEDS A COAT AND YOU HAVE TWO, THEN GIVE HIM ONE. IF HE IS HUNGRY, FEED HIM. YOUR HEAVENLY FATHER WILL SEE AND BLESS YOU FOR IT.
YOU HAVE HEARD IT SAID THAT YOU SHOULD NOT MURDER, BUT I SAY UNTO YOU THAT IF YOU ARE ANGRY WITH YOUR BROTHER WITHOUT JUST CAUSE, YOU WILL BE IN DANGER OF THE JUDGMENT OF GOD.

MATTHEW 5:8, 21–22, 38–44, 6:12; MARK 1:34; LUKE 4:39–41

YOU HAVE HEARD IT SAID THAT A MAN SHOULD NOT COMMIT *ADULTERY*, BUT I SAY UNTO YOU THAT IF YOU SO MUCH AS *LOOK* UPON A WOMAN TO *LUST* AFTER HER, YOU HAVE COMMITTED *ADULTERY* WITH HER ALREADY IN YOUR HEART.

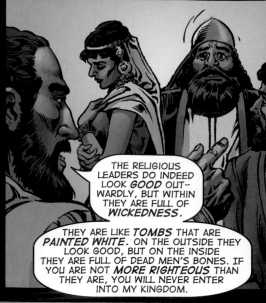

THE RELIGIOUS LEADERS DO INDEED LOOK *GOOD* OUTWARDLY, BUT WITHIN THEY ARE FULL OF *WICKEDNESS*.

THEY ARE LIKE *TOMBS* THAT ARE *PAINTED WHITE*. ON THE OUTSIDE THEY LOOK GOOD, BUT ON THE INSIDE THEY ARE FULL OF DEAD MEN'S BONES. IF YOU ARE NOT *MORE RIGHTEOUS* THAN THEY ARE, YOU WILL NEVER ENTER INTO MY KINGDOM.

THERE IS A BROAD WAY THAT LEADS TO *DESTRUCTION* AND MANY ARE TRAVELING IT.

I AM THE DOOR TO HEAVEN. IF YOU ENTER IN THROUGH *ME* YOU WILL HAVE *ETERNAL* LIFE. IF YOU TRY TO GO ANY OTHER WAY, YOU WILL DIE IN YOUR SINS.

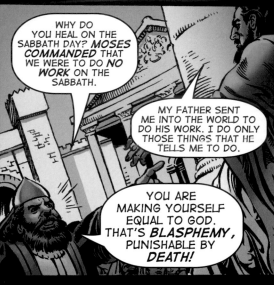

WHY DO YOU HEAL ON THE SABBATH DAY? *MOSES COMMANDED* THAT WE WERE TO DO *NO WORK* ON THE SABBATH.

MY FATHER SENT ME INTO THE WORLD TO DO HIS WORK. I DO ONLY THOSE THINGS THAT HE TELLS ME TO DO.

YOU ARE MAKING YOURSELF EQUAL TO GOD. THAT'S *BLASPHEMY*, PUNISHABLE BY *DEATH!*

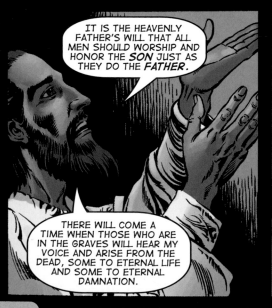

IT IS THE HEAVENLY FATHER'S WILL THAT ALL MEN SHOULD WORSHIP AND HONOR THE *SON* JUST AS THEY DO THE *FATHER*.

THERE WILL COME A TIME WHEN THOSE WHO ARE IN THE GRAVES WILL HEAR MY VOICE AND ARISE FROM THE DEAD, SOME TO ETERNAL LIFE AND SOME TO ETERNAL DAMNATION.

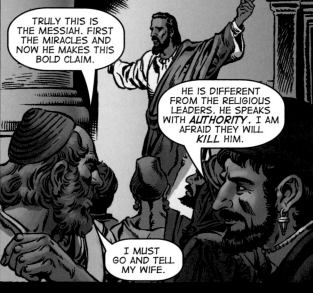

TRULY THIS IS THE MESSIAH. FIRST THE MIRACLES AND NOW HE MAKES THIS BOLD CLAIM.

HE IS DIFFERENT FROM THE RELIGIOUS LEADERS. HE SPEAKS WITH *AUTHORITY*. I AM AFRAID THEY WILL *KILL* HIM.

I MUST GO AND TELL MY WIFE.

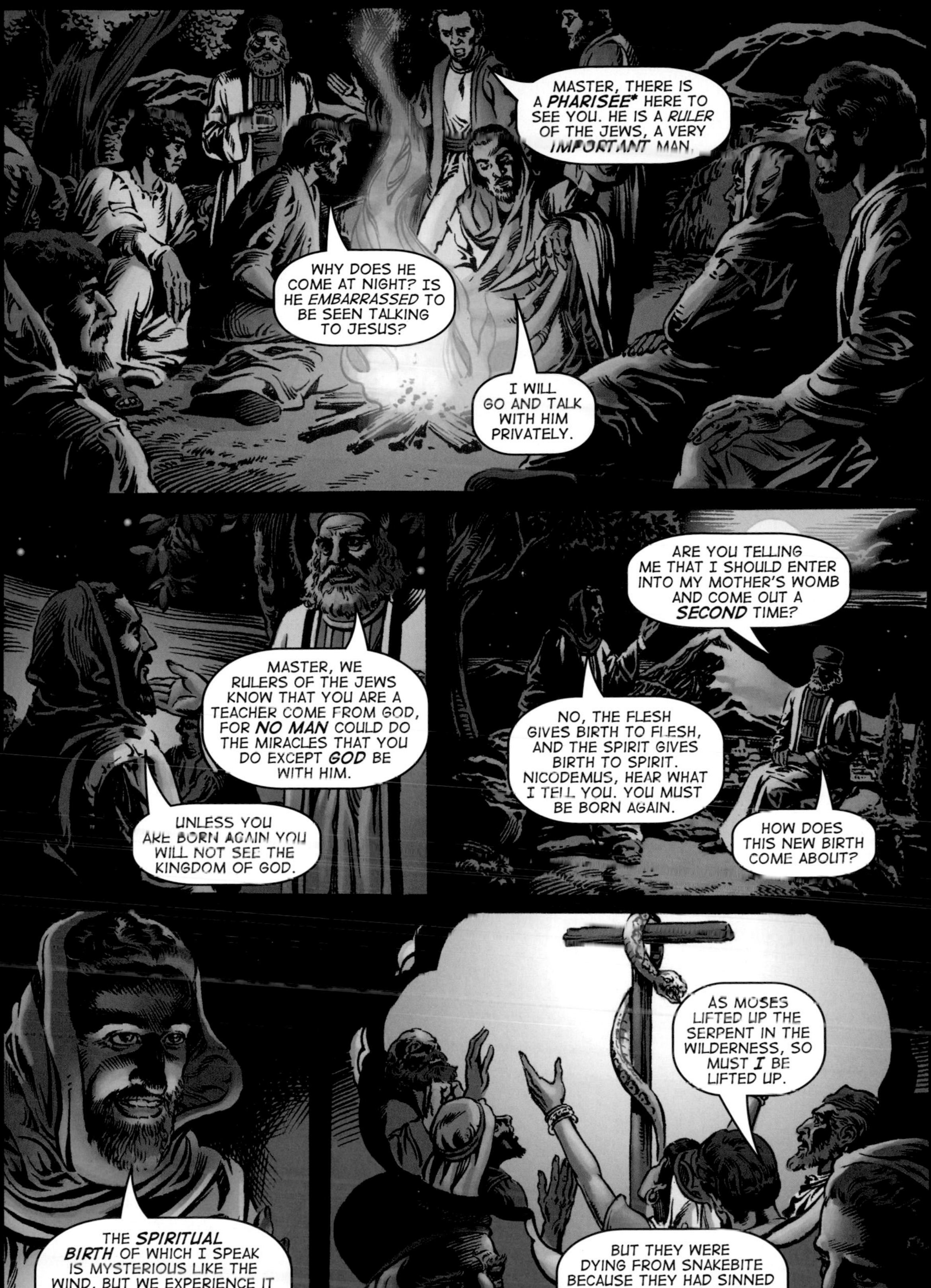
MASTER, THERE IS A PHARISEE* HERE TO SEE YOU. HE IS A RULER OF THE JEWS, A VERY IMPORTANT MAN.
WHY DOES HE COME AT NIGHT? IS HE EMBARRASSED TO BE SEEN TALKING TO JESUS?
I WILL GO AND TALK WITH HIM PRIVATELY.
MASTER, WE RULERS OF THE JEWS KNOW THAT YOU ARE A TEACHER COME FROM GOD, FOR NO MAN COULD DO THE MIRACLES THAT YOU DO EXCEPT GOD BE WITH HIM.
UNLESS YOU ARE BORN AGAIN YOU WILL NOT SEE THE KINGDOM OF GOD.
ARE YOU TELLING ME THAT I SHOULD ENTER INTO MY MOTHER'S WOMB AND COME OUT A SECOND TIME?
NO, THE FLESH GIVES BIRTH TO FLESH, AND THE SPIRIT GIVES BIRTH TO SPIRIT. NICODEMUS, HEAR WHAT I TELL YOU. YOU MUST BE BORN AGAIN.
HOW DOES THIS NEW BIRTH COME ABOUT?
THE SPIRITUAL BIRTH OF WHICH I SPEAK IS MYSTERIOUS LIKE THE WIND, BUT WE EXPERIENCE IT JUST THE SAME. YOU MUST HAVE THIS BIRTH FROM ABOVE IF YOU ARE TO ENTER INTO THE KINGDOM OF GOD.
AS MOSES LIFTED UP THE SERPENT IN THE WILDERNESS, SO MUST I BE LIFTED UP.
BUT THEY WERE DYING FROM SNAKEBITE BECAUSE THEY HAD SINNED AGAINST GOD. WHEN THEY LOOKED AT THE BRASS SERPENT THEY WERE INSTANTLY HEALED.

NUMBERS 21:5–9; JOHN 3:1–14
*A MEMBER OF AN ANCIENT JEWISH SECT NOTED FOR STRICT OBEDIENCE TO JEWISH TRADITIONS.

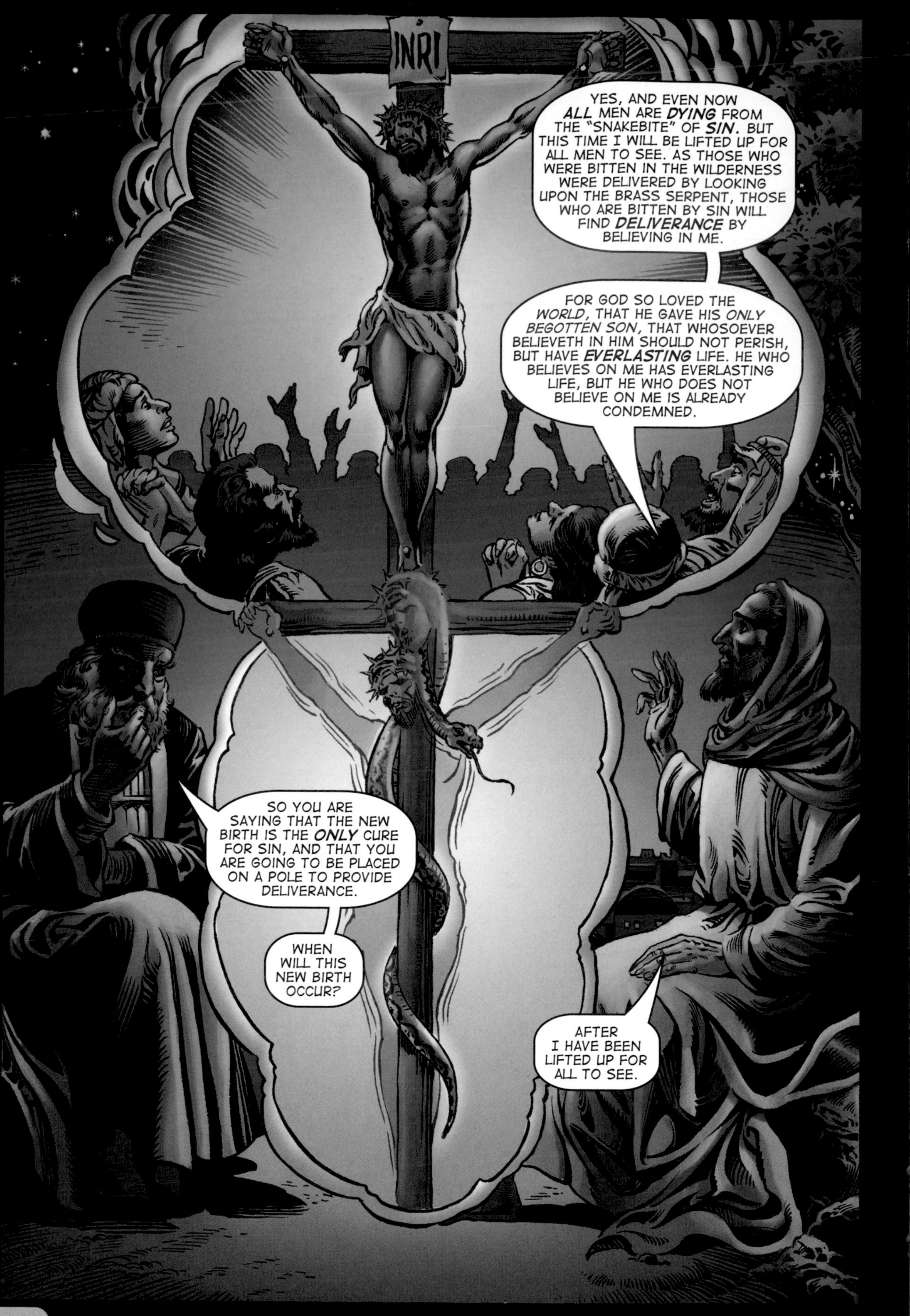
INRI
YES, AND EVEN NOW ALL MEN ARE DYING FROM THE "SNAKEBITE" OF SIN. BUT THIS TIME I WILL BE LIFTED UP FOR ALL MEN TO SEE. AS THOSE WHO WERE BITTEN IN THE WILDERNESS WERE DELIVERED BY LOOKING UPON THE BRASS SERPENT, THOSE WHO ARE BITTEN BY SIN WILL FIND DELIVERANCE BY BELIEVING IN ME.
FOR GOD SO LOVED THE WORLD, THAT HE GAVE HIS ONLY BEGOTTEN SON, THAT WHOSOEVER BELIEVETH IN HIM SHOULD NOT PERISH, BUT HAVE EVERLASTING LIFE. HE WHO BELIEVES ON ME HAS EVERLASTING LIFE, BUT HE WHO DOES NOT BELIEVE ON ME IS ALREADY CONDEMNED.
SO YOU ARE SAYING THAT THE NEW BIRTH IS THE ONLY CURE FOR SIN, AND THAT YOU ARE GOING TO BE PLACED ON A POLE TO PROVIDE DELIVERANCE.
WHEN WILL THIS NEW BIRTH OCCUR?
AFTER I HAVE BEEN LIFTED UP FOR ALL TO SEE.

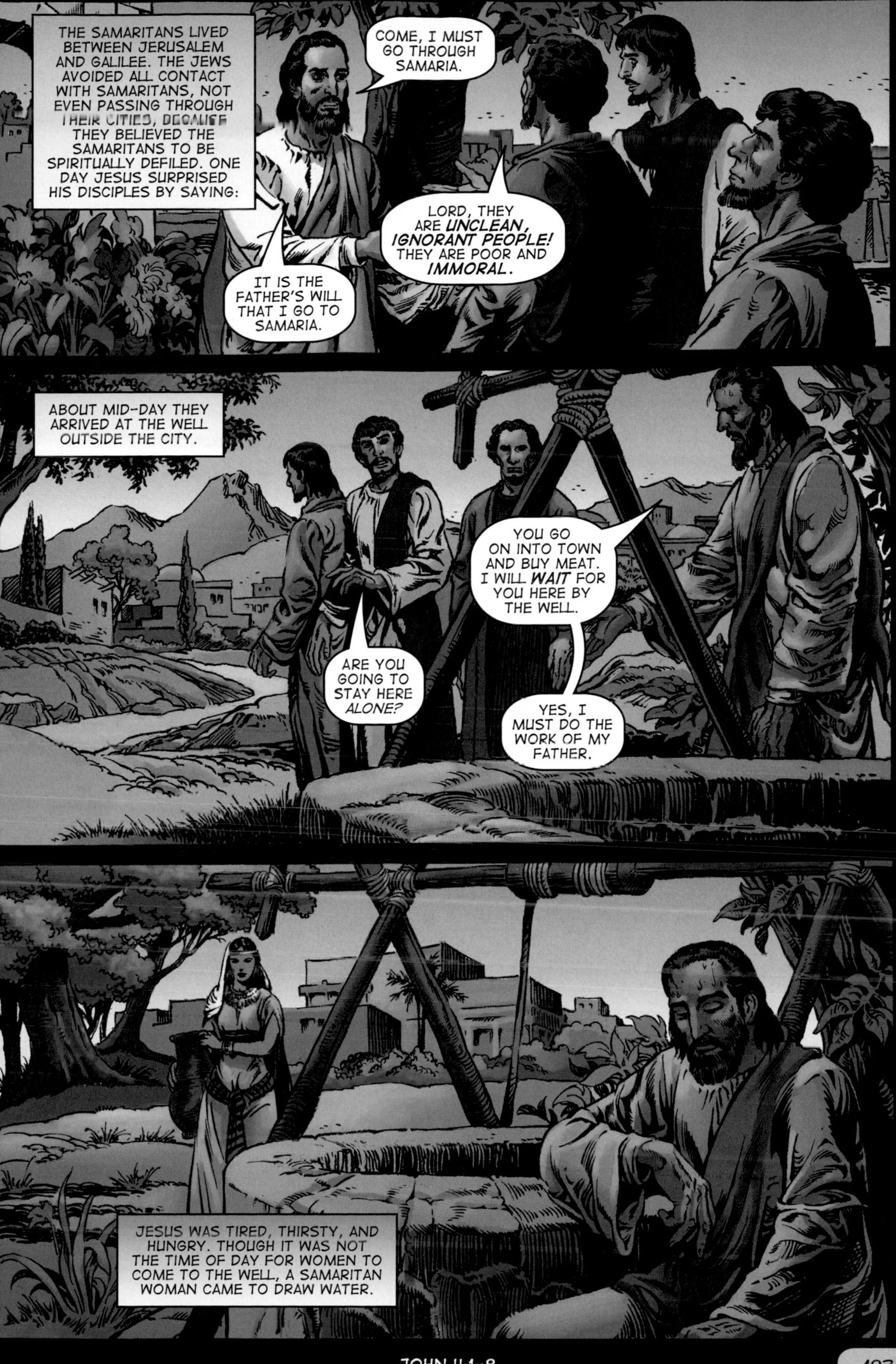
THE SAMARITANS LIVED BETWEEN JERUSALEM AND GALILEE. THE JEWS AVOIDED ALL CONTACT WITH SAMARITANS, NOT EVEN PASSING THROUGH THEIR CITIES, BECAUSE THEY BELIEVED THE SAMARITANS TO BE SPIRITUALLY DEFILED. ONE DAY JESUS SURPRISED HIS DISCIPLES BY SAYING:
COME, I MUST GO THROUGH SAMARIA.
LORD, THEY ARE UNCLEAN, IGNORANT PEOPLE! THEY ARE POOR AND IMMORAL.
IT IS THE FATHER'S WILL THAT I GO TO SAMARIA.
ABOUT MID-DAY THEY ARRIVED AT THE WELL OUTSIDE THE CITY.
YOU GO ON INTO TOWN AND BUY MEAT. I WILL WAIT FOR YOU HERE BY THE WELL.
ARE YOU GOING TO STAY HERE ALONE?
YES, I MUST DO THE WORK OF MY FATHER.
JESUS WAS TIRED, THIRSTY, AND HUNGRY. THOUGH IT WAS NOT THE TIME OF DAY FOR WOMEN TO COME TO THE WELL, A SAMARITAN WOMAN CAME TO DRAW WATER.

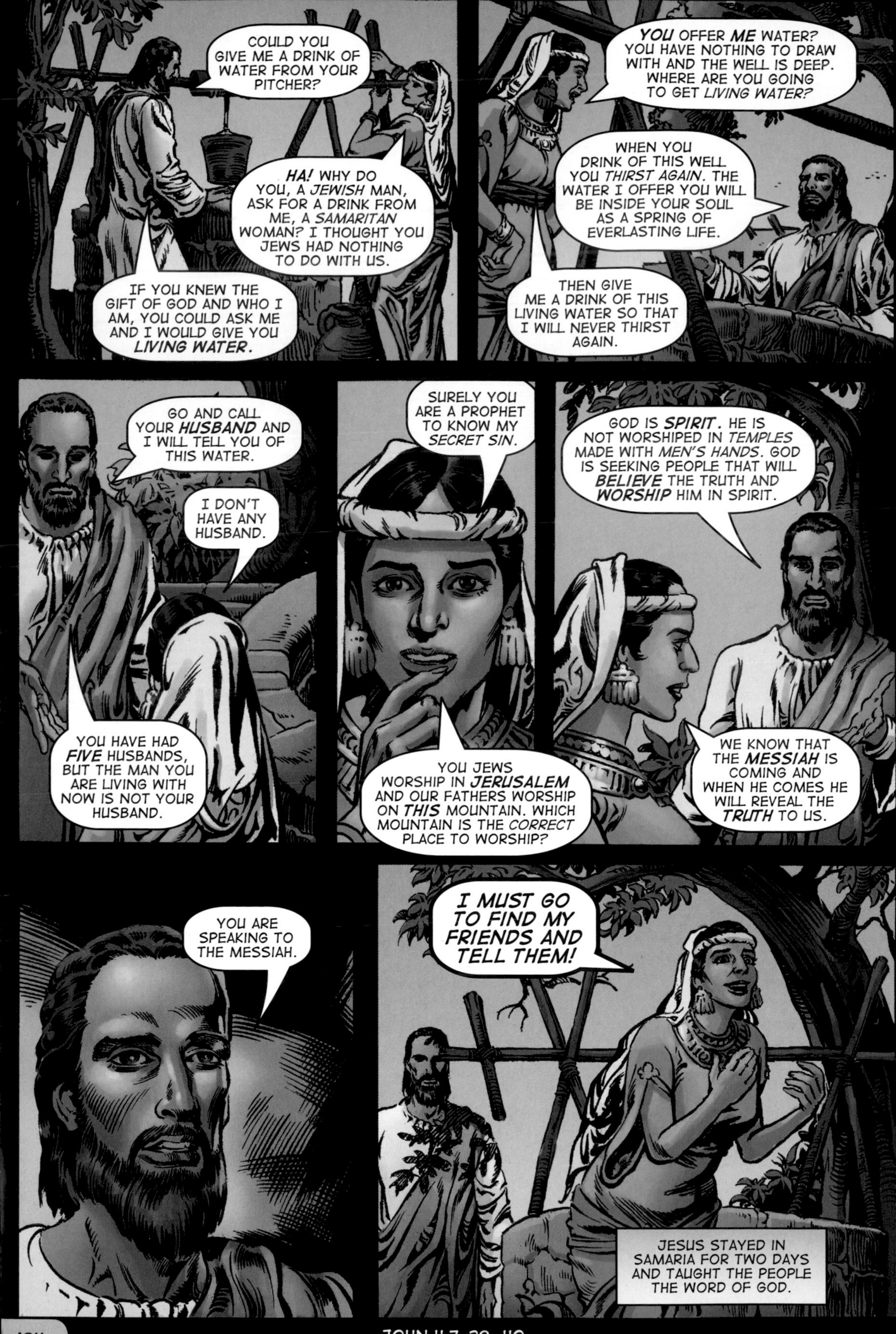
COULD YOU GIVE ME A DRINK OF WATER FROM YOUR PITCHER?
HA! WHY DO YOU, A JEWISH MAN, ASK FOR A DRINK FROM ME, A SAMARITAN WOMAN? I THOUGHT YOU JEWS HAD NOTHING TO DO WITH US.
IF YOU KNEW THE GIFT OF GOD AND WHO I AM, YOU COULD ASK ME AND I WOULD GIVE YOU LIVING WATER.
YOU OFFER ME WATER? YOU HAVE NOTHING TO DRAW WITH AND THE WELL IS DEEP. WHERE ARE YOU GOING TO GET LIVING WATER?
WHEN YOU DRINK OF THIS WELL YOU THIRST AGAIN. THE WATER I OFFER YOU WILL BE INSIDE YOUR SOUL AS A SPRING OF EVERLASTING LIFE.
THEN GIVE ME A DRINK OF THIS LIVING WATER SO THAT I WILL NEVER THIRST AGAIN.
GO AND CALL YOUR HUSBAND AND I WILL TELL YOU OF THIS WATER.
I DON'T HAVE ANY HUSBAND.
YOU HAVE HAD FIVE HUSBANDS, BUT THE MAN YOU ARE LIVING WITH NOW IS NOT YOUR HUSBAND.
SURELY YOU ARE A PROPHET TO KNOW MY SECRET SIN.
YOU JEWS WORSHIP IN JERUSALEM AND OUR FATHERS WORSHIP ON THIS MOUNTAIN. WHICH MOUNTAIN IS THE CORRECT PLACE TO WORSHIP?
GOD IS SPIRIT. HE IS NOT WORSHIPED IN TEMPLES MADE WITH MEN'S HANDS. GOD IS SEEKING PEOPLE THAT WILL BELIEVE THE TRUTH AND WORSHIP HIM IN SPIRIT.
WE KNOW THAT THE MESSIAH IS COMING AND WHEN HE COMES HE WILL REVEAL THE TRUTH TO US.
YOU ARE SPEAKING TO THE MESSIAH.
I MUST GO TO FIND MY FRIENDS AND TELL THEM!
JESUS STAYED IN SAMARIA FOR TWO DAYS AND TAUGHT THE PEOPLE THE WORD OF GOD.

JOHN 4:7-29, 40

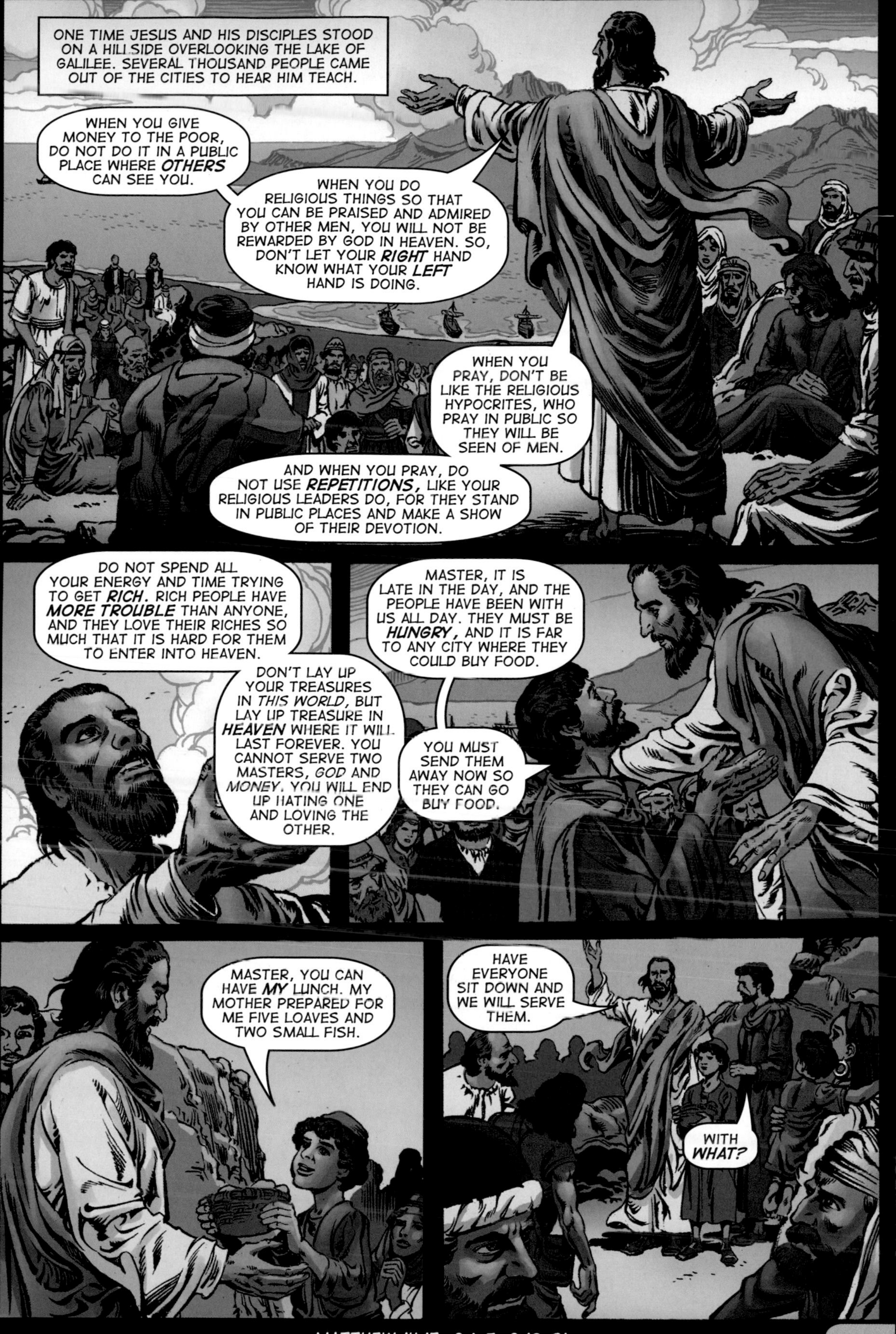
ONE TIME JESUS AND HIS DISCIPLES STOOD ON A HILLSIDE OVERLOOKING THE LAKE OF GALILEE. SEVERAL THOUSAND PEOPLE CAME OUT OF THE CITIES TO HEAR HIM TEACH.
WHEN YOU GIVE MONEY TO THE POOR, DO NOT DO IT IN A PUBLIC PLACE WHERE OTHERS CAN SEE YOU.
WHEN YOU DO RELIGIOUS THINGS SO THAT YOU CAN BE PRAISED AND ADMIRED BY OTHER MEN, YOU WILL NOT BE REWARDED BY GOD IN HEAVEN. SO, DON'T LET YOUR RIGHT HAND KNOW WHAT YOUR LEFT HAND IS DOING.
WHEN YOU PRAY, DON'T BE LIKE THE RELIGIOUS HYPOCRITES, WHO PRAY IN PUBLIC SO THEY WILL BE SEEN OF MEN.
AND WHEN YOU PRAY, DO NOT USE REPETITIONS, LIKE YOUR RELIGIOUS LEADERS DO, FOR THEY STAND IN PUBLIC PLACES AND MAKE A SHOW OF THEIR DEVOTION.
DO NOT SPEND ALL YOUR ENERGY AND TIME TRYING TO GET RICH. RICH PEOPLE HAVE MORE TROUBLE THAN ANYONE, AND THEY LOVE THEIR RICHES SO MUCH THAT IT IS HARD FOR THEM TO ENTER INTO HEAVEN.
DON'T LAY UP YOUR TREASURES IN THIS WORLD, BUT LAY UP TREASURE IN HEAVEN WHERE IT WILL LAST FOREVER. YOU CANNOT SERVE TWO MASTERS, GOD AND MONEY. YOU WILL END UP HATING ONE AND LOVING THE OTHER.
MASTER, IT IS LATE IN THE DAY, AND THE PEOPLE HAVE BEEN WITH US ALL DAY. THEY MUST BE HUNGRY, AND IT IS FAR TO ANY CITY WHERE THEY COULD BUY FOOD.
YOU MUST SEND THEM AWAY NOW SO THEY CAN GO BUY FOOD.
MASTER, YOU CAN HAVE MY LUNCH. MY MOTHER PREPARED FOR ME FIVE LOAVES AND TWO SMALL FISH.
HAVE EVERYONE SIT DOWN AND WE WILL SERVE THEM.
WITH WHAT?

MATTHEW 14:15, 6:1-7, 6:19-21

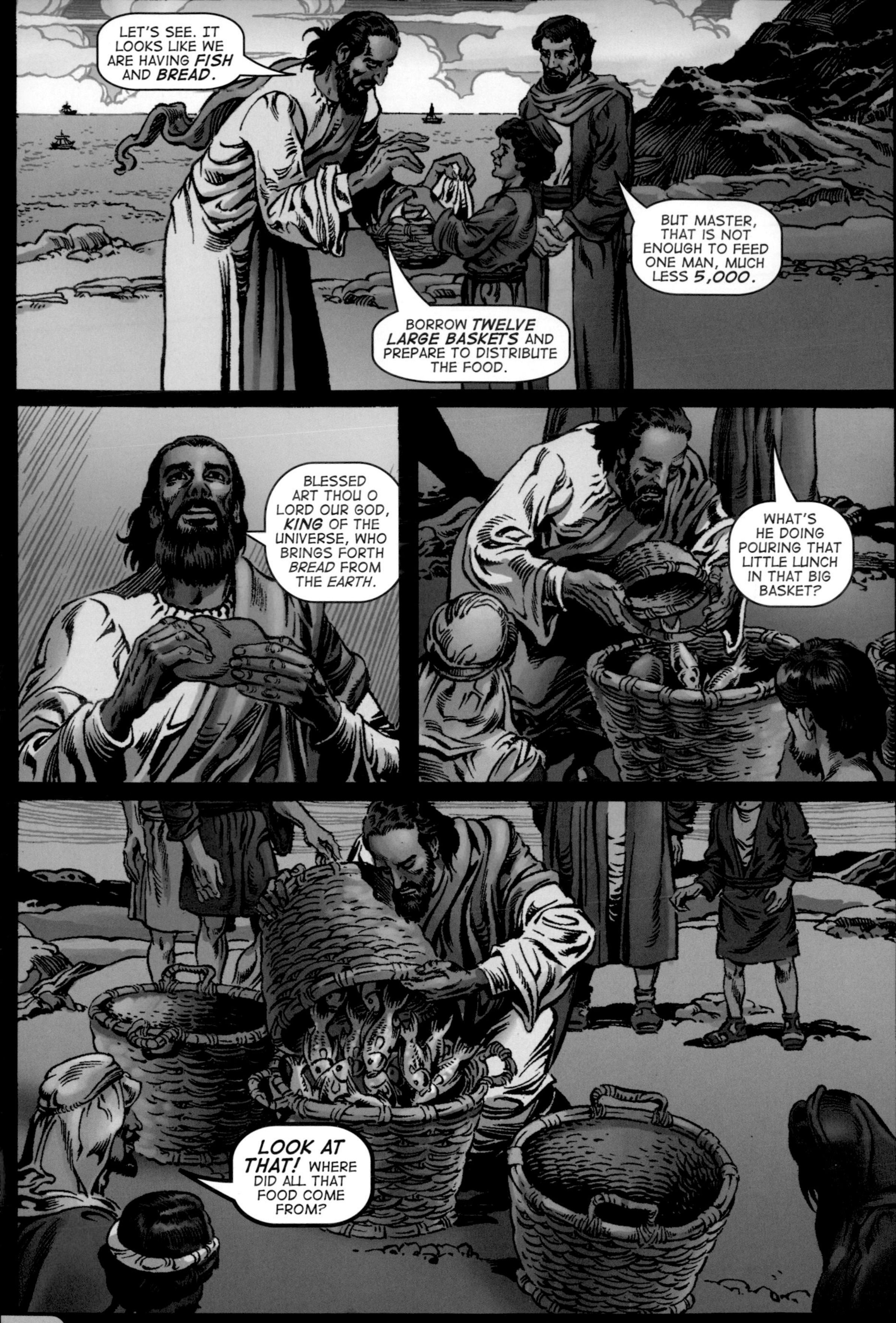

LET'S SEE. IT LOOKS LIKE WE ARE HAVING *FISH* AND *BREAD*.
BUT MASTER, THAT IS NOT ENOUGH TO FEED ONE MAN, MUCH LESS **5,000**.
BORROW ***TWELVE LARGE BASKETS*** AND PREPARE TO DISTRIBUTE THE FOOD.
BLESSED ART THOU O LORD OUR GOD, ***KING*** OF THE UNIVERSE, WHO BRINGS FORTH *BREAD* FROM THE *EARTH*.
WHAT'S HE DOING POURING THAT LITTLE LUNCH IN THAT BIG BASKET?
LOOK AT THAT! WHERE DID ALL THAT FOOD COME FROM?

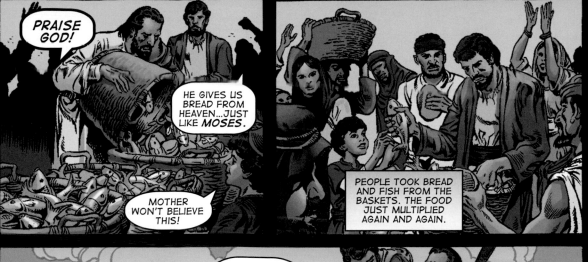

PRAISE GOD!

HE GIVES US BREAD FROM HEAVEN...JUST LIKE *MOSES*.

MOTHER WON'T BELIEVE THIS!

PEOPLE TOOK BREAD AND FISH FROM THE BASKETS. THE FOOD JUST MULTIPLIED AGAIN AND AGAIN.

MASTER, EVERYONE HAS EATEN, AND STILL THE BASKETS ARE FULL. *WE CANNOT EMPTY THEM!*

GATHER UP WHAT IS LEFT, AND THEN YOU AND THE OTHERS TAKE A SHIP TO THE OTHER SIDE OF THE LAKE. I WILL SEE YOU LATER. I MUST GO INTO THE MOUNTAIN TO PRAY.

JESUS WENT UP INTO THE MOUNTAIN ALONE, AND HIS DISCIPLES ALL GOT INTO A SHIP AND LEFT FOR THE OTHER SIDE OF THE LAKE.

JESUS OFTEN WENT ALONE INTO THE WILDERNESS TO PRAY.

MATTHEW 14:20-23

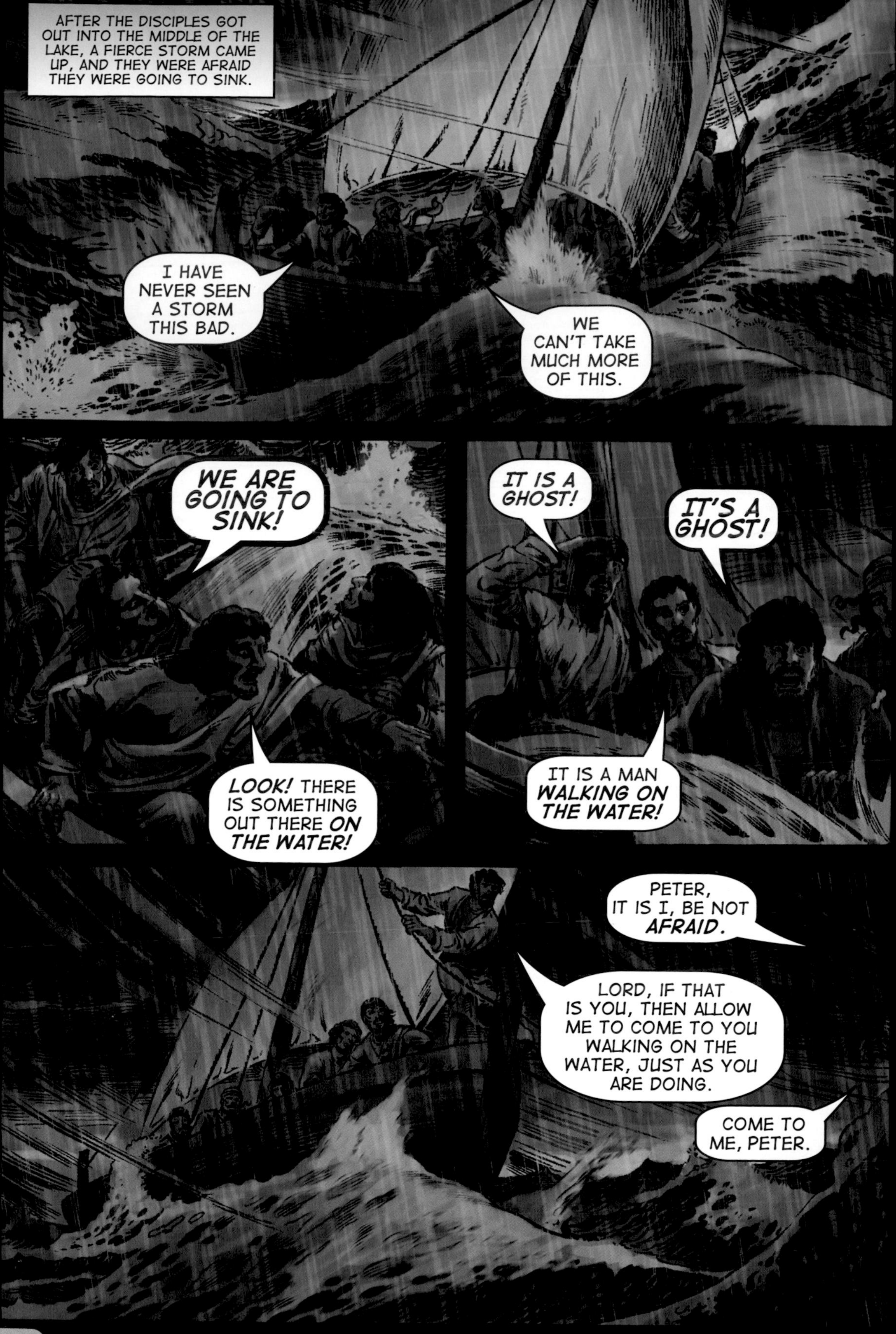
AFTER THE DISCIPLES GOT OUT INTO THE MIDDLE OF THE LAKE, A FIERCE STORM CAME UP, AND THEY WERE AFRAID THEY WERE GOING TO SINK.
I HAVE NEVER SEEN A STORM THIS BAD.
WE CAN'T TAKE MUCH MORE OF THIS.
WE ARE GOING TO SINK!
LOOK! THERE IS SOMETHING OUT THERE ON THE WATER!
IT IS A GHOST!
IT'S A GHOST!
IT IS A MAN WALKING ON THE WATER!
PETER, IT IS I, BE NOT AFRAID.
LORD, IF THAT IS YOU, THEN ALLOW ME TO COME TO YOU WALKING ON THE WATER, JUST AS YOU ARE DOING.
COME TO ME, PETER.

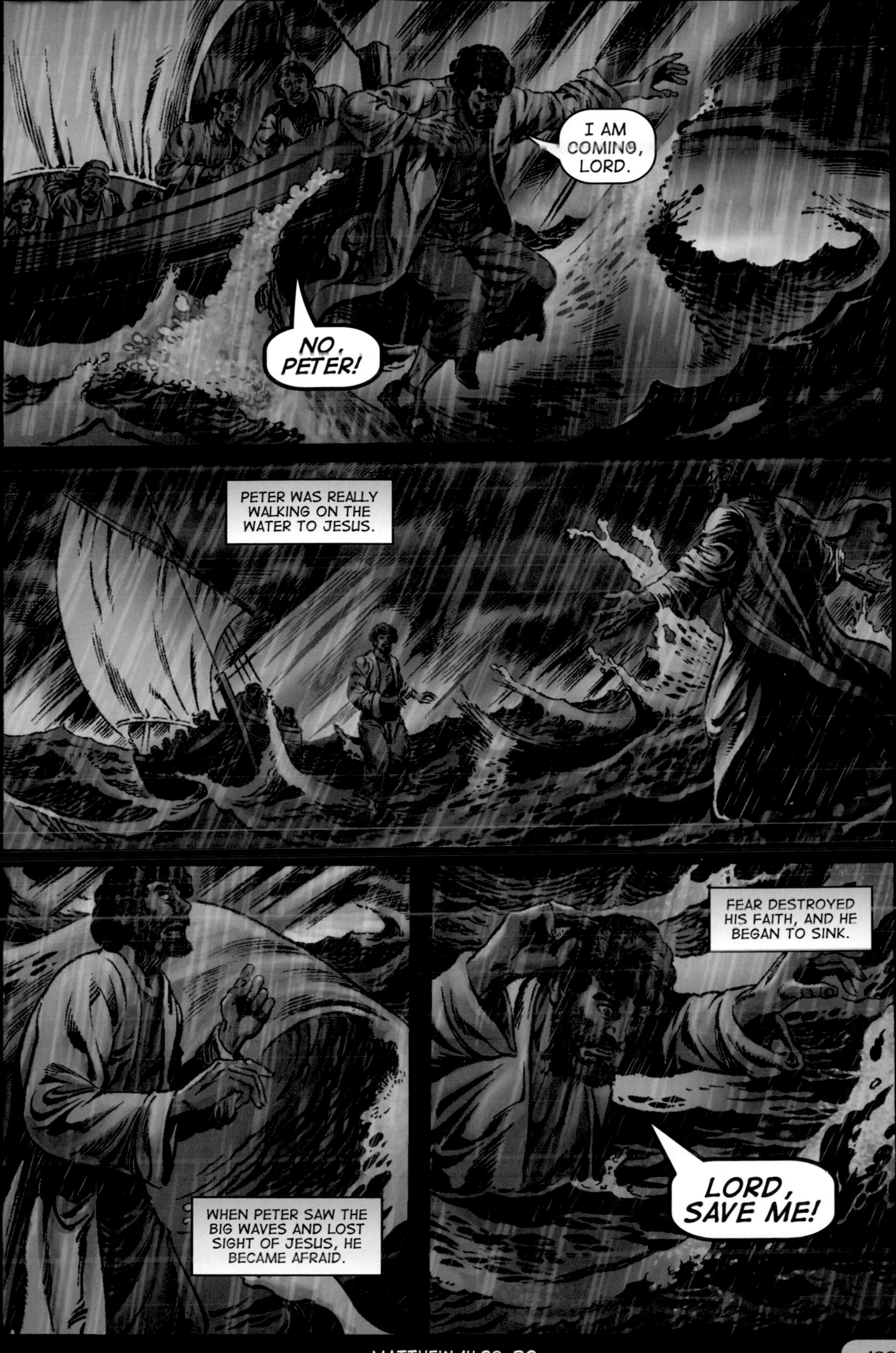
I AM COMING, LORD.
NO, PETER!
PETER WAS REALLY WALKING ON THE WATER TO JESUS.
WHEN PETER SAW THE BIG WAVES AND LOST SIGHT OF JESUS, HE BECAME AFRAID.
FEAR DESTROYED HIS FAITH, AND HE BEGAN TO SINK.
LORD, SAVE ME!

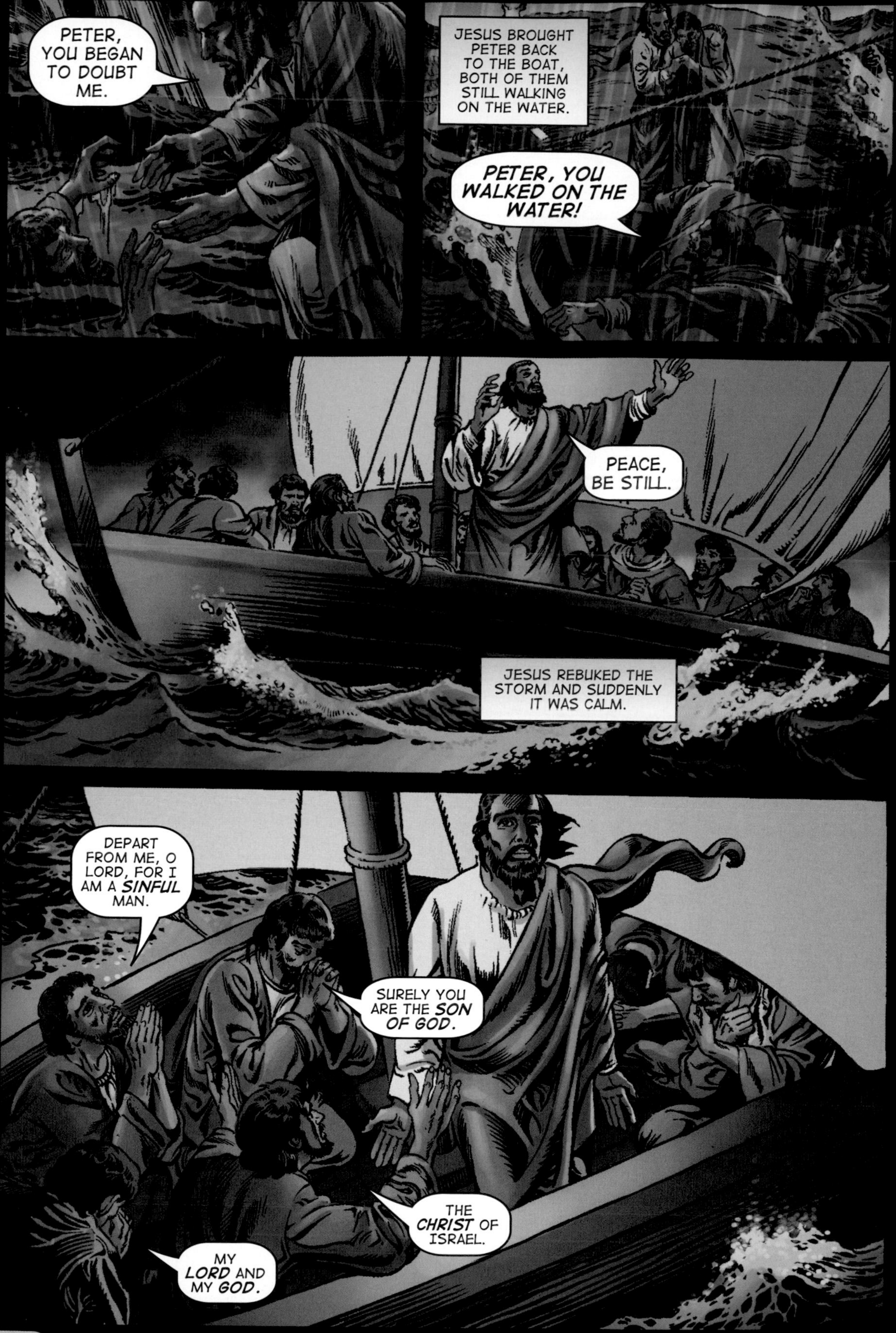
PETER, YOU BEGAN TO DOUBT ME.
JESUS BROUGHT PETER BACK TO THE BOAT, BOTH OF THEM STILL WALKING ON THE WATER.
PETER, YOU WALKED ON THE WATER!
PEACE, BE STILL.
JESUS REBUKED THE STORM AND SUDDENLY IT WAS CALM.
DEPART FROM ME, O LORD, FOR I AM A *SINFUL* MAN.
SURELY YOU ARE THE *SON OF GOD*.
THE *CHRIST* OF ISRAEL.
MY *LORD* AND MY *GOD*.

MATTHEW 14:31–33; 4:38–41

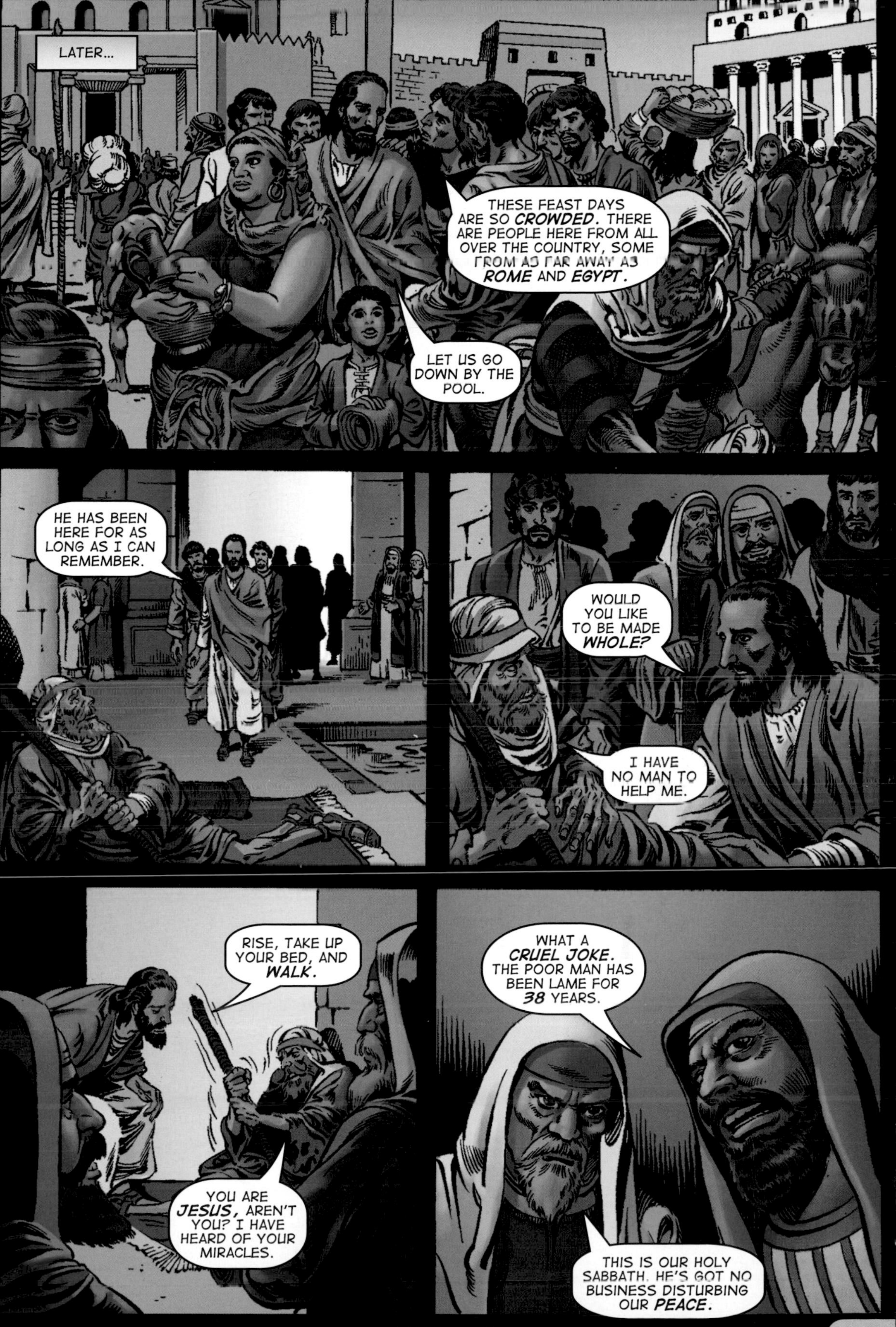
LATER...
THESE FEAST DAYS ARE SO CROWDED. THERE ARE PEOPLE HERE FROM ALL OVER THE COUNTRY, SOME FROM AS FAR AWAY AS ROME AND EGYPT.
LET US GO DOWN BY THE POOL.
HE HAS BEEN HERE FOR AS LONG AS I CAN REMEMBER.
WOULD YOU LIKE TO BE MADE WHOLE?
I HAVE NO MAN TO HELP ME.
RISE, TAKE UP YOUR BED, AND WALK.
YOU ARE JESUS, AREN'T YOU? I HAVE HEARD OF YOUR MIRACLES.
WHAT A CRUEL JOKE. THE POOR MAN HAS BEEN LAME FOR 38 YEARS.
THIS IS OUR HOLY SABBATH. HE'S GOT NO BUSINESS DISTURBING OUR PEACE.

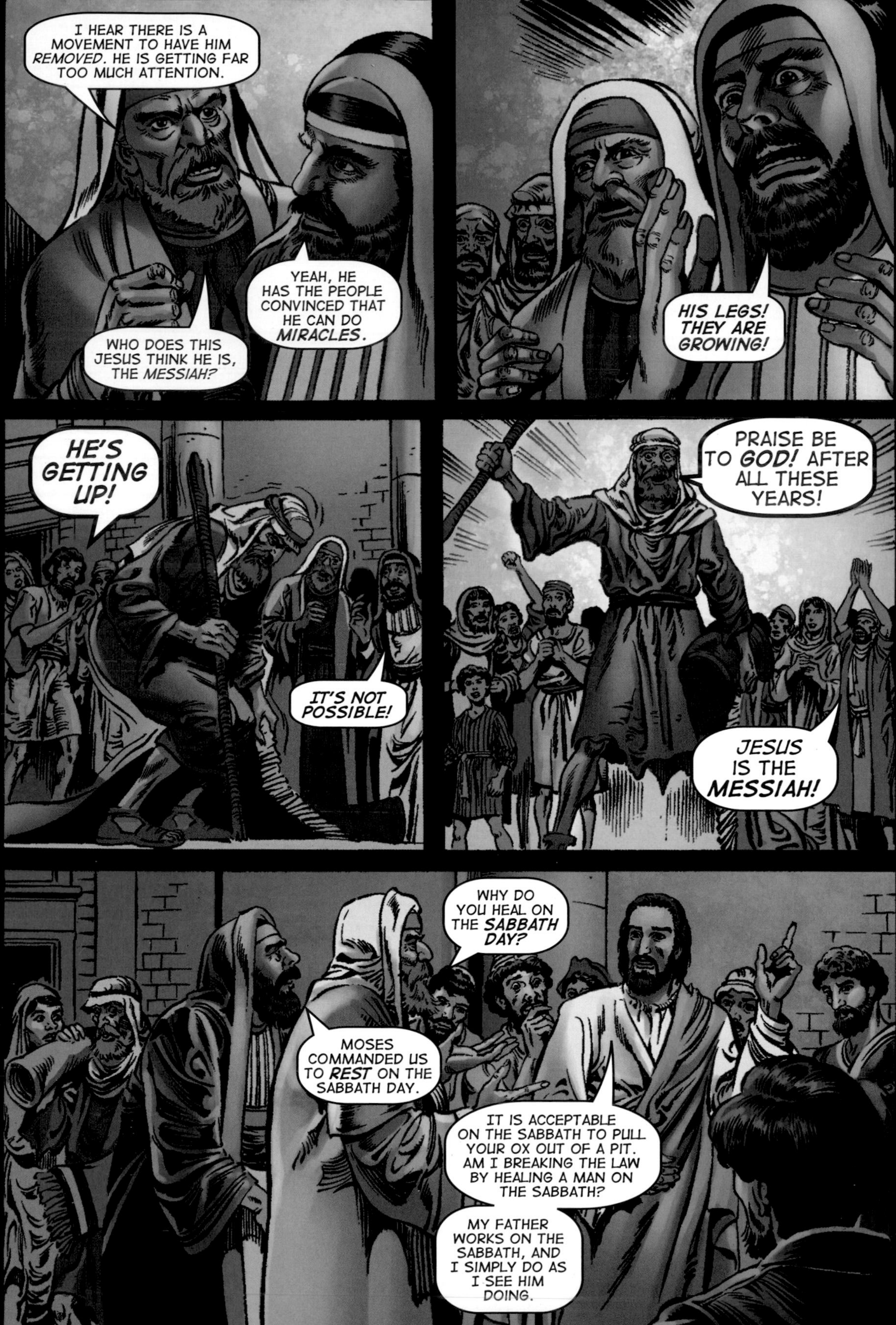
I HEAR THERE IS A MOVEMENT TO HAVE HIM *REMOVED*. HE IS GETTING FAR TOO MUCH ATTENTION.
WHO DOES THIS JESUS THINK HE IS, THE *MESSIAH?*
YEAH, HE HAS THE PEOPLE CONVINCED THAT HE CAN DO ***MIRACLES***.
HIS LEGS! THEY ARE GROWING!
HE'S GETTING UP!
IT'S NOT POSSIBLE!
PRAISE BE TO ***GOD!*** AFTER ALL THESE YEARS!
JESUS IS THE ***MESSIAH!***
WHY DO YOU HEAL ON THE ***SABBATH DAY?***
MOSES COMMANDED US TO ***REST*** ON THE SABBATH DAY.
IT IS ACCEPTABLE ON THE SABBATH TO PULL YOUR OX OUT OF A PIT. AM I BREAKING THE LAW BY HEALING A MAN ON THE SABBATH?
MY FATHER WORKS ON THE SABBATH, AND I SIMPLY DO AS I SEE HIM DOING.

LUKE 14:5–6; JOHN 5:9–17

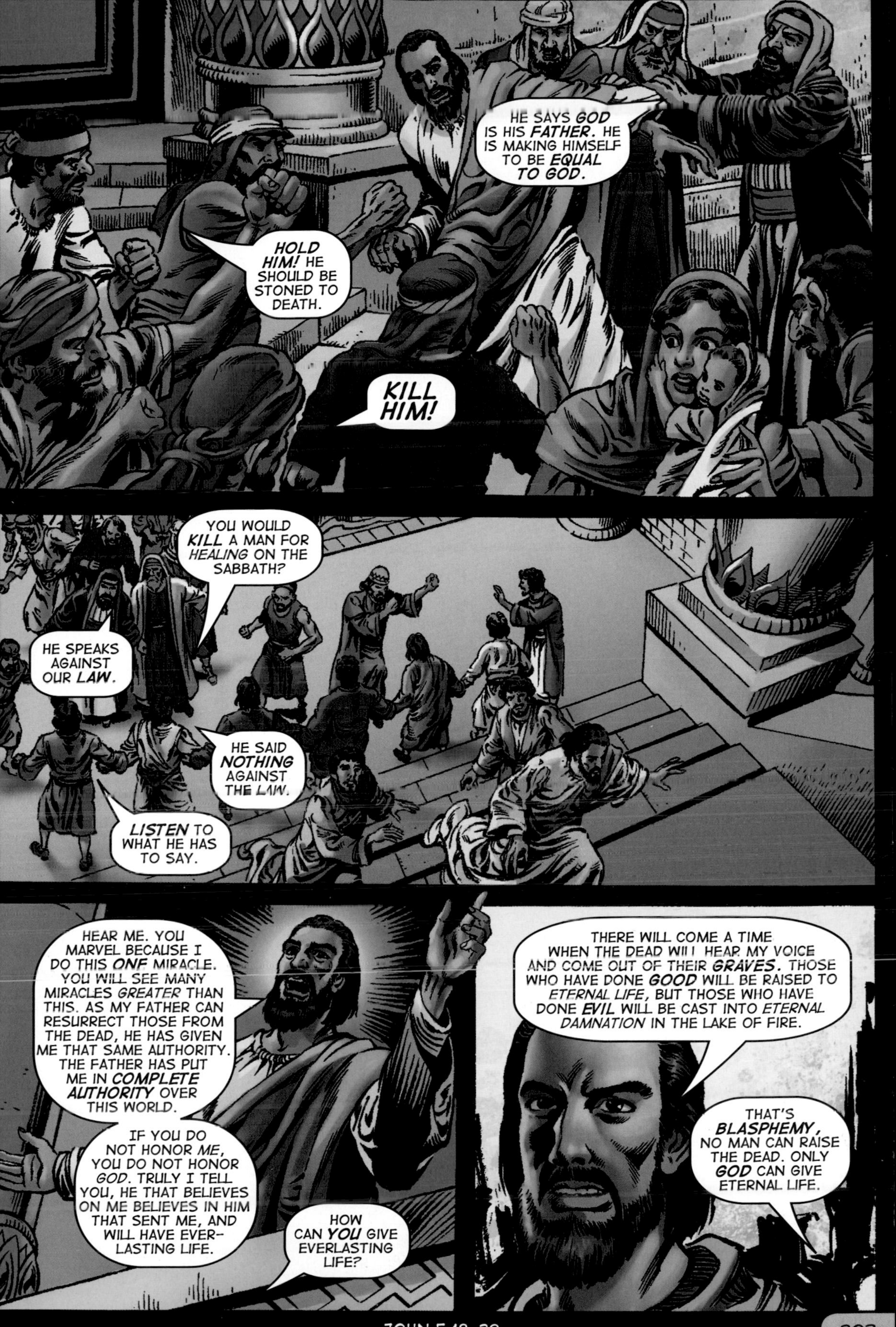
HE SAYS GOD IS HIS FATHER. HE IS MAKING HIMSELF TO BE EQUAL TO GOD.
HOLD HIM! HE SHOULD BE STONED TO DEATH.
KILL HIM!
YOU WOULD KILL A MAN FOR HEALING ON THE SABBATH?
HE SPEAKS AGAINST OUR LAW.
HE SAID NOTHING AGAINST THE LAW.
LISTEN TO WHAT HE HAS TO SAY.
HEAR ME. YOU MARVEL BECAUSE I DO THIS ONE MIRACLE. YOU WILL SEE MANY MIRACLES GREATER THAN THIS. AS MY FATHER CAN RESURRECT THOSE FROM THE DEAD, HE HAS GIVEN ME THAT SAME AUTHORITY. THE FATHER HAS PUT ME IN COMPLETE AUTHORITY OVER THIS WORLD.
IF YOU DO NOT HONOR ME, YOU DO NOT HONOR GOD. TRULY I TELL YOU, HE THAT BELIEVES ON ME BELIEVES IN HIM THAT SENT ME, AND WILL HAVE EVER-LASTING LIFE.
HOW CAN YOU GIVE EVERLASTING LIFE?
THERE WILL COME A TIME WHEN THE DEAD WILL HEAR MY VOICE AND COME OUT OF THEIR GRAVES. THOSE WHO HAVE DONE GOOD WILL BE RAISED TO ETERNAL LIFE, BUT THOSE WHO HAVE DONE EVIL WILL BE CAST INTO ETERNAL DAMNATION IN THE LAKE OF FIRE.
THAT'S BLASPHEMY, NO MAN CAN RAISE THE DEAD. ONLY GOD CAN GIVE ETERNAL LIFE.

JOHN 5:18-29

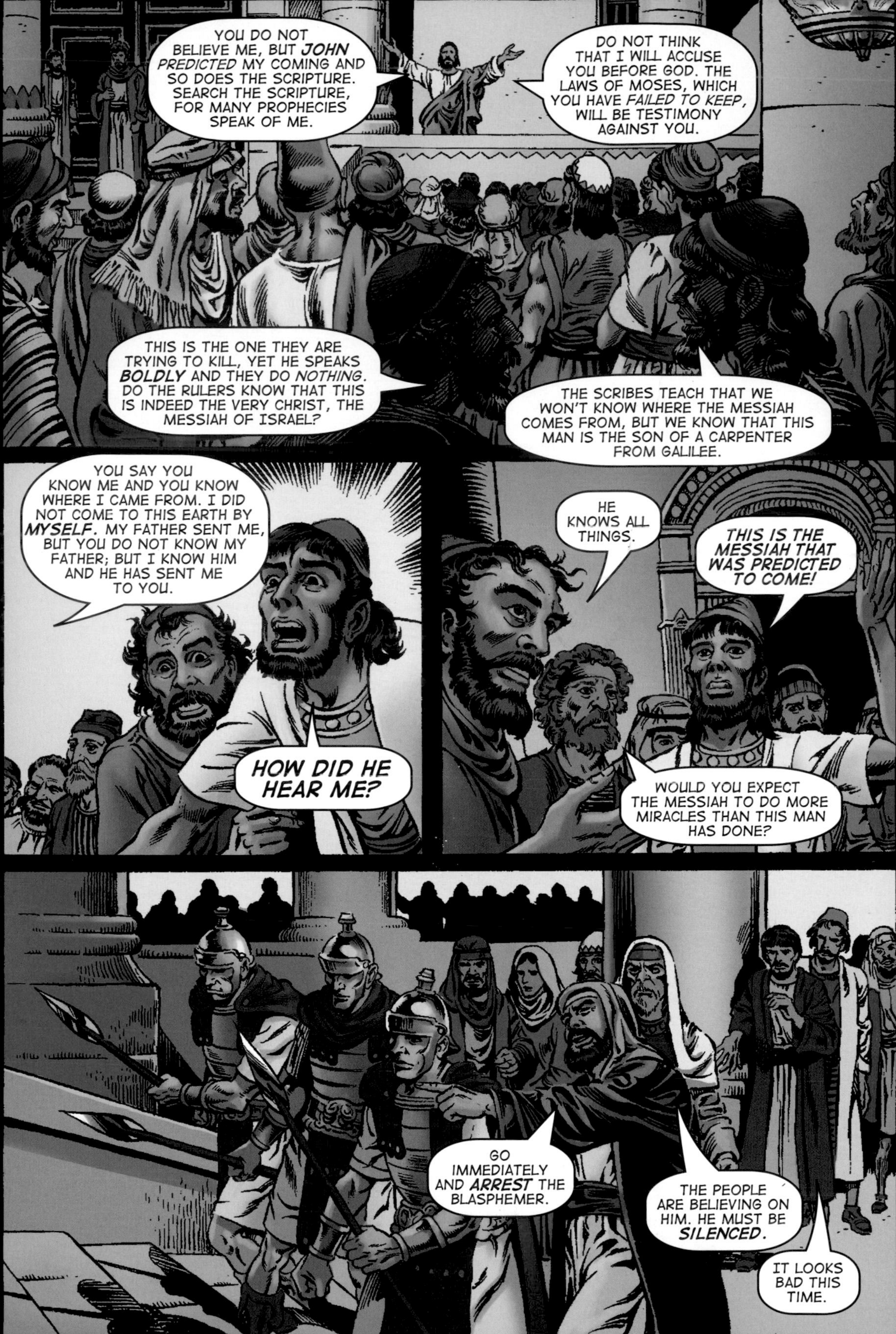
YOU DO NOT BELIEVE ME, BUT *JOHN PREDICTED* MY COMING AND SO DOES THE SCRIPTURE. SEARCH THE SCRIPTURE, FOR MANY PROPHECIES SPEAK OF ME.
DO NOT THINK THAT I WILL ACCUSE YOU BEFORE GOD. THE LAWS OF MOSES, WHICH YOU HAVE *FAILED TO KEEP*, WILL BE TESTIMONY AGAINST YOU.
THIS IS THE ONE THEY ARE TRYING TO KILL, YET HE SPEAKS **BOLDLY** AND THEY DO *NOTHING*. DO THE RULERS KNOW THAT THIS IS INDEED THE VERY CHRIST, THE MESSIAH OF ISRAEL?
THE SCRIBES TEACH THAT WE WON'T KNOW WHERE THE MESSIAH COMES FROM, BUT WE KNOW THAT THIS MAN IS THE SON OF A CARPENTER FROM GALILEE.
YOU SAY YOU KNOW ME AND YOU KNOW WHERE I CAME FROM. I DID NOT COME TO THIS EARTH BY **MYSELF**. MY FATHER SENT ME, BUT YOU DO NOT KNOW MY FATHER; BUT I KNOW HIM AND HE HAS SENT ME TO YOU.
HOW DID HE HEAR ME?
HE KNOWS ALL THINGS.
THIS IS THE MESSIAH THAT WAS PREDICTED TO COME!
WOULD YOU EXPECT THE MESSIAH TO DO MORE MIRACLES THAN THIS MAN HAS DONE?
GO IMMEDIATELY AND **ARREST** THE BLASPHEMER.
THE PEOPLE ARE BELIEVING ON HIM. HE MUST BE **SILENCED**.
IT LOOKS BAD THIS TIME.

JOHN 5:30-39, 45, 6:42-43, 7:25-32, 40-41

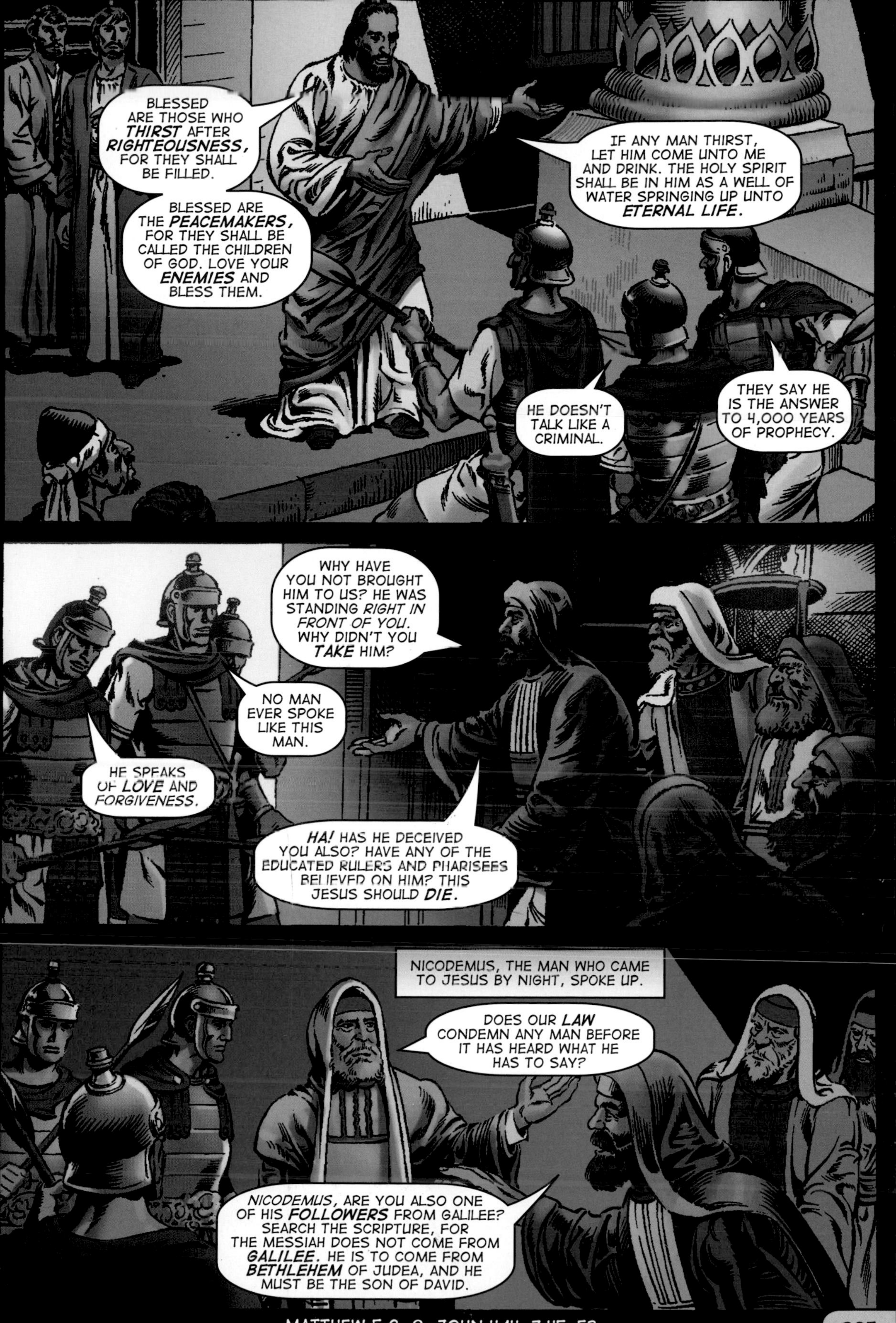
BLESSED ARE THOSE WHO THIRST AFTER RIGHTEOUSNESS, FOR THEY SHALL BE FILLED.
BLESSED ARE THE PEACEMAKERS, FOR THEY SHALL BE CALLED THE CHILDREN OF GOD. LOVE YOUR ENEMIES AND BLESS THEM.
IF ANY MAN THIRST, LET HIM COME UNTO ME AND DRINK. THE HOLY SPIRIT SHALL BE IN HIM AS A WELL OF WATER SPRINGING UP UNTO ETERNAL LIFE.
HE DOESN'T TALK LIKE A CRIMINAL.
THEY SAY HE IS THE ANSWER TO 4,000 YEARS OF PROPHECY.
WHY HAVE YOU NOT BROUGHT HIM TO US? HE WAS STANDING RIGHT IN FRONT OF YOU. WHY DIDN'T YOU TAKE HIM?
NO MAN EVER SPOKE LIKE THIS MAN.
HE SPEAKS OF LOVE AND FORGIVENESS.
HA! HAS HE DECEIVED YOU ALSO? HAVE ANY OF THE EDUCATED RULERS AND PHARISEES BELIEVED ON HIM? THIS JESUS SHOULD DIE.
NICODEMUS, THE MAN WHO CAME TO JESUS BY NIGHT, SPOKE UP.
DOES OUR LAW CONDEMN ANY MAN BEFORE IT HAS HEARD WHAT HE HAS TO SAY?
NICODEMUS, ARE YOU ALSO ONE OF HIS FOLLOWERS FROM GALILEE? SEARCH THE SCRIPTURE, FOR THE MESSIAH DOES NOT COME FROM GALILEE. HE IS TO COME FROM BETHLEHEM OF JUDEA, AND HE MUST BE THE SON OF DAVID.

MATTHEW 5:6, 9; JOHN 4:14, 7:45-52

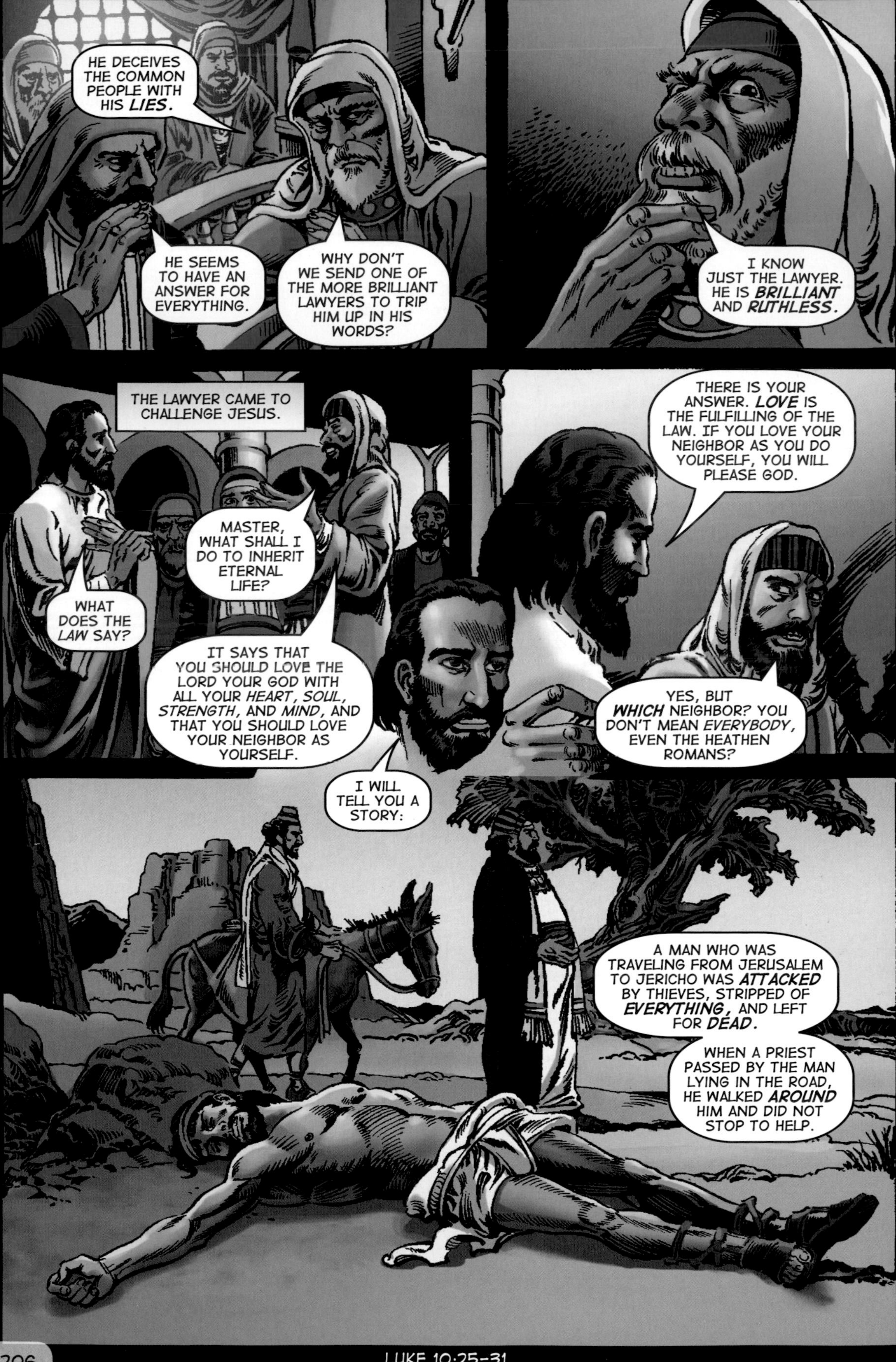
HE DECEIVES THE COMMON PEOPLE WITH HIS **LIES**.
HE SEEMS TO HAVE AN ANSWER FOR EVERYTHING.
WHY DON'T WE SEND ONE OF THE MORE BRILLIANT LAWYERS TO TRIP HIM UP IN HIS WORDS?
I KNOW JUST THE LAWYER. HE IS ***BRILLIANT*** AND ***RUTHLESS***.
THE LAWYER CAME TO CHALLENGE JESUS.
MASTER, WHAT SHALL I DO TO INHERIT ETERNAL LIFE?
WHAT DOES THE *LAW* SAY?
IT SAYS THAT YOU SHOULD LOVE THE LORD YOUR GOD WITH ALL YOUR *HEART*, *SOUL*, *STRENGTH*, AND *MIND*, AND THAT YOU SHOULD LOVE YOUR NEIGHBOR AS YOURSELF.
THERE IS YOUR ANSWER. ***LOVE*** IS THE FULFILLING OF THE LAW. IF YOU LOVE YOUR NEIGHBOR AS YOU DO YOURSELF, YOU WILL PLEASE GOD.
YES, BUT ***WHICH*** NEIGHBOR? YOU DON'T MEAN *EVERYBODY*, EVEN THE HEATHEN ROMANS?
I WILL TELL YOU A STORY:
A MAN WHO WAS TRAVELING FROM JERUSALEM TO JERICHO WAS ***ATTACKED*** BY THIEVES, STRIPPED OF ***EVERYTHING***, AND LEFT FOR ***DEAD***.
WHEN A PRIEST PASSED BY THE MAN LYING IN THE ROAD, HE WALKED ***AROUND*** HIM AND DID NOT STOP TO HELP.

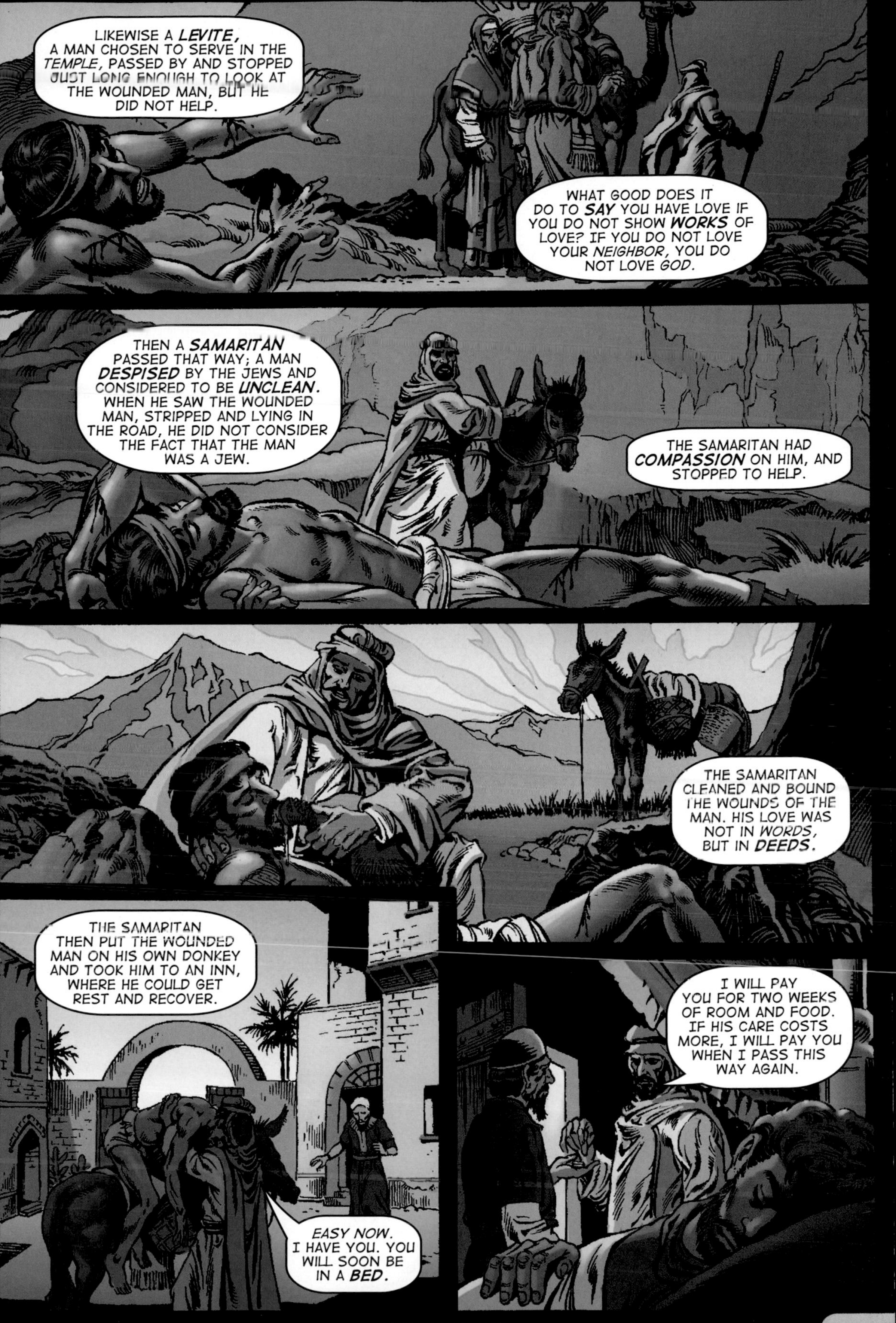
LIKEWISE A LEVITE, A MAN CHOSEN TO SERVE IN THE TEMPLE, PASSED BY AND STOPPED JUST LONG ENOUGH TO LOOK AT THE WOUNDED MAN, BUT HE DID NOT HELP.
WHAT GOOD DOES IT DO TO SAY YOU HAVE LOVE IF YOU DO NOT SHOW WORKS OF LOVE? IF YOU DO NOT LOVE YOUR NEIGHBOR, YOU DO NOT LOVE GOD.
THEN A SAMARITAN PASSED THAT WAY; A MAN DESPISED BY THE JEWS AND CONSIDERED TO BE UNCLEAN. WHEN HE SAW THE WOUNDED MAN, STRIPPED AND LYING IN THE ROAD, HE DID NOT CONSIDER THE FACT THAT THE MAN WAS A JEW.
THE SAMARITAN HAD COMPASSION ON HIM, AND STOPPED TO HELP.
THE SAMARITAN CLEANED AND BOUND THE WOUNDS OF THE MAN. HIS LOVE WAS NOT IN WORDS, BUT IN DEEDS.
THE SAMARITAN THEN PUT THE WOUNDED MAN ON HIS OWN DONKEY AND TOOK HIM TO AN INN, WHERE HE COULD GET REST AND RECOVER.
EASY NOW. I HAVE YOU. YOU WILL SOON BE IN A BED.
I WILL PAY YOU FOR TWO WEEKS OF ROOM AND FOOD. IF HIS CARE COSTS MORE, I WILL PAY YOU WHEN I PASS THIS WAY AGAIN.

LUKE 10:32-35

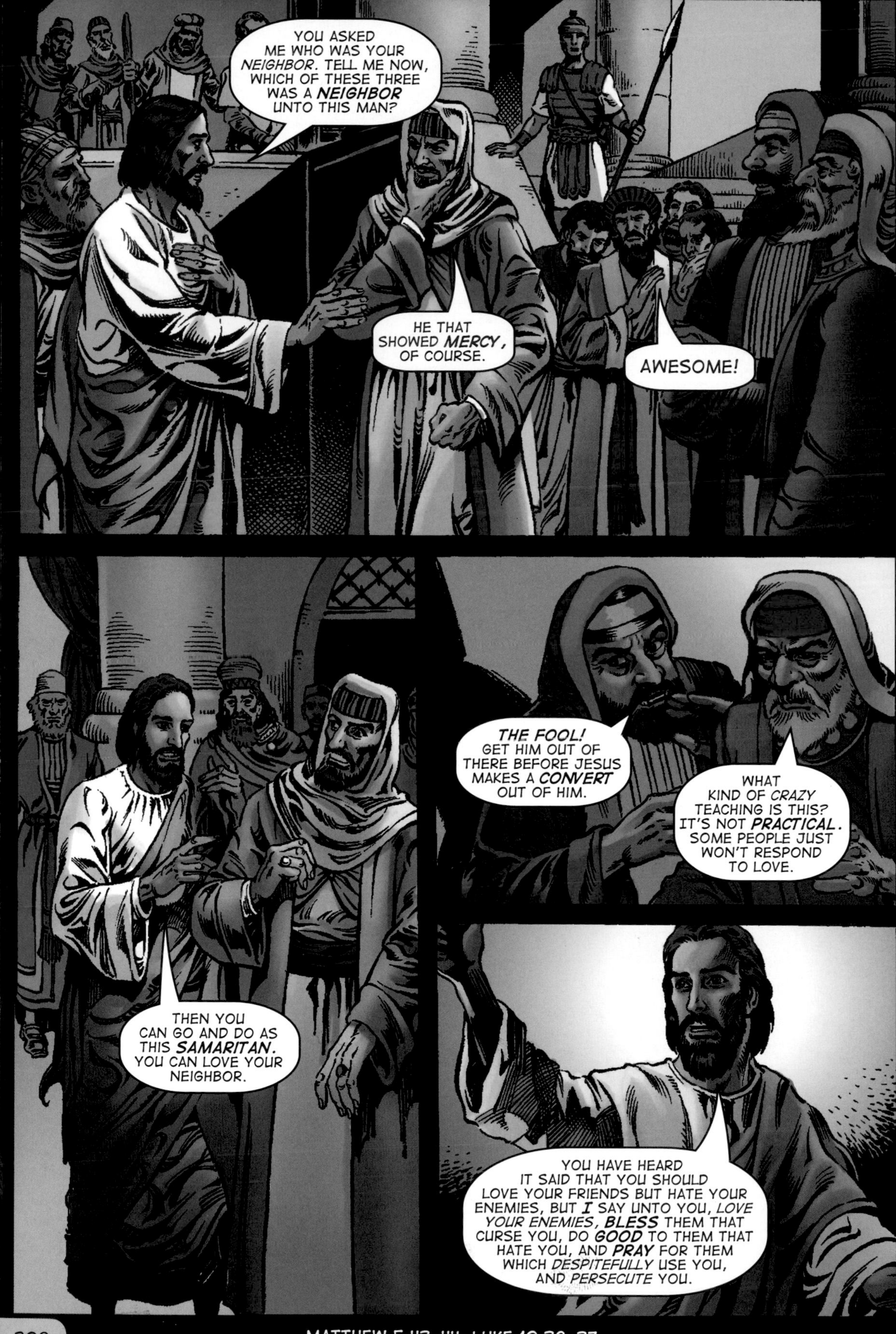
YOU ASKED ME WHO WAS YOUR *NEIGHBOR*. TELL ME NOW, WHICH OF THESE THREE WAS A ***NEIGHBOR*** UNTO THIS MAN?
HE THAT SHOWED ***MERCY***, OF COURSE.
AWESOME!
THEN YOU CAN GO AND DO AS THIS ***SAMARITAN.*** YOU CAN LOVE YOUR NEIGHBOR.
THE FOOL! GET HIM OUT OF THERE BEFORE JESUS MAKES A ***CONVERT*** OUT OF HIM.
WHAT KIND OF *CRAZY* TEACHING IS THIS? IT'S NOT ***PRACTICAL.*** SOME PEOPLE JUST WON'T RESPOND TO LOVE.
YOU HAVE HEARD IT SAID THAT YOU SHOULD LOVE YOUR FRIENDS BUT HATE YOUR ENEMIES, BUT ***I*** SAY UNTO YOU, *LOVE YOUR ENEMIES*, ***BLESS*** THEM THAT CURSE YOU, DO ***GOOD*** TO THEM THAT HATE YOU, AND ***PRAY*** FOR THEM WHICH *DESPITEFULLY* USE YOU, AND *PERSECUTE* YOU.

MATTHEW 5:43–44; LUKE 10:36–37

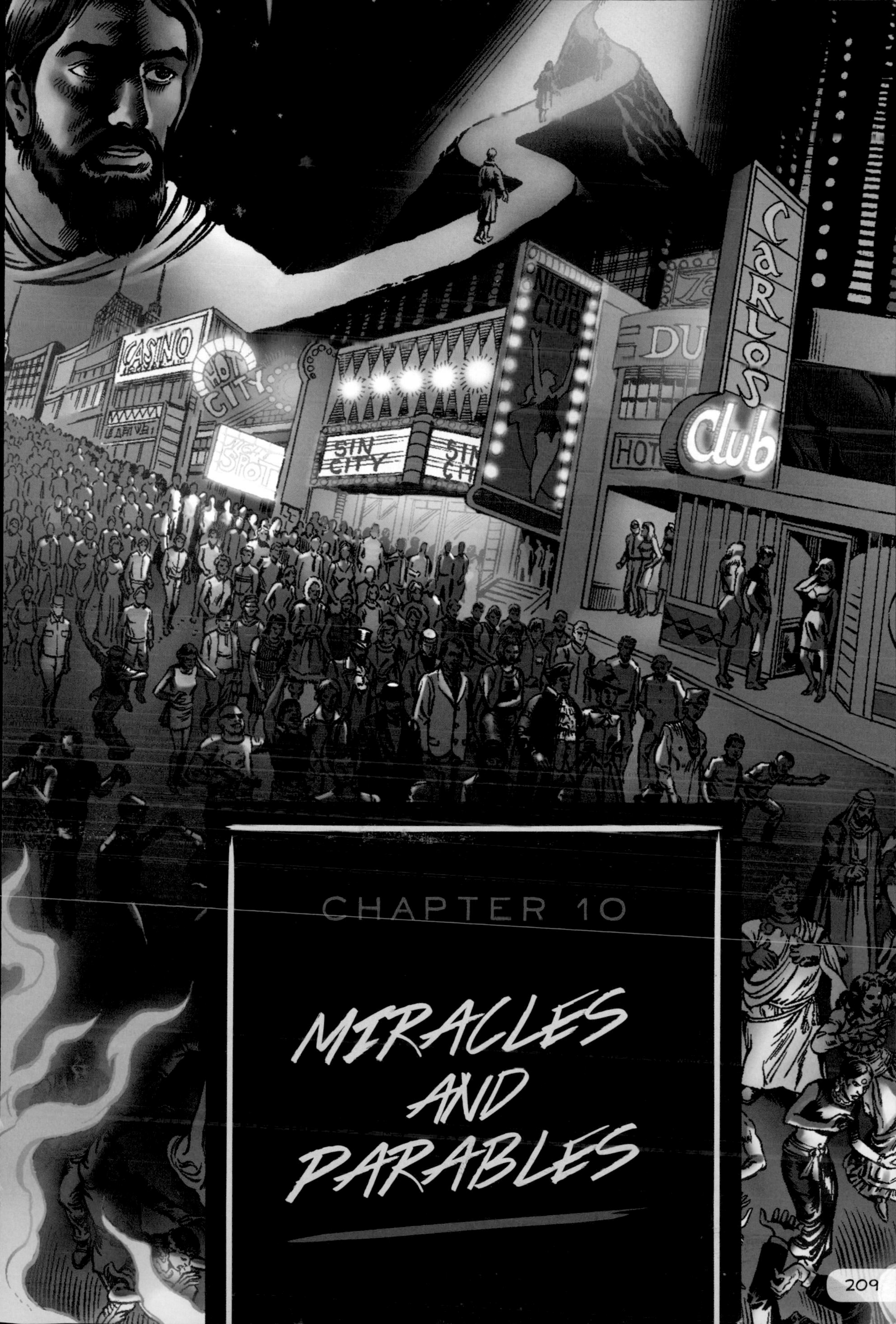
CASINO
HOT CITY
SIN CITY
SIN CITY
NIGHT CLUB
CARLOS
Club

CHAPTER 10

MIRACLES AND PARABLES

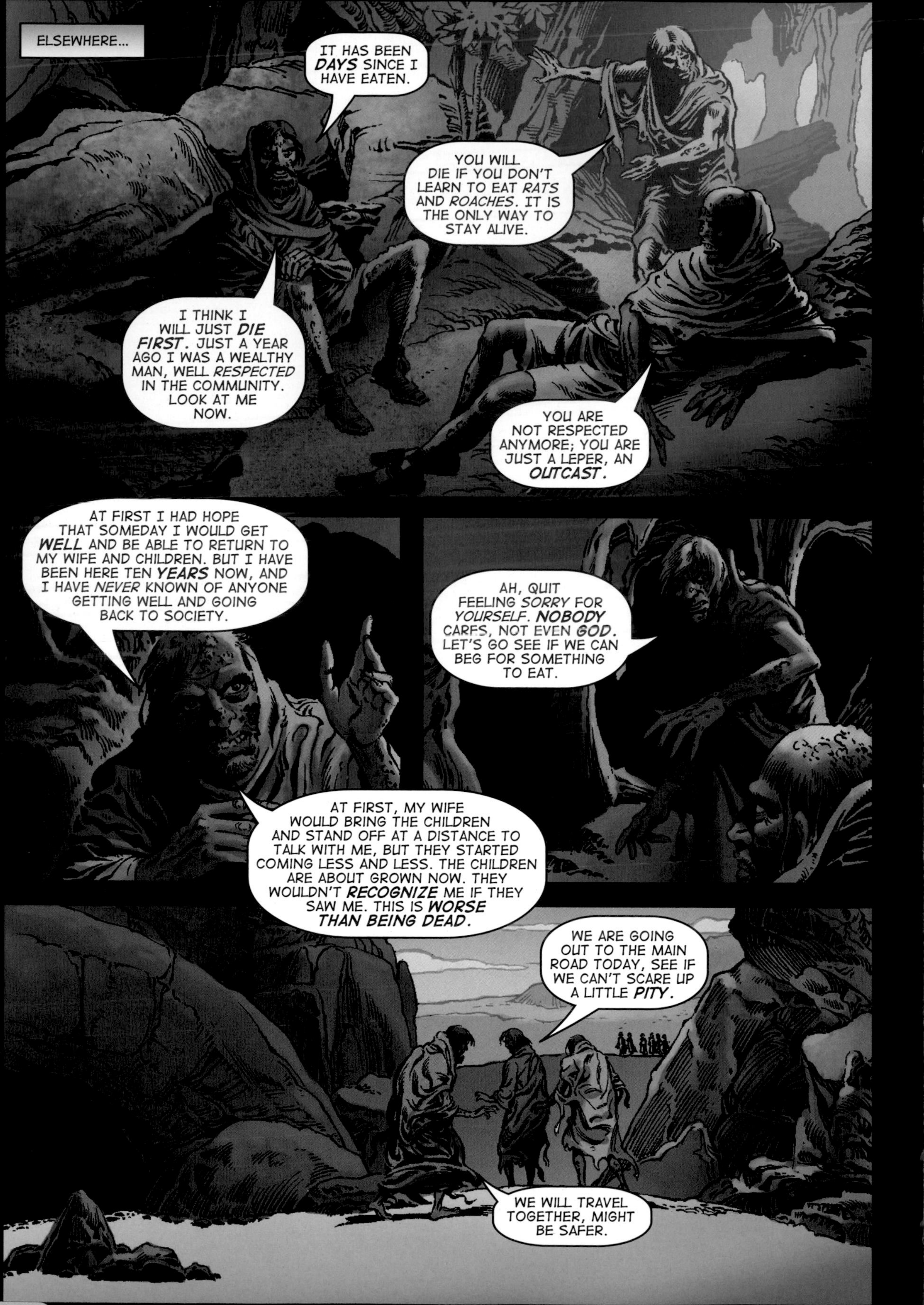
ELSEWHERE...
IT HAS BEEN DAYS SINCE I HAVE EATEN.
YOU WILL DIE IF YOU DON'T LEARN TO EAT RATS AND ROACHES. IT IS THE ONLY WAY TO STAY ALIVE.
I THINK I WILL JUST DIE FIRST. JUST A YEAR AGO I WAS A WEALTHY MAN, WELL RESPECTED IN THE COMMUNITY. LOOK AT ME NOW.
YOU ARE NOT RESPECTED ANYMORE; YOU ARE JUST A LEPER, AN OUTCAST.
AT FIRST I HAD HOPE THAT SOMEDAY I WOULD GET WELL AND BE ABLE TO RETURN TO MY WIFE AND CHILDREN. BUT I HAVE BEEN HERE TEN YEARS NOW, AND I HAVE NEVER KNOWN OF ANYONE GETTING WELL AND GOING BACK TO SOCIETY.
AH, QUIT FEELING SORRY FOR YOURSELF. NOBODY CARES, NOT EVEN GOD. LET'S GO SEE IF WE CAN BEG FOR SOMETHING TO EAT.
AT FIRST, MY WIFE WOULD BRING THE CHILDREN AND STAND OFF AT A DISTANCE TO TALK WITH ME, BUT THEY STARTED COMING LESS AND LESS. THE CHILDREN ARE ABOUT GROWN NOW. THEY WOULDN'T RECOGNIZE ME IF THEY SAW ME. THIS IS WORSE THAN BEING DEAD.
WE ARE GOING OUT TO THE MAIN ROAD TODAY, SEE IF WE CAN'T SCARE UP A LITTLE PITY.
WE WILL TRAVEL TOGETHER, MIGHT BE SAFER.

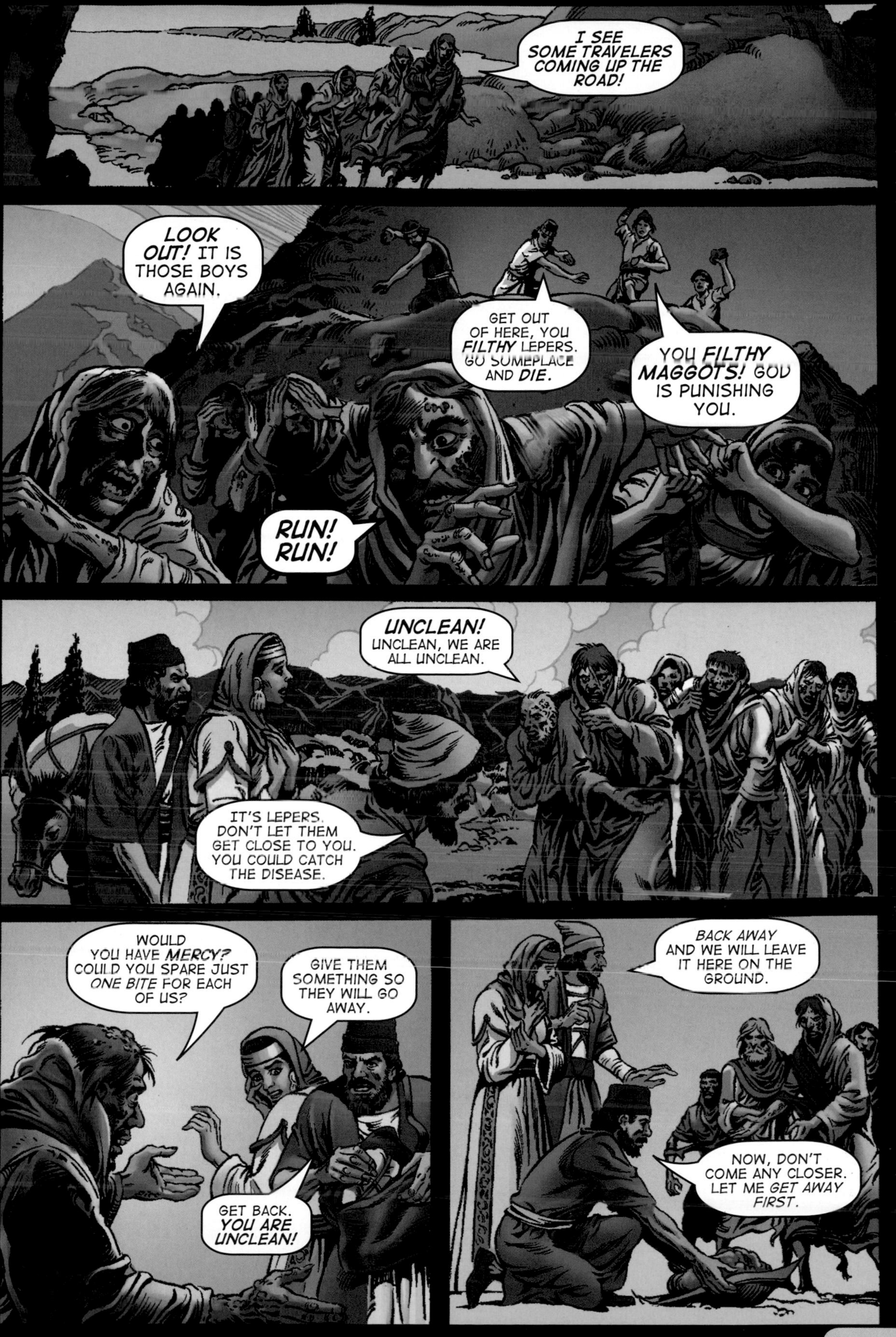
I SEE SOME TRAVELERS COMING UP THE ROAD!
LOOK OUT! IT IS THOSE BOYS AGAIN.
GET OUT OF HERE, YOU FILTHY LEPERS. GO SOMEPLACE AND DIE.
YOU FILTHY MAGGOTS! GOD IS PUNISHING YOU.
RUN! RUN!
UNCLEAN! UNCLEAN, WE ARE ALL UNCLEAN.
IT'S LEPERS. DON'T LET THEM GET CLOSE TO YOU. YOU COULD CATCH THE DISEASE.
WOULD YOU HAVE MERCY? COULD YOU SPARE JUST ONE BITE FOR EACH OF US?
GIVE THEM SOMETHING SO THEY WILL GO AWAY.
GET BACK. YOU ARE UNCLEAN!
BACK AWAY AND WE WILL LEAVE IT HERE ON THE GROUND.
NOW, DON'T COME ANY CLOSER. LET ME GET AWAY FIRST.

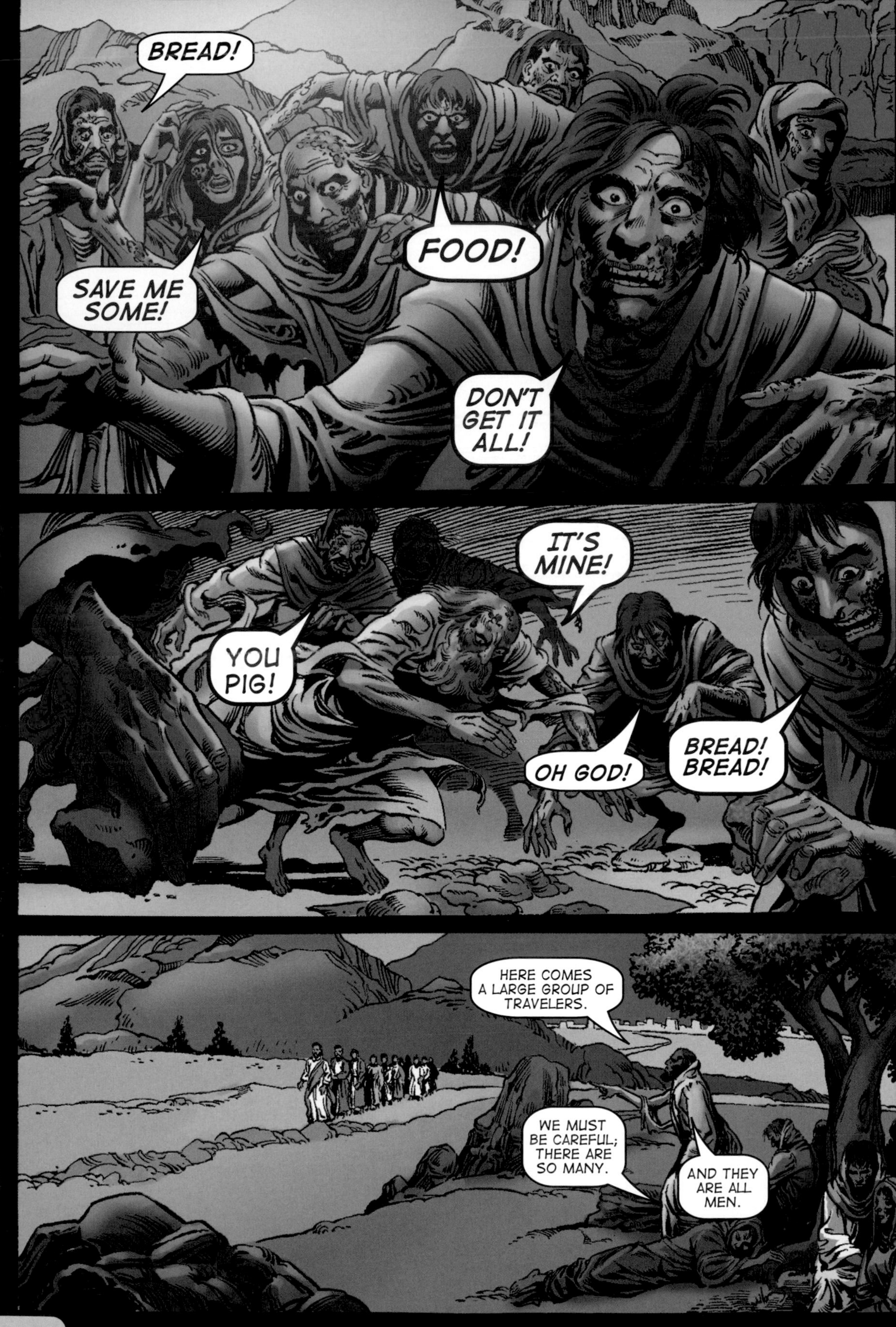
BREAD!
FOOD!
SAVE ME SOME!
DON'T GET IT ALL!
IT'S MINE!
YOU PIG!
OH GOD!
BREAD! BREAD!
HERE COMES A LARGE GROUP OF TRAVELERS.
WE MUST BE CAREFUL; THERE ARE SO MANY.
AND THEY ARE ALL MEN.

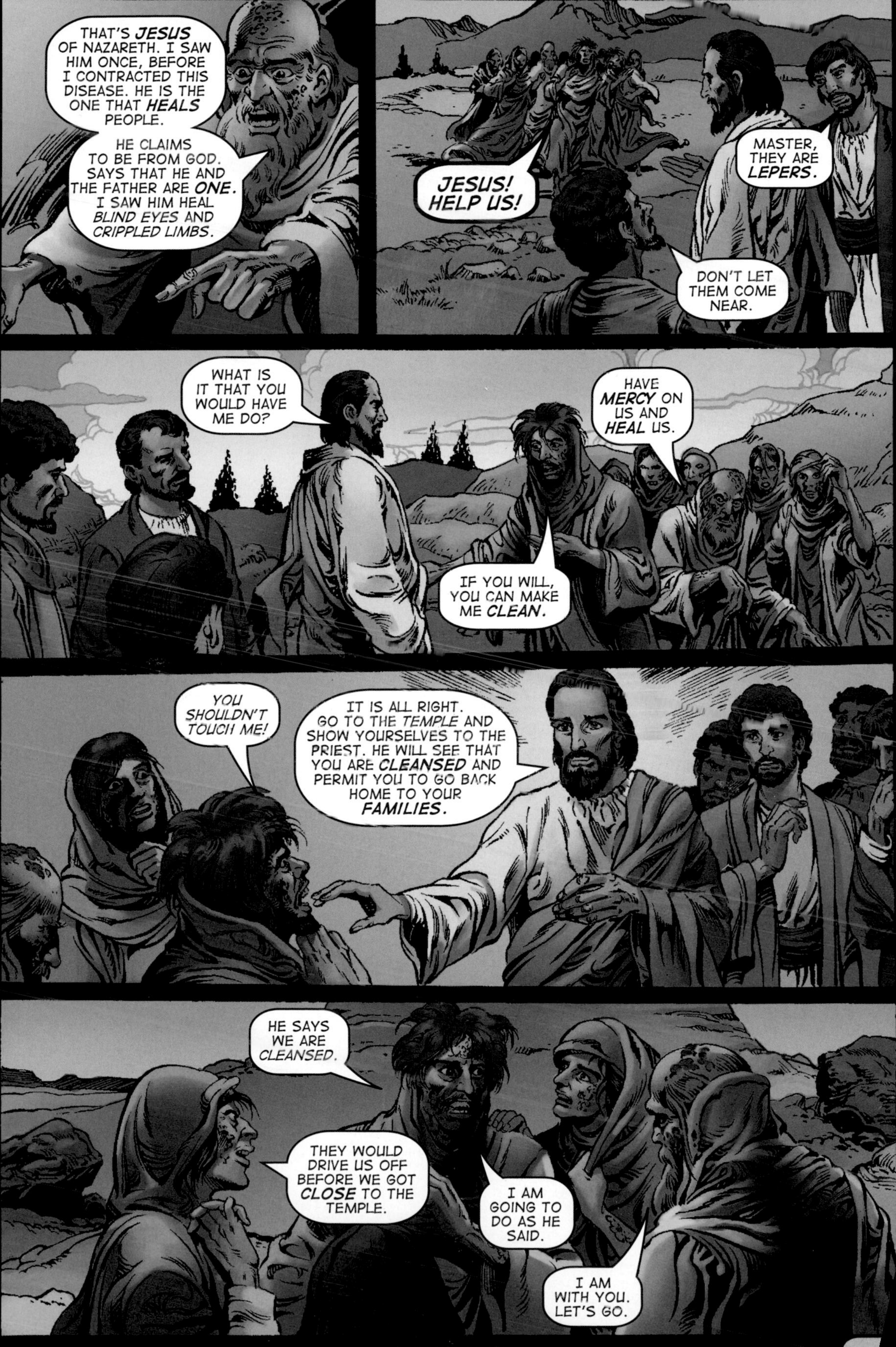
THAT'S JESUS OF NAZARETH. I SAW HIM ONCE, BEFORE I CONTRACTED THIS DISEASE. HE IS THE ONE THAT HEALS PEOPLE.
HE CLAIMS TO BE FROM GOD. SAYS THAT HE AND THE FATHER ARE ONE. I SAW HIM HEAL BLIND EYES AND CRIPPLED LIMBS.
JESUS! HELP US!
MASTER, THEY ARE LEPERS.
DON'T LET THEM COME NEAR.
WHAT IS IT THAT YOU WOULD HAVE ME DO?
HAVE MERCY ON US AND HEAL US.
IF YOU WILL, YOU CAN MAKE ME CLEAN.
YOU SHOULDN'T TOUCH ME!
IT IS ALL RIGHT. GO TO THE TEMPLE AND SHOW YOURSELVES TO THE PRIEST. HE WILL SEE THAT YOU ARE CLEANSED AND PERMIT YOU TO GO BACK HOME TO YOUR FAMILIES.
HE SAYS WE ARE CLEANSED.
THEY WOULD DRIVE US OFF BEFORE WE GOT CLOSE TO THE TEMPLE.
I AM GOING TO DO AS HE SAID.
I AM WITH YOU. LET'S GO.

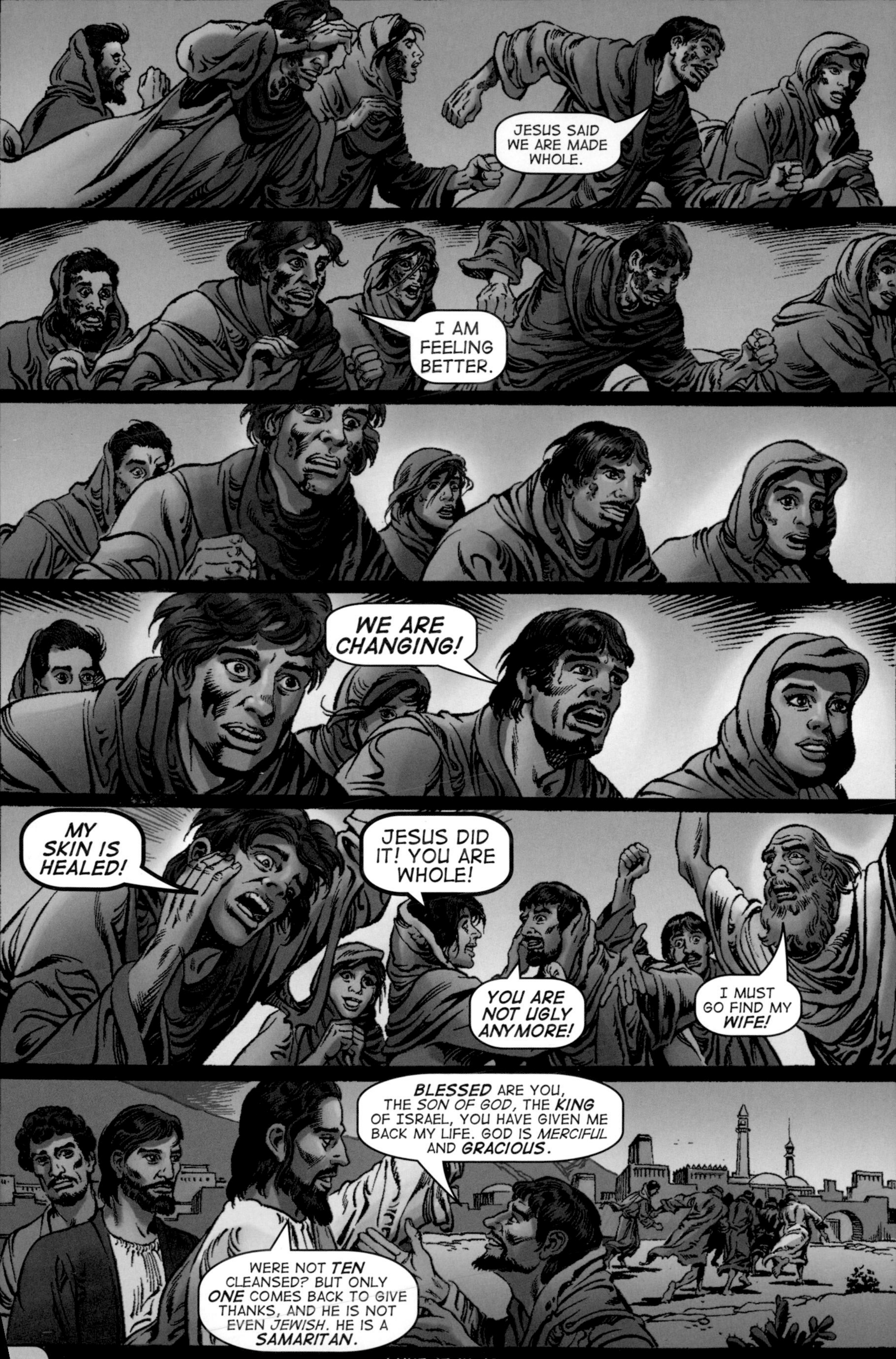

JESUS SAID WE ARE MADE WHOLE.
I AM FEELING BETTER.
WE ARE CHANGING!
MY SKIN IS HEALED!
JESUS DID IT! YOU ARE WHOLE!
YOU ARE NOT UGLY ANYMORE!
I MUST GO FIND MY WIFE!
BLESSED ARE YOU, THE SON OF GOD, THE KING OF ISRAEL, YOU HAVE GIVEN ME BACK MY LIFE. GOD IS MERCIFUL AND GRACIOUS.
WERE NOT TEN CLEANSED? BUT ONLY ONE COMES BACK TO GIVE THANKS, AND HE IS NOT EVEN JEWISH. HE IS A SAMARITAN.

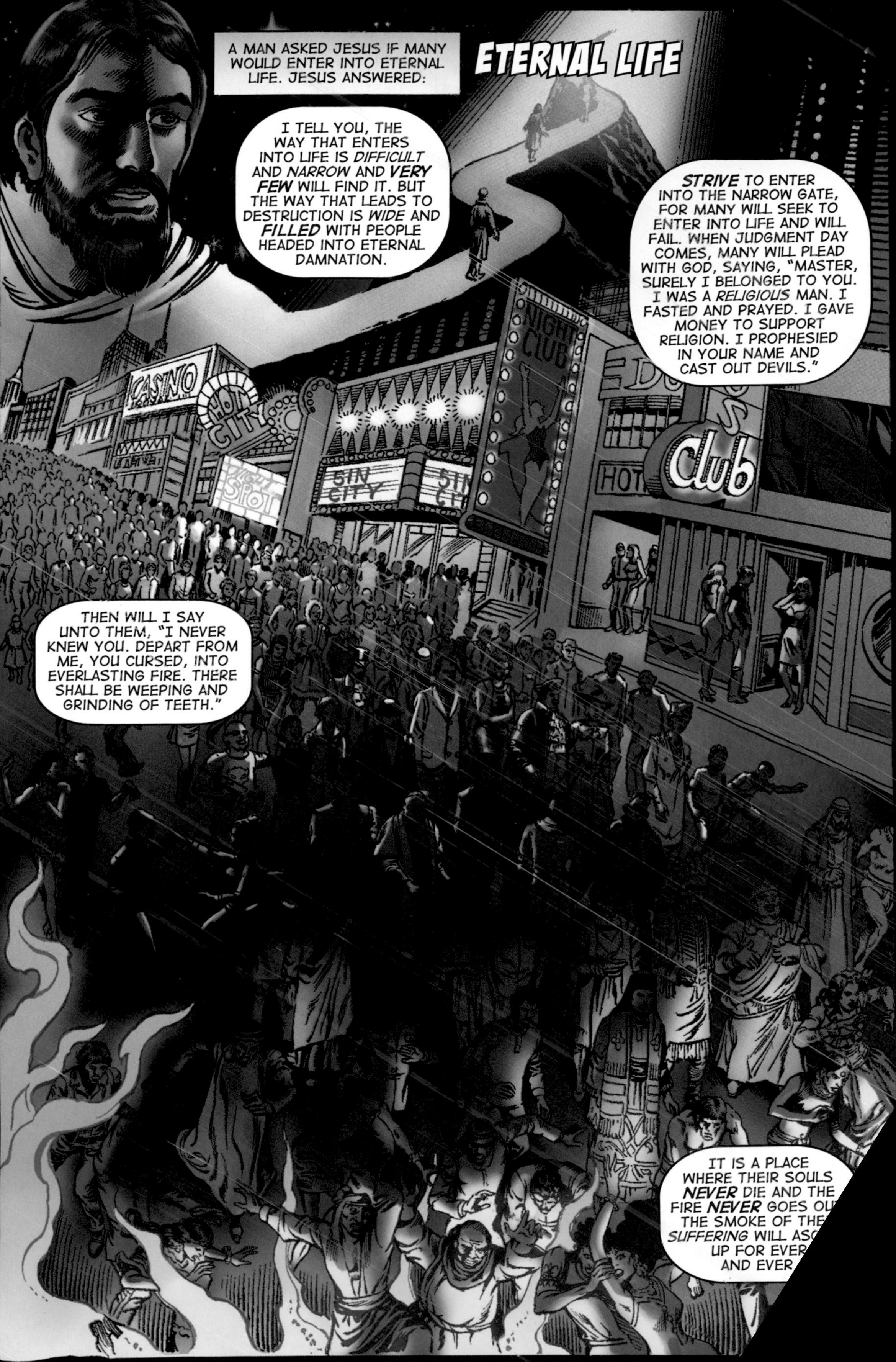
ETERNAL LIFE
A MAN ASKED JESUS IF MANY WOULD ENTER INTO ETERNAL LIFE. JESUS ANSWERED:
I TELL YOU, THE WAY THAT ENTERS INTO LIFE IS *DIFFICULT* AND *NARROW* AND ***VERY FEW*** WILL FIND IT. BUT THE WAY THAT LEADS TO DESTRUCTION IS *WIDE* AND ***FILLED*** WITH PEOPLE HEADED INTO ETERNAL DAMNATION.
STRIVE TO ENTER INTO THE NARROW GATE, FOR MANY WILL SEEK TO ENTER INTO LIFE AND WILL FAIL. WHEN JUDGMENT DAY COMES, MANY WILL PLEAD WITH GOD, SAYING, "MASTER, SURELY I BELONGED TO YOU. I WAS A *RELIGIOUS* MAN. I FASTED AND PRAYED. I GAVE MONEY TO SUPPORT RELIGION. I PROPHESIED IN YOUR NAME AND CAST OUT DEVILS."
CASINO
HOT CITY
NIGHT CLUB
club
SIN CITY
THEN WILL I SAY UNTO THEM, "I NEVER KNEW YOU. DEPART FROM ME, YOU CURSED, INTO EVERLASTING FIRE. THERE SHALL BE WEEPING AND GRINDING OF TEETH."
IT IS A PLACE WHERE THEIR SOULS ***NEVER*** DIE AND THE FIRE ***NEVER*** GOES OU THE SMOKE OF THE *SUFFERING* WILL ASC UP FOR EVER AND EVER

MATTHEW 7:13-14, 22-23; REVELATION 14:11

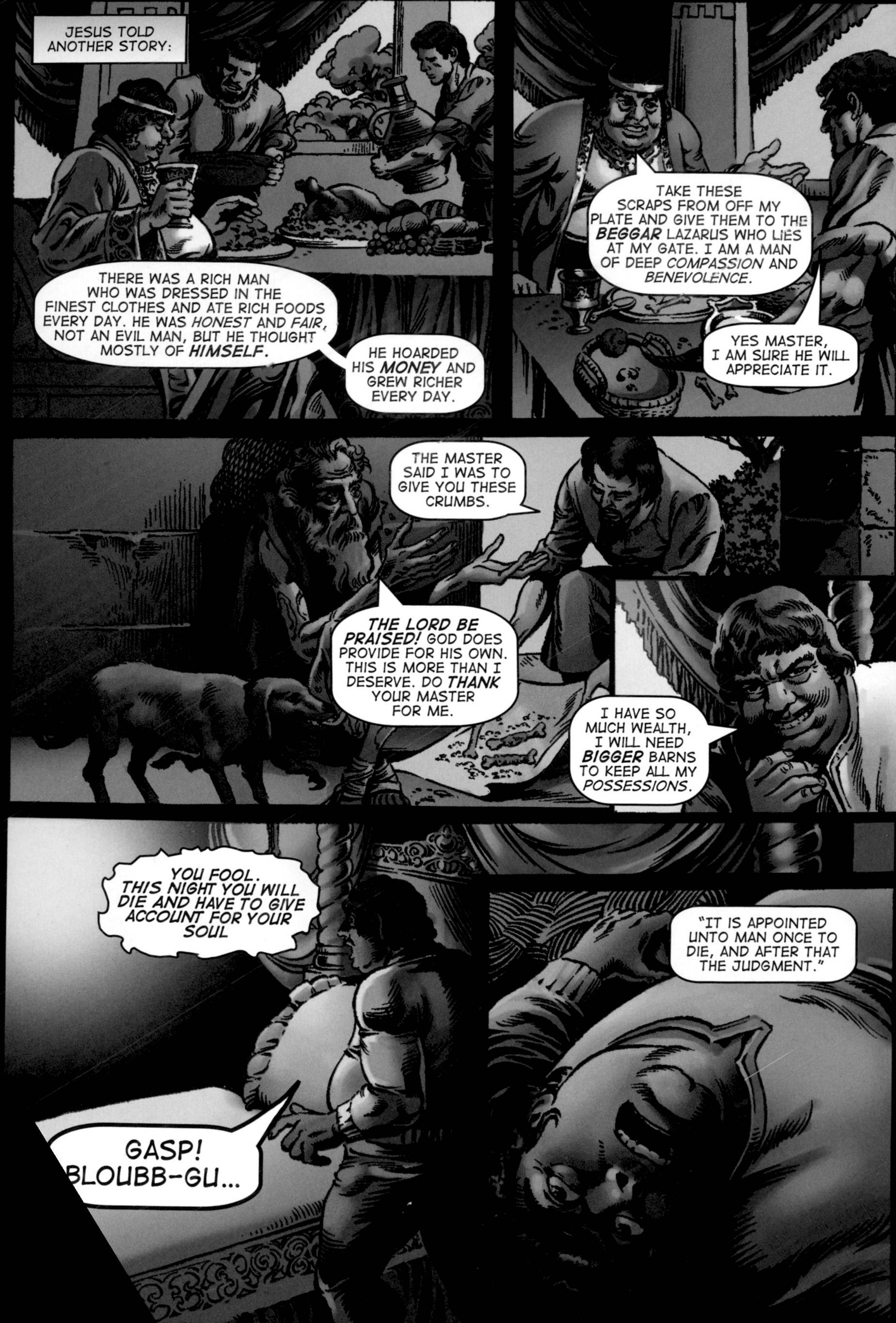
JESUS TOLD ANOTHER STORY:
THERE WAS A RICH MAN WHO WAS DRESSED IN THE FINEST CLOTHES AND ATE RICH FOODS EVERY DAY. HE WAS *HONEST* AND *FAIR*, NOT AN EVIL MAN, BUT HE THOUGHT MOSTLY OF **HIMSELF**.
HE HOARDED HIS **MONEY** AND GREW RICHER EVERY DAY.
TAKE THESE SCRAPS FROM OFF MY PLATE AND GIVE THEM TO THE **BEGGAR** LAZARUS WHO LIES AT MY GATE. I AM A MAN OF DEEP *COMPASSION* AND *BENEVOLENCE*.
YES MASTER, I AM SURE HE WILL APPRECIATE IT.
THE MASTER SAID I WAS TO GIVE YOU THESE CRUMBS.
THE LORD BE PRAISED! GOD DOES PROVIDE FOR HIS OWN. THIS IS MORE THAN I DESERVE. DO **THANK** YOUR MASTER FOR ME.
I HAVE SO MUCH WEALTH, I WILL NEED **BIGGER** BARNS TO KEEP ALL MY *POSSESSIONS*.
YOU FOOL. THIS NIGHT YOU WILL DIE AND HAVE TO GIVE ACCOUNT FOR YOUR SOUL
"IT IS APPOINTED UNTO MAN ONCE TO DIE, AND AFTER THAT THE JUDGMENT."
GASP! BLOUBB-GU...

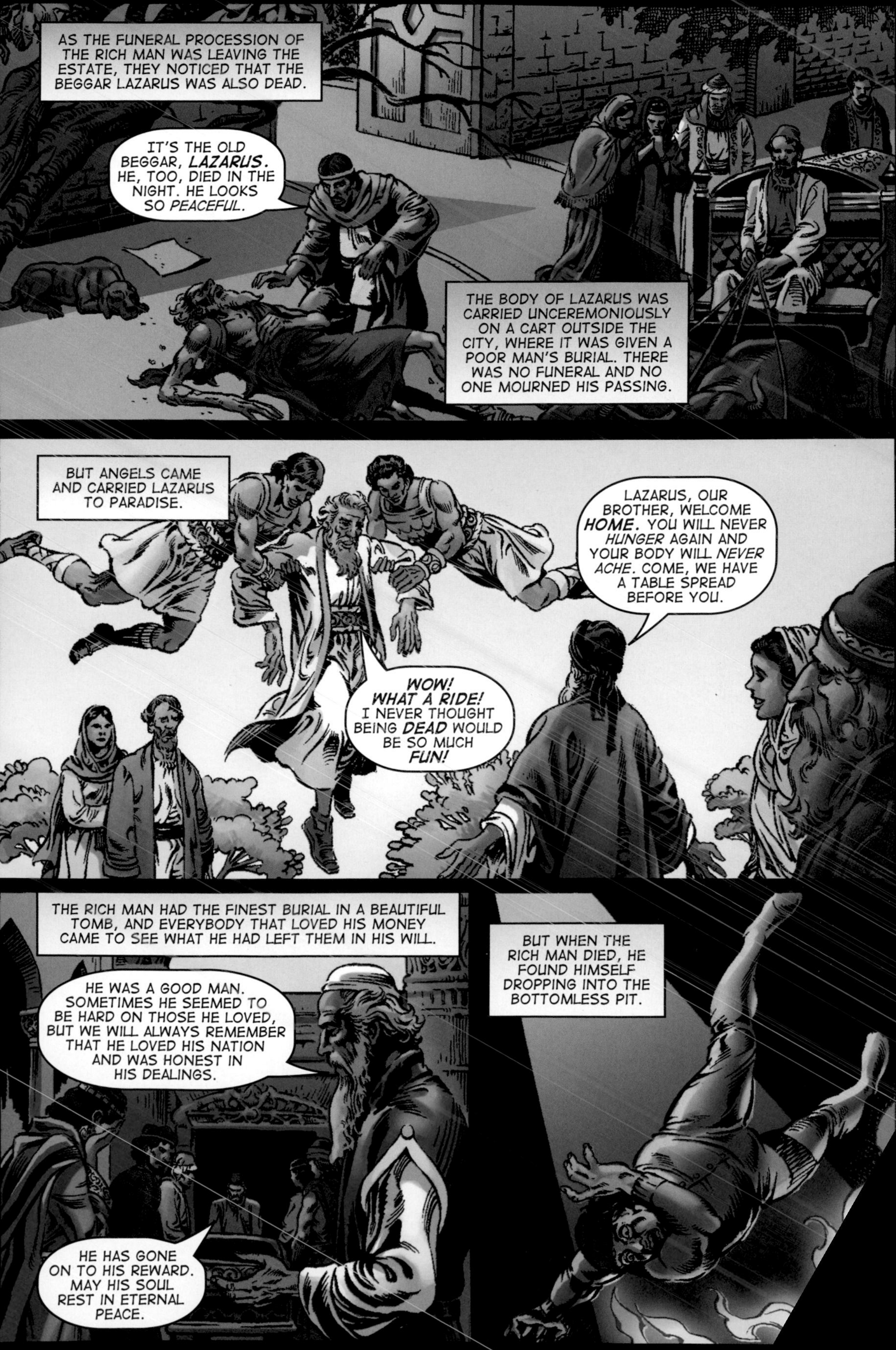
AS THE FUNERAL PROCESSION OF THE RICH MAN WAS LEAVING THE ESTATE, THEY NOTICED THAT THE BEGGAR LAZARUS WAS ALSO DEAD.
IT'S THE OLD BEGGAR, **LAZARUS.** HE, TOO, DIED IN THE NIGHT. HE LOOKS SO *PEACEFUL.*
THE BODY OF LAZARUS WAS CARRIED UNCEREMONIOUSLY ON A CART OUTSIDE THE CITY, WHERE IT WAS GIVEN A POOR MAN'S BURIAL. THERE WAS NO FUNERAL AND NO ONE MOURNED HIS PASSING.
BUT ANGELS CAME AND CARRIED LAZARUS TO PARADISE.
LAZARUS, OUR BROTHER, WELCOME **HOME.** YOU WILL NEVER *HUNGER* AGAIN AND YOUR BODY WILL *NEVER ACHE*. COME, WE HAVE A TABLE SPREAD BEFORE YOU.
WOW! WHAT A RIDE! I NEVER THOUGHT BEING ***DEAD*** WOULD BE SO MUCH ***FUN!***
THE RICH MAN HAD THE FINEST BURIAL IN A BEAUTIFUL TOMB, AND EVERYBODY THAT LOVED HIS MONEY CAME TO SEE WHAT HE HAD LEFT THEM IN HIS WILL.
HE WAS A GOOD MAN. SOMETIMES HE SEEMED TO BE HARD ON THOSE HE LOVED, BUT WE WILL ALWAYS REMEMBER THAT HE LOVED HIS NATION AND WAS HONEST IN HIS DEALINGS.
HE HAS GONE ON TO HIS REWARD. MAY HIS SOUL REST IN ETERNAL PEACE.
BUT WHEN THE RICH MAN DIED, HE FOUND HIMSELF DROPPING INTO THE BOTTOMLESS PIT.

LUKE 16:22

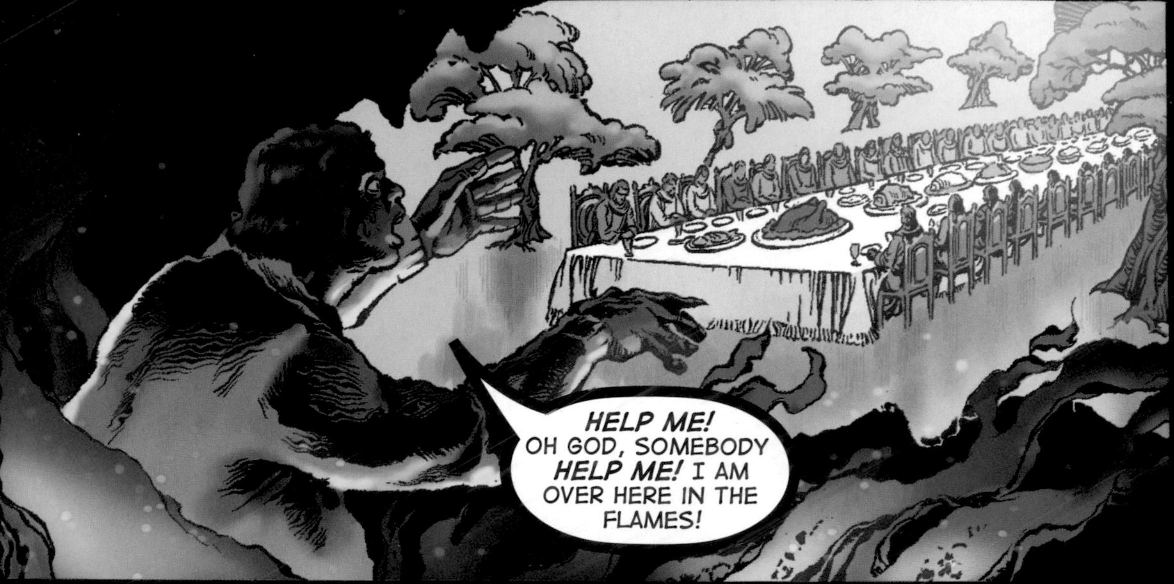
HELP ME! OH GOD, SOMEBODY HELP ME! I AM OVER HERE IN THE FLAMES!

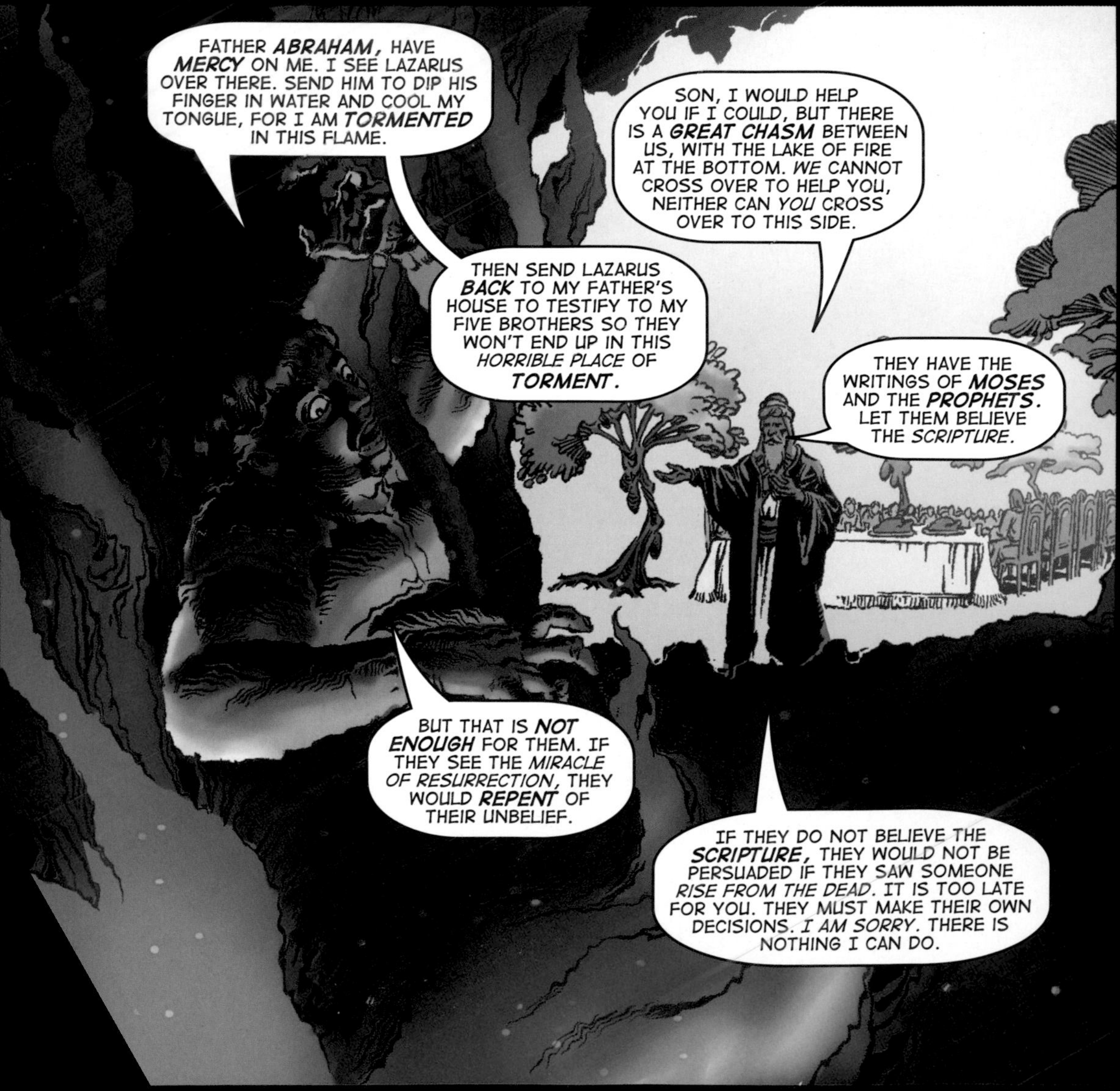
FATHER ABRAHAM, HAVE MERCY ON ME. I SEE LAZARUS OVER THERE. SEND HIM TO DIP HIS FINGER IN WATER AND COOL MY TONGUE, FOR I AM TORMENTED IN THIS FLAME.
SON, I WOULD HELP YOU IF I COULD, BUT THERE IS A GREAT CHASM BETWEEN US, WITH THE LAKE OF FIRE AT THE BOTTOM. WE CANNOT CROSS OVER TO HELP YOU, NEITHER CAN YOU CROSS OVER TO THIS SIDE.
THEN SEND LAZARUS BACK TO MY FATHER'S HOUSE TO TESTIFY TO MY FIVE BROTHERS SO THEY WON'T END UP IN THIS HORRIBLE PLACE OF TORMENT.
THEY HAVE THE WRITINGS OF MOSES AND THE PROPHETS. LET THEM BELIEVE THE SCRIPTURE.
BUT THAT IS NOT ENOUGH FOR THEM. IF THEY SEE THE MIRACLE OF RESURRECTION, THEY WOULD REPENT OF THEIR UNBELIEF.
IF THEY DO NOT BELIEVE THE SCRIPTURE, THEY WOULD NOT BE PERSUADED IF THEY SAW SOMEONE RISE FROM THE DEAD. IT IS TOO LATE FOR YOU. THEY MUST MAKE THEIR OWN DECISIONS. I AM SORRY. THERE IS NOTHING I CAN DO.

LUKE 16:22-31

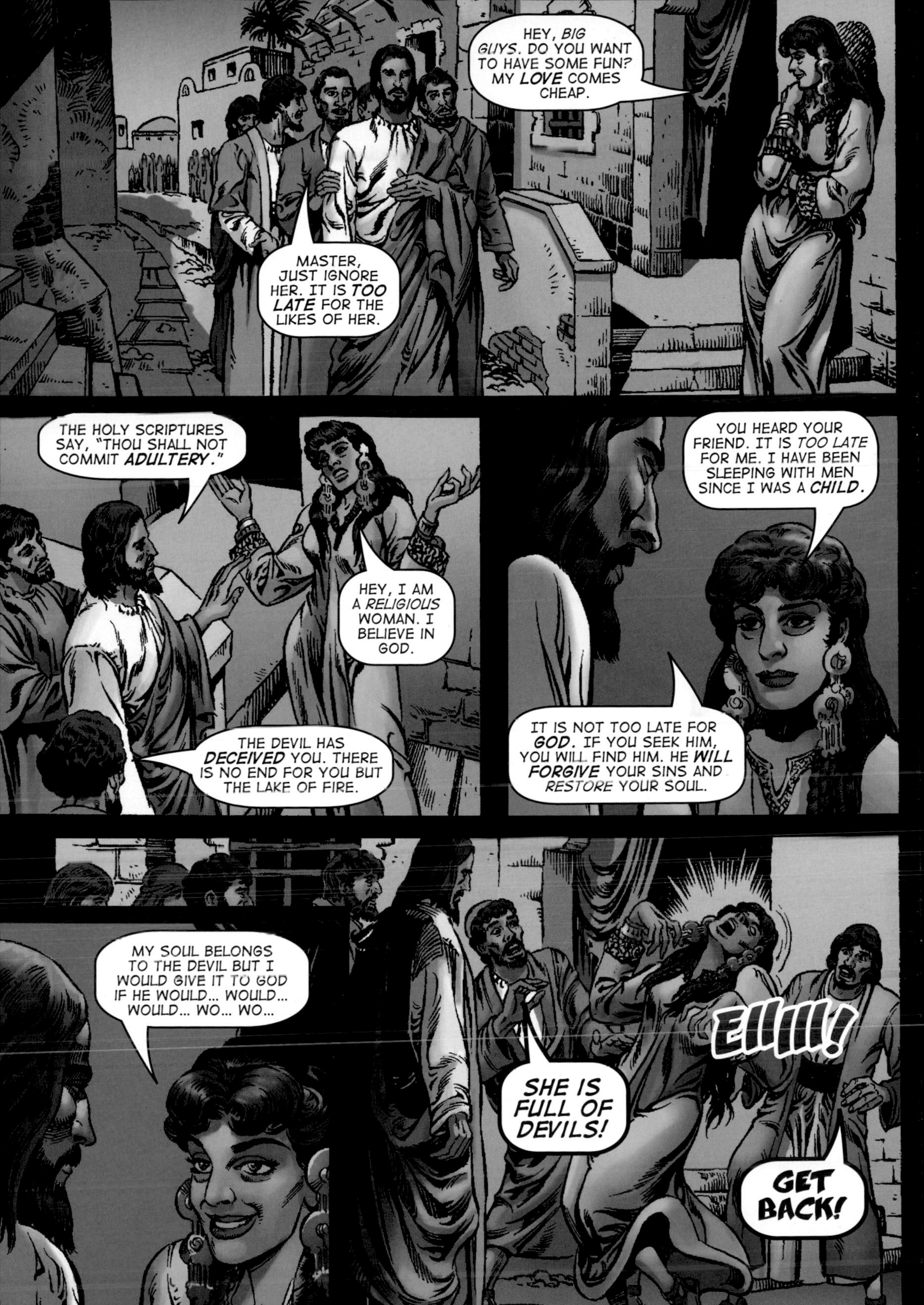
HEY, BIG GUYS. DO YOU WANT TO HAVE SOME FUN? MY LOVE COMES CHEAP.
MASTER, JUST IGNORE HER. IT IS TOO LATE FOR THE LIKES OF HER.
THE HOLY SCRIPTURES SAY, "THOU SHALL NOT COMMIT ADULTERY."
HEY, I AM A RELIGIOUS WOMAN. I BELIEVE IN GOD.
THE DEVIL HAS DECEIVED YOU. THERE IS NO END FOR YOU BUT THE LAKE OF FIRE.
YOU HEARD YOUR FRIEND. IT IS TOO LATE FOR ME. I HAVE BEEN SLEEPING WITH MEN SINCE I WAS A CHILD.
IT IS NOT TOO LATE FOR GOD. IF YOU SEEK HIM, YOU WILL FIND HIM. HE WILL FORGIVE YOUR SINS AND RESTORE YOUR SOUL.
MY SOUL BELONGS TO THE DEVIL BUT I WOULD GIVE IT TO GOD IF HE WOULD... WOULD... WOULD... WO... WO...
EIIIII!
SHE IS FULL OF DEVILS!
GET BACK!

EXODUS 20:14; LUKE 8:2; 1 JOHN 1:9

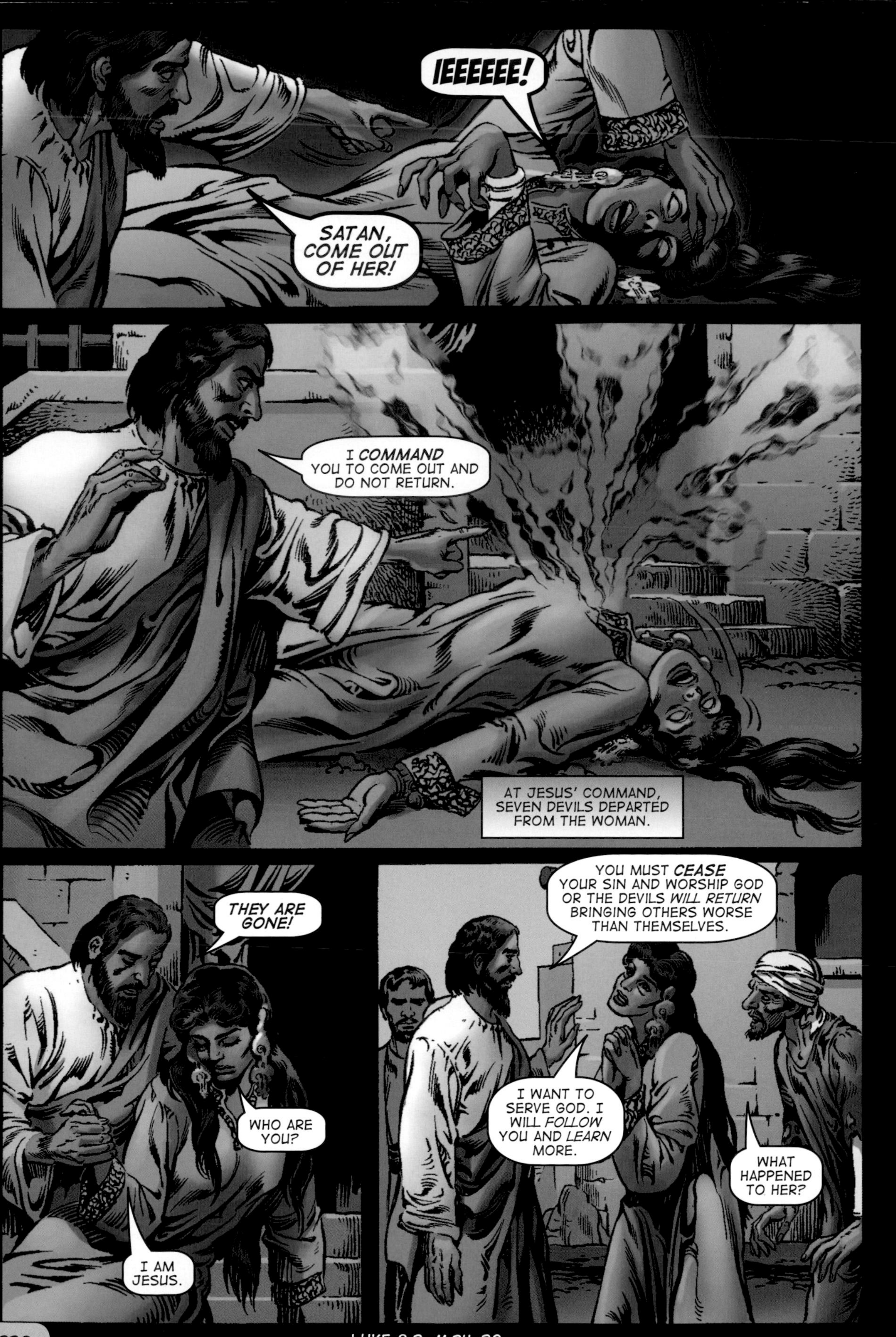

IEEEEEE!
SATAN, COME OUT OF HER!
I COMMAND YOU TO COME OUT AND DO NOT RETURN.
AT JESUS' COMMAND, SEVEN DEVILS DEPARTED FROM THE WOMAN.
THEY ARE GONE!
WHO ARE YOU?
I AM JESUS.
YOU MUST CEASE YOUR SIN AND WORSHIP GOD OR THE DEVILS WILL RETURN BRINGING OTHERS WORSE THAN THEMSELVES.
I WANT TO SERVE GOD. I WILL FOLLOW YOU AND LEARN MORE.
WHAT HAPPENED TO HER?

LUKE 8:2, 11:24-26

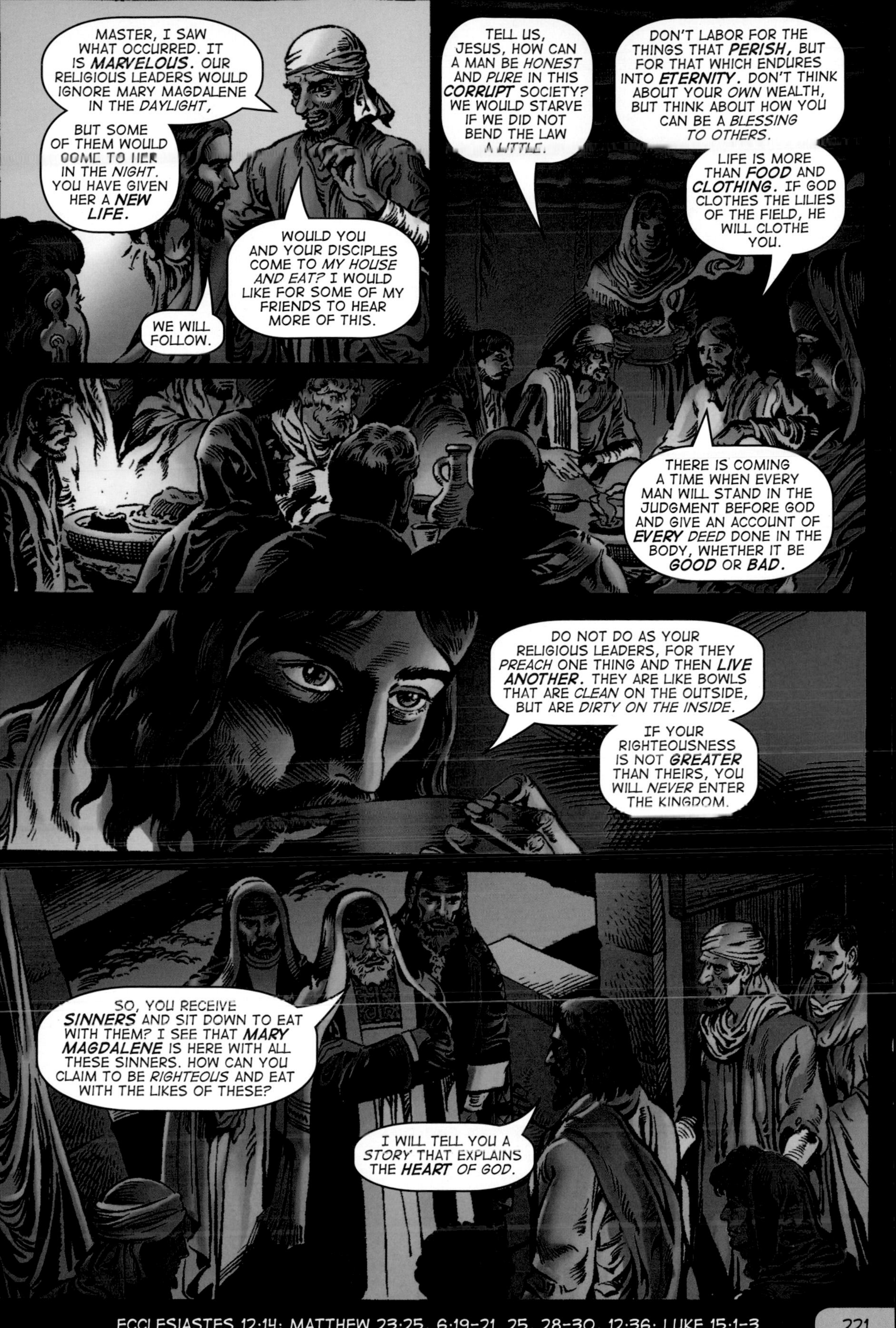
MASTER, I SAW WHAT OCCURRED. IT IS MARVELOUS. OUR RELIGIOUS LEADERS WOULD IGNORE MARY MAGDALENE IN THE DAYLIGHT,
BUT SOME OF THEM WOULD COME TO HER IN THE NIGHT. YOU HAVE GIVEN HER A NEW LIFE.
WOULD YOU AND YOUR DISCIPLES COME TO MY HOUSE AND EAT? I WOULD LIKE FOR SOME OF MY FRIENDS TO HEAR MORE OF THIS.
WE WILL FOLLOW.
TELL US, JESUS, HOW CAN A MAN BE HONEST AND PURE IN THIS CORRUPT SOCIETY? WE WOULD STARVE IF WE DID NOT BEND THE LAW A LITTLE.
DON'T LABOR FOR THE THINGS THAT PERISH, BUT FOR THAT WHICH ENDURES INTO ETERNITY. DON'T THINK ABOUT YOUR OWN WEALTH, BUT THINK ABOUT HOW YOU CAN BE A BLESSING TO OTHERS.
LIFE IS MORE THAN FOOD AND CLOTHING. IF GOD CLOTHES THE LILIES OF THE FIELD, HE WILL CLOTHE YOU.
THERE IS COMING A TIME WHEN EVERY MAN WILL STAND IN THE JUDGMENT BEFORE GOD AND GIVE AN ACCOUNT OF EVERY DEED DONE IN THE BODY, WHETHER IT BE GOOD OR BAD.
DO NOT DO AS YOUR RELIGIOUS LEADERS, FOR THEY PREACH ONE THING AND THEN LIVE ANOTHER. THEY ARE LIKE BOWLS THAT ARE CLEAN ON THE OUTSIDE, BUT ARE DIRTY ON THE INSIDE.
IF YOUR RIGHTEOUSNESS IS NOT GREATER THAN THEIRS, YOU WILL NEVER ENTER THE KINGDOM.
SO, YOU RECEIVE SINNERS AND SIT DOWN TO EAT WITH THEM? I SEE THAT MARY MAGDALENE IS HERE WITH ALL THESE SINNERS. HOW CAN YOU CLAIM TO BE RIGHTEOUS AND EAT WITH THE LIKES OF THESE?
I WILL TELL YOU A STORY THAT EXPLAINS THE HEART OF GOD.

ECCLESIASTES 12:14; MATTHEW 23:25, 6:19-21, 25, 28-30, 12:36; LUKE 15:1-3

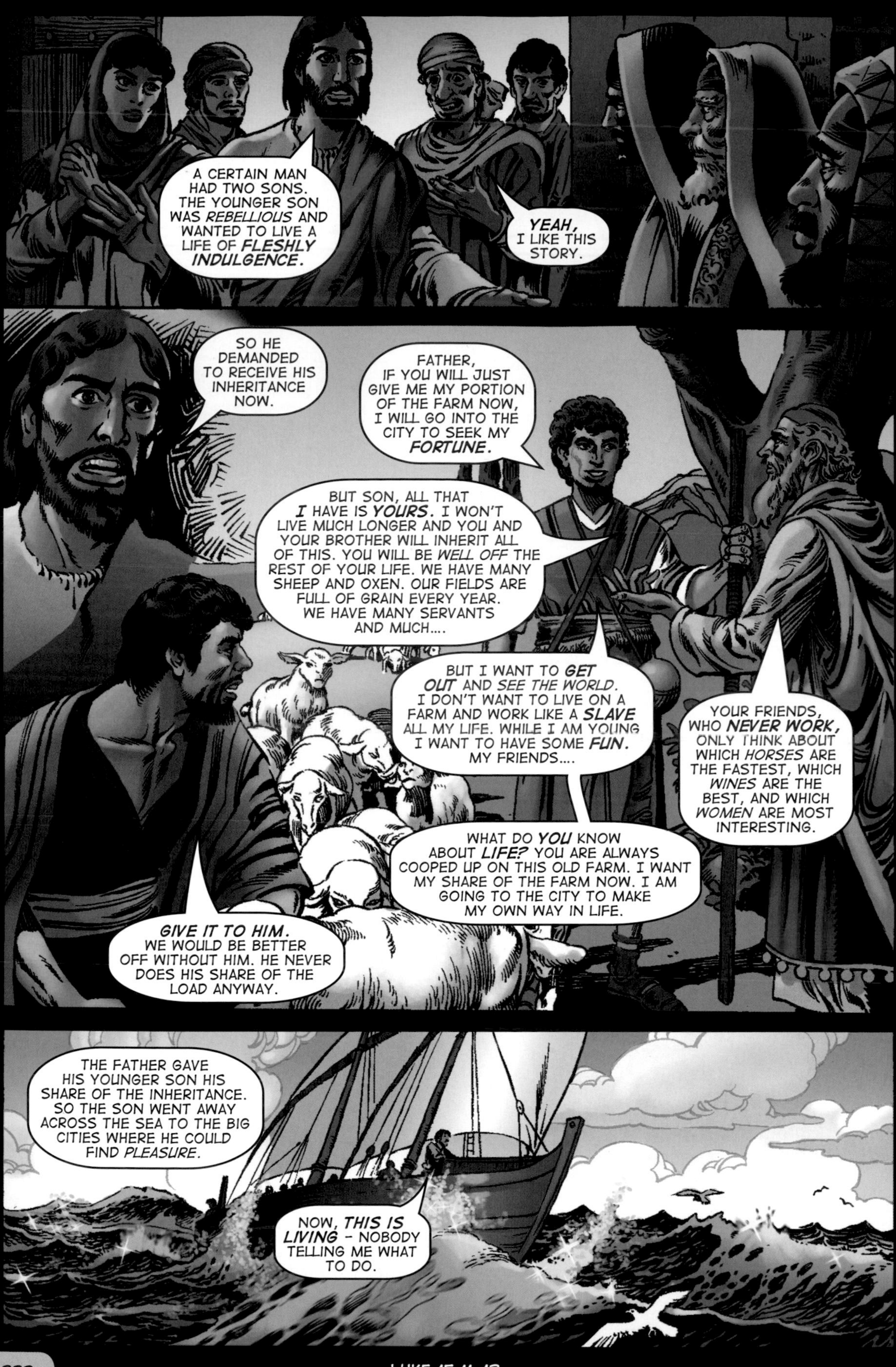
A CERTAIN MAN HAD TWO SONS. THE YOUNGER SON WAS REBELLIOUS AND WANTED TO LIVE A LIFE OF FLESHLY INDULGENCE.
YEAH, I LIKE THIS STORY.
SO HE DEMANDED TO RECEIVE HIS INHERITANCE NOW.
FATHER, IF YOU WILL JUST GIVE ME MY PORTION OF THE FARM NOW, I WILL GO INTO THE CITY TO SEEK MY FORTUNE.
BUT SON, ALL THAT I HAVE IS YOURS. I WON'T LIVE MUCH LONGER AND YOU AND YOUR BROTHER WILL INHERIT ALL OF THIS. YOU WILL BE WELL OFF THE REST OF YOUR LIFE. WE HAVE MANY SHEEP AND OXEN. OUR FIELDS ARE FULL OF GRAIN EVERY YEAR. WE HAVE MANY SERVANTS AND MUCH....
BUT I WANT TO GET OUT AND SEE THE WORLD. I DON'T WANT TO LIVE ON A FARM AND WORK LIKE A SLAVE ALL MY LIFE. WHILE I AM YOUNG I WANT TO HAVE SOME FUN. MY FRIENDS....
YOUR FRIENDS, WHO NEVER WORK, ONLY THINK ABOUT WHICH HORSES ARE THE FASTEST, WHICH WINES ARE THE BEST, AND WHICH WOMEN ARE MOST INTERESTING.
WHAT DO YOU KNOW ABOUT LIFE? YOU ARE ALWAYS COOPED UP ON THIS OLD FARM. I WANT MY SHARE OF THE FARM NOW. I AM GOING TO THE CITY TO MAKE MY OWN WAY IN LIFE.
GIVE IT TO HIM. WE WOULD BE BETTER OFF WITHOUT HIM. HE NEVER DOES HIS SHARE OF THE LOAD ANYWAY.
THE FATHER GAVE HIS YOUNGER SON HIS SHARE OF THE INHERITANCE. SO THE SON WENT AWAY ACROSS THE SEA TO THE BIG CITIES WHERE HE COULD FIND PLEASURE.
NOW, THIS IS LIVING - NOBODY TELLING ME WHAT TO DO.

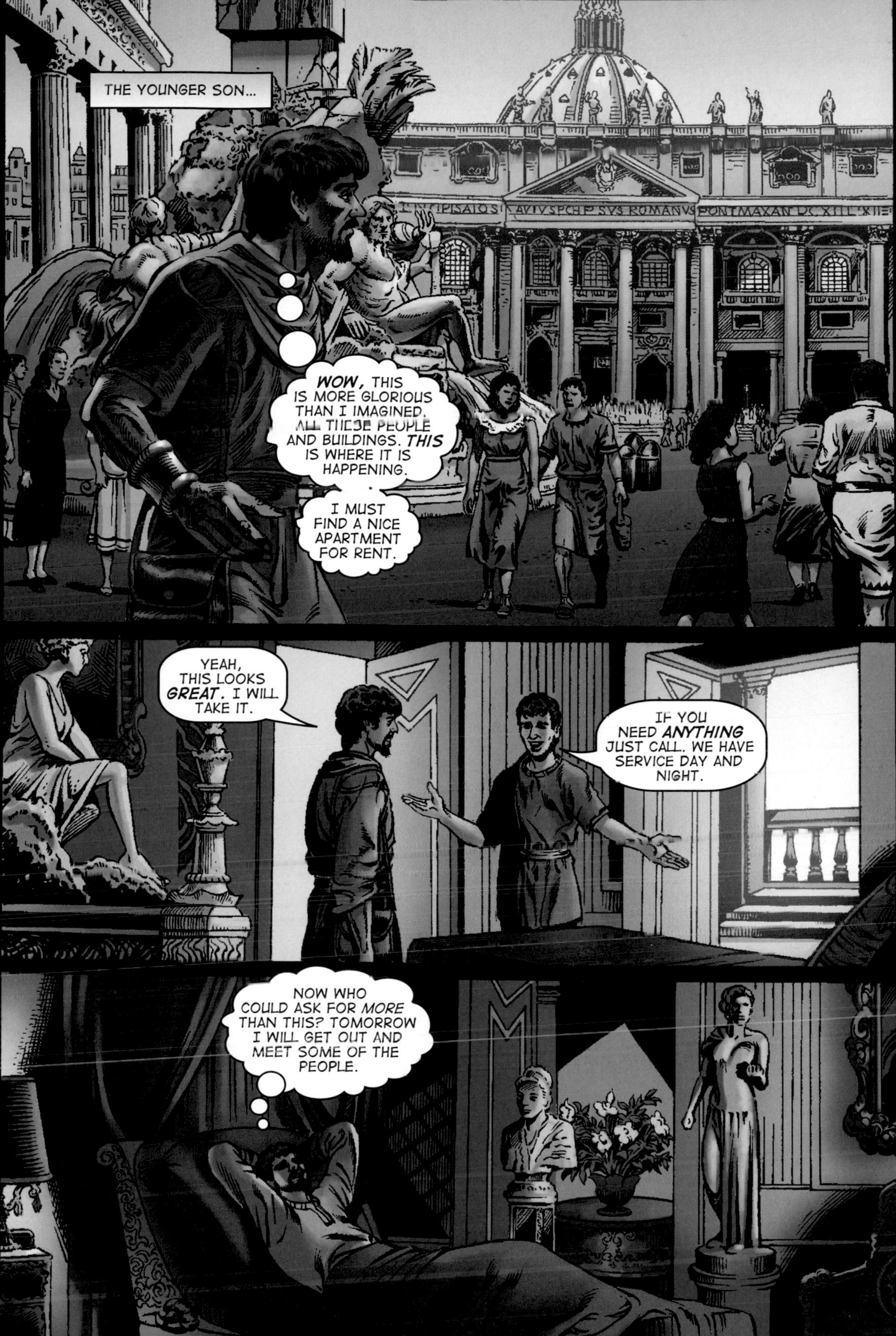
THE YOUNGER SON...
WOW, THIS IS MORE GLORIOUS THAN I IMAGINED. ALL THESE PEOPLE AND BUILDINGS. THIS IS WHERE IT IS HAPPENING.
I MUST FIND A NICE APARTMENT FOR RENT.
YEAH, THIS LOOKS GREAT. I WILL TAKE IT.
IF YOU NEED ANYTHING JUST CALL. WE HAVE SERVICE DAY AND NIGHT.
NOW WHO COULD ASK FOR MORE THAN THIS? TOMORROW I WILL GET OUT AND MEET SOME OF THE PEOPLE.

LUKE 15:13

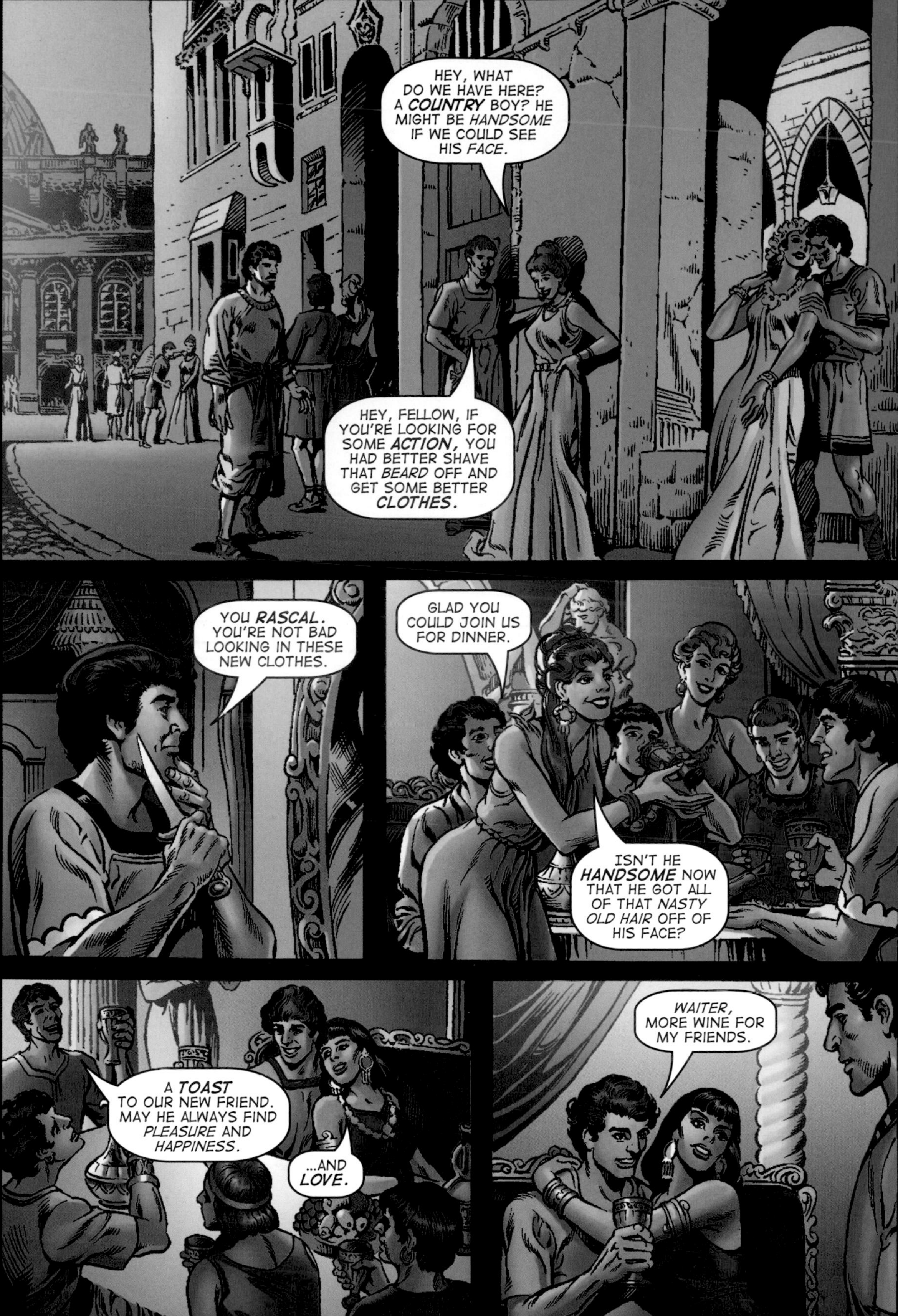
HEY, WHAT DO WE HAVE HERE? A COUNTRY BOY? HE MIGHT BE HANDSOME IF WE COULD SEE HIS FACE.
HEY, FELLOW, IF YOU'RE LOOKING FOR SOME ACTION, YOU HAD BETTER SHAVE THAT BEARD OFF AND GET SOME BETTER CLOTHES.
YOU RASCAL. YOU'RE NOT BAD LOOKING IN THESE NEW CLOTHES.
GLAD YOU COULD JOIN US FOR DINNER.
ISN'T HE HANDSOME NOW THAT HE GOT ALL OF THAT NASTY OLD HAIR OFF OF HIS FACE?
A TOAST TO OUR NEW FRIEND. MAY HE ALWAYS FIND PLEASURE AND HAPPINESS.
...AND LOVE.
WAITER, MORE WINE FOR MY FRIENDS.

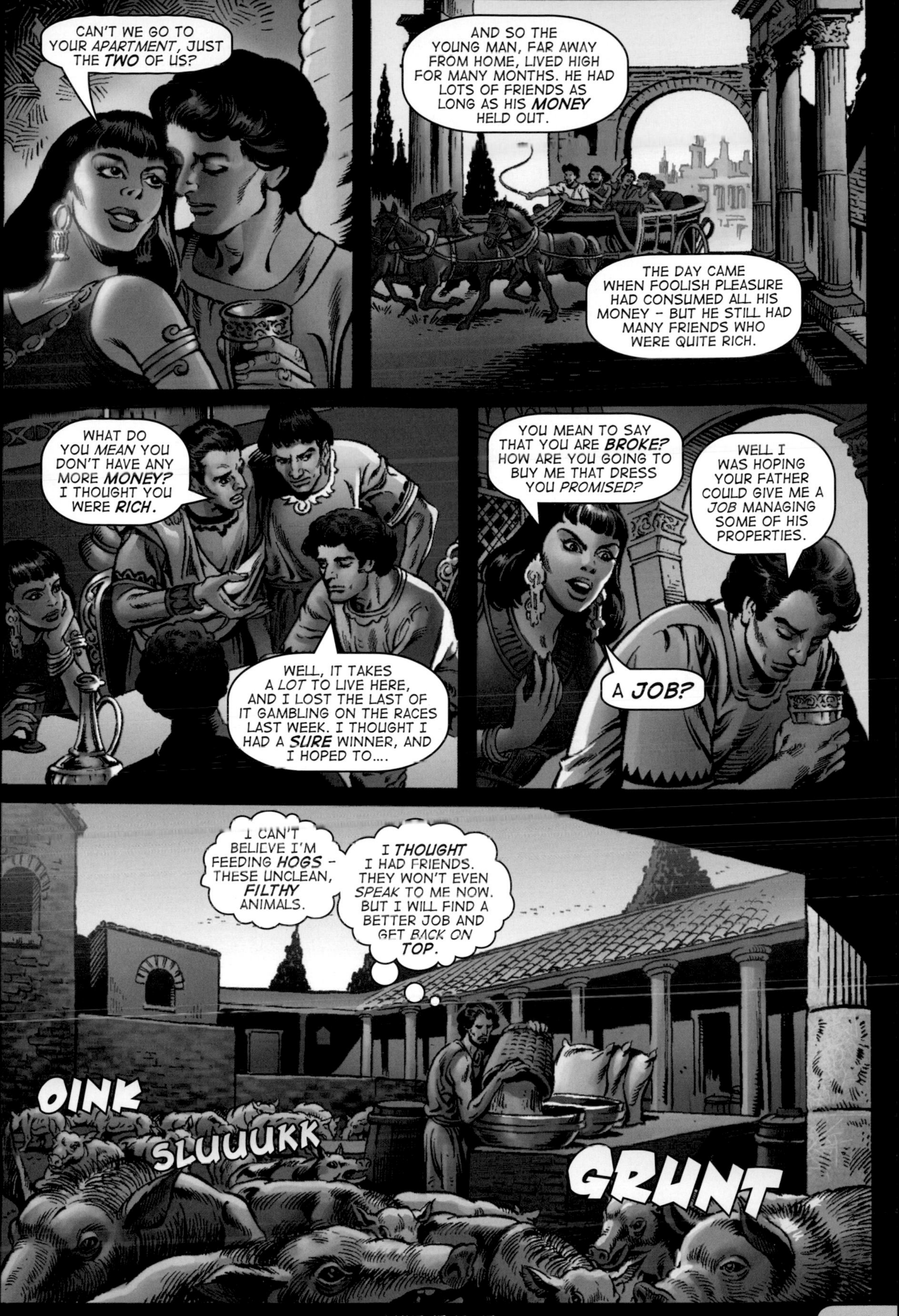

CAN'T WE GO TO YOUR *APARTMENT*, JUST THE *TWO* OF US?
AND SO THE YOUNG MAN, FAR AWAY FROM HOME, LIVED HIGH FOR MANY MONTHS. HE HAD LOTS OF FRIENDS AS LONG AS HIS **MONEY** HELD OUT.
THE DAY CAME WHEN FOOLISH PLEASURE HAD CONSUMED ALL HIS MONEY – BUT HE STILL HAD MANY FRIENDS WHO WERE QUITE RICH.
WHAT DO YOU *MEAN* YOU DON'T HAVE ANY MORE **MONEY?** I THOUGHT YOU WERE **RICH**.
WELL, IT TAKES A *LOT* TO LIVE HERE, AND I LOST THE LAST OF IT GAMBLING ON THE RACES LAST WEEK. I THOUGHT I HAD A **SURE** WINNER, AND I HOPED TO....
YOU MEAN TO SAY THAT YOU ARE **BROKE?** HOW ARE YOU GOING TO BUY ME THAT DRESS YOU *PROMISED?*
WELL I WAS HOPING YOUR FATHER COULD GIVE ME A *JOB* MANAGING SOME OF HIS PROPERTIES.
A **JOB?**
I CAN'T BELIEVE I'M FEEDING **HOGS** – THESE UNCLEAN, **FILTHY** ANIMALS.
I **THOUGHT** I HAD FRIENDS. THEY WON'T EVEN *SPEAK* TO ME NOW. BUT I WILL FIND A BETTER JOB AND GET *BACK ON* **TOP**.
OINK
SLUUUKK
GRUNT

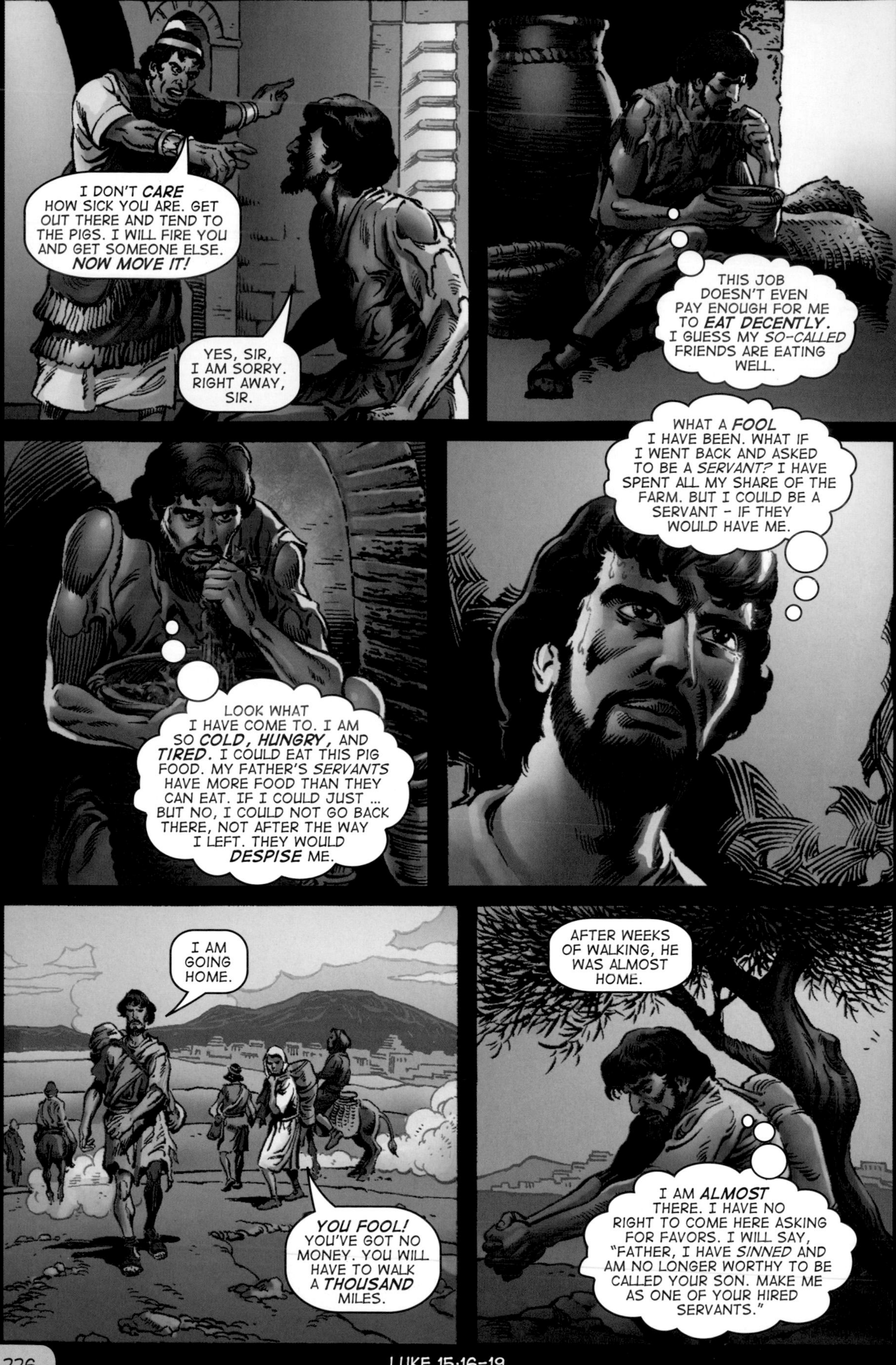
I DON'T CARE HOW SICK YOU ARE. GET OUT THERE AND TEND TO THE PIGS. I WILL FIRE YOU AND GET SOMEONE ELSE. NOW MOVE IT!
YES, SIR, I AM SORRY. RIGHT AWAY, SIR.
THIS JOB DOESN'T EVEN PAY ENOUGH FOR ME TO EAT DECENTLY. I GUESS MY SO-CALLED FRIENDS ARE EATING WELL.
LOOK WHAT I HAVE COME TO. I AM SO COLD, HUNGRY, AND TIRED. I COULD EAT THIS PIG FOOD. MY FATHER'S SERVANTS HAVE MORE FOOD THAN THEY CAN EAT. IF I COULD JUST ... BUT NO, I COULD NOT GO BACK THERE, NOT AFTER THE WAY I LEFT. THEY WOULD DESPISE ME.
WHAT A FOOL I HAVE BEEN. WHAT IF I WENT BACK AND ASKED TO BE A SERVANT? I HAVE SPENT ALL MY SHARE OF THE FARM. BUT I COULD BE A SERVANT - IF THEY WOULD HAVE ME.
I AM GOING HOME.
YOU FOOL! YOU'VE GOT NO MONEY. YOU WILL HAVE TO WALK A THOUSAND MILES.
AFTER WEEKS OF WALKING, HE WAS ALMOST HOME.
I AM ALMOST THERE. I HAVE NO RIGHT TO COME HERE ASKING FOR FAVORS. I WILL SAY, "FATHER, I HAVE SINNED AND AM NO LONGER WORTHY TO BE CALLED YOUR SON. MAKE ME AS ONE OF YOUR HIRED SERVANTS."

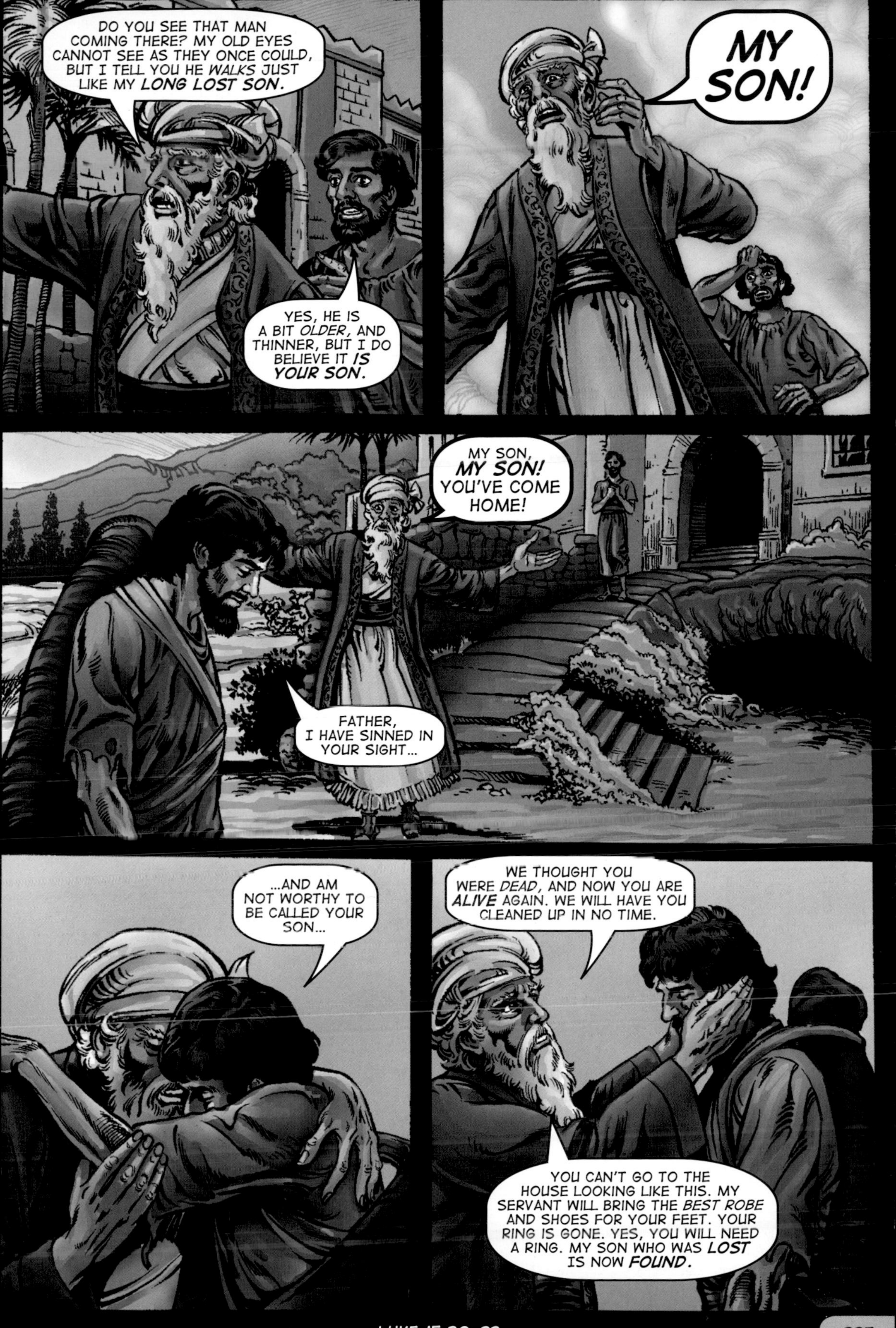
DO YOU SEE THAT MAN COMING THERE? MY OLD EYES CANNOT SEE AS THEY ONCE COULD, BUT I TELL YOU HE *WALKS* JUST LIKE MY ***LONG LOST SON***.
YES, HE IS A BIT *OLDER*, AND THINNER, BUT I DO BELIEVE IT ***IS YOUR SON***.
MY SON!
MY SON, ***MY SON!*** YOU'VE COME HOME!
FATHER, I HAVE SINNED IN YOUR SIGHT...
...AND AM NOT WORTHY TO BE CALLED YOUR SON...
WE THOUGHT YOU WERE *DEAD*, AND NOW YOU ARE ***ALIVE*** AGAIN. WE WILL HAVE YOU CLEANED UP IN NO TIME.
YOU CAN'T GO TO THE HOUSE LOOKING LIKE THIS. MY SERVANT WILL BRING THE *BEST ROBE* AND SHOES FOR YOUR FEET. YOUR RING IS GONE. YES, YOU WILL NEED A RING. MY SON WHO WAS ***LOST*** IS NOW ***FOUND***.

LUKE 15:20-22

KILL THE FATTED CALF, PREPARE A *BANQUET*, INVITE GUESTS, AND WE WILL MAKE *MERRY*, FOR THIS IS A DAY OF *REJOICING*.

I AM SO GLAD YOU ARE ALL HERE TO REJOICE WITH ME ON THIS *WONDERFUL OCCASION*. MY SON IS STILL WEAK FROM HIS ORDEAL, BUT WITH GOOD FOOD HE WILL SOON GROW STRONG. THIS IS THE *BEST DAY OF MY LIFE*.

THE OLDER BROTHER HAD BEEN GONE FOR SEVERAL DAYS. WHEN HE RETURNED HOME, HE FOUND A PARTY IN PROGRESS.

WHAT IS ALL THIS *MUSIC* AND *DANCING* I HEAR?

YOUR LITTLE BROTHER HAS *RETURNED HOME* IN A MOST PITIFUL SHAPE. HE IS SICK AND POOR. YOUR FATHER IS *REJOICING* TO HAVE HIM HOME AGAIN. HURRY INSIDE.

I WILL NOT PARTICIPATE IN THIS *FOOLISHNESS*. HE HAS LIVED A LIFE OF *SIN* AND *SHAME*.

THE SERVANT TOLD THE FATHER WHAT HIS SON HAD SAID, AND HE CAME OUT TO SPEAK WITH HIS SON.

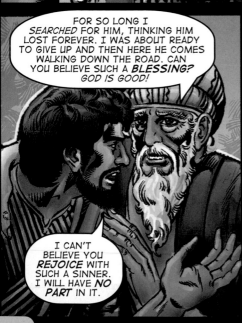

FOR SO LONG I *SEARCHED* FOR HIM, THINKING HIM LOST FOREVER. I WAS ABOUT READY TO GIVE UP AND THEN HERE HE COMES WALKING DOWN THE ROAD. CAN YOU BELIEVE SUCH A *BLESSING*? *GOD IS GOOD!*

I CAN'T BELIEVE YOU *REJOICE* WITH SUCH A SINNER. I WILL HAVE *NO PART* IN IT.

THAT IS A *LOVELY* STORY, BUT ARE YOU SUGGESTING THAT *WE* ARE LIKE THE OLDER BROTHER?

HE WHO HAS *EARS* TO HEAR, LET HIM *HEAR*.

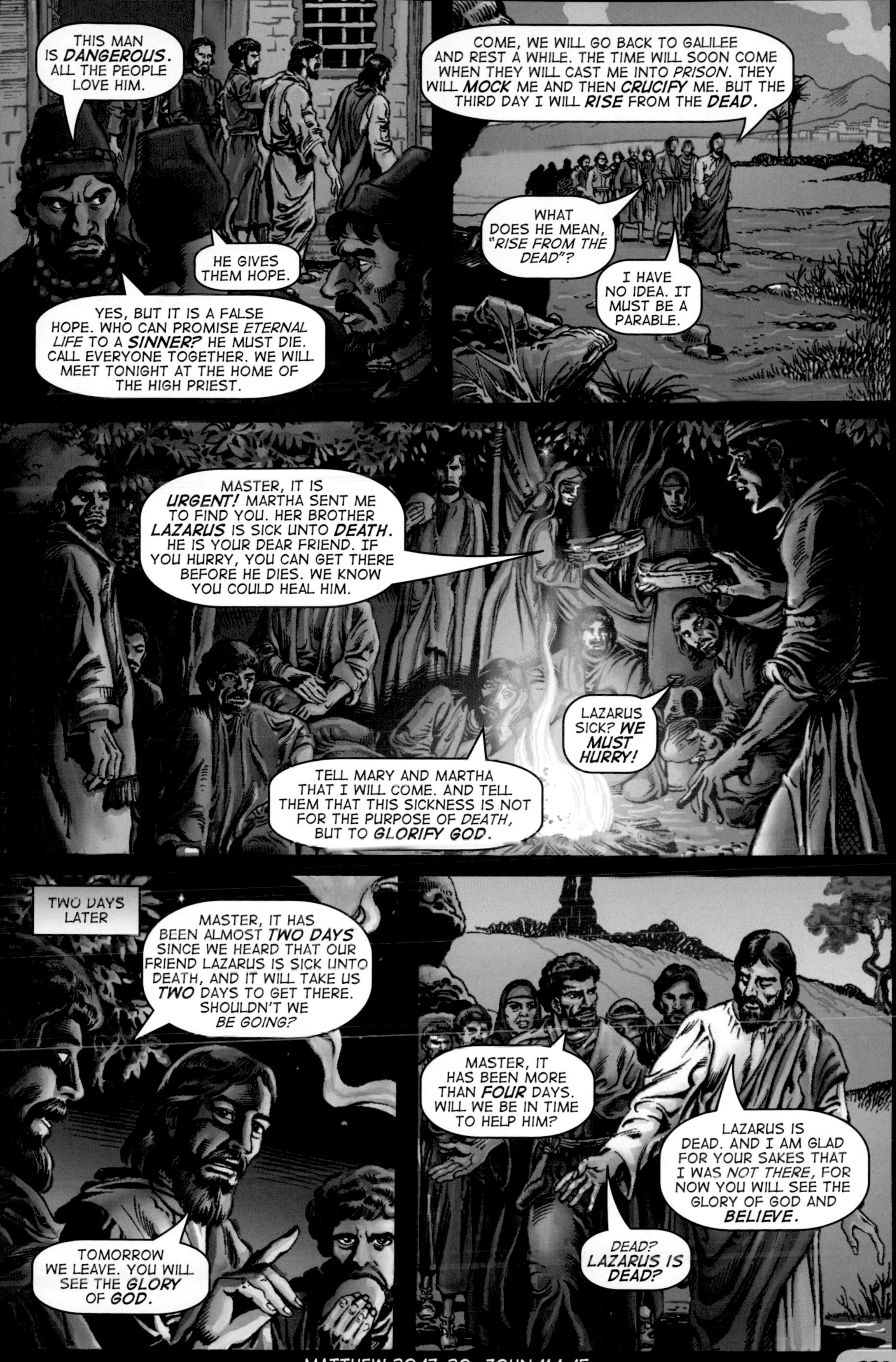
THIS MAN IS DANGEROUS. ALL THE PEOPLE LOVE HIM.
HE GIVES THEM HOPE.
YES, BUT IT IS A FALSE HOPE. WHO CAN PROMISE ETERNAL LIFE TO A SINNER? HE MUST DIE. CALL EVERYONE TOGETHER. WE WILL MEET TONIGHT AT THE HOME OF THE HIGH PRIEST.
COME, WE WILL GO BACK TO GALILEE AND REST A WHILE. THE TIME WILL SOON COME WHEN THEY WILL CAST ME INTO PRISON. THEY WILL MOCK ME AND THEN CRUCIFY ME. BUT THE THIRD DAY I WILL RISE FROM THE DEAD.
WHAT DOES HE MEAN, "RISE FROM THE DEAD"?
I HAVE NO IDEA. IT MUST BE A PARABLE.
MASTER, IT IS URGENT! MARTHA SENT ME TO FIND YOU. HER BROTHER LAZARUS IS SICK UNTO DEATH. HE IS YOUR DEAR FRIEND. IF YOU HURRY, YOU CAN GET THERE BEFORE HE DIES. WE KNOW YOU COULD HEAL HIM.
LAZARUS SICK? WE MUST HURRY!
TELL MARY AND MARTHA THAT I WILL COME. AND TELL THEM THAT THIS SICKNESS IS NOT FOR THE PURPOSE OF DEATH, BUT TO GLORIFY GOD.
TWO DAYS LATER
MASTER, IT HAS BEEN ALMOST TWO DAYS SINCE WE HEARD THAT OUR FRIEND LAZARUS IS SICK UNTO DEATH, AND IT WILL TAKE US TWO DAYS TO GET THERE. SHOULDN'T WE BE GOING?
TOMORROW WE LEAVE. YOU WILL SEE THE GLORY OF GOD.
MASTER, IT HAS BEEN MORE THAN FOUR DAYS. WILL WE BE IN TIME TO HELP HIM?
LAZARUS IS DEAD. AND I AM GLAD FOR YOUR SAKES THAT I WAS NOT THERE, FOR NOW YOU WILL SEE THE GLORY OF GOD AND BELIEVE.
DEAD? LAZARUS IS DEAD?

MATTHEW 20:17-20; JOHN 11:1-15

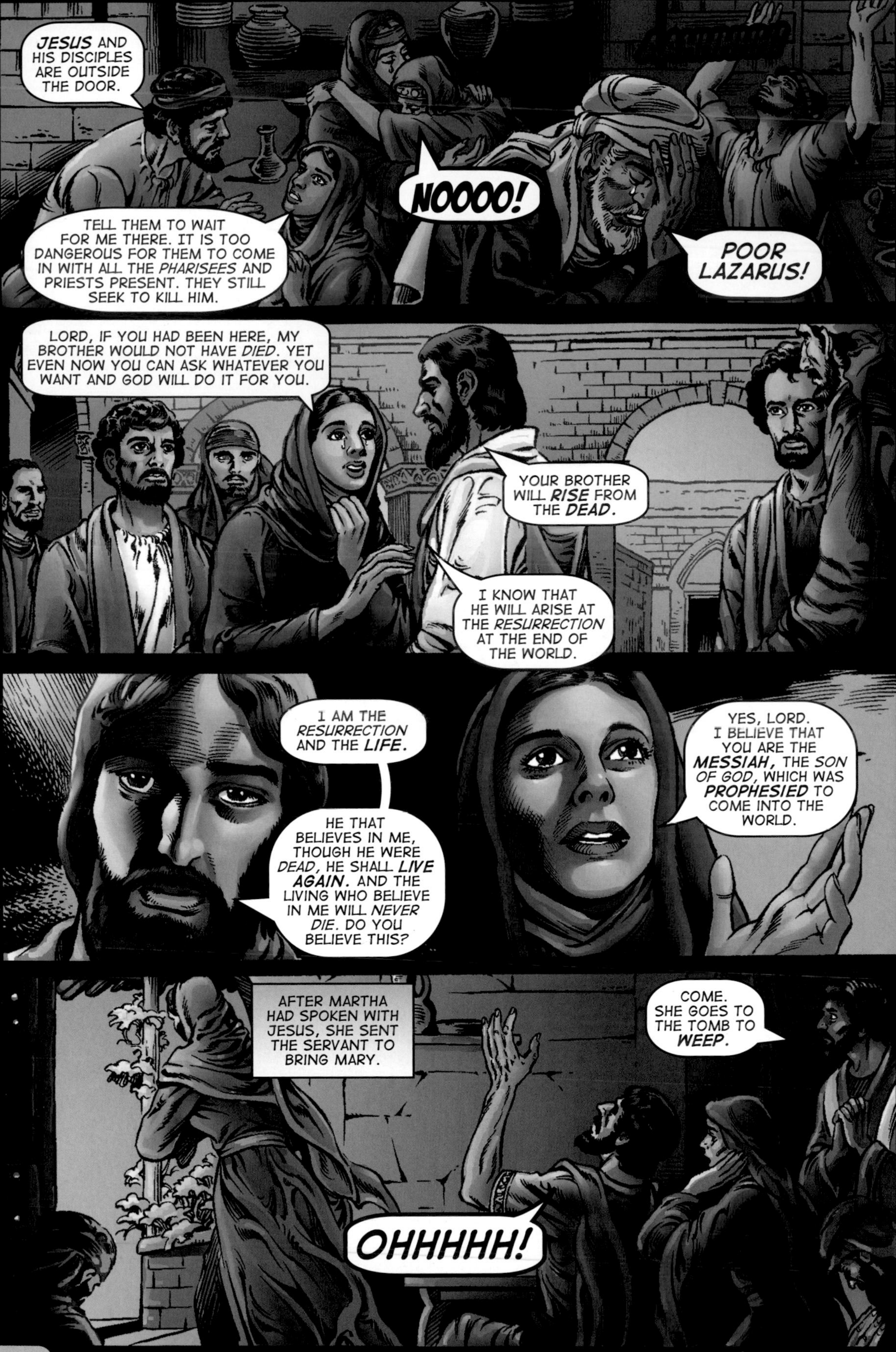
JESUS AND HIS DISCIPLES ARE OUTSIDE THE DOOR.
TELL THEM TO WAIT FOR ME THERE. IT IS TOO DANGEROUS FOR THEM TO COME IN WITH ALL THE PHARISEES AND PRIESTS PRESENT. THEY STILL SEEK TO KILL HIM.
NOOOO!
POOR LAZARUS!
LORD, IF YOU HAD BEEN HERE, MY BROTHER WOULD NOT HAVE DIED. YET EVEN NOW YOU CAN ASK WHATEVER YOU WANT AND GOD WILL DO IT FOR YOU.
YOUR BROTHER WILL RISE FROM THE DEAD.
I KNOW THAT HE WILL ARISE AT THE RESURRECTION AT THE END OF THE WORLD.
I AM THE RESURRECTION AND THE LIFE.
HE THAT BELIEVES IN ME, THOUGH HE WERE DEAD, HE SHALL LIVE AGAIN. AND THE LIVING WHO BELIEVE IN ME WILL NEVER DIE. DO YOU BELIEVE THIS?
YES, LORD. I BELIEVE THAT YOU ARE THE MESSIAH, THE SON OF GOD, WHICH WAS PROPHESIED TO COME INTO THE WORLD.
AFTER MARTHA HAD SPOKEN WITH JESUS, SHE SENT THE SERVANT TO BRING MARY.
COME. SHE GOES TO THE TOMB TO WEEP.
OHHHHH!

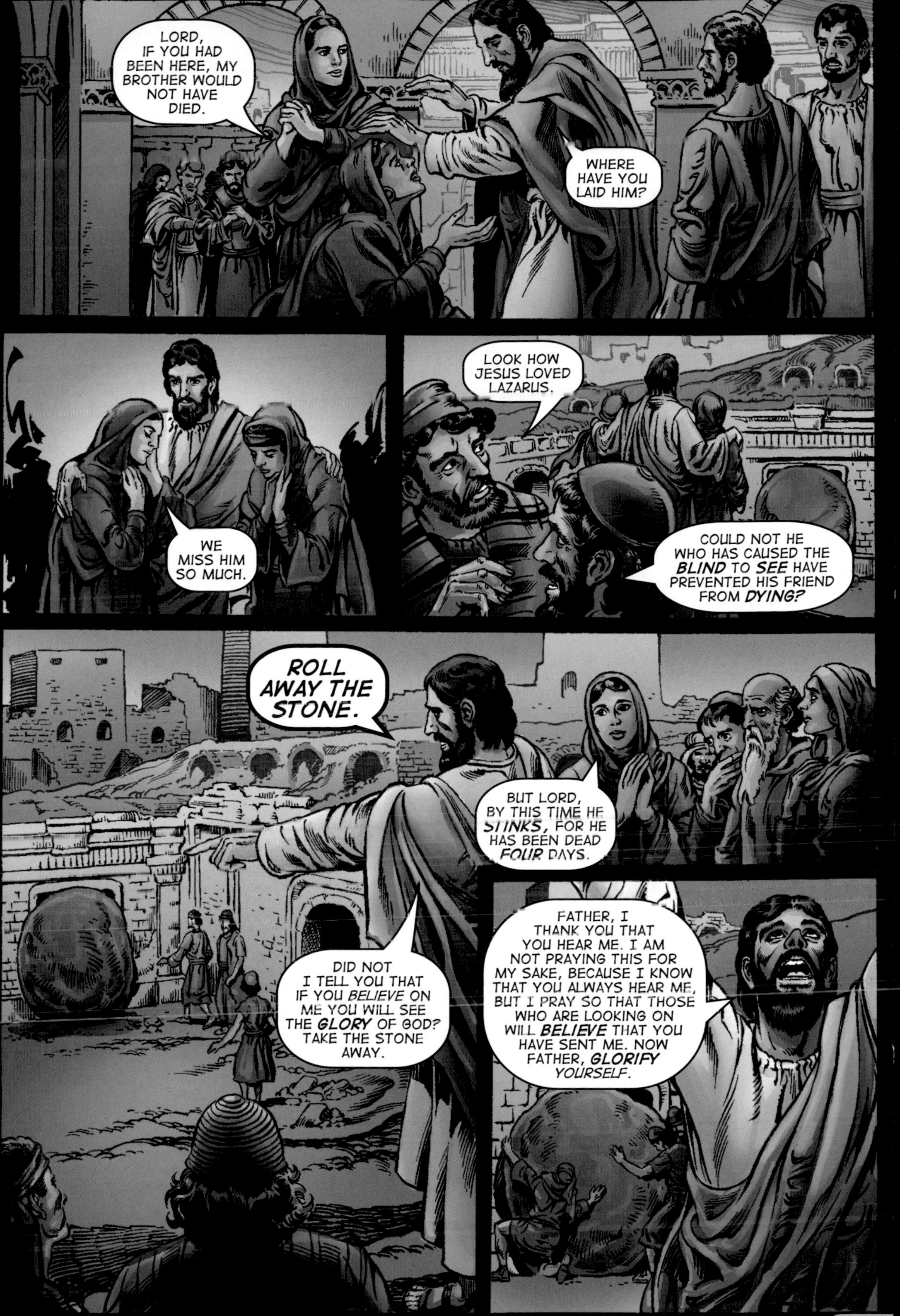
LORD, IF YOU HAD BEEN HERE, MY BROTHER WOULD NOT HAVE DIED.
WHERE HAVE YOU LAID HIM?
WE MISS HIM SO MUCH.
LOOK HOW JESUS LOVED LAZARUS.
COULD NOT HE WHO HAS CAUSED THE ***BLIND*** TO ***SEE*** HAVE PREVENTED HIS FRIEND FROM ***DYING?***
ROLL AWAY THE STONE.
BUT LORD, BY THIS TIME HE ***STINKS,*** FOR HE HAS BEEN DEAD ***FOUR*** DAYS.
DID NOT I TELL YOU THAT IF YOU *BELIEVE* ON ME YOU WILL SEE THE ***GLORY*** OF GOD? TAKE THE STONE AWAY.
FATHER, I THANK YOU THAT YOU HEAR ME. I AM NOT PRAYING THIS FOR MY SAKE, BECAUSE I KNOW THAT YOU ALWAYS HEAR ME, BUT I PRAY SO THAT THOSE WHO ARE LOOKING ON WILL ***BELIEVE*** THAT YOU HAVE SENT ME. NOW FATHER, ***GLORIFY*** *YOURSELF.*

JOHN 11:32–42

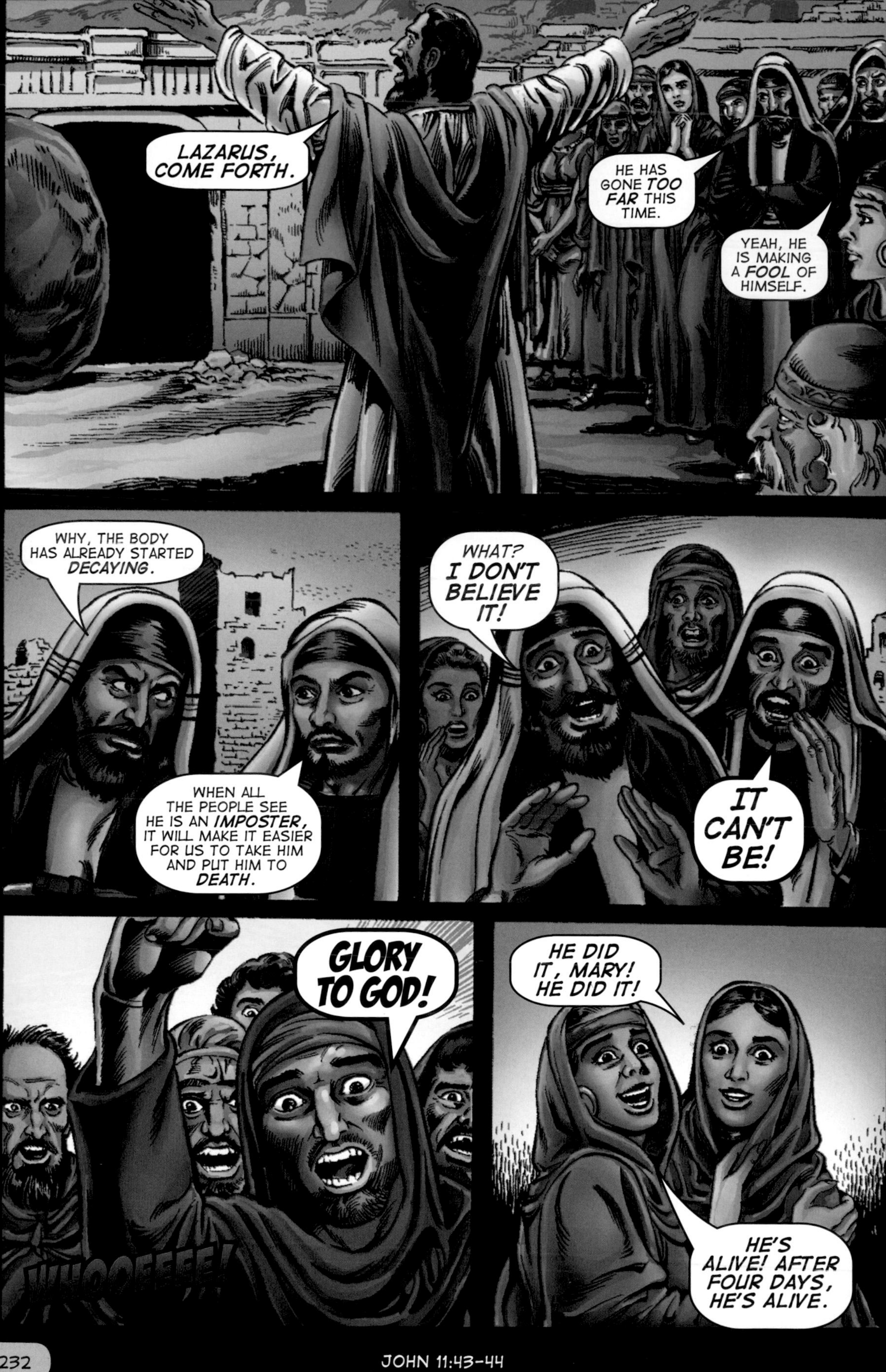
LAZARUS, COME FORTH.
HE HAS GONE TOO FAR THIS TIME.
YEAH, HE IS MAKING A FOOL OF HIMSELF.
WHY, THE BODY HAS ALREADY STARTED DECAYING.
WHEN ALL THE PEOPLE SEE HE IS AN IMPOSTER, IT WILL MAKE IT EASIER FOR US TO TAKE HIM AND PUT HIM TO DEATH.
WHAT? I DON'T BELIEVE IT!
IT CAN'T BE!
GLORY TO GOD!
HE DID IT, MARY! HE DID IT!
HE'S ALIVE! AFTER FOUR DAYS, HE'S ALIVE.

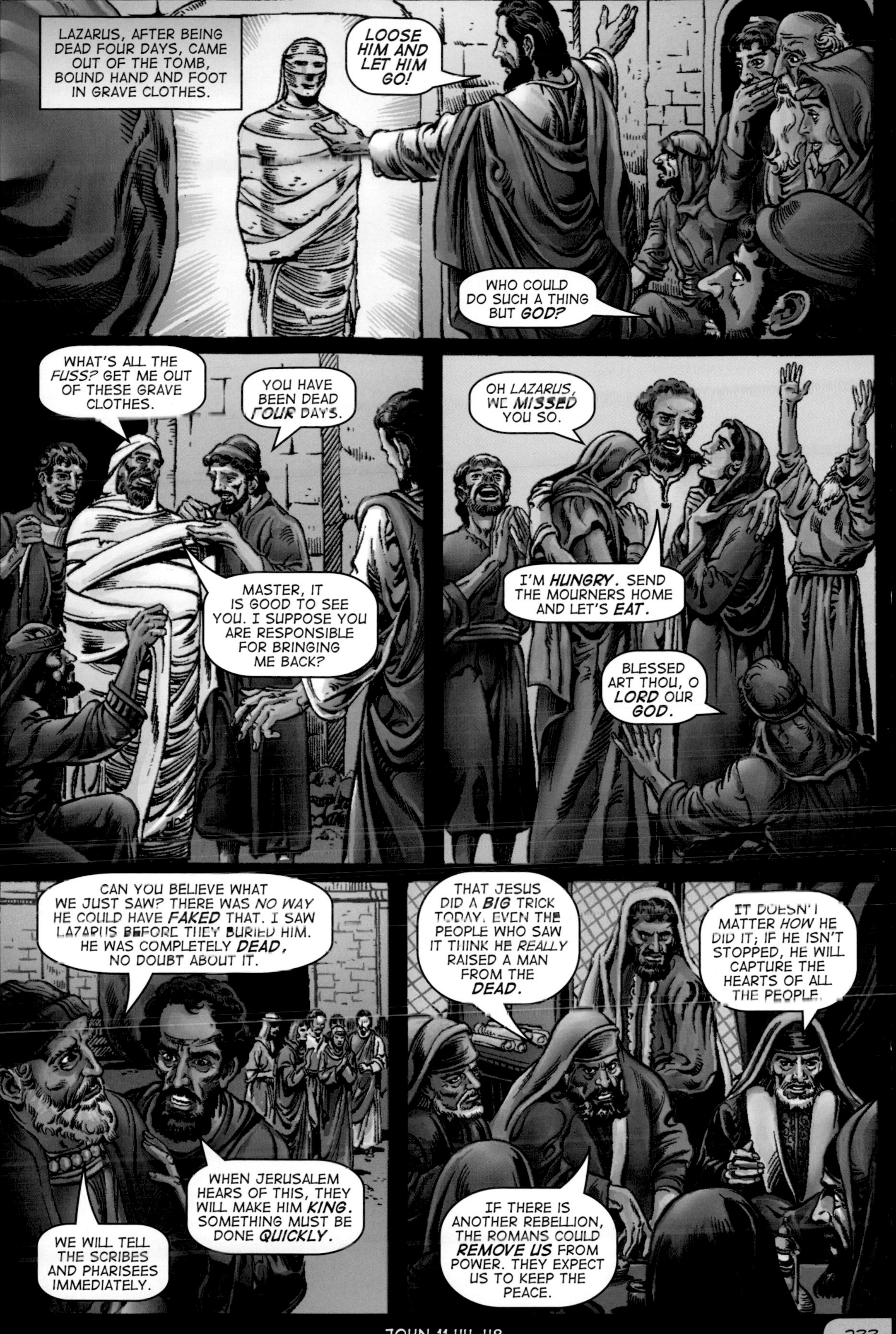
LAZARUS, AFTER BEING DEAD FOUR DAYS, CAME OUT OF THE TOMB, BOUND HAND AND FOOT IN GRAVE CLOTHES.
LOOSE HIM AND LET HIM GO!
WHO COULD DO SUCH A THING BUT GOD?
WHAT'S ALL THE FUSS? GET ME OUT OF THESE GRAVE CLOTHES.
YOU HAVE BEEN DEAD FOUR DAYS.
MASTER, IT IS GOOD TO SEE YOU. I SUPPOSE YOU ARE RESPONSIBLE FOR BRINGING ME BACK?
OH LAZARUS, WE MISSED YOU SO.
I'M HUNGRY. SEND THE MOURNERS HOME AND LET'S EAT.
BLESSED ART THOU, O LORD OUR GOD.
CAN YOU BELIEVE WHAT WE JUST SAW? THERE WAS NO WAY HE COULD HAVE FAKED THAT. I SAW LAZARUS BEFORE THEY BURIED HIM. HE WAS COMPLETELY DEAD, NO DOUBT ABOUT IT.
WHEN JERUSALEM HEARS OF THIS, THEY WILL MAKE HIM KING. SOMETHING MUST BE DONE QUICKLY.
WE WILL TELL THE SCRIBES AND PHARISEES IMMEDIATELY.
THAT JESUS DID A BIG TRICK TODAY. EVEN THE PEOPLE WHO SAW IT THINK HE REALLY RAISED A MAN FROM THE DEAD.
IT DOESN'T MATTER HOW HE DID IT; IF HE ISN'T STOPPED, HE WILL CAPTURE THE HEARTS OF ALL THE PEOPLE.
IF THERE IS ANOTHER REBELLION, THE ROMANS COULD REMOVE US FROM POWER. THEY EXPECT US TO KEEP THE PEACE.

JOHN 11:44-48

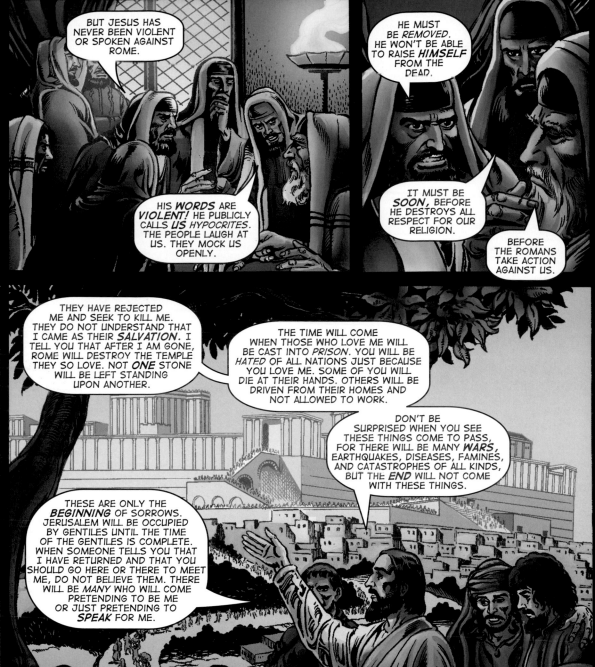

BUT JESUS HAS NEVER BEEN VIOLENT OR SPOKEN AGAINST ROME.

HIS *WORDS* ARE *VIOLENT!* HE PUBLICLY CALLS *US* HYPOCRITES. THE PEOPLE LAUGH AT US. THEY MOCK US OPENLY.

HE MUST BE *REMOVED.* HE WON'T BE ABLE TO RAISE *HIMSELF* FROM THE DEAD.

IT MUST BE *SOON*, BEFORE HE DESTROYS ALL RESPECT FOR OUR RELIGION.

BEFORE THE ROMANS TAKE ACTION AGAINST US.

THEY HAVE REJECTED ME AND SEEK TO KILL ME. THEY DO NOT UNDERSTAND THAT I CAME AS THEIR *SALVATION*. I TELL YOU THAT AFTER I AM GONE, ROME WILL DESTROY THE TEMPLE THEY SO LOVE. NOT *ONE* STONE WILL BE LEFT STANDING UPON ANOTHER.

THE TIME WILL COME WHEN THOSE WHO LOVE ME WILL BE CAST INTO *PRISON*. YOU WILL BE *HATED* OF ALL NATIONS JUST BECAUSE YOU LOVE ME. SOME OF YOU WILL DIE AT THEIR HANDS. OTHERS WILL BE DRIVEN FROM THEIR HOMES AND NOT ALLOWED TO WORK.

DON'T BE SURPRISED WHEN YOU SEE THESE THINGS COME TO PASS, FOR THERE WILL BE MANY *WARS*, EARTHQUAKES, DISEASES, FAMINES, AND CATASTROPHES OF ALL KINDS, BUT THE *END* WILL NOT COME WITH THESE THINGS.

THESE ARE ONLY THE *BEGINNING* OF SORROWS. JERUSALEM WILL BE OCCUPIED BY GENTILES UNTIL THE TIME OF THE GENTILES IS COMPLETE. WHEN SOMEONE TELLS YOU THAT I HAVE RETURNED AND THAT YOU SHOULD GO HERE OR THERE TO MEET ME, DO NOT BELIEVE THEM. THERE WILL BE *MANY* WHO WILL COME PRETENDING TO BE ME OR JUST PRETENDING TO *SPEAK* FOR ME.

BUT WHEN I COME BACK, I WILL COME LIKE *LIGHTNING*. EVERY EYE SHALL SEE ME. THE DEAD WILL BE RAISED AND I WILL SET UP MY KINGDOM ON THE EARTH. BUT BEFORE THIS THERE WILL BE A TIME OF *GREAT TRIBULATION*, WORSE THAN ANYTHING THE WORLD HAS EVER SEEN.

MATTHEW 10:22, 24:2, 5-9, 21, 27-31; LUKE 19:43-44, 21:8; JOHN 11:49-53; REVELATION 2:10

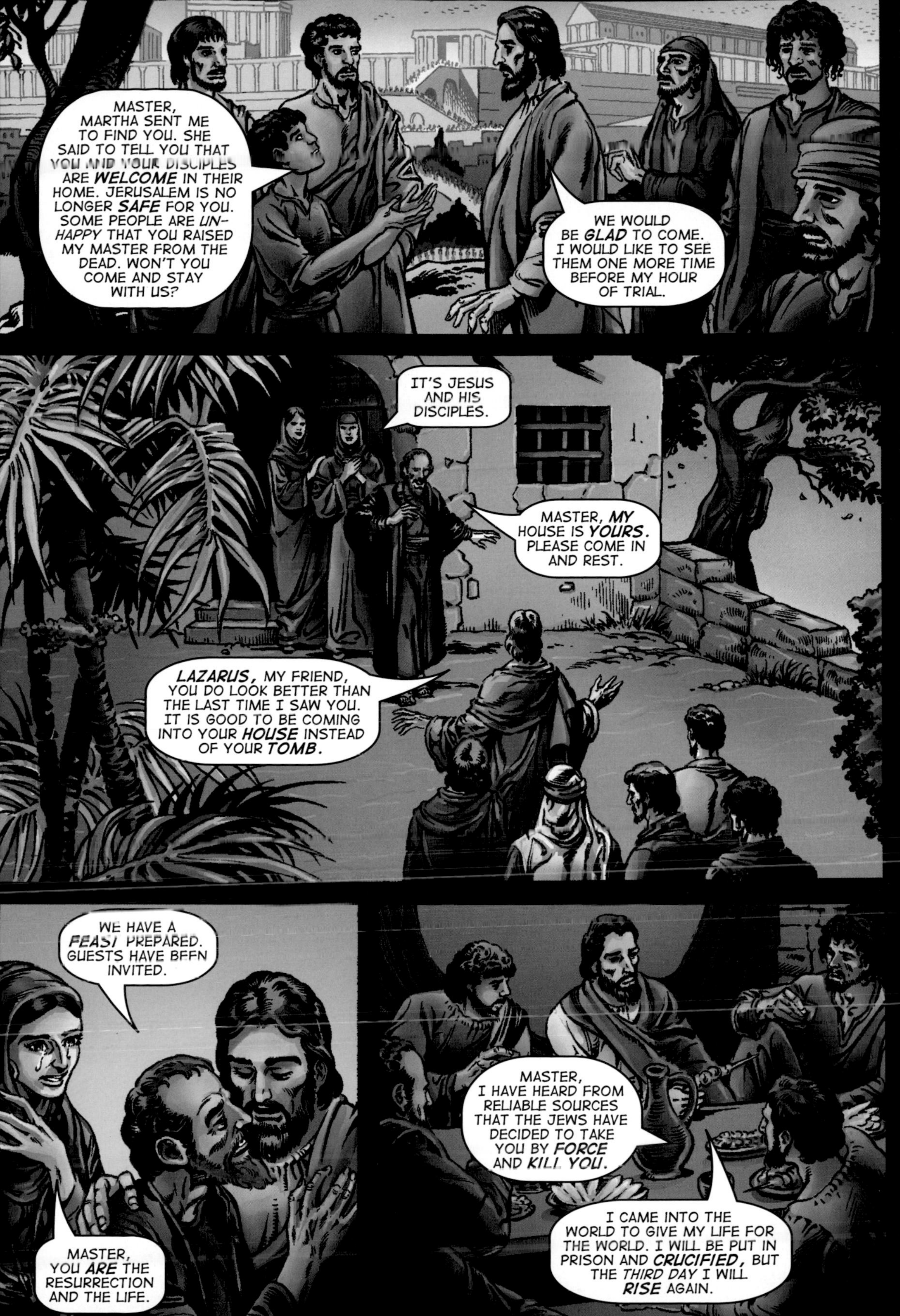

MASTER, MARTHA SENT ME TO FIND YOU. SHE SAID TO TELL YOU THAT YOU AND YOUR DISCIPLES ARE WELCOME IN THEIR HOME. JERUSALEM IS NO LONGER SAFE FOR YOU. SOME PEOPLE ARE UNHAPPY THAT YOU RAISED MY MASTER FROM THE DEAD. WON'T YOU COME AND STAY WITH US?
WE WOULD BE GLAD TO COME. I WOULD LIKE TO SEE THEM ONE MORE TIME BEFORE MY HOUR OF TRIAL.
IT'S JESUS AND HIS DISCIPLES.
MASTER, MY HOUSE IS YOURS. PLEASE COME IN AND REST.
LAZARUS, MY FRIEND, YOU DO LOOK BETTER THAN THE LAST TIME I SAW YOU. IT IS GOOD TO BE COMING INTO YOUR HOUSE INSTEAD OF YOUR TOMB.
WE HAVE A FEAST PREPARED. GUESTS HAVE BEEN INVITED.
MASTER, YOU ARE THE RESURRECTION AND THE LIFE.
MASTER, I HAVE HEARD FROM RELIABLE SOURCES THAT THE JEWS HAVE DECIDED TO TAKE YOU BY FORCE AND KILL YOU.
I CAME INTO THE WORLD TO GIVE MY LIFE FOR THE WORLD. I WILL BE PUT IN PRISON AND CRUCIFIED, BUT THE THIRD DAY I WILL RISE AGAIN.

MATTHEW 20:19, 26:2; JOHN 12:1-2, 14:6

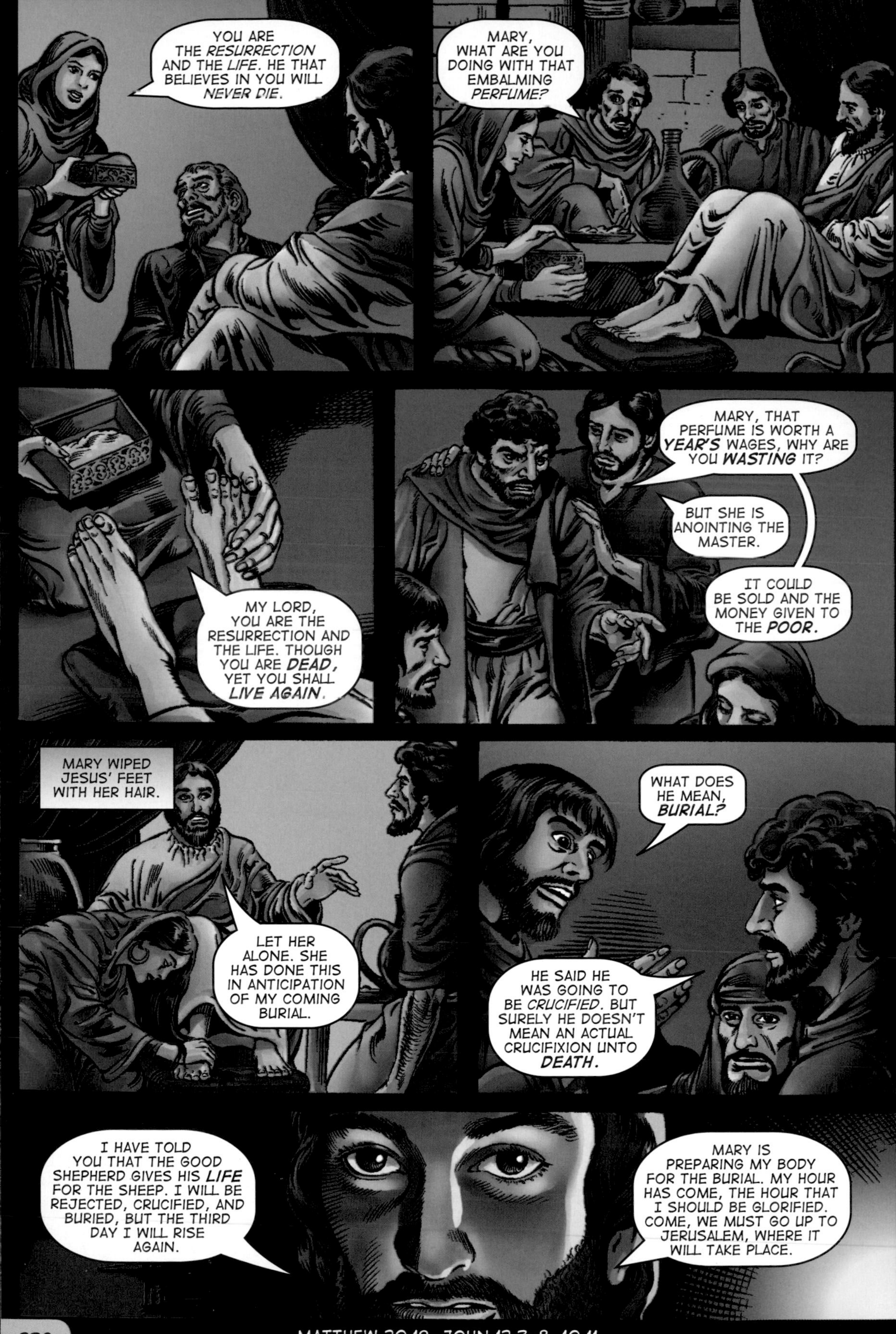

YOU ARE THE RESURRECTION AND THE LIFE. HE THAT BELIEVES IN YOU WILL NEVER DIE.
MARY, WHAT ARE YOU DOING WITH THAT EMBALMING PERFUME?
MY LORD, YOU ARE THE RESURRECTION AND THE LIFE. THOUGH YOU ARE DEAD, YET YOU SHALL LIVE AGAIN.
MARY, THAT PERFUME IS WORTH A YEAR'S WAGES, WHY ARE YOU WASTING IT?
BUT SHE IS ANOINTING THE MASTER.
IT COULD BE SOLD AND THE MONEY GIVEN TO THE POOR.
MARY WIPED JESUS' FEET WITH HER HAIR.
LET HER ALONE. SHE HAS DONE THIS IN ANTICIPATION OF MY COMING BURIAL.
WHAT DOES HE MEAN, BURIAL?
HE SAID HE WAS GOING TO BE CRUCIFIED. BUT SURELY HE DOESN'T MEAN AN ACTUAL CRUCIFIXION UNTO DEATH.
I HAVE TOLD YOU THAT THE GOOD SHEPHERD GIVES HIS LIFE FOR THE SHEEP. I WILL BE REJECTED, CRUCIFIED, AND BURIED, BUT THE THIRD DAY I WILL RISE AGAIN.
MARY IS PREPARING MY BODY FOR THE BURIAL. MY HOUR HAS COME, THE HOUR THAT I SHOULD BE GLORIFIED. COME, WE MUST GO UP TO JERUSALEM, WHERE IT WILL TAKE PLACE.

MATTHEW 20:19; JOHN 12:3-8, 10:11

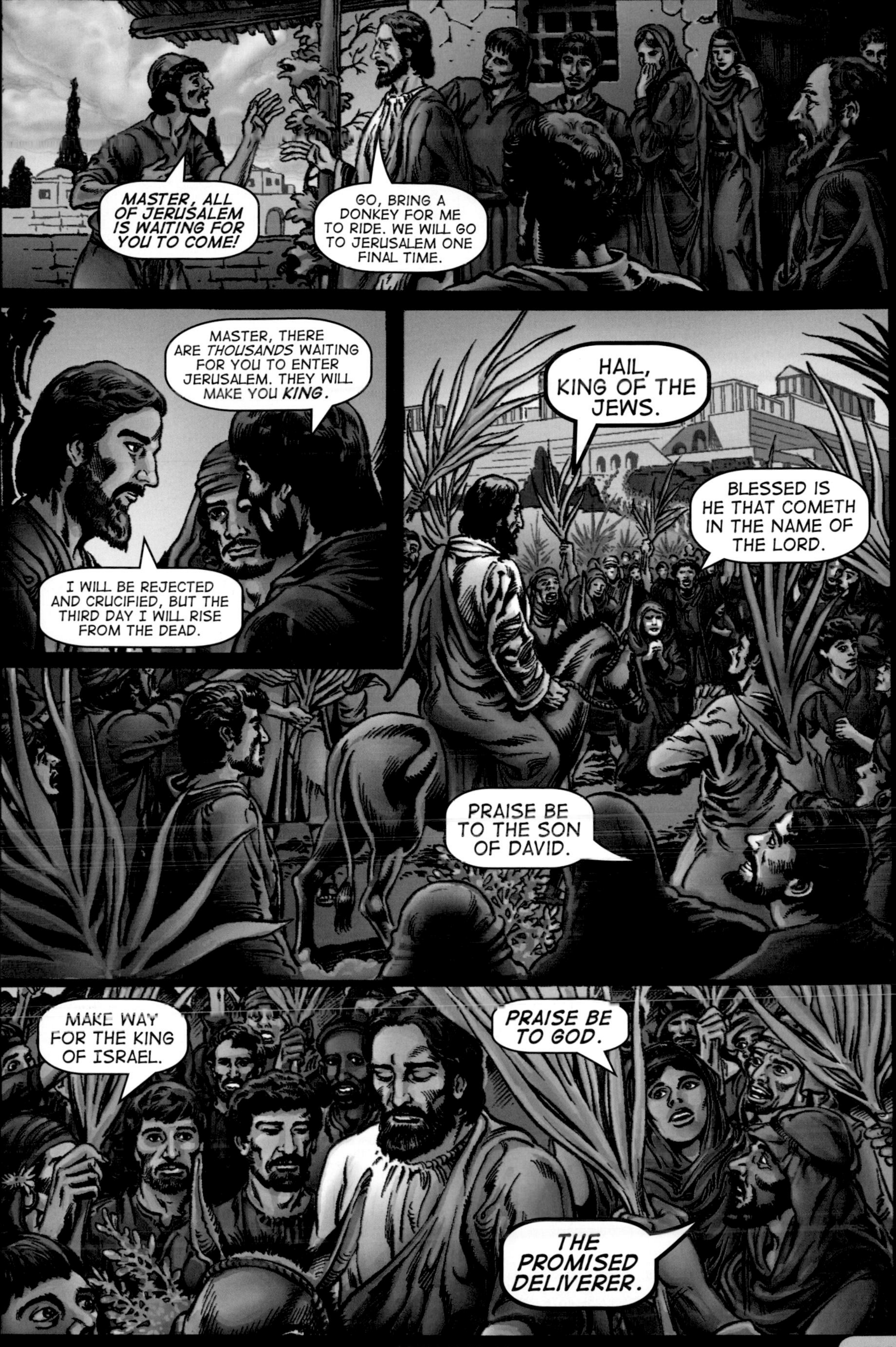
MASTER, ALL OF JERUSALEM IS WAITING FOR YOU TO COME!
GO, BRING A DONKEY FOR ME TO RIDE. WE WILL GO TO JERUSALEM ONE FINAL TIME.
MASTER, THERE ARE THOUSANDS WAITING FOR YOU TO ENTER JERUSALEM. THEY WILL MAKE YOU KING.
I WILL BE REJECTED AND CRUCIFIED, BUT THE THIRD DAY I WILL RISE FROM THE DEAD.
HAIL, KING OF THE JEWS.
BLESSED IS HE THAT COMETH IN THE NAME OF THE LORD.
PRAISE BE TO THE SON OF DAVID.
MAKE WAY FOR THE KING OF ISRAEL.
PRAISE BE TO GOD.
THE PROMISED DELIVERER.

JOHN 12:12–13

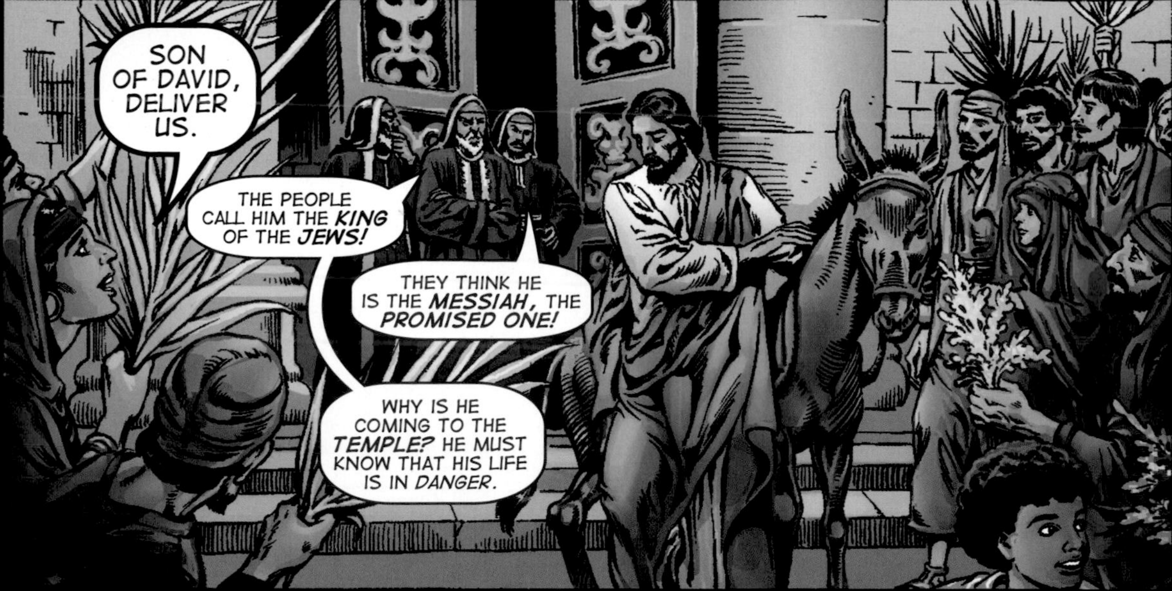
SON OF DAVID, DELIVER US.
THE PEOPLE CALL HIM THE *KING* OF THE *JEWS!*
THEY THINK HE IS THE *MESSIAH,* THE *PROMISED ONE!*
WHY IS HE COMING TO THE *TEMPLE?* HE MUST KNOW THAT HIS LIFE IS IN *DANGER*.

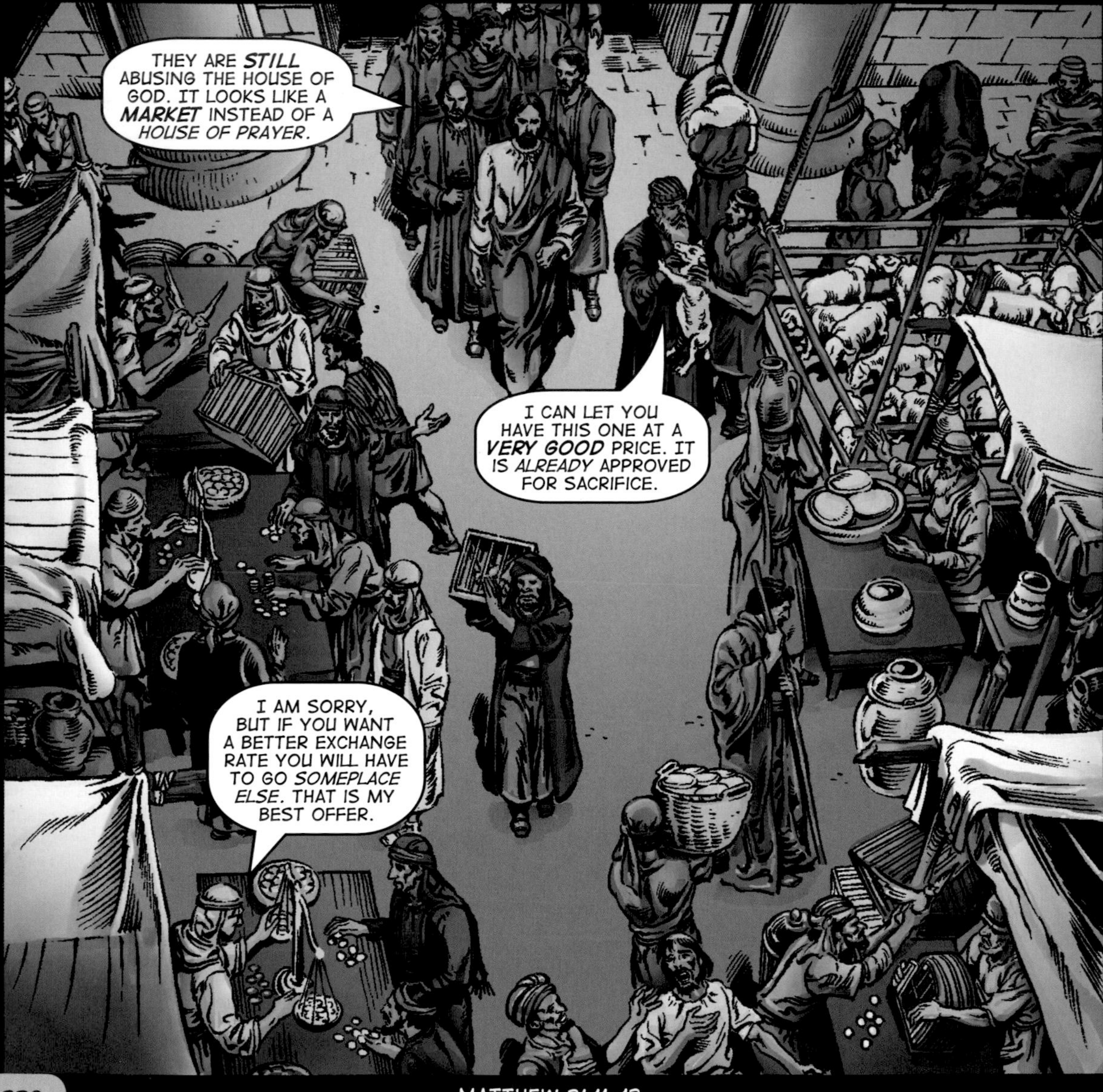
THEY ARE *STILL* ABUSING THE HOUSE OF GOD. IT LOOKS LIKE A *MARKET* INSTEAD OF A *HOUSE OF PRAYER*.
I CAN LET YOU HAVE THIS ONE AT A *VERY GOOD* PRICE. IT IS *ALREADY* APPROVED FOR SACRIFICE.
I AM SORRY, BUT IF YOU WANT A BETTER EXCHANGE RATE YOU WILL HAVE TO GO *SOMEPLACE ELSE*. THAT IS MY BEST OFFER.

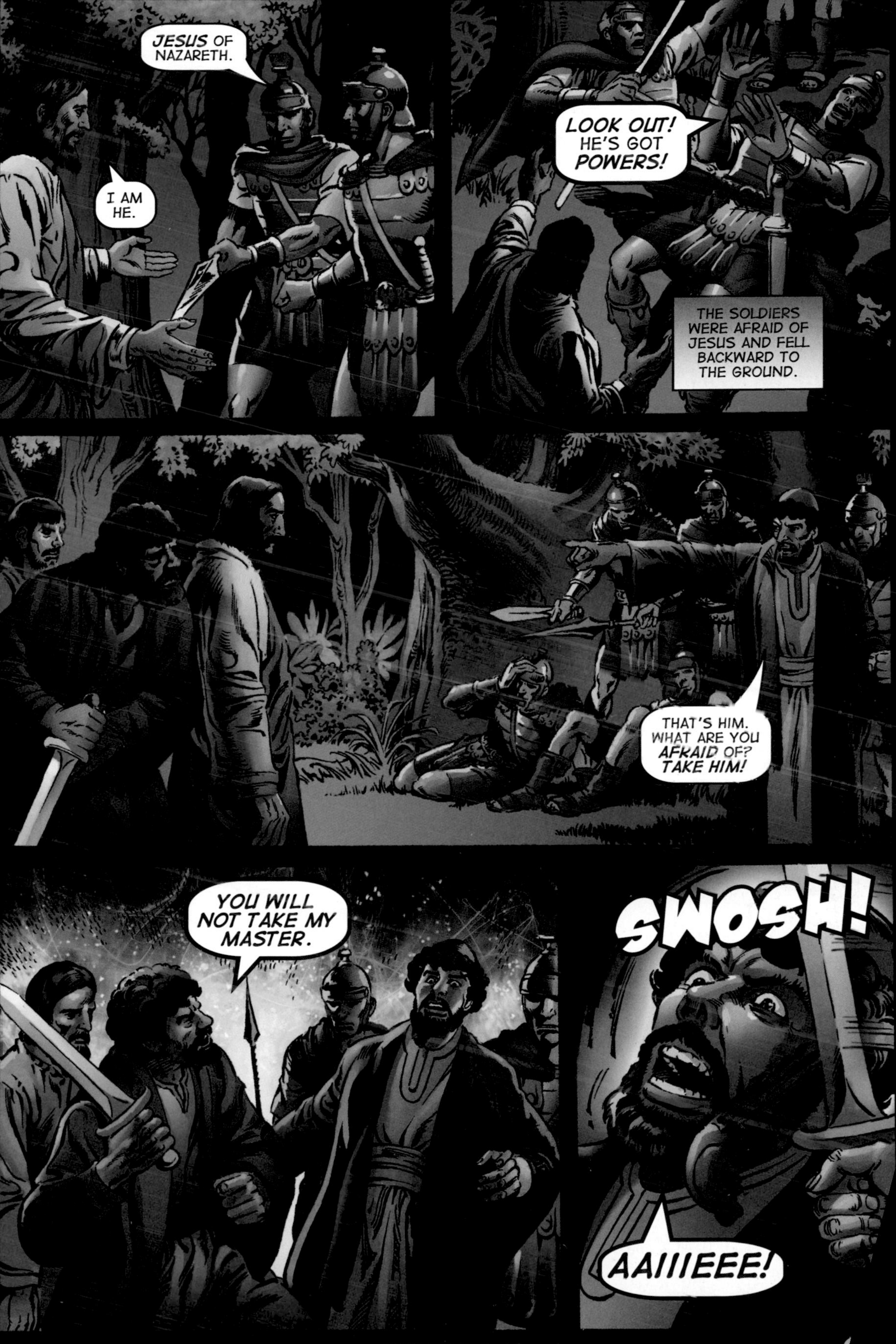
JESUS OF NAZARETH.
I AM HE.
LOOK OUT! HE'S GOT POWERS!
THE SOLDIERS WERE AFRAID OF JESUS AND FELL BACKWARD TO THE GROUND.
THAT'S HIM. WHAT ARE YOU AFRAID OF? TAKE HIM!
YOU WILL NOT TAKE MY MASTER.
SWOSH!
AAIIIEEE!

JOHN 18:4–6, 10

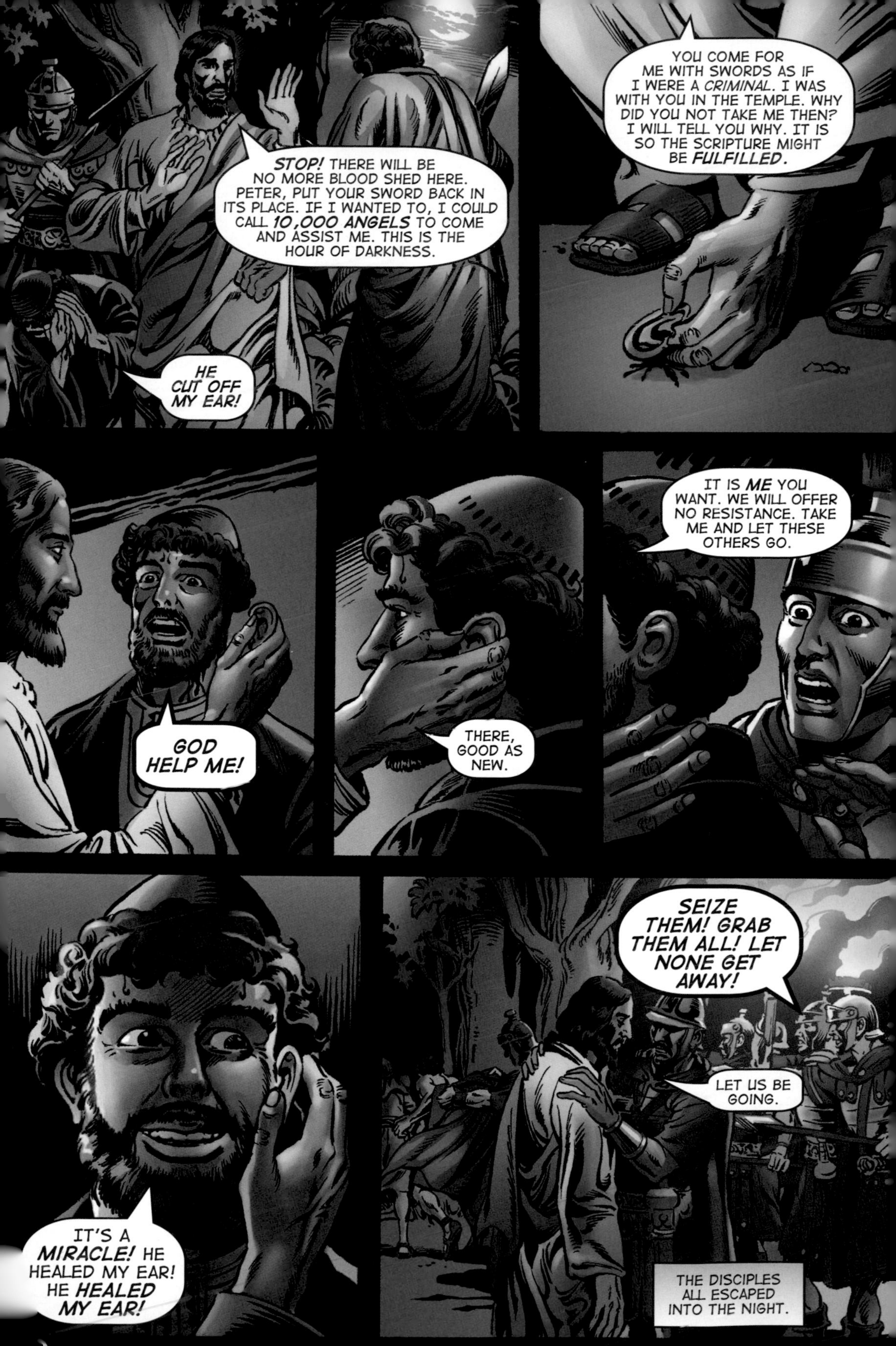
STOP! THERE WILL BE NO MORE BLOOD SHED HERE. PETER, PUT YOUR SWORD BACK IN ITS PLACE. IF I WANTED TO, I COULD CALL 10,000 ANGELS TO COME AND ASSIST ME. THIS IS THE HOUR OF DARKNESS.
HE CUT OFF MY EAR!
YOU COME FOR ME WITH SWORDS AS IF I WERE A CRIMINAL. I WAS WITH YOU IN THE TEMPLE. WHY DID YOU NOT TAKE ME THEN? I WILL TELL YOU WHY. IT IS SO THE SCRIPTURE MIGHT BE FULFILLED.
GOD HELP ME!
THERE, GOOD AS NEW.
IT IS ME YOU WANT. WE WILL OFFER NO RESISTANCE. TAKE ME AND LET THESE OTHERS GO.
IT'S A MIRACLE! HE HEALED MY EAR! HE HEALED MY EAR!
SEIZE THEM! GRAB THEM ALL! LET NONE GET AWAY!
LET US BE GOING.
THE DISCIPLES ALL ESCAPED INTO THE NIGHT.

MATTHEW 26:52-57; MARK 14:51-52; LUKE 22:50-51

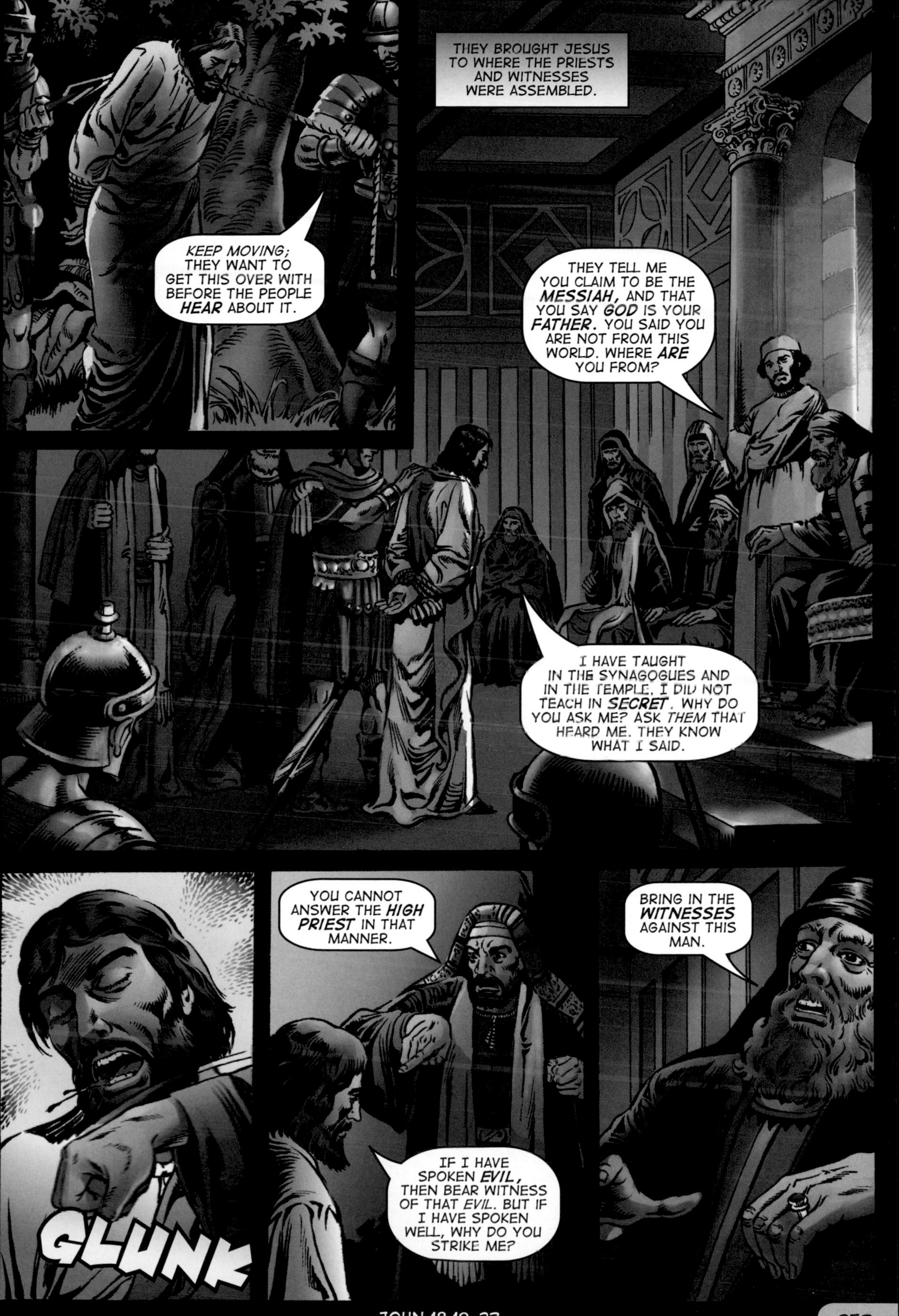
KEEP MOVING; THEY WANT TO GET THIS OVER WITH BEFORE THE PEOPLE HEAR ABOUT IT.
THEY BROUGHT JESUS TO WHERE THE PRIESTS AND WITNESSES WERE ASSEMBLED.
THEY TELL ME YOU CLAIM TO BE THE MESSIAH, AND THAT YOU SAY GOD IS YOUR FATHER. YOU SAID YOU ARE NOT FROM THIS WORLD. WHERE ARE YOU FROM?
I HAVE TAUGHT IN THE SYNAGOGUES AND IN THE TEMPLE. I DID NOT TEACH IN SECRET. WHY DO YOU ASK ME? ASK THEM THAT HEARD ME. THEY KNOW WHAT I SAID.
GLUNK
YOU CANNOT ANSWER THE HIGH PRIEST IN THAT MANNER.
IF I HAVE SPOKEN EVIL, THEN BEAR WITNESS OF THAT EVIL. BUT IF I HAVE SPOKEN WELL, WHY DO YOU STRIKE ME?
BRING IN THE WITNESSES AGAINST THIS MAN.

HE SAID HE WOULD DESTROY THE TEMPLE AND REBUILD IT IN *THREE DAYS* WITHOUT HIS HANDS.

NO, HE SAID IF *SOMEONE ELSE* DESTROYED THE TEMPLE THEN HE WOULD REBUILD IT.

YOU WEREN'T EVEN *THERE.* I HEARD WHAT HE SAID. HE POINTED TO HIMSELF WHEN HE TALKED ABOUT DESTROYING THE TEMPLE. I THINK HE WAS TALKING ABOUT HIS OWN *BODY* BEING DESTROYED.

THAT'S *RIDICULOUS.* HOW COULD HE REBUILD HIS OWN BODY AFTER THREE DAYS?

I DON'T KNOW. HOW COULD HE RAISE THE TEMPLE UP IN THREE DAYS?

DON'T YOU HEAR THEM ACCUSING YOU? AREN'T YOU GOING TO *ANSWER* FOR YOURSELF?

JESUS REMAINED SILENT.

THE FOOL WON'T ANSWER.

I *COMMAND* YOU BY THE *LIVING GOD* TO SPEAK UP AND ANSWER WHETHER YOU ARE THE *CHRIST,* THE SON OF THE LIVING GOD.

I *AM* THE SON OF GOD. AND YOU WILL SEE ME SITTING ON THE RIGHT HAND OF POWER AND COMING BACK TO THIS EARTH IN THE CLOUDS OF HEAVEN.

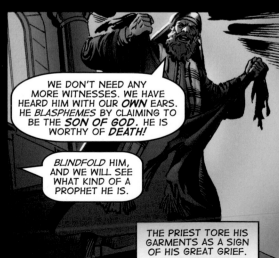

WE DON'T NEED ANY MORE WITNESSES. WE HAVE HEARD HIM WITH OUR *OWN* EARS. HE *BLASPHEMES* BY CLAIMING TO BE THE *SON OF GOD.* HE IS WORTHY OF *DEATH!*

BLINDFOLD HIM, AND WE WILL SEE WHAT KIND OF A PROPHET HE IS.

THE PRIEST TORE HIS GARMENTS AS A SIGN OF HIS GREAT GRIEF.

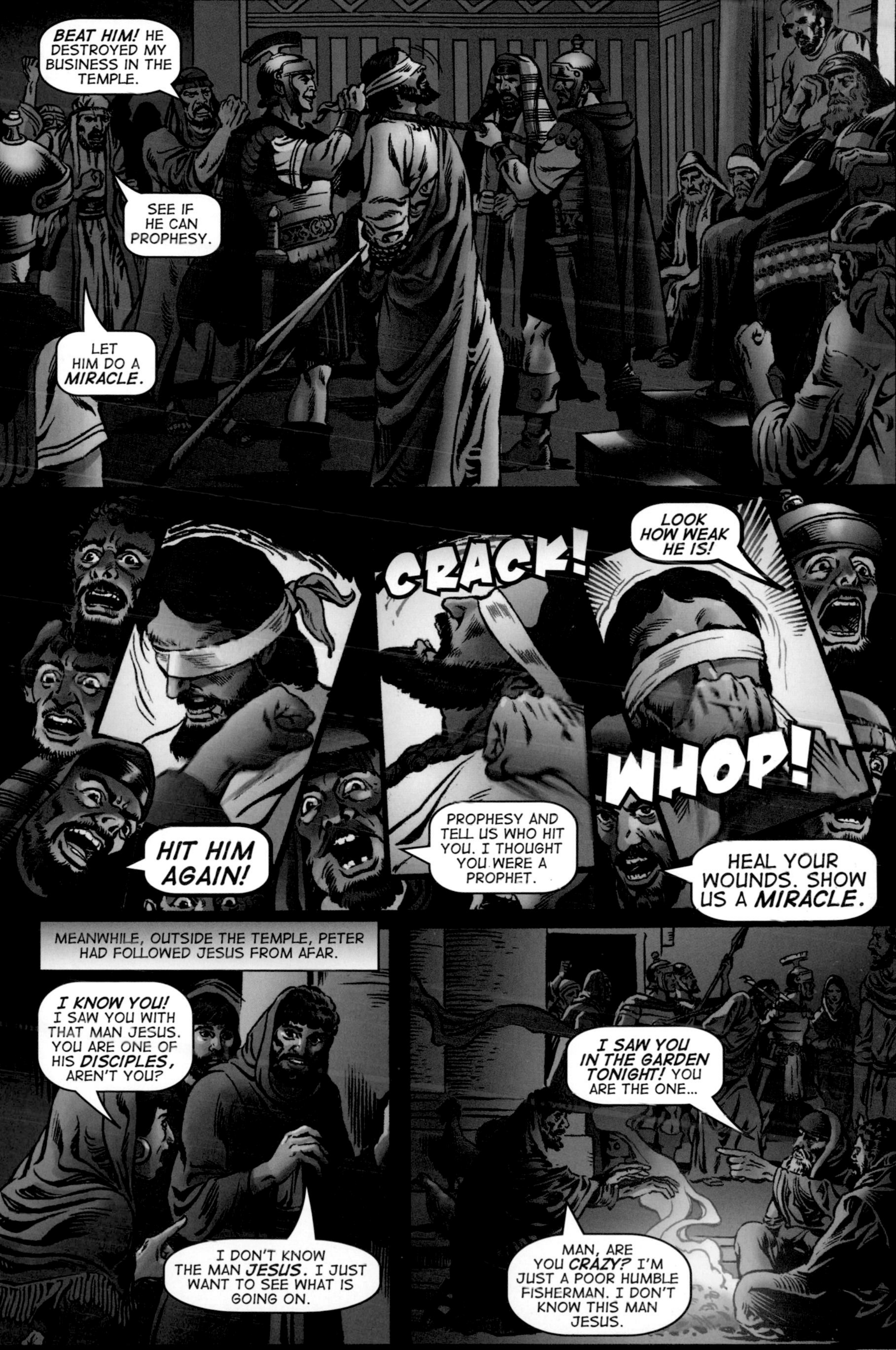
BEAT HIM! HE DESTROYED MY BUSINESS IN THE TEMPLE.
SEE IF HE CAN PROPHESY.
LET HIM DO A MIRACLE.
HIT HIM AGAIN!
CRACK!
PROPHESY AND TELL US WHO HIT YOU. I THOUGHT YOU WERE A PROPHET.
LOOK HOW WEAK HE IS!
WHOP!
HEAL YOUR WOUNDS. SHOW US A MIRACLE.
MEANWHILE, OUTSIDE THE TEMPLE, PETER HAD FOLLOWED JESUS FROM AFAR.
I KNOW YOU! I SAW YOU WITH THAT MAN JESUS. YOU ARE ONE OF HIS DISCIPLES, AREN'T YOU?
I DON'T KNOW THE MAN JESUS. I JUST WANT TO SEE WHAT IS GOING ON.
I SAW YOU IN THE GARDEN TONIGHT! YOU ARE THE ONE...
MAN, ARE YOU CRAZY? I'M JUST A POOR HUMBLE FISHERMAN. I DON'T KNOW THIS MAN JESUS.

MATTHEW 26:67-70; LUKE 22:64-65

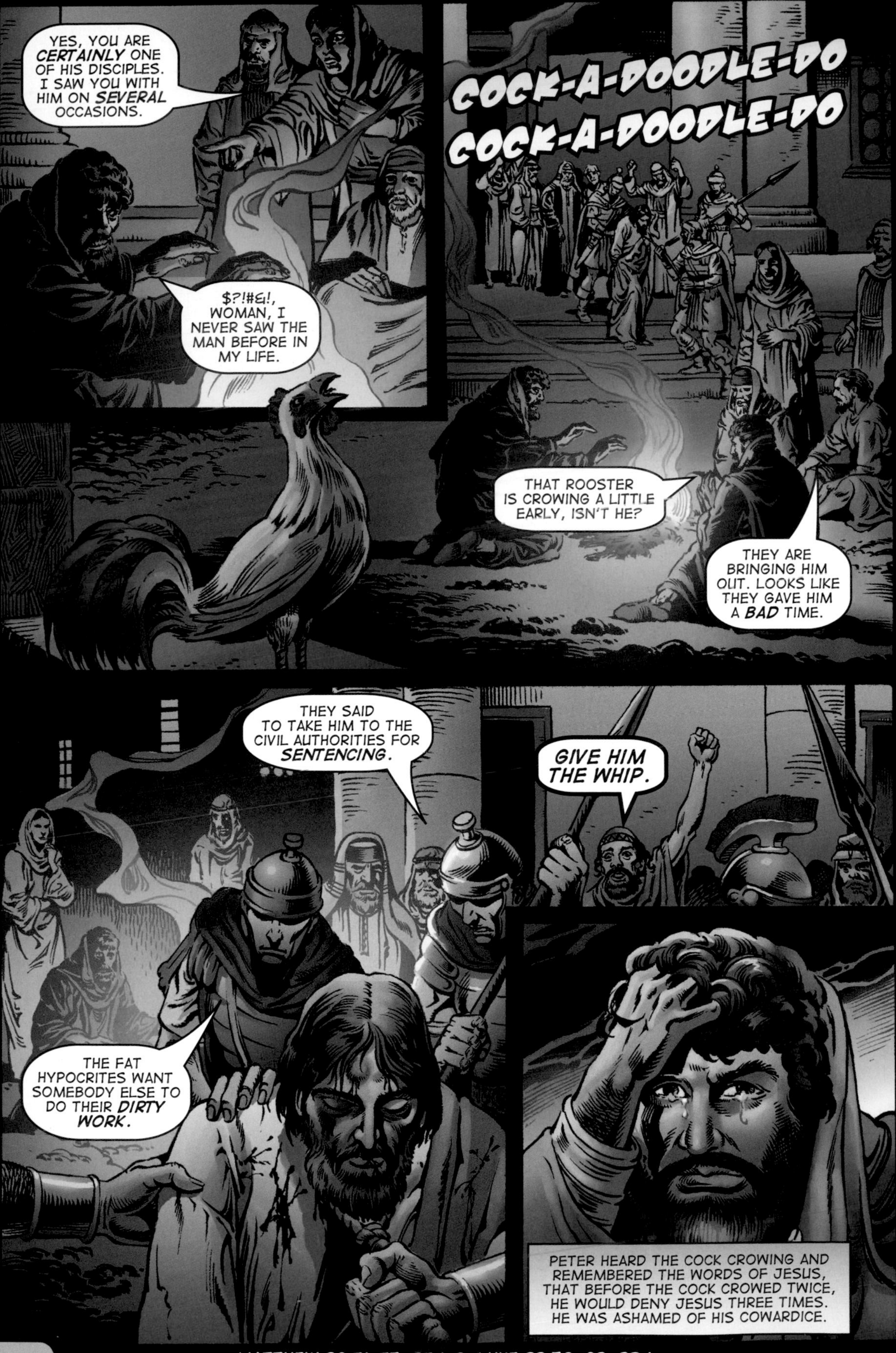
YES, YOU ARE *CERTAINLY* ONE OF HIS DISCIPLES. I SAW YOU WITH HIM ON *SEVERAL* OCCASIONS.
$?!#&!, WOMAN, I NEVER SAW THE MAN BEFORE IN MY LIFE.
COCK-A-DOODLE-DO
COCK-A-DOODLE-DO
THAT ROOSTER IS CROWING A LITTLE EARLY, ISN'T HE?
THEY ARE BRINGING HIM OUT. LOOKS LIKE THEY GAVE HIM A *BAD* TIME.
THEY SAID TO TAKE HIM TO THE CIVIL AUTHORITIES FOR *SENTENCING*.
GIVE HIM THE WHIP.
THE FAT HYPOCRITES WANT SOMEBODY ELSE TO DO THEIR *DIRTY WORK*.
PETER HEARD THE COCK CROWING AND REMEMBERED THE WORDS OF JESUS, THAT BEFORE THE COCK CROWED TWICE, HE WOULD DENY JESUS THREE TIMES. HE WAS ASHAMED OF HIS COWARDICE.

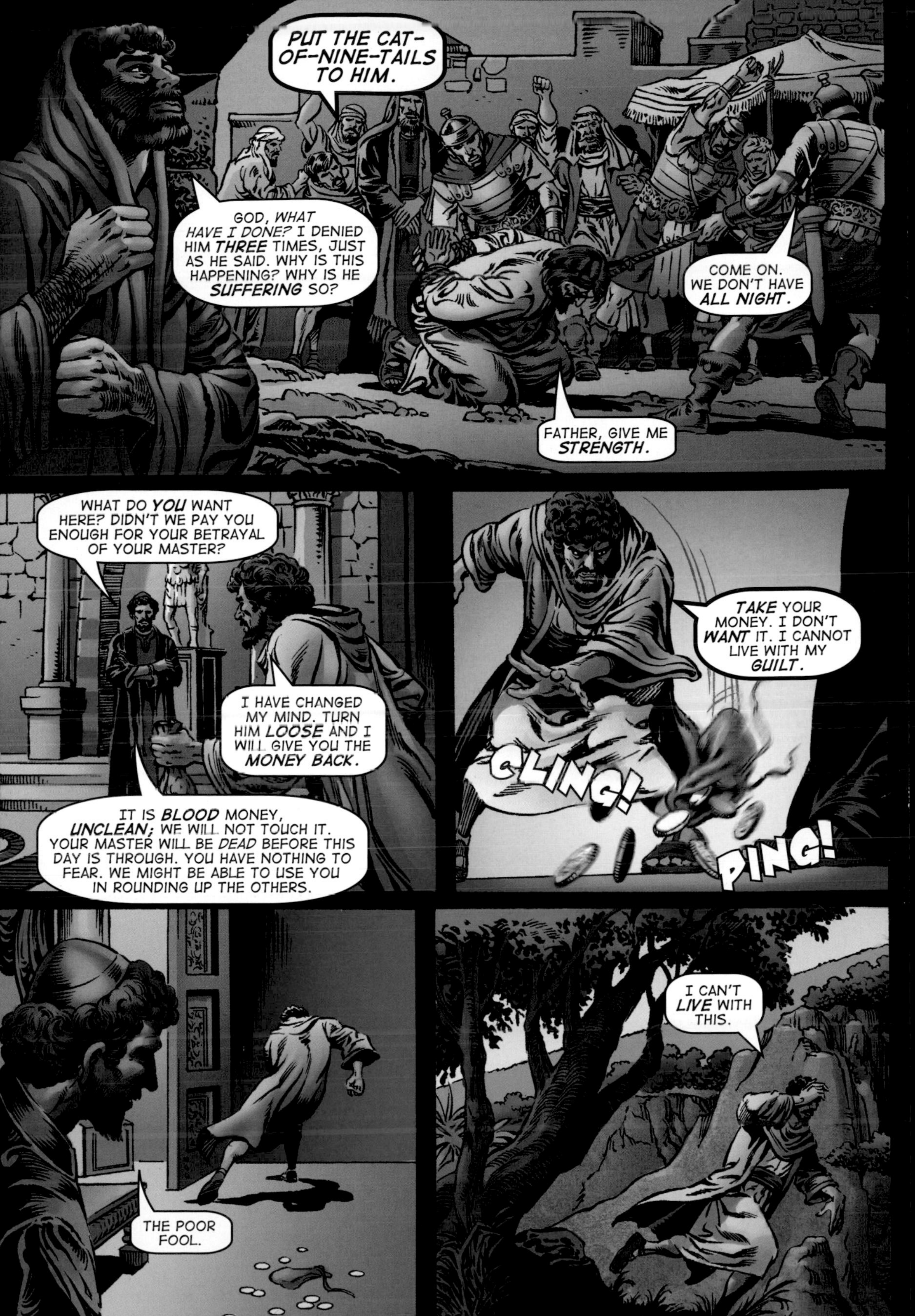
PUT THE CAT-OF-NINE-TAILS TO HIM.
GOD, WHAT HAVE I DONE? I DENIED HIM THREE TIMES, JUST AS HE SAID. WHY IS THIS HAPPENING? WHY IS HE SUFFERING SO?
COME ON. WE DON'T HAVE ALL NIGHT.
FATHER, GIVE ME STRENGTH.
WHAT DO YOU WANT HERE? DIDN'T WE PAY YOU ENOUGH FOR YOUR BETRAYAL OF YOUR MASTER?
I HAVE CHANGED MY MIND. TURN HIM LOOSE AND I WILL GIVE YOU THE MONEY BACK.
IT IS BLOOD MONEY, UNCLEAN; WE WILL NOT TOUCH IT. YOUR MASTER WILL BE DEAD BEFORE THIS DAY IS THROUGH. YOU HAVE NOTHING TO FEAR. WE MIGHT BE ABLE TO USE YOU IN ROUNDING UP THE OTHERS.
TAKE YOUR MONEY. I DON'T WANT IT. I CANNOT LIVE WITH MY GUILT.
CLING!
PING!
THE POOR FOOL.
I CAN'T LIVE WITH THIS.

MATTHEW 27:3-6

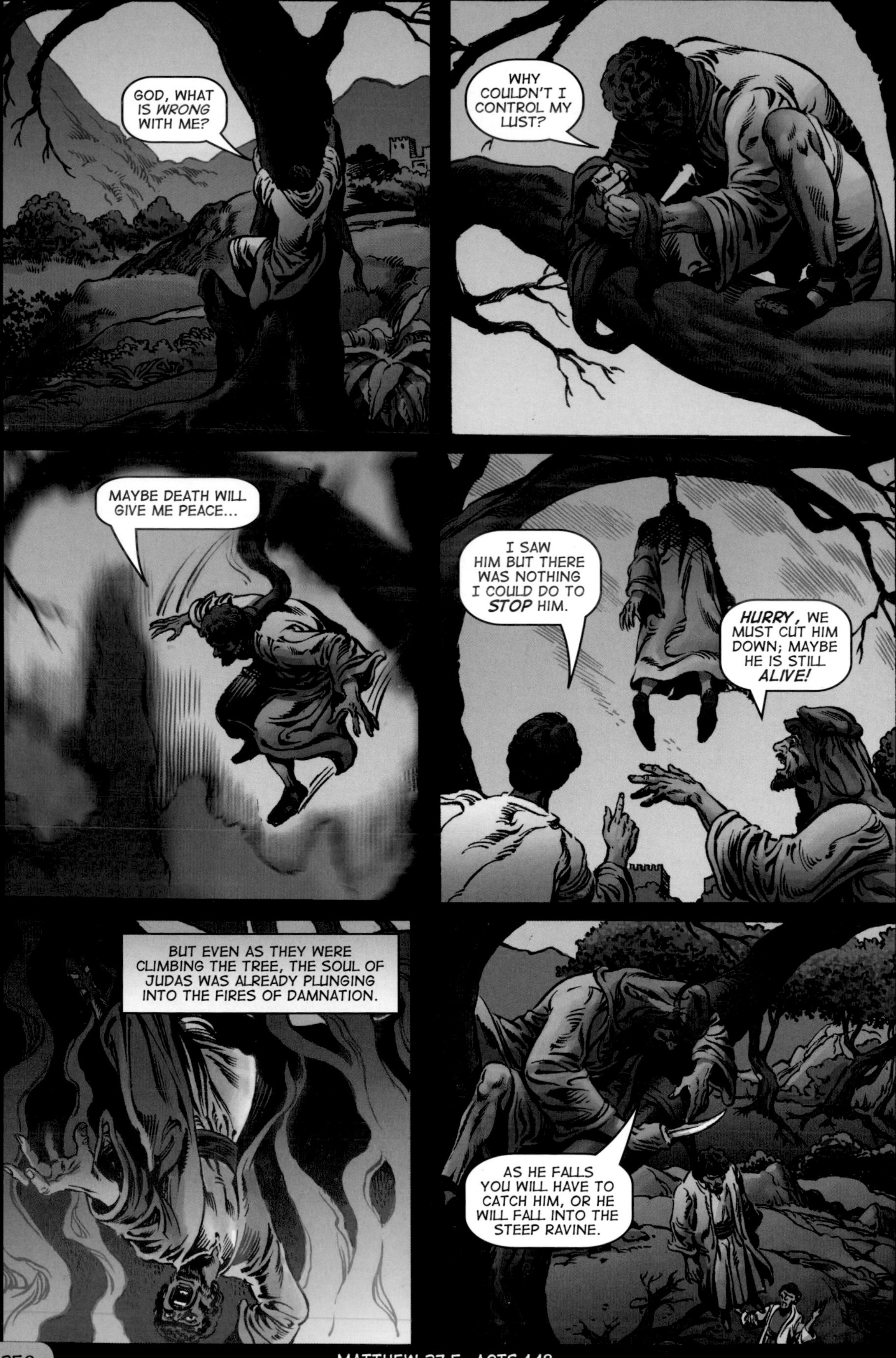
GOD, WHAT IS *WRONG* WITH ME?
WHY COULDN'T I CONTROL MY LUST?
MAYBE DEATH WILL GIVE ME PEACE...
I SAW HIM BUT THERE WAS NOTHING I COULD DO TO **STOP** HIM.
HURRY, WE MUST CUT HIM DOWN; MAYBE HE IS STILL **ALIVE!**
BUT EVEN AS THEY WERE CLIMBING THE TREE, THE SOUL OF JUDAS WAS ALREADY PLUNGING INTO THE FIRES OF DAMNATION.
AS HE FALLS YOU WILL HAVE TO CATCH HIM, OR HE WILL FALL INTO THE STEEP RAVINE.

MATTHEW 27:5; ACTS 1:18

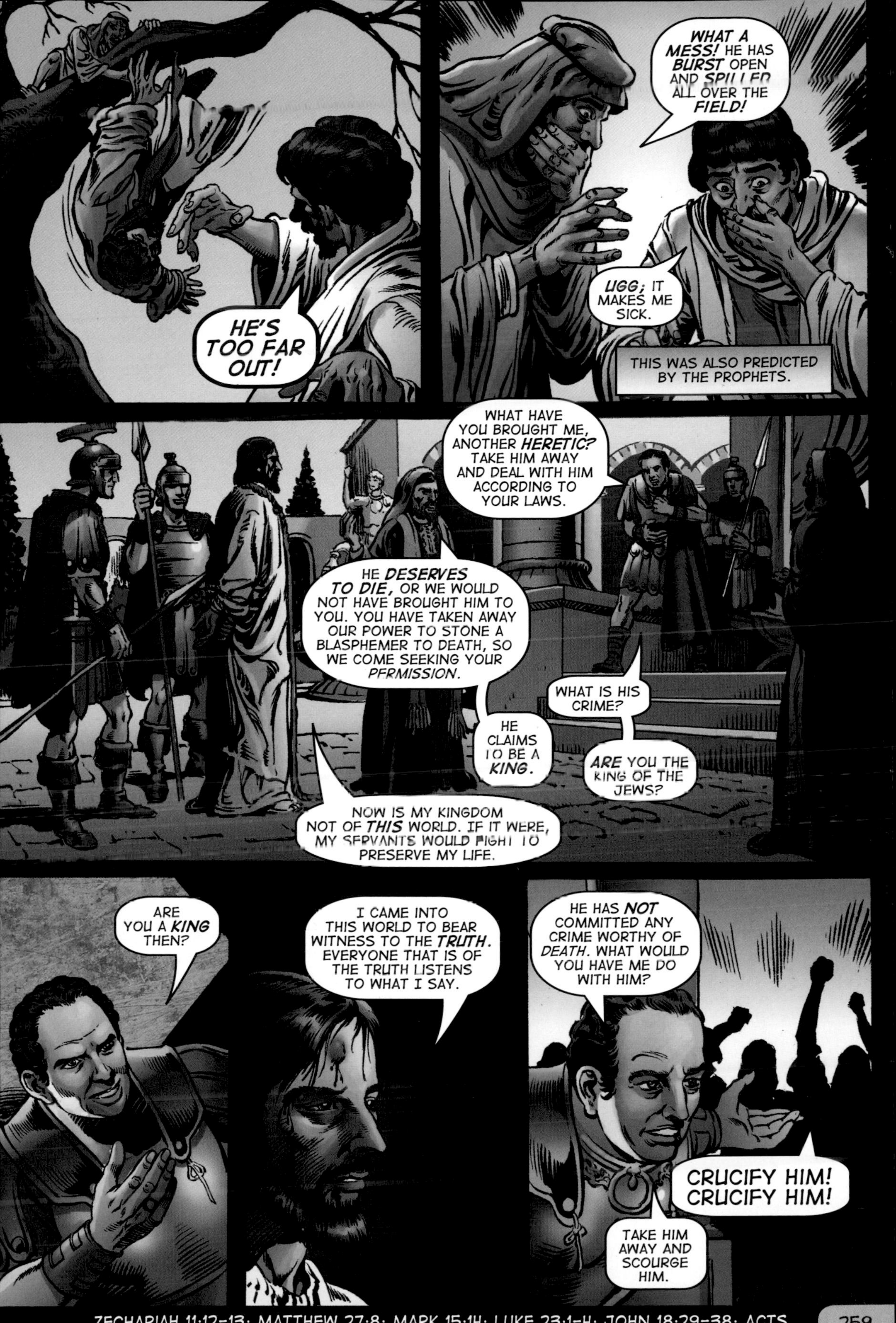
HE'S TOO FAR OUT!
WHAT A MESS! HE HAS BURST OPEN AND SPILLED ALL OVER THE FIELD!
UGG; IT MAKES ME SICK.
THIS WAS ALSO PREDICTED BY THE PROPHETS.
WHAT HAVE YOU BROUGHT ME, ANOTHER HERETIC? TAKE HIM AWAY AND DEAL WITH HIM ACCORDING TO YOUR LAWS.
HE DESERVES TO DIE, OR WE WOULD NOT HAVE BROUGHT HIM TO YOU. YOU HAVE TAKEN AWAY OUR POWER TO STONE A BLASPHEMER TO DEATH, SO WE COME SEEKING YOUR PERMISSION.
WHAT IS HIS CRIME?
HE CLAIMS TO BE A KING.
ARE YOU THE KING OF THE JEWS?
NOW IS MY KINGDOM NOT OF THIS WORLD. IF IT WERE, MY SERVANTS WOULD FIGHT TO PRESERVE MY LIFE.
ARE YOU A KING THEN?
I CAME INTO THIS WORLD TO BEAR WITNESS TO THE TRUTH. EVERYONE THAT IS OF THE TRUTH LISTENS TO WHAT I SAY.
HE HAS NOT COMMITTED ANY CRIME WORTHY OF DEATH. WHAT WOULD YOU HAVE ME DO WITH HIM?
CRUCIFY HIM! CRUCIFY HIM!
TAKE HIM AWAY AND SCOURGE HIM.

ZECHARIAH 11:12-13; MATTHEW 27:8; MARK 15:14; LUKE 23:1-4; JOHN 18:29-38; ACTS 1:18

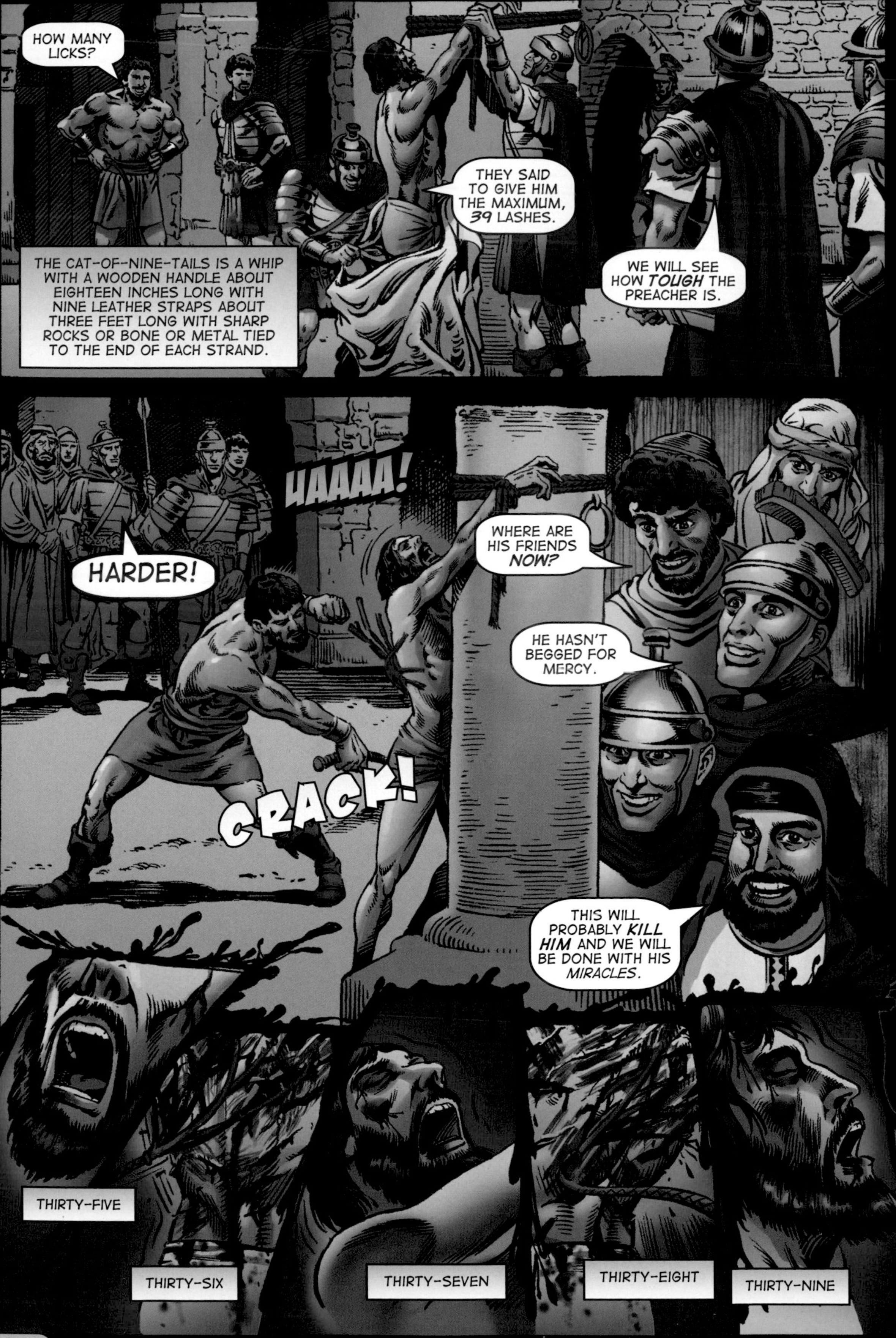
HOW MANY LICKS?
THEY SAID TO GIVE HIM THE MAXIMUM, 39 LASHES.
THE CAT-OF-NINE-TAILS IS A WHIP WITH A WOODEN HANDLE ABOUT EIGHTEEN INCHES LONG WITH NINE LEATHER STRAPS ABOUT THREE FEET LONG WITH SHARP ROCKS OR BONE OR METAL TIED TO THE END OF EACH STRAND.
WE WILL SEE HOW TOUGH THE PREACHER IS.
UAAAA!
HARDER!
WHERE ARE HIS FRIENDS NOW?
HE HASN'T BEGGED FOR MERCY.
CRACK!
THIS WILL PROBABLY KILL HIM AND WE WILL BE DONE WITH HIS MIRACLES.
THIRTY-FIVE
THIRTY-SIX
THIRTY-SEVEN
THIRTY-EIGHT
THIRTY-NINE

LUKE 23:11; JOHN 19:1-2

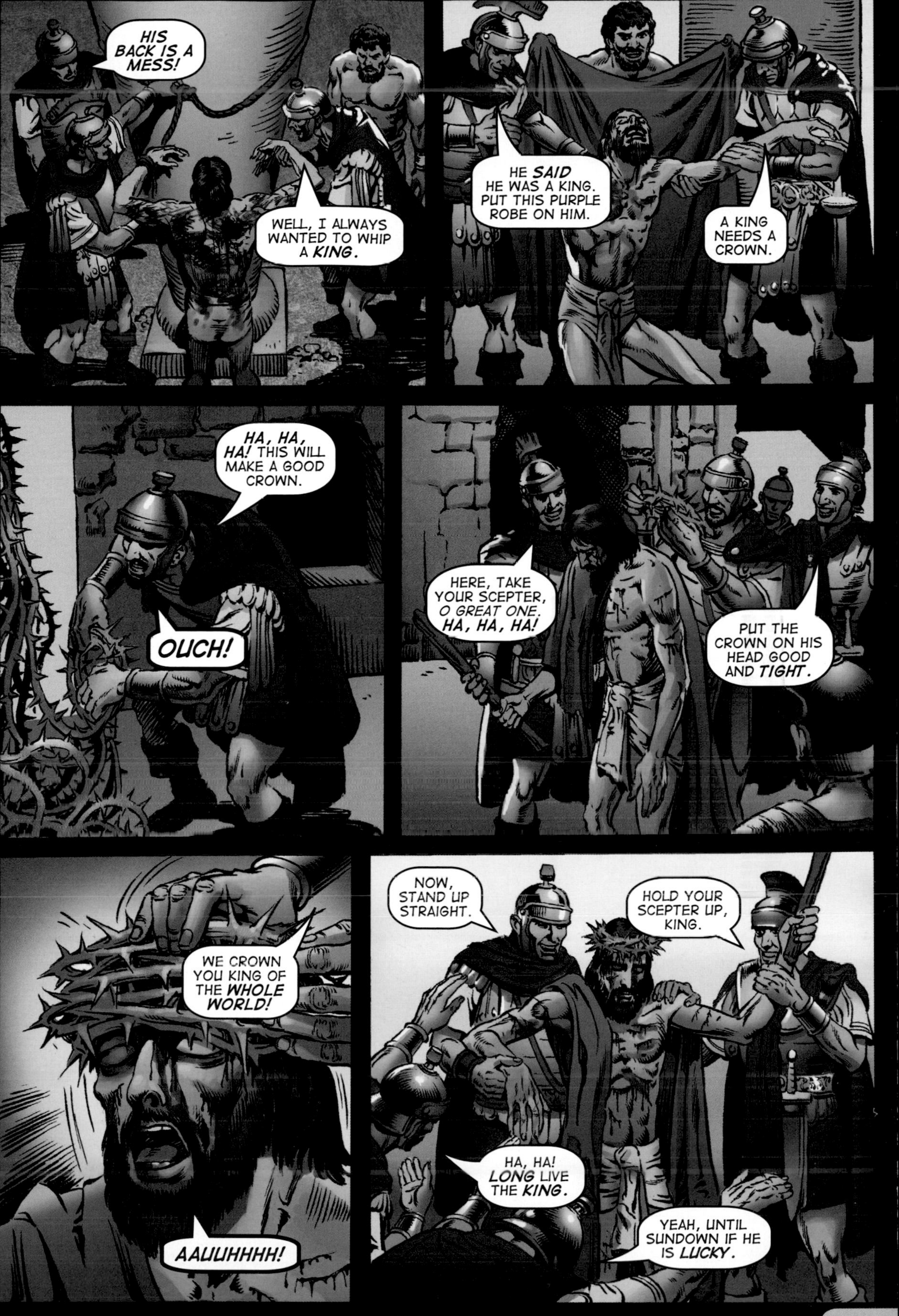
HIS BACK IS A MESS!
WELL, I ALWAYS WANTED TO WHIP A KING.
HE SAID HE WAS A KING. PUT THIS PURPLE ROBE ON HIM.
A KING NEEDS A CROWN.
HA, HA, HA! THIS WILL MAKE A GOOD CROWN.
OUCH!
HERE, TAKE YOUR SCEPTER, O GREAT ONE. HA, HA, HA!
PUT THE CROWN ON HIS HEAD GOOD AND TIGHT.
WE CROWN YOU KING OF THE WHOLE WORLD!
AAUUHHHH!
NOW, STAND UP STRAIGHT.
HOLD YOUR SCEPTER UP, KING.
HA, HA! LONG LIVE THE KING.
YEAH, UNTIL SUNDOWN IF HE IS LUCKY.

JOHN 19:1-3

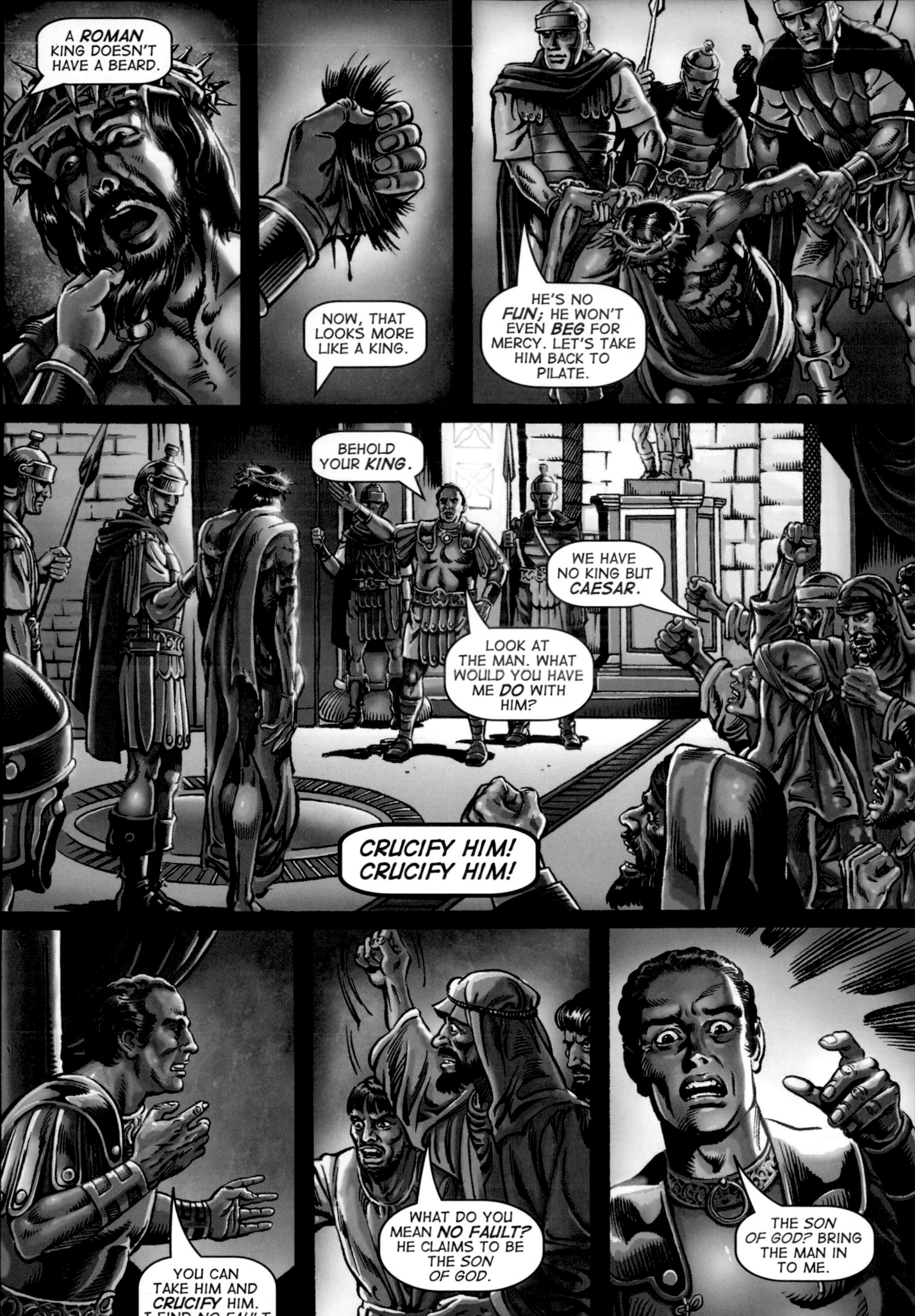
A ROMAN KING DOESN'T HAVE A BEARD.
NOW, THAT LOOKS MORE LIKE A KING.
HE'S NO FUN; HE WON'T EVEN BEG FOR MERCY. LET'S TAKE HIM BACK TO PILATE.
BEHOLD YOUR KING.
LOOK AT THE MAN. WHAT WOULD YOU HAVE ME DO WITH HIM?
WE HAVE NO KING BUT CAESAR.
CRUCIFY HIM! CRUCIFY HIM!
YOU CAN TAKE HIM AND CRUCIFY HIM. I FIND NO FAULT IN THIS MAN.
WHAT DO YOU MEAN NO FAULT? HE CLAIMS TO BE THE SON OF GOD.
THE SON OF GOD? BRING THE MAN IN TO ME.

PSALM 22; ISAIAH 50:6, 53:5, 7; LUKE 23:13–22; JOHN 19:4–8

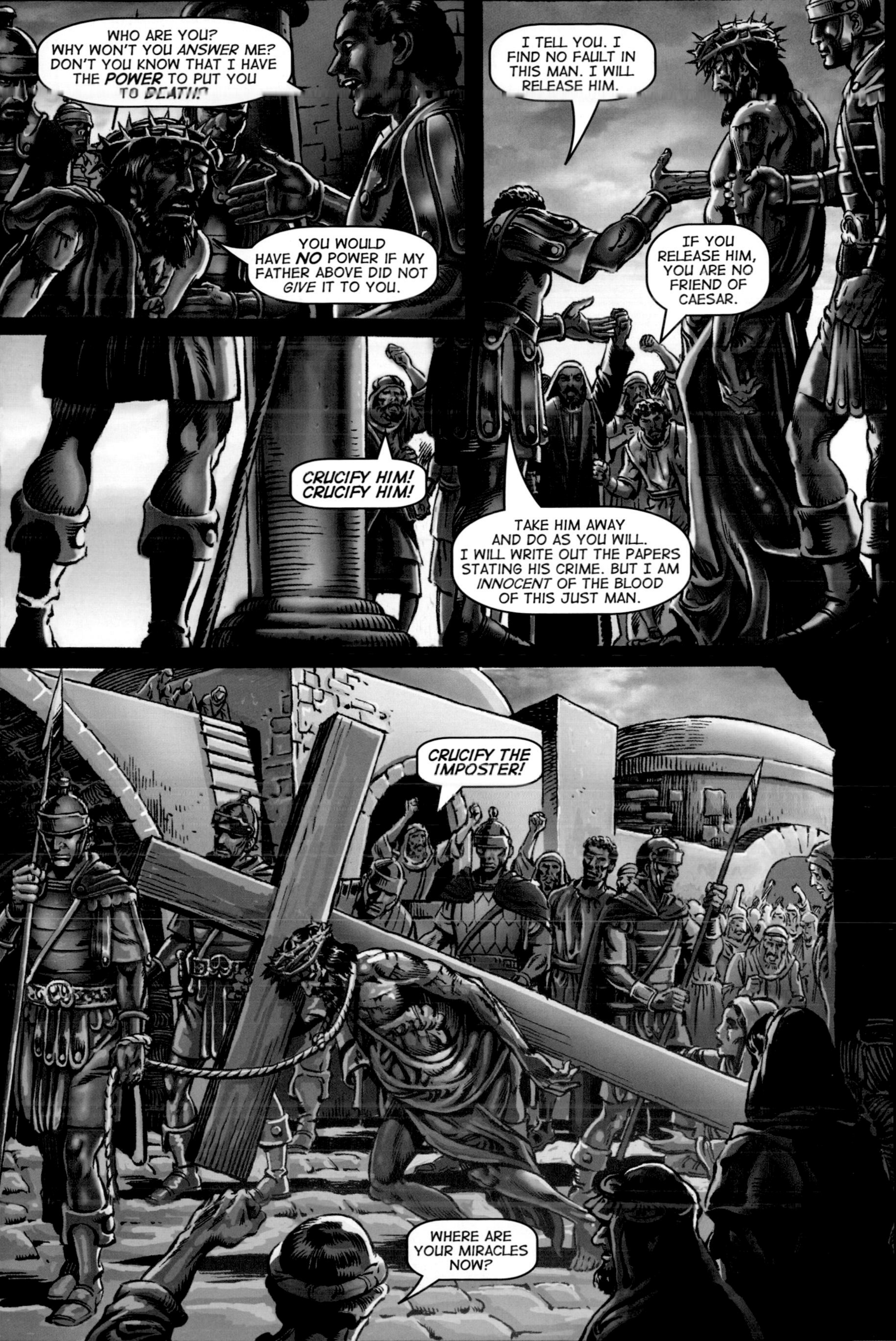
WHO ARE YOU? WHY WON'T YOU *ANSWER* ME? DON'T YOU KNOW THAT I HAVE THE **POWER** TO PUT YOU TO **DEATH!?**
YOU WOULD HAVE **NO** POWER IF MY FATHER ABOVE DID NOT *GIVE* IT TO YOU.
I TELL YOU. I FIND NO FAULT IN THIS MAN. I WILL RELEASE HIM.
IF YOU RELEASE HIM, YOU ARE NO FRIEND OF CAESAR.
CRUCIFY HIM! CRUCIFY HIM!
TAKE HIM AWAY AND DO AS YOU WILL. I WILL WRITE OUT THE PAPERS STATING HIS CRIME. BUT I AM *INNOCENT* OF THE BLOOD OF THIS JUST MAN.
CRUCIFY THE IMPOSTER!
WHERE ARE YOUR MIRACLES NOW?

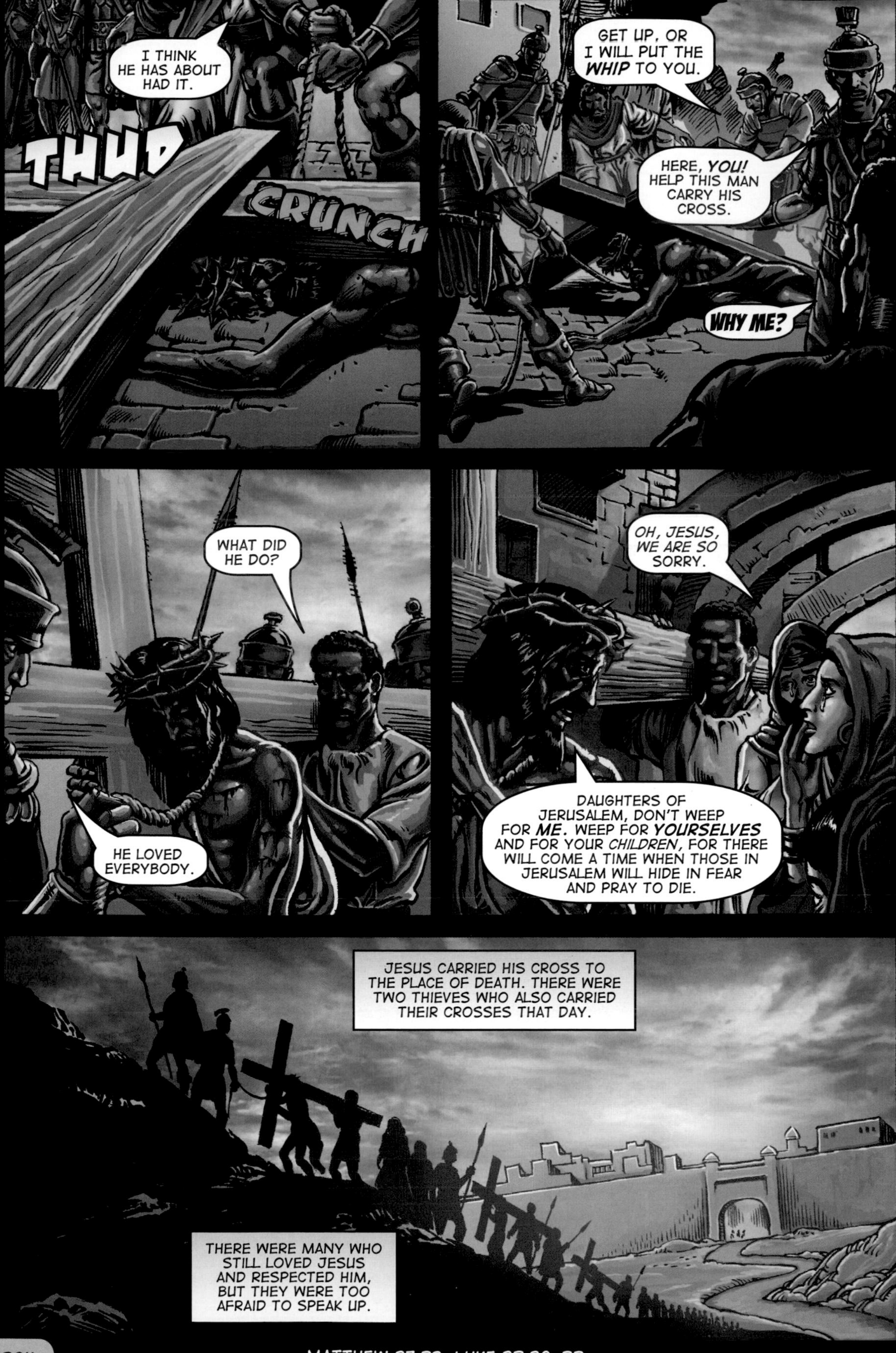
I THINK HE HAS ABOUT HAD IT.
THUD
CRUNCH
GET UP, OR I WILL PUT THE *WHIP* TO YOU.
HERE, *YOU!* HELP THIS MAN CARRY HIS CROSS.
WHY ME?
WHAT DID HE DO?
HE LOVED EVERYBODY.
OH, JESUS, WE ARE SO SORRY.
DAUGHTERS OF JERUSALEM, DON'T WEEP FOR *ME*. WEEP FOR *YOURSELVES* AND FOR YOUR *CHILDREN*, FOR THERE WILL COME A TIME WHEN THOSE IN JERUSALEM WILL HIDE IN FEAR AND PRAY TO DIE.
JESUS CARRIED HIS CROSS TO THE PLACE OF DEATH. THERE WERE TWO THIEVES WHO ALSO CARRIED THEIR CROSSES THAT DAY.
THERE WERE MANY WHO STILL LOVED JESUS AND RESPECTED HIM, BUT THEY WERE TOO AFRAID TO SPEAK UP.

MATTHEW 27:32; LUKE 23:26-33

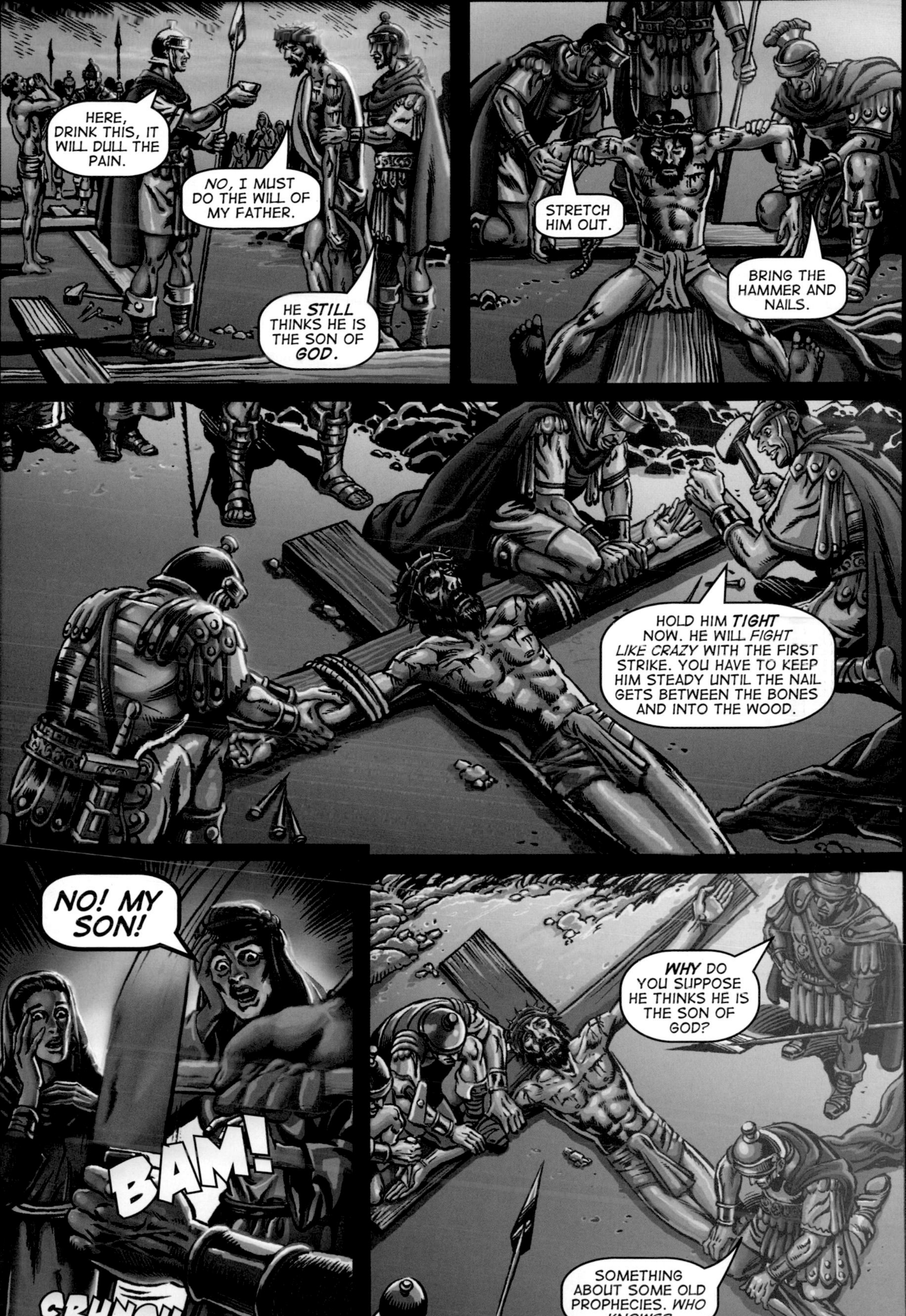
HERE, DRINK THIS, IT WILL DULL THE PAIN.
NO, I MUST DO THE WILL OF MY FATHER.
HE STILL THINKS HE IS THE SON OF GOD.
STRETCH HIM OUT.
BRING THE HAMMER AND NAILS.
HOLD HIM TIGHT NOW. HE WILL FIGHT LIKE CRAZY WITH THE FIRST STRIKE. YOU HAVE TO KEEP HIM STEADY UNTIL THE NAIL GETS BETWEEN THE BONES AND INTO THE WOOD.
NO! MY SON!
BAM!
CRUNCH
WHY DO YOU SUPPOSE HE THINKS HE IS THE SON OF GOD?
SOMETHING ABOUT SOME OLD PROPHECIES. WHO KNOWS?

PSALM 22; ISAIAH 52; MATTHEW 27:33-34

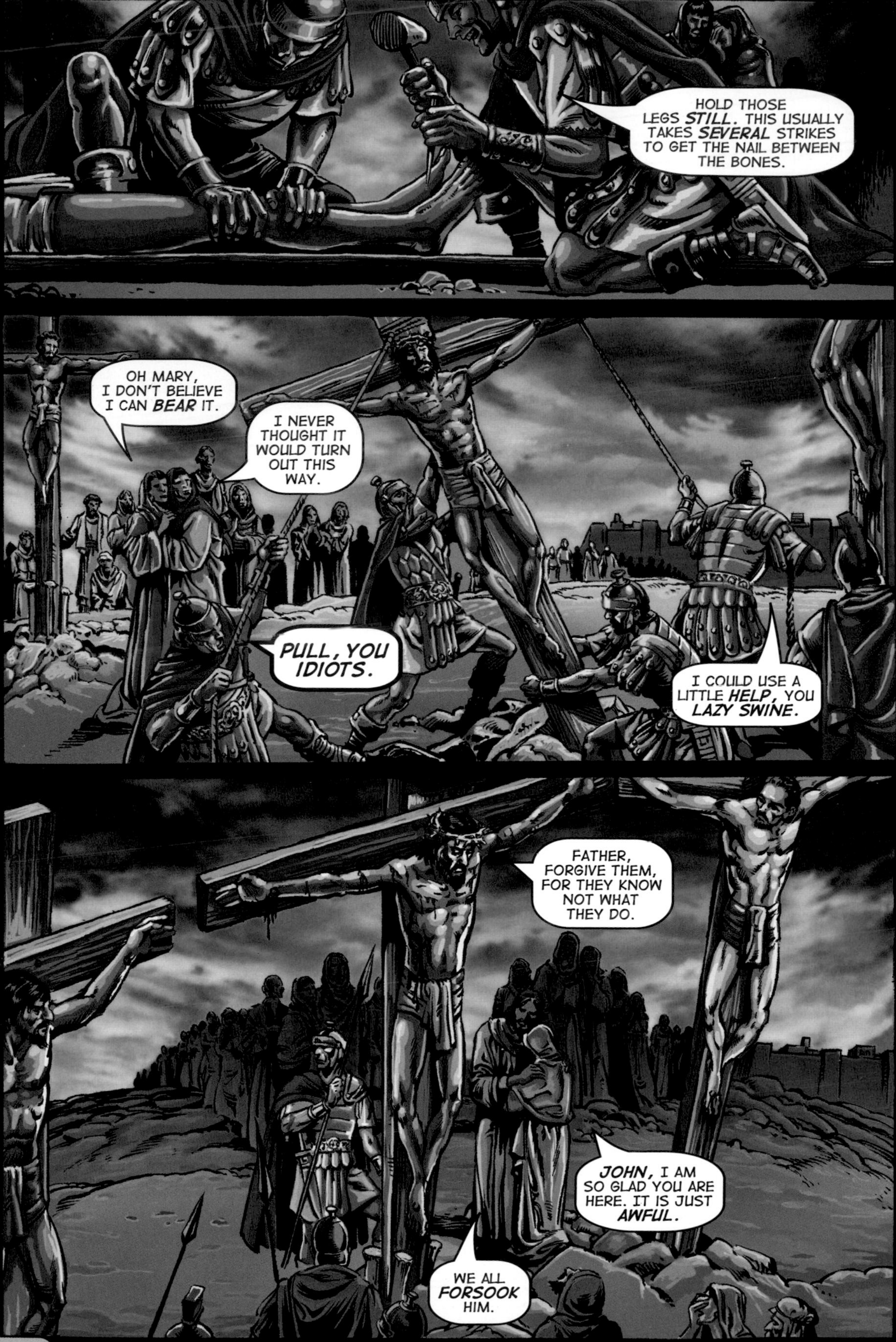
HOLD THOSE LEGS STILL. THIS USUALLY TAKES SEVERAL STRIKES TO GET THE NAIL BETWEEN THE BONES.
OH MARY, I DON'T BELIEVE I CAN BEAR IT.
I NEVER THOUGHT IT WOULD TURN OUT THIS WAY.
PULL, YOU IDIOTS.
I COULD USE A LITTLE HELP, YOU LAZY SWINE.
FATHER, FORGIVE THEM, FOR THEY KNOW NOT WHAT THEY DO.
JOHN, I AM SO GLAD YOU ARE HERE. IT IS JUST AWFUL.
WE ALL FORSOOK HIM.

ZECHARIAH 13:6; LUKE 23:32-34

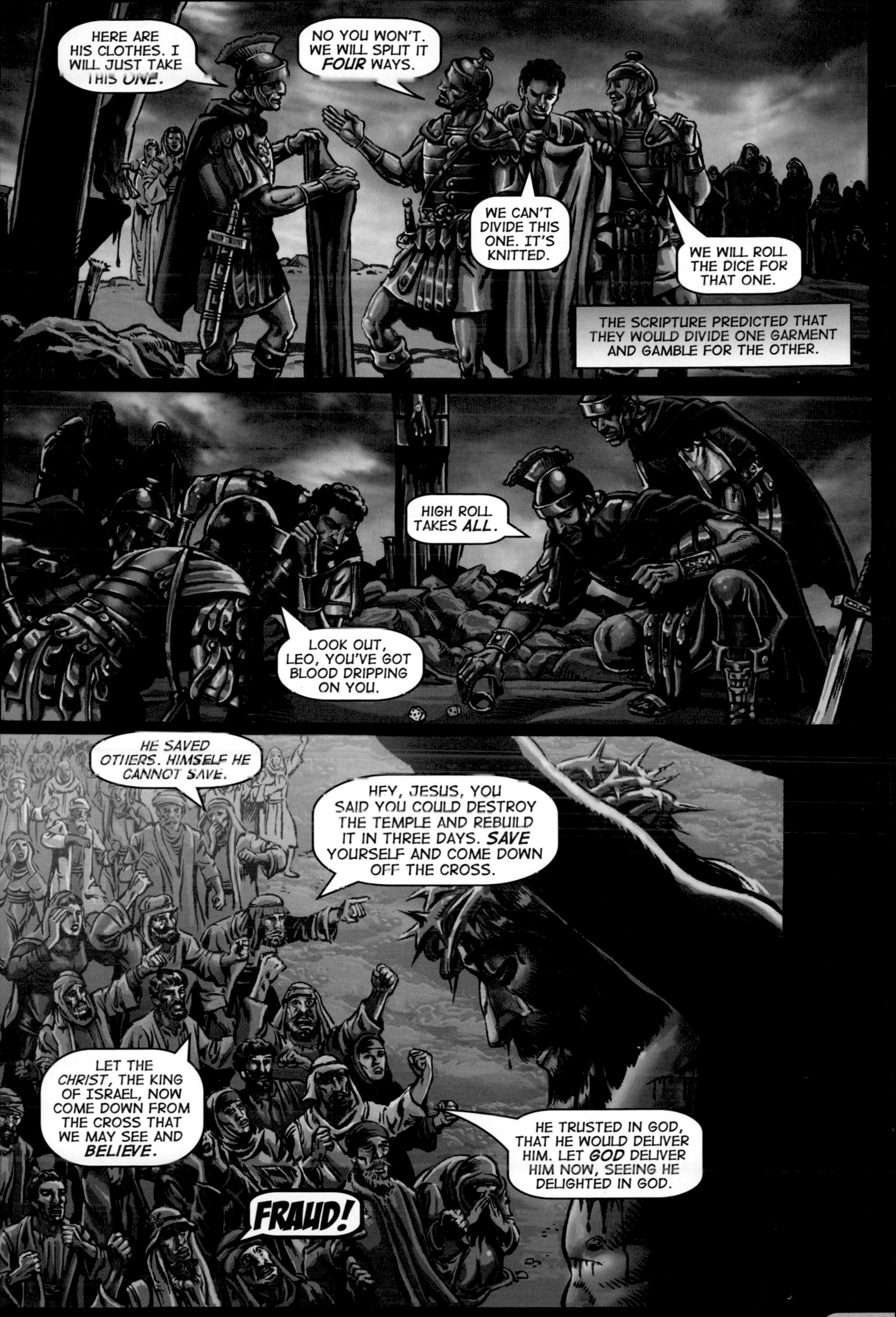
HERE ARE HIS CLOTHES. I WILL JUST TAKE THIS ONE.
NO YOU WON'T. WE WILL SPLIT IT FOUR WAYS.
WE CAN'T DIVIDE THIS ONE. IT'S KNITTED.
WE WILL ROLL THE DICE FOR THAT ONE.
THE SCRIPTURE PREDICTED THAT THEY WOULD DIVIDE ONE GARMENT AND GAMBLE FOR THE OTHER.
HIGH ROLL TAKES ALL.
LOOK OUT, LEO, YOU'VE GOT BLOOD DRIPPING ON YOU.
HE SAVED OTHERS. HIMSELF HE CANNOT SAVE.
HEY, JESUS, YOU SAID YOU COULD DESTROY THE TEMPLE AND REBUILD IT IN THREE DAYS. SAVE YOURSELF AND COME DOWN OFF THE CROSS.
LET THE CHRIST, THE KING OF ISRAEL, NOW COME DOWN FROM THE CROSS THAT WE MAY SEE AND BELIEVE.
HE TRUSTED IN GOD, THAT HE WOULD DELIVER HIM. LET GOD DELIVER HIM NOW, SEEING HE DELIGHTED IN GOD.
FRAUD!

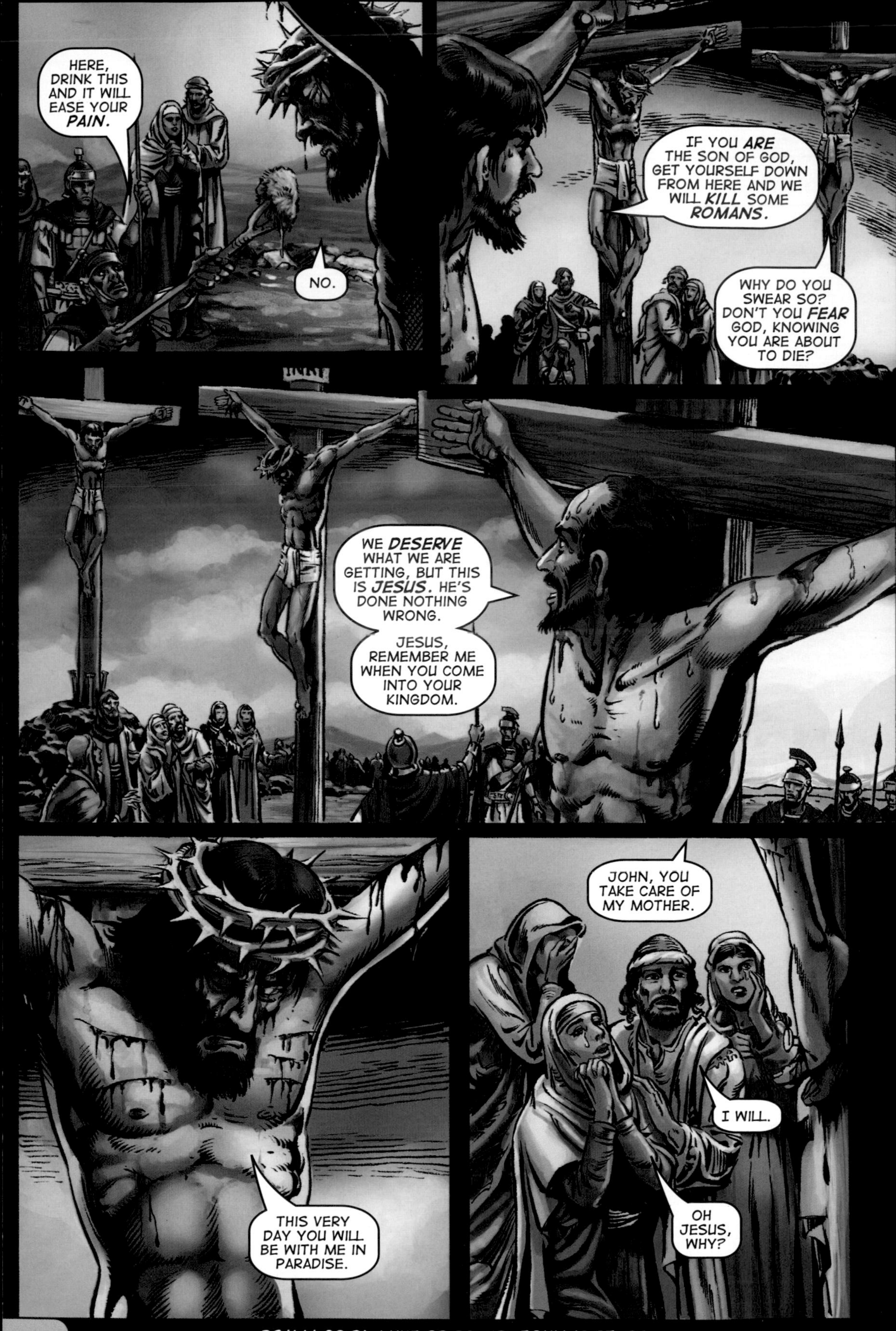
HERE, DRINK THIS AND IT WILL EASE YOUR PAIN.
NO.
IF YOU ARE THE SON OF GOD, GET YOURSELF DOWN FROM HERE AND WE WILL KILL SOME ROMANS.
WHY DO YOU SWEAR SO? DON'T YOU FEAR GOD, KNOWING YOU ARE ABOUT TO DIE?
WE DESERVE WHAT WE ARE GETTING, BUT THIS IS JESUS. HE'S DONE NOTHING WRONG.
JESUS, REMEMBER ME WHEN YOU COME INTO YOUR KINGDOM.
THIS VERY DAY YOU WILL BE WITH ME IN PARADISE.
JOHN, YOU TAKE CARE OF MY MOTHER.
I WILL.
OH JESUS, WHY?

PSALM 69:21; LUKE 23:36-43; JOHN 19:25-27

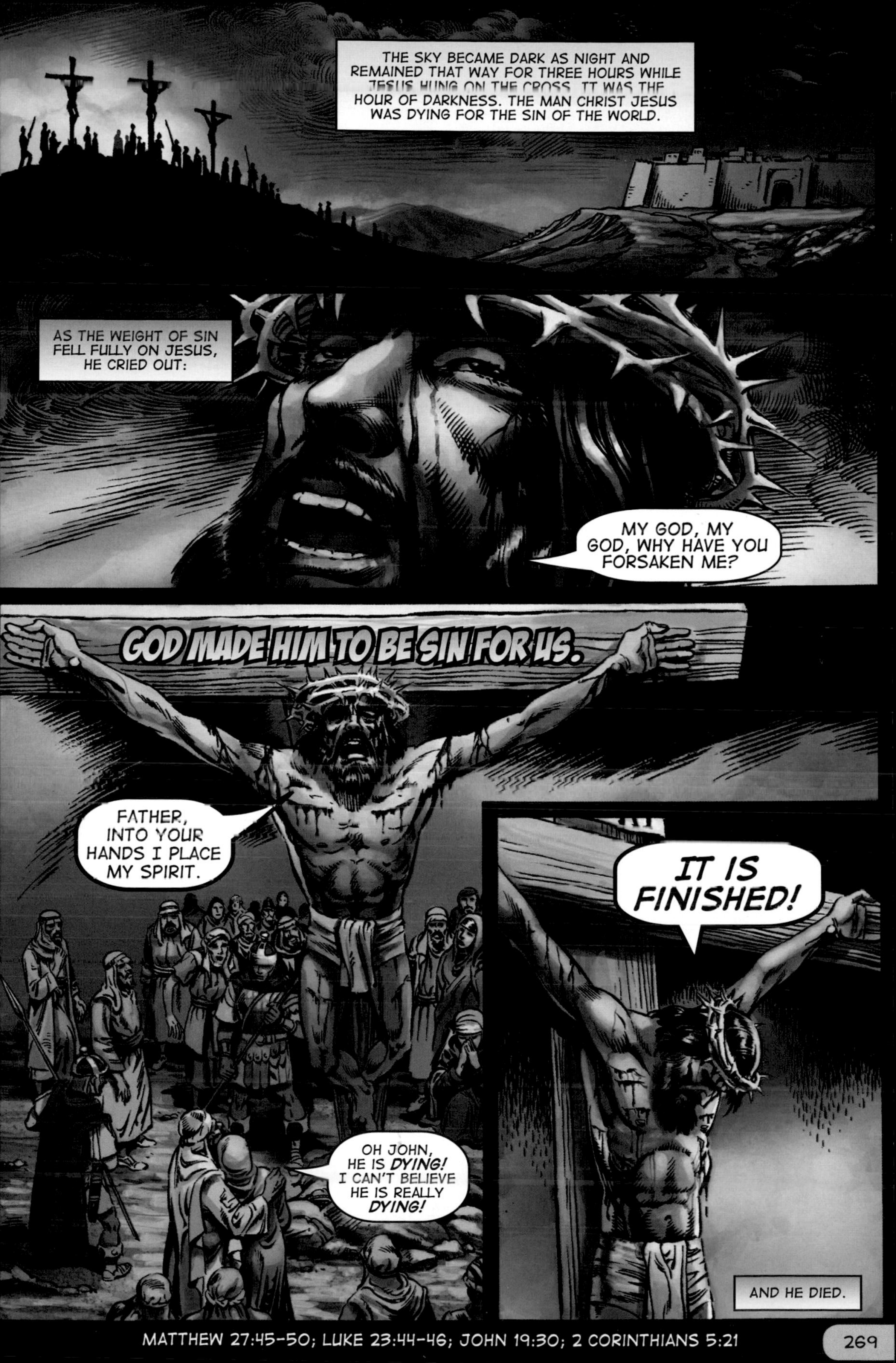
THE SKY BECAME DARK AS NIGHT AND REMAINED THAT WAY FOR THREE HOURS WHILE JESUS HUNG ON THE CROSS. IT WAS THE HOUR OF DARKNESS. THE MAN CHRIST JESUS WAS DYING FOR THE SIN OF THE WORLD.
AS THE WEIGHT OF SIN FELL FULLY ON JESUS, HE CRIED OUT:
MY GOD, MY GOD, WHY HAVE YOU FORSAKEN ME?
GOD MADE HIM TO BE SIN FOR US.
FATHER, INTO YOUR HANDS I PLACE MY SPIRIT.
OH JOHN, HE IS *DYING!* I CAN'T BELIEVE HE IS REALLY *DYING!*
IT IS FINISHED!
AND HE DIED.

MATTHEW 27:45-50; LUKE 23:44-46; JOHN 19:30; 2 CORINTHIANS 5:21

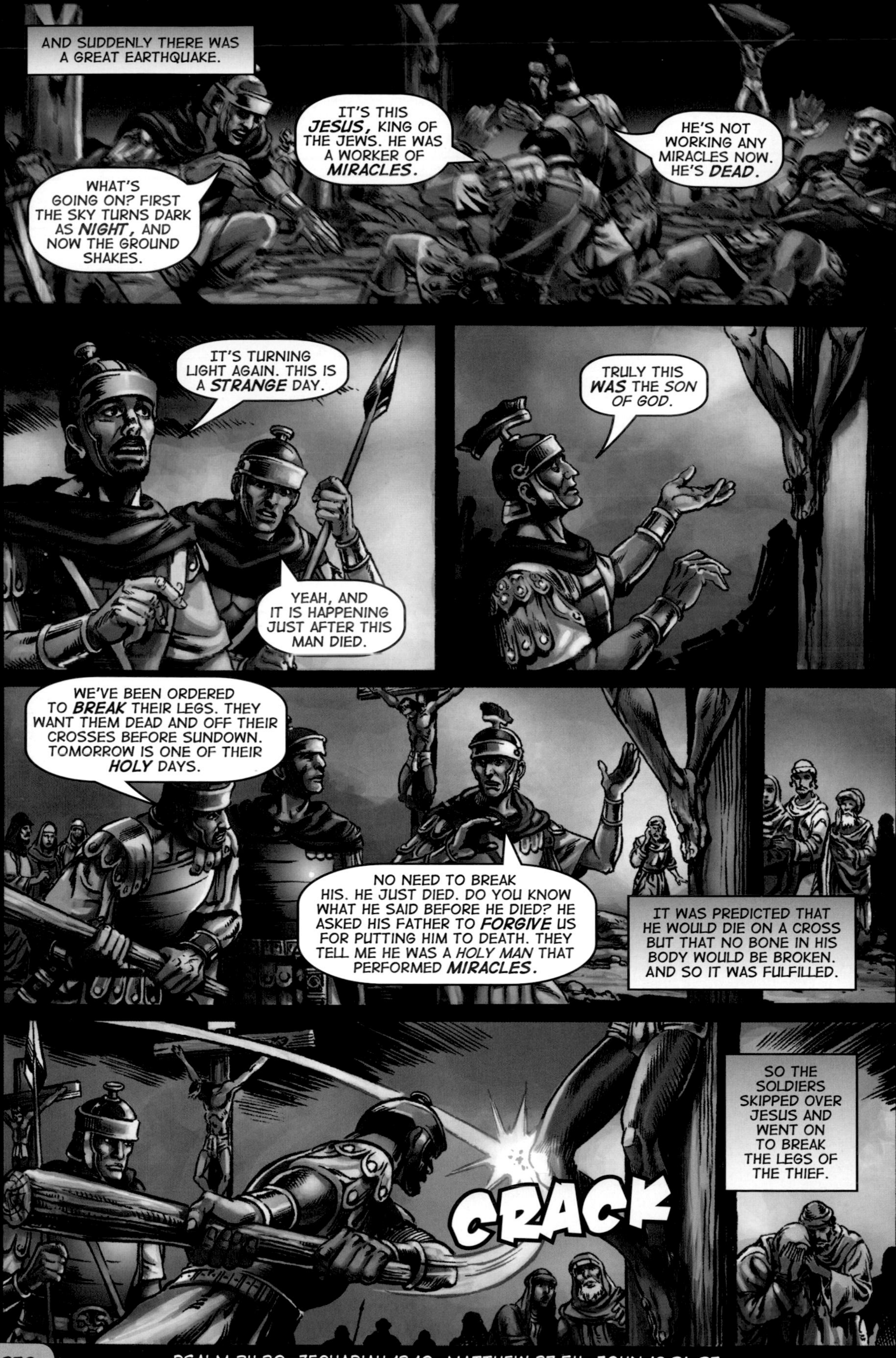
AND SUDDENLY THERE WAS A GREAT EARTHQUAKE.
WHAT'S GOING ON? FIRST THE SKY TURNS DARK AS NIGHT, AND NOW THE GROUND SHAKES.
IT'S THIS JESUS, KING OF THE JEWS. HE WAS A WORKER OF MIRACLES.
HE'S NOT WORKING ANY MIRACLES NOW. HE'S DEAD.
IT'S TURNING LIGHT AGAIN. THIS IS A STRANGE DAY.
YEAH, AND IT IS HAPPENING JUST AFTER THIS MAN DIED.
TRULY THIS WAS THE SON OF GOD.
WE'VE BEEN ORDERED TO BREAK THEIR LEGS. THEY WANT THEM DEAD AND OFF THEIR CROSSES BEFORE SUNDOWN. TOMORROW IS ONE OF THEIR HOLY DAYS.
NO NEED TO BREAK HIS. HE JUST DIED. DO YOU KNOW WHAT HE SAID BEFORE HE DIED? HE ASKED HIS FATHER TO FORGIVE US FOR PUTTING HIM TO DEATH. THEY TELL ME HE WAS A HOLY MAN THAT PERFORMED MIRACLES.
IT WAS PREDICTED THAT HE WOULD DIE ON A CROSS BUT THAT NO BONE IN HIS BODY WOULD BE BROKEN. AND SO IT WAS FULFILLED.
SO THE SOLDIERS SKIPPED OVER JESUS AND WENT ON TO BREAK THE LEGS OF THE THIEF.
CRACK

PSALM 34:20; ZECHARIAH 12:10; MATTHEW 27:54; JOHN 19:31–37

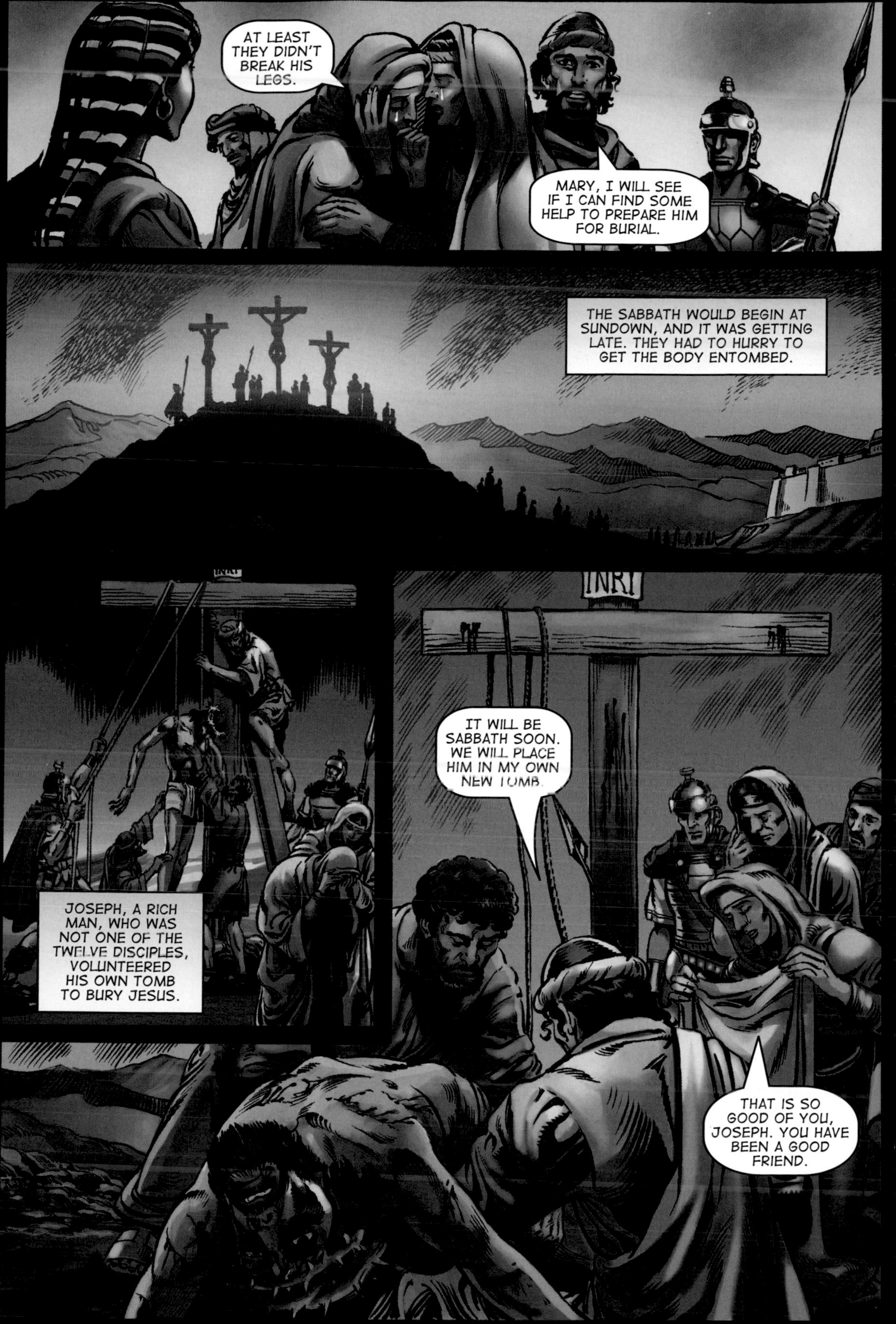
AT LEAST THEY DIDN'T BREAK HIS LEGS.
MARY, I WILL SEE IF I CAN FIND SOME HELP TO PREPARE HIM FOR BURIAL.
THE SABBATH WOULD BEGIN AT SUNDOWN, AND IT WAS GETTING LATE. THEY HAD TO HURRY TO GET THE BODY ENTOMBED.
INRI
JOSEPH, A RICH MAN, WHO WAS NOT ONE OF THE TWELVE DISCIPLES, VOLUNTEERED HIS OWN TOMB TO BURY JESUS.
IT WILL BE SABBATH SOON. WE WILL PLACE HIM IN MY OWN NEW TOMB.
THAT IS SO GOOD OF YOU, JOSEPH. YOU HAVE BEEN A GOOD FRIEND.

JOHN 19:31, 38

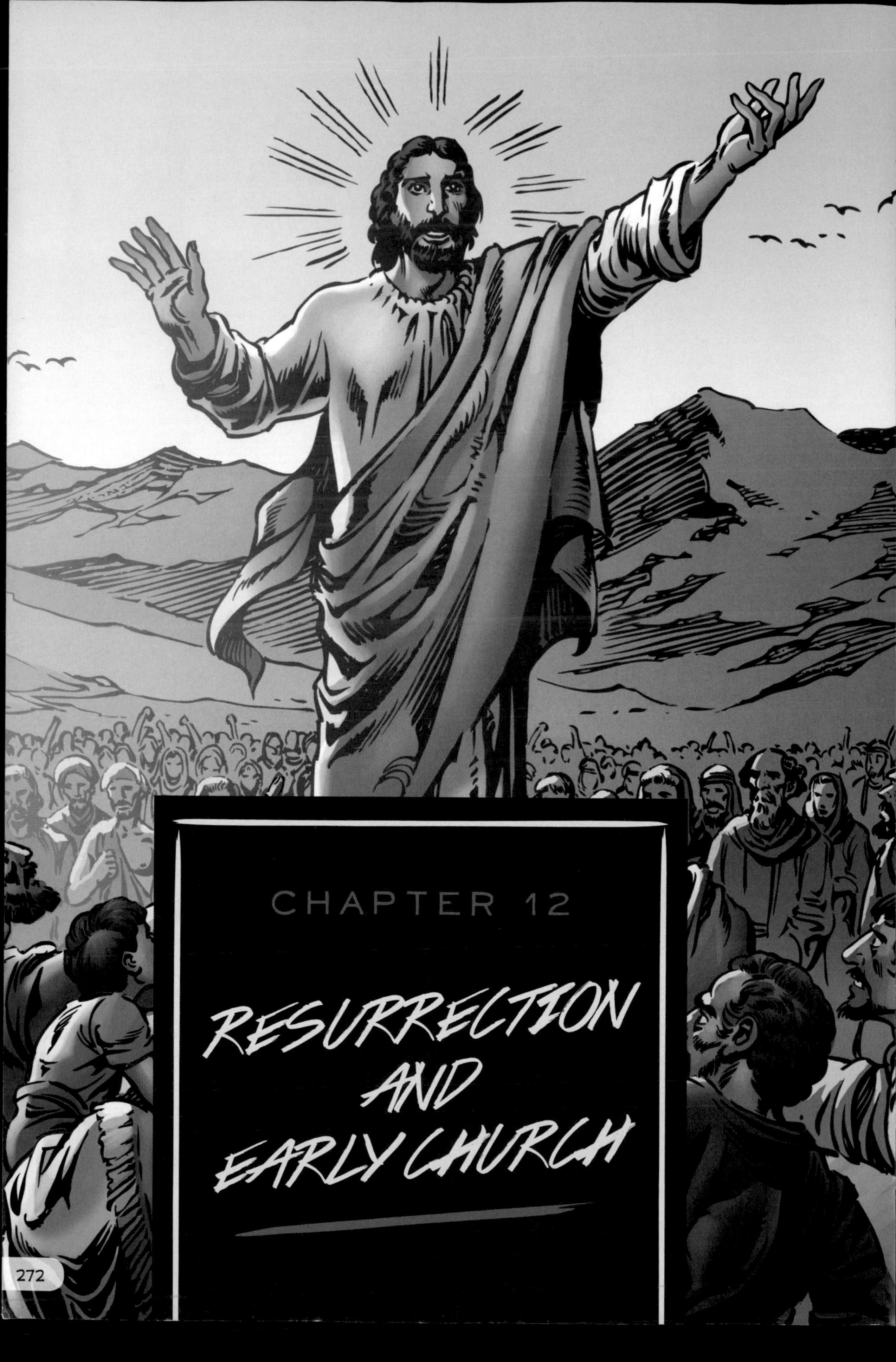

CHAPTER 12

RESURRECTION AND EARLY CHURCH

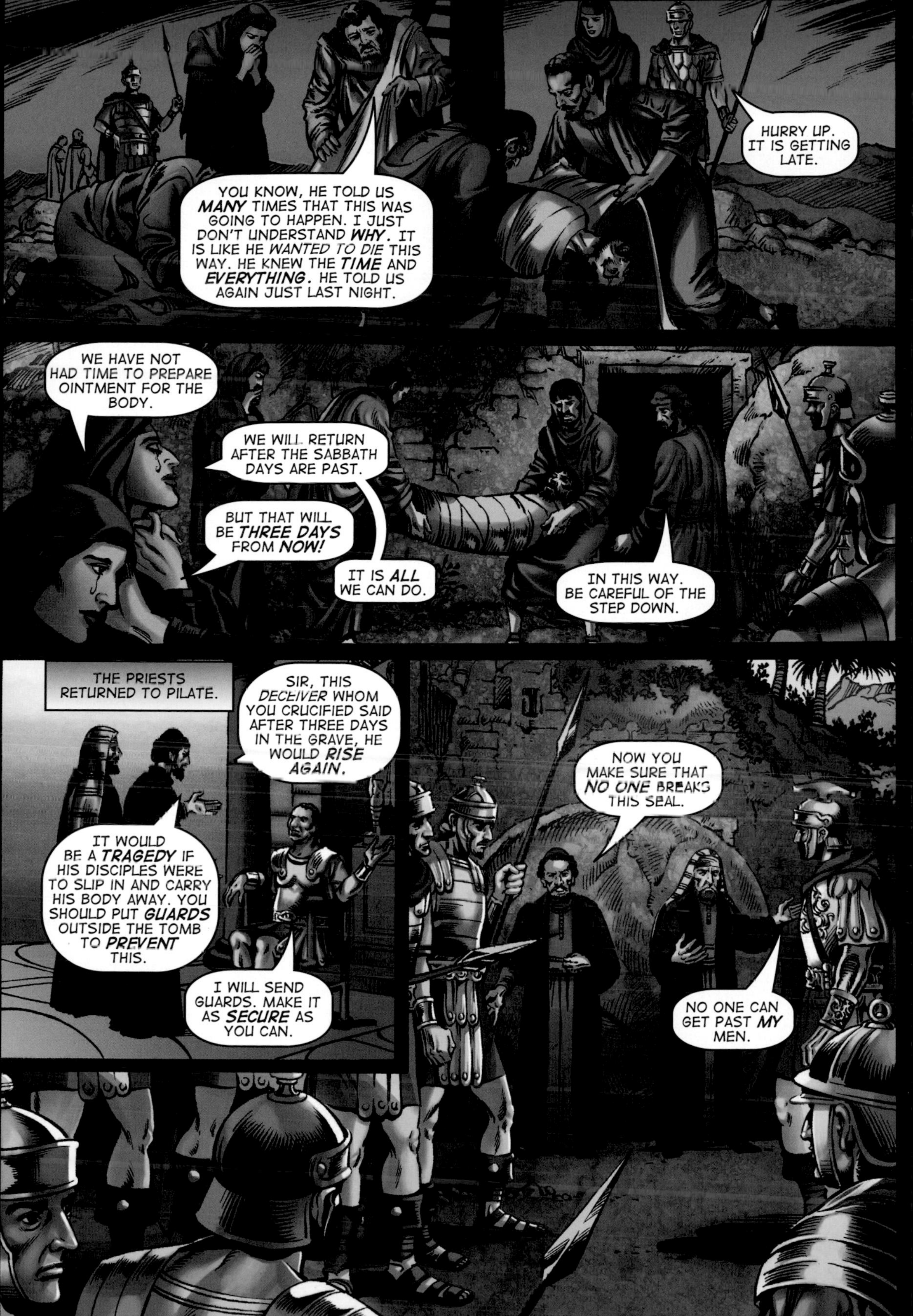
YOU KNOW, HE TOLD US MANY TIMES THAT THIS WAS GOING TO HAPPEN. I JUST DON'T UNDERSTAND WHY. IT IS LIKE HE WANTED TO DIE THIS WAY. HE KNEW THE TIME AND EVERYTHING. HE TOLD US AGAIN JUST LAST NIGHT.
HURRY UP. IT IS GETTING LATE.
WE HAVE NOT HAD TIME TO PREPARE OINTMENT FOR THE BODY.
WE WILL RETURN AFTER THE SABBATH DAYS ARE PAST.
BUT THAT WILL BE THREE DAYS FROM NOW!
IT IS ALL WE CAN DO.
IN THIS WAY. BE CAREFUL OF THE STEP DOWN.
THE PRIESTS RETURNED TO PILATE.
SIR, THIS DECEIVER WHOM YOU CRUCIFIED SAID AFTER THREE DAYS IN THE GRAVE, HE WOULD RISE AGAIN.
IT WOULD BE A TRAGEDY IF HIS DISCIPLES WERE TO SLIP IN AND CARRY HIS BODY AWAY. YOU SHOULD PUT GUARDS OUTSIDE THE TOMB TO PREVENT THIS.
I WILL SEND GUARDS. MAKE IT AS SECURE AS YOU CAN.
NOW YOU MAKE SURE THAT NO ONE BREAKS THIS SEAL.
NO ONE CAN GET PAST MY MEN.

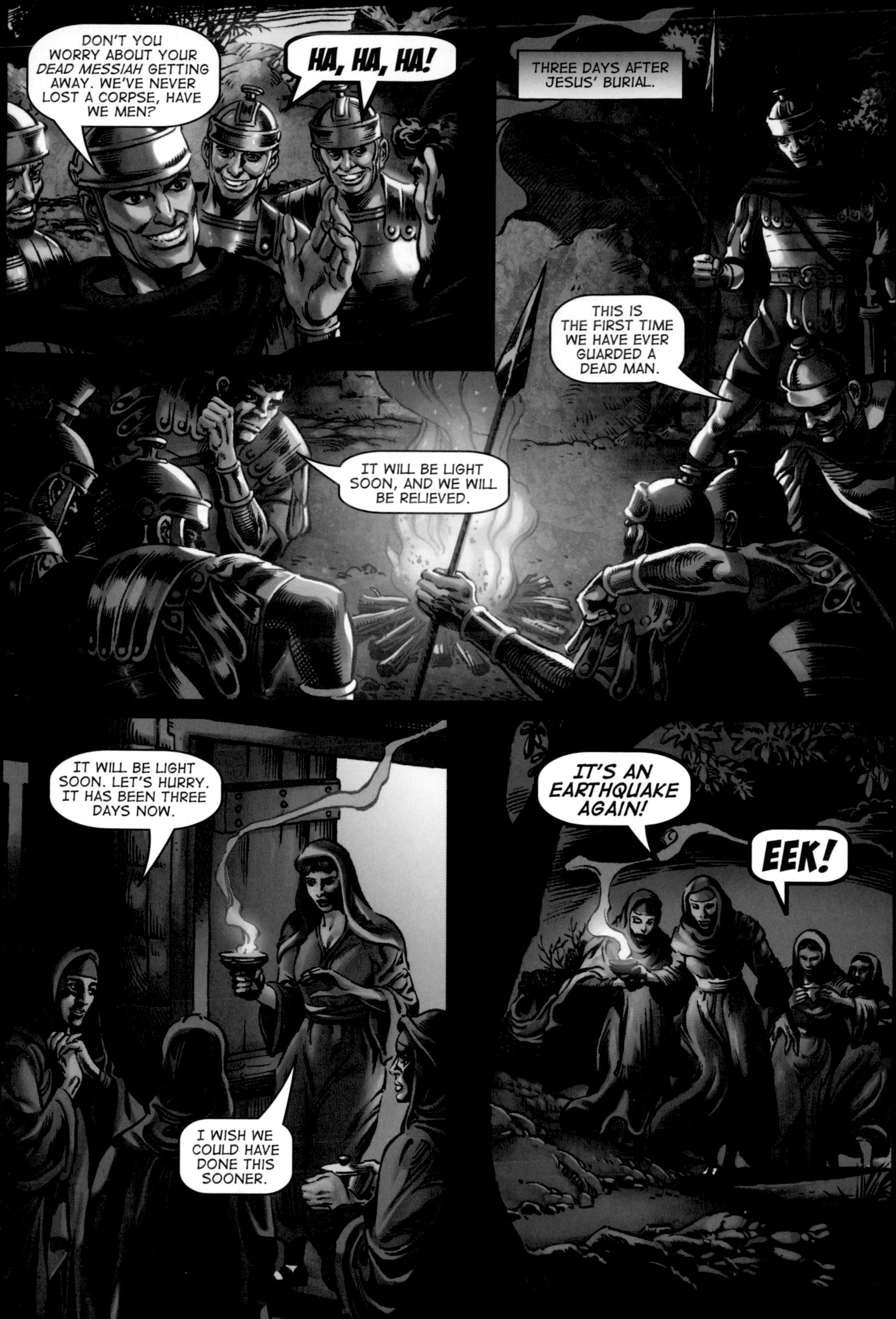
DON'T YOU WORRY ABOUT YOUR *DEAD MESSIAH* GETTING AWAY. WE'VE NEVER LOST A CORPSE, HAVE WE MEN?
HA, HA, HA!
THREE DAYS AFTER JESUS' BURIAL.
THIS IS THE FIRST TIME WE HAVE EVER GUARDED A DEAD MAN.
IT WILL BE LIGHT SOON, AND WE WILL BE RELIEVED.
IT WILL BE LIGHT SOON. LET'S HURRY. IT HAS BEEN THREE DAYS NOW.
I WISH WE COULD HAVE DONE THIS SOONER.
IT'S AN EARTHQUAKE AGAIN!
EEK!

MATTHEW 28:1–2; LUKE 24:1

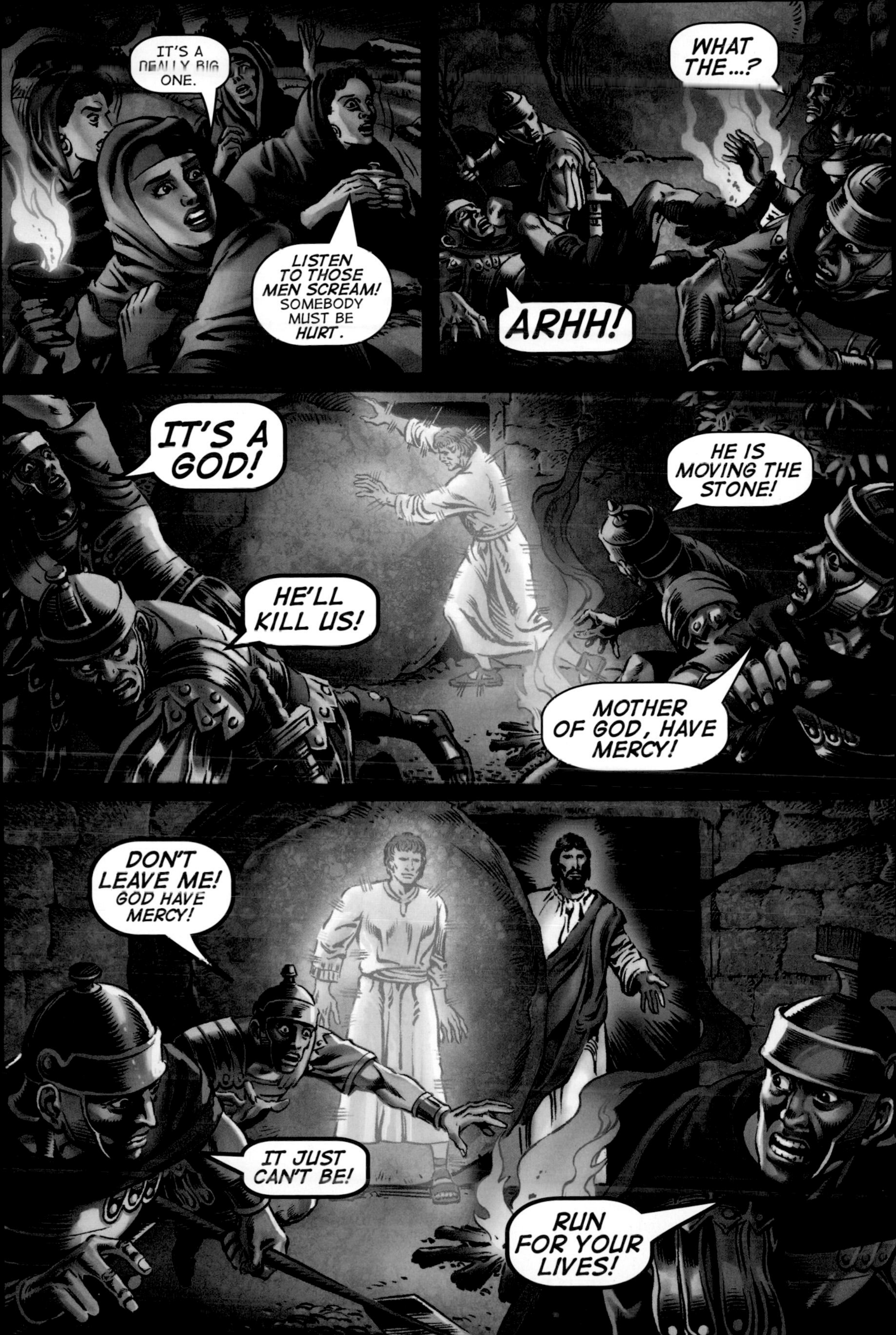
IT'S A REALLY BIG ONE.
LISTEN TO THOSE MEN SCREAM! SOMEBODY MUST BE HURT.
WHAT THE...?
ARHH!
IT'S A GOD!
HE IS MOVING THE STONE!
HE'LL KILL US!
MOTHER OF GOD, HAVE MERCY!
DON'T LEAVE ME! GOD HAVE MERCY!
IT JUST CAN'T BE!
RUN FOR YOUR LIVES!

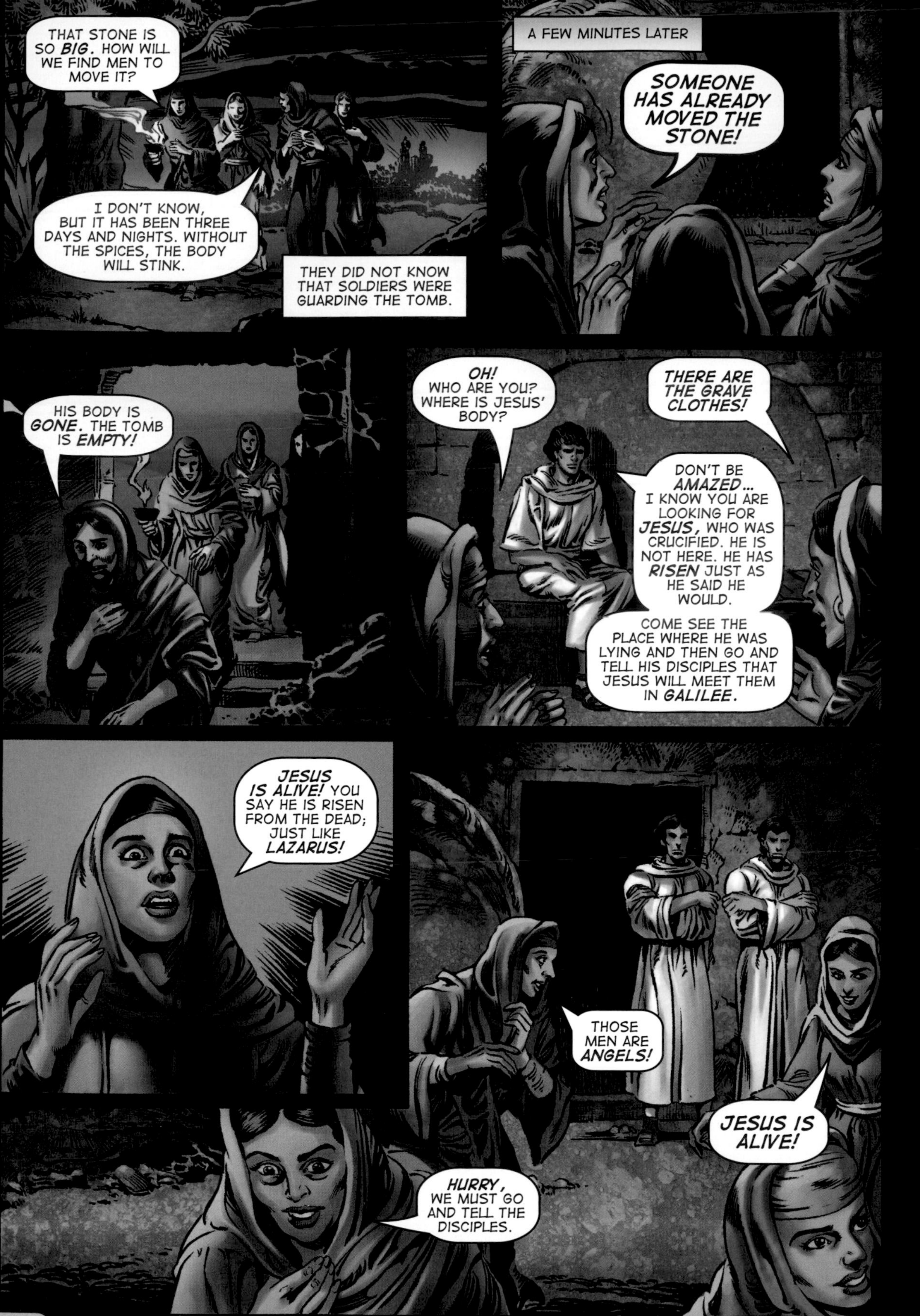
THAT STONE IS SO *BIG*. HOW WILL WE FIND MEN TO MOVE IT?
I DON'T KNOW, BUT IT HAS BEEN THREE DAYS AND NIGHTS. WITHOUT THE SPICES, THE BODY WILL STINK.
THEY DID NOT KNOW THAT SOLDIERS WERE GUARDING THE TOMB.
A FEW MINUTES LATER
SOMEONE HAS ALREADY MOVED THE STONE!
HIS BODY IS *GONE*. THE TOMB IS *EMPTY!*
OH! WHO ARE YOU? WHERE IS JESUS' BODY?
THERE ARE THE GRAVE CLOTHES!
DON'T BE *AMAZED*... I KNOW YOU ARE LOOKING FOR *JESUS*, WHO WAS CRUCIFIED. HE IS NOT HERE. HE HAS *RISEN* JUST AS HE SAID HE WOULD.
COME SEE THE PLACE WHERE HE WAS LYING AND THEN GO AND TELL HIS DISCIPLES THAT JESUS WILL MEET THEM IN *GALILEE*.
JESUS IS ALIVE! YOU SAY HE IS RISEN FROM THE DEAD; JUST LIKE *LAZARUS!*
THOSE MEN ARE *ANGELS!*
JESUS IS ALIVE!
HURRY, WE MUST GO AND TELL THE DISCIPLES.

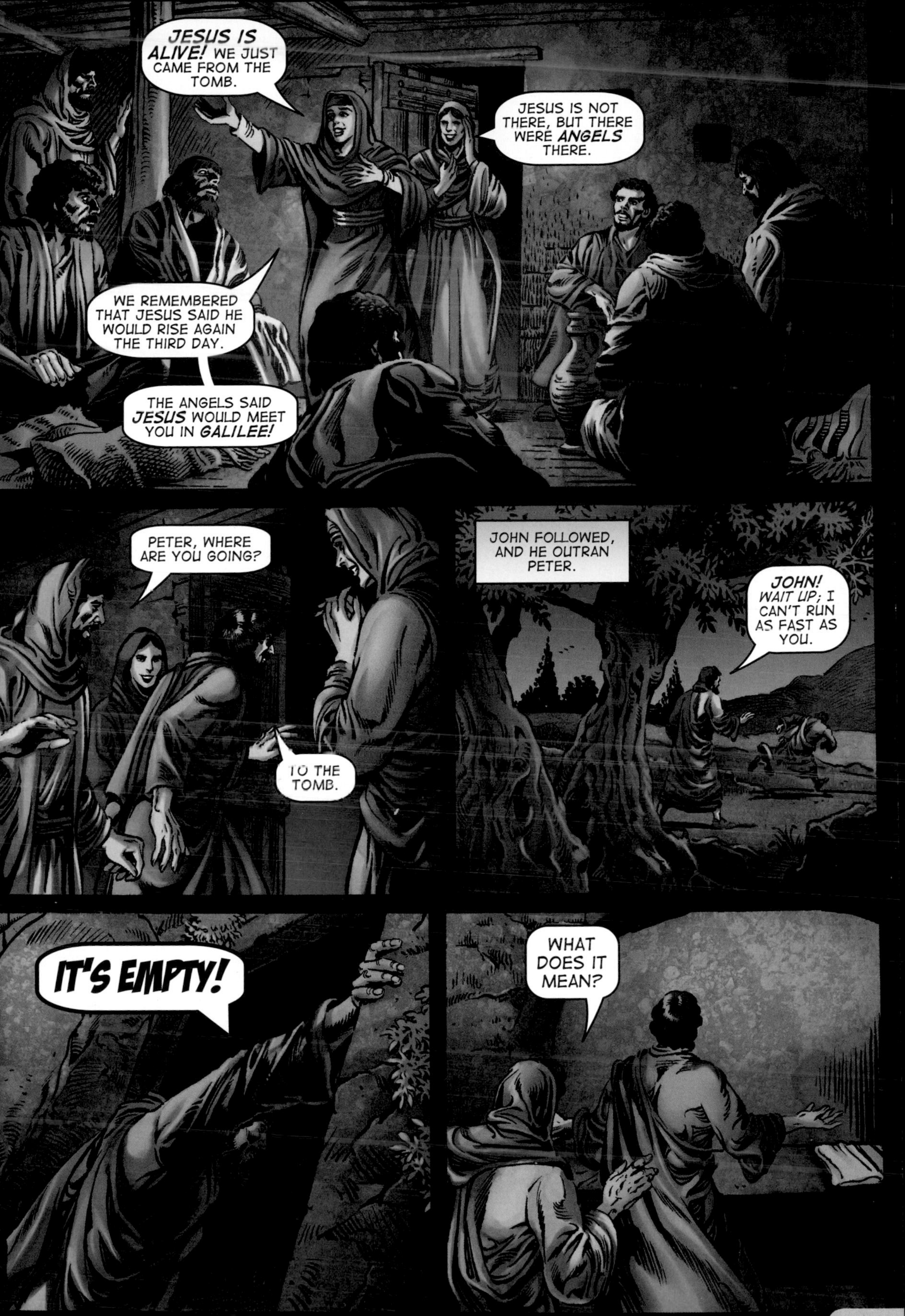
JESUS IS ALIVE! WE JUST CAME FROM THE TOMB.
JESUS IS NOT THERE, BUT THERE WERE ANGELS THERE.
WE REMEMBERED THAT JESUS SAID HE WOULD RISE AGAIN THE THIRD DAY.
THE ANGELS SAID JESUS WOULD MEET YOU IN GALILEE!
PETER, WHERE ARE YOU GOING?
TO THE TOMB.
JOHN FOLLOWED, AND HE OUTRAN PETER.
JOHN! WAIT UP; I CAN'T RUN AS FAST AS YOU.
IT'S EMPTY!
WHAT DOES IT MEAN?

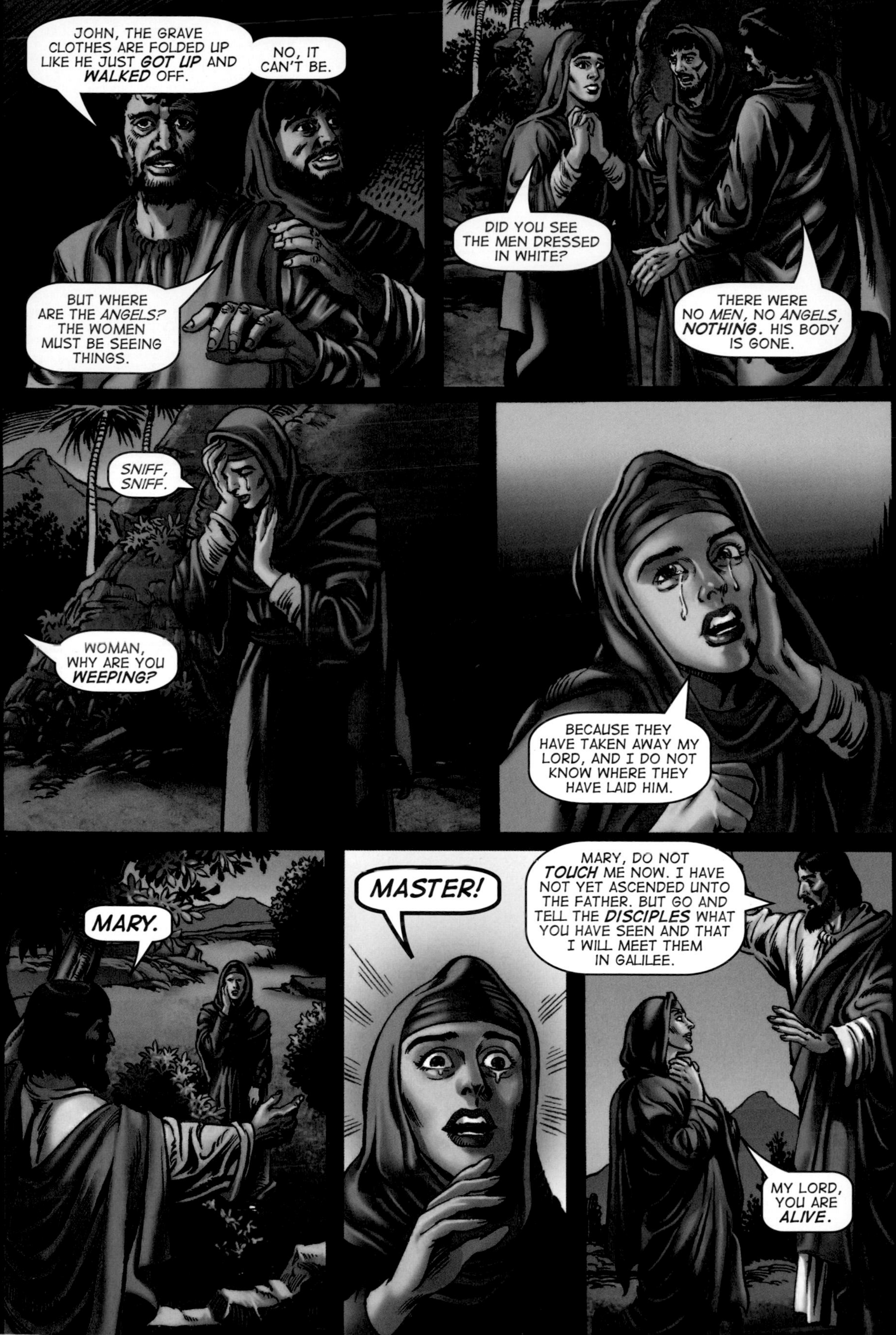
JOHN, THE GRAVE CLOTHES ARE FOLDED UP LIKE HE JUST GOT UP AND WALKED OFF.
NO, IT CAN'T BE.
BUT WHERE ARE THE ANGELS? THE WOMEN MUST BE SEEING THINGS.
DID YOU SEE THE MEN DRESSED IN WHITE?
THERE WERE NO MEN, NO ANGELS, NOTHING. HIS BODY IS GONE.
SNIFF, SNIFF.
WOMAN, WHY ARE YOU WEEPING?
BECAUSE THEY HAVE TAKEN AWAY MY LORD, AND I DO NOT KNOW WHERE THEY HAVE LAID HIM.
MARY.
MASTER!
MARY, DO NOT TOUCH ME NOW. I HAVE NOT YET ASCENDED UNTO THE FATHER. BUT GO AND TELL THE DISCIPLES WHAT YOU HAVE SEEN AND THAT I WILL MEET THEM IN GALILEE.
MY LORD, YOU ARE ALIVE.

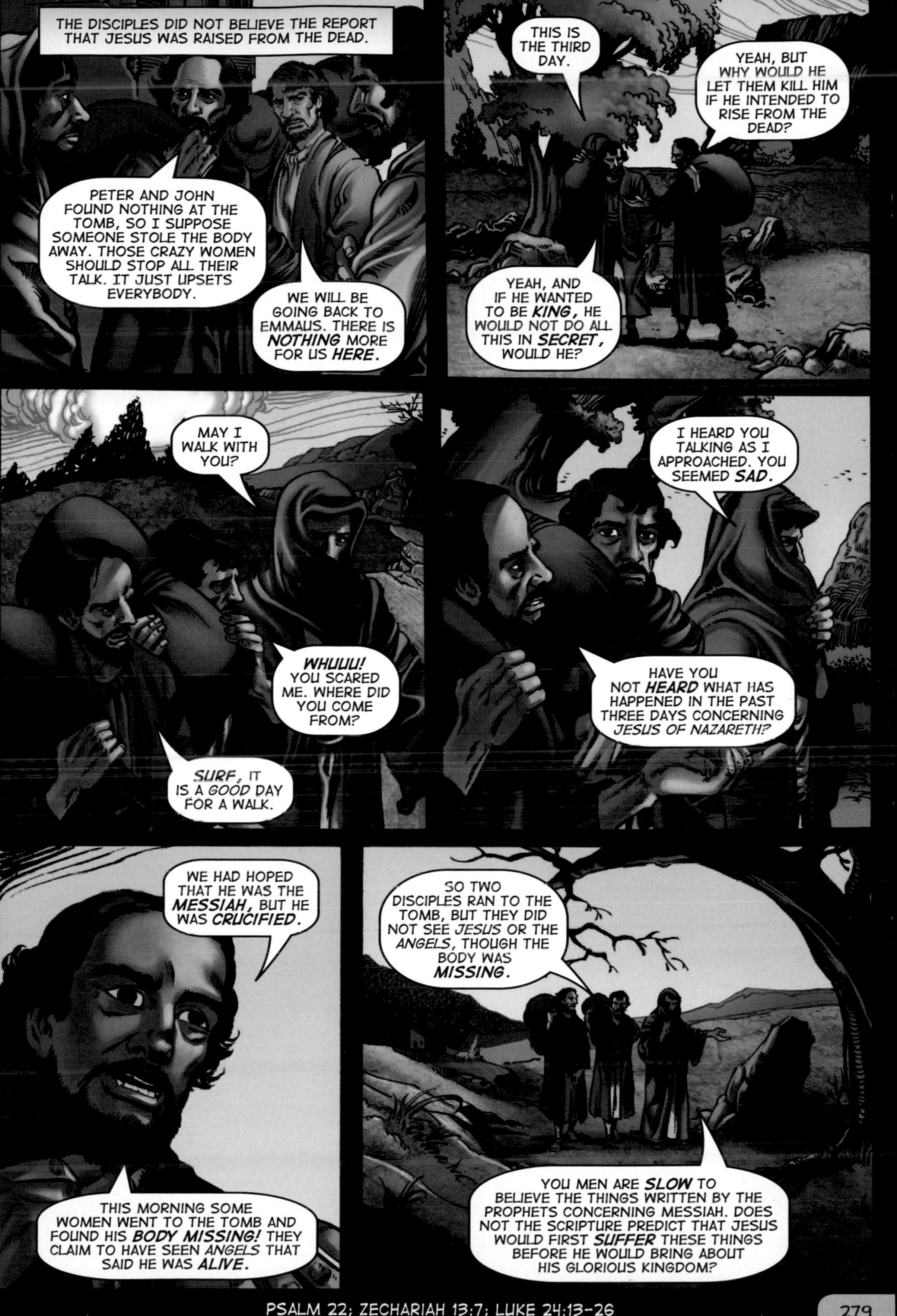
THE DISCIPLES DID NOT BELIEVE THE REPORT THAT JESUS WAS RAISED FROM THE DEAD.
PETER AND JOHN FOUND NOTHING AT THE TOMB, SO I SUPPOSE SOMEONE STOLE THE BODY AWAY. THOSE CRAZY WOMEN SHOULD STOP ALL THEIR TALK. IT JUST UPSETS EVERYBODY.
WE WILL BE GOING BACK TO EMMAUS. THERE IS NOTHING MORE FOR US HERE.
THIS IS THE THIRD DAY.
YEAH, BUT WHY WOULD HE LET THEM KILL HIM IF HE INTENDED TO RISE FROM THE DEAD?
YEAH, AND IF HE WANTED TO BE KING, HE WOULD NOT DO ALL THIS IN SECRET, WOULD HE?
MAY I WALK WITH YOU?
WHUUU! YOU SCARED ME. WHERE DID YOU COME FROM?
SURE, IT IS A GOOD DAY FOR A WALK.
I HEARD YOU TALKING AS I APPROACHED. YOU SEEMED SAD.
HAVE YOU NOT HEARD WHAT HAS HAPPENED IN THE PAST THREE DAYS CONCERNING JESUS OF NAZARETH?
WE HAD HOPED THAT HE WAS THE MESSIAH, BUT HE WAS CRUCIFIED.
THIS MORNING SOME WOMEN WENT TO THE TOMB AND FOUND HIS BODY MISSING! THEY CLAIM TO HAVE SEEN ANGELS THAT SAID HE WAS ALIVE.
SO TWO DISCIPLES RAN TO THE TOMB, BUT THEY DID NOT SEE JESUS OR THE ANGELS, THOUGH THE BODY WAS MISSING.
YOU MEN ARE SLOW TO BELIEVE THE THINGS WRITTEN BY THE PROPHETS CONCERNING MESSIAH. DOES NOT THE SCRIPTURE PREDICT THAT JESUS WOULD FIRST SUFFER THESE THINGS BEFORE HE WOULD BRING ABOUT HIS GLORIOUS KINGDOM?

PSALM 22; ZECHARIAH 13:7; LUKE 24:13–26

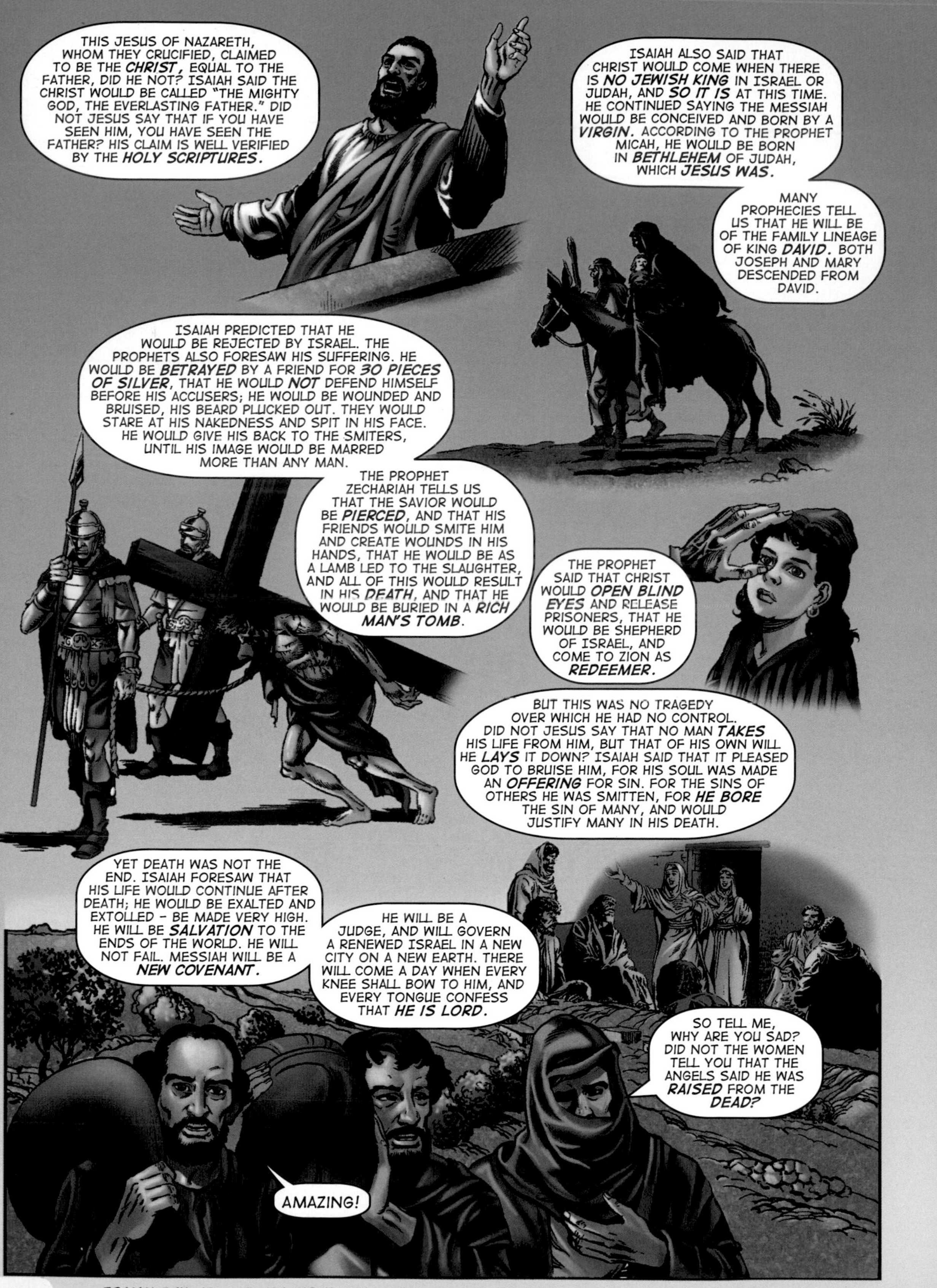
THIS JESUS OF NAZARETH, WHOM THEY CRUCIFIED, CLAIMED TO BE THE CHRIST, EQUAL TO THE FATHER, DID HE NOT? ISAIAH SAID THE CHRIST WOULD BE CALLED "THE MIGHTY GOD, THE EVERLASTING FATHER." DID NOT JESUS SAY THAT IF YOU HAVE SEEN HIM, YOU HAVE SEEN THE FATHER? HIS CLAIM IS WELL VERIFIED BY THE HOLY SCRIPTURES.
ISAIAH ALSO SAID THAT CHRIST WOULD COME WHEN THERE IS NO JEWISH KING IN ISRAEL OR JUDAH, AND SO IT IS AT THIS TIME. HE CONTINUED SAYING THE MESSIAH WOULD BE CONCEIVED AND BORN BY A VIRGIN. ACCORDING TO THE PROPHET MICAH, HE WOULD BE BORN IN BETHLEHEM OF JUDAH, WHICH JESUS WAS.
MANY PROPHECIES TELL US THAT HE WILL BE OF THE FAMILY LINEAGE OF KING DAVID. BOTH JOSEPH AND MARY DESCENDED FROM DAVID.
ISAIAH PREDICTED THAT HE WOULD BE REJECTED BY ISRAEL. THE PROPHETS ALSO FORESAW HIS SUFFERING. HE WOULD BE BETRAYED BY A FRIEND FOR 30 PIECES OF SILVER, THAT HE WOULD NOT DEFEND HIMSELF BEFORE HIS ACCUSERS; HE WOULD BE WOUNDED AND BRUISED, HIS BEARD PLUCKED OUT. THEY WOULD STARE AT HIS NAKEDNESS AND SPIT IN HIS FACE. HE WOULD GIVE HIS BACK TO THE SMITERS, UNTIL HIS IMAGE WOULD BE MARRED MORE THAN ANY MAN.
THE PROPHET ZECHARIAH TELLS US THAT THE SAVIOR WOULD BE PIERCED, AND THAT HIS FRIENDS WOULD SMITE HIM AND CREATE WOUNDS IN HIS HANDS, THAT HE WOULD BE AS A LAMB LED TO THE SLAUGHTER, AND ALL OF THIS WOULD RESULT IN HIS DEATH, AND THAT HE WOULD BE BURIED IN A RICH MAN'S TOMB.
THE PROPHET SAID THAT CHRIST WOULD OPEN BLIND EYES AND RELEASE PRISONERS, THAT HE WOULD BE SHEPHERD OF ISRAEL, AND COME TO ZION AS REDEEMER.
BUT THIS WAS NO TRAGEDY OVER WHICH HE HAD NO CONTROL. DID NOT JESUS SAY THAT NO MAN TAKES HIS LIFE FROM HIM, BUT THAT OF HIS OWN WILL HE LAYS IT DOWN? ISAIAH SAID THAT IT PLEASED GOD TO BRUISE HIM, FOR HIS SOUL WAS MADE AN OFFERING FOR SIN. FOR THE SINS OF OTHERS HE WAS SMITTEN, FOR HE BORE THE SIN OF MANY, AND WOULD JUSTIFY MANY IN HIS DEATH.
YET DEATH WAS NOT THE END. ISAIAH FORESAW THAT HIS LIFE WOULD CONTINUE AFTER DEATH; HE WOULD BE EXALTED AND EXTOLLED - BE MADE VERY HIGH. HE WILL BE SALVATION TO THE ENDS OF THE WORLD. HE WILL NOT FAIL. MESSIAH WILL BE A NEW COVENANT.
HE WILL BE A JUDGE, AND WILL GOVERN A RENEWED ISRAEL IN A NEW CITY ON A NEW EARTH. THERE WILL COME A DAY WHEN EVERY KNEE SHALL BOW TO HIM, AND EVERY TONGUE CONFESS THAT HE IS LORD.
SO TELL ME, WHY ARE YOU SAD? DID NOT THE WOMEN TELL YOU THAT THE ANGELS SAID HE WAS RAISED FROM THE DEAD?
AMAZING!

ISAIAH 7:14, 16, 9:6, 11:1, 40:11, 42:7, 49:7, 53:1, 3, 59:20; MICAH 5:2; JEREMIAH 23:5-6; PSALM 11:1, 4, 22:15, 41:9, 42:4, 6-7, 45:23, 49:6-7, 50:6, 52:13-14, 53:1, 3, 5, 9-10, 12; ZECHARIAH 11:12-13, 12:10, 13:6-7, 50:6, 52:14, 53:5, 7, 9, 12; JOHN 10:18

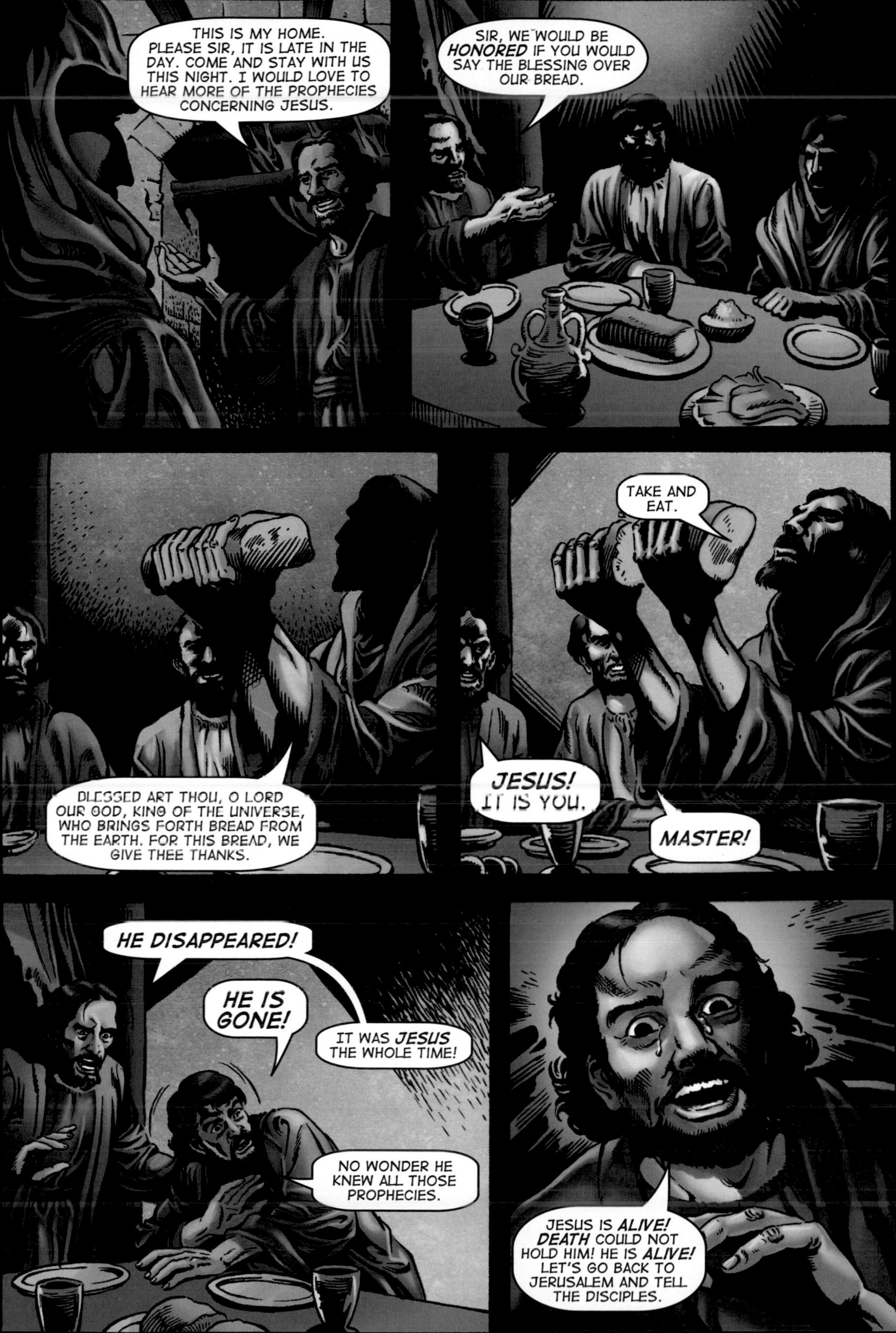
THIS IS MY HOME. PLEASE SIR, IT IS LATE IN THE DAY. COME AND STAY WITH US THIS NIGHT. I WOULD LOVE TO HEAR MORE OF THE PROPHECIES CONCERNING JESUS.
SIR, WE WOULD BE HONORED IF YOU WOULD SAY THE BLESSING OVER OUR BREAD.
BLESSED ART THOU, O LORD OUR GOD, KING OF THE UNIVERSE, WHO BRINGS FORTH BREAD FROM THE EARTH. FOR THIS BREAD, WE GIVE THEE THANKS.
TAKE AND EAT.
JESUS! IT IS YOU.
MASTER!
HE DISAPPEARED!
HE IS GONE!
IT WAS JESUS THE WHOLE TIME!
NO WONDER HE KNEW ALL THOSE PROPHECIES.
JESUS IS ALIVE! DEATH COULD NOT HOLD HIM! HE IS ALIVE! LET'S GO BACK TO JERUSALEM AND TELL THE DISCIPLES.

LUKE 24:28-32

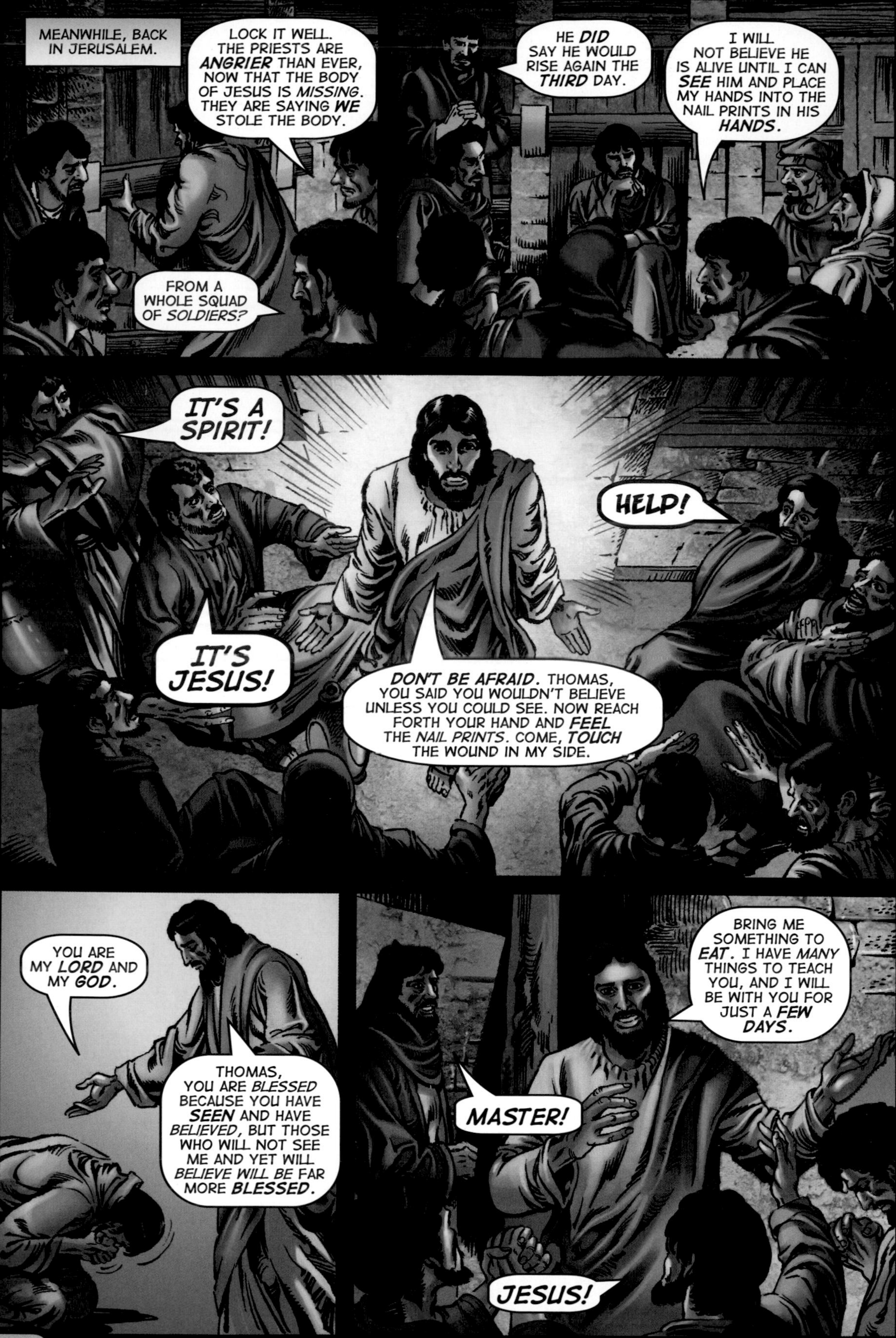

MEANWHILE, BACK IN JERUSALEM.
LOCK IT WELL. THE PRIESTS ARE ANGRIER THAN EVER, NOW THAT THE BODY OF JESUS IS MISSING. THEY ARE SAYING WE STOLE THE BODY.
FROM A WHOLE SQUAD OF SOLDIERS?
HE DID SAY HE WOULD RISE AGAIN THE THIRD DAY.
I WILL NOT BELIEVE HE IS ALIVE UNTIL I CAN SEE HIM AND PLACE MY HANDS INTO THE NAIL PRINTS IN HIS HANDS.
IT'S A SPIRIT!
HELP!
IT'S JESUS!
DON'T BE AFRAID. THOMAS, YOU SAID YOU WOULDN'T BELIEVE UNLESS YOU COULD SEE. NOW REACH FORTH YOUR HAND AND FEEL THE NAIL PRINTS. COME, TOUCH THE WOUND IN MY SIDE.
YOU ARE MY LORD AND MY GOD.
THOMAS, YOU ARE BLESSED BECAUSE YOU HAVE SEEN AND HAVE BELIEVED, BUT THOSE WHO WILL NOT SEE ME AND YET WILL BELIEVE WILL BE FAR MORE BLESSED.
BRING ME SOMETHING TO EAT. I HAVE MANY THINGS TO TEACH YOU, AND I WILL BE WITH YOU FOR JUST A FEW DAYS.
MASTER!
JESUS!

JOHN 20:26-31; LUKE 24:36-43

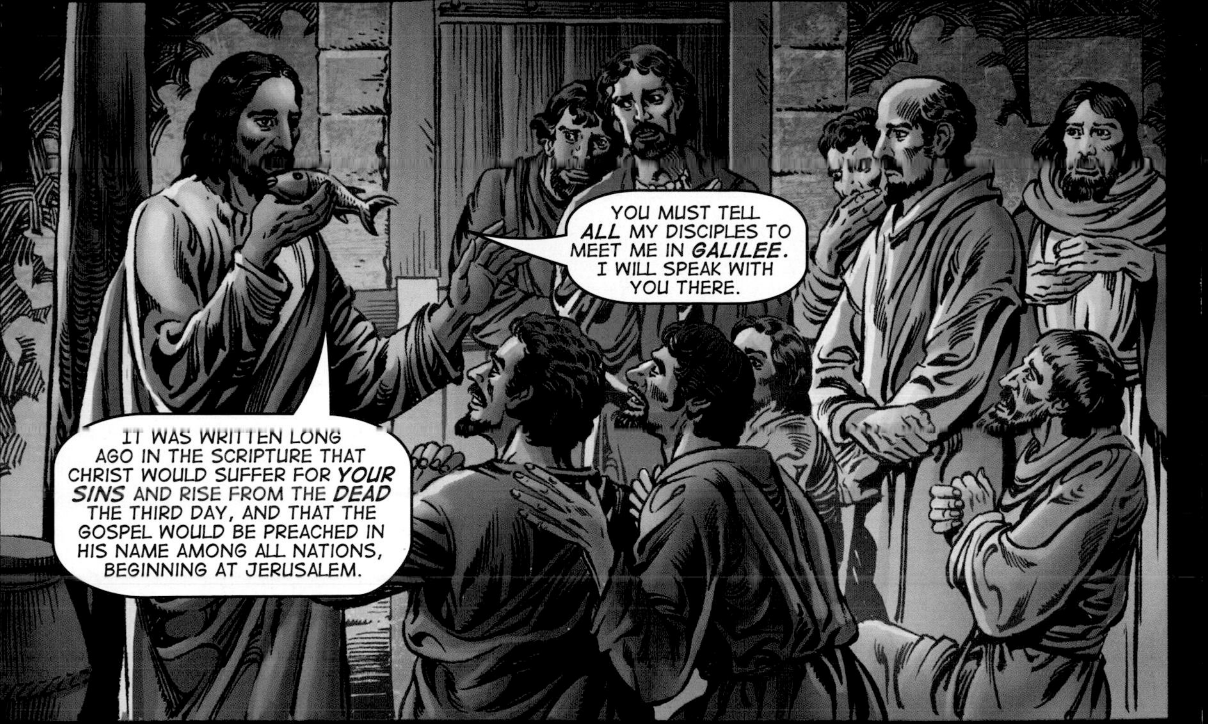
YOU MUST TELL ALL MY DISCIPLES TO MEET ME IN GALILEE. I WILL SPEAK WITH YOU THERE.
IT WAS WRITTEN LONG AGO IN THE SCRIPTURE THAT CHRIST WOULD SUFFER FOR YOUR SINS AND RISE FROM THE DEAD THE THIRD DAY, AND THAT THE GOSPEL WOULD BE PREACHED IN HIS NAME AMONG ALL NATIONS, BEGINNING AT JERUSALEM.

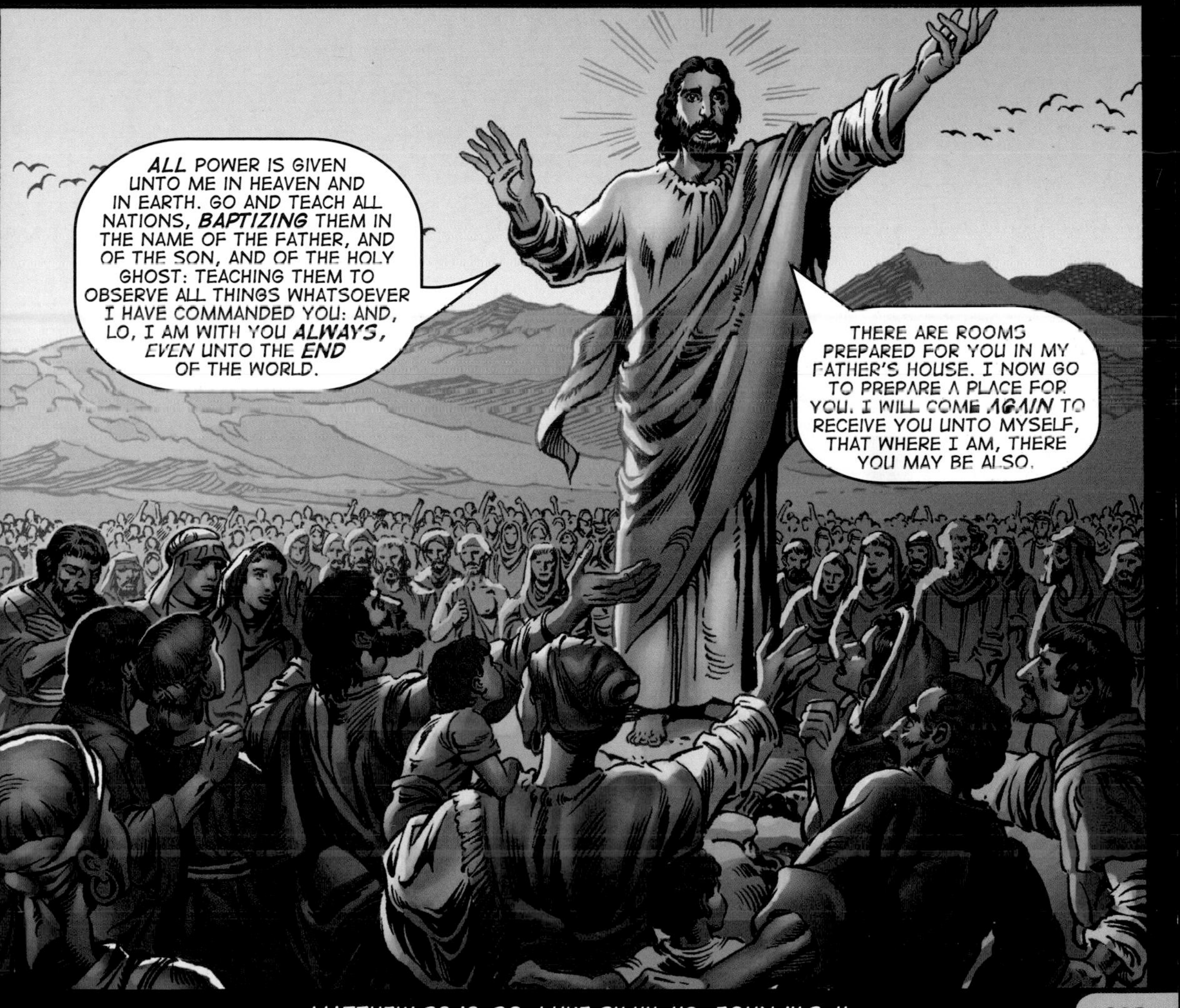
ALL POWER IS GIVEN UNTO ME IN HEAVEN AND IN EARTH. GO AND TEACH ALL NATIONS, BAPTIZING THEM IN THE NAME OF THE FATHER, AND OF THE SON, AND OF THE HOLY GHOST: TEACHING THEM TO OBSERVE ALL THINGS WHATSOEVER I HAVE COMMANDED YOU: AND, LO, I AM WITH YOU ALWAYS, EVEN UNTO THE END OF THE WORLD.
THERE ARE ROOMS PREPARED FOR YOU IN MY FATHER'S HOUSE. I NOW GO TO PREPARE A PLACE FOR YOU. I WILL COME AGAIN TO RECEIVE YOU UNTO MYSELF, THAT WHERE I AM, THERE YOU MAY BE ALSO.

MATTHEW 28:18-20; LUKE 24:44-49; JOHN 14:2-4

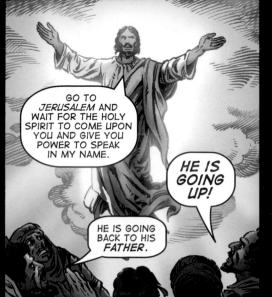

GO TO *JERUSALEM* AND WAIT FOR THE HOLY SPIRIT TO COME UPON YOU AND GIVE YOU POWER TO SPEAK IN MY NAME.

HE IS GOING UP!

HE IS GOING BACK TO HIS *FATHER*.

I AM WITH YOU ALWAYS, UNTO THE *END* OF THE *WORLD*.

HE IS GONE. HE *WENT BACK TO HEAVEN*.

WHY ARE YOU STILL LOOKING IN THE SKY?

WHAT? WHO IS THAT?

IT IS THE SAME TWO ANGELS I SAW AT THE TOMB.

SOMEDAY JESUS WILL COME BACK IN A CLOUD JUST AS YOU HAVE SEEN HIM GO.

HE HAS RETURNED TO HIS FATHER IN HEAVEN.

GO BACK TO JERUSALEM AND WAIT FOR THE SPIRIT.

LUKE 24:49-51; ACTS 1:7-11

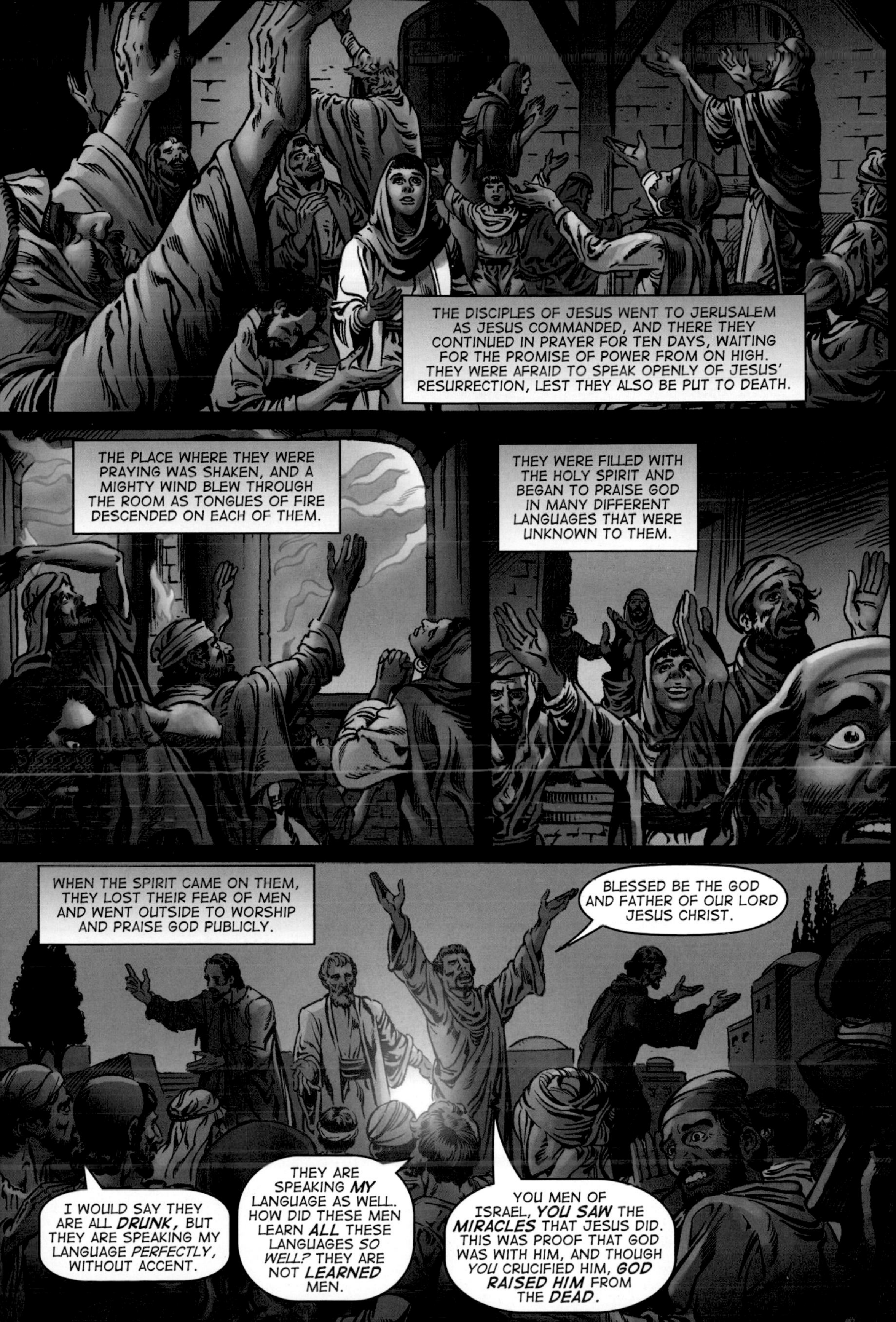
THE DISCIPLES OF JESUS WENT TO JERUSALEM AS JESUS COMMANDED, AND THERE THEY CONTINUED IN PRAYER FOR TEN DAYS, WAITING FOR THE PROMISE OF POWER FROM ON HIGH. THEY WERE AFRAID TO SPEAK OPENLY OF JESUS' RESURRECTION, LEST THEY ALSO BE PUT TO DEATH.
THE PLACE WHERE THEY WERE PRAYING WAS SHAKEN, AND A MIGHTY WIND BLEW THROUGH THE ROOM AS TONGUES OF FIRE DESCENDED ON EACH OF THEM.
THEY WERE FILLED WITH THE HOLY SPIRIT AND BEGAN TO PRAISE GOD IN MANY DIFFERENT LANGUAGES THAT WERE UNKNOWN TO THEM.
WHEN THE SPIRIT CAME ON THEM, THEY LOST THEIR FEAR OF MEN AND WENT OUTSIDE TO WORSHIP AND PRAISE GOD PUBLICLY.
BLESSED BE THE GOD AND FATHER OF OUR LORD JESUS CHRIST.
I WOULD SAY THEY ARE ALL ***DRUNK***, BUT THEY ARE SPEAKING MY LANGUAGE *PERFECTLY*, WITHOUT ACCENT.
THEY ARE SPEAKING ***MY*** LANGUAGE AS WELL. HOW DID THESE MEN LEARN ***ALL*** THESE LANGUAGES *SO WELL?* THEY ARE NOT ***LEARNED*** MEN.
YOU MEN OF ISRAEL, ***YOU SAW*** THE ***MIRACLES*** THAT JESUS DID. THIS WAS PROOF THAT GOD WAS WITH HIM, AND THOUGH *YOU* CRUCIFIED HIM, ***GOD RAISED HIM*** FROM THE ***DEAD***.

ACTS 1:12-14, 2:1-13, 32, 36

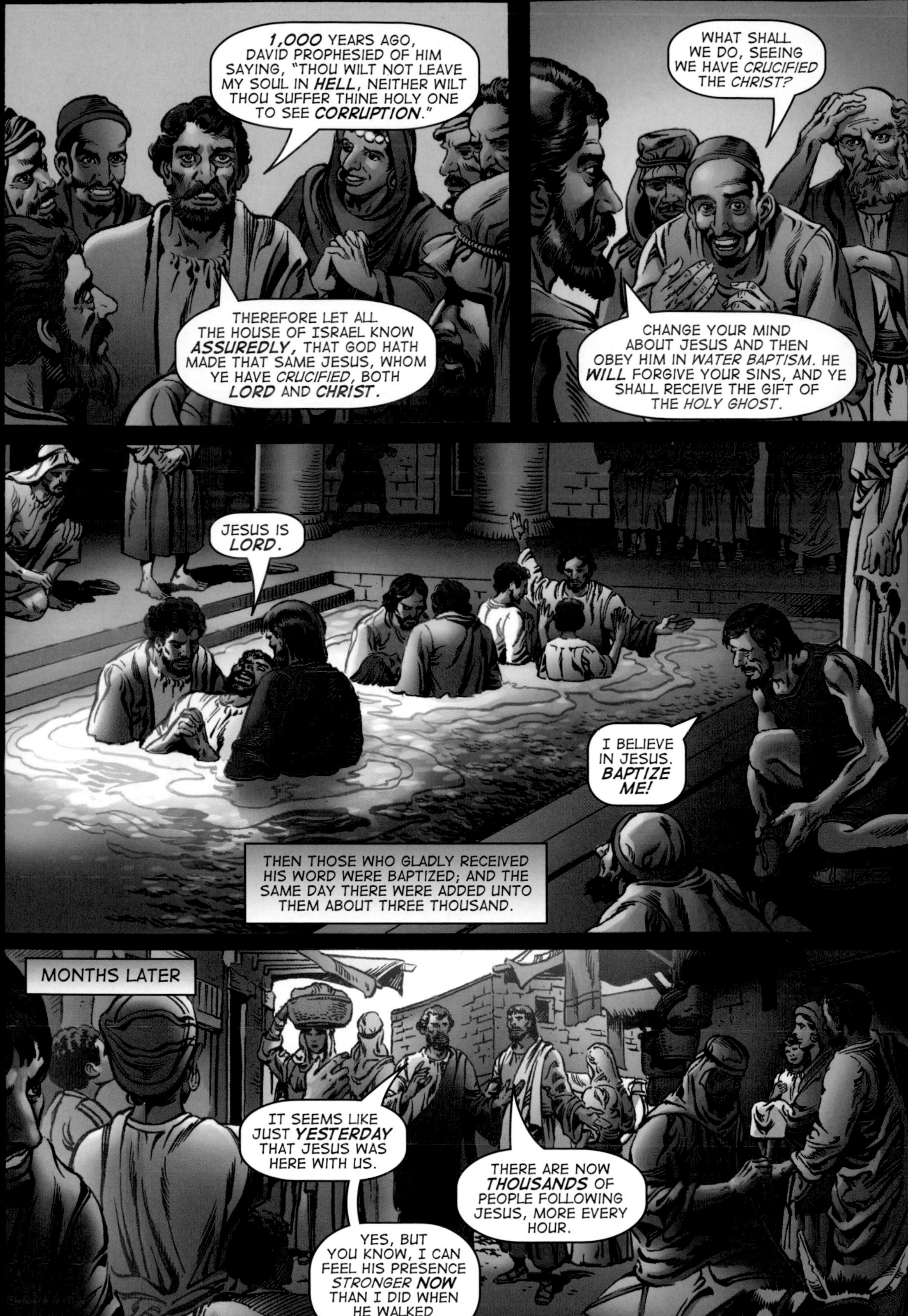
1,000 YEARS AGO, DAVID PROPHESIED OF HIM SAYING, "THOU WILT NOT LEAVE MY SOUL IN HELL, NEITHER WILT THOU SUFFER THINE HOLY ONE TO SEE CORRUPTION."
THEREFORE LET ALL THE HOUSE OF ISRAEL KNOW ASSUREDLY, THAT GOD HATH MADE THAT SAME JESUS, WHOM YE HAVE CRUCIFIED, BOTH LORD AND CHRIST.
WHAT SHALL WE DO, SEEING WE HAVE CRUCIFIED THE CHRIST?
CHANGE YOUR MIND ABOUT JESUS AND THEN OBEY HIM IN WATER BAPTISM. HE WILL FORGIVE YOUR SINS, AND YE SHALL RECEIVE THE GIFT OF THE HOLY GHOST.
JESUS IS LORD.
I BELIEVE IN JESUS. BAPTIZE ME!
THEN THOSE WHO GLADLY RECEIVED HIS WORD WERE BAPTIZED; AND THE SAME DAY THERE WERE ADDED UNTO THEM ABOUT THREE THOUSAND.
MONTHS LATER
IT SEEMS LIKE JUST YESTERDAY THAT JESUS WAS HERE WITH US.
YES, BUT YOU KNOW, I CAN FEEL HIS PRESENCE STRONGER NOW THAN I DID WHEN HE WALKED WITH US.
THERE ARE NOW THOUSANDS OF PEOPLE FOLLOWING JESUS, MORE EVERY HOUR.

PSALM 2, 16:2; ACTS 2:27, 37-41

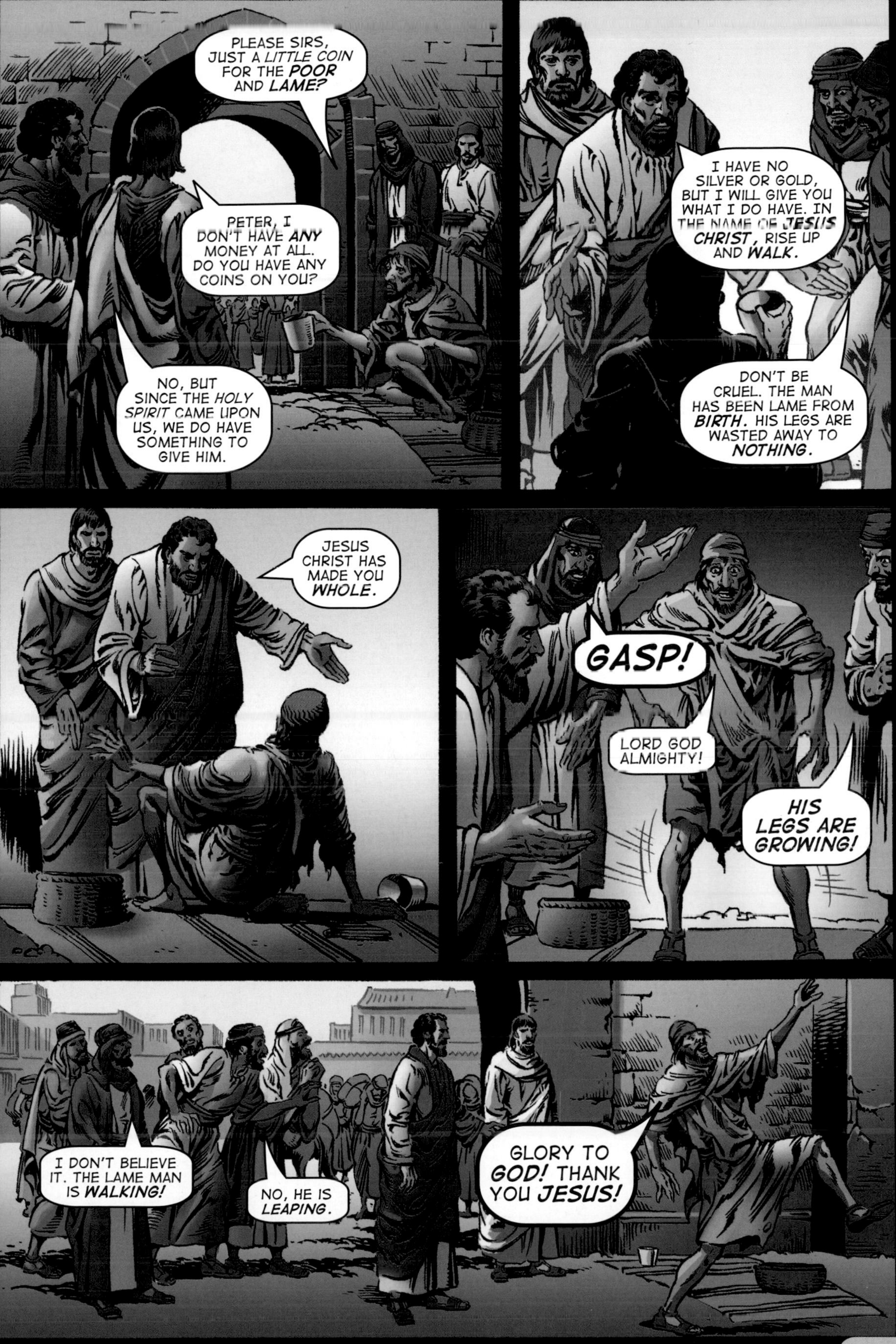
PLEASE SIRS, JUST A LITTLE COIN FOR THE POOR AND LAME?
PETER, I DON'T HAVE ANY MONEY AT ALL. DO YOU HAVE ANY COINS ON YOU?
NO, BUT SINCE THE HOLY SPIRIT CAME UPON US, WE DO HAVE SOMETHING TO GIVE HIM.
I HAVE NO SILVER OR GOLD, BUT I WILL GIVE YOU WHAT I DO HAVE. IN THE NAME OF JESUS CHRIST, RISE UP AND WALK.
DON'T BE CRUEL. THE MAN HAS BEEN LAME FROM BIRTH. HIS LEGS ARE WASTED AWAY TO NOTHING.
JESUS CHRIST HAS MADE YOU WHOLE.
GASP!
LORD GOD ALMIGHTY!
HIS LEGS ARE GROWING!
I DON'T BELIEVE IT. THE LAME MAN IS WALKING!
NO, HE IS LEAPING.
GLORY TO GOD! THANK YOU JESUS!

ACTS 3:1–11

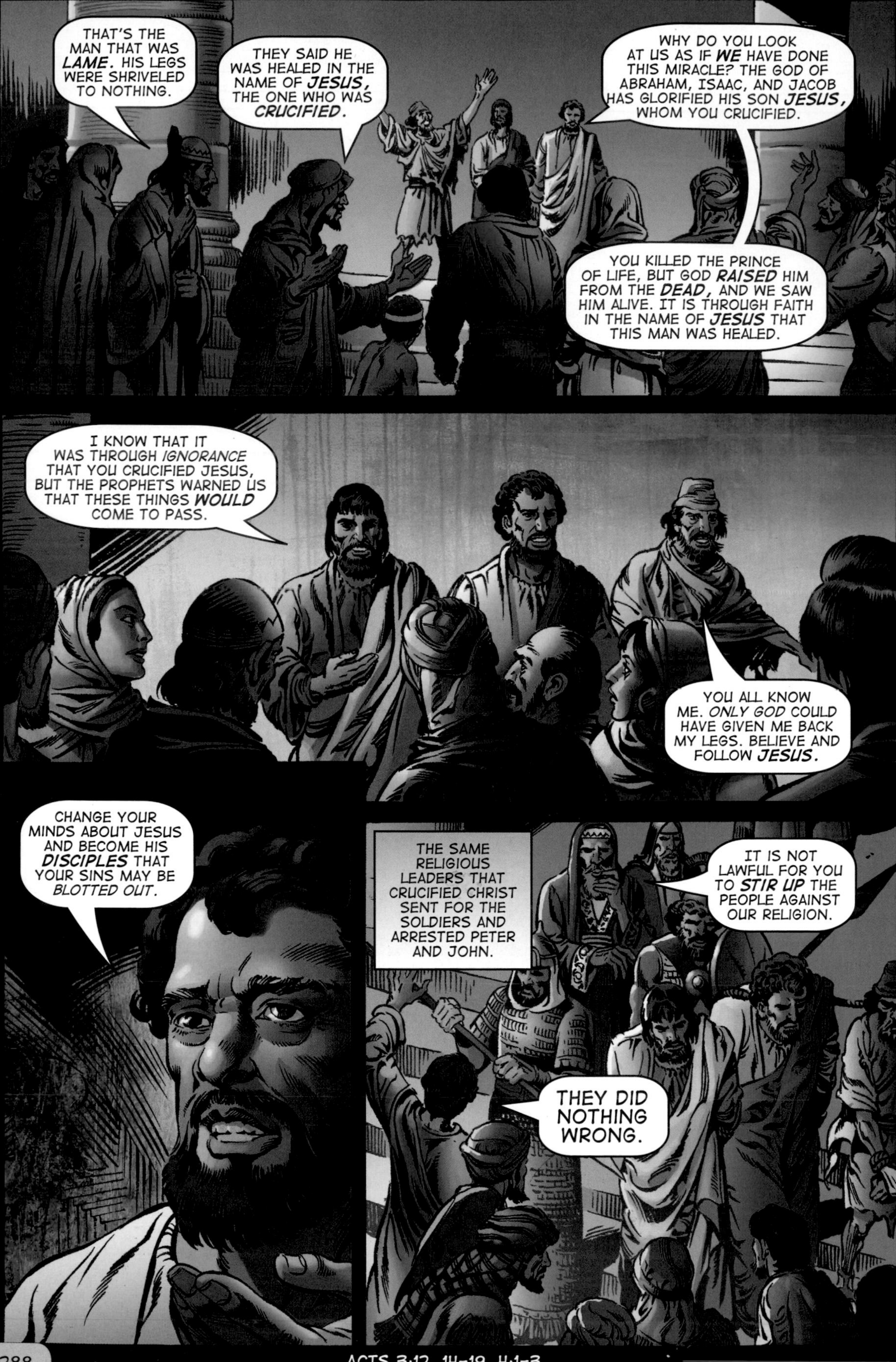
THAT'S THE MAN THAT WAS LAME. HIS LEGS WERE SHRIVELED TO NOTHING.
THEY SAID HE WAS HEALED IN THE NAME OF JESUS, THE ONE WHO WAS CRUCIFIED.
WHY DO YOU LOOK AT US AS IF WE HAVE DONE THIS MIRACLE? THE GOD OF ABRAHAM, ISAAC, AND JACOB HAS GLORIFIED HIS SON JESUS, WHOM YOU CRUCIFIED.
YOU KILLED THE PRINCE OF LIFE, BUT GOD RAISED HIM FROM THE DEAD, AND WE SAW HIM ALIVE. IT IS THROUGH FAITH IN THE NAME OF JESUS THAT THIS MAN WAS HEALED.
I KNOW THAT IT WAS THROUGH IGNORANCE THAT YOU CRUCIFIED JESUS, BUT THE PROPHETS WARNED US THAT THESE THINGS WOULD COME TO PASS.
YOU ALL KNOW ME. ONLY GOD COULD HAVE GIVEN ME BACK MY LEGS. BELIEVE AND FOLLOW JESUS.
CHANGE YOUR MINDS ABOUT JESUS AND BECOME HIS DISCIPLES THAT YOUR SINS MAY BE BLOTTED OUT.
THE SAME RELIGIOUS LEADERS THAT CRUCIFIED CHRIST SENT FOR THE SOLDIERS AND ARRESTED PETER AND JOHN.
IT IS NOT LAWFUL FOR YOU TO STIR UP THE PEOPLE AGAINST OUR RELIGION.
THEY DID NOTHING WRONG.

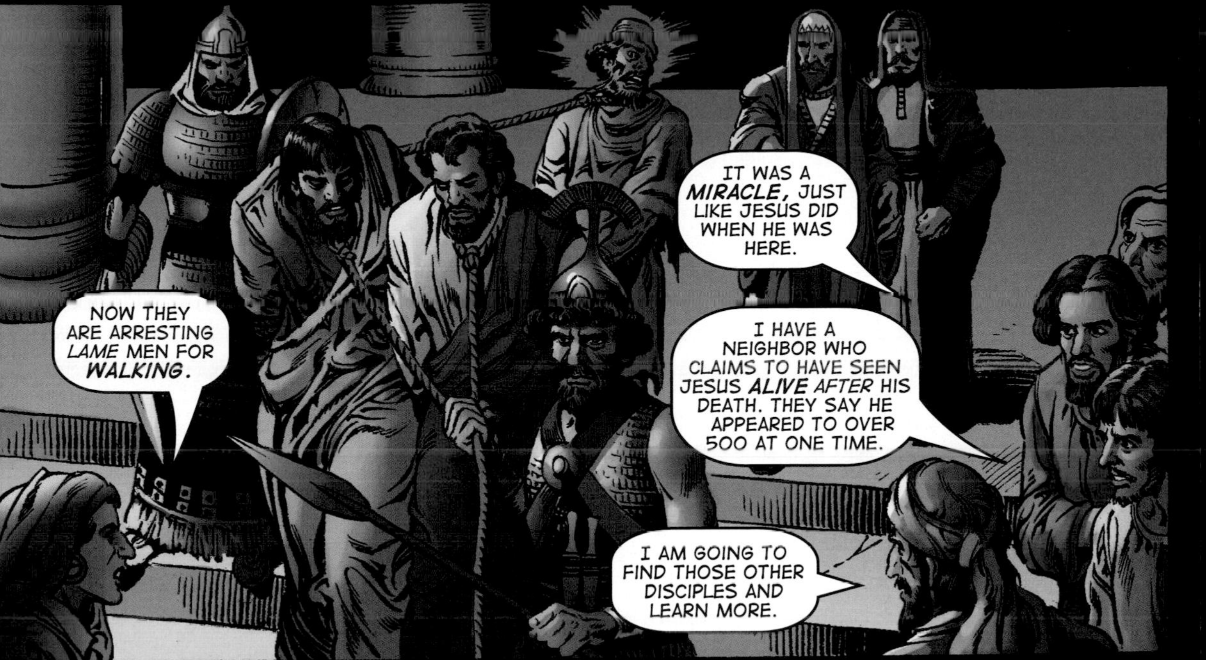
IT WAS A MIRACLE, JUST LIKE JESUS DID WHEN HE WAS HERE.
NOW THEY ARE ARRESTING LAME MEN FOR WALKING.
I HAVE A NEIGHBOR WHO CLAIMS TO HAVE SEEN JESUS ALIVE AFTER HIS DEATH. THEY SAY HE APPEARED TO OVER 500 AT ONE TIME.
I AM GOING TO FIND THOSE OTHER DISCIPLES AND LEARN MORE.

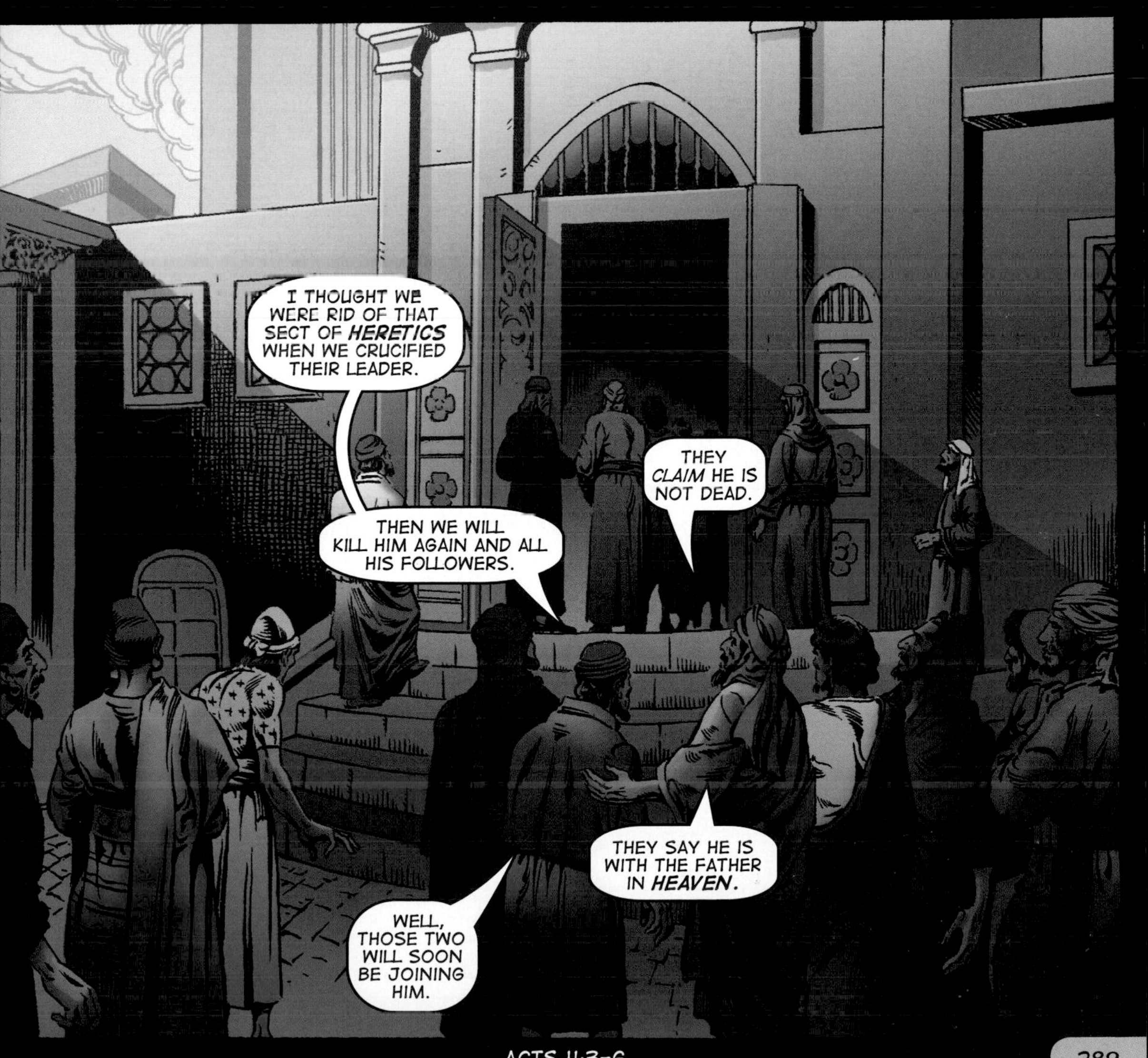
I THOUGHT WE WERE RID OF THAT SECT OF HERETICS WHEN WE CRUCIFIED THEIR LEADER.
THEY CLAIM HE IS NOT DEAD.
THEN WE WILL KILL HIM AGAIN AND ALL HIS FOLLOWERS.
THEY SAY HE IS WITH THE FATHER IN HEAVEN.
WELL, THOSE TWO WILL SOON BE JOINING HIM.

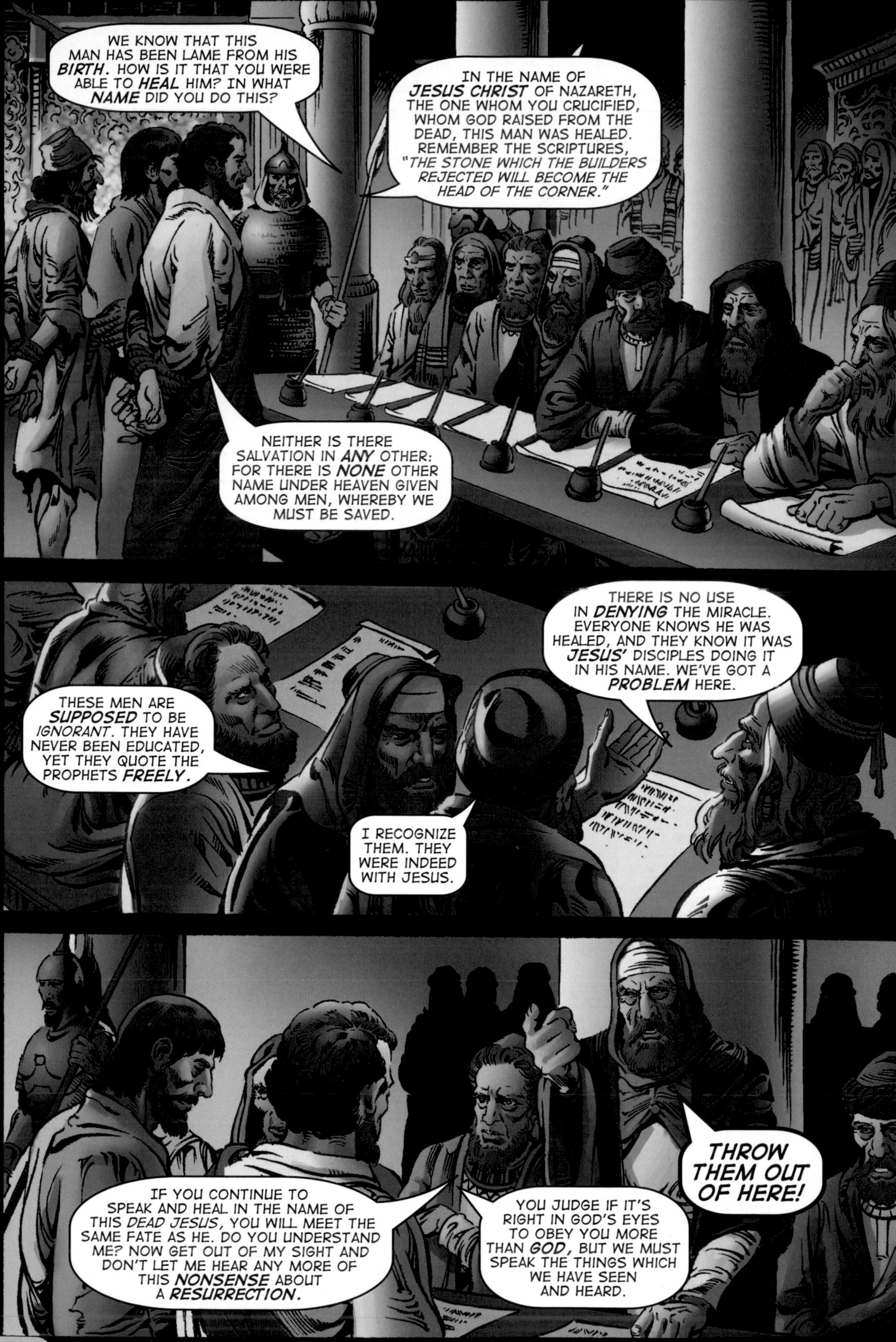
WE KNOW THAT THIS MAN HAS BEEN LAME FROM HIS BIRTH. HOW IS IT THAT YOU WERE ABLE TO HEAL HIM? IN WHAT NAME DID YOU DO THIS?
IN THE NAME OF JESUS CHRIST OF NAZARETH, THE ONE WHOM YOU CRUCIFIED, WHOM GOD RAISED FROM THE DEAD, THIS MAN WAS HEALED. REMEMBER THE SCRIPTURES, "THE STONE WHICH THE BUILDERS REJECTED WILL BECOME THE HEAD OF THE CORNER."
NEITHER IS THERE SALVATION IN ANY OTHER: FOR THERE IS NONE OTHER NAME UNDER HEAVEN GIVEN AMONG MEN, WHEREBY WE MUST BE SAVED.
THESE MEN ARE SUPPOSED TO BE IGNORANT. THEY HAVE NEVER BEEN EDUCATED, YET THEY QUOTE THE PROPHETS FREELY.
I RECOGNIZE THEM. THEY WERE INDEED WITH JESUS.
THERE IS NO USE IN DENYING THE MIRACLE. EVERYONE KNOWS HE WAS HEALED, AND THEY KNOW IT WAS JESUS' DISCIPLES DOING IT IN HIS NAME. WE'VE GOT A PROBLEM HERE.
IF YOU CONTINUE TO SPEAK AND HEAL IN THE NAME OF THIS DEAD JESUS, YOU WILL MEET THE SAME FATE AS HE. DO YOU UNDERSTAND ME? NOW GET OUT OF MY SIGHT AND DON'T LET ME HEAR ANY MORE OF THIS NONSENSE ABOUT A RESURRECTION.
YOU JUDGE IF IT'S RIGHT IN GOD'S EYES TO OBEY YOU MORE THAN GOD, BUT WE MUST SPEAK THE THINGS WHICH WE HAVE SEEN AND HEARD.
THROW THEM OUT OF HERE!

PSALM 118:22; ACTS 4:7-21

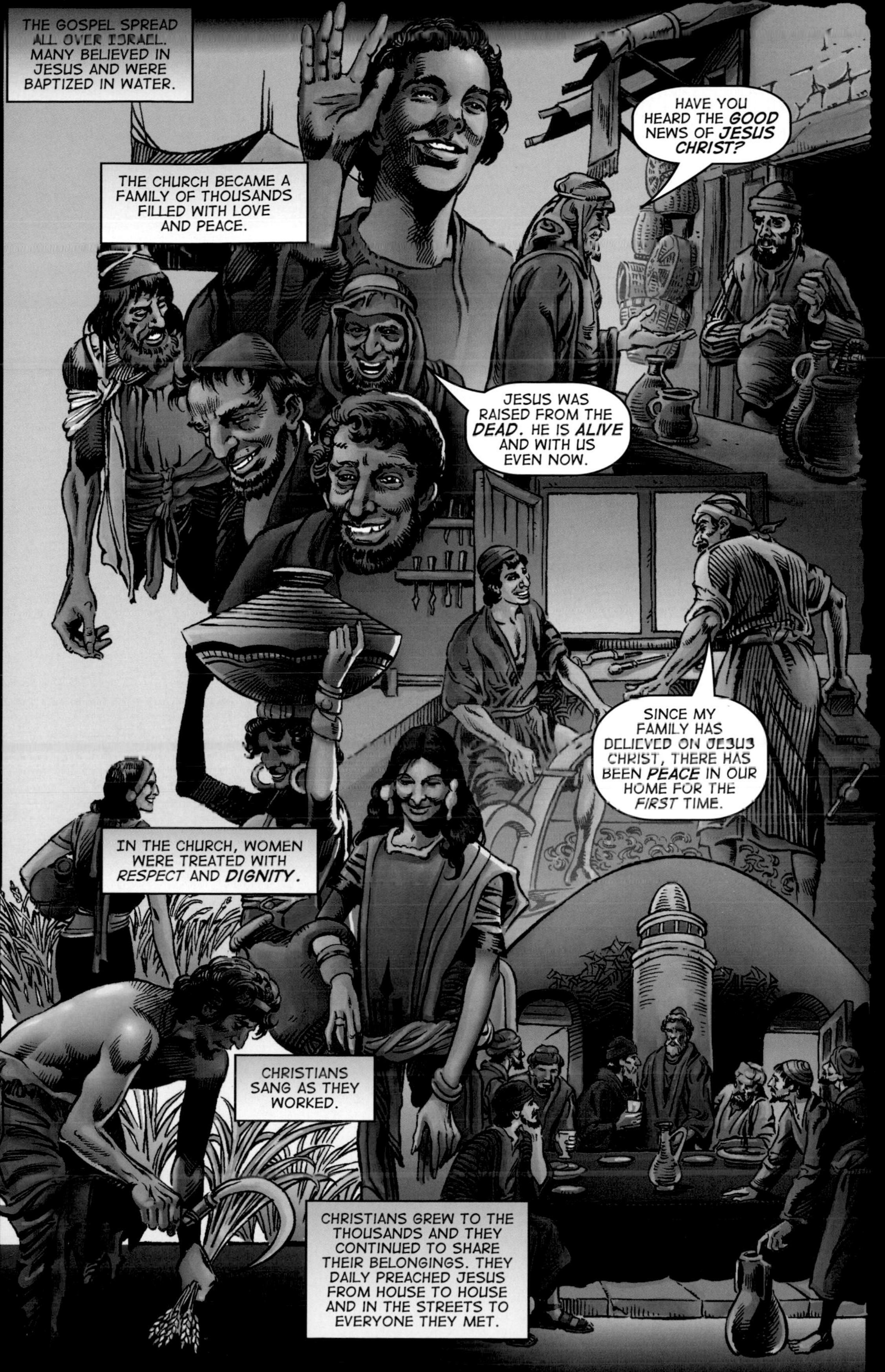
THE GOSPEL SPREAD ALL OVER ISRAEL. MANY BELIEVED IN JESUS AND WERE BAPTIZED IN WATER.
HAVE YOU HEARD THE GOOD NEWS OF JESUS CHRIST?
THE CHURCH BECAME A FAMILY OF THOUSANDS FILLED WITH LOVE AND PEACE.
JESUS WAS RAISED FROM THE DEAD. HE IS ALIVE AND WITH US EVEN NOW.
SINCE MY FAMILY HAS BELIEVED ON JESUS CHRIST, THERE HAS BEEN PEACE IN OUR HOME FOR THE FIRST TIME.
IN THE CHURCH, WOMEN WERE TREATED WITH RESPECT AND DIGNITY.
CHRISTIANS SANG AS THEY WORKED.
CHRISTIANS GREW TO THE THOUSANDS AND THEY CONTINUED TO SHARE THEIR BELONGINGS. THEY DAILY PREACHED JESUS FROM HOUSE TO HOUSE AND IN THE STREETS TO EVERYONE THEY MET.

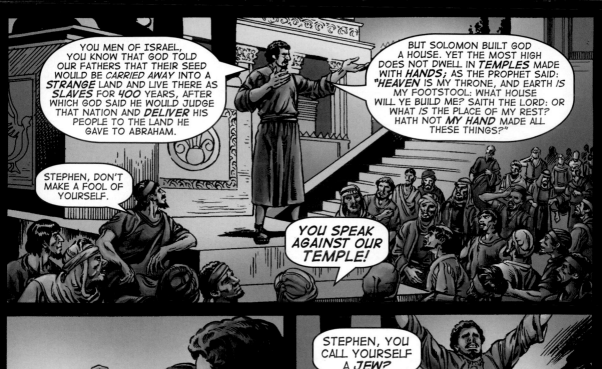

YOU MEN OF ISRAEL, YOU KNOW THAT GOD TOLD OUR FATHERS THAT THEIR SEED WOULD BE *CARRIED AWAY* INTO A *STRANGE* LAND AND LIVE THERE AS *SLAVES* FOR *400* YEARS, AFTER WHICH GOD SAID HE WOULD JUDGE THAT NATION AND *DELIVER* HIS PEOPLE TO THE LAND HE GAVE TO ABRAHAM.

BUT SOLOMON BUILT GOD A HOUSE. YET THE MOST HIGH DOES NOT DWELL IN *TEMPLES* MADE WITH *HANDS;* AS THE PROPHET SAID: "*HEAVEN* IS MY THRONE, AND EARTH *IS* MY FOOTSTOOL: WHAT HOUSE WILL YE BUILD ME? SAITH THE LORD: OR WHAT *IS* THE PLACE OF MY REST? HATH NOT *MY HAND* MADE ALL THESE THINGS?"

STEPHEN, DON'T MAKE A FOOL OF YOURSELF.

YOU SPEAK AGAINST OUR *TEMPLE!*

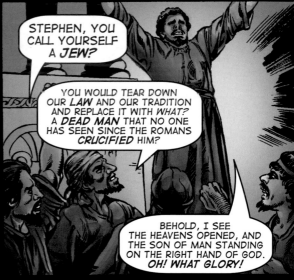

STEPHEN, YOU CALL YOURSELF A *JEW?*

YOU WOULD TEAR DOWN OUR *LAW* AND OUR TRADITION AND REPLACE IT WITH *WHAT?* A *DEAD MAN* THAT NO ONE HAS SEEN SINCE THE ROMANS *CRUCIFIED* HIM?

YOU ARE *STUBBORN* AND *REBELLIOUS.* YOUR HEART IS NOT RIGHT WITH GOD. YOU *RESIST* THE HOLY GHOST JUST AS YOUR FATHERS DID. YOU AND YOUR FATHERS HAVE PERSECUTED AND SLAIN THE PROPHETS WHO PREDICTED THE COMING OF JESUS CHRIST, BUT YOU BETRAYED AND MURDERED HIM ALSO.

BEHOLD, I SEE THE HEAVENS OPENED, AND THE SON OF MAN STANDING ON THE RIGHT HAND OF GOD. *OH! WHAT GLORY!*

PUT YOUR HANDS OVER YOUR EARS. DO NOT LISTEN TO SUCH *BLASPHEMY!*

HE DESERVES TO DIE!

TAKE HIM OUT OF THE CITY AND *STONE* HIM TO DEATH.

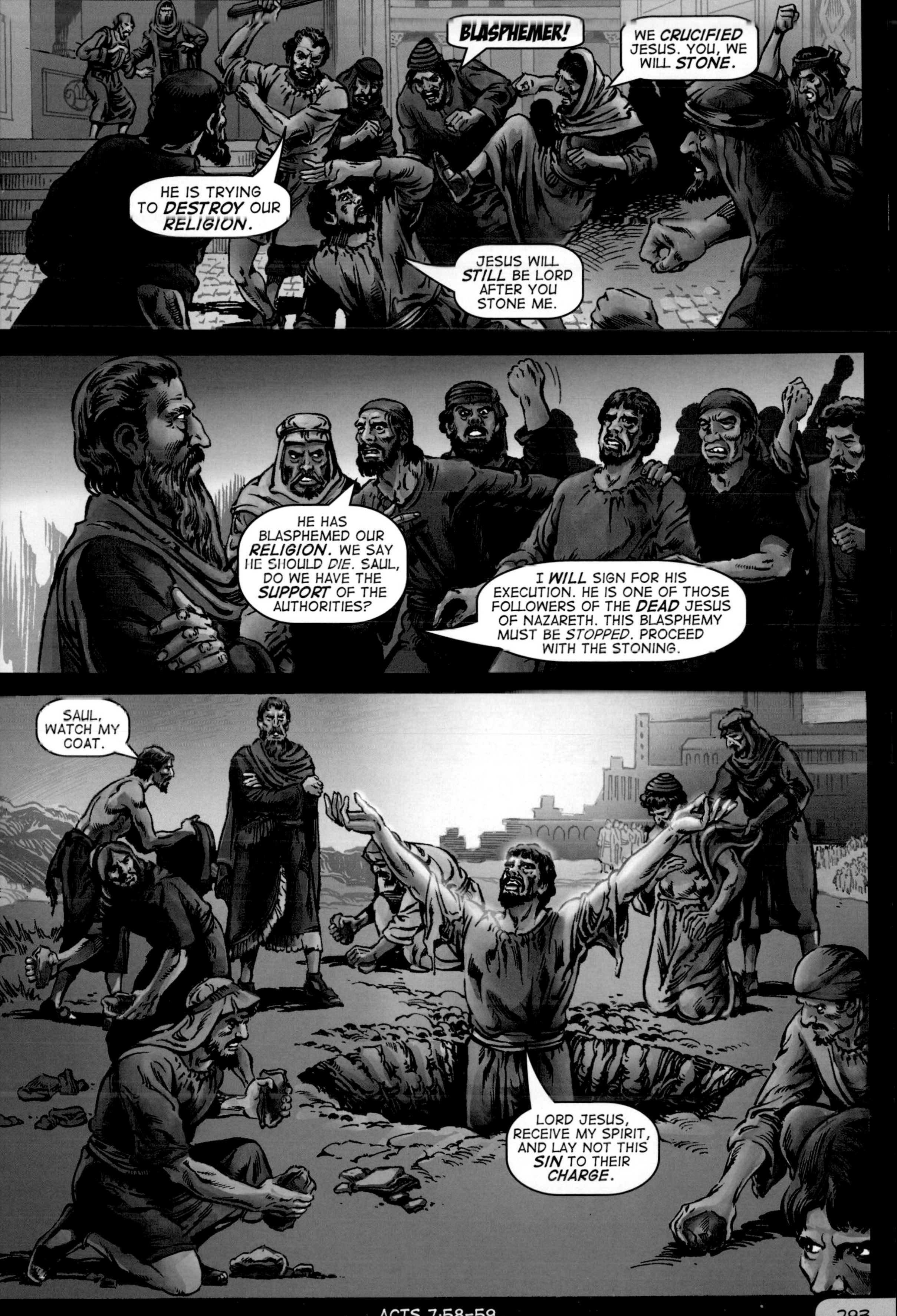
BLASPHEMER!
WE CRUCIFIED JESUS. YOU, WE WILL STONE.
HE IS TRYING TO DESTROY OUR RELIGION.
JESUS WILL STILL BE LORD AFTER YOU STONE ME.
HE HAS BLASPHEMED OUR RELIGION. WE SAY HE SHOULD DIE. SAUL, DO WE HAVE THE SUPPORT OF THE AUTHORITIES?
I WILL SIGN FOR HIS EXECUTION. HE IS ONE OF THOSE FOLLOWERS OF THE DEAD JESUS OF NAZARETH. THIS BLASPHEMY MUST BE STOPPED. PROCEED WITH THE STONING.
SAUL, WATCH MY COAT.
LORD JESUS, RECEIVE MY SPIRIT, AND LAY NOT THIS SIN TO THEIR CHARGE.

ACTS 7:58-59

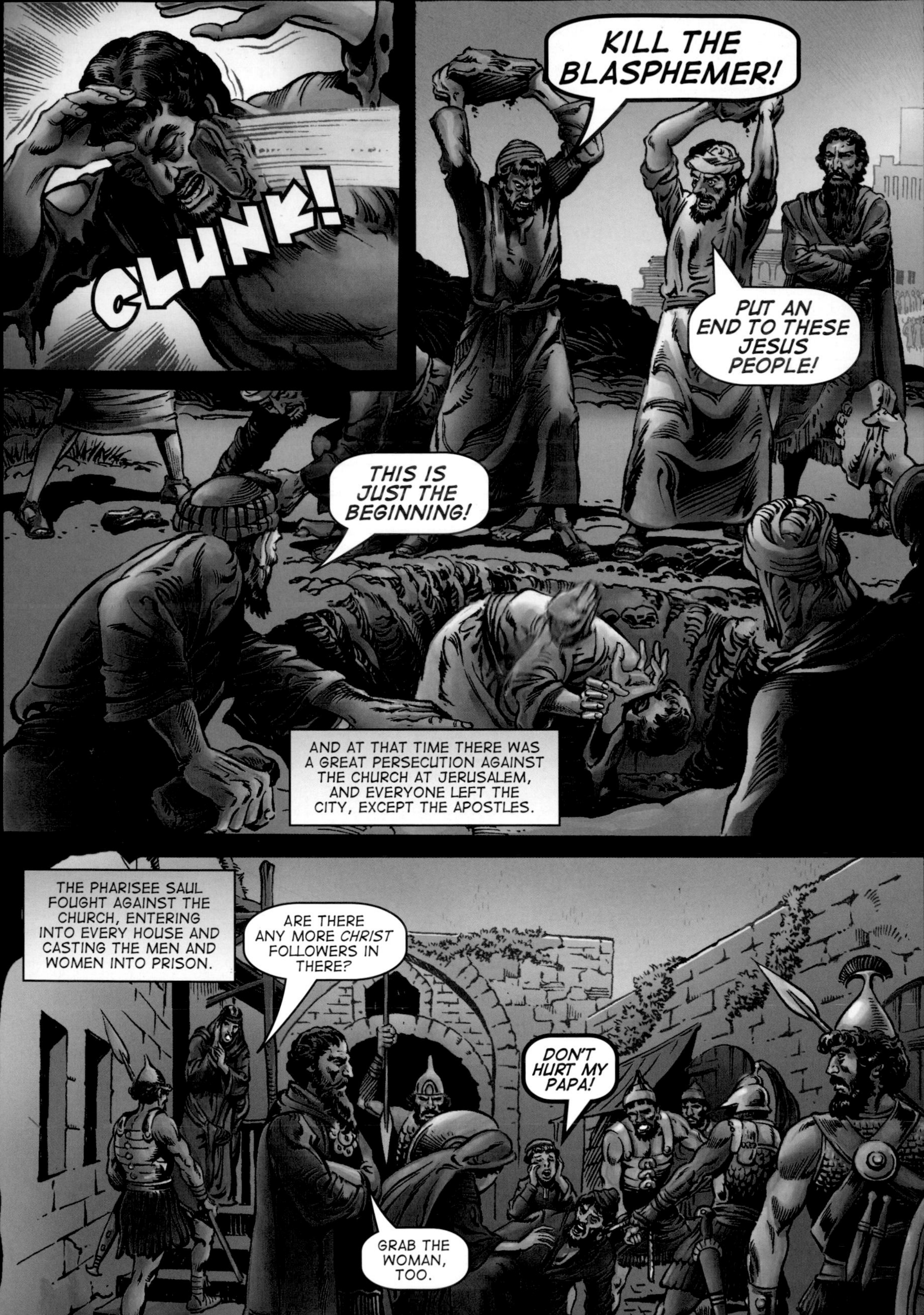
CLUNK!
KILL THE BLASPHEMER!
PUT AN END TO THESE JESUS PEOPLE!
THIS IS JUST THE BEGINNING!
AND AT THAT TIME THERE WAS A GREAT PERSECUTION AGAINST THE CHURCH AT JERUSALEM, AND EVERYONE LEFT THE CITY, EXCEPT THE APOSTLES.
THE PHARISEE SAUL FOUGHT AGAINST THE CHURCH, ENTERING INTO EVERY HOUSE AND CASTING THE MEN AND WOMEN INTO PRISON.
ARE THERE ANY MORE *CHRIST* FOLLOWERS IN THERE?
DON'T HURT MY PAPA!
GRAB THE WOMAN, TOO.

ACTS 7:59–8:3

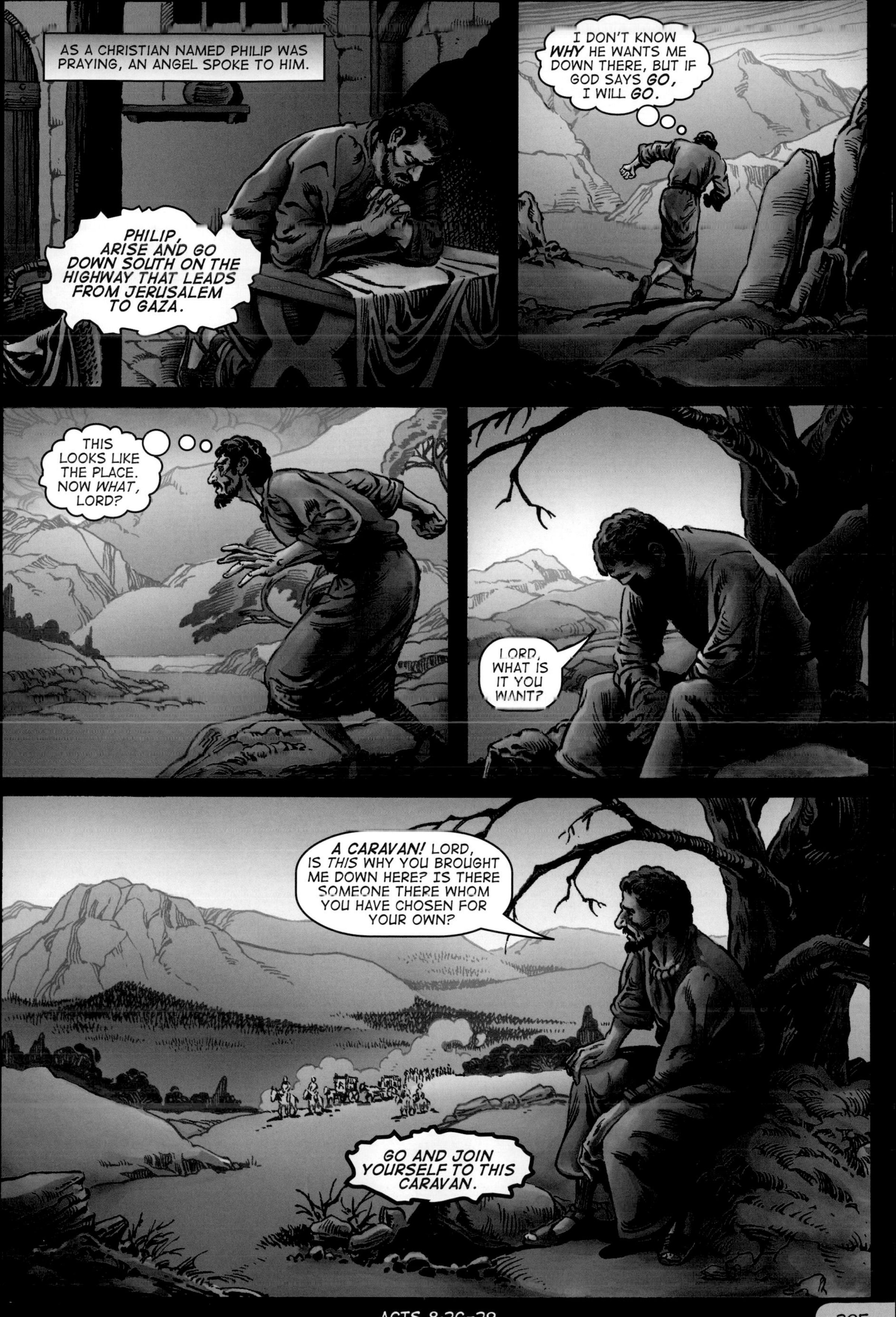
AS A CHRISTIAN NAMED PHILIP WAS PRAYING, AN ANGEL SPOKE TO HIM.
PHILIP, ARISE AND GO DOWN SOUTH ON THE HIGHWAY THAT LEADS FROM JERUSALEM TO GAZA.
I DON'T KNOW WHY HE WANTS ME DOWN THERE, BUT IF GOD SAYS GO, I WILL GO.
THIS LOOKS LIKE THE PLACE. NOW WHAT, LORD?
LORD, WHAT IS IT YOU WANT?
A CARAVAN! LORD, IS THIS WHY YOU BROUGHT ME DOWN HERE? IS THERE SOMEONE THERE WHOM YOU HAVE CHOSEN FOR YOUR OWN?
GO AND JOIN YOURSELF TO THIS CARAVAN.

ACTS 8:26-29

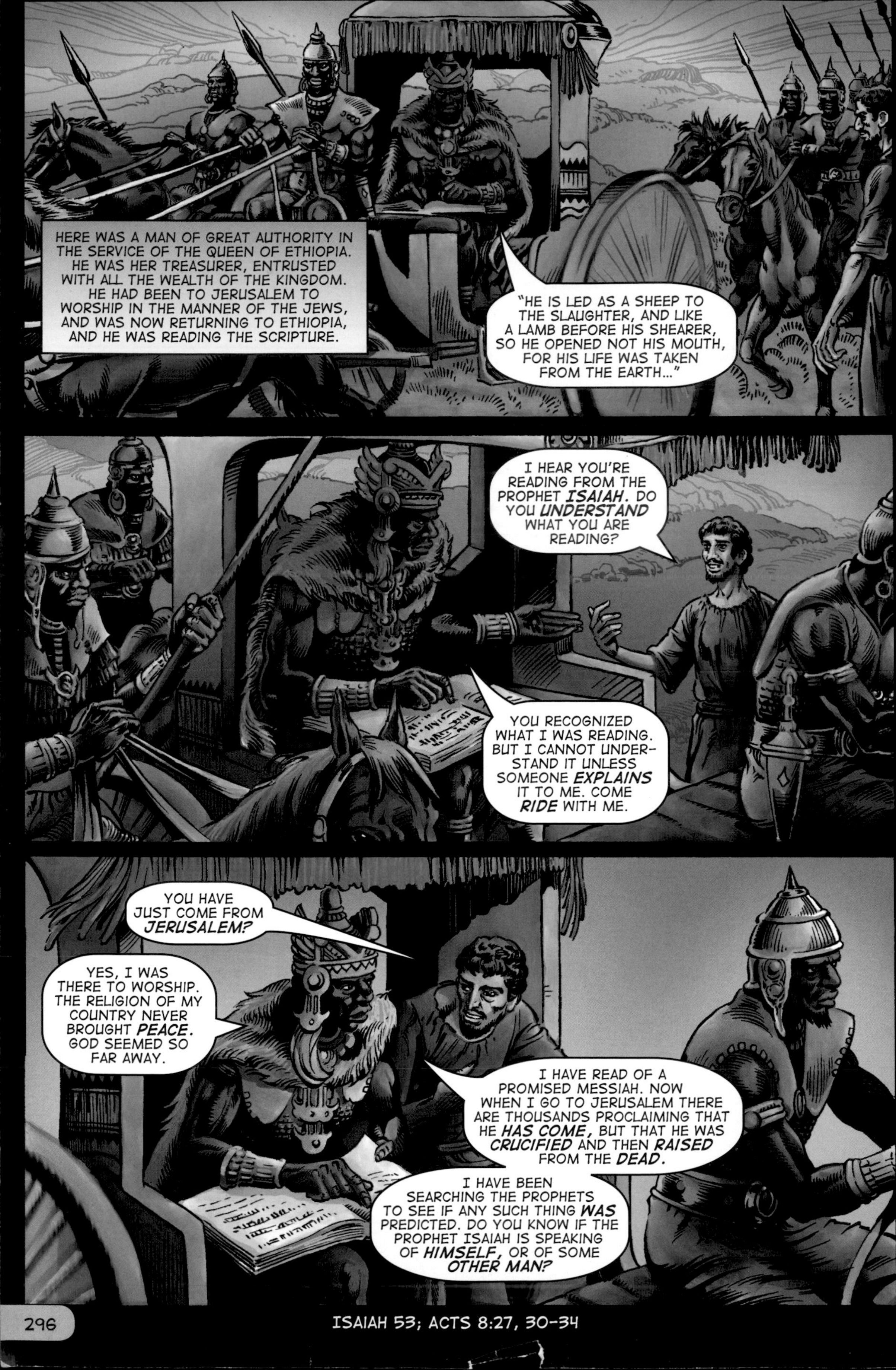
HERE WAS A MAN OF GREAT AUTHORITY IN THE SERVICE OF THE QUEEN OF ETHIOPIA. HE WAS HER TREASURER, ENTRUSTED WITH ALL THE WEALTH OF THE KINGDOM. HE HAD BEEN TO JERUSALEM TO WORSHIP IN THE MANNER OF THE JEWS, AND WAS NOW RETURNING TO ETHIOPIA, AND HE WAS READING THE SCRIPTURE.
"HE IS LED AS A SHEEP TO THE SLAUGHTER, AND LIKE A LAMB BEFORE HIS SHEARER, SO HE OPENED NOT HIS MOUTH, FOR HIS LIFE WAS TAKEN FROM THE EARTH..."
I HEAR YOU'RE READING FROM THE PROPHET ISAIAH. DO YOU UNDERSTAND WHAT YOU ARE READING?
YOU RECOGNIZED WHAT I WAS READING. BUT I CANNOT UNDERSTAND IT UNLESS SOMEONE EXPLAINS IT TO ME. COME RIDE WITH ME.
YOU HAVE JUST COME FROM JERUSALEM?
YES, I WAS THERE TO WORSHIP. THE RELIGION OF MY COUNTRY NEVER BROUGHT PEACE. GOD SEEMED SO FAR AWAY.
I HAVE READ OF A PROMISED MESSIAH. NOW WHEN I GO TO JERUSALEM THERE ARE THOUSANDS PROCLAIMING THAT HE HAS COME, BUT THAT HE WAS CRUCIFIED AND THEN RAISED FROM THE DEAD.
I HAVE BEEN SEARCHING THE PROPHETS TO SEE IF ANY SUCH THING WAS PREDICTED. DO YOU KNOW IF THE PROPHET ISAIAH IS SPEAKING OF HIMSELF, OR OF SOME OTHER MAN?

ISAIAH 53; ACTS 8:27, 30-34

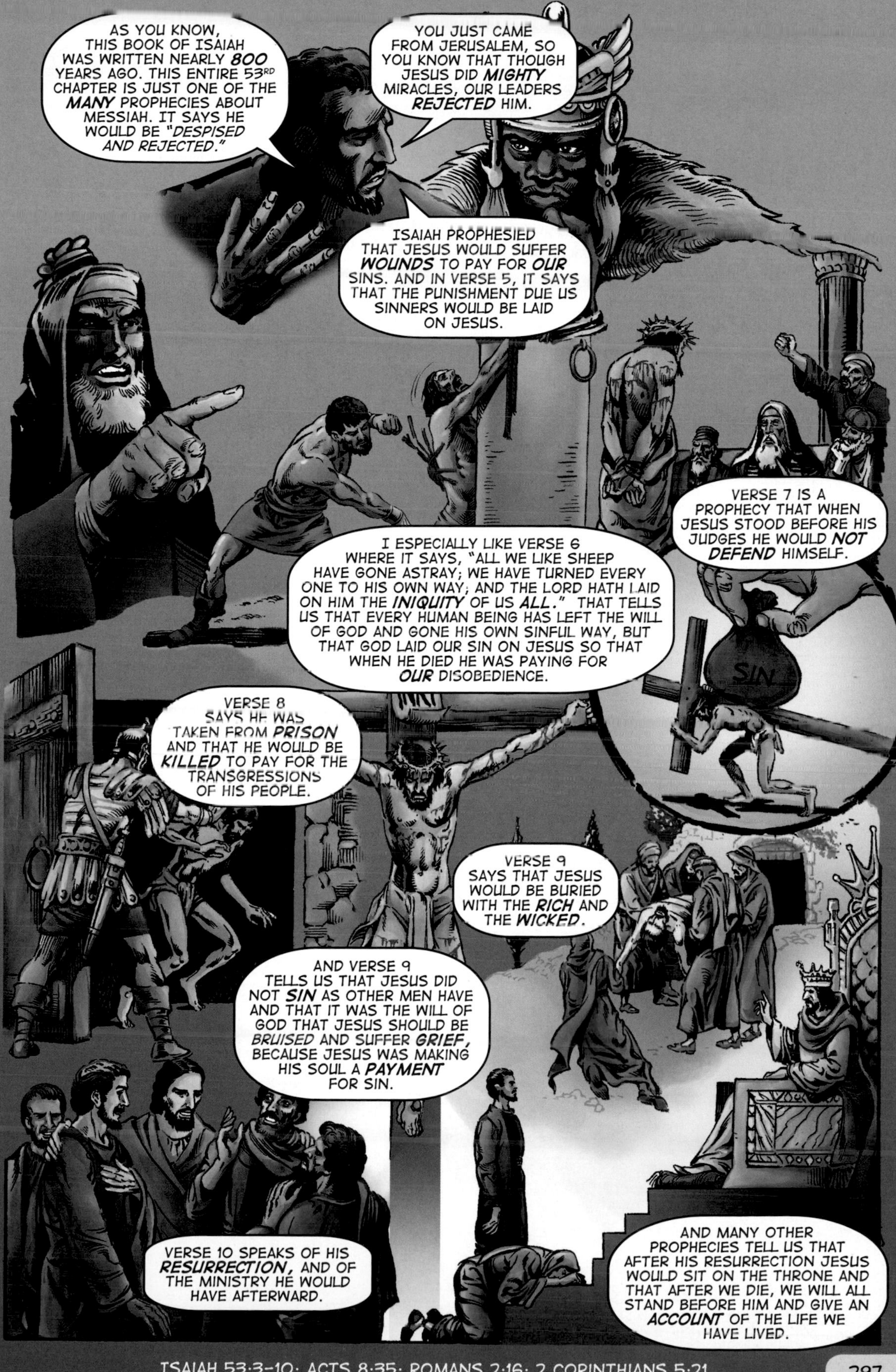
AS YOU KNOW, THIS BOOK OF ISAIAH WAS WRITTEN NEARLY 800 YEARS AGO. THIS ENTIRE 53RD CHAPTER IS JUST ONE OF THE MANY PROPHECIES ABOUT MESSIAH. IT SAYS HE WOULD BE "DESPISED AND REJECTED."
YOU JUST CAME FROM JERUSALEM, SO YOU KNOW THAT THOUGH JESUS DID MIGHTY MIRACLES, OUR LEADERS REJECTED HIM.
ISAIAH PROPHESIED THAT JESUS WOULD SUFFER WOUNDS TO PAY FOR OUR SINS. AND IN VERSE 5, IT SAYS THAT THE PUNISHMENT DUE US SINNERS WOULD BE LAID ON JESUS.
VERSE 7 IS A PROPHECY THAT WHEN JESUS STOOD BEFORE HIS JUDGES HE WOULD NOT DEFEND HIMSELF.
I ESPECIALLY LIKE VERSE 6 WHERE IT SAYS, "ALL WE LIKE SHEEP HAVE GONE ASTRAY; WE HAVE TURNED EVERY ONE TO HIS OWN WAY; AND THE LORD HATH LAID ON HIM THE INIQUITY OF US ALL." THAT TELLS US THAT EVERY HUMAN BEING HAS LEFT THE WILL OF GOD AND GONE HIS OWN SINFUL WAY, BUT THAT GOD LAID OUR SIN ON JESUS SO THAT WHEN HE DIED HE WAS PAYING FOR OUR DISOBEDIENCE.
SIN
VERSE 8 SAYS HE WAS TAKEN FROM PRISON AND THAT HE WOULD BE KILLED TO PAY FOR THE TRANSGRESSIONS OF HIS PEOPLE.
VERSE 9 SAYS THAT JESUS WOULD BE BURIED WITH THE RICH AND THE WICKED.
AND VERSE 9 TELLS US THAT JESUS DID NOT SIN AS OTHER MEN HAVE AND THAT IT WAS THE WILL OF GOD THAT JESUS SHOULD BE BRUISED AND SUFFER GRIEF, BECAUSE JESUS WAS MAKING HIS SOUL A PAYMENT FOR SIN.
VERSE 10 SPEAKS OF HIS RESURRECTION, AND OF THE MINISTRY HE WOULD HAVE AFTERWARD.
AND MANY OTHER PROPHECIES TELL US THAT AFTER HIS RESURRECTION JESUS WOULD SIT ON THE THRONE AND THAT AFTER WE DIE, WE WILL ALL STAND BEFORE HIM AND GIVE AN ACCOUNT OF THE LIFE WE HAVE LIVED.

ISAIAH 53:3–10; ACTS 8:35; ROMANS 2:16; 2 CORINTHIANS 5:21

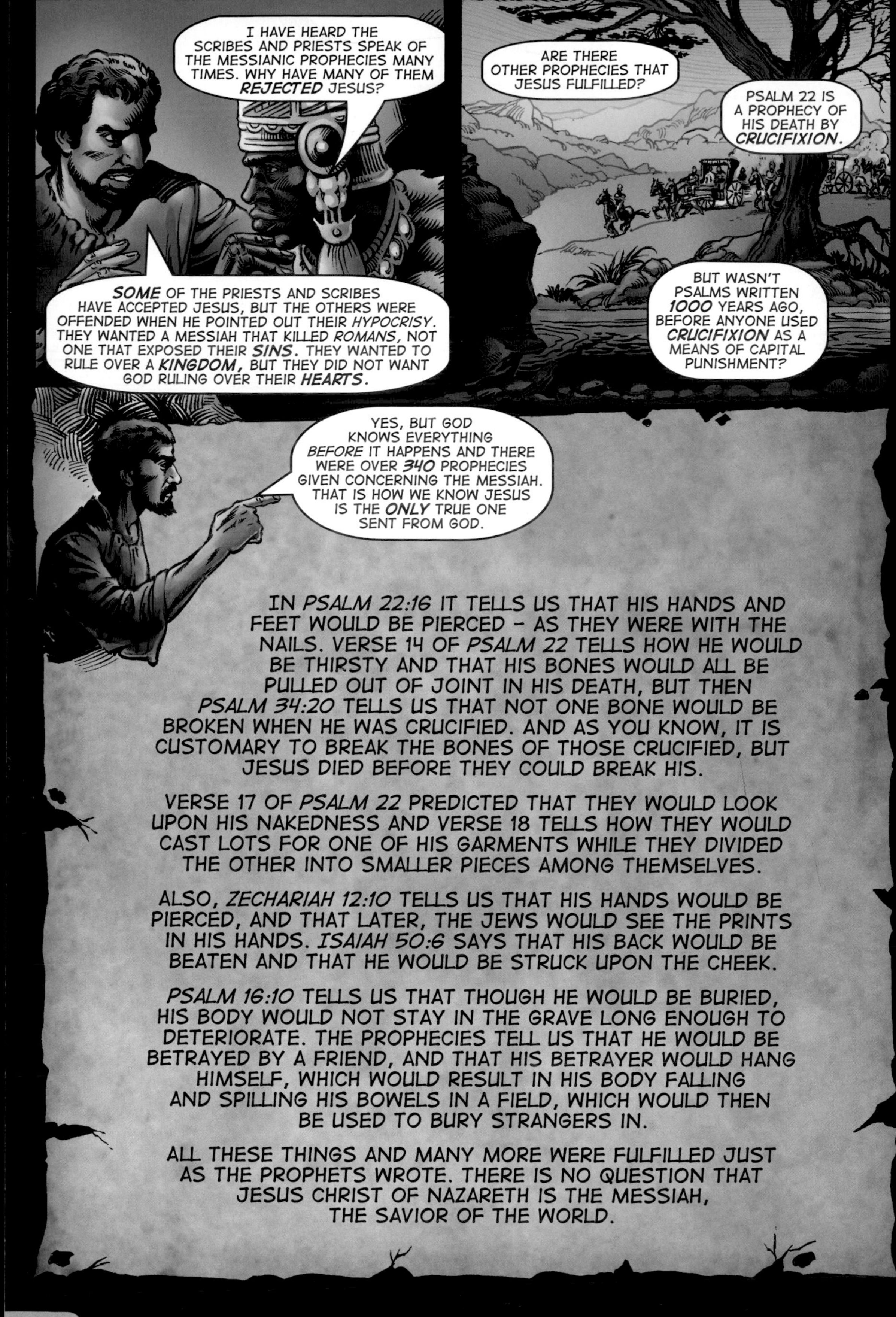
I HAVE HEARD THE SCRIBES AND PRIESTS SPEAK OF THE MESSIANIC PROPHECIES MANY TIMES. WHY HAVE MANY OF THEM REJECTED JESUS?
SOME OF THE PRIESTS AND SCRIBES HAVE ACCEPTED JESUS, BUT THE OTHERS WERE OFFENDED WHEN HE POINTED OUT THEIR HYPOCRISY. THEY WANTED A MESSIAH THAT KILLED ROMANS, NOT ONE THAT EXPOSED THEIR SINS. THEY WANTED TO RULE OVER A KINGDOM, BUT THEY DID NOT WANT GOD RULING OVER THEIR HEARTS.
ARE THERE OTHER PROPHECIES THAT JESUS FULFILLED?
PSALM 22 IS A PROPHECY OF HIS DEATH BY CRUCIFIXION.
BUT WASN'T PSALMS WRITTEN 1000 YEARS AGO, BEFORE ANYONE USED CRUCIFIXION AS A MEANS OF CAPITAL PUNISHMENT?
YES, BUT GOD KNOWS EVERYTHING BEFORE IT HAPPENS AND THERE WERE OVER 340 PROPHECIES GIVEN CONCERNING THE MESSIAH. THAT IS HOW WE KNOW JESUS IS THE ONLY TRUE ONE SENT FROM GOD.
IN PSALM 22:16 IT TELLS US THAT HIS HANDS AND FEET WOULD BE PIERCED - AS THEY WERE WITH THE NAILS. VERSE 14 OF PSALM 22 TELLS HOW HE WOULD BE THIRSTY AND THAT HIS BONES WOULD ALL BE PULLED OUT OF JOINT IN HIS DEATH, BUT THEN PSALM 34:20 TELLS US THAT NOT ONE BONE WOULD BE BROKEN WHEN HE WAS CRUCIFIED. AND AS YOU KNOW, IT IS CUSTOMARY TO BREAK THE BONES OF THOSE CRUCIFIED, BUT JESUS DIED BEFORE THEY COULD BREAK HIS.
VERSE 17 OF PSALM 22 PREDICTED THAT THEY WOULD LOOK UPON HIS NAKEDNESS AND VERSE 18 TELLS HOW THEY WOULD CAST LOTS FOR ONE OF HIS GARMENTS WHILE THEY DIVIDED THE OTHER INTO SMALLER PIECES AMONG THEMSELVES.
ALSO, ZECHARIAH 12:10 TELLS US THAT HIS HANDS WOULD BE PIERCED, AND THAT LATER, THE JEWS WOULD SEE THE PRINTS IN HIS HANDS. ISAIAH 50:6 SAYS THAT HIS BACK WOULD BE BEATEN AND THAT HE WOULD BE STRUCK UPON THE CHEEK.
PSALM 16:10 TELLS US THAT THOUGH HE WOULD BE BURIED, HIS BODY WOULD NOT STAY IN THE GRAVE LONG ENOUGH TO DETERIORATE. THE PROPHECIES TELL US THAT HE WOULD BE BETRAYED BY A FRIEND, AND THAT HIS BETRAYER WOULD HANG HIMSELF, WHICH WOULD RESULT IN HIS BODY FALLING AND SPILLING HIS BOWELS IN A FIELD, WHICH WOULD THEN BE USED TO BURY STRANGERS IN.
ALL THESE THINGS AND MANY MORE WERE FULFILLED JUST AS THE PROPHETS WROTE. THERE IS NO QUESTION THAT JESUS CHRIST OF NAZARETH IS THE MESSIAH, THE SAVIOR OF THE WORLD.

PSALM 22:6, 17-18, 16:10, 34:20; ISAIAH 50:6, ZECHARIAH 12:10

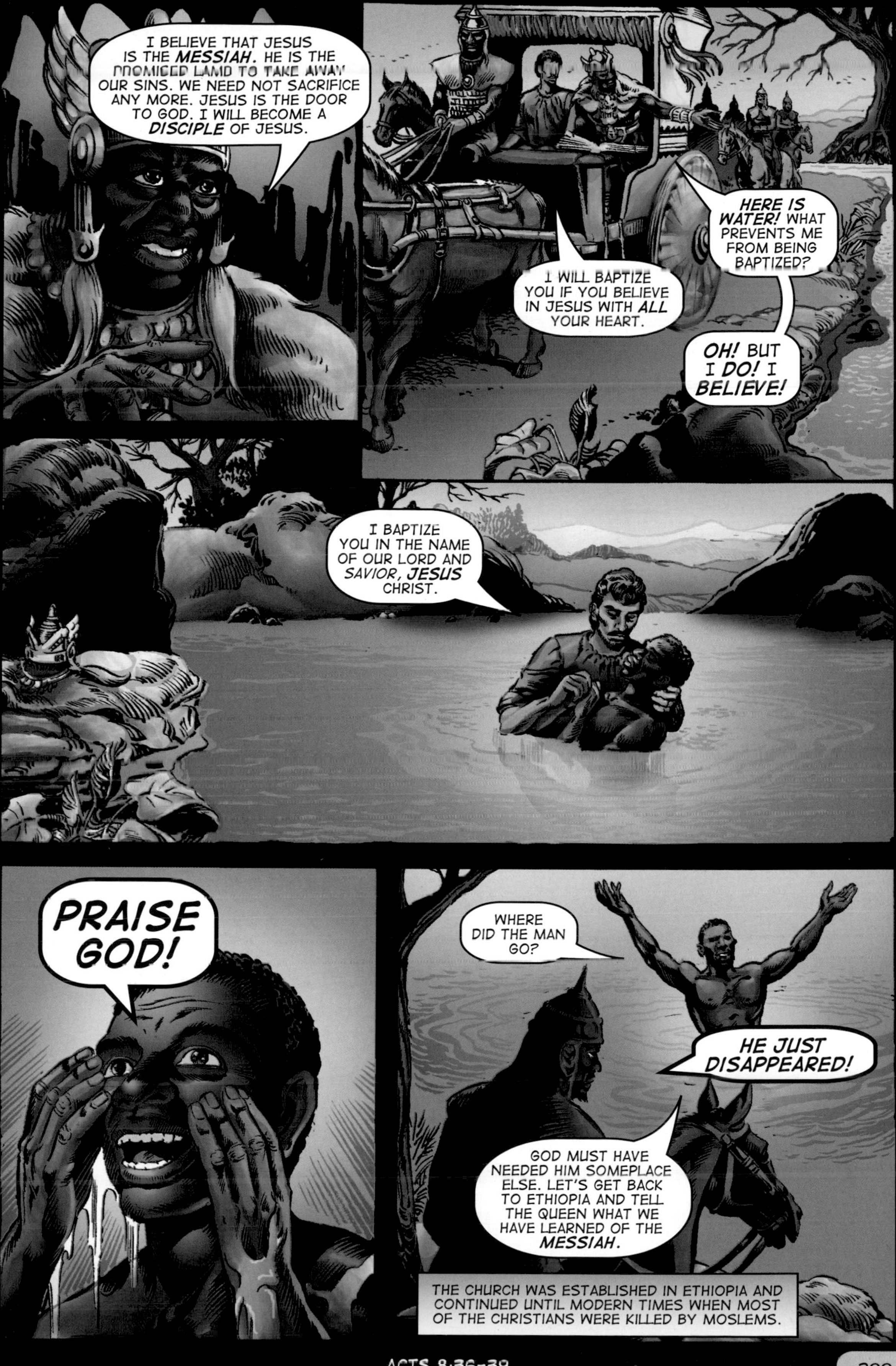
I BELIEVE THAT JESUS IS THE MESSIAH. HE IS THE PROMISED LAMB TO TAKE AWAY OUR SINS. WE NEED NOT SACRIFICE ANY MORE. JESUS IS THE DOOR TO GOD. I WILL BECOME A DISCIPLE OF JESUS.
HERE IS WATER! WHAT PREVENTS ME FROM BEING BAPTIZED?
I WILL BAPTIZE YOU IF YOU BELIEVE IN JESUS WITH ALL YOUR HEART.
OH! BUT I DO! I BELIEVE!
I BAPTIZE YOU IN THE NAME OF OUR LORD AND SAVIOR, JESUS CHRIST.
PRAISE GOD!
WHERE DID THE MAN GO?
HE JUST DISAPPEARED!
GOD MUST HAVE NEEDED HIM SOMEPLACE ELSE. LET'S GET BACK TO ETHIOPIA AND TELL THE QUEEN WHAT WE HAVE LEARNED OF THE MESSIAH.
THE CHURCH WAS ESTABLISHED IN ETHIOPIA AND CONTINUED UNTIL MODERN TIMES WHEN MOST OF THE CHRISTIANS WERE KILLED BY MOSLEMS.

ACTS 8:36-39

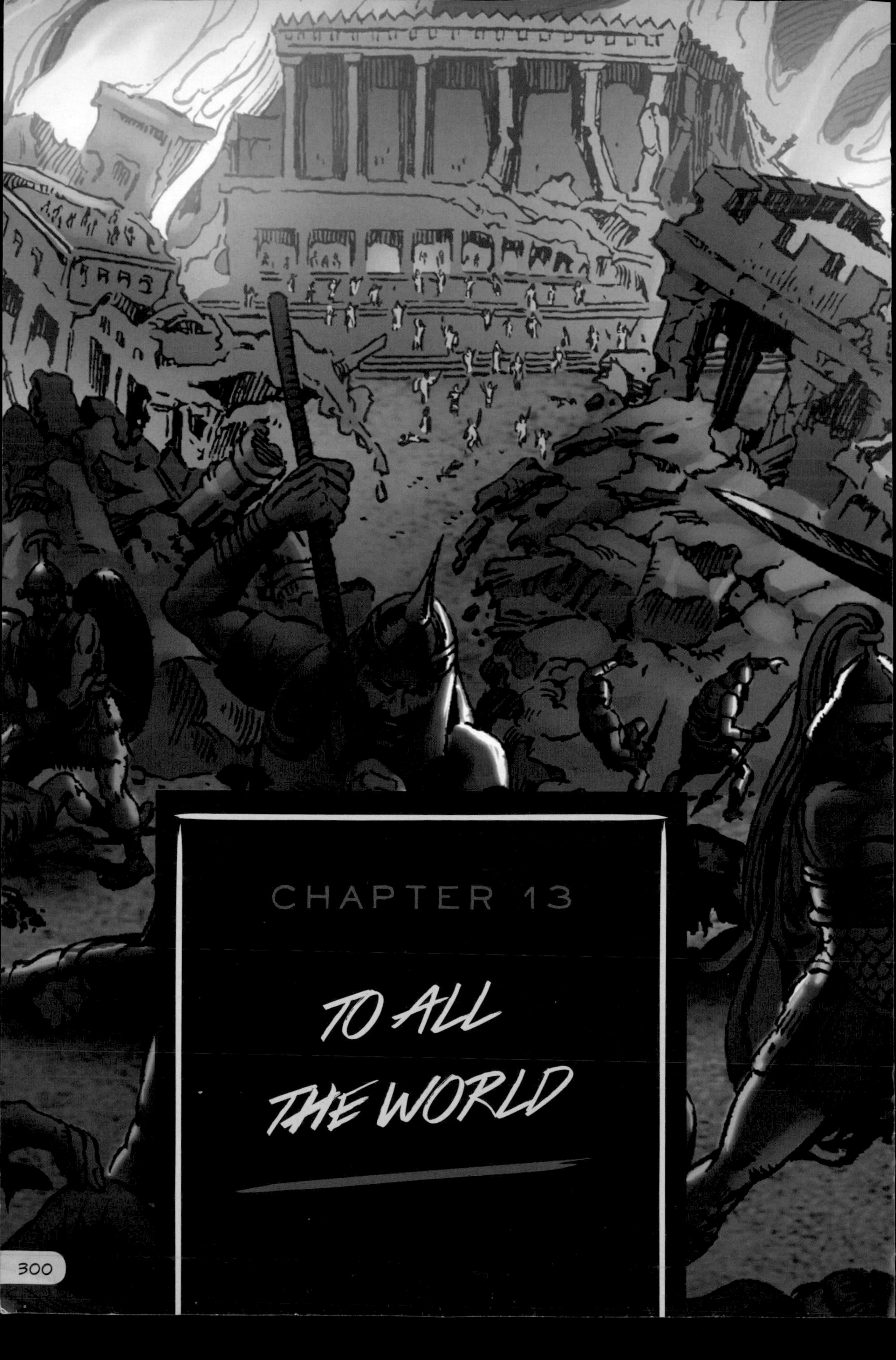

CHAPTER 13

TO ALL THE WORLD

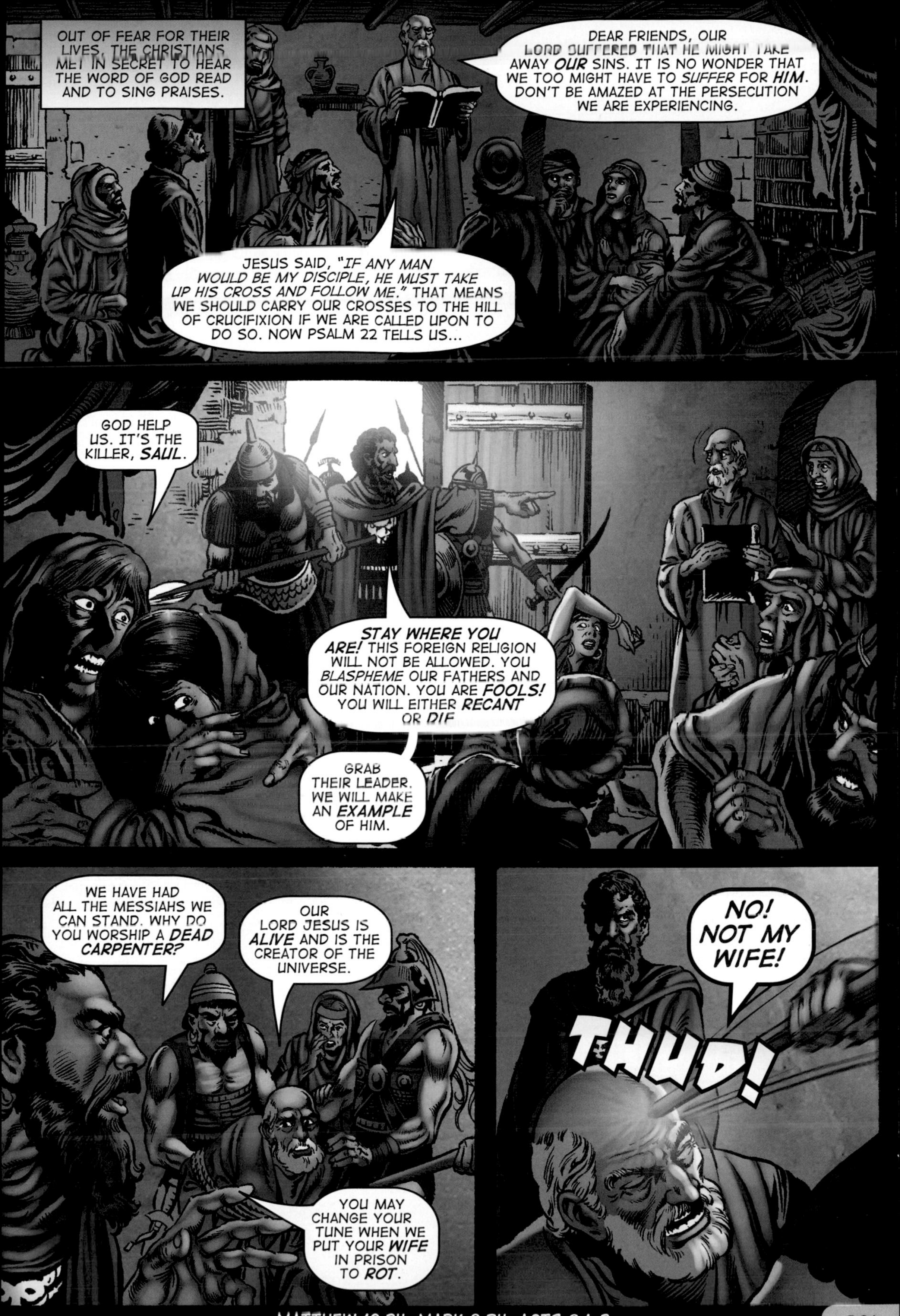
OUT OF FEAR FOR THEIR LIVES, THE CHRISTIANS MET IN SECRET TO HEAR THE WORD OF GOD READ AND TO SING PRAISES.
DEAR FRIENDS, OUR LORD SUFFERED THAT HE MIGHT TAKE AWAY OUR SINS. IT IS NO WONDER THAT WE TOO MIGHT HAVE TO SUFFER FOR HIM. DON'T BE AMAZED AT THE PERSECUTION WE ARE EXPERIENCING.
JESUS SAID, "IF ANY MAN WOULD BE MY DISCIPLE, HE MUST TAKE UP HIS CROSS AND FOLLOW ME." THAT MEANS WE SHOULD CARRY OUR CROSSES TO THE HILL OF CRUCIFIXION IF WE ARE CALLED UPON TO DO SO. NOW PSALM 22 TELLS US...
GOD HELP US. IT'S THE KILLER, SAUL.
STAY WHERE YOU ARE! THIS FOREIGN RELIGION WILL NOT BE ALLOWED. YOU BLASPHEME OUR FATHERS AND OUR NATION. YOU ARE FOOLS! YOU WILL EITHER RECANT OR DIE.
GRAB THEIR LEADER. WE WILL MAKE AN EXAMPLE OF HIM.
WE HAVE HAD ALL THE MESSIAHS WE CAN STAND. WHY DO YOU WORSHIP A DEAD CARPENTER?
OUR LORD JESUS IS ALIVE AND IS THE CREATOR OF THE UNIVERSE.
YOU MAY CHANGE YOUR TUNE WHEN WE PUT YOUR WIFE IN PRISON TO ROT.
NO! NOT MY WIFE!
THUD!

MATTHEW 16:24; MARK 8:34; ACTS 9:1-2

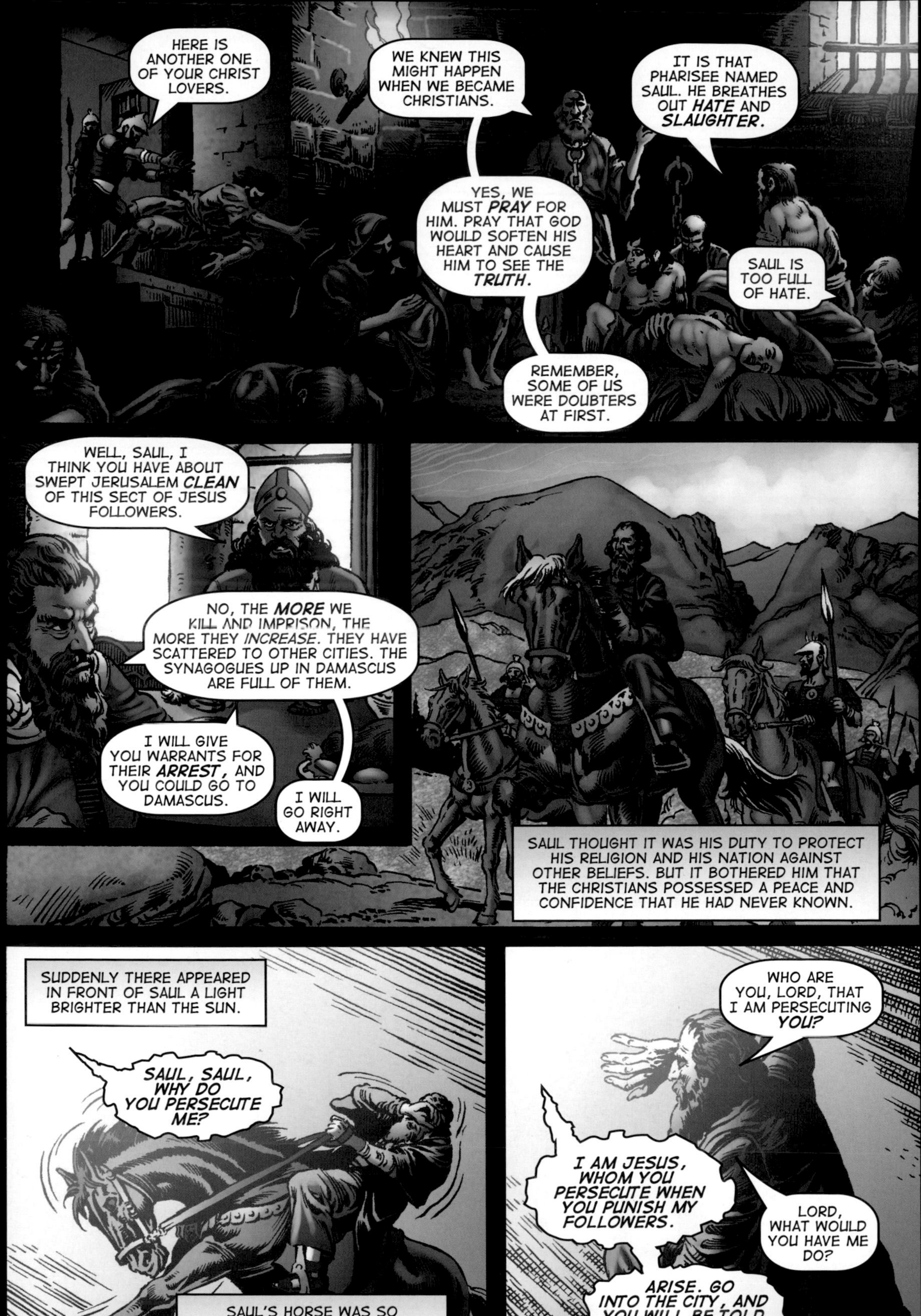

HERE IS ANOTHER ONE OF YOUR CHRIST LOVERS.
WE KNEW THIS MIGHT HAPPEN WHEN WE BECAME CHRISTIANS.
IT IS THAT PHARISEE NAMED SAUL. HE BREATHES OUT HATE AND SLAUGHTER.
YES, WE MUST PRAY FOR HIM. PRAY THAT GOD WOULD SOFTEN HIS HEART AND CAUSE HIM TO SEE THE TRUTH.
SAUL IS TOO FULL OF HATE.
REMEMBER, SOME OF US WERE DOUBTERS AT FIRST.
WELL, SAUL, I THINK YOU HAVE ABOUT SWEPT JERUSALEM CLEAN OF THIS SECT OF JESUS FOLLOWERS.
NO, THE MORE WE KILL AND IMPRISON, THE MORE THEY INCREASE. THEY HAVE SCATTERED TO OTHER CITIES. THE SYNAGOGUES UP IN DAMASCUS ARE FULL OF THEM.
I WILL GIVE YOU WARRANTS FOR THEIR ARREST, AND YOU COULD GO TO DAMASCUS.
I WILL GO RIGHT AWAY.
SAUL THOUGHT IT WAS HIS DUTY TO PROTECT HIS RELIGION AND HIS NATION AGAINST OTHER BELIEFS. BUT IT BOTHERED HIM THAT THE CHRISTIANS POSSESSED A PEACE AND CONFIDENCE THAT HE HAD NEVER KNOWN.
SUDDENLY THERE APPEARED IN FRONT OF SAUL A LIGHT BRIGHTER THAN THE SUN.
SAUL, SAUL, WHY DO YOU PERSECUTE ME?
SAUL'S HORSE WAS SO FRIGHTENED THAT IT THREW HIM INTO THE ROAD AND RAN AWAY.
WHO ARE YOU, LORD, THAT I AM PERSECUTING YOU?
I AM JESUS, WHOM YOU PERSECUTE WHEN YOU PUNISH MY FOLLOWERS.
LORD, WHAT WOULD YOU HAVE ME DO?
ARISE. GO INTO THE CITY, AND YOU WILL BE TOLD WHAT TO DO.

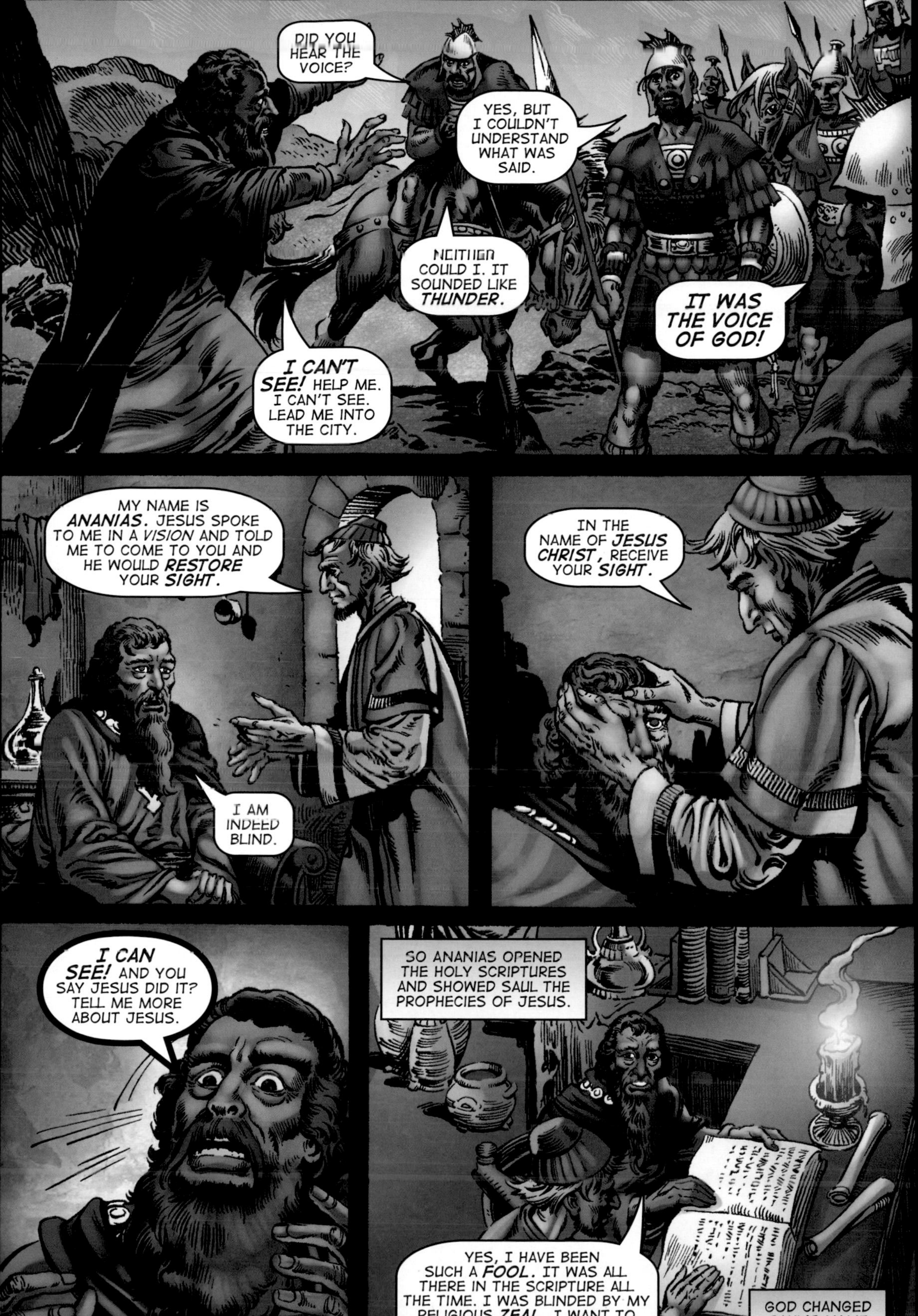
DID YOU HEAR THE VOICE?
YES, BUT I COULDN'T UNDERSTAND WHAT WAS SAID.
NEITHER COULD I. IT SOUNDED LIKE THUNDER.
IT WAS THE VOICE OF GOD!
I CAN'T SEE! HELP ME. I CAN'T SEE. LEAD ME INTO THE CITY.
MY NAME IS ANANIAS. JESUS SPOKE TO ME IN A VISION AND TOLD ME TO COME TO YOU AND HE WOULD RESTORE YOUR SIGHT.
I AM INDEED BLIND.
IN THE NAME OF JESUS CHRIST, RECEIVE YOUR SIGHT.
I CAN SEE! AND YOU SAY JESUS DID IT? TELL ME MORE ABOUT JESUS.
SO ANANIAS OPENED THE HOLY SCRIPTURES AND SHOWED SAUL THE PROPHECIES OF JESUS.
YES, I HAVE BEEN SUCH A FOOL. IT WAS ALL THERE IN THE SCRIPTURE ALL THE TIME. I WAS BLINDED BY MY RELIGIOUS ZEAL. I WANT TO BE BAPTIZED AND BECOME A FOLLOWER OF JESUS.
GOD CHANGED SAUL'S NAME TO PAUL.

ACTS 9:7–19

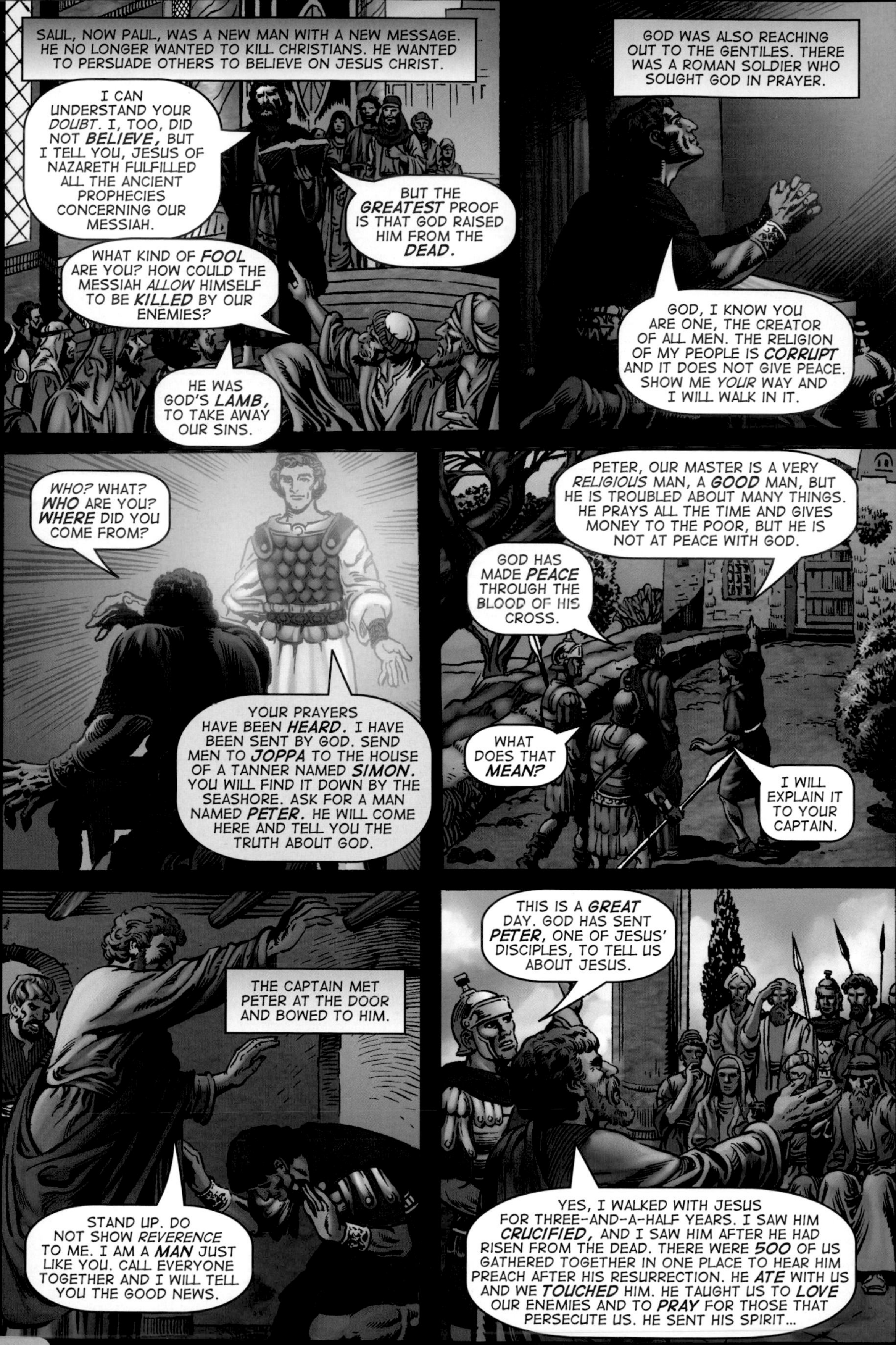
SAUL, NOW PAUL, WAS A NEW MAN WITH A NEW MESSAGE. HE NO LONGER WANTED TO KILL CHRISTIANS. HE WANTED TO PERSUADE OTHERS TO BELIEVE ON JESUS CHRIST.
I CAN UNDERSTAND YOUR *DOUBT*. I, TOO, DID NOT ***BELIEVE,*** BUT I TELL YOU, JESUS OF NAZARETH FULFILLED ALL THE ANCIENT PROPHECIES CONCERNING OUR MESSIAH.
BUT THE ***GREATEST*** PROOF IS THAT GOD RAISED HIM FROM THE ***DEAD.***
WHAT KIND OF ***FOOL*** ARE YOU? HOW COULD THE MESSIAH *ALLOW* HIMSELF TO BE ***KILLED*** BY OUR ENEMIES?
HE WAS GOD'S ***LAMB,*** TO TAKE AWAY OUR SINS.
GOD WAS ALSO REACHING OUT TO THE GENTILES. THERE WAS A ROMAN SOLDIER WHO SOUGHT GOD IN PRAYER.
GOD, I KNOW YOU ARE ONE, THE CREATOR OF ALL MEN. THE RELIGION OF MY PEOPLE IS ***CORRUPT*** AND IT DOES NOT GIVE PEACE. SHOW ME *YOUR* WAY AND I WILL WALK IN IT.
WHO? WHAT? ***WHO*** ARE YOU? ***WHERE*** DID YOU COME FROM?
YOUR PRAYERS HAVE BEEN ***HEARD.*** I HAVE BEEN SENT BY GOD. SEND MEN TO ***JOPPA*** TO THE HOUSE OF A TANNER NAMED ***SIMON.*** YOU WILL FIND IT DOWN BY THE SEASHORE. ASK FOR A MAN NAMED ***PETER.*** HE WILL COME HERE AND TELL YOU THE TRUTH ABOUT GOD.
PETER, OUR MASTER IS A VERY *RELIGIOUS* MAN, A ***GOOD*** MAN, BUT HE IS TROUBLED ABOUT MANY THINGS. HE PRAYS ALL THE TIME AND GIVES MONEY TO THE POOR, BUT HE IS NOT AT PEACE WITH GOD.
GOD HAS MADE ***PEACE*** THROUGH THE BLOOD OF HIS CROSS.
WHAT DOES THAT ***MEAN?***
I WILL EXPLAIN IT TO YOUR CAPTAIN.
THE CAPTAIN MET PETER AT THE DOOR AND BOWED TO HIM.
STAND UP. DO NOT SHOW *REVERENCE* TO ME. I AM A ***MAN*** JUST LIKE YOU. CALL EVERYONE TOGETHER AND I WILL TELL YOU THE GOOD NEWS.
THIS IS A ***GREAT*** DAY. GOD HAS SENT ***PETER,*** ONE OF JESUS' DISCIPLES, TO TELL US ABOUT JESUS.
YES, I WALKED WITH JESUS FOR THREE-AND-A-HALF YEARS. I SAW HIM ***CRUCIFIED,*** AND I SAW HIM AFTER HE HAD RISEN FROM THE DEAD. THERE WERE ***500*** OF US GATHERED TOGETHER IN ONE PLACE TO HEAR HIM PREACH AFTER HIS RESURRECTION. HE ***ATE*** WITH US AND WE ***TOUCHED*** HIM. HE TAUGHT US TO ***LOVE*** OUR ENEMIES AND TO ***PRAY*** FOR THOSE THAT PERSECUTE US. HE SENT HIS SPIRIT...

ACTS 9:20-22, 10:1-27, 38-41

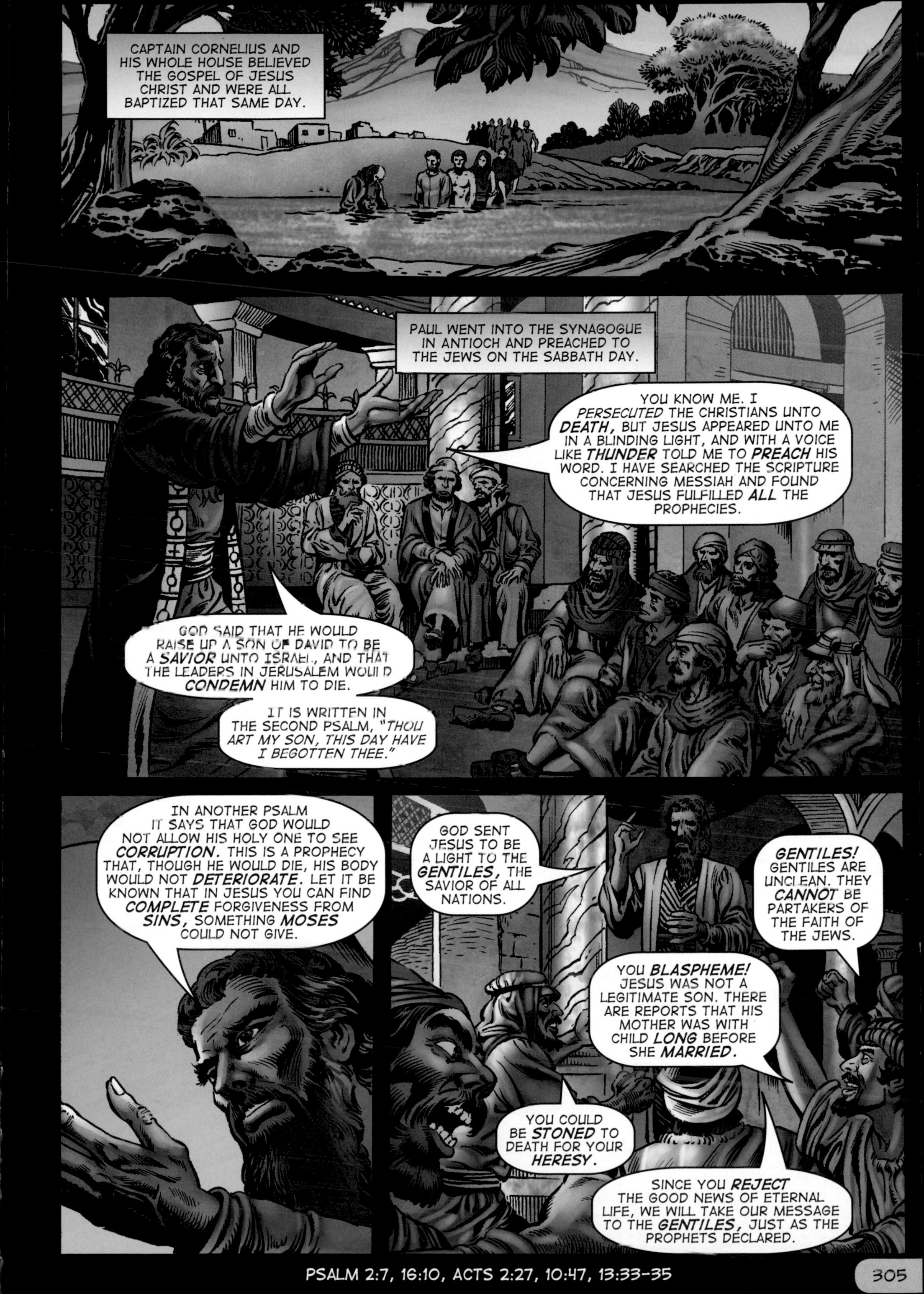
CAPTAIN CORNELIUS AND HIS WHOLE HOUSE BELIEVED THE GOSPEL OF JESUS CHRIST AND WERE ALL BAPTIZED THAT SAME DAY.
PAUL WENT INTO THE SYNAGOGUE IN ANTIOCH AND PREACHED TO THE JEWS ON THE SABBATH DAY.
YOU KNOW ME. I *PERSECUTED* THE CHRISTIANS UNTO **DEATH**, BUT JESUS APPEARED UNTO ME IN A BLINDING LIGHT, AND WITH A VOICE LIKE **THUNDER** TOLD ME TO **PREACH** HIS WORD. I HAVE SEARCHED THE SCRIPTURE CONCERNING MESSIAH AND FOUND THAT JESUS FULFILLED **ALL** THE PROPHECIES.
GOD SAID THAT HE WOULD RAISE UP A SON OF DAVID TO BE A **SAVIOR** UNTO ISRAEL, AND THAT THE LEADERS IN JERUSALEM WOULD **CONDEMN** HIM TO DIE.
IT IS WRITTEN IN THE SECOND PSALM, "*THOU ART MY SON, THIS DAY HAVE I BEGOTTEN THEE.*"
IN ANOTHER PSALM IT SAYS THAT GOD WOULD NOT ALLOW HIS HOLY ONE TO SEE **CORRUPTION**. THIS IS A PROPHECY THAT, THOUGH HE WOULD DIE, HIS BODY WOULD NOT **DETERIORATE**. LET IT BE KNOWN THAT IN JESUS YOU CAN FIND **COMPLETE** FORGIVENESS FROM **SINS**, SOMETHING **MOSES** COULD NOT GIVE.
GOD SENT JESUS TO BE A LIGHT TO THE **GENTILES**, THE SAVIOR OF ALL NATIONS.
GENTILES! GENTILES ARE UNCLEAN. THEY **CANNOT** BE PARTAKERS OF THE FAITH OF THE JEWS.
YOU **BLASPHEME!** JESUS WAS NOT A LEGITIMATE SON. THERE ARE REPORTS THAT HIS MOTHER WAS WITH CHILD **LONG** BEFORE SHE **MARRIED**.
YOU COULD BE **STONED** TO DEATH FOR YOUR **HERESY**.
SINCE YOU **REJECT** THE GOOD NEWS OF ETERNAL LIFE, WE WILL TAKE OUR MESSAGE TO THE **GENTILES**, JUST AS THE PROPHETS DECLARED.

PSALM 2:7, 16:10, ACTS 2:27, 10:47, 13:33-35

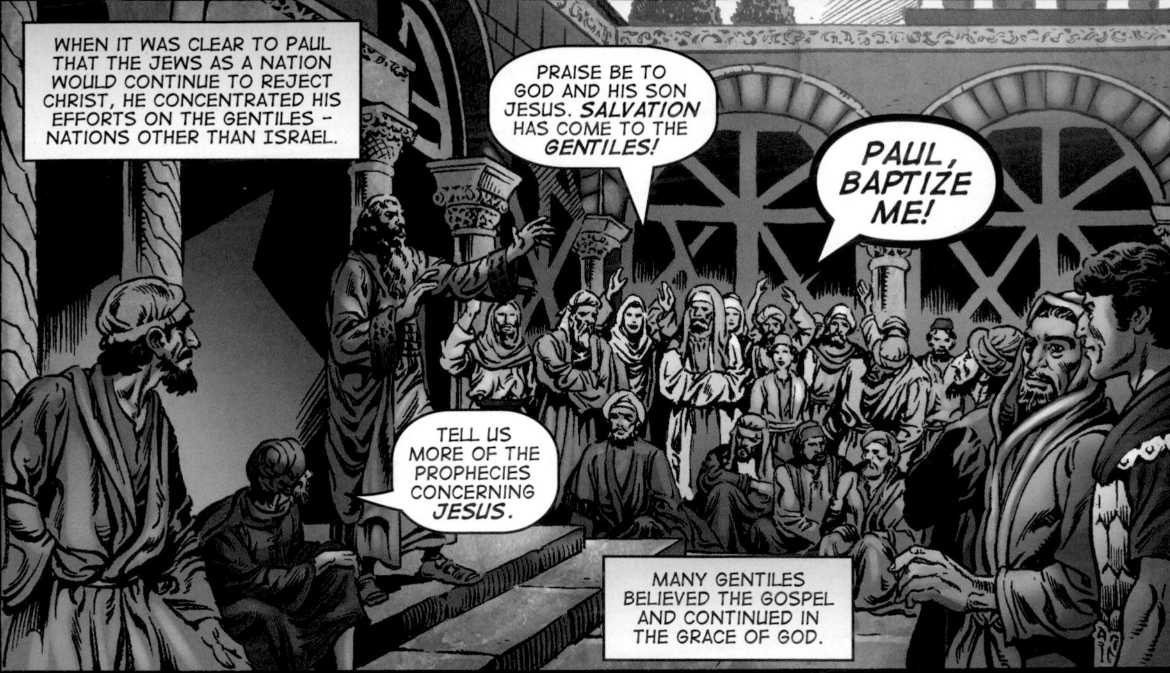
WHEN IT WAS CLEAR TO PAUL THAT THE JEWS AS A NATION WOULD CONTINUE TO REJECT CHRIST, HE CONCENTRATED HIS EFFORTS ON THE GENTILES - NATIONS OTHER THAN ISRAEL.
PRAISE BE TO GOD AND HIS SON JESUS. *SALVATION* HAS COME TO THE *GENTILES!*
PAUL, BAPTIZE ME!
TELL US MORE OF THE PROPHECIES CONCERNING *JESUS*.
MANY GENTILES BELIEVED THE GOSPEL AND CONTINUED IN THE GRACE OF GOD.

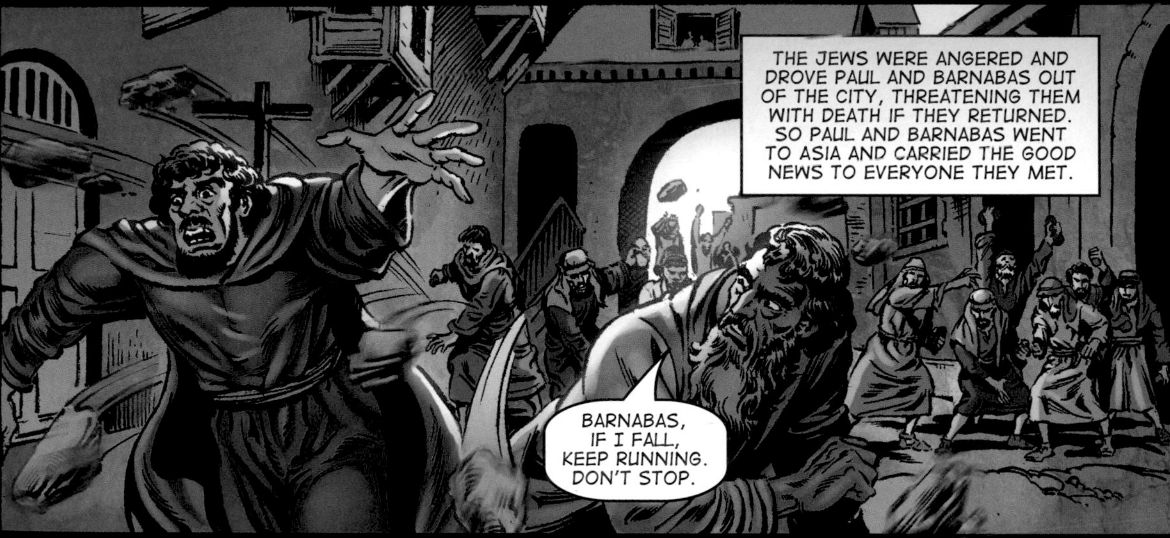
THE JEWS WERE ANGERED AND DROVE PAUL AND BARNABAS OUT OF THE CITY, THREATENING THEM WITH DEATH IF THEY RETURNED. SO PAUL AND BARNABAS WENT TO ASIA AND CARRIED THE GOOD NEWS TO EVERYONE THEY MET.
BARNABAS, IF I FALL, KEEP RUNNING. DON'T STOP.

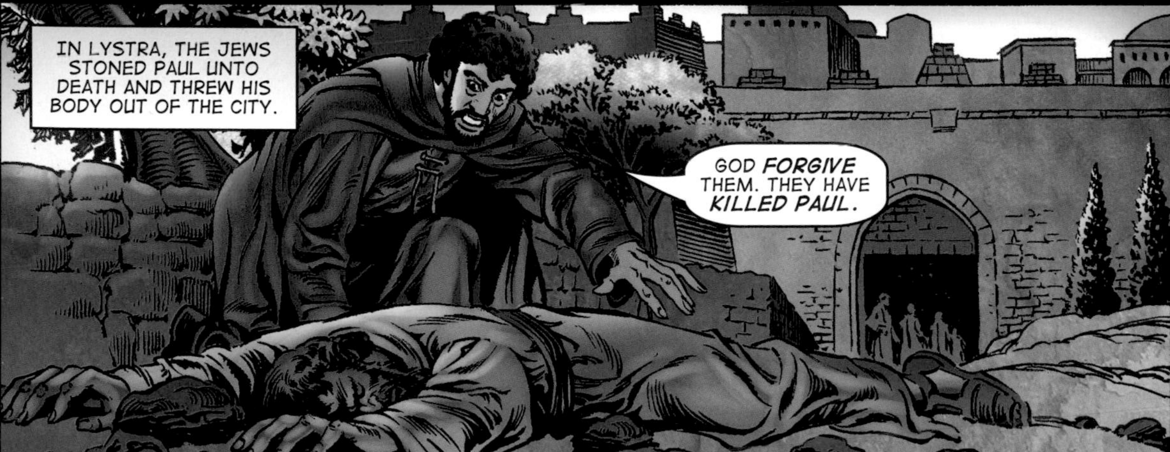
IN LYSTRA, THE JEWS STONED PAUL UNTO DEATH AND THREW HIS BODY OUT OF THE CITY.
GOD *FORGIVE* THEM. THEY HAVE *KILLED PAUL*.

ACTS 14:18-20

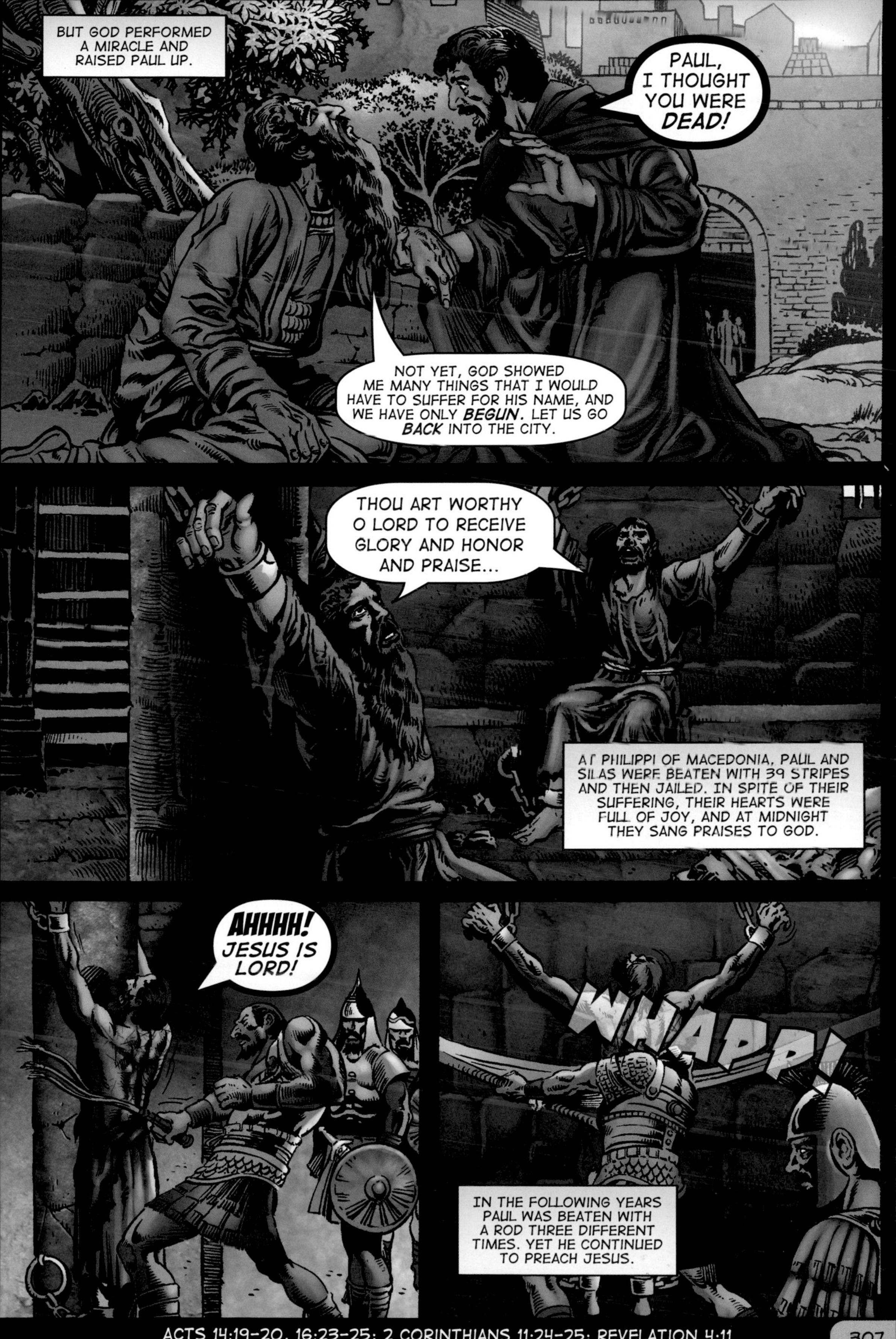
BUT GOD PERFORMED A MIRACLE AND RAISED PAUL UP.
PAUL, I THOUGHT YOU WERE DEAD!
NOT YET, GOD SHOWED ME MANY THINGS THAT I WOULD HAVE TO SUFFER FOR HIS NAME, AND WE HAVE ONLY BEGUN. LET US GO BACK INTO THE CITY.
THOU ART WORTHY O LORD TO RECEIVE GLORY AND HONOR AND PRAISE...
AT PHILIPPI OF MACEDONIA, PAUL AND SILAS WERE BEATEN WITH 39 STRIPES AND THEN JAILED. IN SPITE OF THEIR SUFFERING, THEIR HEARTS WERE FULL OF JOY, AND AT MIDNIGHT THEY SANG PRAISES TO GOD.
AHHHH! JESUS IS LORD!
WHAPP!
IN THE FOLLOWING YEARS PAUL WAS BEATEN WITH A ROD THREE DIFFERENT TIMES. YET HE CONTINUED TO PREACH JESUS.

ACTS 14:19-20, 16:23-25; 2 CORINTHIANS 11:24-25; REVELATION 4:11

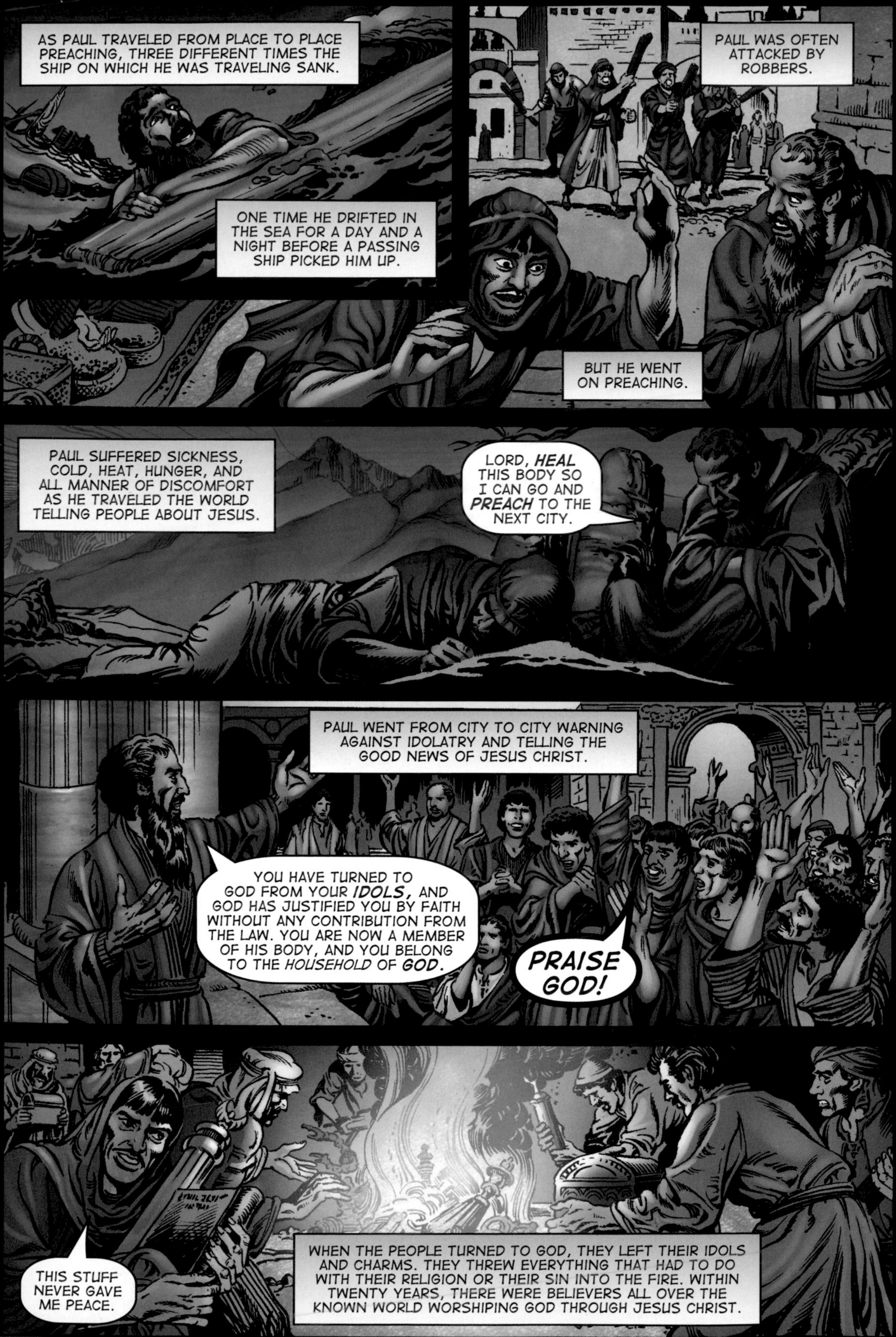
AS PAUL TRAVELED FROM PLACE TO PLACE PREACHING, THREE DIFFERENT TIMES THE SHIP ON WHICH HE WAS TRAVELING SANK.
ONE TIME HE DRIFTED IN THE SEA FOR A DAY AND A NIGHT BEFORE A PASSING SHIP PICKED HIM UP.
PAUL WAS OFTEN ATTACKED BY ROBBERS.
BUT HE WENT ON PREACHING.
PAUL SUFFERED SICKNESS, COLD, HEAT, HUNGER, AND ALL MANNER OF DISCOMFORT AS HE TRAVELED THE WORLD TELLING PEOPLE ABOUT JESUS.
LORD, **HEAL** THIS BODY SO I CAN GO AND ***PREACH*** TO THE NEXT CITY.
PAUL WENT FROM CITY TO CITY WARNING AGAINST IDOLATRY AND TELLING THE GOOD NEWS OF JESUS CHRIST.
YOU HAVE TURNED TO GOD FROM YOUR ***IDOLS,*** AND GOD HAS JUSTIFIED YOU BY FAITH WITHOUT ANY CONTRIBUTION FROM THE LAW. YOU ARE NOW A MEMBER OF HIS BODY, AND YOU BELONG TO THE *HOUSEHOLD* OF **GOD**.
PRAISE GOD!
THIS STUFF NEVER GAVE ME PEACE.
WHEN THE PEOPLE TURNED TO GOD, THEY LEFT THEIR IDOLS AND CHARMS. THEY THREW EVERYTHING THAT HAD TO DO WITH THEIR RELIGION OR THEIR SIN INTO THE FIRE. WITHIN TWENTY YEARS, THERE WERE BELIEVERS ALL OVER THE KNOWN WORLD WORSHIPING GOD THROUGH JESUS CHRIST.

1 CORINTHIANS 10:14, 12:12–13, 18; 2 CORINTHIANS 11:25; GALATIANS 2:6; EPHESIANS 2:19

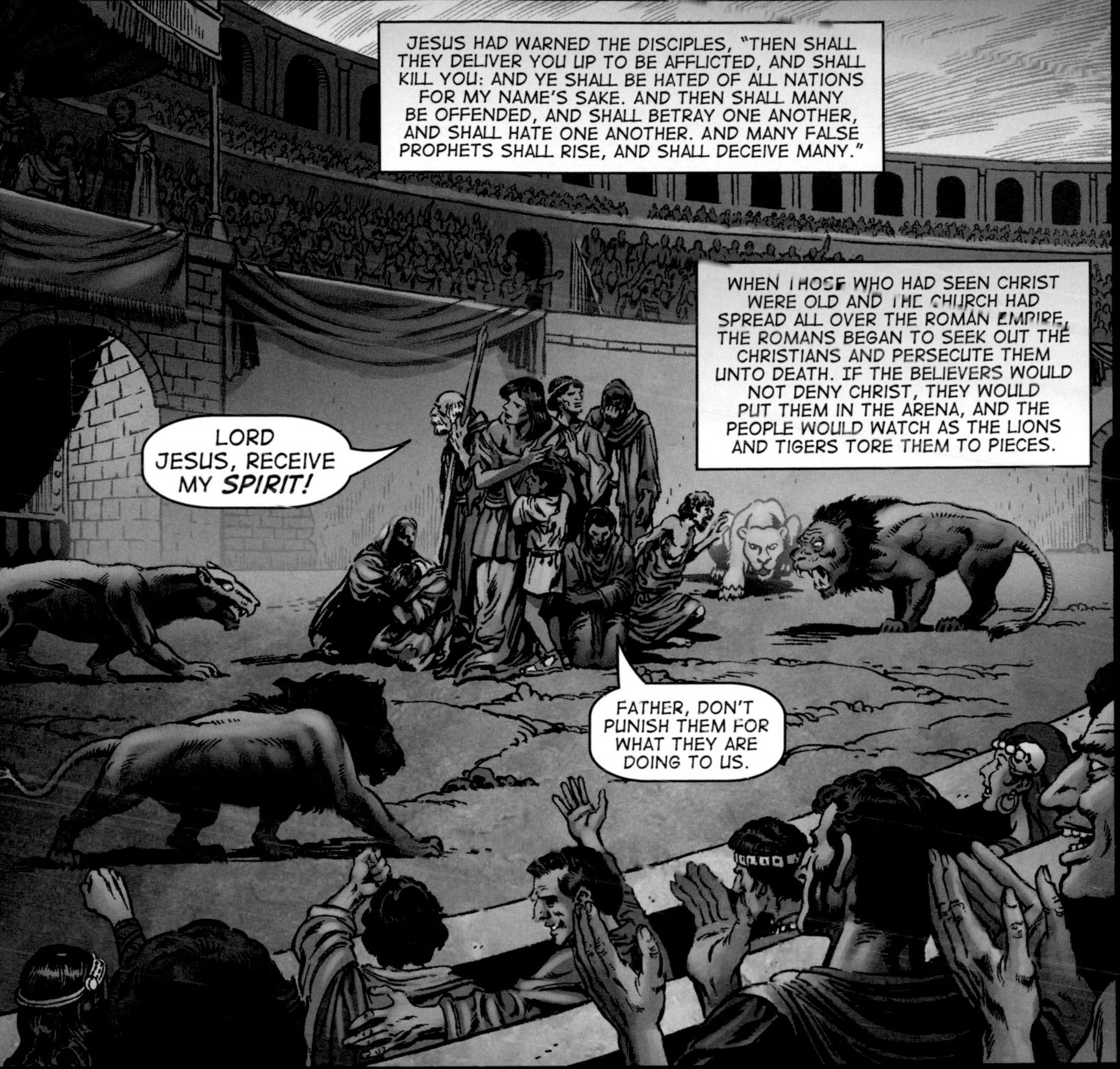
JESUS HAD WARNED THE DISCIPLES, "THEN SHALL THEY DELIVER YOU UP TO BE AFFLICTED, AND SHALL KILL YOU: AND YE SHALL BE HATED OF ALL NATIONS FOR MY NAME'S SAKE. AND THEN SHALL MANY BE OFFENDED, AND SHALL BETRAY ONE ANOTHER, AND SHALL HATE ONE ANOTHER. AND MANY FALSE PROPHETS SHALL RISE, AND SHALL DECEIVE MANY."
WHEN THOSE WHO HAD SEEN CHRIST WERE OLD AND THE CHURCH HAD SPREAD ALL OVER THE ROMAN EMPIRE, THE ROMANS BEGAN TO SEEK OUT THE CHRISTIANS AND PERSECUTE THEM UNTO DEATH. IF THE BELIEVERS WOULD NOT DENY CHRIST, THEY WOULD PUT THEM IN THE ARENA, AND THE PEOPLE WOULD WATCH AS THE LIONS AND TIGERS TORE THEM TO PIECES.
LORD JESUS, RECEIVE MY *SPIRIT!*
FATHER, DON'T PUNISH THEM FOR WHAT THEY ARE DOING TO US.

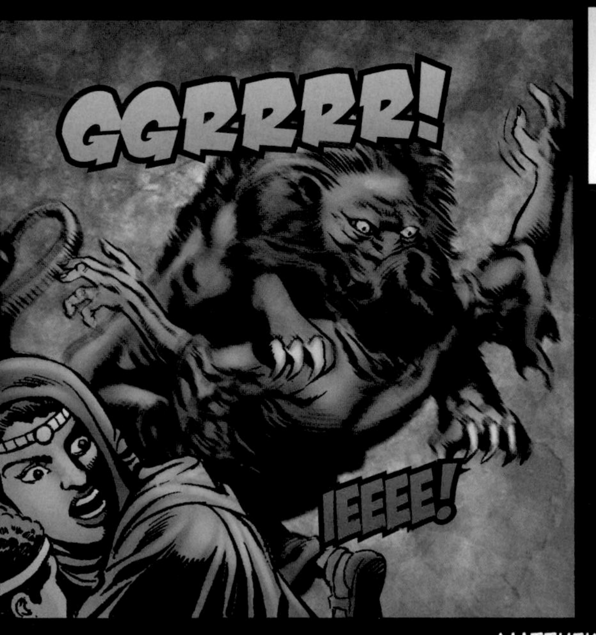
GGRRRR!
IEEEE!

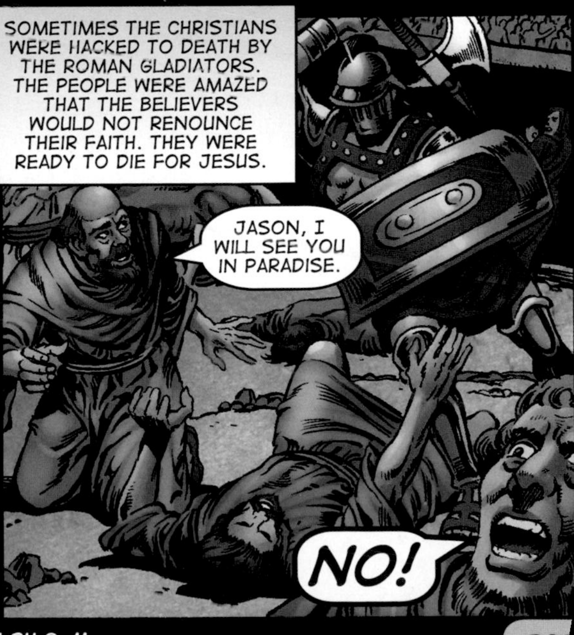
SOMETIMES THE CHRISTIANS WERE HACKED TO DEATH BY THE ROMAN GLADIATORS. THE PEOPLE WERE AMAZED THAT THE BELIEVERS WOULD NOT RENOUNCE THEIR FAITH. THEY WERE READY TO DIE FOR JESUS.
JASON, I WILL SEE YOU IN PARADISE.
NO!

MATTHEW 24:9–11

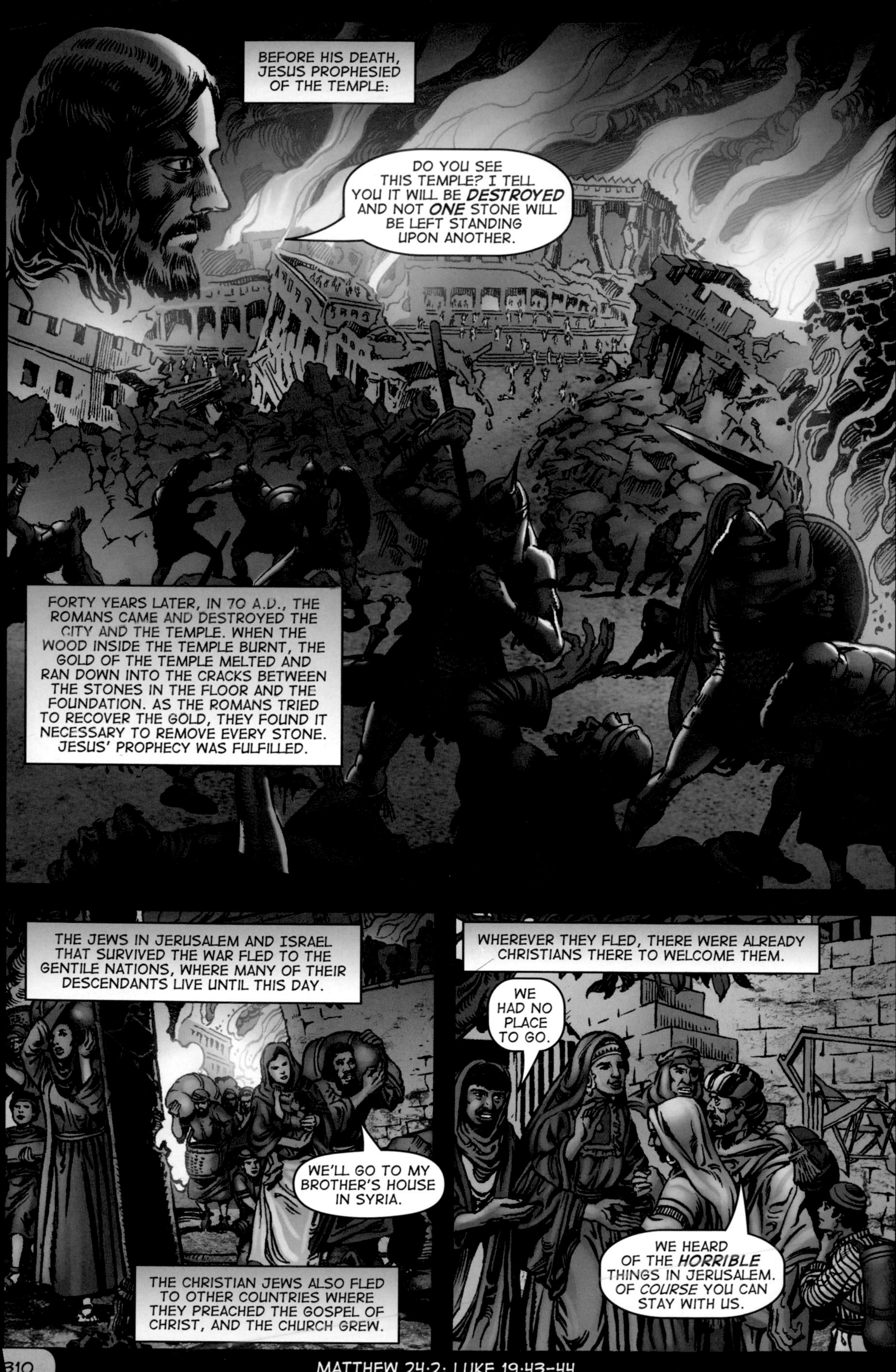
BEFORE HIS DEATH, JESUS PROPHESIED OF THE TEMPLE:
DO YOU SEE THIS TEMPLE? I TELL YOU IT WILL BE DESTROYED AND NOT ONE STONE WILL BE LEFT STANDING UPON ANOTHER.
FORTY YEARS LATER, IN 70 A.D., THE ROMANS CAME AND DESTROYED THE CITY AND THE TEMPLE. WHEN THE WOOD INSIDE THE TEMPLE BURNT, THE GOLD OF THE TEMPLE MELTED AND RAN DOWN INTO THE CRACKS BETWEEN THE STONES IN THE FLOOR AND THE FOUNDATION. AS THE ROMANS TRIED TO RECOVER THE GOLD, THEY FOUND IT NECESSARY TO REMOVE EVERY STONE. JESUS' PROPHECY WAS FULFILLED.
THE JEWS IN JERUSALEM AND ISRAEL THAT SURVIVED THE WAR FLED TO THE GENTILE NATIONS, WHERE MANY OF THEIR DESCENDANTS LIVE UNTIL THIS DAY.
WE'LL GO TO MY BROTHER'S HOUSE IN SYRIA.
THE CHRISTIAN JEWS ALSO FLED TO OTHER COUNTRIES WHERE THEY PREACHED THE GOSPEL OF CHRIST, AND THE CHURCH GREW.
WHEREVER THEY FLED, THERE WERE ALREADY CHRISTIANS THERE TO WELCOME THEM.
WE HAD NO PLACE TO GO.
WE HEARD OF THE HORRIBLE THINGS IN JERUSALEM. OF COURSE YOU CAN STAY WITH US.

MATTHEW 24:2; LUKE 19:43-44

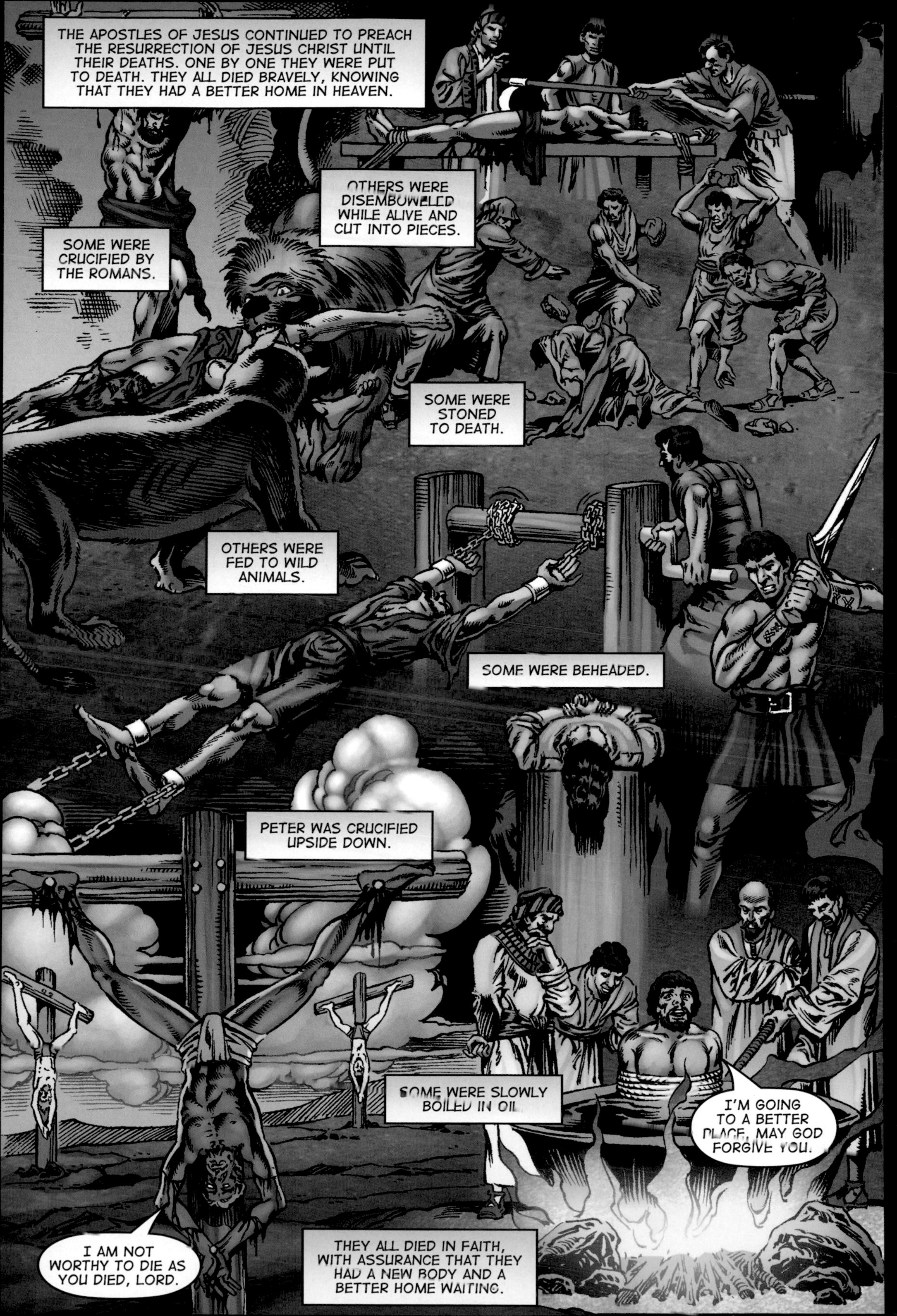
THE APOSTLES OF JESUS CONTINUED TO PREACH THE RESURRECTION OF JESUS CHRIST UNTIL THEIR DEATHS. ONE BY ONE THEY WERE PUT TO DEATH. THEY ALL DIED BRAVELY, KNOWING THAT THEY HAD A BETTER HOME IN HEAVEN.
SOME WERE CRUCIFIED BY THE ROMANS.
OTHERS WERE DISEMBOWELED WHILE ALIVE AND CUT INTO PIECES.
SOME WERE STONED TO DEATH.
OTHERS WERE FED TO WILD ANIMALS.
SOME WERE BEHEADED.
PETER WAS CRUCIFIED UPSIDE DOWN.
SOME WERE SLOWLY BOILED IN OIL.
I'M GOING TO A BETTER PLACE, MAY GOD FORGIVE YOU.
I AM NOT WORTHY TO DIE AS YOU DIED, LORD.
THEY ALL DIED IN FAITH, WITH ASSURANCE THAT THEY HAD A NEW BODY AND A BETTER HOME WAITING.

MATTHEW 14:10; JOHN 21:18

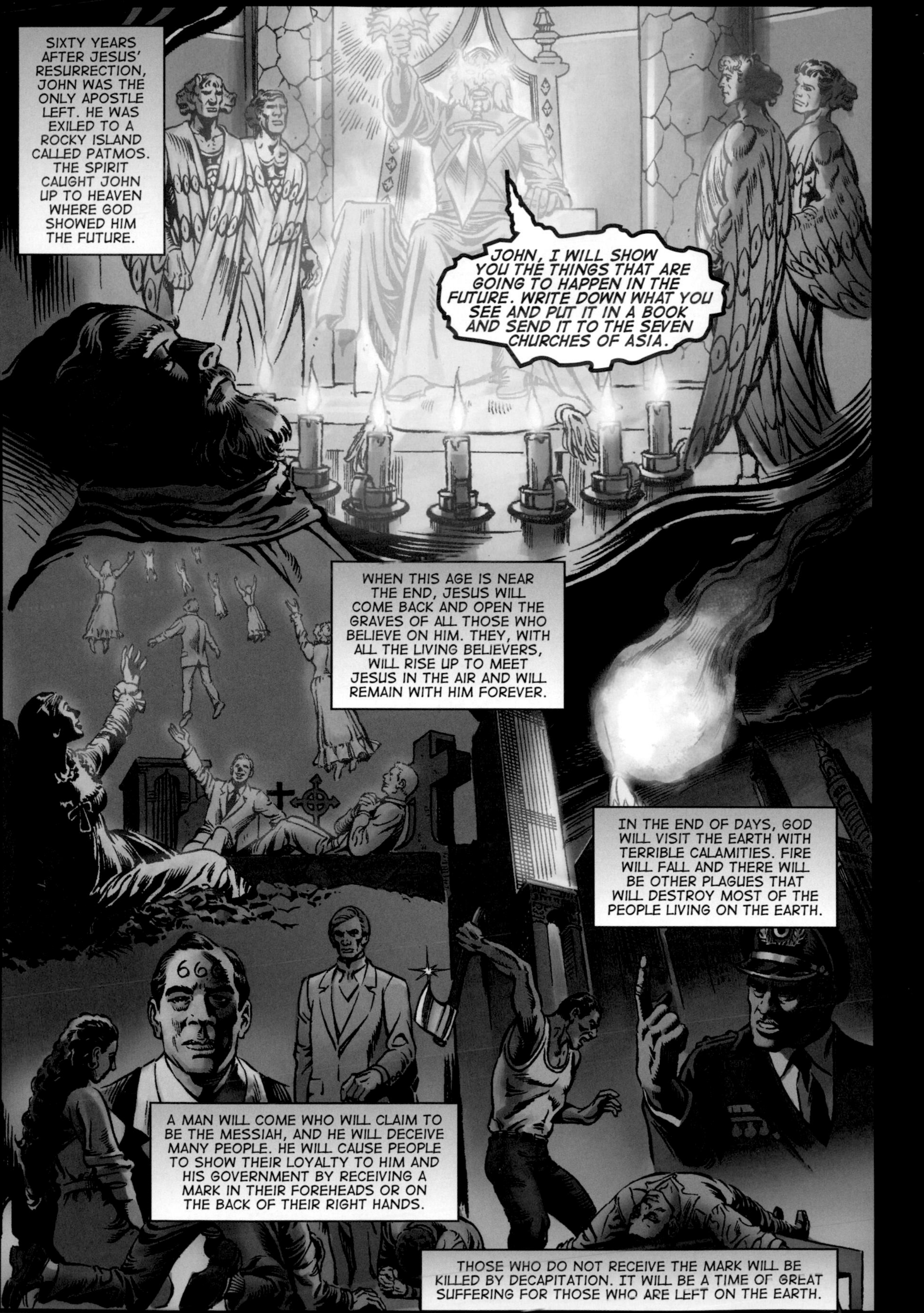

SIXTY YEARS AFTER JESUS' RESURRECTION, JOHN WAS THE ONLY APOSTLE LEFT. HE WAS EXILED TO A ROCKY ISLAND CALLED PATMOS. THE SPIRIT CAUGHT JOHN UP TO HEAVEN WHERE GOD SHOWED HIM THE FUTURE.
JOHN, I WILL SHOW YOU THE THINGS THAT ARE GOING TO HAPPEN IN THE FUTURE. WRITE DOWN WHAT YOU SEE AND PUT IT IN A BOOK AND SEND IT TO THE SEVEN CHURCHES OF ASIA.
WHEN THIS AGE IS NEAR THE END, JESUS WILL COME BACK AND OPEN THE GRAVES OF ALL THOSE WHO BELIEVE ON HIM. THEY, WITH ALL THE LIVING BELIEVERS, WILL RISE UP TO MEET JESUS IN THE AIR AND WILL REMAIN WITH HIM FOREVER.
IN THE END OF DAYS, GOD WILL VISIT THE EARTH WITH TERRIBLE CALAMITIES. FIRE WILL FALL AND THERE WILL BE OTHER PLAGUES THAT WILL DESTROY MOST OF THE PEOPLE LIVING ON THE EARTH.
A MAN WILL COME WHO WILL CLAIM TO BE THE MESSIAH, AND HE WILL DECEIVE MANY PEOPLE. HE WILL CAUSE PEOPLE TO SHOW THEIR LOYALTY TO HIM AND HIS GOVERNMENT BY RECEIVING A MARK IN THEIR FOREHEADS OR ON THE BACK OF THEIR RIGHT HANDS.
THOSE WHO DO NOT RECEIVE THE MARK WILL BE KILLED BY DECAPITATION. IT WILL BE A TIME OF GREAT SUFFERING FOR THOSE WHO ARE LEFT ON THE EARTH.

1 THESSALONIANS 4:14, 4:16-17; 2 THESSALONIANS 2:3-4; REVELATION 1:9, 11, 8:1-13, 9:18, 13:16, 20:4

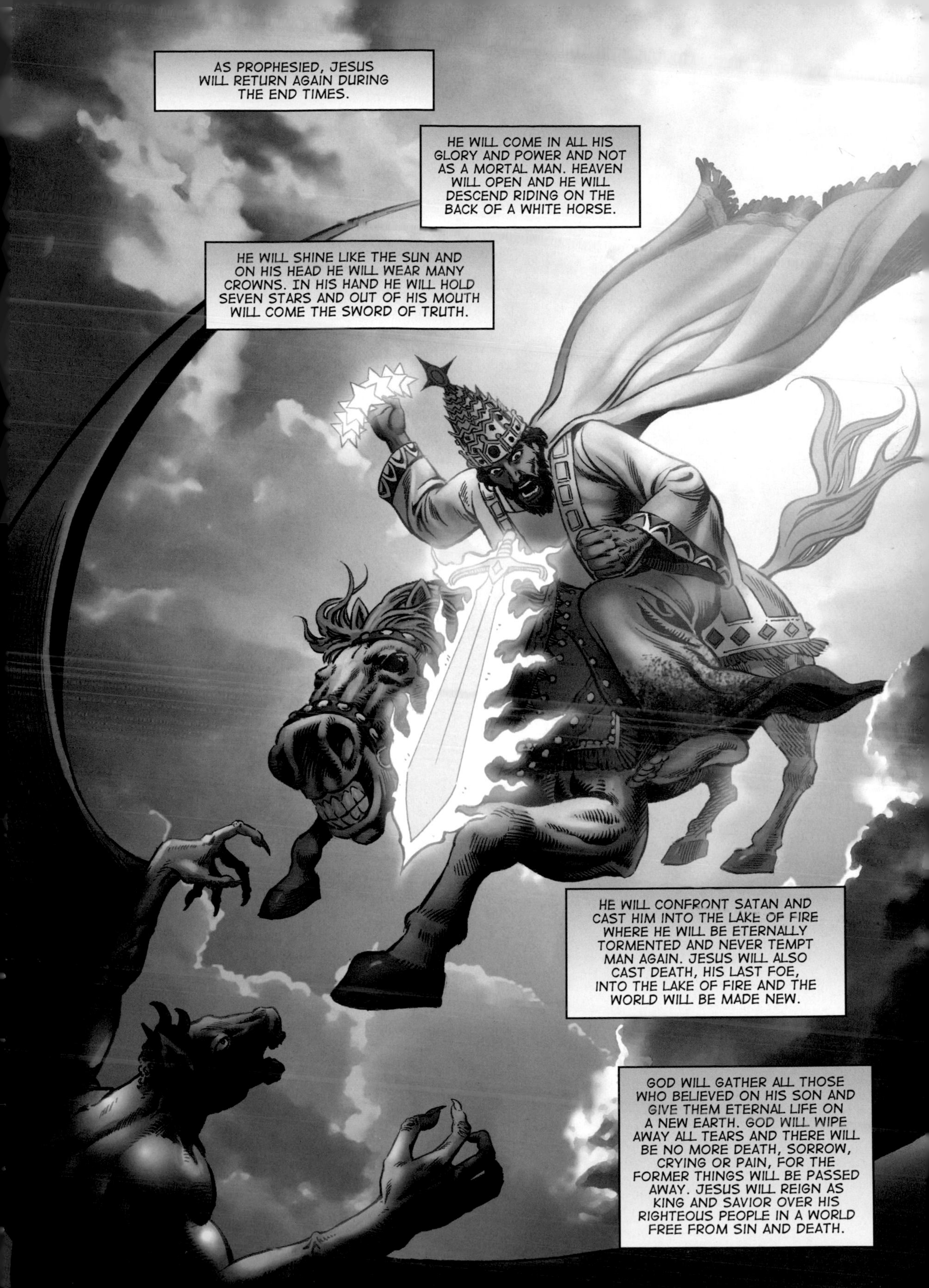
AS PROPHESIED, JESUS WILL RETURN AGAIN DURING THE END TIMES.
HE WILL COME IN ALL HIS GLORY AND POWER AND NOT AS A MORTAL MAN. HEAVEN WILL OPEN AND HE WILL DESCEND RIDING ON THE BACK OF A WHITE HORSE.
HE WILL SHINE LIKE THE SUN AND ON HIS HEAD HE WILL WEAR MANY CROWNS. IN HIS HAND HE WILL HOLD SEVEN STARS AND OUT OF HIS MOUTH WILL COME THE SWORD OF TRUTH.
HE WILL CONFRONT SATAN AND CAST HIM INTO THE LAKE OF FIRE WHERE HE WILL BE ETERNALLY TORMENTED AND NEVER TEMPT MAN AGAIN. JESUS WILL ALSO CAST DEATH, HIS LAST FOE, INTO THE LAKE OF FIRE AND THE WORLD WILL BE MADE NEW.
GOD WILL GATHER ALL THOSE WHO BELIEVED ON HIS SON AND GIVE THEM ETERNAL LIFE ON A NEW EARTH. GOD WILL WIPE AWAY ALL TEARS AND THERE WILL BE NO MORE DEATH, SORROW, CRYING OR PAIN, FOR THE FORMER THINGS WILL BE PASSED AWAY. JESUS WILL REIGN AS KING AND SAVIOR OVER HIS RIGHTEOUS PEOPLE IN A WORLD FREE FROM SIN AND DEATH.

1 THESSALONIANS 4:16; REVELATION 1:16, 19:11-21, 20:10-15, 21:1-4

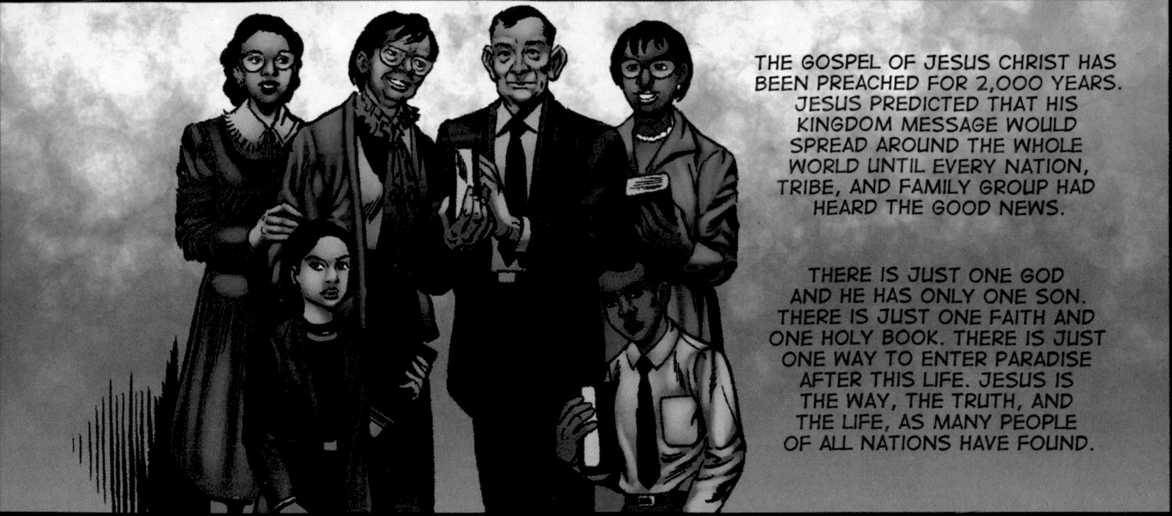
THE GOSPEL OF JESUS CHRIST HAS BEEN PREACHED FOR 2,000 YEARS. JESUS PREDICTED THAT HIS KINGDOM MESSAGE WOULD SPREAD AROUND THE WHOLE WORLD UNTIL EVERY NATION, TRIBE, AND FAMILY GROUP HAD HEARD THE GOOD NEWS.
THERE IS JUST ONE GOD AND HE HAS ONLY ONE SON. THERE IS JUST ONE FAITH AND ONE HOLY BOOK. THERE IS JUST ONE WAY TO ENTER PARADISE AFTER THIS LIFE. JESUS IS THE WAY, THE TRUTH, AND THE LIFE, AS MANY PEOPLE OF ALL NATIONS HAVE FOUND.

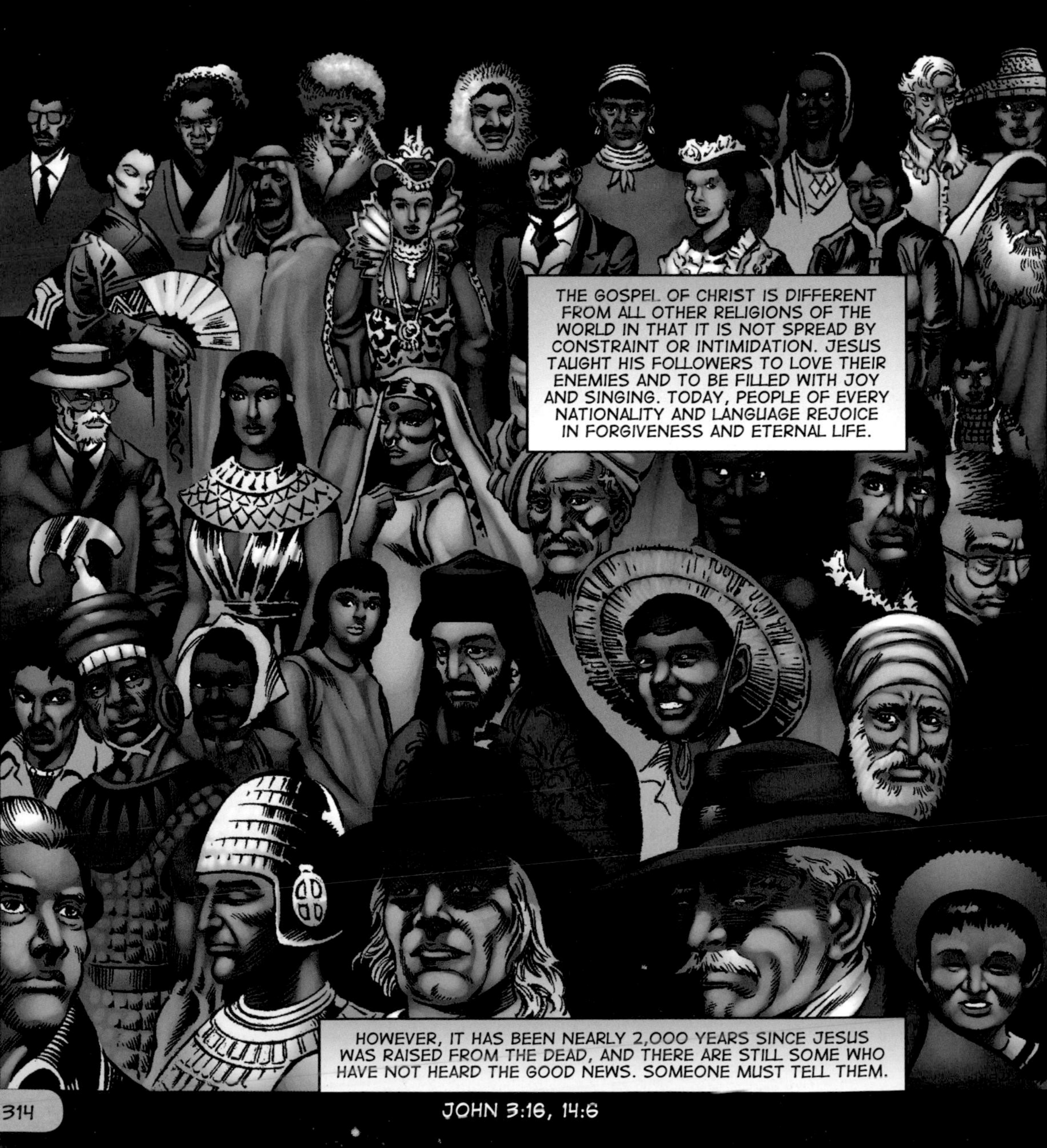
THE GOSPEL OF CHRIST IS DIFFERENT FROM ALL OTHER RELIGIONS OF THE WORLD IN THAT IT IS NOT SPREAD BY CONSTRAINT OR INTIMIDATION. JESUS TAUGHT HIS FOLLOWERS TO LOVE THEIR ENEMIES AND TO BE FILLED WITH JOY AND SINGING. TODAY, PEOPLE OF EVERY NATIONALITY AND LANGUAGE REJOICE IN FORGIVENESS AND ETERNAL LIFE.
HOWEVER, IT HAS BEEN NEARLY 2,000 YEARS SINCE JESUS WAS RAISED FROM THE DEAD, AND THERE ARE STILL SOME WHO HAVE NOT HEARD THE GOOD NEWS. SOMEONE MUST TELL THEM.

JOHN 3:16, 14:6

THE GREAT WHITE THRONE JUDGMENT

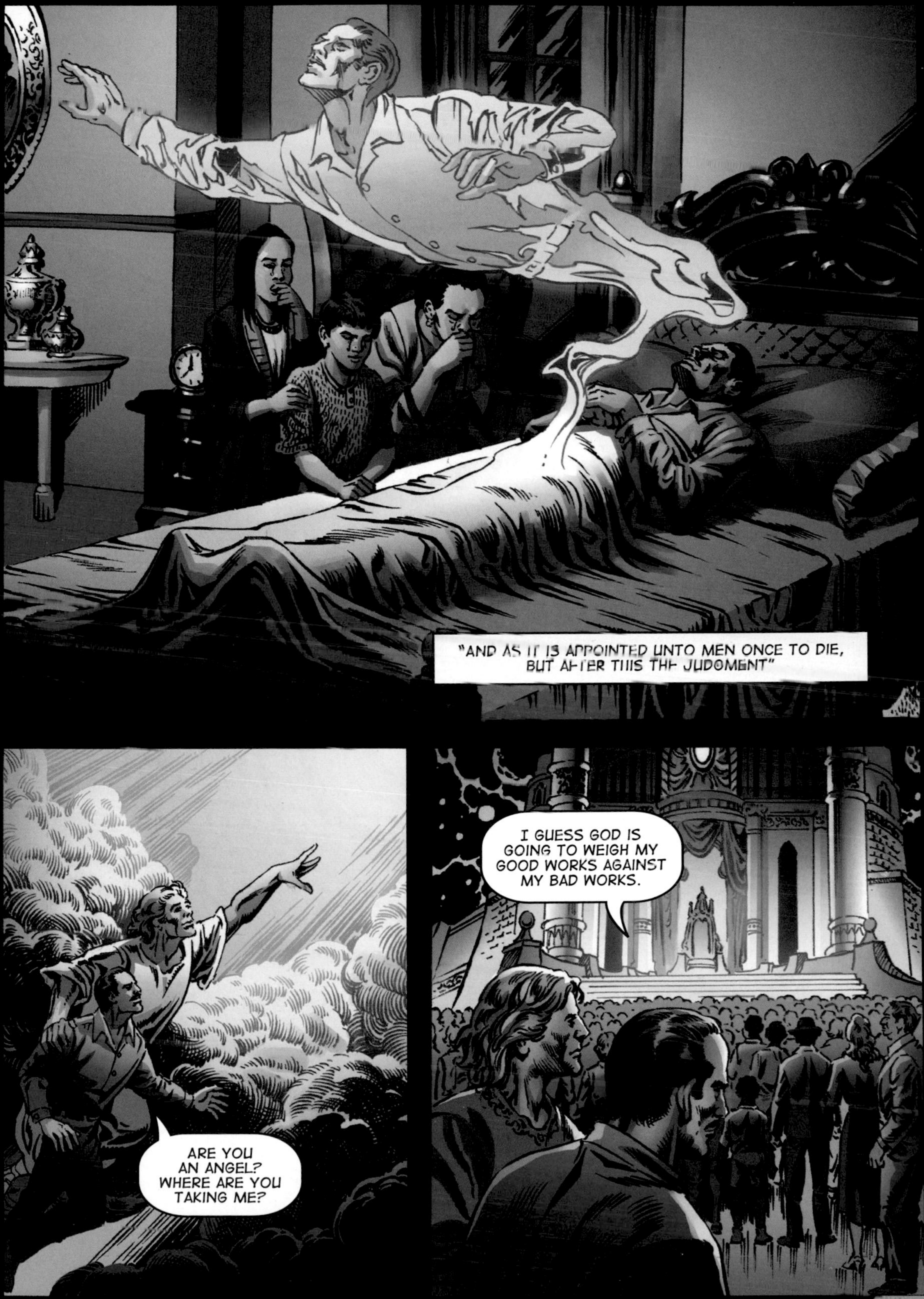
"AND AS IT IS APPOINTED UNTO MEN ONCE TO DIE, BUT AFTER THIS THE JUDGMENT"
ARE YOU AN ANGEL? WHERE ARE YOU TAKING ME?
I GUESS GOD IS GOING TO WEIGH MY GOOD WORKS AGAINST MY BAD WORKS.

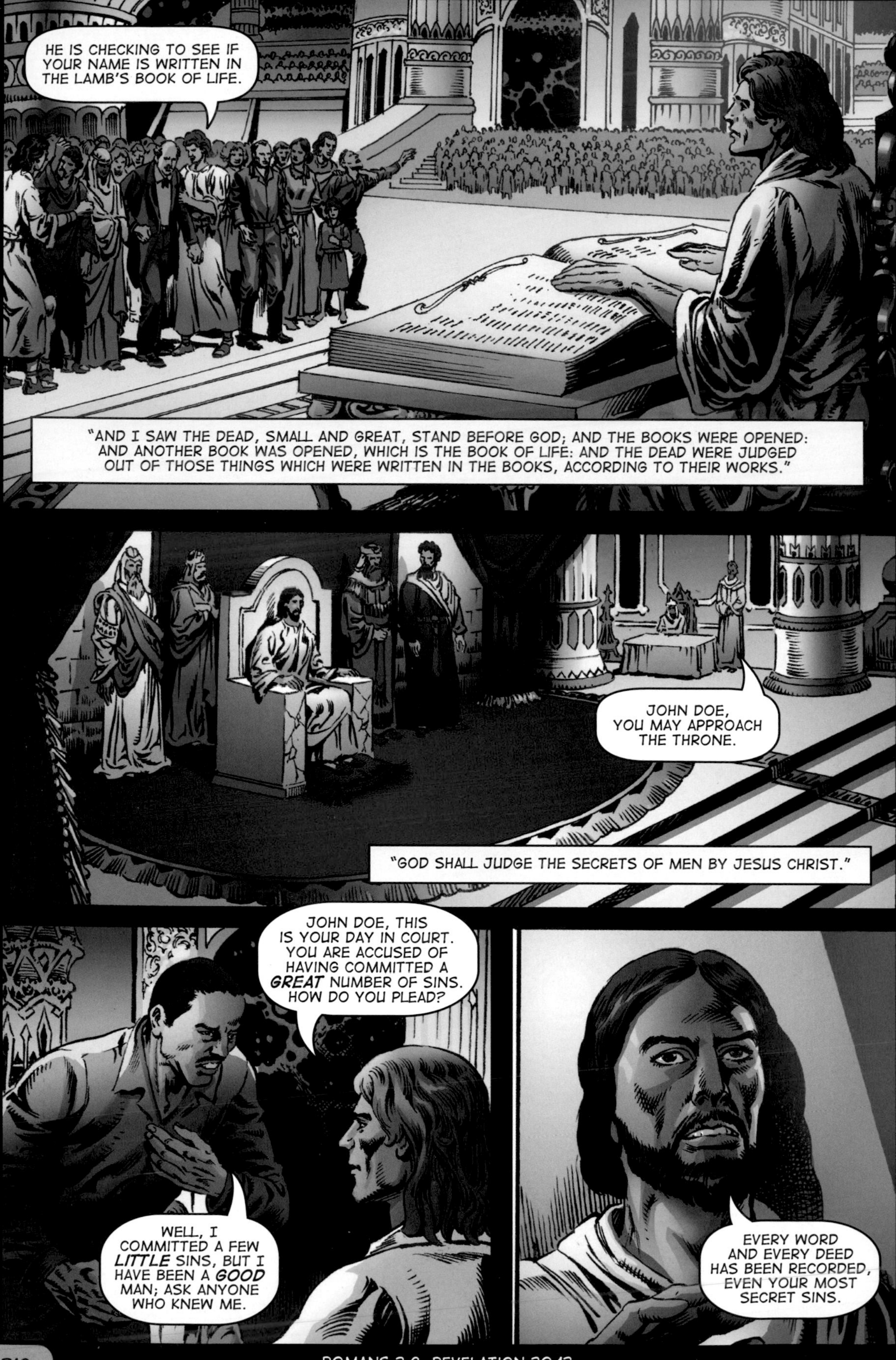

HE IS CHECKING TO SEE IF YOUR NAME IS WRITTEN IN THE LAMB'S BOOK OF LIFE.
"AND I SAW THE DEAD, SMALL AND GREAT, STAND BEFORE GOD; AND THE BOOKS WERE OPENED: AND ANOTHER BOOK WAS OPENED, WHICH IS THE BOOK OF LIFE: AND THE DEAD WERE JUDGED OUT OF THOSE THINGS WHICH WERE WRITTEN IN THE BOOKS, ACCORDING TO THEIR WORKS."
JOHN DOE, YOU MAY APPROACH THE THRONE.
"GOD SHALL JUDGE THE SECRETS OF MEN BY JESUS CHRIST."
JOHN DOE, THIS IS YOUR DAY IN COURT. YOU ARE ACCUSED OF HAVING COMMITTED A *GREAT* NUMBER OF SINS. HOW DO YOU PLEAD?
WELL, I COMMITTED A FEW *LITTLE* SINS, BUT I HAVE BEEN A *GOOD* MAN; ASK ANYONE WHO KNEW ME.
EVERY WORD AND EVERY DEED HAS BEEN RECORDED, EVEN YOUR MOST SECRET SINS.

ROMANS 2:6; REVELATION 20:12

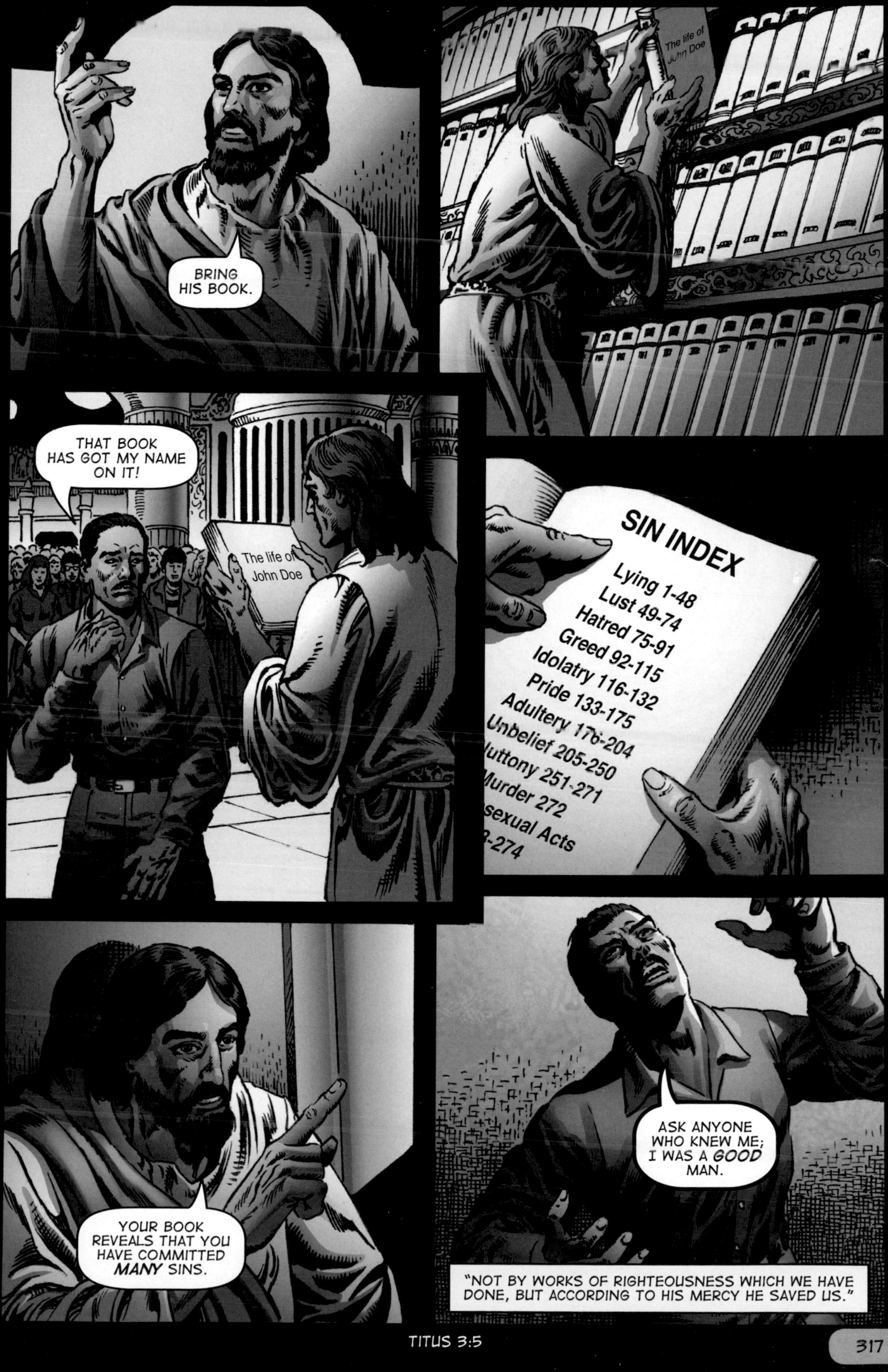

BRING HIS BOOK.
The life of John Doe
THAT BOOK HAS GOT MY NAME ON IT!
The life of John Doe
SIN INDEX
Lying 1-48
Lust 49-74
Hatred 75-91
Greed 92-115
Idolatry 116-132
Pride 133-175
Adultery 176-204
Unbelief 205-250
luttony 251-271
Murder 272
sexual Acts
-274
YOUR BOOK REVEALS THAT YOU HAVE COMMITTED *MANY* SINS.
ASK ANYONE WHO KNEW ME; I WAS A *GOOD* MAN.
"NOT BY WORKS OF RIGHTEOUSNESS WHICH WE HAVE DONE, BUT ACCORDING TO HIS MERCY HE SAVED US."

TITUS 3:5

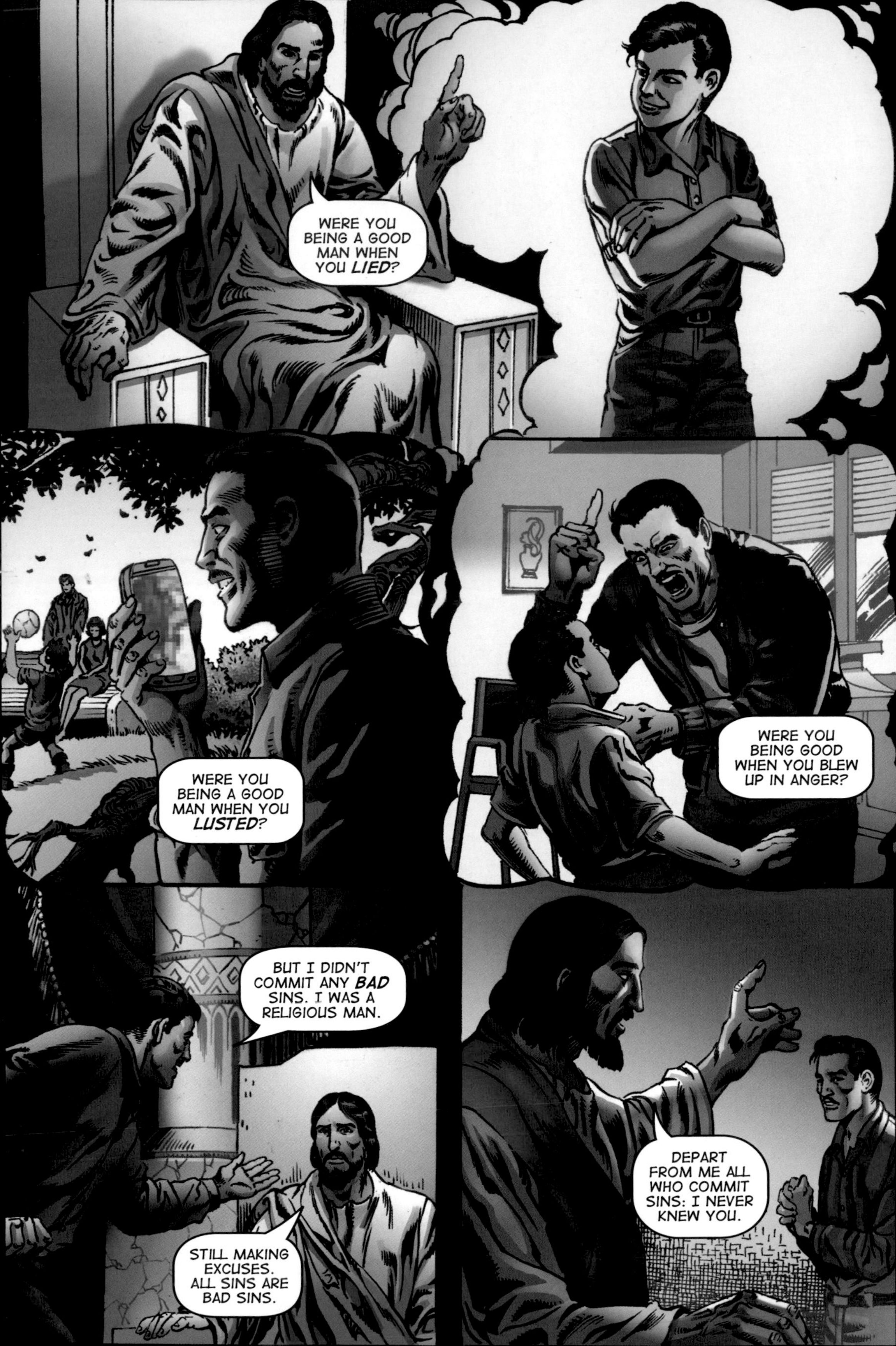
WERE YOU BEING A GOOD MAN WHEN YOU LIED?
WERE YOU BEING A GOOD MAN WHEN YOU LUSTED?
WERE YOU BEING GOOD WHEN YOU BLEW UP IN ANGER?
BUT I DIDN'T COMMIT ANY BAD SINS. I WAS A RELIGIOUS MAN.
STILL MAKING EXCUSES. ALL SINS ARE BAD SINS.
DEPART FROM ME ALL WHO COMMIT SINS: I NEVER KNEW YOU.

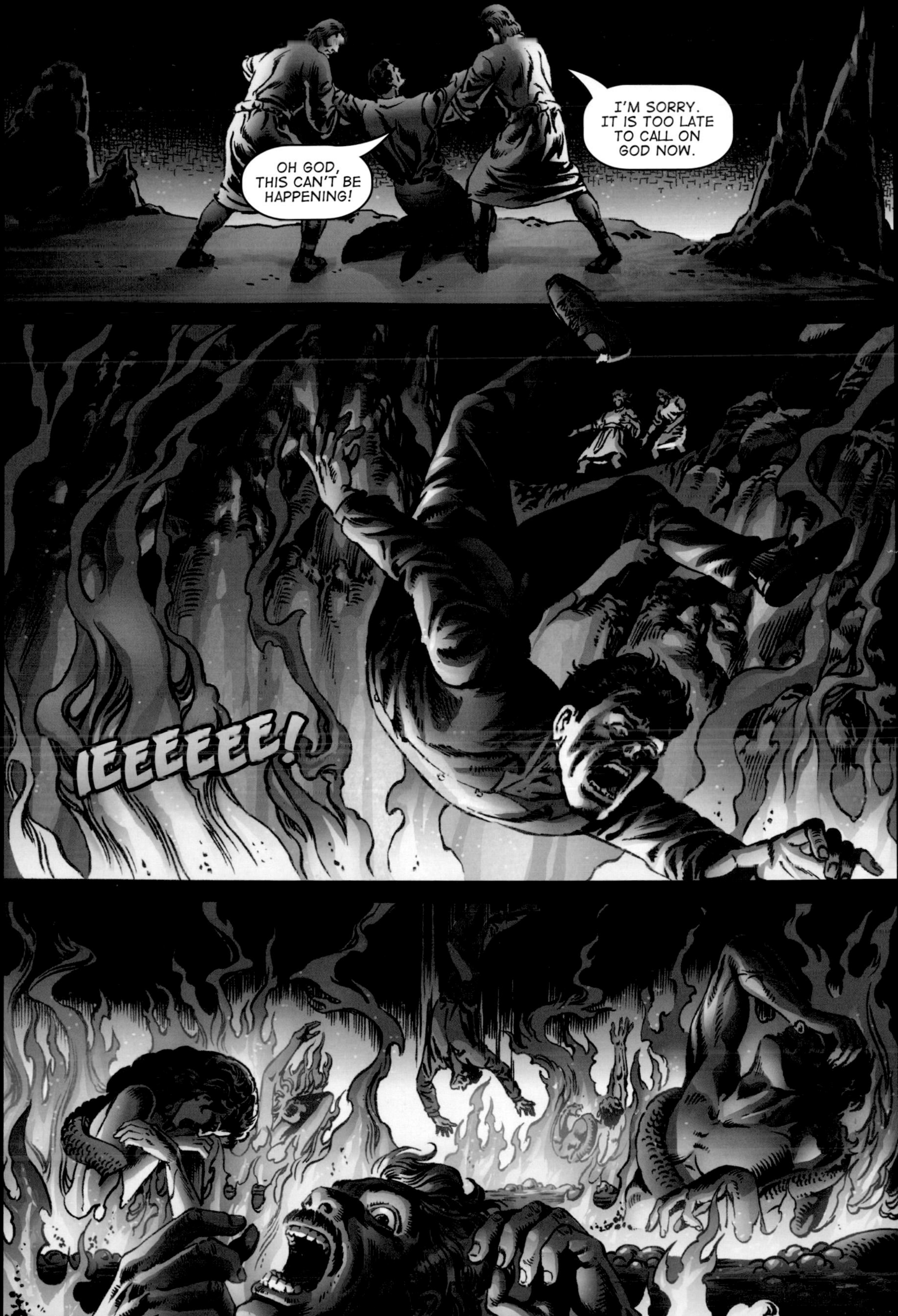
OH GOD, THIS CAN'T BE HAPPENING!
I'M SORRY. IT IS TOO LATE TO CALL ON GOD NOW.
IEEEEEE!

THE WICKED...SHALL BE CAST INTO THE FURNACE OF FIRE:
THERE SHALL BE WAILING AND GNASHING OF TEETH. MATTHEW 13:49-50

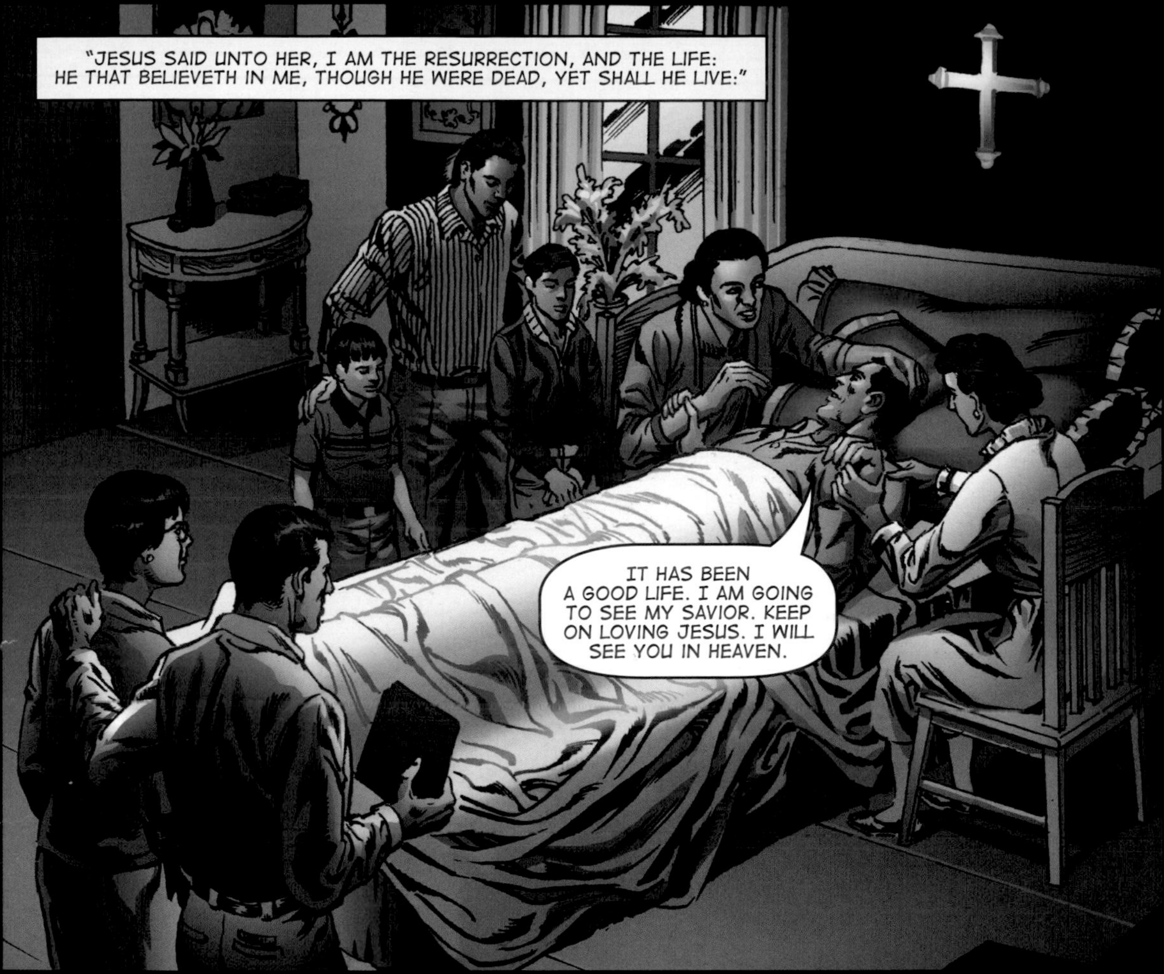
"JESUS SAID UNTO HER, I AM THE RESURRECTION, AND THE LIFE: HE THAT BELIEVETH IN ME, THOUGH HE WERE DEAD, YET SHALL HE LIVE:"
IT HAS BEEN A GOOD LIFE. I AM GOING TO SEE MY SAVIOR. KEEP ON LOVING JESUS. I WILL SEE YOU IN HEAVEN.

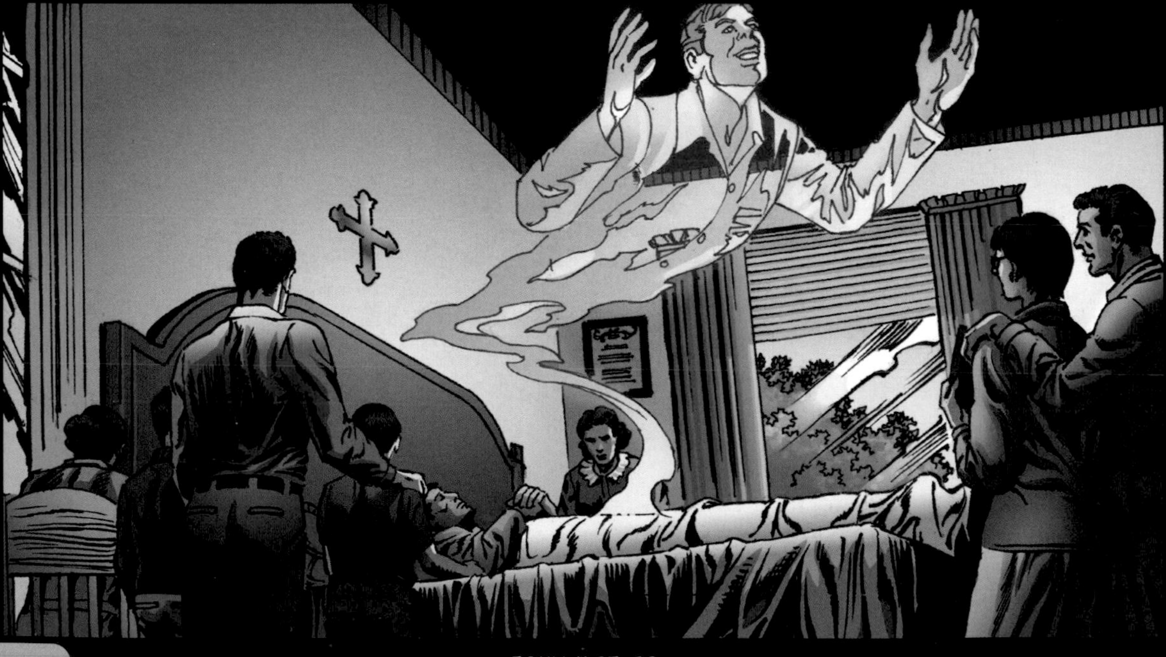

JOHN 11:25-26

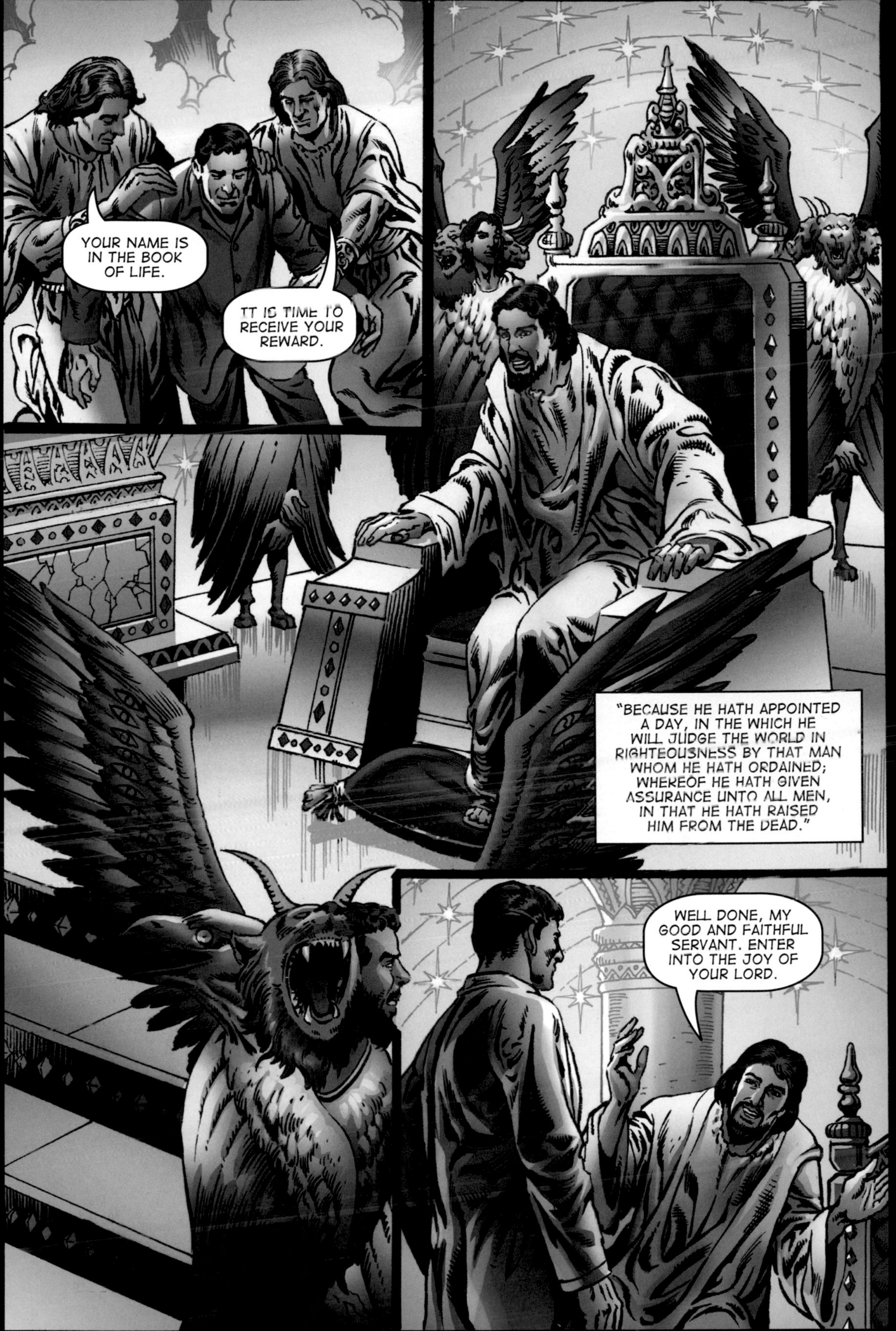
YOUR NAME IS IN THE BOOK OF LIFE.
IT IS TIME TO RECEIVE YOUR REWARD.
"BECAUSE HE HATH APPOINTED A DAY, IN THE WHICH HE WILL JUDGE THE WORLD IN RIGHTEOUSNESS BY THAT MAN WHOM HE HATH ORDAINED; WHEREOF HE HATH GIVEN ASSURANCE UNTO ALL MEN, IN THAT HE HATH RAISED HIM FROM THE DEAD."
WELL DONE, MY GOOD AND FAITHFUL SERVANT. ENTER INTO THE JOY OF YOUR LORD.

THE SUPERHERO AMONG BOOKS

The "Bible," or "Scriptures," or "the Word of God" is the basis of faith for the Christian religion. It is also the most influential book ever written. An extraordinary composition, the Bible is a collection of 66 individual books written by some 40 different authors. All were from the continent of Asia, and with a possible exception or two, all were Jewish. The authors' differences, though, are more profound than their similarities. Their professions covered an extreme range of ancient possibilities. Some were kings, others tax collectors. There were fishermen, doctors, farmers, servants, lawyers, and more. They also wrote during radically different time periods, spanning roughly 15 centuries from just after 1500 B.C. until about 100 A.D. Most of them didn't know each other, and yet when the different books of the Bible were finally joined together, the Bible told the same story throughout.

This supernatural character of the Bible is because the Holy Spirit of God inspired these men to write. As a result, this ancient work remains the most popular book in the world today. It was the first book ever produced on a movable type printing press and is still more widely distributed every year than any other book. The complete Bible has been translated into more than 500 languages, and there are nearly 3,000 translations of at least a portion of Scripture.

The Bible is divided into two main parts: the Old Testament and the New Testament. The Old Testament consists of 39 individual books comprised of 927 chapters. Much of it was written in the Hebrew language, which looks like this:

בראשית ברא אלהים את השמים ואת הארץ

In addition to being central to the Christian faith, the Old Testament is still sacred to the Jewish People.

As for the New Testament, it is made up of 27 books in 260 chapters. The writers of this portion of the Bible used several languages including Greek, which looks like this:

εν αρχη ην ο λογος και ο λογος ην προς τον θεον και θεος ην ο λογος

The Bible recounts the history of the world, showing that God is the Author of all that happens. Unlike other history books, however, Scripture also foretells the end of times, and it explains the reasons why events unfold as they do.

From the Bible, we learn about the origin of mankind, the cause of sin and evil, and the reality of heaven and hell. The Bible has repeatedly prophesied the future, and the prophecies have always turned out to be true—which means we can count on the accuracy of its account of events yet to happen.

As a guide for life, the Bible provides the correct answers for your most important questions, such as:

- Is there really a God?
- Why are we here, and what is our purpose?
- Why do we have to die?
- What happens to us after we die?
- After death, will we be re-incarnated?
- Are devils different than the spirits of people who have died?
- How are humans different from animals?
- What, exactly, is sin?
- What do we have to do to be saved out of the cycle of sin and karma?
- How can we live forever in heaven?
- Why does mankind experience suffering and disappointment, and then finally die?

The answers to these questions, and many others, can be found in the Bible. Read it for yourself!

that delivers the saving message of the Gospel of Christ through innovative, technologically savvy media.

Good and Evil International produces and distributes print, electronic, and video versions of the *Good and Evil* graphic Bible storybook and other communication products. Our target audiences include specific sociographic groups, and we offer ways for supporters to actively participate in mission opportunities.

THESE ARE OUR PRIMARY TARGETS FOR EXPOSURE TO THE GOSPEL:

Unreached people around the globe;
People already exposed through other forms of mission outreach but only marginally penetrated for the cause of Christ;
"Forgotten" people such as prisoners, homeless, and similarly disconnected people within otherwise "reached" populations;
Children and young adults;
"Over-exposed" audiences for whom traditional Gospel presentations have become ineffective, such as military personnel, schools, hospitals, and other such identifiable groups.

In pursuit of our mission, Good and Evil International has set a goal of seeing *Good and Evil* translated and distributed into at least 100 different languages. To do that, we're looking for translation and publishing partners. If you share our vision and think you may be in a position to have this book translated into one of the languages not yet in print, we would like to help you help us. While we retain the copyright in any and all languages, and are the sole distributorship in English, we make available the resources you need to translate and format the book.

a translation is complete, we reserve the right to make that translation available to other missionaries who can print and distribute it through their networks.

If you are interested in translating, please contact us by writing or emailing:

Good and Evil International, Inc.
1000 Pearl Road
Pleasantville, TN 37033-1796
mel@comicbook.bible

So far, *Good and Evil* has been translated into 45 languages with dozens more in progress. The color version is now available for purchase and immediate shipping in English, Spanish, Chinese, and Russian. Over 40 additional languages, including Arabic, Hindi, Vietnamese, and Ukrainian can be purchased in black and white by print on demand (POD).

For more information on how you can distribute *Good and Evil*, contact Mel Cohen at mel@comicbook.bible or by calling 931-593-2484.

WITH YOUR HELP, WE'LL GET THE GOOD GUYS "OUT THERE."

TAKE THE RIGHT(S) APPROACH TO MISSIONS

Through our international rights agent, Good and Evil International has negotiated dozens of contracts to have publishers in Africa, Asia, Europe, North America, and South America print and distribute Good and Evil in indigenous languages. The 45 translations currently available include Spanish, Chinese, German, Polish, Russian, French, Afrikaans, Zulu, and many others.

For a complete list, go to **www.comicbook.bible/languages**
Another three dozen translations are underway—including Hebrew, Finnish, Dutch, Malay, Lahu, Portuguese, and Urdu—but we are seeking additional international partners for translation and distribution.

With a distribution rights agreement, you can publish the Good and Evil translation of your choice under your organization's logo. These agreements are an efficient way to make Good and Evil available in countries outside America in the indigenous language and avoid the high cost of freight shipments from the United States.

FOR MORE INFORMATION ABOUT RIGHTS AGREEMENTS, CONTACT:

Mel Cohen, general manager
Email: mel@comicbook.bible
Or call 931-593-2484.

HOME MISSIONS FOR THE HOME

While many of us are called to the far reaches to share Christ, most are not. And that means your greatest mission field is likely your own home. Raising children of Light in a world of deepening darkness is a crucial task, and a kid-friendly presentation of God's truth can be one of your most valuable tools for the job. In addition to this graphic-novel-style book, *Good and Evil* is available in a lively, 13-episode animated video.

Children and young adults alike can spend hours with *Good and Evil,* and the truth soaks in as they do. The book and DVD series also make great gifts for other family or friends who need a fresh exposure to God's truth. To order the *Good and Evil* book or DVD series, go to www.comicbook.bible. When it comes to winning your family and friends, nothing could be more mission critical.

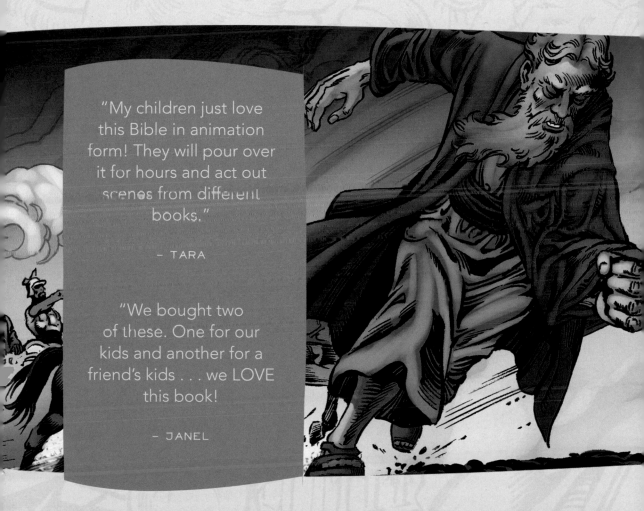

"My children just love this Bible in animation form! They will pour over it for hours and act out scenes from different books."

– TARA

"We bought two of these. One for our kids and another for a friend's kids . . . we LOVE this book!

– JANEL

TO ORDER THE *GOOD AND EVIL* BOOK OR DVD SERIES,
GO TO WWW.COMICBOOK.BIBLE

John 1:1-37 (KJV)

1 In the beginning was the Word, and the Word was with God, and the Word was God.

2 The same was in the beginning with God.

3 All things were made by him; and without him was not any thing made that was made.

4 In him was life; and the life was the light of men.

5 And the light shineth in darkness; and the darkness comprehended it not.

6 There was a man sent from God, whose name was John.

7 The same came for a witness, to bear witness of the Light, that all men through him might believe.

8 He was not that Light, but was sent to bear witness of that Light.

9 That was the true Light, which lighteth every man that cometh into the world.

10 He was in the world, and the world was made by him, and the world knew him not.

11 He came unto his own, and his own received him not.

12 But as many as received him, to them gave he power to become the sons of God, even to them that believe on his name:

13 Which were born, not of blood, nor of the will of the flesh, nor of the will of man, but of God.

14 And the Word was made flesh, and dwelt among us, (and we beheld his glory, the glory as of the only begotten of the Father,) full of grace and truth.

15 John bare witness of him, and cried, saying, This was he of whom I spake, He that cometh after me is preferred before me: for he was before me.

16 And of his fulness have all we received, and grace for grace.

17 For the law was given by Moses, but grace and truth came by Jesus Christ.

18 No man hath seen God at any time, the only begotten Son, which is in the bosom of the Father, he hath declared him.

19 And this is the record of John, when the Jews sent priests and Levites from Jerusalem to ask him, Who art thou?

20 And he confessed, and denied not; but confessed, I am not the Christ.

21 And they asked him, What then? Art thou Elias? And he saith, I am not. Art thou that prophet? And he answered, No.

22 Then said they unto him, Who art thou? that we may give an answer to them that sent us. What sayest thou of thyself?

23 He said, I am the voice of one crying in the wilderness, Make straight the way of the Lord, as said the prophet Esaias.

24 And they which were sent were of the Pharisees.

25 And they asked him, and said unto him, Why baptizest thou then, if thou be not that Christ, nor Elias, neither that prophet?

26 John answered them, saying, I baptize with water: but there standeth one among you, whom ye know not;

27 He it is, who coming after me is preferred before me, whose shoe's latchet I am not worthy to unloose.

28 These things were done in Bethabara beyond Jordan, where John was baptizing.

29 The next day John seeth Jesus coming unto him, and saith, Behold the Lamb of God, which taketh away the sin of the world.

30 This is he of whom I said, After me cometh a man which is preferred before me: for he was before me.

31 And I knew him not: but that he should be made manifest to Israel, therefore am I come baptizing with water.

32 And John bare record, saying, I saw the Spirit descending from heaven like a dove, and it abode upon him.

33 And I knew him not: but he that sent me to baptize with water, the same said unto me, Upon whom thou shalt see the Spirit descending, and remaining on him, the same is he which baptizeth with the Holy Ghost.

34 And I saw, and bare record that this is the Son of God.

35 Again the next day after John stood, and two of his disciples;

36 And looking upon Jesus as he walked, he saith, Behold the Lamb of God!

37 And the two disciples heard him speak, and they followed Jesus.

Job 38 (KJV)

1 Then the Lord answered Job out of the whirlwind, and said,

2 Who is this that darkeneth counsel by words without knowledge?

3 Gird up now thy loins like a man; for I will demand of thee, and answer thou me.

4 Where wast thou when I laid the foundations of the earth? declare, if thou hast understanding.

5 Who hath laid the measures thereof, if thou knowest? or who hath stretched the line upon it?

6 Whereupon are the foundations thereof fastened? or who laid the corner stone thereof;

7 When the morning stars sang together, and all the sons of God shouted for joy?

8 Or who shut up the sea with doors, when it brake forth, as if it had issued out of the womb?

9 When I made the cloud the garment thereof, and thick darkness a swaddlingband for it,

10 And brake up for it my decreed place, and set bars and doors,

11 And said, Hitherto shalt thou come, but no further: and here shall thy proud waves be stayed?

12 Hast thou commanded the morning since thy days; and caused the dayspring to know his place;

13 That it might take hold of the ends of the earth, that the wicked might be shaken out of it?

14 It is turned as clay to the seal; and they stand as a garment.

15 And from the wicked their light is withholden, and the high arm shall be broken.

16 Hast thou entered into the springs of the sea? or hast thou walked in the search of the depth?

17 Have the gates of death been opened unto thee? or hast thou seen the doors of the shadow of death?

18 Hast thou perceived the breadth of the earth? declare if thou knowest it all.

19 Where is the way where light dwelleth? and as for darkness, where is the place thereof,

20 That thou shouldest take it to the bound thereof, and

that thou shouldest know the paths to the house thereof?

21 Knowest thou it, because thou wast then born? or because the number of thy days is great?

22 Hast thou entered into the treasures of the snow? or hast thou seen the treasures of the hail,

23 Which I have reserved against the time of trouble, against the day of battle and war?

24 By what way is the light parted, which scattereth the east wind upon the earth?

25 Who hath divided a watercourse for the overflowing of waters, or a way for the lightning of thunder;

26 To cause it to rain on the earth, where no man is; on the wilderness, wherein there is no man;

27 To satisfy the desolate and waste ground; and to cause the bud of the tender herb to spring forth?

28 Hath the rain a father? or who hath begotten the drops of dew?

29 Out of whose womb came the ice? and the hoary frost of heaven, who hath gendered it?

30 The waters are hid as with a stone, and the face of the deep is frozen.

31 Canst thou bind the sweet influences of Pleiades,

or loose the bands of Orion?

32 Canst thou bring forth Mazzaroth in his season? or canst thou guide Arcturus with his sons?

33 Knowest thou the ordinances of heaven? canst thou set the dominion thereof in the earth?

34 Canst thou lift up thy voice to the clouds, that abundance of waters may cover thee?

35 Canst thou send lightnings, that they may go and say unto thee, Here we are?

36 Who hath put wisdom in the inward parts? or who hath given understanding to the heart?

37 Who can number the clouds in wisdom? or who can stay the bottles of heaven,

38 When the dust groweth into hardness, and the clods cleave fast together?

39 Wilt thou hunt the prey for the lion? or fill the appetite of the young lions,

40 When they couch in their dens, and abide in the covert to lie in wait?

41 Who provideth for the raven his food? when his young ones cry unto God, they wander for lack of meat.

BIBLE FIRST!

FAITH COMETH BY HEARING

Bible First! is a correspondence Bible study built on the premise that God's Word is the most powerful Gospel witness in the world. The primary purpose of this course is to introduce students to the Lord Jesus Christ through the book of Genesis. ***Bible First!*** consists of 20 lessons and takes students one chapter at a time from Creation, through the stories of Adam and Eve, Cain and Abel, Noah, Abraham, Sodom and Gomorrah, Isaac, Jacob and Joseph. In each story, the lessons point them to Jesus, drawing on the types and parallels that God Himself built into Genesis for that very purpose.

Did You Know?
The Bible Is for Us

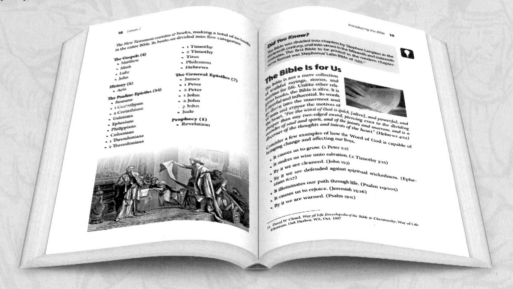

Prepare to be amazed, shocked, thrilled and transformed as you embark on a journey that will introduce you not only to the greatest Book ever written, but also to its Author.

TO SIGN UP AND ORDER THIS 20-LESSON COURSE, GO TO:

www.getbiblefirst.com